THE FRENCH RENAISSANCE
IN ENGLAND

THE
FRENCH RENAISSANCE
IN ENGLAND

AN ACCOUNT OF THE LITERARY RELATIONS
OF ENGLAND AND FRANCE IN THE
SIXTEENTH CENTURY

BY

SIDNEY LEE

1968
OCTAGON BOOKS, INC.
New York

Originally published in 1910 by The Clarendon Press, Oxford

Reprinted 1968
by special arrangement with Oxford University Press, Inc.

OCTAGON BOOKS, INC.
175 FIFTH AVENUE
NEW YORK, N. Y. 10010

LIBRARY OF CONGRESS CATALOG CARD NUMBER: 68-23977

Printed in U.S.A. by
NOBLE OFFSET PRINTERS, INC.
NEW YORK 3, N. Y.

PREFACE

THIS volume is based on a series of six lectures which I delivered, under the title of 'The Literary Relations of England and France during the Sixteenth Century', before the University of Oxford during the summer term of 1909. My thanks are due to the Delegates of the Common University Fund, on whose invitation the lectures were undertaken.

In the course of preparation for the press, the lectures have been largely rewritten and expanded. The change in the main title is justified not merely by considerations of brevity, but also by the fact that the French Renaissance was known in England almost exclusively through its written word, and only slightly and subsidiarily through its art.

Although I have not attempted to deal exhaustively with all the aspects of the theme, I hope that I have succeeded in bringing home to my readers not merely the extent of the debt which English literature, thought, and scholarship of the Tudor epoch owes to the French Renaissance, but also the interest attaching to that comparative study of European literature, on which I have sought to lift a corner of the curtain.

It is as a tentative contribution to a comparative study of literature that I wish the work mainly to be judged. That study has been pursued in this country on a smaller scale and less systematically than abroad. Yet the comparative study of literature is to my thinking a needful complement of those philological and aesthetic studies which chiefly occupy the attention of English scholars. The serious student of literature can never safely ignore the suggestive phrases of Walter Pater : 'Producers of great literature do not live in isolation, but catch light and heat from each other's thought. A people without intellectual commerce with other peoples has never done anything conspicuous in literature.' Nor is it wise to neglect the sagacious counsel of Matthew Arnold: 'The criticism which alone can much help us for the future is a criticism which regards Europe as being, for intellectual and spiritual purposes, one great confederation, bound to a joint action and working to a common result.' In other words, every great national literature is a fruit of much foreign sustenance and refreshment, however capable the national spirit may prove of mastering the foreign element. The comparative study should therefore form an integral part of any sound analysis of literary achievement. Students of literature who keep their sight fixed exclusively on a single nation's literary work run the risk of narrowing and distorting their critical judgement. No literature can be viewed in a just perspective until the comparative study has brought foreign literary effort within the range of vision. My purpose in this volume will have been fulfilled if I convince discerning students of English literature of the sixteenth century that knowledge of the coeval literature of France is required to verify their estimates of the value and originality of wellnigh all the literary endeavour of Tudor England.

My main results are due to a long-continued parallel study of the literary work of the two countries. At the same time a little complementary research which I have pursued in historic manuscripts has yielded some unexpected fruit. I cannot find, for example, that there has been printed before the letter in which Montaigne's intimate friend and neighbour, Pierre de Brach, announced, immediately after the event, the great essayist's death to Francis Bacon's brother, Anthony Bacon.[1] But while I have done what I could to explore much of the field for myself, I have to acknowledge numerous obligations to earlier workers in very varied directions. The modern critical editions of the French and English writings of the epoch, and the many recent literary and biographical monographs which bear on them and their work, are my chief

---

[1] The original is at Lambeth: see p. 173.

authorities, and these I specify in detail in my notes.[1]   General
works, which I have found of constant service, are C. A. Sainte-
Beuve's *Tableau historique et critique de la poésie française au
XVIe siècle*, 1893; Arsène Darmesteter and Adolphe Hatz-
feld's *Le XVIe siècle en France : littérature et langue*, 1893;
Louis Petit de Julleville's *Histoire de la langue et de la littérature françaises*, tom. iii, Seizième siècle, 1897; M. Gustave
Lanson's *Manuel bibliographique de la littérature française moderne*, I. Seizième siècle, 1909; together with the suggestive volumes of M. Emile Faguet, viz.: *La Tragédie française
au XVIe siècle* (1550–1600), 1897; his *Seizième siècle: études
littéraires*, 1898; and his *Histoire de la littérature française*, tom. 1, Jusqu'à la fin du XVIe siècle, 1900.[2]   Among
English books which deal generally with the literary history of
sixteenth-century France, by far the most useful and complete
is Mr. Arthur Tilley's *Literature of the French Renaissance*
(2 vols., 1904).   I am grateful, too, for the help which I have
derived from the writings of my friend of five-and-twenty
years' standing, M. Jusserand, now French ambassador at
Washington.   It is barely possible to overpraise M. Jusserand's
exhaustive contributions to the history of English literature.

[1] The text of Ronsard's poetry, which I quote freely, presents some
difficulties.   I have used Blanchemain's edition in the *Bibliothèque Elzé-
virienne* (8 vols., Paris, 1857–1867), which follows, for the early and most
important work of the poet, the first collected edition of 1560 (4 vols.).
Blanchemain depends for Ronsard's later poetry on the many succeeding
collective editions, which Ronsard superintended in his declining years.
The poet liberally corrected his text after its first publication.   Marty-
Laveaux's fine edition of Ronsard (6 vols., Paris, 1887) adopts the text of
the collective edition of 1584, the last to be issued in Ronsard's lifetime.
There are consequently several discrepancies between my citations of
Ronsard and Marty-Laveaux's versions.   Ronsard's early poetry was
chiefly familiar to the Elizabethans, and they seem to have used the early
editions.   The textual variations are not material to my argument, but
this word of warning is necessary.   By far the best study of the complicated history of Ronsard's text is supplied by M. Hugues Vaganay's
edition of the first book of Ronsard's *Amours*, based on the edition of 1578.
This volume was published in 1910, with a preface by Prof. Joseph Vianey,
and an ample *apparatus criticus* by the editor.   No close student of
Ronsard's poetry can dispense with this valuable work.   Mr. St. John
Lucas's interesting *Selected Poems of Pierre de Ronsard* (Oxford, 1908)
follows Marty-Laveaux's text.
[2] An English translation of the whole of this work entitled *A Literary
History of France* was published by Fisher Unwin in 1907.

With some of his conclusions I disagree, but I am none the
less certain that no critic of Tudor literature can hope for salvation if he fail to master M. Jusserand's *English Novel in the
Time of Shakespeare* (1890), his *Shakespeare in France
under the Ancien Régime* (1899), or his *Literary History
of the English People from the Origins to the Civil War*
(1895–1906). The three books charm the reader almost
equally in the original French and in the English translation.

In subsidiary study of French political complications of the
era, I have been aided by Henry Martyn Baird's *History of
the rise of the Huguenots* (1880), and his *Huguenots and
Henry of Navarre* (1886), as well as by Mr. Edward Armstrong's *The French Wars of Religion* (1892).

It was only after my own labours were well advanced that
I enjoyed the benefit of reading M. Louis Charlanne's *L'influence française en Angleterre au XVIIᵉ siècle*, Paris, 1906,
and Dr. Alfred Horatio Upham's *The French Influence in
English Literature from the Accession of Elizabeth to the
Restoration* (New York, Columbia University Press, 1908).
M. Charlanne's literary survey starts where I end. But his
chapters on social life have given me useful suggestions. Dr.
Upham begins his research at a somewhat later period than
myself and continues his inquiry long after the close of the sixteenth century, beyond which I do not venture. But we cover in
somewhat different fashion a substantial part of the same ground,
and I have specified at various points my debt to Dr. Upham's
researches. I have also benefited by Prof. L. E. Kastner's
papers in the *Modern Language Review* (1907–10) on the
heavy loans which Elizabethan poets levied on the verse of the
Pléiade. I had previously treated this branch of the theme in
my Introduction to *Elizabethan Sonnets* (in Constable's *English Garner*, 1904), and in a paper on Chapman's *Amorous
Zodiacke* in *Modern Philology* (Chicago University Press,
October, 1905). The latter essay I reprint in Appendix II of
this volume, under the title *George Chapman and Gilles
Durant*, and I make in Appendix I some fresh additions to
the Elizabethan poems whose French originals I have identified by my unaided effort. But Prof. Kastner's industry and

learning have brought to light numerous concrete examples
of the Elizabethan poets' direct indebtedness which I had
overlooked.

The poetry and prose of the French Renaissance would
seem to have attracted rather wider attention and a warmer
appreciation among English writers of a past generation
than among those of the present. Louisa Stuart Costello's
Specimens of the Early Poetry of France (1835); Father
Prout's *Reliques* (1836); and Henry Francis Cary's *Early
French Poets* (1846), are all suggestive, if somewhat discursive
and slender, memorials of early nineteenth-century enthusiasm for French poetry of the sixteenth century. Prof.
Henry Morley's biographies of Palissy the Potter (1852) and of
Clément Marot (1871) are biased by Protestant feeling, but both
are interesting efforts of a mid-Victorian student to deal with
the literary and artistic influence of the Huguenots. More
lively and enlightened are the studies of Sir Walter Besant in
his *Early French Poetry* (1868), *The French Humorists
from the Twelfth to the Nineteenth Century* (1873), and his
brief monograph on *Rabelais* (1885).

During the second half of the last century four members
of the University of Oxford illustrated, to more scholarly and
satisfying purpose, the great place that the French Renaissance fills in the history of modern scholarship and culture.
The early volumes of Algernon Charles Swinburne testify to
his wide and sympathetic reading in French poetry, chiefly
of the era of the Renaissance. The Victorian poet did much
to familiarize his generation with the manner and sentiment
of the sixteenth-century poetry of France. Mark Pattison's essays on French scholars and scholarship (*Essays*,
collected in two vols., Oxford, 1889) which were crowned
by his biography of Isaac Casaubon (1875), learnedly expound the value of the contribution which France of the
Renaissance made to the elucidation of Greek language
and literature. Walter Pater in his *Studies in the History
of the Renaissance* (1873), and in his unfinished romance
of *Gaston de Latour* (1896), defined with rare insight
the aesthetic quality of French literature in the sixteenth

century ; while Richard Copley Christie, in his elaborate biography of Étienne Dolet (1880), ably supplemented Mark Pattison's earlier exposition of the achievements of French humanism. With these four writers it is not unfitting to associate the name of the late Lady Dilke, whose *Renaissance of Art in France* (1879) proved the first of an important series of volumes on French art and artists.

Although the tradition of appreciative study of the French Renaissance has shown of late years in England signs of decay, it is incumbent on me to add to those books by living English writers which I have mentioned already as giving me assistance and suggestion, Mr. Andrew Lang's *Ballads and Lyrics of Old France* (new edition, 1907), Mr. George Wyndham's *Ronsard and the Pléiade* (1906), Prof. Dowden's *Michel de Montaigne* (1905), Mr. John C. Bailey's *The Claims of French Poetry* (1907), and Mr. Rowland E. Prothero's *The Pleasant Land of France* (1908).

In spite of my efforts to test my facts and dates, I cannot hope to have escaped error in handling a theme which demands an acquaintance with very varied topics in the literary history of two great peoples and a grasp of an infinitude of historical and bibliographical detail. Nor have I found it easy to avoid the occasional repetition of information which seemed to need examination from more points of view and under more headings than one. For sins of commission or omission I crave my readers' indulgence. I have to thank Mr. W. B. Owen, B.A., formerly scholar of St. Catharine's College, Cambridge, for helping me to compile the comparative chronological table of the progress in culture and politics of the two countries, which will, I hope, be of some graphic service. Mr. Owen has also prepared the index, and given me much zealous aid in correcting the whole work for the press.

S. L.

August 31, 1910.

CONTENTS

CONTENTS

BOOK III

FRENCH INFLUENCE ON ELIZABETHAN PROSE

BOOK IV

FRENCH INFLUENCE ON THE ELIZABETHAN LYRIC

BOOK V

THE MESSAGE OF THE HUGUENOTS

BOOK VI

FRENCH INFLUENCE ON ELIZABETHAN DRAMA

APPENDIX

CHRONOLOGICAL TABLE

OF LEADING EVENTS IN THE HISTORY OF FRENCH AND
ENGLISH CULTURE AND POLITICS FROM THE BIRTH
OF ERASMUS IN 1466 TILL THE DEATH OF SHAKE-
SPEARE IN 1616[1]

FRANCE.	ENGLAND.
1466 [Birth of Erasmus.]	
1467 Birth of Budé.	
1468 Death of Alain Chartier.	
1470 First printing press in Paris.	
1472 University of Bordeaux founded.	
1477	Caxton sets up printing press at Westminster; prints *Moral Proverbs* of Christine de Pisan.
1478	Birth of Sir Thomas More.
1479 Birth of Jean Grolier.	
1483 Death of Louis XII. Accession of Charles VIII. Birth of Rabelais. [Birth of Luther.]	Death of Edward IV. Accession of Richard III.
1484 Birth of Julius Caesar Scaliger ('the elder Scaliger').	
1485 *Maistre Pierre Pathelin* (written about 1469) first published.	Death of Richard III. Accession of Henry VII. Linacre goes to Italy. Malory's *Le Morte Arthur.*
1487 French paraphrase of the Bible published at Paris.	
1489 Villon's *Le Grand Testament et le Petit.*	
1492 Birth of Margaret of Angoulême (afterwards Queen Margaret of Navarre). Martial de Paris, *Vigilles de . . . Charles VII.*	James IV becomes King of Scotland.
1494 French invade Italy. [Sebastian Brant, *Narrenschiff.*]	
1496	Colet and Erasmus in Paris. [Birth of Holbein.]
1497 Birth of Clément Marot. Christine de Pisan, *La Cité des Dames. La Nef des folz,* verse translation of Brant's satire.	
1498 Death of Charles VIII. Accession of Louis XII. [Columbus discovers the American continent.]	Erasmus first visits England; resides at Oxford.
1499 Gringoire, *Le Château de Labour.*	
1500	Barclay's *Castell of Labour* from Gringoire's French.

[1] A few events (other than French) of European moment are inserted between
square brackets. Where authors' names and titles of books are given without
added word, the year to which the entry is attached is that of first publication
of the cited works.

FRANCE.	ENGLAND.
1501 Henri Étienne sets up press at Paris.	
1502	Lady Margaret Beaufort founds professorships of Divinity at Oxford and Cambridge.
1504 Le Maire de Belges, *Le Temple d'Honneur et de Vertu.* Gringoire, *Les Abus du Monde.*	
1508	Lady Margaret Beaufort endows St. John's College, Cambridge. Barclay's *Ship of Fooles*—translation of Brant's satire.
1509 Birth of Calvin.	Death of Henry VII. Accession of Henry VIII. Death of Lady Margaret Beaufort. Colet founds St. Paul's School. Richard Pynson first royal printer. Erasmus's *Encomium Moriae.* Hawes's *Passetyme of Pleasure.*
1510 Le Maire de Belges, *L'Amant vert.*	
1511 Gringoire's *Le Jeu du Prince des Sots* played before Louis XII.	
1513 [Machiavelli's *Prince* composed.] Birth of Amyot.	James V becomes King of Scotland.
1514	Henry VIII's sister Mary marries Louis XII of France.
1515 Death of Louis XII. Accession of Francis I.	More in Flanders.
1516 Budé writes *Institution du Prince.*	More's *Utopia* published at Antwerp.
1517 Budé, *De Asse et partibus eius.*	Erasmus finally leaves England. London riots against foreigners ('Evil May Day').
1518	Linacre founds the College of Physicians in London.
1519 [Charles V elected Emperor of Germany.] Birth of Theodore Beza.	Death of Colet. Erasmus's *Colloquia.*
1520	Meeting of Henry VIII and Francis I at the 'Field of the Cloth of Gold'.
1521 [Luther translates Bible into German.]	Barclay's *Introductorie to write and to pronounce French.*
1522 Budé appointed librarian to Francis I ; begins royal collection of Greek MSS.	
1523	Lord Berners' translation of Froissart's *Chronicles,* vol. i (vol. ii, 1525).
1524 Birth of Ronsard. Rabelais's *Pantagruel* possibly published.	Death of Linacre and Stephen Hawes. Skelton's *Garlande of Laurell.*
1525 Battle of Pavia, defeat of French, and capture of Francis I. End of the French invasion of Italy.	Tyndale's New Testament in English.
1527 Margaret of Angoulême marries as second husband Henry d'Albret, King of Navarre, and opens her literary court. Francis I's reconstruction and decoration of Fontainebleau and the Louvre begins.	Holbein visits England. William Lily's *Grammatices Rudimenta.*

FRANCE.

1529 Treaty of Cambray between Francis I and the Emperor Charles V. Budé's *Commentarii Linguae Graecae*. Tory's *Champ-Fleury*. Foundation of the Collège de France.

1530 Flight of Florentine scholars to France on fall of the republic. Le Fèvre's French translation of the Bible.

1531

1532 Alamanni's *Opere Toscane* (Lyons). Machiavelli's *Il Principe*. Rabelais's *Pantagruel*, first extant edition. Birth of J. A. de Baïf. First collection of Marot's *Œuvres*. Margaret of Navarre, *Le Miroir de l'âme pécheresse*.

1533 Birth of Montaigne. Marot's edition of Villon's *Œuvres*. Collège de Guienne opened at Bordeaux. Catherine de' Medici marries the dauphin, afterwards Henry II.

1534 Rabelais's *Gargantua*. Death of Gringoire (?). François Clouet's portrait of Francis I. Protestants of Paris denounce the Mass. Cartier explores North America.

1535 Olivetan's French Bible.

1536 Ramus attacks Aristotelian logic at Paris. [Death of Erasmus at Basle.] Calvin's *Christianae Religionis Institutio*.

1537

1538 Marot's Poems collected. Dolet sets up press at Lyons.

1539 The acting brotherhood 'Les Confrères de la Passion' installed at the Hôtel de Flandres. University of Nismes founded chiefly by Margaret of Navarre.

1540 Death of Budé. Birth of Joseph Justus Scaliger (the younger Scaliger). Dolet's *La manière de bien traduire*.

1541 Calvin's *Institution de la religion Chrestienne* (first French edition). Calvin finally establishes his religious autocracy at Geneva. Queen Margaret of Navarre begins the *Heptameron*.

ENGLAND.

Death of John Skelton.

Palsgrave's *L'Esclarcissement de la langue françoyse*. Death of Pynson.

Sir Thomas Elyot's *Governour*. Henry VIII, with Anne Boleyn, visits Francis I.

Henry VIII divorces Queen Catherine of England and marries Anne Boleyn.

Lord Berners's translation of *Huon of Burdeux*. Henry VIII declared supreme head of the Church in England.

Execution of Sir Thomas More. Coverdale's Bible (first complete English translation). Death of Tyndale.

Matthew's English Bible. James V of Scotland marries Marie of Guise. The 'Great' Bible in English.

Udall's *Ralph Roister Doister*, the first English comedy, acted at Eton. Nonesuch Palace near Cheam begun by Henry VIII. Regius professorships founded by Henry VIII at Oxford.

FRANCE.

1542 Antoine Heroet's *La Parfaicte Amye*. Persecution of French Protestants begins. Buchanan's *Jephthes* acted by students at Bordeaux. Ariosto's *Gli Suppositi* in French translation. Dolet's translation of Cicero's Letters.

1543 Ramus's *Aristotelicae Animadversiones* published and suppressed.

1544 Death of Marot. New edition of his *Œuvres*. [Birth of Tasso.] Birth of Du Bartas. Scève's *Délie*.

1545 Le Maçon's French translation of the *Decameron*. French translation of Ariosto's *Gli Suppositi*.

1546 Étienne Dolet burnt. [Death of Luther.] Birth of Desportes. Budé's *Institution du Prince*. Rabelais's *Pantagruel* (Book III).

1547 Death of Francis II. Accession of Henry II. Margaret of Navarre's *Les Marguerites de la Marguerite des princesses*. Saint-Gelais's *Œuvres*. Amyot's *L'Histoire Æthiopique*. Ramus's *Institutionum dialecticarum libri tres*.

1548 Sibilet's *Art poëtique*. Rabelais's *Pantagruel* (Book IV). Religious drama prohibited in Paris. The actors 'Les Confrères de la Passion' occupy and rebuild the Hôtel de Bourgogne in Paris.

1549 Death of Queen Margaret of Navarre. Birth of Du Plessis. Formation of the Pléiade. Du Bellay's *Deffense et illustration de la langue françoise, Olive*, and *Recueil*.

1550 More's *Utopia* in French translation. Ronsard's *Odes*. Théodore de Bèze's *Abraham sacrifiant*. Birth of Aubigné.

1551 Jean Brétog's *Tragédie françoise* produced in Paris. The Geneva Psalter.

1552 Rabelais's *Pantagruel* (Book IV completed). Ronsard's *Amours*. Baïf's *Amours*. Jodelle's *Cléopâtre* and *Eugène* first performed before Charles IX in Paris. Ambroise Paré appointed surgeon to the French King.

ENGLAND.

1542 Death of James V of Scotland. Accession of Mary Queen of Scots. Death of Sir Thomas Wyatt.

1543 Death of Holbein in London. First Greek book printed in England by Reginald Wolf.

1544 Henry VIII invades France and takes Boulogne.

1546 Treaty of Ardres between England and France.

1547 Death of Henry VIII. Accession of Edward VI. Death of the Earl of Surrey.

1548 Foreign Protestants welcomed to England. Mary Queen of Scots sent to France.

1549 English Book of Common Prayer.

1551 More's *Utopia* translated into English. Shrewsbury School founded.

1552 Birth of Edmund Spenser and Sir Walter Raleigh. Death of Alexander Barclay.

FRANCE.

ENGLAND.

1553 Birth of Henry of Navarre (Henry IV of France). Birth of De Thou. Death of Rabelais. Magny's *Amours*. [Servetus burnt at Geneva.]

Death of Edward VI. Accession of Mary. Wilson's *Arte of Rhetorique*.

1554 Magny's *Gayetes*. Henri Étienne's editio princeps of *Anacreon*.

Birth of Sir Philip Sidney.

1555 Huguenot settlement in Brazil. The sculptor Goujon begins work at the Louvre. Ronsard's *Hymnes* and *Amours de Marie*. Louise Labé's *Œuvres*. Vauquelin de la Fresnaie's *Foresteries* (Books I and II). Ramus's *Dialectique*.

1557 Magny's *Les Soupirs*. La Peruse's *Médée*.

Tottel's *Miscellany*. Nonesuch Palace completed. Incorporation of the Stationers' Company in London.

1558 Death of Julius Caesar Scaliger (Scaliger the Elder). Death of Melin de Saint-Gelais. Queen Margaret's *Histoire des Amans Fortunez* (reissued next year as the *L'Heptameron*). Perlin's Description of England (Paris). Du Bellay's *Regrets*. Germain Pilon, the sculptor, begins work on royal tombs at St. Denis.

Loss of Calais. Death of Queen Mary. Accession of Queen Elizabeth. Mary Queen of Scots marries Francis II of France.

1559 Peace of Cateau Cambrésis between France, Spain, and England. Death of Henry II. Accession of Francis II. Catherine de' Medici, queen-mother. Amyot's translations of Plutarch's *Lives* and of Longus's *Daphnis and Chloe*. Magny's *Odes*. Du Bellay's *Le poète courtisan*. Bandello's *Les Histoires tragiques* (translated by Boaistuau and Belleforest).

Mirror for Magistrates, first part.

1560 Death of Francis II. Accession of Charles IX. L'Hôpital becomes Chancellor of France. Conspiracy of Amboise. Death of Du Bellay. Pasquier's *Recherches de la France* (Book I). Ronsard's *Œuvres* (first collective edition). Hotman's *Le Tigre*, an attack on Cardinal de Lorraine.

The 'Genevan' Bible in English. Westminster School founded.

1561 Death of Magny. Scaliger's *Poetics*. Grévin's *Théâtre* including his *César*.

Birth of Bacon. Norton's translation of Calvin's *Institution of Christian Religion*. English version of the Genevan Psalter.

FRANCE.	ENGLAND.
1562 Outbreak of Religious War in France. Huguenots defeated at Dreux. Huguenot settlement in Florida. Ronsard's *Discours des misères de ce temps*.	English army supports Huguenots in Normandy. *Gorboduc* acted at the Inner Temple.
1563 Duke of Guise killed at siege of Orléans (18 Feb.). Peace of Amboise (19 March). Death of La Boëtie.	Ascham's *Schoolmaster* written. Ribaut's *Description of Florida* from the French.
1564 Death of Calvin (27 May). Rabelais' *Pantagruel* (Book V).	Treaty of Troyes between France and England. Birth of Marlowe and Shakespeare.
1565 [Cinthio's *Hecatommithi*.] Ronsard's *Abrégé de l'art poëtique françois* and *Elegies*. Pasquier's *Recherches* (Books I–II). Death of Grolier.	Mary Queen of Scots marries Henry Stewart, Earl of Darnley.
1566 Death of Louise Labé. Louis des Masures' *David combattant, David fugitif*, and *David triomphant*.	Birth of James VI of Scotland. Udall's *Ralph Roister Doister* printed. Painter's *Palace of Pleasure*. Gascoigne's *Supposes* acted at Gray's Inn.
1567 Defeat of Huguenots at battle of St. Denis (10 Nov.). Ronsard's *Œuvres* (6 vols.). Baïf's *Le Brave* performed.	James VI becomes king of Scotland. Rugby School founded. Golding's translation of Ovid's *Metamorphoses*. George Turberville's translation of Mantuanus' *Eclogues*.
1568 Garnier's *Porcie*.	The 'Bishops' Bible in English. Skelton's *Poems* (complete edition).
1569 Huguenots defeated at Jarnac (March). Death of Condé. Defeat of Coligny at Moncontour (October). Du Bellay's *Œuvres*. Scévole de Saint-Marthe's *Premières Œuvres*.	*A Theatre for Worldlings* (containing Spenser's renderings of Du Bellay and Marot). Heywood's *Four P's* first printed.
1570 Peace of St. Germain (August). Death of Grévin. Baïf opens his Académie de Poésie et de Musique.	Ascham's *Schoolmaster*. Royal Exchange opened in London (begun 1566).
1571 De la Porte's *Les Epithètes*. Visit of 'I Gelosi' (Italian actors) to Paris. [Battle of Lepanto.]	
1572 The St. Bartholomew Massacre in Paris (24 Aug.). Murder of Coligny and Ramus. Death of Goujon. Amyot translates Plutarch's *Moralia*. Ronsard's *Franciade*. Belleau's *Bergeries*. Baïf's *Poems* (collective edition). Jean de la Taille's *Saül le furieux*. Henri Étienne's *Thesaurus Graecae Linguae*.	
1573 Sieges of Rochelle and Sancerre. Death of Jodelle. Death of L'Hôpital. Du Bartas's *La Muse Chrestienne*. Desportes' *Les premières œuvres*. Jean de la Taille's *La Famine* and *Les Corrivaux*. Garnier's *Hippolyte*. Belleau's *La Reconnue*. Hotman's *Franco-Gallia*.	Birth of Inigo Jones and John Donne.

FRANCE.   ENGLAND.

1574 Death of Charles IX. Henry III becomes King of France. [Death of Cinthio.] Jodelle's *Œuvres.* Garnier's *Cornélie. Discours merveilleux,* an attack on Queen Catherine de' Medici.

Negotiations begun for marriage of the Duke of Alençon with Queen Elizabeth.

1575 Palissy's public lectures inaugurate the science of Geology. Jamyn's *Œuvres poétiques.* Vauquelin de la Fresnaie's *L'Art poétique françois* begun. Duplessis-Mornay's *Discours de la vie et de la mort.* Birth of Montchrétien.

George Gascoigne's *Posies.*

1576 Henry of Navarre heads the Protestants in France. Pierre de Brach's *Poèmes.* Belleau's *Pierres précieuses.* Baïf's *Mimes* (Book I). Bodin's *République* (six books). Boëtie's *Contr' Un.* Gentillet's attack on Machiavelli's creed.

First public theatre in London.

1577 Death of Belleau. 'I Gelosi' (Italian actors) again visit Paris. Aubigné's *Les Tragiques* begun (published 1617).

Kendall's *Flowers of Epigrammes.* Golding's translation of Beza's *Abraham sacrifiant.* Patrick's *Discourse upon the meanes of wel governing,* written (a translation of Gentillet's tract against Machiavelli).

1578 Du Bartas's *La Semaine.* Ronsard's *Œuvres* (5 vols).. Henri Étienne's *Deux dialogues du nouveau françois italianisé.* Garnier's *Marc - Antoine.* French translation of Montemayor's *Diana.*

Mirror for Magistrates (complete edition).

1579 Larivey's *Six premières comédies.* Garnier's *La Troade.* Du Plessis - Mornay's *Vindiciae contra tyrannos.* Henri Étienne's *De la Précellence du Langage françois.* Pontoux's *L'Idée.*

Gosson's *School of Abuse.* North's translation of Plutarch's *Lives* (from Amyot's French). Spenser's *Shepheard's Calender.* Gabriel Harvey, Sidney, and Spenser form society of the *Areopagus.* Lyly's *Euphues, the Anatomy of Wit.* Birth of John Fletcher. First Scotch Bible. Lyly's *Euphues and his England.*

1580 Montaigne's *Essais* (two books). Garnier's *Antigone.* Bodin's *Démonomanie des Sorciers.* Beza's *Icones.*

1581 Du Plessis's *De la verité de la religion chrestienne.*

Francis, Duke of Anjou, in England to sue for hand in marriage of Queen Elizabeth. Sidney's *Arcadia* finished ; *Sonnets* and *Apologie for Poetrie* begun.

1582 Garnier's *Bradamante.* Montaigne's *Essais* (2nd edition). Belleforest's *Histoires tragiques* (from Bandello), new edition completed. Tessier's *Premier Livre d'Airs.*

Thomas Watson's *Hecatompathia or Passionate Centurie of Love.* Permanent printing press established at Cambridge University. Hakluyt's *Divers Voyages.* Beza's *Christian Meditations.*

FRANCE.	ENGLAND.
1583 Garnier's *Les Juives*. J. J. Scaliger's *De Emendatione Temporum*.	
1584 Death of the Duke of Alençon (June). The Holy League formed. Du Bartas's *La Seconde Semaine*. Ronsard's *Œuvres* (1 vol. folio). French translation of Tasso's *Aminta*. Death of François Clouet the painter.	Birth of Francis Beaumont. John Soothern's *Pandora* (an imitation of Ronsard). Lyly's *Campaspe* produced at Court. Munday's *Two Italian Gentlemen*. Thomas Hudson's translation of Du Bartas's *Judith*. Scot's *Discoverie of Witchcraft*. Temple's annotated edition of Ramus's *Dialectica*.
1585 Death of Ronsard (27 Dec.). Garnier's *Tragédies*.	Permanent printing press established at Oxford University. Raleigh's endeavours to colonize Virginia.
1586 Pasquier's *Letters* (ten books).	English army supports Protestants of Low Countries. Death of Sir Philip Sidney. Hooker's *Ecclesiastical Polity* begun.
1587 Henry of Navarre's victory at Coutras. La Noue's *Discours politiques et militaires*. Du Bartas visits James VI at Edinburgh.	Execution of Mary Queen of Scots. Thomas Nashe's *Unfortunate Traveller*. Greene's *Debate between Follie and Loue*, a rendering of Louise Labé's *Débat*. Marlowe, Lodge, Greene, and Peele begin writing for the English stage. Marlowe's *Tamberlaine* produced.
1588 Murder of Henry of Guise and the Cardinal of Guise (December). Montaigne's *Essais* (Book III).	Defeat of the Spanish Armada. Part of Du Plessis's *Vindiciae*, published in English. Yonge's *Musica Transalpina*. Greene's *Pandosto*.
1589 Death of Catherine de' Medici (January). Henry III assassinated (July 31). Henry IV claims French crown. Death of J. A. de Baïf. Pierre Matthieu's play of *La Guisiade* popular in Paris.	Puttenham's *Arte of English Poesie*. Arthur Golding completes and publishes Sidney's translation of Du Plessis's 'Truth of Christianity'. Hakluyt's *Principall Navigations*.
1590 Henry IV's victory at Ivry (March 14). Death of Charles X, claimant to the throne (May). Death of Paré, Palissy, Du Bartas, Cujas, and Hotman.	Sidney's *Arcadia*. Spenser's *Faerie Queene* (Books I–III). Lodge's *Rosalynde*. Countess of Pembroke translates Garnier's *Marc-Antoine*.
1591 Death of La Noue.	Two English armies support Henry IV of France in Northern France, one under Earl of Essex. Sidney's *Astrophel and Stella*. Spenser's *Daphnaida* and *Complaints*. Shakespeare's *Love's Labour's Lost* written.
1592 Death of Montaigne. Death of Alexander of Parma (Dec. 8). *Le Guysien* produced.	Shakespeare remodels *Henry VI*. Constable's *Diana* and Daniel's *Delia* (first editions).
1593 Henry IV becomes a Catholic (July 25). French translation of Guarini's *Il Pastor Fido*. J. J. Scaliger appointed professor at Leyden. Death of Amyot.	Death of Marlowe. Lodge's *William Longbeard* and *Phillis*. Shakespeare's *Venus and Adonis*. Drayton's *Idea*. Watson's *Tears of Fancie*. Countess of Pembroke's translation of Du Plessis's *Discourse of Life and Death*.

FRANCE.	ENGLAND.
1594 Henry IV enters Paris, and is crowned King (Feb. 27). *La Satyre Ménippée.* Jean Godard's *Les Déguisés.* Durant's *Œuvres poétiques,* including *Le Zodiac Amoureux* (first printed 1587).	Shakespeare's *Lucrece.* Daniel's *Cleopatra.* Marlowe's *Dido* and *Edward II.* Kyd's version of Garnier's *Cornélie.* Chapman's *Shadow of Night.* Tasso's *Melancholy* produced at the Rose Theatre.
1595 [Death of Tasso.]	Death of Thomas Kyd. The Countess of Pembroke's version of Garnier's *Marc-Antoine.* English translation of *La Satyre Ménippée* (*A Pleasant Satyre—A Satyre Menippized*). Sidney's *Apologie for Poetrie.* Spenser's *Colin Clout, Amoretti,* and *Epithalamion.* Chapman's *Ovids Banquet of Sence* (including *The Amorous Zodiacke*).
1596 Death of Bodin.	Spenser's *View of the State of Ireland* completed. Spenser's *Faerie Queene* (Books IV–VI) and *Prothalamion.* Lodge's *Margarite of America.* Death of Sir Francis Drake.
1597 Passerat's *Poèmes* (Book I).	Bacon's *Essays* (1st edition). Hooker's *Ecclesiastical Polity* (five books). Shakespeare writes 1 *Henry IV.*
1598 Edict of Nantes. Henry IV grants toleration to the Protestants. Installation of professional actors at the Hôtel de Bourgogne, with Alexandre Hardy as playright. Death of Henri Étienne.	Globe Theatre built. Sidney's *Arcadia* in folio. Jonson's *Every Man in his Humour* acted. Chapman completes Marlowe's *Hero and Leander.* *Love's Labour's Lost* in quarto.
1599	Death of Edmund Spenser. Peele's *David and Bethsabe.*
1600 Death of Garnier.	Earl of Essex's rebellion and execution. Fairfax's translation of Tasso's *Jerusalem Delivered.* Sir William Cornwallis's *Essays.* Marlowe's *Massacre at Paris.* Death of Hooker.
1601 Biron's conspiracy. Montchrétien's *Tragédies.* Bertaut's *Œuvres poétiques.*	*Two tragedies in one* published. Webster's *The Guise* produced.
1602 Execution of Biron. Bertaut's *Vers amoureux.* Death of Passerat.	Shakespeare's *Hamlet* produced. Davison's *Poetical Rhapsody.* Bodley's Library opened at Oxford.
1603	Death of Queen Elizabeth. Accession of James I. Florio's translation of Montaigne's *Essais.* *Hamlet,* the First Quarto.
1604 De Thou's *History* (Part I). Death of Beza at Geneva.	England makes peace with Spain. *Hamlet,* the Second Quarto.
1605 [Cervantes' *Don Quixote* (Part I).] Vauquelin de la Fresnaie's *Diverses poésies.* Hardy's *Alphée.*	Bacon's *Advancement of Learning.* Ben Jonson's *Volpone* produced.
1606 Death of Desportes. Passerat's *Œuvres Poétiques.* Birth of Corneille.	English translation of Bodin's *République* by Richard Knolles.

FRANCE.	ENGLAND.
1607 Death of Vauquelin de la Fresnaie. Hardy's *Coriolan*.	Ben Jonson's *Volpone*. Alexander's *Monarchicke Tragedies*. Chapman's *Bussy d'Ambois*. Tomkis's *Lingua*. First collective edition of Sylvester's translation of Du Bartas's *La Semaine* complete.
1608	*King Lear* in quarto. Chapman's *Byron's Conspiracy and Tragedy*. Birth of Milton.
1609 Henry IV assassinated. Accession of Louis XIII. Regnier's *Satires* (I–XII). Death of J. J. Scaliger.	Spenser's *Works* published in quarto. Shakespeare's *Sonnets*, *Troilus and Cressida*, and *Pericles* in quarto. *Antony and Cleopatra* and *Coriolanus* probably produced.
1611 Death of Bertaut. Larivey's *Comedies* (Part II).	Cotgrave's *French-English Dictionary*. Coryat's *Crudities*. Shakespeare's *Tempest* written. The Authorised Version of the Bible.
1612 Regnier's *Satires* (revised edition).	Bacon's *Essays* (2nd edition). Death of Robert Cecil, Earl of Salisbury.
1613 [Death of Guarini.]	Chapman's *Revenge of Bussy d'Ambois*.
1614	Raleigh's *History of the World*.
1615 [Cervantes' *Don Quixote* (Part II).] Montchrétien, *Traité de l'Œconomie politique*.	
1616 [Death of Cervantes.] Aubigné's *Les Tragiques* published (written in 1577).	Death of Hakluyt, Francis Beaumont, and Shakespeare. William Drummond of Hawthornden's *Poems*.

BOOK I

THE DEBT OF TUDOR CULTURE
TO FRANCE

I

The Renaissance in Italy, France, and England

ENGLISH literature of the sixteenth century reached its ultimate triumph in the drama and poetry of Shakespeare. On this fact the historian and the critic dwell with a just persistence. Less attention is commonly bestowed on the equally instructive truth that English literature of the sixteenth century was no spontaneous, no merely local or isolated manifestation, but a late and slowly maturing fruit of the widespread European movement which is known as the Renaissance. Elizabethan literature has an unassailable line of foreign descent and kinship. Whatever justification historian or critic may allege for the prevalent disregard of the pedigree, there lurks in the apathy a risk of distorting the historical vision, of clouding the critical judgement.

The Renaissance may be defined in its broadest aspect as a strenuous effort on the part of Western Europe to eliminate barbarism and rusticity from the field of man's thought, and to substitute humanism and liberal culture of infinite scope. The discovery of Greek literature and the renewed study of the Latin classics were the exciting causes of the movement. But the Renaissance was far more than a literary revival; it was a regeneration of human sentiment, a new birth of intellectual, aesthetic, and spiritual aspiration. Life throughout its sweep was invested with a new significance and a new potentiality. While sympathy was awakening with the ideas and forms of Greek and Latin literature, other forces were helping to kindle a sense of joy, a love of beauty, a lively interest in animate and inanimate nature—of an unprecedented quality. The past fails to account for all the new growth of artistic sensibility, of intellectual and spiritual curiosity. The present, with its discovery of the new western world

and the recasting of cosmography, bred a novel and an independent stimulus.   Never before was seen so versatile an
ingenuity in adapting old forms of expression to changed
conceptions of mind and matter.   The fertilizing forces of the
Renaissance begot a new world of art and letters, which was
fired by a double ardour of revolution and of restoration.

It was in Italy that the stirring movement was born and
nurtured.   It crossed the Alps somewhat sluggishly.   Thence
it passed at varying intervals and at different rates of progress
into France, Germany, Spain, and England.

England was slow to enlist in this triumphant advance of
humanism, in this mighty march of mind.   The culture of the
Renaissance blossomed late in the British isle, far later than
in Italy, or indeed in France.   Nor did the English soil prove
equal to fostering the humanist development in all the fields
of artistic endeavour which the new spirit fructified abroad.
No original painting, no original music, no original architecture of Renaissance inspiration was cradled in Tudor
England.   There the Renaissance sought distinctive expression
in literature and poetry alone.

Near two hundred years separate the great first-fruits of
the literary and artistic movement in Italy from the full
English harvest of literary treasure.   As early as the fourteenth century, Giotto in painting and Petrarch in poetry
preached in Northern Italy the new doctrine of the Renaissance, and inaugurated in their native country a humanist
enthusiasm, which maintained its energy in the twin paths of
art and letters till the sixteenth century closed.   The opening
scenes of the Italian Renaissance in the fourteenth century
gave earnest of a glorious perfection, and the sixteenth
century, to which the last episodes of the Italian movement
belong, is still familiarly known as 'the golden age' of
Italian literature as well as of Italian art.   Through three
centuries humanism animated the whole range of artistic
effort in Italy.   During the first quarter of the sixteenth
century new paths of glory were conquered by Ariosto in
Italian poetry, by Machiavelli and Guicciardini in Italian
prose, by Raphael, Correggio, and Titian in Italian painting :

a generation later Italian art and letters acknowledged the sovereignty of Michelangelo, and Michelangelo's immediate successors on the thrones of his country's poetry and art were of the calibre of Guarini and Tasso, of Tintoretto and Paolo Veronese. The latest of the three centuries in the history of the Italian Renaissance was the era of Machiavelli and Tasso, no less than of Michelangelo and Tintoretto. The Renaissance in Italy shows a tenacity and an enduring breadth and brilliance which have no precise parallel elsewhere. It came into being earlier, and lived longer and in more versatile strength than in any other country of Europe.

The French Renaissance is far younger than the Italian movement; the scope of its triumph was narrower; its career was briefer. But the French Renaissance was of older standing than the English; it ranged over wider fields of art; its history is longer; it ran a more continuous and less fitful course; it sprang into active life in the early years of the sixteenth century, and only lost its energy in the latest years. Though the zenith of Renaissance inspiration was reached by French poetry in the work of Ronsard during the sixth decade, the spirit glowed in Ronsard's senior, Rabelais, three decades earlier, and in his junior, Montaigne, three decades later. Meanwhile the French Renaissance yielded rich stores of art as well as literature. Places among the masterpieces of the world have been accorded portraits from the easels of the Clouets; the French sculptors Pilon and Goujon rank with the heroes of Italy.

In both artistic and literary branches of aesthetic effort the French no less than the Italian Renaissance won unfading laurels before the literature which was the sole fruit of the English Renaissance acquired genuine coherence of form or aim. In both France and Italy humanism reached its final stage of perfection in art and letters while Spenser and Shakespeare were very young men, before their spurs were fairly won. Ronsard died just before Shakespeare came of age. Tasso, though he was Spenser's senior by no more than eight years, enjoyed a universal fame long before the *Faerie Queene* was sent to press. The Italian Renaissance and the French Renaissance put forth their finest flowers before the Elizabethan era was well in leaf.

At the outset there was promise in England of a different issue. At the end of the fifteenth and the beginning of the sixteenth century England saw bright flashes of humanist development. The scholarship and speculation of Thomas Linacre and of Sir Thomas More illumined the darkness for a brief season. At no long interval the poets Wyatt and Surrey brought another touch of radiance into the scene. To sanguine observers of Henry VIII's reign exploits seemed at hand which might challenge comparison with those of their great European contemporaries, Ariosto and Machiavelli in Italy, Rabelais and Clément Marot in France. But the promise proved delusive. Attractive as were the first emanations of Tudor humanism and Tudor poetry, they were gleams only, and quickly faded. When Surrey's muse was silenced, near half a century of darkness or hazy light intervened before the literary flame was to burn in England with ample or lasting glow.

Only from the year 1579, when Spenser and Sir Philip Sidney first gave earnest of their genius, did the stream of great literature flow in England continuously or with sustained force. The impulse grew in strength for thirty years and then decayed. The flourishing period of English Renaissance literature was not only belated, but was of short duration compared with that of France or Italy. At the extreme end of the sixteenth century the drama of the Renaissance in England scaled through one generation heights of which the movement alike in Italy and in France fell short. It is no insularity on the part of the English critic, there is no proof that he is 'sick of self-love', in the acknowledgement that the best Elizabethan drama betrays a more affluent inspiration and a deeper emotion than any drama of French or Italian workmanship. Yet this glorious compensation does not obscure the comparatively restricted bounds of English artistic energy during the era, nor may the historian overlook the tardiness of the English Renaissance in proving its strength, or the brevity of the period of its prosperity.

On the threshold of our present study of literary history we must divest ourselves of many modern prepossessions. Not till the eighteenth century opened, can England be said to have marched in the European van of intellectual progress. The supreme work of Shakespeare and Bacon belongs for the most part to the seventeenth rather than to the sixteenth century, and their pre-eminence gives them perhaps a place apart, but on any showing they were the youngest heirs of the spirit of the continental Renaissance. They were giants in the rearguard of the advancing host.

Through eight decades of the sixteenth century the intellectual activity of England lagged behind not only France and Italy, but even Germany and Spain. From Germany, Tudor England was content to borrow a reformed theology and much of her knowledge of art and science. The lessons that Spain had more especially to teach her seemed for near a century beyond her intellectual or political grasp. Spain's pioneer colonization of America implied a rare mental alertness. Whatever errors may be imputed to the Spanish occupation of the New World, the mighty exploit was born of a robust imagination and an intuitive command of the two complex sciences of navigation and government. England followed the guidance of Spain in this colonizing sphere of activity with tardiness and reluctance. Richard Hakluyt and Sir Walter Raleigh, who preached to England in the epoch of Shakespeare's manhood the duty of sustained colonial endeavour, bear ample testimony to their country's failure to appreciate the meaning of the Spanish example. They are eloquent in regrets of English unwillingness to learn the lesson that Spain was teaching. The French mind seized the Spanish hint more quickly than the English. Though French experiments in American colonization and exploration lacked the steady persistence of Spain, Frenchmen none the less made resolute endeavours to plant the French flag in Brazil, in Florida, and in Canada. These French designs compare favourably in their aims and results with the bold but ineffectual expeditions of Martin Frobisher, of Sir Humphrey Gilbert, and of Sir Walter

Raleigh's agents in Virginia.   There is nothing, at any rate, in the colonial history of Tudor England quite analogous to the fruitful achievements of Jacques Cartier or of his younger disciple, Samuel Champlain, on the northern confines of the American continent.[1]

The backwardness of England in the exploration and settlement of the newly discovered hemisphere oddly contrasts with the forwardness of Spain and even with the relatively modest activity of France.   Such discrepancies point a comprehensive moral.   Through all but the very close of the sixteenth century, the English mind proved less alert or less pliant than the continental mind, when confronted by the new conceptions of the era.   In love of political independence, in physical bravery and endurance, in mercantile aptitude, Tudor England never feared rivalry with foreign nations.   But slowness to appreciate nascent ideas and mistrust of artistic sentiment made it difficult for her during the epoch of the Renaissance to keep fully abreast of the intellectual culture of the other peoples of Western Europe.

II

ENGLAND'S INTELLECTUAL COMMERCE

It is needless to repeat the warning against treating sixteenth-century English literature, and Elizabethan literature more especially, as an isolated growth, as a plant rooted in English soil and drawing its sustenance from English earth. No argument or evidence can gainsay the fact that Elizabethan, like all Tudor literature, was an organism of varied fibre, much of which was rooted in foreign mould.

Although the spirit of the Renaissance came to fruition in England late, intellectual commerce with the Continent was active throughout the era, in varying degrees of intensity. Links to bind England to the great confederation of in-

[1] Cf. ' The Call of the West '— four articles by the present writer in *Scribner's Magazine* for 1907.

tellectual Europe were in existence from the outset, and, if often slender in texture, were never incapable, under due incitement, of increasing their strength.   Through the eight decades of her quiescence, Tudor England was absorbing, however slackly, foreign sustenance ; she was garnering, however inertly, foreign stimulus to future exertion.

No contemporary observer at any time underrated the debt that Tudor England owed to foreign culture.   Queen Elizabeth was regarded at home as the standard type of England's intellectual development, and one of the many compliments on the width of her intellectual horizon well interprets the general situation.   A poetic eulogist congratulated her on being

> not only in her mother-voice
> Rich in oration,

but he pointed out that she

> with phrases choice
> So on the sudden can discourse in Greek,
> French, Latin, Tuscan, Dutch, and Spanish, eke
> That Rome, Rhine, Rhone, Greece, Spain, and Italy
> Plead all for right in her nativity.[1]

Here we have a characteristically rough and irregular, but an almost exhaustive, enumeration of the foreign influences at work, not merely on the Queen, but on the best intellects among her subjects.   All these six tongues and literatures— Greek, French, Latin, Spanish, Dutch (i.e. German), and Tuscan—plead of right for recognition in casting the nativity of Tudor and, more especially, of Elizabethan literature.

A doctrine of the universal brotherhood of literary effort

---

[1] Joshua Sylvester's translation of Du Bartas's *Second Week* (4th edit. 1613, p. 333).   Queen Elizabeth's varied linguistic faculty, which is well attested by Ascham (*The Scholemaster*, ed. Mayor, p. 63), was noticed by many other French poets.   Ronsard (Book IV, § ii *infra*) together with the Huguenot poets Aubigné (Book V, § vii) and Grévin (Book VI, § iii) all write as admiringly on the subject as Du Bartas.   The great scholar, J. J. Scaliger, who visited England about 1590, wrote : 'Elisabeth Reyne sçavoit plus que tous les Grands de son vivant, & parloit Italien, François, Alemand, Latin, Grec & Anglois' (*Scaligeriana*, Cologne, 1695, p. 134).

was vaguely formulated by the literary profession in Elizabethan England. The cosmopolitan tendencies of the
Elizabethan world of letters were recognized by critics of
the day with perfect equanimity. The poet, Samuel Daniel,
who was under a large debt to the foreign muses, sought
a more or less philosophic interpretation of the hydra-headed
alien force which vitalized the Shakespearean era. Writing
in 1603, Daniel warily argued that it was

> the proportion [i. e. property] of a happy pen,
> Not to b' invassal'd to one monarchy,
> But dwell with all the better world of men
> Whose spirits all are of one community.

Culture, according to Daniel, declines to be hemmed in by
the barriers of nationality. On the contrary, Genius

> vents her treasure in all lands
> And doth a most secure commercement find.[1]

Varied was the argument which affirmed the benefits deriv-
able from commerce with foreign literature. Elizabethans
of philological proclivities boasted of the readiness of their
language to adapt foreign words to literary purposes. The
learned antiquary, Richard Carew, attributed to foreign reinforcements at the end of the sixteenth century 'the excellence
of the English tongue'. 'Seeing then we borrow,' Carew
wrote to his friend and fellow-archaeologist Camden, '(and
that not shamefully) from the Dutch, the Briton, the Roman,
the Dane, the French, the Italian, and Spaniard, how can our
stock be other than exceeding plentiful?' The dangers to be
apprehended from a polyglot vocabulary were easily exaggerated. 'It may be objected that such patching maketh
Littleton's hotch-pot of our tongue, and in effect brings the
same rather to a Babelish confusion than any one entire language.'[2] But the writer reaches the complacent conclusion of
every able and impartial judgement that the English tongue
owes to the foreign elements in its composition most of its
significance, ease, copiousness, and melody.

---

[1] Daniel's *Works*, ed. Grosart, vol. i, p. 287.
[2] Camden, *Remains Concerning Britain* (1870 edition), p. 47.

Ample evidence is available of the zeal with which Elizabethan men of letters scanned the achievements of the literary
heroes of the European Renaissance for literary suggestion.
A graphic illustration is worth offering here of the active
interest which the English public showed, when the English
Renaissance was flowering, in the personal experience of great
contemporary leaders of continental literature.   Much may be
gauged from the fact that the melancholy fortunes of Tasso's
concluding years were, while he was yet alive, the subject of
a play, which was several times performed at the chief theatre
in Elizabethan London.   The piece called *Tasso's Melancholy*
may well have had Ophelia's words for motto :

> O what a noble mind is here o'erthrown ! . . .
> The observed of all observers quite, quite down.

Goethe unconsciously followed in the Elizabethan playwright's
footsteps and proved a cognate breadth of interest by penning
a play on the same theme.   The text of the Elizabethan drama
no longer survives, but there is an extant record of its first
production by the theatrical manager Philip Henslowe at the
Rose Theatre in London on August 11, 1594.[1]   The play
proved exceptionally popular and profitable.   It was repeated
six times before the end of the year and at least four times
next year.   Tasso worked out his sad destiny while Shakespeare's genius was first proving its strength.   On April 25,
1595, the great Italian poet died, and within three weeks—on
May 14, 1595—the English piece of which he was the hero
was acted in London for at least the tenth time.   Nor did its
theatrical life then cease.   Six years later, early in 1601,
Dekker, a writer of genuine Elizabethan vigour, was employed to revise this play of *Tasso's Melancholy*, and it
would seem to have been revived at the London playhouse
while Shakespeare was planning his great tragedy of *Hamlet*.
' Tasso's Robe ' and ' Tasso's Picture ' long figured among the
properties of the Rose Theatre.   The stir that the Italian
master's personal tragedy roused in the sphere of Elizabethan
drama near the heyday of its activity points to only one

---

[1] Henslowe's *Diary*, ed. Greg, vol. i, pp. 19–22.

conclusion.   It is luminous proof of the briskness of the
literary and intellectual commerce of Elizabethan England
with the European continent at the end of the sixteenth
century.

III

THE INTERPRETATIVE FACULTY OF FRANCE

In estimating, with precision, the influence that France, our
sole immediate concern, exerted on England in this era of
intellectual stir, it is needful to define the part that France
played in the mighty movement of the European Renaissance,
and to apprehend the distinguishing features of the humanist
development within the bounds of her own territory.   It has
to be remembered that France was only one of the countries
whose influence helped to cast the nativity of Tudor culture.
There were many other influences at work—classical influences,
Italian and Spanish influences, and in the sphere of scholarship, art, and theology, German and Flemish influences.
'Rome, Rhine, Rhone, Greece, Spain, and Italy,' all plead for
recognition.

Yet I am prepared to defend the position that French culture
has a bearing on the development of Tudor culture, which
neither the classics nor Italian art and literature nor German
art and literature can on a broad survey be said to equal.
Two external kinds of considerations support this conclusion :
firstly, the political, social, and geographical relations between
the two countries, and secondly, the constitution or composition
of French culture.   Intercourse between England and France
was on the one hand closer than between England and any
other foreign country, and on the other hand France's
idiosyncrasy or individuality had unique qualification for
quickening England's imitative and assimilative instinct, when
the two were brought into conjunction.

It was the mission of France to bring to England something
more than the harvest of her own soil.   Though France had
not yet attained the military and political ascendancy over
Europe which marked the era of Louis XIV, she first became

in the sixteenth century that home or storehouse of culture and ideas, she first acquired those powers of collecting and transmitting culture and ideas, which soon led Paris to be styled the artistic and intellectual capital, not alone of France, but of Europe. Lucidity, clarity, precision of statement, together with a notable measure of urbanity, blitheness, and gaiety, became commanding characteristics of the French intellect during the sixteenth century. Such traits fitted her for a rôle of interpreter and tutor to other nations, not merely of her own culture and ideas, but of the culture and ideas which she absorbed from others. She had, then and later, great moments of original inspiration. But in the history of modern European civilization her interpretative faculty, her capacity for teaching without preaching, have given her as high a title to external fame and gratitude as any of her original contributions to thought or art. Her expository power has constituted her for fully three centuries a universal court of taste, an apostolate of humanism *urbi et orbi*, the world's *arbiter elegantiarum*. Such offices she first filled with effect in the sixteenth century, and her prentice hand of civilizing missionary was conspicuously exercised on Tudor England.

IV

The Culture of the French Renaissance

The culture of the French Renaissance is like Jacques's melancholy, 'compounded of many simples, extracted from many objects.' It is an amalgam of Attic grace and simplicity, of Latin directness, of Italian sensuousness, but it owes much of its colour to Gallic alertness and inventiveness of mind, to the Gallic spirit of airy mockery. The term which is often applied to the main idiosyncrasy of the French character, *l'esprit gaulois*, is a phrase which is difficult to translate. It is often confused unjustly with humorous obscenity. In its original manifestations, *l'esprit gaulois* implies three enviable qualities: firstly, flexibility of thought; secondly, gaiety, tending at times to levity and coarseness, but readily yielding to

pathetic tenderness; and thirdly, a melodious ease of frank
and simple utterance. Its main power comes from the volatile
wit, the good-natured raillery, of the native temperament, which
is never readily repressed even in serious situations. The
religious drama of mediaeval France has its episodes of banter
and laughter. There was no monotony about *l'esprit gaulois*;
it was impatient of stagnation; it was prone to favour change
of form and hue. Greece and modern Italy are the main
sources of inspiration for the French Renaissance. But the
native French soil which Greece and modern Italy fertilized,
contributed rich sustenance and fascinating iridescence of its
own.

There was no lack of literature in France of the fifteenth
century. Lyric and allegory, history and epic, farce and
religious drama flourished in France before the Renaissance
dawned. The school of Gallic literature, which immediately
preceded the Renaissance, was for the most part of a primitive
allegorical, or chivalric type. It deserves the attention of
English students because the pioneers of Tudor prose and
poetry, and even of Tudor drama, eagerly gleaned some direction and some energy from the literary harvest of late mediaeval
France. Tudor pioneers were often uncritical and unadven-
turous in their choice of French models. At the outset, at
any rate, they overlooked the vigorous freshness of Villon or
Comines, preferring the more torpid industry of Alan Chartier
and Christine de Pisan, whose fame was fanned at home and
abroad by royal and noble patronage. Better taste and judgement prevailed with a later generation of Tudor England,
which worshipped at the veteran shrine of Froissart and
also paid tribute to the contemporary vogue of Clément
Marot. Yet, despite the fact that Villon and Comines
lacked recognition across St. George's Channel, their achievement illustrates the sort of literary influence which mediaeval
France was capable of exerting. Villon was mainly a national
poet in whom racial or local sentiment was, perhaps, too
strongly developed to gain easily the ear of foreign readers.
Much of his verse is couched in a Parisian dialect, and is
addressed to the populace of Paris. But his original poetic

insight enabled him to interpret the blitheness, the frankness, the sensibility of his country's genius. He described what he felt and saw without disguise or restraint, and gave expression to a full-blooded humanity, frequently in terms of a savage coarseness. At the same time his poems are occasionally woven of that golden texture which is destined to make a universal appeal. Delicate metre and language clothe genuine pathos. Very touchingly does the poet hymn the transience of fame and beauty. Rarely have the regrets of reminiscence been more artistically phrased than in Villon's 'Ballade des dames du temps jadis' (Ballade of old-time Ladies), or in his 'Ballade des seigneurs du temps jadis' (Ballade of old-time Lords), with the two tuneful refrains 'Mais où sont les neiges d'antan ?' and ' Mais où est le preux Charlemaigne ?'

Something of the French breadth of sentiment which inspired Villon appears in the almost contemporary chronicle of Philippe de Comines, who, although born on the Flemish border of France, was a thorough Frenchman by temperament and domicile. Comines's chronicle shows how the old French spirit fostered the gift of vivacious, fluent, picturesque narrative. Comines combines with his power of vivid description a piquant irony and a reflective energy, which enable him convincingly to depict character and suggest motive. If Comines's predecessor Froissart may be compared with Livy, to Comines may be assigned some affinity with Tacitus. The erudition of the Renaissance ultimately brought French verse and prose, under Greek and Latin influence, to rare perfection of point and ease. Verse and prose were largely purged of turbidity, from which no mediaeval effort was quite free ; they acquired a more uniform polish. Nevertheless, the faculty of lively and piquant narrative, which Comines possessed in abundance, echoed, like Villon's poetic blitheness and sensibility, a veteran native note.

The ancient literary dispensation was not peremptorily rejected when the fresh dispensation of the Renaissance first claimed French allegiance. In the exuberant genius of Rabelais, the junior of Villon by fifty years, the tradition of Villon, in its unregeneracy and immodesty, joins hands for a season with the alien learning and insight of Greece and Italy. The poet Clément Marot, a pious editor of Villon's work, made, too, a humbler effort to reconcile the old spirit with the new. The result of the compromise was something of a patchwork, which challenged many canons of art.

But while the past poetry was not quickly dispossessed, it became plain, when the sixteenth century was nearing middle age, that the old Gallic taste and temper were to pass for the time under the sway of a new poetic inspiration, and were to adapt themselves to new poetic channels. When Rabelais and Marot laid down their pens, the old forces in the French literary arena showed exhaustion, and the literary activity of France ceased to pursue the ancient ways. The French Renaissance finally proclaimed drastic innovations and de-creed divorce with the domestic tradition. Graeco-Italian influences took control of the literary and poetic stage. In the work of Ronsard and his friends of the Pléiade, all the innovating temper of the French Renaissance came by its own. Ronsard and his friends deliberately rejected as vulgar and barbarous the old French idiom and the pre-scriptive usages of the Gallic spirit. They deliberately grafted the nation's poetry on Greek and Italian stocks. Pindar became a French hero. Anacreon, whom French scholars first discovered, and Petrarch, whom they naturalized, were gods of the new idolatry. Ronsard and his allies counted themselves reformers, and claimed to be moved by a patriotic ardour. Their pretensions were not ques-tioned. Gallic ' saltness' often lent zest to their labours, but the old crudity was effaced. The silvery melodies and clas-sical refinement of the new lyric outburst won instant popularity and caught not merely their fellow countrymen's ear, but many a foreign ear as well. The Elizabethan poets admitted that they fetched a new elegance from France ; they quaffed, one said, copious draughts of the new French Helicon.[1] With what measure of truth such words were spoken will presently appear.

---

[1] Cf. *Returne from Parnassus*, 1606, Act I. Sc. ii. 275 (ed. Macray, p. 86), and Joseph Hall's *Satires*, Book VI, Sat. i, 1598 (ed. Singer, 1824, p. 159).

V

FRENCH DISCIPLESHIP TO GREECE AND ROME

The processes at work in the evolution of Ronsard and the Graeco-Italian school of the French Renaissance were perfectly plain and natural. At the end of the fifteenth century the newly-discovered Greek literature gripped the finest French intellect with the hold of passion, nor was the grip relaxed through the sixteenth century. At the end of the fifteenth century there was inaugurated in France that golden age of pure scholarship which is identified with the names of Budaeus, the Scaligers, and the Étiennes (or Stephenses). A dozen others deserve mention in the same breath. Greek professorships were founded not in Paris alone, but in numerous provincial universities. Greek manuscripts were collected for Francis I's royal library.

French classical scholarship, like all branches of modern culture, owed much to Italy. It was in Italy that almost all the great classical authors were printed for the first time. A few were first printed in Germany, and only four or five in France. But France vastly improved on the Italian type of classical scholarship. The Gallic spirit even there was active, and relieved learning of most of the burden of dullness.

Although French original editions of the great classics are not numerous, France quickly excelled Italy in its faculty for textual criticism and interpretation, and above all for translation into the vernacular. Anacreon, Phaedrus, and Plutarch in his rôle of philosopher, are the most notable authors which France first rescued from manuscripts. But the French recensions and annotations of the text of authors of the rank of Aeschylus and Plato first brought the Hellenic genius home to the intelligence of modern Europe. The first effective textual criticism of the Greek Testament came from French pens.

The earliest French printers were scholars of repute, and were themselves skilful editors. One practical service which the French printers rendered European scholarship is especially characteristic of the genius of the French Renaissance; they refashioned with fine taste Greek typography. They set the European pattern of Greek print for two hundred years.

As scholars, Tudor England fell lamentably behind their French neighbours. According to Sir Richard Jebb, Richard Bentley, the Greek scholar of the end of the seventeenth and the beginning of the eighteenth century, was the first Englishman who can be classed with the great scholars of the French Renaissance. Sixteenth-century English scholars were few, and their steps were halting. Nearly all their inspiration came from the energetic humanism of France.

A larger benefit which the French humanists offered foreigners as well as their own countrymen was that of translating the great Latin and Greek classics into vernacular French. Not the most erudite professors of Greek or Latin disdained this work, with the result that wellnigh every great Latin or Greek author was, before the sixteenth century was very old, at the disposal of the French people in accurate and idiomatic French. An interesting and popular critical tract of the period by the classical scholar and printer of Lyons, Étienne Dolet, which was first published in 1540 and was many times reprinted, was entitled *La manière de bien traduire d'une langue en autres* (On the manner of translating well from one language into others). Dolet's laws of translation are wonderfully modern and illuminating. His sagacious injunctions to the translator loyally to study the idiom of the language from which, as well as the language into which, he translates, may now sound obvious and commonplace, but they are not obsolete. They were obeyed with such skill by Dolet and his contemporaries that one or two Greek authors— notably Plutarch—became in the French translation of the sixteenth century, and have since remained, standard works of French literature. Plutarch's *Lives* also became in an English translation an Elizabethan classic. But it is significant to remember that the Elizabethan translation of Plutarch was rendered not from the Greek original, but from the contemporary French. That fact, I think I shall be able to show, illustrates a widely-distributed feature of the literary relations between the two countries in the sixteenth century.

It was not only in scholarship or in pure literature that the classical studies of Renaissance France bore luxurious fruit. The intellectual energy of the nation was seeking a wider field of exercise. Roman history and Roman law stimulated and stirred the French intellect hardly less than Greek language and literature.

Though Renaissance study of Roman law was begun in Italy, it was perfected in France. Andrea Alciati (1492–1550), a native of Milan, did his most notable work as professor of law at the universities of Avignon (from 1521) and of Bourges (from 1522 onwards). From him Europe is commonly credited with deriving a true apprehension of the significance of Roman law. He was the first to appraise the value of the legal system of Rome, and he first brought to the effort literary grace and perspicuity. Erasmus, most eminent and enlightened of critics, applied to Alciati the eulogy which Cicero passed on Q. Mutius Scaevola, the prince of jurists of ancient Rome, ' iurisperitorum eloquentissimus.'[1] Hardly less distinguished than Alciati was Jacques de Cujas (1522–90), professor of law at Bourges, a Frenchman who evolved modern juridical science out of his investigation into Roman codes. Cujas, the junior of Alciati by thirty years, survived him by more than forty, and the prolonged era of their joint labours identified the French Renaissance through nearly all its course with brilliant revelations of the significance of law in both principle and practice. A third French professor of the period, Jean Bodin (1530–96), was led by similar classical avenues to a new political philosophy, to a formal theory of government. Bodin's

---

[1] Alciati was also famous as the earliest and most popular of modern emblem writers, and as the inventor thereby of an ingenious literary relaxation, which was characteristic of the Renaissance temper. Alciati's *Emblems* are proverbs in Italian verse symbolically illustrated. They were first published at Milan in 1522, and soon achieved a very large circulation in France, where a translation came out in 1536. The continental editions of the sixteenth century are said to have numbered more than fifty. Though no edition appeared in England, eighty-six of Alciati's emblems are adopted by Geffrey Whitney in his *Choice of Emblems*, Leyden, 1586. (See reprint, edited by Henry Green, 1866, pp. 245-6.)

systematic survey of political ideas was fresh and vigorous enough to give the cue to many of Montesquieu's generalizations. Not until the extreme end of the sixteenth century, when Hooker made the attempt from an Anglican Churchman's point of view, did any Englishman venture to treat politics on such comprehensive lines. Elizabethan students were long content to make Bodin's exposition of political theory an academic text-book.

The political literature of the Renaissance was, like almost all Renaissance effort, born in Italy. *Il Principe* of Machiavelli was the earliest manifesto of Renaissance polity. A strenuous plea for autocracy, it long enjoyed a universal vogue; in spite of obvious prejudice and partisanship, its authority was not readily effaced. Though Bodin and the French Renaissance school of political thought ranged beyond the limits of Machiavelli's masterly defence of despotism, Machiavelli's illiberal argument colours Bodin's theoretic disquisitions. But as the century waned, Machiavelli's credit in France dwindled. The Huguenots directly challenged the Machiavellian principle of politics. Concentrating their vision on the history of the Roman Republic, the Huguenot thinkers elaborated a practical scheme of constitutional government, which adapted to monarchical conditions the republican conception of liberty. Some of the Huguenot pamphleteers advocated incidentally tyrannicide as an instrument of political reform, but the main importance of the Huguenot political doctrine lay in a frank recognition of popular right and in an assumption of the reasonableness of democracy. English critics of the policy of the first two Stuart kings found serviceable arguments in the Huguenot literature of sixteenth-century France.

Yet broad and deep as was the debt of the French Renaissance to classical teaching, the classical lesson was not always accepted quite submissively. Many a phase of classical speculation was exposed to censorious scrutiny. The Gallic spirit set up a barrier against philosophical servility, and guaranteed independence of thought. Revolution was always in process as well as restoration.

Numerous Frenchmen of the Renaissance in their philosophical, ethical, or logical inquiries, boldly questioned the
classical tradition.   Peter Ramus, or Pierre de la Ramée
(1515–72), startled the University of Paris in 1536 with a thesis
professing to demonstrate that whatever Aristotle had sought
to establish was wrong.   It was on what he viewed as the
ruins of Aristotelianism that Ramus laid the foundation of a
new system of logic which Bacon learned at Cambridge.   The
youngest hero of the French Renaissance, Michel de Montaigne (1533–92), created a new type of literature and speculation in those familiar essays which Bacon echoed with the zeal
of a disciple.   Montaigne, who discussed in the Pagan spirit
ethics and religion, declined with a charming frankness to
bow the head to any authority, ancient or modern.   Innovators like Ramus and Montaigne were classicists by training.
Latin was the language of their daily life.   Yet their work
proved that a revolutionary tendency coloured the intellectual
enfranchisement which issued under the spell of the Gallic
spirit from sympathetic study of Greek and Latin literature.

VI

The Italian Element

The debt of the French Renaissance to modern Italy is
hardly less conspicuous than its debt to Greece or Rome.
The course of politics quickened those racial affinities which
made France an easy prey to the sensuous charm of modern
Italian art and poetry.

It was a thirty years' war which France waged on Italy that
brought French culture largely under Italian sway.   The
military invasion of Italy by France was inaugurated by
the French king Charles VIII in 1494.   Full thirty years
later it reached a close which wrought physical disaster on
the invading host.   Yet the French rout under the walls of
Pavia in 1525 merely served to tighten the bonds which
linked France to Italian culture.   The last of the royal French
invaders, Francis I, who was taken prisoner in the fatal

contest, was enslaved by Italian taste. The king loved the
fanciful titles of 'le père des Muses' and 'le restaurateur des
lettres'. Ronsard hailed him as 'Nourrisson de Phébus, des
Muses le mignon'.[1] The Phoebus who nurtured Francis I
was of Roman lineage, and the Muses of whom he was the
darling were denizens of Tuscany.

During Francis I's long reign (1515–47), court and society in
France fostered an extravagant adoration of Italian art as well
as of Italian letters. Leonardo da Vinci, the most catholically
endowed of Italian artists, Andrea del Sarto, one of the most
skilful of Italian colourists, and Benvenuto Cellini, the
greatest of Italian artificers, were among the French king's
guests. At his bidding Italian architects converted the
feudal castle of Fontainebleau into a sumptuous Italian palace,
which became a paradise of Italian art. Francis I's son,
Henry II; his grandsons, Francis II, Henry III, and Charles IX;
and their successor, Henry IV, all vied with one another in
embellishing that edifice with noble ornament of sculpture
and metal work, with parks and gardens, which enhanced the
beauty of Francis I's design, and strengthened its Italian spirit.
When the Republic of Florence, the chief home of the Italian
Renaissance, fell in 1530, and was finally merged in the Duchy
of Tuscany, Florentine refugees found no warmer welcome
than in Paris. Much Italian literature was penned in the French
capital under the patronage of 'le monarque François', and
was printed at French presses. The Italian conquest of French
taste was sealed in 1533 by the marriage of Francis I's son and
successor, Henry II, with Catherine de' Medici. The Italian
consort of the French prince was the daughter of Lorenzo de'
Medici, Duke of Urbino, the last representative of the most
cultured of Florentine families, whose features Michelangelo
has immortalized in his famous statue of Il Pensieroso. After
Queen Catherine's husband died in 1539, her three sons filled
in succession the French throne, and during those thirty years
(1559–89), she found as Queen Mother full scope for her
dominating temper. Her political ambition was nurtured by

----

[1] Ronsard, Œuvres, vii. 178.

study of Machiavelli's *Prince*—that stimulating Italian plea for despotism which its author had dedicated to her father. But, in spite of political distraction, she never ceased to worship the muses of her native land. The Louvre under her sovereignty was illumined by foreign art and learning. Her fellow countrymen, Aretino and Tasso, greeted her as a queen of Parnassus; Ronsard and his comrades saluted her as an Italian Pallas, a worthy scion of the Medicean race which had preserved Athens from oblivion.[1] The Queen Mother's two younger sons, Charles IX and Henry III, were carefully educated in the spirit of the Italian Renaissance under her direction, and they kept the Italian temper of the French court well alive till near the end of the century.

No unmixed good issued from the Italian predominance. Italian culture cherished classical scholarship and speculation. The classical sympathies of France were reinforced by Italian example. Italian predilections were not prejudicial to Frenchmen's enthusiasm for classical study. But there were elements of density and of preciosity in the Italian temper which tended to cloud the scholarly vision and to cloak the lucidity of the Greek or Latin. In the vernacular poetry of France Italian influence encroached on Hellenism as the century aged. Vicious affectation and confused pedantry threatened the well-being of poetic effort, and checked the native impulse, which made for clearer light.

In 1589 the Italianate House of Valois fell with the assassination of Henry III. The kindred house of Bourbon filled the vacant throne in the person of Henry of Navarre. The new king owed his fame to his chieftainship of the Huguenots. The versatile culture which his grandmother, Margaret of Navarre, cherished, coloured his mind, but the aesthetic code of Italy which swayed the fashionable world of

---

[1] Cf. Ronsard's *Œuvres*, iii. 379 (Le Bocage Royal) :

> Elle, se souvenant des vertus de sa race . . .
> Laquelle a remis sus les lettres et les arts . . .
> Sans cette noble race en oubli fust Athènes.

In *Les Poésies inédites de Catherine de Médicis* (Paris, 1884), M. Édouard Fremy gives a good sketch of Queen Catherine's varied accomplishments.

orthodox France made smaller appeal to him than to his predecessors.

A sense of nationality deepened in France with the peaceful solution of her internal strife. Henry of Navarre, who brought the century's civil and religious warfare to an end, invigorated the sense of patriotism and discouraged dependence on the foreigner. The epoch closed amid cries of revolt against the French poets' servitude to Italian conceits. Patriotic critics denounced as treason the literary habit of assimilating Italian forms of speech. There was a vigorous attempt to dethrone Petrarch and Tasso, acknowledged masters of the poetic realm in France as well as in Italy. But the raising of the standard of rebellion produced no sudden collapse of the old régime. The Italian tide ebbed slowly in French literature. It was flowing most strongly when Elizabethan literature was born, and the French poetry which flourished contemporaneously with the Elizabethan was deeply tinged with Italian hues.

VII

The Diffusion of Renaissance Culture in France

The culture of the French Renaissance repays examination from many points of view. Not merely do its constituent elements and the manner of their intermingling offer much food for critical study, but the dissemination or geographical distribution of Renaissance refinement through the country contributed to its general effect, and invites inquiry. With almost magical celerity the culture of the Renaissance diffused itself through the length and breadth of France. The force and influence of the movement were thereby strengthened abroad as well as at home.

Paris was the main focus of light in the glow of the French Renaissance. The great capital had rare powers of attraction for the rest of France and for the world.[1] None the less the country outside Paris fed the flame of culture with a signal

[1] Cf. James Howell's *Instructions for Forreine Travell*, 1642 (ed. Arber, p. 28), 'Paris, that huge though dirty theatre of all nations.' Howell is writing of Paris as he knew it in 1618.

efficiency. The provinces, with their local parliaments and local
traditions, encouraged a sentiment of local independence and of
neighbourly rivalry, without seriously imperilling the country's
homogeneity.   The political divisions gave cultured energy a
series of competing rallying-points. A small district of the south
formed during most of the century the affiliated kingdom of
Navarre, and that *imperium in imperio* played a noble part in
the development of the new enlightenment. From 1527 to
1549 Margaret, Queen Consort of Navarre, Francis I's sister
and Henry of Navarre's grandmother, made her palace at
Nérac a nursery of art and letters, which was hardly second
in brilliance to the Louvre or to Fontainebleau. The court
of Navarre, whose accomplished and liberal-minded queen
divided her enthusiasm between light-hearted Boccaccio and
austere Calvin, brought into the sphere of taste a genuinely
catholic tolerance. Nor did such a provincial centre as Nérac
stand alone. France was honeycombed with citadels of culture,
which helped to broaden, fortify, and vivify national sympathy
with art and literature.

Well might Marot liken the cultured eminence of the town
of Lyons, for example, to Troy or Mount Pelion. From
the early days of the century many cities boasted annual
poetic competitions—*Grands Jours*—which were seasons and
ceremonies of popular holiday. Ronsard, the kingly poet of
the Renaissance, ranked above all his many honours the silver
statuette of Minerva which the city of Toulouse awarded him in
place of the customary sprig of eglantine at its annual literary
tournament of 'Les Jeux Floraux'. Nearly three hundred years
after Ronsard, Victor Hugo won the like prize at a subsequent
celebration of the same festival of Toulouse ; so inveterate was
the literary tradition of provincial France, and so deep were
its roots planted during the epoch of the Renaissance. Truthfully Ronsard apostrophized ' toute la France ' as ' terre pleine
de villes ' and ' d'hommes aux Muses accorts '. With his gaze
fixed beyond Paris the national poet may win pardon for the
exaggeration in his hymn to his fatherland (*Œuvres*, v. 287) :

> Dedans l'enclos de nos belles citez
> Mille et mille arts y sont exercitez.

The activity of provincial universities made twenty towns
rivals of Paris in the promotion of humanist education. Many
provincial French universities enjoyed, indeed, in specialized
lines of study a world-wide repute which Paris failed to reach.
The religious wars threatened the prosperity of some of the
southern seats of learning. The course of study was interrupted, and their pecuniary resources diminished. But
reverses proved only temporary, and almost all the universities
of France can boast a record of sixteenth-century achievement
to which Oxford and Cambridge were during the period
strangers. The medical school of Montpellier and the law
school of Bourges drew its students from all Europe. Of
Lyons and Bordeaux, Toulouse and Poitiers, Orleans and
Caen, a like story can be told. Provincial professors often
held the ear of the civilized world.

No less worthy of commemoration is the fact that in some
forty French provincial towns printing presses were at work
without intermission from the earliest years of the sixteenth
century, and were in constant process of multiplication in the
hundred years that followed. Scholars and men of letters
invariably directed these typographic enterprises. Such a
phase of the intellectual history of France strangely contrasts
with the circumstance that in England London alone can
claim an uninterrupted succession of printers during the same
era. Neither Oxford nor Cambridge, England's only two
universities at the time, saw a printing press permanently
established within its boundaries till the eighth decade of the
sixteenth century. Nor is it irrelevant to notice that itinerant
sellers of printed leaflets, mainly popular songs or satires, made
their first appearance in France at the end of the fifteenth
century. ' Les bisouarts,' as these ballad-mongers and pedlars
in printed wares were called, are of older standing in France
than in any other country of Europe. Thus few French
towns through the sixteenth century lacked their coteries of
humanists, their poetic schools, their learned presses, or their
colporteurs. There is nothing in the annals of the English
Renaissance which can compare with this diffusion of
intellectual energy and ambition.

The roots of Renaissance culture were planted deep in France and fertilized all the land. Therein probably lies the key to the mystery why the progress of the French Renaissance was neither perceptibly retarded nor prejudiced by the rapid growth in France of the reformed religious doctrine or by the desperate and absorbing struggle for supremacy which was long waged between it and the old faith. The problem is puzzling. The tenacity of the Renaissance spirit which came of the dissemination of the movement through France may suggest a solution. The greatest Frenchman of the century, Calvin, invented an austere formula, which denied salvation to intellectual or artistic enthusiasm. Calvin's disciples in foreign lands anathematized profane art and letters unreservedly. Calvin himself, a humanist by education, liberally qualified in practice his philistine creed, even after his migration to Geneva. Huguenots, who remained in France, reconciled acceptance of his dogma with the pursuit of intellectual and artistic ideals.

Much will be said of the contribution of the Huguenots to French literature at a later stage. Here I will only point out that humanism and the Reformed religion on French soil remained, in spite of the Calvinist's dismal inhibition, for the most part loyal allies. At the outset almost every humanist favoured the Reformed faith. At any rate, the humanist shared with the Reformer a common suspicion of mediaeval convention. The cultured court of Navarre was wholly identified with the religious Reformation. At the outset humanism found no such warm welcome in the orthodox circles of Paris as among the French Reformers. The Sorbonne in early days detected in the new Greek scholarship a menace of orthodoxy. But the anti-humanist prejudice soon decayed among French lovers of ancient dogma, and the progress of humanism enjoyed the sanction of Roman Catholicism. Both French Protestant and French Catholic found indeed a practicable way of reconciling humanism with their religious convictions. Despite the patent fact that humanist principles of intellectual freedom were inimical to the rule alike of Rome and Geneva, neither religious party in France could resist the humanist fascination. Followers of both creeds found a means of accommodating their conceptions of religious truth with humanist ambitions. When civil war broke out between French Catholics and Huguenots, humanism continued to flourish in both camps. If Ronsard and the leaders of the Pléiade were Catholic laymen loyal enough to the faith to fill abbacies and other ecclesiastical benefices,—Palissy the potter, Goujon the sculptor, Goudimel the musician, Ramus the logician, the Étiennes the scholar-printers, Scaliger the Greek critic, were all frank in their avowal of Huguenot or Reformation sympathies.

Calvin, the high-priest of the French Reformation, for all his own and his followers' perverse professions to the contrary, bore, to the last, traces of his humanist training and of his intellectual affinity with humanism. He rendered French humanism the immense service of first investing French prose with a definitely logical precision. Nor did Calvin's ingrained sense of scholarship stop there. Under his auspices, Henri Étienne was suffered to pursue at Geneva those scholarly studies which conspicuously dignified the humanist cause, while there was devised in Geneva at Calvin's suggestion a system of education which owed its triumph to its humanist leaven. No fact bears more graphic testimony to the strength of the impression which Renaissance sentiment made on the French mind, and no fact is of greater significance in the study of French influence on Elizabethan literature, than this liberal identification of French humanism with French Protestantism. The pervasive influence of French humanism penetrated the dense walls of Calvin's theocratic state. French humanism derived a hallowing grace in the sight of English puritans from the sanction of the French Reformers.

A kindred inference may be drawn from the respect for literature which the French Renaissance fostered among wealthy men of a middle station in life. Humanism moulded the lives and immortalized the names of many Frenchmen who made no bid for the professional credit of authorship and whose activities were largely absorbed by the practical pursuit of non-literary vocations.

Jean Grolier and Jacques Auguste De Thou are still regarded through the civilized world as emperors of taste among lovers of books, and their careers help to indicate the alluring versatility of the culture of the French Renaissance. Book-collecting was the pursuit through which Grolier and De Thou reached their enviable eminence in the annals of French civilization. They are now perhaps best remembered by the artistic beauty of the bookbinding, which distinguished their private libraries. But both men were amateur critics of literature and admitted no volumes to their shelves that lacked intrinsic literary interest. Their ambitions were many-sided. The elder of the two, Grolier, a friend of Francis I, spent much time as a diplomatic agent in Rome and other cities of Italy. It was in Italy that he laid the foundations of his great collection. The younger of the two, De Thou, was a lawyer and the president of the Paris Parlement. A history of his own time, from his pen, is a sagacious contribution to historical and autobiographical literature, but he belongs professionally to men of affairs and not to men of letters. These two standard-bearers of culture in the citizen army of the Renaissance were not, strictly speaking, contemporaries. Grolier was born in 1479 and died in 1565, when he was in his eighty-sixth year. De Thou was born in 1553, and lived on till 1617. Their two lives cover a consecutive period of one hundred and thirty-eight years, and are conterminous with the course of the French Renaissance wellnigh from start to finish. From the opening to the closing of the sixteenth century the humanist spirit of the Renaissance continuously commended itself through its comprehensiveness of aim to legal, official, and mercantile society of France no less than to royalty, nobility, and academic or professedly literary circles.

VIII

Tudor Politics: the Loss of Calais

In the comparative study of the literature of two countries it is especially necessary to take due note of the sort of intercourse, political and social, which was carried on between the peoples, before the attempt be made to measure the literary indebtedness of the one to the other. Literary ideas, poetic ideas, often circulate through the world in so mysteriously detached and isolated a way that, when a definite process of transference is alleged, it is prudent to ascertain whether or no the hard material fact of historical intercommunications will support the allegation of borrowing. Certain historical conditions must accompany transference of literary example and suggestion. Avowed translation stands on an obvious footing of its own. No miscalculation of cause and effect is possible there. But imitation, adaptation, assimilation of suggestion, all of which mould literary composition, are more stealthy and more subtly penetrating agents than frankly direct translation. They are factors which call for circumspect handling. It is not only avowed translation from the French which in my belief largely fashioned Tudor literature, but adaptation, imitation, and assimilation of suggestion as well. Agents so insidious and elusive cannot be confidently analysed until we apprehend the political and social atmospheres which envelop their working.

The political and diplomatic relations of France and Tudor England are pertinent topics of preliminary study. Through the middle ages England and France had waged almost constant battle. The conclusion of the 100 years' war in 1453 is not marked by much cordiality between the peoples. Yet even then something might have been said for Pope's epigram, which was suggested long afterwards by the dependence of England on French taste in Charles II's reign:

> We conquered France, but felt our captive's charms,
> Her arts victorious triumphed o'er our arms.

In the course of the strife of the fourteenth and fifteenth centuries England had claimed the whole and occupied much of French territory. The only French land which she held at the peace of 1453 was Calais and the adjoining Marches. This strip of France remained an English possession through the first eight-and-fifty years of the sixteenth century. For two hundred and eleven years Calais was a material and substantial link between the two countries. It was a stronghold of English commerce, and a military fortress which was reckoned an impregnable protection of the English coast from invasion and a valuable starting-point for her own foreign aggressions. To it the city of Boulogne was temporarily added for nine middle years of the sixteenth century. For a season Tudor England fervently hugged the old national ambition of becoming a continental power. Tudor England was reluctant to acknowledge political advantage in her natural title to insularity.

Political or diplomatic isolation was never indeed deemed either practicable or quite reputable by English statesmanship, and the changed aims and conceptions of international policy which gained strength through Europe in the sixteenth century shortened the dividing lines between England and the continent. During the reign of Henry VII new diplomatic theories of the balance of power were inaugurated in Europe, and France and England, despite preliminary threatenings of warfare, were, through the early years of the sixteenth century, brought into alliance, for the first of many times, against a common rival, the Emperor. The diplomatic turnings of the political wheel, which issued in the protracted duel between Elizabethan England and Spain, fostered a political understanding between France and England during a great part of Henry VIII's reign and during nearly the whole of Queen Elizabeth's reign. Henry VIII frankly acknowledged the principle of the balance of power when he devised, according to popular tradition, his bold motto, *cui adhaereo praeest*, —'the party to which I adhere getteth the upper hand.' There was a growing sentiment throughout the century that England was politically bound to the continent by a loose federal tie. An Elizabethan observer remarked, 'France and Spain are, as it were, the scales in the balance of Europe, and England the tongue or holder of the balance.'[1] The English 'tongue' habitually inclined to the French scale rather than to the Spanish.

Such breaches of the peace as interrupted the flow of

[1] Camden's *Annals*, edit. 1688, p. 223.

diplomatic cordiality between France and Tudor England quickly led, like lovers' quarrels, to new assurances of political affection. When Henry VIII ascended the throne there was a general belief that an era of peace was securely installed. The millennium was confidently anticipated at no distant date. But the omens proved deceitful, and a new Anglo-French war belied peaceful anticipations. The brief struggle was not, however, reopened for some thirty years, and a marked avowal of friendliness filled that pacific interval. From 1513 to 1543 the diplomatic atmosphere powerfully encouraged the passage of French culture into England. A notable event opened the auspicious period. The marriage of the French king Louis XII to Henry VIII's sister, Mary, made the French court, for the short season that the monarch survived his marriage, a rendezvous of English nobility and gentry. The English princess's chamberlain was Lord Berners, who proved his French sympathies by translating Froissart. Palsgrave, the author of the first exhaustive French - English grammar, was her chaplain. Moreover, among the new French queen's personal attendants was Anne Boleyn, who prolonged her stay in the French Palace for seven years, and subsequently, as Henry VIII's second wife, infected the English court with markedly French predilections. Anne Boleyn, who was Queen Elizabeth's mother, ranks high among English apostles of French culture.

Meanwhile, the splendid meeting of Francis I, that magnifico of the Renaissance, with the English king near Calais, on the Field of the Cloth of Gold in 1521, worthily inaugurated Henry VIII's loyal discipleship to the French king in matters of taste. Henry wrote French verse on the rather limping model which was set by his French brother. With his eyes fixed on the recent building of Fontainebleau, he superintended the erection of his gorgeous palace of Nonsuch near Cheam in Surrey, and like the French king, he brought architects and artificers from Italy. Henry VIII's endowment of regius professors in Greek, Latin, and Hebrew at both Cambridge and Oxford in 1540 imitated in spirit and closely followed in point of time Francis I's establishment of like chairs in his new foundation of the Collège de France in 1530. Henry VIII sent his natural son, the Earl of Richmond, to Francis's court to share the education of the French king's sons, and the English youth's tutor and companion was that Earl of Surrey who, with Sir Thomas Wyatt, inaugurated Renaissance poetry in England. The trend of diplomacy encouraged Henry VIII and his French court to accept French guidance in matters of culture.

Towards the end of Henry VIII's reign the ancient military strife between the two countries was resumed. Diplomatic pressure brought the English king into a fresh alliance with the Emperor, and France fomented Scottish enmity of England. The main result for the time was an extension of English hold on French soil. France surrendered Boulogne, and for seven years the two seaports of Boulogne and Calais were both under English dominion. But the conquest was not maintained. France chafed under the indignity and recovered Boulogne of Henry VIII's son and successor, Edward VI. Within another eight years, at the close of the brief succeeding reign of Henry VIII's eldest daughter Mary, France and England were at war for a third time in the century. The short campaign robbed England of Calais for ever. In 1558, for the first time for two hundred years, England was deprived of all footing on the European continent.

The unexpected humiliation was a source of deep grief to the English people, and overwhelmed the English sovereign, Queen Mary, with a fatal melancholy. The English crown, she said, had lost its brightest jewel. But the heavy cloud had for England a silver lining. Although Elizabethan diplomacy long nursed the delusive hope that the lost dependency might be restored to England, the transference of the territory to France was in the interest of harmony. It cancelled a French grievance and removed an old source of international discord.

The capture of Calais stirred the French muse, and the poetic celebrations of the event deserve a passing notice. It is the only military episode involving French and English interests jointly, which has left much impression on French

poetry of the era, and the chastened note was of happy
augury. The English defeat evoked from French poets a
patriotic demonstration whose tone shows sober complacency
and little vindictive vaunting. The most thoughtful of French
poets of the age, Joachim Du Bellay, whose sentiment towards
England was less charitable than that of his colleagues,
went no further in his *Hymne au roy sur la prinse de Calais*
than an assurance that the body of France, long mutilated by
' le furieux Anglois', was now made whole.[1] A popular
French versifier of the Renaissance school, Olivier de
Magny, gave, in an ode, gentler expression of the patriotic
elation which 'la prise de Calais' excited in France. The
good news seemed to the poet almost too good to be
true:

> Ce Calais inexpugnable,
> Ce vieil rampart des Angloys,
> Qu'on disoit tant imprenable,
> Est-il pris a ceste fois?

Through forty-six such stanzas the Frenchman modestly ex-
patiated on the glorious miracle.[2] French humanism of the
strictest classical type shared the general jubilation, and
Adrian Turnebus, the eminent Greek professor at Paris,
voiced the national satisfaction at this dismissal of England
from French soil in a voluble, but temperate, *Panegyricus
de Calisio capto*:

> Nunc naufragus Anglus
> Eiectusque miserque suae est illisus arenae.[3]

The event left clearer trace on the popular chanson, and even
on French drama. At least six popular songs on the triumph
of France and sorrow of England were hawked about Paris
and the provinces.

> Calais, ville imprenable,
> Recognois ton seigneur,

[1] Du Bellay, *Œuvres*, 1597, ff. 170 et seq.
[2] De Magny, *Odes*, 1876, ii. p. 24.
[3] Gruter, *Delitiae C. Poetarum Gallorum* (1619), pars iii, 1014. There
was another Latin poem by a Frenchman, Guillaume Paradin, which bore
the title : ' De Motibus Galliae et expugnato receptoque Itio Caletorum,
Anno MD.LVIII.' Leyden, 1558, 4to.

was chanted in street and lane.[1]   A morality play, *La Reprise de Calais*, mainly consisting of a placid conversation between an Englishman and a Frenchman, was popular on the Paris stage.   There the Frenchman piously assigns the national victory to God:

> De ceste victoire
> Or doncques la gloire
>   Fault a Dieu donner,
> Qui Calais nous donne.
> C'est l'antique bourne,
>   Pour France bourner.[2]

In England the humiliation went unsung.   A ballad in defence of Lord Wentworth, the English commander who was put on his trial for the loss of the French town, is the sole poetic record in English of the disaster, and that unique declaration is no longer extant.[3]

The crisis of Calais left no lasting resentment on either English or French minds, in spite of the passing thrill in French poetry.   None of the subtler ties of cultured sentiment or diplomatic interest which bound England to her neighbour were effectively loosened by the shock.   The French poets were content with the victory and cherished no animosity against the vanquished.   Near the beginning of Queen Elizabeth's reign the English queen sent an army into France to support a domestic revolt of French Protestants against the established government.   But this somewhat hesitating act of war was followed immediately by 'an honourable and joyful peace betwixt the queen's majesty and the French king, their realms dominions and subjects'.   The treaty was signed at Troyes on April 12, 1564, eleven days before Shakespeare's birth, and on his birthday it was proclaimed in France amid general rejoicings.   Throughout the

---

[1] Le Roux de Lincy, *Recueil des Chants Historiques Français depuis le XIIe jusqu'au XVIIIe siècle*, ii. 211. M. de Lincy cites a Parisian publication of 1559, *Recueil des plus belles Chansons de ce temps mis en trois parties*, for the chief chansons on the capture of Calais.

[2] L. Petit de Julleville, *La Comédie et les mœurs en France au moyen âge*. Paris, 1886, p. 183.

[3] A ballad called *The Purgacion of . . . Lord Wentworth* was licensed for publication in April, 1559. See Arber's *Registers*, i. 101.

dramatist's lifetime the political relations of England and France were mainly governed by this convention. In June, 1564, splendid fêtes took place at Lyons, when the French king, Charles IX, received the Order of the Garter from the English queen's ambassadors. French poets greeted the union of French and English hearts. Within six years of the English loss of Calais the poetic leader of the French Renaissance, Ronsard, was vowing to Sir William Cecil, the prime minister of England, that the heavenly powers had long since promised to

> . . . joindre un jour par fidelle alliance
> Vostre Angleterre avecques nostre France.[1]

IX

The Elizabethan Political Links

As soon as England's last territorial link with France was broken, there were framed fresh political attachments which notably facilitated the exertion on England of French intellectual influence. Religious sympathy combined with official diplomacy to forge new political bonds. The religious reformers in France towards the end of Francis I's reign became the organized community of Huguenots; the French government endeavoured to suppress the Protestant organization by brute force, and the quarrel issued in civil war. The French kings and their advisers justly perceived in the Huguenot doctrine a menace not only to established religion, but to established political principles, and more especially to the pretensions of monarchical absolutism. The English Lutherans from the first welcomed the spread of their faith in France. English Protestants claimed French Protestants as brothers in the divine spirit. The persecution of the Huguenots greatly stimulated English sympathy with their French neighbours. The cry of liberty never

---

[1] Ronsard, *Œuvres*, iii. 395 (le Bocage Royal); cf. Paul Laumonier's *Ronsard, Poète Lyrique*, 1909, pp. 214–15.

failed to awaken some echo in English hearts. English Protestants came either tacitly or openly to applaud the political sentiment of the Huguenots as well as their spiritual dogma.

When Edward VI's reign made England a distinctively Protestant country, the English people eagerly acknowledged a new fellow feeling with an energetic and alert-minded section of the French people. Englishmen eagerly offered hospitality to French refugees from Catholic tyranny. Early in Edward VI's reign the door of England was opened to French Huguenots, and save for the short interval of Queen Mary's rule, it was not closed for the rest of the century. Persecuted Protestants from the Low Countries, from Italy, and even from Spain, likewise sought an asylum in Elizabethan England. Flemings who spoke both French and Flemish were perhaps more numerous than natives of France or than Flemings who spoke both German and Flemish. Italians and Spaniards of the reformed faith were fewer. But the French-speaking Walloons showed so many of the characteristics of Frenchmen that such influence as they exerted may be accounted French. The Huguenots who made their homes in sixteenth-century England were for the most part skilled artisans or professional men, silk-weavers or practitioners in medicine. The refinements of life benefited in all directions by their presence. Tudor England was backward in manufacturing or scientific ingenuity, and the alien Protestant invasion was well fitted to offer her useful instruction in science and manufacture. Religious sympathy checked effective jealousy in commercial circles, and restrained the mob's suspicion of foreign custom and speech. Scholarship, too, was well represented among Huguenot visitors. The French refugees who attended Edward VI's court included Henri Étienne, the scholar printer, who did more than any man in Europe for the scholarly study of Greek and the dissemination of scholarly culture. The greatest of French scholars, the younger Scaliger, was a later visitor. Tudor Englishmen who were conscious of intellectual aspirations fervently blessed the arrival of the Huguenots.

With the ripening of the Huguenot alliance opportunities

increased for English intercourse with all ranks of the French reforming party. As the civil and religious strife in France waxed more furious, the Huguenots repeatedly appealed for English intervention under arms. Twice in Elizabeth's reign, near the beginning and near the end, English armies joined Huguenot soldiers on the field of battle in France. A brilliant file of Huguenot leaders—Odet de Châtillon, Coligny's brother, whom Ronsard acclaimed as 'l'Hercule Chrétien', François de la Noue, general and military writer, Du Plessis Mornay, apologist for Protestantism—came to the English court to petition the queen for military help. In all these men humanist sympathies enlivened religious zeal. Elizabethan courtiers delighted in personal friendship with the flower of the Huguenot fraternity. The chief Elizabethan champion of the Renaissance, Sir Philip Sidney, lived in closest intimacy with the most enlightened of French Protestants throughout his short career of manhood.

The development of the French Reformation helped, somewhat illogically, to ratify in public opinion political alliance with a Catholic power, as well as to confirm the hold of French culture on Elizabethan England. A diplomatic episode which supplemented the Protestant influence curiously illustrates the paradoxical workings of the international situation. An efficient factor in the promotion of the friendly intercourse between the two countries, which the Huguenot movement encouraged, was the prolonged negotiation for the marriage of the English Protestant queen to a French Catholic prince. This strange scheme of diplomatic matrimony was pursued intermittently but without disruption for thirteen years. Religious differences did not deter Queen Elizabeth from serious contemplation of a matrimonial union with a Catholic prince of France. Indeed, she encouraged the advances not of one heir of French royalty but of two in succession. Her first French wooer was Francis I's grandson, Henry, Duke of Anjou, and when he ascended the French throne as Henry III he yielded his place of Queen Elizabeth's suitor to his younger brother Francis, the Duke of Alençon. Both princes were sons of Catherine de' Medici, and were in sympathy with the

Italian leanings of the French world of art and letters. Indulgent to every sensual vice they were neither physically nor morally deserving of respect, but their temperaments were responsive to the call of art and letters. Each was a writer of verse and a patron of painters and sculptors. Like her mother, Anne Boleyn, Queen Elizabeth was devoted to French literature. As a child she translated into English prose a French poem by Margaret, the cultivated Queen of Navarre, her suitor's great-aunt. It was a pious lucubration of Huguenot tendency, 'Le miroir de l'âme pécheresse' (The mirror of the sinful soul). Ronsard was at one time the English sovereign's guest, and his poetic glorification of her personal and intellectual charm ranks with the most adroit and graceful of poetic tributes to royalty. 'Royalle,' 'douce,' 'courtoise,' 'honneste,' 'liberalle,' 'jeune de face,' and 'vieille de prudence,' are among the epithets which the French courtier-poet showered on Queen Elizabeth. His poetic adulation was wisely rewarded with a diamond jewel.

With the French princes who paid their addresses to her Elizabeth professed herself in complete aesthetic sympathy, and for the Duke of Alençon she soon pretended a consuming passion. She charitably pardoned his ugliness, and her playful blandishments led him to accept with a cheerful acquiescence the appellation of 'little frog' which she bestowed on him. Twice he visited her court without modifying the royal enthusiasm, and in his brilliant retinue came many representatives of current French thought and fashion, who helped to keep England loyal to French Renaissance culture, and to check any exclusive dependence on humanism of the Huguenot tinge. One of the French duke's companions was Pierre de Bourdeilles, titular Abbé de Brantôme, the blithe biographer of contemporary French gallantry. Of another of the duke's attendants, Jean Bodin, the political philosopher of the Renaissance, an illustrative story is told. The learned visitor, after sojourning in the University of Cambridge, visited a nobleman's mansion in London, and he found in each place young English students reading his standard treatise *De la République* in a Latin translation. On examining the version, which he assigned to the pen of an incompetent French tutor in England, he judged it to be so inefficient that he hurried home to turn his work into scholarly Latin.[1] The anecdote suggests how the presence in England of Bodin's master, the Duke of Alençon, served incidentally to quicken the development of English scholarship and learning.

The premature death of the dissipated hero of this royal romance brought it to an untimely end. But the general belief in England for so long a period as thirteen years that a Frenchman was to become King Consort of England, invigorated the Gallic enthusiasm of the English upper classes. In the straitest circles of Protestantism the expectation bred dismay and complaint which steadily grew. But the plan was credited with political advantage; there were liberal-minded Protestants who acquiesced in it with missionary hope, and the bitter-tongued opposition was reduced to impotent clamour. The personal constitution of the duke's escort, while he was in England, lent the project a graceful note of culture.

A third link between the English and French nations, although less direct, was hardly less efficient than the queen's matrimonial designs or the Huguenot intercourse. The strong political and social tie which bound France to Scotland, the independent northern half of the British island, stimulated the tendency to make English culture tributary to France. The political and social intimacy of France and Scotland was long a supreme factor in Scottish history, and it worked as an active solvent of English insularity. Domestic bonds united the rulers of the French and Scottish nations. There were many inter-marriages between the royal houses of the two kingdoms, and the royal family of the Stuarts eagerly imbibed French culture, in both the fifteenth and sixteenth centuries. Much French poetry bears witness to the intimacy of French and Scottish royal circles. James I's daughter, Margaret, who was wife of Louis XI while he was Dauphin, penned some touching French rondeaus, and was patron of French men of letters.

[1] Preface to the English translation of Bodin's *Commonweale*, by Richard Knolles, 1606.

James V, great-great-grandson of James I, married twice, and both his queens were French princesses.   One, Madeleine, was Francis I's daughter, and moved the youthful adoration of Ronsard, who as a boy was page at her husband's Scottish court.   The second of James V's two queens, Marie de Guise, was daughter of the great Catholic house, and was treated by Francis I as an adopted daughter ; she was the mother of Mary Stuart.   Mary Queen of Scots was thus half a Frenchwoman. French was practically her mother-tongue, and the French accent with which she spoke Scottish made the tongue, otherwise most cacophonous to French ears, graceful and harmonious.   French poetry was Mary Stuart's chief reading. Ronsard and Du Bellay devoted their finest powers to glowing eulogies of her fascinating beauty, and the French verse which she loved to pen on their pattern moved the hearts of her French admirers.[1]   Her son James, whom Henry of Navarre called ' captain of arts and clerk of arms ', welcomed French poets to his court with all his mother's ardour.

The flame of French culture burnt very briskly at sixteenth-century Edinburgh, and French influence farther south was thereby quickened.   The promising youth of Scotland was educated in France.   Scottish students distinguished themselves as professors at French Universities.   Scottish hospitality was constantly offered to French guests, and England lay within the lines of communication.[2]   The Gallic sentiment which was woven into the web of Scottish culture had opportunities of communicating itself to the English side of the Tweed.   At the end of Elizabeth's reign political parties were vying with one another in advocacy of the Scottish king's claim to the English throne, and the strong Scottish party in England saw an advantage in championing French standards of taste.   When the sixteenth century came to a close, French breezes played perceptibly on Elizabethan England from the Cheviot Hills

[1] Cf. Brantôme, *Vies des Dames Illustres*, No. III, Marie Stuart, Reyne d'Escosse.

[2] The first road-book for England was published at Paris in 1579, and was prepared by Jean Bernard chiefly for travellers from France to Scotland.   The title ran : *La Guide des Chemins d'Angleterre fort necessaire à ceux qui y voyagent ou qui passent de France en Escosse.*

as well as from the English Channel. Politics in England, whether they be examined in their ecclesiastical, their diplomatic, or their dynastic aspect, tended through the era of the French Renaissance to familiarize Englishmen with the culture of France.

X

THE STUDY OF FRENCH IN TUDOR SOCIETY

The political conditions, which brought France and England in the sixteenth century into familiar intimacy, find a natural reflection in the social usages of Tudor England. English society had through mediaeval times cherished a predilection for French modes and manners. In Tudor England knowledge of the French language and sympathy with French social habits finally became accepted badges of gentility. Taste in dress, in recreation, and in culinary matters, was dictated for the most part by French example. The insular prejudice against foreigners was not extinguished, and the notorious riot in London on 'Evil May-day' of 1517, when the lives and property of foreign visitors were menaced with destruction, proved the strength of the hate of foreigners among the trading and labouring classes of the capital. The antipathy was rarely shared by the upper classes, but it lingered on in the middle and the lower orders. The authorities found means of holding mob violence in check, but suspicion and dislike of the alien found constant voice in both literary satire and the illiterate scurrility of the street. The penetrating charm—'le douceur'—of French culture could, however, be relied on to quench the flames of merely insular jealousy.

Throughout the century young Englishmen of good family invariably completed their education in foreign travel and by attendance at a foreign university. In many quarters the practice was deemed to be perilous to the students' religion and morals. The foundation of Trinity College, Dublin, in 1592 was justified on the ground ' that many of our people have usually heretofore used to travel into France, Italy, and Spain, to get learning in such foreign universities, whereby they have been infected with popery and other ill qualities '.[1] But the usage of youthful peregrination was barely affected by such suspicions. The young Englishman's educational tour often extended to Italy and Germany as well as to France, but France was rarely omitted, and many youths confined their excursions to French territory. Neither Francis Bacon nor his brother Anthony passed in their *Wanderjahre* beyond French bounds. As far as we know, Francis went no further afield than Paris. Anthony chiefly spent his time in the south of France, and while sojourning at Bordeaux he became the intimate friend of Montaigne. Almost every French university had some English students. The main aim of these visitors to France was to acquire a good French accent, always a matter of difficulty with Englishmen, and to learn manners, of which Tudor Englishmen were commonly held to be congenitally innocent. ' The first country,' wrote James Howell, who had a keen eye for deportment, ' that it is requisite for the English to know is France.'

Nor was provision of a very adequate kind for acquiring the French language wanting at home. The tradition of French study was of old standing in England. But never before the Tudor epoch did the French teacher fill a commanding place in English society.

From early days of the French Renaissance French philologists prophesied that the French tongue would become the universal language of culture. Many Frenchmen proudly claimed, while the century was yet young, that, as far as England was concerned, that consummation was already reached. ' In England French is spoken,' writes a French grammarian about 1550, ' at any rate among the princes and their courts in all their talk.'[2] In 1552, Étienne Pasquier, a poet and

---

[1] J. W. Stubbs's *History of the University of Dublin*, 1889, p. 354.
[2] Jacques Peletier du Mans, *Dialogues de l'Ortografe*, p. 60 (1550): ' En Angleterre, amoins entre les Princes e en leurs cours, iz parle[n]t François en tous leurs propos.' Of the distribution of ' la tres-noble et

critic who lived on friendly terms with Montaigne and other princes of French literature and confidently foretold a world-wide adoption of the French language, wrote to Adrian Turnebus, the Greek scholar of Paris, that 'there is no nobleman's house in England, Scotland, or Germany without a tutor to teach the children French '.[1]

Through the early part of the century Tudor England was peculiarly distinguished by the number of French humanists —Frenchmen of literary distinction—who faced the task of teaching French to English boys and girls of royal or gentle birth. These visitors played a prominent part on the social stage. At the very opening of the epoch Henry VII appointed Bernard André, a native of Toulouse, tutor to his sons, Arthur and Henry. André was so facile a writer of French and Latin verse that by a paradoxical freak of fortune he became Poet Laureate at the English court. Among other French tutors in Tudor England was Nicolas Bourbon, a protégé of Queen Anne Boleyn. He was a humanist of wide repute, whose friends included Rabelais and Marot. From Bourbon, Robert Dudley, Earl of Leicester, with his brothers and their kinsfolk learnt French as children. Bourbon mingled with leaders of the reforming party while in England during Henry VIII's reign, and eulogized in facile epigrams Cromwell and Cranmer, while he discourteously taunted Sir Thomas More with his lowly origin and the resemblance of his surname to the Greek word for 'fool'. On re-settling in France, Bourbon abandoned the church of the Reformers and re-entered the orthodox fold, but his humanist sympathy and reputation knew no decay, and distinguished him in both camps.

---

tres-parfaite langue Française', Mellema, author of a Dictionnaire flamand-français, 1591, writes somewhat later : ' Puis grande partie d'Alemaigne, du pays de Levant, de Muscovie, de Pologne, *d'Angleterre et d'Ecosse* usent de ladite langue.'

[1] *Les Lettres d'Estienne Pasquier*, Amsterdam, 1723, Liv. i, p. 5 : ' Presque en toute l'Allemagne (que dy-je, l'Allemagne, si l'Angleterre et l'Escosse y sont comprises) il ne se trouve maison noble qui n'ait pre-cepteur pour instruire ses enfans en nostre langue Françoise. Donques l'Allemand, l'Anglois et l'Ecossois se paissent de la douceur de nostre vulgaire.'

Of a third French tutor in England an even more interesting story may be told. A French poet of modest attainments, with an equal capacity for art and poetry, Nicolas Denisot (1515–59) was French tutor of the three daughters of Protector Somerset, the Protestant statesman.   Under Denisot's guidance the young English ladies wrote Latin elegies on the queen of contemporary French literature, Margaret of Navarre.   The labour of love was welcomed with enthusiasm in Paris.   The Latin verses—one hundred quatrains—were published in Paris in 1550 under Denisot's editorship.   The poetic essay moved the sympathy of Denisot's poetic friends—*plusieurs des excellentz poètes de la France.* A volume of translations from French pens in Greek and Italian as well as in French was issued by Denisot next year.[1] Denisot's triumph in bringing his English pupils under the banner of French humanism deeply impressed Frenchmen. Ronsard was then approaching the throne of French poetry, and in one of the great poet's earliest odes he salutes the ladies Seymour with charming buoyancy. If Orpheus had heard

> . . . . le luth des Sirenes
> Qui sonne aux bords escumeux
> Des Albionnes arenes,

the Greek lyrist would have forsaken his own pagan key and learned of the Englishwomen their Christian note.   Ronsard exuberantly credits Denisot with drawing England into alliance with France in the war which the Renaissance waged on barbarism.

> Denisot se vante heuré [i.e. heureux]
> D'avoir oublié sa terre
> Et passager demeuré
> Trois ans en vostre Angleterre . . .
>
> . . . . les esprits
> D'Angleterre et de la France,
> Bandez d'une ligue, ont pris
> Le fer contre l'ignorance.

---

[1] The rare volume is entitled *Le tombeau de Marguerite de Valois royne de Navarre faict premierement en distiques Latins par les trois sœurs Anne, Marguerite et Jeanne de Seymour, princesses en Angleterre* (Paris, 1551).

All that was needed to seal the union, in Ronsard's gallant fancy, was for one of Denisot's English scholars to cross the sea and find a French husband.

> Lors vos escrits avancez
> Se verront recompensez
> D'une chanson mieux sonnée
> Qui crîra vostre hymenée.[1]

The missionaries of French humanism among the Tudor nobility did not live without honour in their own country. Bernard André, Nicolas Bourbon, and Nicolas Denisot were all faithful servants in the temple of French scholarship, if they did not pass beyond the outer courts. Their presence in England is a notable episode in the international story.

Nor was the teaching of French confined to the children of the nobility. At the Grammar School of Southampton a refugee from French Flanders was appointed head master early in Elizabeth's reign. There all the boys had to speak French during school-time, under pain of wearing a fool's cap at meals. Professional teachers of French for the middle classes abounded in London at the end of the century. One Claude De-saint-liens, a Bourbon gentleman who anglicized his French name into the English word Holy-band, had his class-rooms at the sign of the Lucrece in St. Paul's Churchyard, above the shop of a leading printer, publisher, and bookseller of the day, Thomas Purfoot. The literary profession in Elizabethan England was disposed to cultivate friendly intercourse with the French tutor.

Many of these French teachers in London were voluminous authors of educational manuals. French grammars, helps to pronunciation, conversation-books for the fit education of young English gentlemen and gentlewomen, flowed from

---

[1] Ronsard, *Odes*, Livre V, No. III. Ronsard addresses Ode X in the same book to Denisot as 'peintre et poète'. Remi Belleau, Ronsard's colleague of the Pléiade, paid Denisot in a sonnet a naïve compliment on his industrious pursuit of the two arts (*Œuvres*, ed. Gouverneur, Paris, 1867, t. i, p. 202):

> Ce double trait, dont l'un industrieux
> Ravit notre œil, l'autre doux notre oreille ;
> De ta main docte annonce la merveille,
> Et de tes vers l'accent laborieux.

their pens in profusion. On the foundation of French-English vocabularies of recent compilation was based one of the best early efforts in lexicography which Elizabethan England produced—Randle Cotgrave's well-known French-English Dictionary (1611). This masterly effort to make the French language accessible to Elizabethan Englishmen renders modern students the lasting service, hardly designed by its author, of determining the precise meaning of many an obsolete Elizabethan word.

Of early French grammars produced in England, the fullest and best came from the pen of an Englishman, John Palsgrave, who acted as chaplain to Henry VIII's sister while she was Queen of France. Later Palsgrave became tutor of Henry VIII's natural son, the Earl of Richmond. His voluminous *L'Esclarcissement de la langue Françoyse*, which was published in London in 1530, is a philological monument and the acknowledged parent of all French grammars of France. It had no French predecessor. The path to a knowledge of French was never easier for Englishmen than in Tudor times, and the Tudor text-books of the French teachers were nobly crowned by the domestic labours of Palsgrave and Cotgrave.

XI

FRENCH DRESS, FRENCH WINES, AND FRENCH DANCES

There was no phase of social life in which French taste failed to exercise authority in Tudor England. Very widespread was French influence on English costume in the sixteenth century. From a far earlier period French fashions in dress won in England the admiration of the rich. Chaucer in the four-teenth century bears witness to his countrymen's love of the refinements of French garments. From end to end of the sixteenth century the French tailor was the acknowledged arbiter of English fashions in clothes for both men and women.

Of the English gallant, Sir Thomas More wrote, in words often repeated by his successors :

> He struts about
> In cloaks of fashion French. His girdle, purse,
> And sword are French. His hat is French.
> His nether limbs are cased in French costume.
> His shoes are French. In short, from top to toe
> He stands the Frenchman.[1]

The English gallant was not averse to modifying French schemes of apparel by adapting features from Italy and Spain. According to Shakespeare's *Merchant of Venice* (I. ii. 79-81) the young baron of England buys only his round hose in France; he obtains his doublet from Italy, his bonnet from Germany, and his behaviour everywhere. Similarly Dekker remarks that an Englishman's suit of clothes steals patches from every nation ' to piece out his pride'. But French tailors controlled the Tudor scheme of dress. The Porter in *Macbeth* (II. iii. 15) attests that the English tailor's habitual offence was that of ' stealing out of a French hose ' (i. e. of slavishly copying French fashions). ' Bonjour, there 's a French salutation to your French slop,' is one of Mercutio's quips at Romeo's expense. Camden's friend, Richard Carew, may be trusted when at the end of the century he remarks that English fashions, despite their mixed quality, came in substance from our neighbours the French; that every change in the French vogue was faithfully reflected in England, and that the store of French patterns was daily renewed.[2] The best judges in such matters shared Polonius's opinion (*Hamlet*, I. iii. 70-4), when he advised his son—

[1] I quote the efficient English rendering by John Howard Marsden in his *Philomorus : notes on Latin poems of Thomas More*, 2nd edition, 1878, p. 223. In More's *Epigrammata* the satiric poem is headed ' In Anglum Gallicae linguae affectatorem '. The opening verses run :

> Amicus et sodalis est Lalus mihi,
> Britanniaque natus altusque insula.
> At cum Britannos Galliae cultoribus
> Oceanus ingens, lingua, mores dirimant,
> Spernit tamen Lalus Britannica omnia,
> Miratur expetitque cuncta Gallica.

[2] Camden, *Remains* (1870 edition), p. 47 : ' Our neighbours the French have been likewise contented we should take up by retail their fashions : or rather we retain yet but some remnant of that which once here bare all the sway, and daily renew the store.'

> Costly thy habit as thy purse can buy,
> But not expressed in fancy: rich not gaudy . . .
> And they in France of the best rank and station
> Are most select and generous, chief in that.

Tudor costume found in France the surest type of elegance.

Patriotic sentiment exposed the passion for French finery, like all French social usages, to frequent ridicule. Insular moralists detected in the ' viperous ' fascination of the French refinements incentive to every sin. Voluble was the satiric scorn of all foreign affectations in manner and speech, and especially of the homage paid to the French standards of taste. Insular sentiment tended to impute to the Anglo-French vogue a habit of ludicrous braggadocio. When a number of young English noblemen and gentlemen returned home from a visit to the French court in 1518, the chronicler Hall declares that ' they were all French in eating, drinking, and apparel, yea in French vices and brags, so that all estates of England were by them laughed at '. Sir Thomas More in his epigrams, the Puritan divines during the reign of Edward VI, the dramatists and pamphleteers at the extreme end of the century, all vie with one another in quips at the expense of the ' giddy-pated English ', who were always on the watch for ' new French cuts ', and whose doublet, slops, and gloves, were designed on French models. However small was the gallant's knowledge of the French language, it was his habit, according to patriotic censure, to boast familiarity with it. Of the English man of fashion More again writes in language which was often repeated :

> If he speak
> Though but three little words in French, he swells
> And plumes himself on his proficiency,
> And his French failing, then he utters words
> Coined by himself, with widely gaping mouth
> And sound acute, thinking to make at least
> The accent French.

More insists that whatever language the Englishman essays to speak, his bad French controls his tongue and accentuates

the absurdity of his bastard cosmopolitanism. 'With accent
French', More's Englishman

> speaks the Latin tongue,
> With accent French the tongue of Lombardy,
> To Spanish words he gives an accent French,
> German he speaks with the same accent French.
> In truth he seems to speak with accent French,
> All but the French itself. The French he speaks
> With accent British.

More's sarcasm plainly credits France with the function of
missionary of all foreign culture. The satirist Nashe broadly
insinuated that the Englishman who travelled in France gained
no profit save the habit of loose living and of speaking English strangely and insolently.[1]

In no branch of fashionable life was Tudor custom free
from French influence. Ladies of rank who devoted their
leisure to lacemaking and embroidery sought their patterns
in French manuals of needlework, some of which were re-
published in England. France enjoyed in the sixteenth
century a supreme repute for culinary skill, for fantastical
meats and salads, for sumptuous confectionery. The English nobility invariably employed French cooks, who were
reckoned 'to have the best invention of any in Europe', and
their epicurean ingenuity was denounced as unrighteous
alchemy.[2] Of extravagant entertainments among the English
nobility, the gossiping letter-writer, Chamberlain, bitterly
complains early in the seventeenth century, and he lays the

---

[1] Thomas Nashe, *The Unfortunate Traveller*, 1587 (Works, ed.
McKerrow, ii. 300): 'What is there in France to be learned more
than in England, but falsehood in fellowship, perfect slovenry, to love no
man but for my pleasure, to swear 'Ah par la mort Dieu', when a man's
hams are scabbed. For the idle traveller (I mean not for the soldier)
I have known some that have continued there by the space of half a dozen
years, and when they come home, they have hid a little weerish lean face
under a broad hat, kept a terrible coil with the dust in the street in their
long cloaks of gray paper, and spoke English strangely. Nought else
have they profited by their travel, save learned to distinguish between the
true Bordeaux grape, and know a cup of neat Gascoigne wine from wine
of Orleans.'
[2] Moryson's *Itinerary*, 1617, Part III, p. 135; Harrison's *Description*
(1577), i. 144 (New Shakspere Soc.).; Overbury's *Characters*, 1614,
'A French Cook.'

fault at French doors. After describing a series of rich
banquets in London he remarks: 'But, *pour retourner à
nos moutons*, this feasting begins to grow at an excessive rate. The very provisions of cates for this supper,
rising to more than £600; *wherein we are too apish to
imitate the French monkeys in such monstrous waste.*'[1]

French wines seem also to have been reckoned enviable
luxuries for which high prices were paid. The taste for
foreign wines steadily grew through the sixteenth century,
and was gratified by importations from Spain and Germany,
and even from Italy and Greece, as well as from France. But
France easily maintained her supremacy as wine-purveyor for
the English market. In Shakespeare's youth it was stated
that as many as fifty-six sorts of French wine were known in
England, whereas no more than thirty kinds came from the
rest of the Continent.[2] Nashe credits the travelled Englishman
with a capacity to distinguish between the true and false
Bordeaux grape, or at least to know a cup of neat Gascon
from wine of Orleans. French wines were regarded as lighter
than any other. English travellers noticed with surprise the
French habit of mixing water with wine.[3] Rarely could
they be induced to imitate so fantastic a weakness. The
influence which the drinking customs of French society
exerted on the Elizabethans tended to sobriety.

Despite the satirists' shots, which they fired at random
over the whole field of French usage, the embellishments which
France contributed to Tudor life bear unvarying testimony
to the superior artistic sentiment and skill of our neighbours.
It was not solely devices of French birth which France introduced into England. Many Italian and some Spanish accomplishments reached England through France. The Italians
perfected the art of fencing, and several eminent Elizabethan fencing-masters were Italian. Yet the accomplishment in England owed much to French tutors. Shakespeare
in *Hamlet* (IV. vii. 100) mentions Frenchmen as champions

---

[1] *Court of James I*, i. 459.
[2] William Harrison's *Description of England* (1577), i. 149.
[3] Fynes Moryson's *Itinerary*, 1617, Part III, p. 135.

of the exercise, and calls fencing experts 'scrimers'. The term is a colloquial Anglicism of the pure French word 'escrimeurs', and its employment points to the nationality of many instructors in Shakespeare's England. Of the equestrian art of the manège in Elizabethan England—the exercise of 'riding the Great Horse',—much the same story has to be told. The chief riding-masters in London were Frenchmen. Shakespeare grows eloquent over the equestrian feats of 'the French', who 'can well on horseback' (*Hamlet*, IV. vii. 84). French manuals on the equestrian exercise were prized by Queen Elizabeth's courtiers, and the technical terms were French words.[1]

To the French manner of dancing Elizabethan England stands deeply indebted for the chief development of a popular form of recreation, and a valued aid to deportment. One of the earliest Tudor translations from the French was a book on French dancing. To a treatise, which was publshed in London in 1521, on the writing and speaking of French by Alexander Barclay, an indefatigable translator of con- temporary foreign literature, there was appended a short pamphlet on French dancing, which was translated by the printer, Robert Copland.[2] The encyclopaedic writer on education, Sir Thomas Elyot, in his *Governour* (1531), devotes as many as four chapters (xix–xxii) to the his- tory and practice of dancing. He specifies as popular dances of his own day burgenettes and pavanes, tour- dions, galliards, rounds and brawls, all of which are either directly or indirectly of French origin. Often a popular Elizabethan dance reached England through France from more distant lands. Many dances familiar to Elizabethan students, like the pavane, the galliard, and the coranto, have

---

[1] See Lord Herbert of Cherbury's *Autobiography*, ed. Lee, 2nd edition, pp. 39 *seq.*

[2] The treatise on dancing is thus introduced:—' Here foloweth the maner of dauncynge of bace daunces after the use of fraunce and other places translated out of frenche in englysshe by Robert coplande.' Most of the dances are clearly French. Copland's translation was reprinted with Robert Laneham's letter (ed. Furnivall), by the New Shakspere Society in 1890 (pp. clx–clxii).

been traced to Italy or Spain, but France borrowed them
from those countries, and in her familiar rôle imported them
into England.

The names of some very new and fashionable dances of
Shakespeare's day betray a pure French origin. 'The French
brawl,' a kind of cotillon, and the 'cinque pace ' or 'cinq pas '
(i. e. five paces), an anticipation of the minuet, were wholly
of Gallic invention. 'A newe ballade, intytuled " Good
Fellowes must go learne to daunce ",' which was published in
1569, salutes the 'brall' as just 'come out of Fraunce',
and dubs it the 'trickiest' invention of the year.[1] The
Shakespearean student is equally familiar with 'the high
lavolt ', a somewhat violent dance, facility in which was
reckoned a mark of refinement, although the steps approxi-
mated to leaps. Troilus complains that he 'cannot heel *the
high lavolt* or sweeten talk or play at subtle games'.[2]
' Lavolte ', or ' la volta ', was, in spite of its Italian name, of
French, or at any rate of Provençal origin. It achieved
a vast popularity in Parisian society late in the sixteenth
century, just before it reached Elizabethan England.[3] Save
the 'lavolte', these foreign dances are all slow and stately
measures, and strike a suggestive contrast with the boisterous

[1] Lilly's *Ancient Ballads and Broadsides*, p. 221. The name of the
dance, 'brawl,' comes from the Old French word *bransle*, and is altogether
distinct from 'brawl' in the sense of 'quarrel'. The likeness between
the two words encouraged an obvious pun. Cf. Shakespeare's *Love's
Labour 's Lost*, III. i. 9–10 : 'MOTH. Master, will you win your love in
a *French brawl?* ARMAD. How meanest thou ? *brawling in French ?*'

[2] *Troilus and Cressida*, IV. iv. 88 ; see also Shakespeare's *Henry V*, III.
v. 33. Other Elizabethan dramatists attest the vogue of this new dance.

[3] Ronsard, in his poem called *La Charité* (1578), addressed to Marguerite,
Henri III's sister and Henry of Navarre's wife, describes the dance
which he calls ' la volte provençale ':

> Le Roy (i. e. Henri III) dansant la volte Provençalle
> Faisoit sauter la Charité sa Sœur;
> Elle, suivant d'une grave douceur,
> A bonds legers voloit parmy la salle :
>   Ainsi qu'on voit aux grasses nuits d'Automne
> Un prompt Ardant sur les eaux esclairer,
> Tantost deçà, tantost delà virer,
> Et nul repos à sa flame ne donne. (*Œuvres*, iv, pp. 182–3.)

Reginald Scot, in his *Discoverie of Witchcraft* (1584), ridicules the French
writer Bodin for having attributed to witches the recent introduction ' out
of Italie into France of that dance which is called La volta '.

and tumultuous movements of the indigenous English jig.
The Elizabethan Englishman's bearing acquired much new
gravity and dignity in the dancing-schools of France.

XII

The Debt to the Art of Italy and Germany

France never worked quite single-handed in the cause of
English aesthetic progress. She had some coadjutors. A
few refinements of the noblest kind, which swayed Tudor
England hardly less conspicuously than literature moved her,
can scarcely be reckoned among the genuine fruits of French
influence. Tudor music, Tudor architecture, Tudor painting,
owed much to the inspiration of Europe, but other countries
than France offered England incentive in those branches of
culture.

Music roused much enthusiasm in Tudor England, but
its most popular developments were dictated by Italian and
not by French example. The great poets of the French
Renaissance were devoted to music, but French musicians
were for the most part pupils of Italy, and gathered their
honey from Tuscan or Neapolitan flowers.[1] The madrigal,
so marked a feature of Elizabethan music that one might
easily mistake it for a domestic invention, was, in spite of
abundant imitations in France, an Italian importation. It
was only in the year 1588 that the term was first employed
in English. An English amateur who had travelled in Italy
then ventured to write of 'certaine Italian madrigales'.[2]
The word had already been naturalized for a generation by
the poets of France, but the text and music of the Elizabethan madrigals were more often drawn direct from
Italian compositions than from French. Elizabethan music-

---

[1] Ronsard, a musical enthusiast, uses this language of Orlando di
Lasso (1532–94), 'divin Orlande,' a musician of French birth who spent
most of his life abroad and was a composer of the first rank.
[2] Nicolas Yonge, *Musica Transalpina* (1588), preface.

books are largely of Italian parentage, and most of the musicians whom Queen Elizabeth and her father took into their service were Italians.

The early date, at which Tudor interest manifested itself in Italian music of the Renaissance, may be gauged by the fact that the organist of St. Mark's, Venice, Fra Dionysius Memo, was brought to England by Henry VIII soon after his accession. Bassano, Lupo, Ferrabosco, are the names of the chief musicians in Queen Elizabeth's service.

French musicians were not wholly unknown to Elizabethan England, and French song-books or books of 'airs' were not ignored by Elizabethan devisers of musical anthologies. The French family of Lanier, which was famous in the seventeenth century for its mingled devotion to music and painting, first settled in England during Elizabeth's reign. The earliest member who is known to have reached England was Jean Lanier of Rouen, a musician who died in London in 1572.[1] But, despite a few French traces, Italians dominated the musical world of Tudor England. The French influence on Elizabethan music is, on the whole, insignificant compared with the Italian.

Building was pursued in Tudor England on a liberal scale, but Renaissance influences were slow to draw English architecture out of its mediaeval mould. A style, which remained Gothic in spite of some skilful qualification, persisted in England long after the forces of the Renaissance had re-created the Gothic vogue abroad or replaced it by another manner. Native architecture was not eager to assimilate

---

[1] The most distinguished member of this family, Nicolas Lanier (1588-1686), whose portrait was painted by Vandyke, was not appointed master of the King's music before 1626. It is possible that G. Tessier, an Italo-French musician who, although he describes himself as a Breton, had learned his art in Italy, was also at one time in Elizabeth's service. In 1582 he published in Paris a book of airs (*Premier Livre d'Airs*) prefaced by an Italian letter addressed to the King of France, Henry III. The opening piece is dedicated to Queen Elizabeth: ' alla serenissima et sacratissima regina d' Inghilterra.' Fifteen years later a book of French airs (*Le Premier Livre de Chansons et Airs*) published in London was described as by Carle Tessier, ' musitien de la chambre du Roy' (i. e. Henry IV). Carle Tessier was possibly a son of G. Tessier, and was likewise apparently an occasional visitor at Queen Elizabeth's court. (Cf. Picot, *Les Français Italianisants*, 1907, vol. ii, pp. 205-7.)

foreign example. St. George's chapel at Windsor and Henry VII's chapel at Westminster, despite a few Italianate details, bear witness in early Tudor England to the conservative tendency. Hampton Court Palace, in which a modified Gothic scheme is applied to domestic purposes, pays small tribute to the classical spirit of the new enlightenment. In houses of moderate size the late mediaeval combination of brick and timber long continued, and the development of fresh artistic feeling was discouraged.

But while the sixteenth century was still young, some architectural innovations of the Renaissance reached England from Italy. Ultimately the Italian Renaissance found luxurious expression in the royal palace of Nonesuch and in a score of noblemen's mansions. Much fine decorative work in Henry VIII's later years was designed and executed by Italian craftsmen or by Englishmen who had studied in Italy. With the progress of the century, German or Flemish influence, which Holbein inaugurated, gained on Italian influence in the architecture of Tudor England. The greatest public building which was erected in Elizabethan England, Sir Thomas Gresham's Royal Exchange in London, reproduced by aid of Flemish workmen the design of the Hôtel des Villes Hanséatiques at Antwerp.

France meanwhile made slender contribution to the architectural activity of her neighbour.[1] Only a little minor ornamentation in Tudor churches or houses is attributable

[1] Cf. Reginald Blomfield's *History of Renaissance Architecture in England*, 1897, i. In Braun's *Urbium Praecipuarum Mundi Theatrum* (1582) there is an engraving of Nonesuch Palace, with the comment that the architects and artificers employed on it included Frenchmen as well as Dutchmen, Italians, and Englishmen. Mr. Blomfield's remark on this statement runs thus (i. 18):—'The mention of Frenchmen is also remarkable. The names of French artists or workmen scarcely ever occur in the State Papers, and there are few instances of Renaissance work in England which can be attributed to them. The capitals to the arch between the More chantry and the chancel of old Chelsea Church are an unusual instance. They closely resemble French work of the early sixteenth century such as is found along the banks of the Seine between Paris and Rouen. The monument in the Oxenbrigge Chapel in Brede Church, Sussex, dated 1537, is another rare example. It is of Caen stone, admirably carved, and was probably made in France and shipped to the port of Rye, some nine miles distant from Brede.'

to French hands. The master-mason or chief architect of
James V of Scotland came from France, and Stirling Castle
and Falkland Palace bear traces of French ingenuity, but
in Scotland, too, the Italian or German vogue prevailed.

In the result, Tudor England remained poorer in specimens of Renaissance architecture than Italy or France. Of
one type of domestic building, which lent a peculiar charm to
sixteenth-century France, Tudor England knew barely anything. There is nothing in Tudor England to compare in
beauty or originality with the wealth of châteaus which
sprang up in the valley of the Loire in the early days of the
French Renaissance. Although Tudor architecture has a
serious and solid attraction of its own, it lacks the buoyant
freedom of French enterprise and invention.

England gave birth to no architect of genius before the
rise of Inigo Jones, the designer of the banqueting-hall of
Whitehall. Jones, born in 1573, was a pupil of a sixteenth-
century Italian master, Palladio. No Englishman before him
grasped the full significance of the art of the Italian Renaissance, which finally established its prestige in England
in James I's reign. The consummate technical skill and
expansiveness of the French Renaissance architecture never
knew an English exponent.

To Germany Tudor England is mainly indebted for its
pictorial art. Though Henry VIII, in loyal discipleship to
Francis I, invited to England a few Italian painters, as well
as Italian architects and musicians, the chief painters of Tudor
England came, like her tutors in theology and her experts
in metallurgy and mechanics, from Germany or the Low
Countries. The greatest painter of Tudor England, Holbein,
was a native of Augsburg. His chief successor here, Sir
Antonio More, was a native of Utrecht. Of the best known
Elizabethan artists, Lucas de Heere came from Ghent, Mark
Gerrard from Bruges, and Zuccharo from the duchy of
Urbino. The French Renaissance school of painting was
even less familiar to Tudor England than its school of
architecture. In 1571 an ambitious art-dealer of Paris wrote
entreating Sir William Cecil, Queen Elizabeth's prime

minister, to submit proposals to his royal mistress for the purchase of his magnificent collection of masterpieces by French as well as by Italian and German artists, but the offer was apparently rejected.[1]

In engraving, Tudor England was very far behind the Continent. The art flourished in Germany for near a century before any effort was made to practise it on English soil. Not until the art of engraving was perfected in Italy, Germany, and the Low Countries were any specimens attempted in England. Copperplate engravers grew numerous in Elizabeth's reign, but they were, for the most part, Flemings or Germans of secondary repute in the world at large. English pupils occasionally did their Teutonic masters' instruction much credit, but Tudor England produced no master capable of emulating the smallest of the achievements of Albrecht Dürer, the German, or of Marcantonio Raimondi, the Italian—the two artists who early in the sixteenth century first set engraving securely among the fine arts.[2]

XIII

THE FRENCH VIEW OF THE ENGLISH NATIONAL CHARACTER

However uncongenial may be the conclusion, we must face with what cheerfulness we may, the historic fact that Tudor England owed the graces of life to foreign influence, and chiefly to the influence of France. After making allowance for inevitable tendencies to national assertiveness and national jealousy, it is to be feared that the French critics who credited Tudor England with barbarism had some justification for their comment. The charge abounds, and is

[1] *Le XVIe siècle et les Valois*, par le Comte de la Ferrière, Paris, 1879, pp. 300–1.

[2] See Sidney Colvin's *Early Engravers and Engraving in England, 1545–1695: A Historical and Critical Essay.* (Printed by order of the Trustees of the British Museum, 1905.) The useful and beautiful art of making 'mill-money' (i. e. coins struck from dies by machinery) was first introduced into the Mint in England by a French immigrant in 1561. The art, which both Da Vinci and Cellini developed, reached France from Italy in 1551 (see W. J. Hocking's *Some Notes on the Early History of Coinage by Machinery*, 1909).

a commonplace in foreign literature. It finds echo in Shakespeare's *Henry V*, where the French officers taunt the English, not only with excessive devotion to great meals of beef, but with deficiency in intellectual armour.[1] Courage and tenacity are the only virtues these censors put to the credit of English nationality. Foreign visitors, even scholars like Scaliger, dwell regretfully on the English people's want of courtesy, and accept the mysterious tradition that the county of Kent, on whose coast foreign travellers landed, was inhabited by men trailing tails behind them. The tradition of Kentish men's tails was widespread among continental authors. The fable seems to have been first formulated in print by the Italian historian of England, Polydore Vergil. The Elizabethan topographer of Kent, William Lambarde, reproaches Polydore with having led foreign nations to 'believe as verely that [Kentishmen] have long tailes and be monsters by nature'.[2]

The English people repaid such insults with liberal interest. If the civility of the English court and nobility was often handsomely acknowledged by French visitors, their patience was tried by the rhetoric of the street-corner, which habitually greeted the stranger as a 'French dog'. Estienne Perlin, a French priest who was a student of Paris University, has left an account of a two-years' visit which he paid England and Scotland at the end of Edward VI's reign.[3] Perlin speaks bitterly of the manners of the English people, and of the superior treatment which English visitors received in France. 'Les gens de ceste nation hayent à mort les Francoys, comme leurs vielz ennemis, et du tout nous appellent *France chenesve, France dogue*, qui est a dire "maraultz Francois", "chiens Francois", et autrement nous appellent *orson* [whoreson], " villains ", " filz de putaing " Il

---

[1] *Henry V*, III. iv. 158-62.

[2] *Perambulation of Kent*, 1587, p. 315. Cf. Fynes Moryson, *Itinerary*, 1617, Part III, p. 53: 'The Kentish men of old were said to have tayles, because trafficking in the Low Countries, they never paid full payments of what they did owe, but still left some part unpaid.' Moryson's hardly satisfactory explanation does not seem to be found elsewhere.

[3] *Description des royaulmes d'Angleterre et d'Escosse*, Paris, 1558; reprinted, London, 1775, pp. 11–12.

me desplait que ces vilains, estans en leur pays, nous crachent a la face, et eulx, estans à la France, on les honore et revere comme petis dieux ; en ce, les Francois se monstrent francs de cœur et noble d'esperit.'

Another French view of Tudor Englishmen deserves citation. In De la Porte's standard thesaurus called *Les Épithètes* (Paris, 1571), more generous terms are employed in an estimate of English character and physiognomy. The following is the curious list of epithets which the French writer declares to be applicable to 'Les Anglois' : ' Blonds, outrecudiz, ennemis des francois, archers, mutins, coués (i. e. tailed), belliqueus, anglo-saxons, superbes, rouges, furieus, hardis, audacieus.' The legend of the ' tails ' is not ignored, but to his list De la Porte appends the charitable note : ' Les Anglois sont beaux et bien proportionnez, hardis a la guerre, et fort bons archers. Le peuple n'aime point les estrangers, et est autant incivil et malgracieus que la noblesse est courtoise et affable.' [1]

Popular ignorance is always the prey of a false patriotism. It was impossible that the temper of the Tudor mob should be completely purged of hostility to foreign customs and to foreign ideas. Travelled Englishmen of cultivation were themselves known frankly to admit that their country was barbarous, its manners rude, and its people uncivil. But however deeply the insular prejudice was rooted in the heart of the common people, there is consolation in the reflection that the Tudor mind at its best was singularly free from the narrowness of national separatism. The Tudor mind at its best had in it a power of receptivity, an assimilative capacity which ultimately purified it of much of its native grossness and adapted its native robustness to great artistic purpose. Tudor literature

---

[1] Page 17. To the Scotch, De la Porte applies the following list of descriptive epithets (p. 92 b): 'Nobles, vaillans, fiers, blonds, hautains, septentrionaus, prompts, guerriers, enuieus, brusques, farouches, beaux, actifs.' There is added the note : ' Ce peuple est beau de visage et bien fait de corps, mais malpropre et peu soigneus de se vestir et parer honnestement, soudain en ses actions, farouche et vindicatif, puissant, robuste, et courageus en guerre, faisant grande parade de sa noblesse.'

caught light and heat from France, or, through France, from Athens and Rome and modern Italy. Sixteenth-century France interpreted to sixteenth-century England Greek and Italian culture and ideas in much the same way as in the eighteenth century France interpreted England's ideas to Germany. France was the chief refining agent in Tudor society. She did much to liberalize Tudor thought.

Some contemporary English observers whose temperament, in spite of education, exposed them to gusts of insular jealousy of the foreigner, expressed a fear that subservience to French or Italian example might hamper the evolution of the national genius. The typical Elizabethan scholar, Gabriel Harvey, when he noticed Cambridge undergraduates steeping their minds, contrary to academic regulations, in current literature of France and Italy, was impulsively moved to the harsh hexameter:

O times, O manners, O French, O Italish England.[1]

The lament was short-sighted. The national genius was absorbing the most healthful sustenance. All that was best in foreign literature was needed to create the new national expression on which Shakespeare set the final seal. The spirit of imitation and adaptation was well alive in Shakespeare, his mind was wrought upon by endless modes of thought and style, but his creative genius refashioned all in a new mould, and his achievement must needs be called national, because it has no parallel in foreign countries.

[1] *Letterbook of Gabriel Harvey*, 1573–80, f. 52 (Camden Soc., 1884, p. 97).

BOOK II

FRENCH INFLUENCE ON ENGLISH LITERATURE 1500–1550

French Light and English Gloom

FRENCH literature of the first half of the sixteenth century has an abiding interest in the way alike of performance and promise. Contemporary English literature makes no pretension to equal vitality. Humanism was advancing with sure step through the length and breadth of France. A golden age of scholarship was inaugurated there. In vernacular literature the influence of the past was still powerful, even if the archaic tendencies were scoring their final victories. In poetry the old Gallic tradition, which Villon had lately glorified, acquired a fresh charm at the hand of Clément Marot, whose buoyancy and versatility were but lightly tinged by classical and Italian colour. The Graeco-Italian spirit was on the point of refashioning French poetry, but it had not yet acquired strength or fervour. The mediaeval temper was not yet exorcised.

In prose, forces of the past were also assertive. Rabelais, who was endowed with the most liberal intelligence of the epoch, sought to fuse the unregenerate turbidity of a former era with the best enlightenment of the present and future. But, outside the bounds of poetry, a new dispensation was already in being. While Rabelais was still jovially blending simples old and new, Calvin was austerely purging French prose of the old-fashioned cloudiness of thought and phraseology, and was steadily seeking a logical precision of utterance, which should initiate a style of vernacular writing new not only to France but to Europe.

Just as the half-century closed, Ronsard and his friends of the Pléiade judicially pronounced the Gallic tradition of the past to be a relic of barbarism. The year 1550 just stops short of the finest development, the greatest triumph, of the

French literature of the Renaissance. At the moment Ronsard (1524-85) had just committed himself to the cause of drastic reform. He had offered no proof of power to give the new plea effect, but he was on the eve of his conquest of the French Parnassus. Montaigne (1533-92) plays a part no less heroic than that of Ronsard on the stage of the French Renaissance ; he was a boy of seventeen in the sixteenth century's midmost year. The new light had dawned, and the noontide was quickly approaching.

In England there was no such sustained intellectual or literary activity, no such imminent capture of the final goal. The flashes of scholarship in early Tudor England kindled no achievement of the first rank. There was a fleeting radiance in the poetry of Wyatt and Surrey, in which Italian inspiration mingled with French, but the glow of Marot's poetic versatility was not matched in England. The ingenious graces and finished harmonies of the school of Ronsard when it was leaving its state of pupilage in France, had no contemporary counterpart across the channel. Nor was there in English prose any blustering championship of humanism to challenge comparison with Rabelais's chronicle of Pantagruel. Translation of more conventional specimens of French mediaeval literature constitutes the chief exploits in English prose of Rabelais's era. An Englishman, Sir Thomas More, made one prose endeavour of supreme originality in his *Utopia*. But in a comparative survey of literature More's masterpiece prompts a paradoxical reflection. The work was written not in English, but in Latin, and England showed no sign of appreciating its imaginative and speculative virtues at their true rate until she slowly learnt their value from continental criticism. More's political and social essay is the only fruit of an English pen, which during the sixteenth century left its impress on the contemporary thought of Europe. But neither the English language nor English appreciation helped the venture to its influence. Its recognition was due to foreign scholarship and foreign insight. More's *Utopia* fanned no flame of culture in the country of its author until at least two younger generations had run their course.

In the year 1550, when France was bright with literary fire, vernacular literature in England was suffering eclipse. Such literary energy as flung a tempered or a muffled light on the previous half-century appeared to be exhausted. The middle years of the century form in English literary annals a period of melancholy gloom which looked incapable of dispersal. Verse sank to the level of doggerel. Prose rarely rose above pedestrian dullness. The literary voice seemed to be dumb. The literary atmosphere appeared to be a smoky and sterilized 'congregation of vapours'. The only hopeful sign was an unqualified acknowledgement, in circles where literary and scholarly ambition still breathed, that foreign example was pointing the way to better things.

II

First Gleams of Tudor Humanism

There is ground for treating the literary stagnation of mid-sixteenth-century England as an abnormal instance of arrested development. The course of events pointed at one moment to a different and more exhilarating issue. At the end of the fifteenth century there was sign in England of a national humanist revival. In that movement, which promised better than it performed, three Oxford men, Colet, Linacre, and More, took the lead.

Before the sixteenth century opened, Linacre and Colet, with half a dozen other Oxford scholars, visited Italy and France. They eagerly studied Greek, and awoke some enthusiasm for the new learning in England. England seemed actively to be seeking affiliation with the European confederacy of humanism. Indeed, Linacre and More personally played distinguishable parts in the European drama of culture. But there were limitations in these Oxford scholars' intellectual affinities and ambitions. The merely aesthetic side of literature or scholarship scarcely moved them. They were no apostles of the Muses, who sought to dispel intellectual darkness with the torch of poetry and imaginative enthusiasm. More was better endowed with the literary instinct than his associates; he delighted in the Greek anthology, and brought a literary touch to illumine social speculation; yet his main interests were absorbed by political economy and theology. Linacre was fascinated by the inquiries of Aristotle and other Greek investigators into natural science; he finally concentrated his attention on the study of Greek medicine, and gained continental fame by a translation into Latin of the work of Galen, the Greek medical writer. At home he is chiefly remembered as the founder of the English College of Physicians. His friend Colet's zeal for educational reform was more vividly coloured by the genuine spirit of the Renaissance. Under the spell of the new learning, Colet founded St. Paul's School in London for the study of Greek as well as of Latin, but his intellectual affinity was mainly with scholastic philosophy and with Neo-Platonic mysticism. These Oxford pioneers won noble personal triumphs in special fields of culture. Yet none of their eminent individual achievements stimulated a national striving after literary perfection, or a national outburst of poetic sentiment. They set flowing no irresistible tide of intellectual or literary energy. They failed to sweep the country into the broad continental flood of liberal culture, even if they deserve the credit of building on English soil one or two outworks of that intellectual empire which ruled beyond the seas.

Foreign impulses moved these early Tudor scholars. Italian influence wrought primarily on them. Most of them sojourned in youth in Florence and Venice. France, however, chiefly gave their aspirations coherent shape and substance. On their way home from Italy, Colet and Linacre paused at Paris, and there they came into touch with the two men who set the seal on the humanist development of Europe. Linked together by ties of close friendship, these two men, whose names are familiar in the classicized forms of Budaeus and Erasmus, exercised a sovereignty in European scholarship which was unquestioned through the first half of the sixteenth century. The first runnings of the Renaissance stream in

England were mainly tributary to the work of these two
foreign masters.

The chief fact in the history of humanism in the early part
of the century is that France became the European centre of
scholarship.   Italy, which first introduced modern Europe to
Greek literature, yielded to France her place as apostle of
classical and notably of Greek culture.   Primarily associated
with the triumph of France is Guillaume Budé, or Budaeus
(1467–1540), who from his twenty-fourth year devoted himself
with an absorbing passion to the cause of the new learning.
As a teacher in the University of Paris he founded Greek
scholarship for modern Europe in the early days of the
sixteenth century, and subsequently acquired European fame
as an author, not merely on Greek philology, but on
Roman law, numismatics, and education.   While librarian to
Francis I, he formed a noble collection of Greek manuscripts,
and, after long years of controversy, he induced the king to
establish the Collège de France for the promotion of the
scholarly study of Greek, Hebrew, and Latin, by way of
a liberalizing counterpoise to the conservative Sorbonne.
Budaeus wrote as ably in French as in the learned tongues.
In his own language he penned his *Institution du Prince*,
which he dedicated to his royal patron, while King Francis I
was a youth of two-and-twenty.[1]   There the scholar
preaches the enlightened doctrine that a king should be a
philosopher and a man of learning; he asserts the superiority
of Greek over Latin as a means of culture, and insists on the
importance of the study of history as well as of philology.
Budaeus's repute finally rested on his discursive *Commentarii*
linguae Graecae, a commentary on the Greek language which
is a standard contribution to classical literature.   It first
interpreted the Greek language systematically and on
scholarly lines.   According to Sir Richard Jebb, Budaeus,
however inferior in literary genius to Erasmus, his intimate
friend and only rival, was a greater scholar and more learned
man.   The highest testimony to Budaeus's eminence

[1] Though written in 1516, Budaeus's *Institution* was not published till
1546.

was given by his younger contemporary, Calvin, who saluted him as 'the foremost glory and support of literature, by whose service our France claims for itself to-day the palm of erudition'. French poets paid in their native tongue no less enthusiastic tributes to the man whom they reckoned the greatest in reputation for learning of every kind.[1]

This verdict was accepted with acclamation in England by the pioneers of the Renaissance. Only one of Linacre's letters survives, and that, half in Greek and half in Latin, is a tribute of admiration addressed by him to Budaeus. More was an unswerving worshipper, and he owed to Budaeus the most encouraging appreciation which his *Utopia* received in its early days. More's contemporary, Sir Thomas Elyot, was one of the earliest English disciples of Budaeus's Greek scholarship, and he declared that the Frenchman's commentaries 'first offered an exact trial [i. e. elucidation] of the native sense of [Greek] words'. From the hand of Budaeus English scholars, like continental scholars, received the key which opened the treasury of Greek letters.

More direct and obvious than the influence of Budaeus on the transient dawn of English humanism was that of Erasmus (1466–1536), who, although a Dutchman, mainly developed in Paris his scholarly genius. His alert and inspiring personality is chiefly responsible for the best fruit of the humanist enlightenment all over Europe. With the Oxford pioneers of Renais-

---

[1] Some of the Latin elegies on the great man's death (in 1540) were rendered into English by poetasters, whose veneration was characteristically masked by a barbaric uncouthness of utterance. Compare, for example:

> All men bewailed Budaeus death;
> the air did also moan;
> The brawling brooks eke wept, because
> Budaeus good was gone.
> So men did wail, that everywhere
> were papers printed seen
> Of verses, threnes, and epitaphs,
> full fraught with tears of teen.

Flowers of Epigrammes, by Timothe Kendall, 1577 (Spenser Society, 1874, pp. 70-1). Kendall here translates one of the many elegies on Budaeus by the humanist disciple of Calvin, Theodore Beza. Cf. Beza's *Juvenilia*, ed. Machard, 1879, p. 60.

sance culture, his relations were continuous and close, and their debt to him scarcely admits of exaggeration. Colet first met Erasmus at Paris at the end of the fifteenth century, when the Dutch scholar was acting as tutor to a young English nobleman, William Blount, Lord Mountjoy. Erasmus was staying in an English boarding-house in the French capital. It was after Colet's introduction to him in Paris that Erasmus first visited England, at the invitation of his noble English pupil. Henceforth England was his frequent home, and he amply rewarded her hospitality by the intellectual impulse which he exerted on his hosts. Erasmus was a brilliant critic of life as well as of letters, and he caught from his Parisian experience a Gallic blitheness, some touch of which he communicated to Sir Thomas More, the most warmly attached of all his English disciples. To Erasmus's eager enthusiasm and social charm, and to the solid virtues of Budaeus's learning, is due most of the fruitfulness which can be allowed early Tudor humanism.

Probably the greatest service that Erasmus rendered to the intellectual renown of England was the stimulus that his friend-ship offered the genius of Colet's Oxford friend, Sir Thomas More. More is by far the greatest figure in the intellectual history of early Tudor England. But his association with the vernacular literature of the secular kind is too small to give him prominence in the history of the written language. The secular verse and the polemical theology which he penned in his native tongue have claims to the attention of students of popular speech and of popular taste, but they have not the supreme touch of style and inventiveness, which makes for vital or permanent influence.

More's political and social romance of *Utopia* stands on a different footing. It does not strictly belong to English literature, for it was written in Latin. Although its topics lie outside the aesthetic field, it interprets with such imaginative faculty most of the social and political ideals of the European Renaissance, that only a thin line separates it from pure literature. A destructive criticism of the social abuses of the old régime prefaces illuminating proposals for the regeneration and reconstruction of society. Cultivation of the intellect, religious toleration, civil liberty, high levels of physical well-being, are the watchwords of More's social reformation.

More's work has varied foreign affinities. The speculative temper is coloured alike by Plato's *Republic*, and by vague reports of aboriginal polity which had reached the writer from the discoverers of the New World. France can only claim indirect influence in its composition. Yet it was while More was engaged on diplomatic business at Antwerp, where French was the language of official circles, it was while he was talking in French with a Portuguese sailor who had voyaged to America, that More's alert imagination conceived his new ideal of society.

More's *Utopia* came into being as a contribution to European rather than to English literature. The greater part was penned in a foreign country. It was developed after the great Dutch apostle of humanism had delivered his message to its author. In no other work from an English pen is the effect of Erasmus's airy insight, playful sarcasm, and enlightened humanity more clearly visible. It was, too, on the Continent and not in England that the *Utopia* found its welcome.

Renaissance teaching had not yet permeated English sentiment, despite the efforts of Linacre and Colet. The fortunes of More's *Utopia* show that England, despite the endeavours of the Oxford pioneers, set small store by the stirring humanist revelation which her own son offered her. The first edition of the romance was printed at Louvain with the commendations of foreign, but of no English, scholars. It was quickly re-issued at Paris with an attractive epistle of kindly appreciation from the scholar Budaeus, which was addressed to a young English pupil, a graduate of the University of Paris, Thomas Lupset.[1] To Budaeus's generous preface the work chiefly owed its continental vogue. Edition after edition in the original Latin came from the Continental presses. No English printer handled the Latin

---

[1] The young Englishman, a protégé of Colet and an enthusiastic student of the New Learning, supervised the proofs.

text till the Oxford Press produced an edition in 1663, nearly 150 years after its first publication.

Nor was English, the native language of the author, the first vernacular into which the work was translated. It was a French version which first popularized More's speculations. The French rendering preceded any English rendering by at least a year. The priority of France in this regard needs no recondite explanation. The *Utopia* had a closer affinity with French intellectual progress than with English. In her association with More's *Utopia* France, too, was true to her rôle of agent-general for European culture. The great French scholar Budaeus may be said to have rendered England as well as Europe the service of interpreting the significance of More's philosophy. The anonymous French translator of 1549, and the Parisian bookseller, Charles Angelier, who in 1550 circulated More's Latin in modern speech, may be credited with giving the unscholarly world the first opportunity of studying at first hand More's social and political gospel.[1] France efficiently relieved More's *Utopia* of the risk of oblivion to which English blindness exposed it.

The paradoxical features which attach to the early fate of More's *Utopia* pass beyond the confines of bibliography. The cold neglect of the book at home, and the magnetic force which it exerted abroad, receive graphic illustration in the most characteristic literature of the early days of the French Renaissance. Not only was More's *Utopia* printed in Paris in the original Latin; not only was it eulogized by foreign scholars; not only was it translated into French before England gave any sign of recognition, it was also read and

---

[1] The terms of the title of the French translation are interesting: ' La Description de l'isle d'Vtopie ou est comprins le miroer des republicques du monde, et l'exemplaire de vie heureuse redigé par escript en stille tres elegant de grand'haultesse et maieste par illustre bon et scaieant personnage Thomas Morus citoyen de Londre & chancelier d'Angleterre. Avec l'Epistre liminaire composée par Monsieur Budé maistre des requestes du feu Roy Françoys premier de ce nom. . . . Les semblables sont à vendre au Palais à Paris au premier pillier de la grand'Salle en la Bouticque de Charles Angelier devant la Chapelle de Messieurs les Presidens.' 1550. The volume opens with a publishing licence of the Parlement of Paris dated 14 Nov. 1549.

assimilated by the most notable prose-writer and most advanced thinker of the early days of the French Renaissance—by Rabelais.   And that at an hour when More was barely known to his own countrymen save in his secondary and conflicting rôle of an heroic martyr of reaction.   Special attention is due to the evidence of familiarity with More's book which Rabelais offers in his buoyant story of Gargantua and of Gargantua's son Pantagruel, because it is a new fact in the comparative study of French and English literature, and one without precise parallel in the period which we are surveying.

Readers of Rabelais may remember how the giant Pantagruel learns that the decadent nation of the Dipsodes had invaded a country of enlightenment, which bore the name Utopia, and that the chief city of Utopia, which is called by Rabelais ' the city of the Amaurots ', was threatened by the Dipsodes with assault.   According to the story, the giant straightway undertakes the defence of the Utopians.   Rabelais's island of Utopia, with ' the great city of the Amaurots ', comes straight from More's romance.   The names are of More's invention.[1] Rabelais devotes four chapters to Pantagruel's warfare with the nation of the Dipsodes in behalf of Utopia and its inhabitants.   We learn that the giant, after taking prisoner Anarchus, the rebel king of the Dipsodes, transports into the conquered land of Dipsody a colony of Utopians to the number of 9,876,543,210 men, women, and children, ' besides artificers of all trades and professors of all sciences, in order to people, cultivate, and improve ' the degenerate country.

Utopia stands in the sight of Rabelais for the perfect state. There the golden age was renewed as it was in the time of Saturn ; and with some wise remarks on the problems of colonization, which oddly contrast with many grotesque and offensive details of the near context, Rabelais brings to a close the account of the colonization of Dipsody by the Utopians.[2]

[1] Prof. Abel Lefranc, in *Les Navigations de Pantagruel : étude sur la géographie rabelaisienne* (Paris, 1905), while pursuing a different line of inquiry, was the first to call attention to Rabelais's indebtedness to More's *Utopia*.

[2] The story of Pantagruel's relations with Utopia and the city of the Amaurots begins in Chapter 23 of Rabelais's second book, and is con-

Rabelais makes a serious appeal to the colonists of a new country to abandon the erroneous opinion of ' some tyrannical spirits ' that the natives should be plundered and ' kept in awe with rods of iron '. For the force of arms Rabelais would substitute ' affability, courtesy, gentleness, and liberality ', so that the conquered people may learn to live well under good laws. ' Nor can a conqueror,' argues Rabelais in the precise vein of Sir Thomas More, ' reign more happily, whether he be a monarch, emperor, king, prince, or philosopher, than by making his justice to second his valour. His valour shows itself in victory and conquest; his justice will appear in the goodwill and affection of the people when he maketh laws, publisheth ordinances, establisheth religion, and doth what is right to every one.'

Rabelais is at one with More at many other points of his humane polity. Their views in matters of education and of toleration for the most part coincide. The grafting of the English humanist's far-sighted speculation on the French humanist's disordered and farcical comedy of life is something of a literary curiosity. The isolated episode in our comparative study clearly invests More with the proud title of

tinued in Chapters 28 and 31, closing in the first chapter of the third book with Rabelais's benevolent remarks on the duties of the conquering colonist. It was not as a contribution to English literature, but to the continental literature of the Renaissance, that Rabelais knew the *Utopia*. Rabelais shows small knowledge of, or interest in, England. Two references, however, suggest that English and Scottish students were familiar figures in the academic society in France which Rabelais frequented. In Book II, Chapter 9, Pantagruel's companion, Panurge, cites a barely intelligible sentence on the inequality of the rewards of virtue, which he pretends to be in English. It is clearly Lowland Scotch derived from some Scotch student in Paris. (See Prof. Ker on ' Panurge's English ' in *An English Miscellany*, presented to Dr. Furnivall, Oxford, 1901, pp. 196-8.) In succeeding chapters of Rabelais's second book (chaps. 18-20) there is a farcical account of a disputation conducted by means of pantomimic signs between Panurge and a vainglorious English scholar called Thaumast. The latter had come out of ' the very heart of England ' to learn in France the secrets of philosophy. Thaumast finally admits that the French disputant has discovered to him ' the very true well, fountain, and abyss of the encyclopedia of learning', and promises to reduce to writing and to print the story of his experience. That promise was, according to Rabelais, duly fulfilled in a ' great book ' ' imprinted at London '.

the only Englishman who made in his day a substantial contribution to the broad stream of European thought.

More's work was done before the tide of European enlightenment had effectively stirred the intellectual waters of England. Of all the great French writers of the epoch Rabelais was least known in Tudor England. Although there was much in his boisterous frankness and intoxicated fooling which adumbrated the Elizabethan spirit, he for a long period escaped the observation of Englishmen. The exuberant sarcasm of some late Elizabethans, like Nashe, may owe something to him. But there was none in the England of his own day to appreciate the meaning of his deliverance as he appreciated the meaning of Sir Thomas More's message. Elizabethans made a tardy and imperfect acknowledgement of kinship with Rabelais. Their fathers were too backward in their study of humanism to spell out his alphabet.

III

French Grammars from Tudor Pens

The French mind under the early impulse of the Renaissance was sensitive to new intellectual or imaginative suggestion and impression. But in the seed-time of the French Renaissance, in the epoch of Rabelais, England had no fuel outside More's Latin prose wherewith to feed her neighbour's literary ardour. France was seeking foreign sustenance elsewhere. Writers in English lacked original inspiration, and literary drudgery satisfied most of their ambitions. Translation from the French mainly occupied their pens ; such industry could be no more than a domestic concern. There was a scanty poetry, which was, for the most part, the child of foreign parents; to foreign observers its dialect seemed inarticulate. As the century aged, and when the impulse of the Renaissance dwindled in France, the spirit of nationalism grew in French literature, and gradually, almost imperceptibly, assimilation of foreign ideas suffered discouragement. When Elizabethan poetry reached its full flood, French literature was passing through a phase of spent glory, which fostered a spirit of exclusiveness. As a consequence Elizabethan poetry won no recognition in France. Had the literary genius of the English Renaissance blossomed half a century earlier, England might have turned the tables on France in the way of literary indebtedness.

In early Tudor days the humble labours of translation and homely verse, which mainly absorbed English literary energy, were occasionally supplemented by experiments in grammar and lexicography. More especially did Tudor study of the French tongue issue in such practical exercises. French receptivity showed here no unreadiness to accept help from English hands. Tudor guidance in French grammar was welcomed in France. But when we close the page of More's *Utopia*, we find English authorship of the sixteenth century offering French students nothing besides the Gibeon-itish service of hewer of grammatical wood or drawer of lexicographic water. In all other fields throughout the period, England was the borrower and France the lender.

The story of the French grammars of Tudor England is a somewhat depressing pendant to the episode of the adventures in France of More's *Utopia*. But the two incidents have the common characteristic that they reverse the prevailing tendency of the Anglo-French literary intercourse and put England in the place of creditor instead of debtor. Grammar was an honoured study in the circle of Colet and his friends. Latin grammars of Linacre and of William Lily, who was the first master of Colet's foundation of St. Paul's school, acquired a foreign as well as a domestic vogue. If they are elementary and not wholly original efforts, Linacre's and Lily's grammars displayed a methodical simplicity which recommended them to teacher and pupil at home and abroad. Long afterwards—in the last quarter of the sixteenth century —an Englishman, Edward Grant, head master of Westminster School, first tried his hand at a Greek grammar for English boys (1575), and this endeavour in a revised version by Grant's successor at Westminster, William Camden (1597), achieved a wide popularity. But the most remarkable grammatical energy of Tudor England was bestowed on the French language, and it was there that English energy mainly won recognition in France. The rooted conviction among the cultivated classes of Tudor England that a familiar knowledge of French was essential to refinement found emphatic expression in a series of grammatical compilations. Caxton published some French-English dialogues. Alexander Barclay, a literary journeyman whose industry was mainly displayed in translation, compiled a French-English grammar as early as 1521. Barclay's efforts to reproduce phonetically French pronunciation is of importance to the study of English and French phonetics alike. For our present purpose the value of Barclay's *Introductorie to Write and Pronounce French* lies in the testimony that it offers to the Englishman's reverence for French speech. The Englishman seems doubtful of his competence to practise original composition in his native language, and seeks to compensate his defect by close study of a foreign tongue.[1]

The two names which are to be mainly associated with the Tudor devotion to French grammar are Giles Dewes and John Palsgrave. Palsgrave's achievement entitles him to the respect of all philologists, and confers distinction on the slavish toil of all grammarians. Dewes seems to have been a Frenchman who came here to teach French to Henry VIII, and then transferred his services to Henry VIII's daughter, Mary Tudor. For the princess Mary he wrote *An Introductorie for to learne to rede, to pronounce, and to speake French trewly*, which was first published about 1528. The work is short. It opens with rules of pronunciation. A grammatical section follows with tables of conjugation. The last part consists of letters and conversations between master and pupil, and between the princess Mary and members of her household. These French and English dialogues occasionally touch on public affairs, and although they are sparing of concrete

[1] It is curious to note that Robert Copland, the printer and publisher, appended to Barclay's French grammar that translation from his own pen of a treatise on French dances to which reference has been made above : see p. 52.

information, suggest by way of compensation the formal quaintness of contemporary conversational style in both languages.

Palsgrave's work is far more impressive. An Englishman,
educated at Paris, he went to the French court as chaplain of
Henry VIII's sister Mary, when she married the French king
Louis XII. But his life was mainly spent in England as
tutor to pupils of good birth, among whom was Henry VIII's
natural son, the Earl of Richmond. Humanism sheds some
brightness on his career. He was a familiar figure in learned
society, and claimed friendly intimacy with More and Erasmus.
His *magnum opus*, which he entitled *L'Esclarcissement de
la langue françoyse,* was prepared by him for the exclusive
use of his pupils, and he deprecated its sale to any one else.
The volume, the first sheets of which were printed in 1530 by
the Norman immigrant Pynson, startles us by its enormous size.
It reaches a total of 1110 large quarto pages. But its system-
atized and exhaustive design almost justifies the remarkable
bulk. Palsgrave makes a sustained endeavour to compare the
idiom and grammatic structure of the two languages. Elaborate rules are devised to govern every French inflection.
The conjugation of all French verbs, according to their
several types, is set out in full. The purposes of lexicography are served hardly less effectively than those of
grammar. There is an elaborate French vocabulary with
interpretations in English. Great stress is laid on the correct
pronunciation and the correct spelling of French. Above all
is it to be noticed that illustrations of verbal usage are liberally
supplied from past and present French writers, whose repute
stood high in Palsgrave's own day. His survey of French
literature is wide. Citations are frequent from the *Roman
de la Rose*, the ample fountain of almost all mediaeval
allegory ; from Alain Chartier, the laureate of French poetry
and prose of the first half of the fifteenth century ; and from
Le Maire des Belges, the popular leader of that prolific
school of French poetry which endeavoured, early in the
sixteenth century, to bind the new spirit of the Renaissance
in mediaeval fetters. Palsgrave, by way of epilogue, expresses
the wish that ' the nobility of this realm and all other persons,

of whatever estate or condition soever they be, may by the means hereof in their tender age the sooner attain unto a knowledge of the French tongue '.

The point best worth remembering about Palsgrave's massive venture is that nothing quite resembling it had been undertaken in France. He, an Englishman, practically gave the French people rules for their own language. Palsgrave's originality has been fully recognized in France. Tudor England set up one monument of literary drudgery which warrants some patriotic exultation. Not only can it claim a genuinely solid merit, but it drew from France the paradoxical acknowledgement that a 'barbarous' neighbour first taught her the grammatical principles of her own tongue.[1]

IV

THE RENAISSANCE PRINTERS OF FRANCE AND ENGLAND

The foremost contribution which was made outside Italy or France to the development of the Renaissance was the German invention of printing. From central Europe came, too, rare manifestations of artistic genius as well as a reformation of theological principle and practice. But the art of typography was the most momentous gift that Germany made to the new culture of Europe. No feature in the intellectual history of this period can compare in practical interest with the progress of the new mechanical contrivance, which stimulated literary effort, and provided means of distributing literary culture. Far-reaching differences marked the early growth of printing in the two countries of France and England, and much significance attaches to the contrast. A suggestive light is thrown on the intellectual qualities and tendencies of the two peoples in the days of Colet and More, of Budaeus and Rabelais, by a summary comparison of the

[1] A reprint in 889 quarto pages which was undertaken in 1852 by the government of Napoleon III does ample justice to Palsgrave's ingenuity. The editor salutes Palsgrave's volume as the only complete and authentic inventory of the French language of the compiler's day.

character, work, aims, and number of the early printers of England and France.

In France printing was introduced and was developed artistically and mechanically by men of learning. The process was deliberately fostered as an instrument of scholarly culture. The distinction to be drawn between the history of the infant presses of England and France may be inferred from such primary facts. In Paris the first French press was set up by two professors at the Sorbonne, who brought from Germany experts in the newly discovered art early in 1470. The craft was first practised within the precincts of the University. The Parisian professors' original object was to reproduce Latin educational manuals for their pupils. But the elementary bounds of the academic curriculum were quickly passed, and in less than two years twenty-two more or less substantial volumes had been issued, including (besides school-books) separate works of Vergil, Cicero, and Plato (in Latin), all the known writings of Terence, Sallust, Juvenal, and Persius, and two contemporary contributions to literature from the accomplished pen of Aeneas Sylvius, who was a pioneer of learning in the fifteenth century, and ended his career as Pope Pius II.[1]

The invention of printing instantly fascinated the cultivated intelligence of France. Within thirty years of its introduction a mass of printed literature in French and Latin was generally accessible, and the observer is amazed by its vastness and variety. Religious service-books and educational manuals were hardly more abundant in the closing years of the fifteenth century than Latin classics, both in the original and in translations, and vernacular prose and poetry. Presses multiplied with bewildering rapidity, not only in Paris, but in the provinces. At the opening of the sixteenth century eighty-five presses were at work in the capital city, and thirty-eight in the country outside. The owners and workers of these numerous presses were nearly all scholars and men of letters. Printing was formally admitted

[1] *The First Paris Press.* An account of the books printed for G. Fichet and J. Heynlin in the Sorbonne, 1470-2, by A. Claudin (Bibliographical Society's Publications, 1898).

at the dawn of the French Renaissance into the circle of the learned professions, if not of the fine arts.

Throughout the sixteenth century French typography retained its scholarly and lettered associations. The demigods of the golden age of French scholarship in the sixteenth century were printers. Henri Étienne the first, Robert Étienne his son, and Henri Étienne the second his grandson, whose surname took on English lips the form Stephens, have many titles to fame. Their careers cover the whole of the sixteenth century. The eldest of the three set up a press at Paris in 1501. The son and grandson edited with rare acumen the chief Greek and Latin texts; they compiled Latin and Greek dictionaries with heroic industry; they criticized current literary effort in admirable French prose; they urged, in the national interest, high ideals and ambitions on those who wrote in the native tongue of France. At the same time they actively shared the labour of putting manuscript into type at the presses which they owned, and energetically endeavoured to improve the mechanical details and artistic temper of their craft.

The Renaissance fostered the association of typography with literature, learning, and art throughout the European continent. Nowhere was the link from the outset so tenacious as in France, and there are no more brilliant examples of the alliance than the three generations of Étiennes supply; yet the Étiennes are stars in a French galaxy of cultured typographers.

The lieutenants need fear no comparisons with the captains in this field. The eminent bookseller and publisher of Paris, Geoffroy Tory, to whose artistic skill the Étiennes' press owed many of its aesthetic improvements, held his own in an almost wider region of culture. Born at Bourges about 1480, and educated in Italy, he was professor of philosophy at Bordeaux and other flourishing universities before he turned to the business of bookselling, printing, and publishing in Paris, where Francis I rewarded his efficiency by conferring on him the title of royal printer. At Paris he not only showed a fine taste in the choice of books for publication and in the superintendence of the typography, but he cut woodblocks with his own hand and devised illuminated miniatures. As an

engraver and miniaturist he won a universal repute. Nor do
such achievements exhaust Tory's characteristic record. Tory
wrote in French, and illustrated with engravings by himself,
an encyclopaedic volume fancifully entitled *Champ-Fleury*,
in which, besides expounding the principles and practice of
typography, grammar, and punctuation, he adjured his fellow
countrymen to eschew foreign fashions and to develop national
taste and habit on independent lines.[1]

Again, Étienne Dolet, the scholar-printer of Lyons, combined, in only a degree less than Tory or the Étiennes, literary
skill and enthusiasm with mechanical and mercantile aptitude.
His scholarly love for the style of Cicero led him to translate Cicero's works into French, and he was a voluminous
original writer alike in his own language and in Latin. Both
Rabelais and Clément Marot honoured him with their friendship. Yet the most effective service which Dolet rendered
to humanism was his work of printer at Lyons in the generation succeeding that of Tory, and he sealed his renown as a
humanist by suffering martyrdom in the Place Maubert at
Paris in the cause of freedom of opinion and of the press.[2]
The French Renaissance printer was no servant nor hireling
of current culture, literature, and opinion. He took his place
among the leaders and masters of scholarship and thought.
His workshop was an intellectual arsenal where he forged
with his own hand weapons of light.

Very different and far less glorious is the early story of
printing in England. The contrast illustrates how far Tudor
England loitered behind France in her intellectual progress
and in her encouragement of culture. William Caxton was an
intelligent silk-mercer of London, whose business took him to
the Low Countries before the middle of the fifteenth century.
During some thirty consecutive years he traded at Bruges.
There he learnt French and took pleasure in reading French

[1] Tory's *Champ-Fleury*, which does not compete with Palsgrave's
treatment of French grammar, was published at Paris in 1529—a year
before Palsgrave's book. The author died in 1533, aged 53.
[2] R. C. Christie's masterly biography of Dolet (2nd edition, 1899)
supplies a graphic detailed picture of the character and achievements
of this representative scholar-printer of the French Renaissance.

books in manuscript.   By way of recreation he translated with
his own pen a French mediaeval chronicle concerning the siege
of Troy. This literary labour he began at Bruges on March 1,
1468, and he completed it on September 19, 1471, while he
was staying on mercantile business at Cologne. That city
had become a year or two earlier a centre of typographic
activity, and there the art, which was of German origin,
came for the first time under English notice. When the
mercer returned to Bruges, he and a friendly Fleming
amused their leisure by putting the translation into type,
and it was published at Bruges in 1476. Thus the first
English book to appear in print was written and published
abroad, and was a rendering from the French. The title lays
stress on its French origin.[1]

Caxton soon repeated his experiment on English soil. He
brought from the continent the needful apparatus in 1477, and
opened a press in Westminster in 1478. The interval between
the beginnings of French and English printing is thus in
point of time only eight years. But the circumstances attending the birth of the art in the two countries and the rates of its
early progress lie very far asunder. In France printing was
deliberately imported from Germany with a view to facilitating
the growth of culture, and scholarship took control of its operations from the first. For England it came into being as the pastime of an English trader who was domiciled abroad, and the
seed which he sowed and watered in his own country developed
slowly and inertly. It is noticeable that Caxton supplied his
press with much 'copy' from his own pen, and that his example
was followed by one or two of his early successors, but the
English printers' literary handiwork was confined to translation from French prose in print or manuscript, and was

[1] The title runs to this effect :—' The volume, entitled and named the
Recueil of the histories of Troy, [was] composed and drawn out of divers
books of Latin into French by the right venerable person and worshipful
man Raoul le Fevre . . . which said translation and work was begun in
Bruges in the county of Flanders the first day of March the year of the
Incarnation of our Lord God a thousand four hundred sixty and eight,
and ended and finished in the holy city of Cologne the nineteenth day of
September the year of our Lord God a thousand four hundred sixty and
eleven.'

designed for popular recreation or edification. Scholarship had small hand in superintending the choice.

There was in the early diffusion of English typography, too, a constraint to which France offers small parallel. By the end of the fifteenth century only three or four presses had been set up in London, and all save Caxton's were small ventures of half-educated foreign mechanics. A German, independently of Caxton, printed a few books at Oxford in Caxton's day, but this enterprise came to an early end and found for near a century no assured successor. The history of the Oxford University Press cannot be traced further back than the year 1585.[1] Of Cambridge University a very similar story has to be told ; there a visitor from Cologne first printed nine or ten books in 1521 and 1522, but no attempt was made to inaugurate a permanent press till 1582. An English schoolmaster made a few typographic experiments at St. Albans in the early days. It was only in London that the art was practised from the fifteenth century without interruption.

Even in the English metropolis, the scope of the operations was modest when they are compared with those of foreign centres. Foreign hands guided the English enterprise. Caxton's chief assistant, Wynkyn de Worde, who came from Alsace, succeeded to his master's position of wellnigh solitary eminence. The thin ranks of London printers were gradually reinforced early in the sixteenth century by further recruits from Germany and the Low Countries. Meanwhile English typography contracted an immense debt to the superior mechanical and literary energy of the French. It is clear that in one or two cases Caxton had his books set up in Paris, and was the importer, and not the manufacturer, of volumes bearing his trade-mark. Of like significance is the fact that the 'copy' with which he largely fed his press was translations by himself or by his patrons which were mainly from recently printed

[1] Cf. F. Madan's *A Chart of Oxford Printing* (Bibliographical Society's Monographs, No. XII), 1904, and his *Early Oxford Press, 1468–1640* (Oxford Historical Society, 1895) ; and Robert Bowes and G. J. Gray, *J. Siberch* (the first Cambridge printer), Cambridge, 1906.

French literature. It is not therefore surprising to learn that, after Wynkyn de Worde's brief reign, the successor to Caxton as chief London printer was a French immigrant into England, Richard Pynson. The name of Pynson looms large in the annals of early English typography. He was a Norman, who learnt the art at Rouen, his native city. Caxton ignored the texts of the classics. In 1497 Pynson gave the English press its first tinge of scholarship by printing for the first time in England a Latin classic.[1] He chose the six plays of Terence. The first Paris press, a quarter of a century before, had rendered France the identical service. The classical tradition which distinguished the continental press since the discovery of the art was thus leisurely inaugurated in England by a Frenchman. But Pynson failed to graft a distinctive note of scholarship on the English effort in typography. To the Frenchman, English typography, however, lies under a substantial obligation. He was the first royal printer in England, receiving the appointment from Henry VIII on his accession in 1509. Thus in his person the new art first received official recognition. Pynson introduced 'the Roman letter' in place of the ancient Gothic or 'black letter', beyond which Caxton had not ventured. But in spite of Pynson's skilful embellishments of his craft, which were generally accepted by the country of his adoption, the superior cunning and activity of French typographers were freely acknowledged in England during his lifetime and long afterwards.

French collaboration was very slowly driven from the field of Tudor typography. In 1538, under the auspices of the minister Cromwell, a complete translation of the Bible, which was known as the Great Bible, was prepared for authorized use in English churches. The manuscript seems to have dismayed the London printers by its bulk, and the 'copy' was sent to Paris to be set up in a printing office there. Though the French government intervened and hindered the completion of the undertaking, the French type and presses were transferred to London. The finished volume—the greatest monument of early printing in England—remains a tribute to

[1] A Cicero, *Pro Milone*, is doubtfully assigned to Oxford, 1480.

French typographical craftsmanship and energy. The subsidiary mechanical appliances of the art long continued to be supplied by aliens. Not for some seventy years after the printing-press was introduced into this country does type seem to have been cast here. For the best part of a century type was imported from the continent. The earliest manufacturer of type in England was a French settler, Hubert Danvillier or Donviley, who received a grant of denization as 'fondeur de lettres' at the end of Edward VI's reign.[1]

French and other foreign printers had their agents in London throughout the early years of the sixteenth century, and French editions not only of the classics but of religious service-books abounded in the English market. The classical texts which were studied by Tudor scholars were invariably foreign importations, and largely came from France, although Germany and Italy were also prolific sources of supply. The French printers gave English scholarship especially valuable and practical aid in a direction of the highest moment. Greek typography was not practised at all in England for many a long year. It was at first a practical monopoly of Italy, and was somewhat slow in reaching France. Not till 1507, when some of Theocritus's poems were produced in Paris, was Greek printing associated with the French press. Soon after that date the French scholar-printers became Greek printers on a great scale and brought Greek typography to perfection. A standard Greek type was invented by Claude Garamond, the royal printer of Francis I, about 1541, and 'French Royal' type long held sway throughout Europe. No Greek book was printed in England before 1543, when Reginald Wolf, a German immigrant, set up an extract from Chrysostom in Greek type of French design.[2] Wolf's volume had few and

---

[1] *Alien Members of the Book Trade during the Tudor Period,* edited by E. J. Worman (Bibliographical Society, 1906), pp. 13–14. The French denizen, Hubert Danvillier, had a kinsman, Antonius Danvillier, also a French subject, who was naturalized in 1567, after having practised, at least since 1562, as a 'fusor typorum' in Blackfriars.

[2] See Robert Proctor's *Printing of Greek in the Fifteenth Century* (Illustrated Monographs, Bibliographical Society, No. VIII, 1900). A few words in Greek type were introduced into Latin texts by Siberch, the printer at Cambridge in 1522, and that example was followed several

undistinguished successors. Tudor England can claim no monument of Greek printing to set beside the scores of great contemporary examples of France. To the artistic ingenuity of French printers the circulation and perusal of Greek literature, a chief source of the new enlightenment, owed almost everything in Tudor England.[1]

The varied advantages which the typographic art derived from foreign guidance and example, never succeeded in investing the profession of printer in England with those noble literary and scholarly traditions which attached to it from the first in France as well as in Italy, Germany, and Holland. John Rastell, a literary lawyer, who was the friend and brother-in-law of Sir Thomas More, set up a press of his own under Wynkyn de Worde's tuition; but Rastell remains an unique instance of a member of a learned profession engaging under a Tudor sovereign in the printing trade, and his career quickly ended in disaster. Probably the nearest approach to a learned printer that Tudor England knew was Reginald Wolf, a native of Strasburg, who came to England in adult years, and was appointed royal printer to King Edward VI. We have just seen that he enjoys the distinction of printing in England the first Greek book. It was he, too, who originally devised and planned the great chronicle of English history which is identified with the name of Holinshed, its chief compiler. Yet Wolf hardly reached the standard of typographic culture with which the literary history of the Continent makes us familiar.

The religious element in the English atmosphere seems to have impaired the printers' enthusiasm for pure scholarship and learning. Foreign printers on settling in England tended to set the sectarian interests of religion above the broader interests

times before 1543, but no complete Greek text appeared in England earlier.

[1] The first great monument of Greek printing in England falls outside the sixteenth century; that was the edition of Chrysostom printed at Eton early in the seventeenth century from Greek type of the French pattern (c. 1610), by Sir Henry Savile, who had studied abroad under the best continental scholars. The French model was followed too in the beautiful Greek type presented to Oxford University by Dr. Fell at the end of the seventeenth century.

of culture. Many French printers, including the Étiennes, were of the Reformed faith, but the Huguenot sentiment worked otherwise than English Puritanism. Wolf came to identify himself wholly with English Protestantism, and his press ultimately served the cause of religious dogma almost to the exclusion of profane letters. There were examples of a like degeneracy on the part of a few printers of English birth, who shared Wolf's literary instinct. Grafton, a Tudor printer of English race, prepared for the press some compilations of English history from his own pen, but his literary activity was afterwards restricted to paths of Puritan theology. John Day, the printer-friend of John Foxe, the martyrologist, controlled a press of high mechanical repute, for which he wrote much; but all his writing was designed to champion the cause of Puritanism and to refute the pretensions of Rome. Thus a religious rather than a scholarly ideal dominated such Tudor printers as cherished any literary ambition through the middle years of the century. Here and there an English printer claimed responsibility for a translation of a popular profane pamphlet from a foreign tongue, but the episode was infrequent and rarely bore witness to a pronounced literary feeling. The choice of text showed indeed less taste than was exhibited by Caxton, the father of English typography, who made small pretension to aesthetic or scholarly aim. Nor did any of Caxton's successors approach him in his translating industry or versatility. From whatever point of view we examine the literary effort of Tudor printers, there emerges the plain fact that the French type of scholar-printer, whose literary skill and sympathy ranked him with the great contemporary men of letters, was unknown to Tudor England. The contrast between the positions assigned by the two countries to the printer and his art in the society of culture was sharply defined by the Stationers' Company of London in the seventeenth century, when Parliament threatened to abolish some mercantile privileges of the trade :

France especially is famous for the value she sets upon that profession and trade of men, whom we in England incorporate by the name of Stationers; for there they are privileged above mere mechanics, and honoured with a habitation, as it were, in the suburbs of literature itself.[1]

V

EARLY TUDOR TRANSLATIONS FROM FRENCH PROSE

Although printers in England of the early sixteenth century were comparatively few and uncultivated, they were not idle. Much literature came quickly from their presses. Caxton's activities marked out the road which most of his early disciples followed. Apart from service-books or missals, which were in Latin, their work was mainly confined to the English language. They ignored the texts of the classics. Mediaeval literature in England was scanty. Caxton put into type the poetry of Chaucer and Lydgate, but most of his abundant energy was absorbed by translation from the French, much of which came from his own pen. Caxton's translations were invariably in prose. A little French poetry was rendered for him by others into English verse. From the date of the introduction of printing into England down to 1550, the bulk of the literature offered by the printers to the English reading public was in prose, and for the most part in prose which was translated from the French. The French source was not always itself an original work; it was often a translation from the classical tongues, or from the Italian or the Spanish. Cicero, Vergil, Seneca, Thucydides were soon printed in English, but the printed text was derived from contemporary French versions. French was the key with which Caxton and his early successors sought to unlock for their clients such literature of the world as seemed deserving of notice.

Caxton was pursuing a veteran tradition in offering English readers a recreative literature from French pens. The taste for French verse and prose was already well alive. The authors of mediaeval France were already vaguely acknowledged in England to be apostles of culture. Caxton's printing press conspicuously reinforced the conservative pre-

[1] Arber, *Stationers' Company Registers*, i. 584.

dilection. French literature of the Renaissance type was unborn in the season of Caxton's activity. The first English printers were bound to have recourse to the expiring literary efforts of mediaeval France. There were voluminous stores in both manuscript and print from which Caxton could glean. The fame of the later mediaeval authors was still strong in France, and the early French presses increased the circulation of their work. The books belonged to a school which the Renaissance was on the point of dismissing to oblivion. The tone of thought was languid, and lacked the stimulus of the new era.

The early Tudor press gave its readers in full measure English versions of French romances of chivalry, of romantic allegories with ethical intention, and of picturesque historical narratives. Many had just been printed in France for the first time. No ampler proof of the readiness and eagerness of the average English mind to assimilate French literature is needed than the mere catalogue of books to which the early English printers devoted their labours.

In the more ancient literary fields Caxton found the richest fuel for his press in translations by his own pen of such French tales of chivalry as *The four Sons of Aymon*, *The Life of Charlemagne*, and the romantic *History of Blanchardin and Eglantine*. Of all Caxton's publications none in the category of French chivalric romance claims a higher interest than his *Morte d'Arthur*, a cycle of Arthurian legend. Sir Thomas Malory had adapted the work from the French some seven years before Caxton set up his press at Westminster. Malory's manuscript was completed before Caxton had learned the printing art at Bruges or Cologne. In publishing it Caxton illustrated his sympathy with a pre-existent vogue. It was in France that the Arthurian tradition, which English literature was to assimilate, had long since received its literary baptism. Such English romances of Arthur, Lancelot, and Guinevere as circulated in mediaeval manuscripts, acknowledged French inspiration. Malory worked almost exclusively on old French versions of the Arthurian story. Fifty-six times does he warn his reader that ' the French book ' is his guide and tutor.   Malory is a compiler on a liberal scale, and brings together scattered stories, but he offers his readers little that cannot be traced to a comparatively early French original. To Caxton's typographic labours on Malory's *Morte d'Arthur* is mainly due the fruitful career which Arthurian romance has since run in English poetry.   There is no more striking testimony either to the continuity of French influence on English literature or to the stimulus which that influence derived from the printing press.

Caxton found other literary material in French composition of more recent date.   Through the early years of Caxton's own fifteenth century a French writer who enjoyed wide vogue was Alain Chartier (1390 – 1458), whose literary industry is attested by massive memorials both in print and manuscript.   He was a voluble philosopher in prose and a fluent poet, delighting in ballades and rondeaus, in melancholy strains of ethical allegory, and in prose disquisitions on the philosophy of life.   For a time he was French ambassador in Scotland, and Margaret of Scotland, the wife of Louis XI while Dauphin, adored him and his work.   Alfred de Musset has written a charming poem on the old anecdote, now unhappily refuted as apocryphal, that the princess publicly in the French court kissed the sleeping philosopher and poet, who was notorious for his ugliness, and excused herself for the breach of etiquette by the remark that she kissed the golden wisdom which issued from the ugly lips.[1]   Chartier died in old age in 1458 after a life spent in the service of Church and State.   But his name had lost

---

[1] The story was first printed by Étienne Pasquier, the poet-historian, in 1560, who illustrates Chartier's 'mots dorez et belles sentences' by a long quotation from his *Curial* (see *Les Recherches de la France*, Livre VI, ch. xvi, in Pasquier's *Œuvres*, Amsterdam, 1723, i. 584-5).   The story was well known to the Elizabethans.   Puttenham relates it somewhat inaccurately in his *Arte of English Poesie*, 1589 (ed. Arber, 1869, p. 35). The English critic assigns the adventure to 'that noble woman twice French queen, Lady Anne of Britain, wife first to King Charles the VIII, and after to Louis the XII, who passing one day from her lodging toward the king's side, saw in a gallery Master Alain Chartier, the king's secretary, an excellent maker or poet, leaning on a table's end asleep, and stooped down to kiss him, saying thus in all their hearings, " we may not of princely courtesy pass by and not honour with our kiss the mouth from whence so many sweet ditties and golden poems have issued." '

none of its repute in the France of Caxton's time.   A French
contemporary of the English printer hailed Chartier as

> Un Poete hault et scientific . . .
> Doux en ses faicts, et plein de rhetorique.
> Clerc excellent, orateur magnifique.

Caxton mainly turned his attention to Chartier's prose, to
his *Curial*, a gently pathetic description of the trials of
a courtier's life.[1]   English readers welcomed the book with
something of the Scottish princess's ardour.

Another French writer, whose fame in England Caxton
rather extended than inaugurated, was Christine de Pisan, wife
of Étienne Castel (1363–1430 ?).   She may almost be regarded
as the earliest of professional authors amongst women, and is
certainly worthy to rank with literary heroines of a later age.
Prose and poetry came with equal fluency from her pen, and
her voluble expositions of mediaeval ethics and ideals gave her
a repute which her contemporary Joan of Arc alone excelled
among the women of her time.   A lyric in praise of the Maid
of Orleans was one of the latest of Christine's songs.   Christine
had declined the invitation of Henry IV of England to visit his
court, but her only son, Jean Castel, learned knightly exercises
from an English master.   In the household of the Earl of
Salisbury Jean Castel was serving when Caxton was a young
man.   The teaching which Christine devised for her son in
her versified *Moral Proverbs* was turned into English by
Earl Rivers, brother of Edward IV's queen Elizabeth, and
was circulated by Caxton in print.   To Christine is ascribed,
moreover, the original French of the chivalric handbook,
Fayts of Arms and Chivalry, which also came in English
from Caxton's press, and enjoyed a wide popularity in social
circles during the early years of Sir Thomas More.   The cult
of old French chivalry was endowed with a new lease of
life by Caxton's typographic energy, and Christine de Pisan
enjoyed in England the honours of its chief priestess.

[1] To Caxton's volume there was prefixed a translation of a ballade of
unexceptionable moral intention with a clumsy burden ('Ne chyer but
of a man Joyous'). The poem, though assigned to Chartier, is from
another pen. See M. Paul Meyer's note in reprint of Caxton's volume
by the Early English Text Society.

A popular venture of Henry Pepwell, one of Caxton's youngest professional pupils, was *The Cyte of Ladyes,* an English rendering of one of Christine's spacious allegories in prose. The original, *Le trésor de la cité des dames,* was first printed in the fifteenth century at the great Paris press of Antoine Verard.[1]

When the sixteenth century opened, Tudor England, at the bidding of Caxton and his disciples, continued to seek sober recreation in French literature of a dead or dying generation. The toil of translation was treated by the first English printers as a normal part of their office-work. They were self-educated, and wrote with rough and ready pen. It was inevitable that their voluminous energy should leave its mark on the style of early Tudor prose. Their syntax was often faulty. They were no grammatical purists. They liberally and literally transferred to their pages French idiom and French vocabulary. But they tended under French sway to fluency. Although they linked their sentences with one another by no more subtle ties than disjointed particles, they helped to make English prose lithe and flexible. Above all, they stimulated the habit of vernacular composition. The late mediaeval French prose, which Caxton and his immediate successors so freely anglicized, lacked that lucidity and logical precision which the French Renaissance was to generate, but it had for the most part a simplicity which often bred a languid charm. English prose of the fifteenth century was, when compared with its French prototype, as small in quantity as in literary quality, but the English printers' energy in translation fitfully brightened the literary prospects of the domestic language, and there was for the time no other clear source of illumination.

Caxton's example was fruitful, and proved a stepping-stone to better achievement. In the generation which embraces the first thirty years of the sixteenth century one English writer pursued Caxton's methods with enhanced ability and pronounced literary effect. Lord Berners has

[1] Cf. *Robert Laneham's Letter*, ed. Furnivall (New Shakspere Soc.), 1890, pp. clxxvii et seq.

higher claims than Caxton to the literary historian's attention. He betrays qualifications for the literary craft to
which Caxton was a stranger, but he can plead no greater
independence of French inspiration. Lord Berners worked
even more exclusively than Caxton under French influence.
Like Palsgrave, he was one of the English courtiers who
accompanied Henry VIII's sister Mary to the brilliant Parisian
court when she married Louis XII. His later life too, was
closely connected with France. It was wholly passed at
Calais, then an English possession. Of Calais and its
marches he was governor. His work brings England's French
outpost into prominence as a literary as well as a territorial
link with France. At Calais Berners first turned to literature,
devoting voluminous industry to rendering French books
into English. Some of the authors whom he introduced to
his own country were Spanish. But he worked not on the
original text, but on French versions.

Lord Berners's translating zeal achieved two triumphs, which
notably helped to maintain English literary effort in its French
mould. He rendered into English two French books of great
length and of surpassing interest in different ways. His first
undertaking was Froissart's *Chronicle* (1523–5). A subsequent
venture was one of the best of the French romances of chivalry,
Huon of Bordeaux. Both works were of veteran standing in
Lord Berners's time. Froissart was a contemporary of Chaucer.
He was a mediaeval poet as well as a mediaeval chronicler,
and his poetry shows that the lyric sense was strong in
him. He was well endowed with the joy of life, with gaiety
of heart, with gifts of observation and an eye for picturesque
incident. All these qualities colour his story of the four-
teenth-century war between France and England, and give
his chronicle the temper of a prose epic and the variety
of a chivalric romance. Lord Berners's literary touch was
heavier than that of his original author. His style caught less
of the Gallic blitheness than could be wished. But his
English version of Froissart opened to the English people
a new vein of historical literature, which was unknown in
England before. Froissart had his precursors in Villehardouin

and Joinville. Mediaeval England was innocent of such masters of historic sensibility.

The romance of *Huon of Bordeaux*, which Berners also communicated to his fellow countrymen in their own tongue about 1530, belongs to another literary category. Its pretences to historic truth are empty flourishes. It is a curious medley of French charm and *naïveté* and of Gothic and grotesque legend. With a welcome inconsistency it imports into feudal scenery the airy figure of Oberon, King of the Fairies. Oberon is an ethereal conception even in Berners's dry presentation of the French, and it stirred the English imagination. Shakespeare drew from Berners's English version his knowledge of the fairy king. If the influence on English literature of mediaeval French fancy were confined to those scenes in *A Midsummer Night's Dream* of which Oberon is the hero, English gratitude to mediaeval France and her Tudor interpreters ought not to be grudging.

But it was not only chivalric history or romance that Tudor England found of interest and service in French prose. The translators from the French supplied Englishmen with much of their first knowledge of practical science. Botany became a popular English study largely under French influence. ' *The Grete Herball*, which giveth parfyt knowlege and understandyng of all maner of herbes and there gracyous vertues,' which was till near the end of the sixteenth century the standard English manual of botany, was a literal rendering ' out of ye Frensshe into Englysshe ' of *Le Grand Herbier*, an early publication of the press of Paris. The English version was first printed 'at London in Southwarke' in 1526, a year after the publication of the second and concluding volume of Lord Berners's notable rendering of Froissart.

VI

Les Rhétoriqueurs

Berners, like Caxton, translated French prose into English. Neither betrayed interest in French verse, nor showed much acquaintance with strictly contemporary French literature.

Both sought their material in work of a past generation. There were, however, poetic writers in England of Berners's generation who stood to French literature in a somewhat different relation. The debt of early Tudor poetry to France was hardly smaller than that of early Tudor prose, but the loans involved no calls on the past; they were levied without exception on the present. The French literature from which the early Tudor poets sought inspiration was of their own epoch, and free adaptation took for the most part the place of direct and avowed translation. A few poetic voices in early Tudor England essayed some original utterance, but they failed to strike a distinctively national note. The native fancy was for the most part a foreign echo, and the metrical form was invariably a foreign suggestion. None the less the obligation to the foreigner usually stopped short of literal transference.

A crowd of poetic pens were active and voluble in France at the end of the fifteenth and through the early decades of the sixteenth century. The printing presses groaned more heavily beneath the weight of freshly penned verse than of freshly penned prose. Elaborate treatises on the art of poetry and on prosody bore witness to the seriousness with which poetic labour was pursued. There was a sportive ingenuity in some new metrical devices, although the light verse often sank to the level of inane punning and did not disdain the verbal quip of the charade. Rondeaus and ballades abounded, for the gay heart of France had not ceased to beat. But Villon's triumphs were not repeated. Dullness was the goddess to which the French contemporaries of early Tudor poets often sacrificed their energies. The French poets of the epoch too often yielded to the torpor of rhetorical and allegorical convention which the *Roman de la Rose* inaugurated more than two centuries before. Rhetorical allegory was the staple of their argument. The view of life is always ethically sound; the warnings against sin and imposture are fervent, but the savour of tediousness is pronounced.

'Les rhétoriqueurs,' as the early poetic school of sixteenth-century France is known to French critics, have

for numbers, fertility, and popularity no counterpart in contemporary England. In them the old mediaeval tradition,
although just tinged with the new humanism, died hard.
Jean le Maire de Belges (1473-1525?), who wrote of
honour and virtue with much allegorical skill and more
variety than is common, was reckoned by charitable friends
the Homer of this band. The grammarian Palsgrave
cites him liberally, and he was confidently placed among the
immortals. There is more reason in the ridicule which
Rabelais bestowed on another eminent member of the
brotherhood, Guillaume Crétin (d. 1525)—*le bon Crétin au
vers équivoque*—the poetic historiographer of Francis I.
Of him, under the grotesque name of Raminagrobis, Panurge
takes humorous counsel on the subject of marriage, quoting
literally one of his serious poems as if it were an effort in
burlesque. In the train of this army there tramped, however, one attractive vagabond figure, Pierre Gringoire, who
lived in somewhat obscure circumstances from 1475 until
about 1534.[1] He was a professional actor, whose main energy
was engaged in penning rudimentary plays, dramatic dialogues
and satires, insolently lampooning current politics and social
life. In the presentation of his social and political burlesques
on the stage he filled the chief parts. But Gringoire was more
versatile than his dramatic essays suggest. He made many
experiments in that allegorical interpretation of virtue and
vice, in which the 'rhétoriqueurs' did homage to the ancient
manner of the *Roman de la Rose*.

It was to Gringoire and to his masters, 'Les Rhétoriqueurs,'
that the early stream of Tudor poetry was largely tributary.
English allegory and satire of Henry VIII's reign were of the
contemporary French pattern. Gringoire and his companions
of the French stage also fed Tudor drama at its birth. John
Heywood's *Four P's* follows closely a French model.[2] But
Heywood and his disciples refrained from confessing their debts
to France. Nor of five English verse-writers of the epoch

[1] Out of the uncertainties of his biography was evolved the little
modern French play by Théodore de Banville, recently familiar on the
English stage under the title of 'The Balladmonger'.
[2] See p. 372, infra.

who merit notice, did more than one frankly avow themselves to be translators of current French or other foreign poetry. Only one plainly announced an ambition to improve Tudor culture by accepting foreign guidance. The other four worked more subtly and less openly, but their labours almost as clearly echoed the French note.

The credit of first openly introducing Tudor readers to French poetry of their own period belongs to Alexander Barclay (1475?–1552). He is a figure of great importance in a comparative study of Tudor literature and the contemporary literature of the Continent. One of the many Scotchmen who were educated in Paris, he passed all his adult career in England, holding ecclesiastical office in Devonshire, Ely, or London. He declared that his aim in life was to ' English such foreign authors as might benefit the mind and morals of English people '. He modestly disclaims ability to do more. Though he did not confine his attention to French literature, his laborious compilation of a French grammar, *The Introductory to Write and to Pronounce French,* shows how high the French language stood in his regard.

All Barclay's translations showed a poetic facility which caught the popular ear, and familiarized a somewhat sluggish audience with the drift of much contemporary foreign effort. Very widely known was Barclay's rendering of the Latin *Eclogues* of the contemporary Italian, Baptista Mantuanus, the ' good old Mantuan ' of Shakespeare's schooldays.[1] Even more acceptable proved Barclay's *Ship of Fools,* which came from the German of the master satirist of the era, Sebastian Brandt. A French rendering of the *Ship of Fools* was printed as early as 1497. French example governed there and elsewhere Barclay's choice of material. It is more pertinent to our present purpose to dwell on Barclay's allegorical poem called *The Castle of Labour,* which came from the contemporary

---

[1] A later translation by George Turberville came out in 1567. Cf. *Love's Labour's Lost,* IV. 2, where Holofernes the schoolmaster quotes the opening words of Mantuanus's *Eclogues* :

' " Fauste, precor gelida quando pecus omne sub umbra
Ruminat,"

and so forth. Ah! good old Mantuan . . . Old Mantuan! old Mantuan! Who understandeth thee not, loves thee not.'

French of Pierre Gringoire, and is peculiarly characteristic of the pre-Renaissance tendency of poetry in France.

Gringoire's *Château de Labour*, which was turned into English verse by Barclay, is cast in the conventional mould. 'Jeune Enfant' (Young Child) is the hero, who after much tuition from personages named respectively Chastisement ('Chastiement'), Free Will ('Franc Arbitre'), and Reason ('Entendement')—the last a very grave old man—is misled by a lady of fashion whom he marries. Legal tricksters involve 'Jeune Enfant' in many misunderstandings with his wife. He is finally led by 'Bon Voulant', 'Boncœur', 'Talent de Bien-Faire' (Desire of Well-doing) to the Castle of Labour, where he finds peace and satisfaction. Hard work is the salvation of man's soul. Such is the moral of the piece, which runs conversely in Barclay's words:

> Idleness, mother of all adversity,
> Her subjects bringeth to extreme poverty.

Barclay's version went through at least two editions. The French muse of Gringoire smoothed the path of allegory in Tudor England.

Alexander Barclay was hardly less well acquainted with Gringoire's master in allegory, Jean Le Maire de Belges, whose fame was made by *Le Temple d'Honneur et de Vertu* (*c.* 1503). The French poet wrote this allegorical poem 'à l'honneur de feu Monseigneur de Bourbon'. In 1513, when Sir Edward Howard, the Lord High Admiral of England, was slain in a sea-fight with the French off the coast of Brittany, Barclay followed closely in the Frenchman's footsteps of elegy, and gave voice to the national mourning in 'The description of the Towre of vertue and honour into the which the noble Howarde contended to enter by worthy actes of chivalry'. Barclay's *Towre* was planned on the model of Le Maire's *Temple*.

The discipleship to foreign masters of the four Tudor poets, John Skelton (1460–1529), Stephen Hawes (1470?–1524), Sir Thomas Wyatt (1503–42), and the Earl of Surrey

---

[1] Mr. Wilfrid P. Mustard, *Modern Language Notes*, Jan., 1909, Vol. xxiv, No. 1, pp. 9–10.

(1517-47), lies less on the surface than in the case of Barclay. Their ambition led them far from the path of mere translation. The little group falls chronologically and critically into two virtually independent pairs. Skelton and Hawes differ much in manner and matter, but they were precise contemporaries, and they are nearly akin with the past in their primitive sentiment. Wyatt and Surrey are of a younger generation, and, for all their uncouthness, had a touch of lyric intensity and a flexible temper which encouraged the pursuit of novel effects. Very distantly they heralded some coming developments. The part they play on the stage of British literary history is somewhat shadowy and solitary. But their affinity is with the future.

The chronological interval between these twin pairs of poets exposed them to French influences of somewhat different kinds. Hawes and Skelton began their work late in the fifteenth century, and were coeval with the latest survivors of French mediaevalism, with the ' rhétoriqueurs ' who, though they absorbed something of the new classical learning drew most of their inspiration from an era that was dying. The current French poetry which offered its stimulus to Hawes and Skelton mainly consisted of allegories on the pattern of Le Maire de Belges or Gringoire, or of verse chronicles of recent and contemporary history, or of crude dramatic satire which attacked with an undiscriminating insolence political and theological opinion or social life.

More promising were the French auspices which smiled on Wyatt and Surrey. They were young enough to witness the glorious advent of Clément Marot (1497-1544), who carried on the mediaevalized tradition of the ' rhétoriqueurs ', but touched it with the hand of genius. Marot's spirit caught the sunset glow of the Middle Age, and fused it with the dawning light of the French Renaissance.

VII

French Influence on Skelton and Hawes

From the days of Chaucer in the fourteenth century Englishmen had acknowledged the fascination of the metrical dexterity and variety of French poetry. The tune often attracted Englishmen more potently than the words. The first Tudor poets were loyal to the Chaucerian traditions of dependence on French metre. They pursued almost involuntarily the old habit of naturalizing French rhyme. The matter was often a loan from France. But the metrical chains which bound early Tudor poetry to the French muse are more promising features of the picture than the links of topic. There was little in contemporary French verse to quicken English poetic thought. But the French metres were capable of increasing the pliability of the English language and of English prosody.

The mediaeval French poets were marvellously fertile in the development of metrical forms, and fully warranted English emulation. Ballades and rondeaus, virelays and chansons, are the best known though by no means the only metrical inventions of mediaeval France, and they were wrought to melodious effect by many generations of French poets before the Renaissance came into being. The French contemporaries of Hawes and Skelton were loyal to the old forms, but were prone to pedantic emendation which often issued in grotesque puerilities, in shallow fopperies of rhyme. The sensitive taste of the full-fledged Renaissance was offended by the 'rhétoriqueurs'' extravagances, and the whole mediaeval usage was quickly involved in an ill repute which was not wholly deserved. The old metrical standards were rejected for new. Skelton and Hawes, came for the most part under the sway of these unregenerate crudities and eccentricities. Both derived inspiration from the French 'rhétoriqueurs', who were their contemporaries.

Skelton, although capable at times of gentle tones, was in the main a bitter and aggressive satirist of persons and things. For Frenchmen he showed small personal friendship. He attacked a distinguished French humanist and historian, Robert Gaguin, who was ambassador at Henry VIII's court. The foreigner had frowned on him 'full angerly and pale'. But despite his insular professions, Skelton's work pays ample tribute to French culture. It abounds in French words and phrases. He christened his diatribe against his French foe

Gaguin with the French substantive *Recule* (i.e. retort). One of his best known poems, an allegorical description of the vices of courtiers, called *The bowge of Court*, employs, oddly but characteristically, an anglicized form of the French word *bouche* (mouth) in the sense of 'rations'. A translation by Skelton of a popular mediaeval ethical treatise, Guillaume de Guilleville's *Pélerinage de la vie humaine*, attests, too, a French affinity, and an involuntary respect for the French mediaeval tradition.[1]

More important are the signs that Skelton gave of the close attention with which he watched the poetic rhetoricians who ruled the French realm of letters in his own time. From them he eagerly caught hints. Le Maire de Belges, the most versatile of the rhetorical poets in France at the opening of the sixteenth century, gained much fame from a playful piece called *L'Amant vert*. There 'the green lover', i.e. a parrot, recites two lively addresses or *contes* in verse to the bird's mistress, a patroness of the poet, Margaret, Duchess of Burgundy. Skelton dedicated to Queen Catherine of Arragon, Henry VIII's first queen, two rambling satires called *Speke, Parrot*, which he also placed in a parrot's lips. It is clear whence came the suggestion. Skelton's voluble bird is no less polyglot than the pet of the Burgundian duchess in Le Maire's narration. 'Dowse (i.e. douce) French of Paris Parrot can cerne (i.e. discern, understand)' is one of Skelton's Anglo-French testimonies to his parrot's accomplishments, and many a descriptive note appended by Skelton to his poem is in ill-printed French. The English parrot has a far more strident note than the French bird, but the kinship is not in doubt.

Yet Skelton's chief debt to French influence only becomes visible when we compare with French verse the English poet's

---

[1] This achievement illustrates the persistent popularity in England of comparatively valueless French mediaeval literature. Skelton here anglicized part of *Le Roman des Trois Pélerinages*, a long moralizing paraphrase of *Le Roman de la Rose* (the old French allegory), which was composed in the fourteenth century and was already popular in Chaucer's England. Skelton's translation is lost, but he mentions it in the list of works which he supplies in *A Garland of Laurel*. Lydgate had already translated the same work. A translation of another portion of Guilleville's gigantic work Caxton printed in 1483 as *The Pilgrimage of the Sowle*.

characteristic metre of short lines which vary in number of
syllables from four to six, and rhyme usually by couplets, but
at times four, five, or six times over. This metre, which is
known in England by the specific epithet Skeltonian, may be
originally a Low Latin invention. Something very like it
reached France in the early middle ages, but Skelton's French
contemporaries gave it a new life, and they may well be
regarded as its parents. No English poet of any earlier
epoch had ventured systematically on lines of fewer syllables
than eight; alternations of lines of seven syllables were occasional but rare. Of Skelton's abbreviated scheme he wrote :

> Though my rime be ragged
> Tattered and jagged,
> Rudely rainbeaten,
> Rusty and motheaten,
> If ye take well therewith
> It hath in it some pith.

It is not difficult to show that the 'pith' of Skeltonian verse
—its short, jolting gallop—is of recent French breeding, or to
show that its most telling features, which have no English
precedents of earlier dates, are matched in popular French
verse of Skelton's own generation.

Probably the most popular French poem which was written
and published in Skelton's early manhood was a spacious
epic on the reign of Charles VII (who died in 1461), *Les
Vigiles de la mort de Charles VII.* The author was
Martial de Paris, who is often called Martial d'Auvergne
(1440–1508). His spirited verse is said to have been sung by
French peasants while they laboured in the field. Martial
specially loved the jog-trot melody of five- and six-syllable
lines, with an ingenious rhyming scheme which pleasingly
relieves the monotony of the brief line :

> Mieux vaut la liesse,
> L'amour et simplesse
> De bergiers pasteurs,
> Qu'avoir à largesse
> Or, argent, richesse,
> Ni la gentilesse
> De ces grans seigneurs :

Car ils ont douleurs
Et des maux greigneurs;
Mais pour nos labeurs
Nous avons sans cesse
Les beaux prés et fleurs,
Fruitaiges, odeurs,
Et joye à nos cœurs,
Sans mal qui nous blesse.

Vivent pastoureaux,
Brebis et agneaux!
Cornez, chalumelles:
Filles et pucelles,
Prenez vos chappeaux
De roses vermeilles,
Et dansez sous treilles,
Au chant des oyseaux.[1]

Skelton emulated such experiments with slight variations. He never reached the French level of grace or gaiety; yet in salutations to his lady patronesses in his *Garland of Laurel*, he essays many a pleasing innovation in English prosody on the French pattern. Here is an example of Martial de Paris's five- and six-syllable lines in Skeltonian English, which the English poet addressed to a well-wisher:

Sterre of the morow gray,
The blossom on the spray,
The freshest flowre of May,
Maydenly demure,
Of womanhode the lure,
Whereof I make you sure,
It were an hevenly helthe,
It were an endless welth,
A lyfe for God himselfe,
To here this nightingale
Amonge the byrdes smale
Warbelying in the vale.

In a cognate strain Skelton apostrophizes 'Maystres Margaret Hussey':

Mirry Margaret,
As mydsomer flowre,
Jentill as fawcon
Or hawke of the towre:

[1] *Les Poètes françois jusqu'à Malherbe* (Paris, 1824, t. II, pp. 282-3).

> With solace and gladnes,
> Moche mirthe and no madnes,
> All good and no badnes.

But Skelton mainly devoted his short rhyming lines to satiric raillery.   Again he echoes the metre, phrase, and sentiment of the brief French verse.   Here is an example of 'Skeltonese' from the poet's abusive censures of Sir Thomas More

> But this bawcock doctor,
> And purgatory proctor,
> Waketh now for wages;
> And, as a man that rages,
> Or overcome with ages,
> Disputeth *per ambages*,
> To help these parasites,
> And naughty hypocrites,
> With legends of lies,
> Feigned fantasies,
> And very vanities,
> Called verities,
> Unwritten and unknown,
> But as they be blown
> From liar to liar;
> Invented by a frier.

In France such irregular truncations of metre were chiefly, although not exclusively, consecrated at the beginning of the sixteenth century to the purposes of the scurrilous drama.   In a French morality penned in Skelton's early life, a character personating a discontented monk attacked the superiors of his monastery in a metrical key which adumbrates Skelton's manner.   The general effect is almost identical:

> Nostre baillif superieur,
> Nostre prieur, et souprieur,
> Nous deffendent de nous galer,
> De rien voir, d'ouïr, de parler,
> De manger ne chair, ne pouesson,
> De boyre de nulle bouesson,
> Sur paines de leurs disciplines;
> Mais eux avant dire matines,
> Leurs lessons et leurs oresmus,
> Ils faisaient tous *gaudeamus*.[1]

[1] Petit de Julleville, *La Comédie et les mœurs en France au moyen âge* (Paris, 1886, pp. 222-3).

Skelton's rough tongue was clearly practising a French tune. The macaronic tags of Latin in both the French and English lines tell their own tale.

Short-syllabled metres were familiar to later generations of Tudor England. Skelton's example was largely responsible for the vogue. Yet the fashion was also maintained for a time in France after Skelton's day, especially by satiric writers for the French stage. Marot, likewise, practised it, with an improved urbanity. There were curious adaptations of it, too, in the supreme developments of French Renaissance poetry. Later French practitioners must share with Skelton whatever credit attaches to the subsequent dissemination of the metre in England. Wyatt's experiments with it are doubtless due to his study of Marot. The uses to which John Heywood and other embryonic dramatists put it were the fruit of his acquaintance with contemporary French drama. In Elizabethan days, when this metrical mode was reckoned grotesque and out of date, it was currently cited among eccentricities that were peculiar to French poetry. An Elizabethan parodist of French verse was guilty of this inanity:

> Down I sat,
> I sat down,
> Where Flora has bestowed her graces;
> Green it was,
> It was green,
> Far passing other places.[1]

The author unjustifiably assigned his imaginary French original to Ronsard. The insolent attribution is merely of interest as evidence that the short trotting verse was recognized to be a French importation.

Skelton's contemporary and chief poetic rival, Stephen Hawes, pursued a more conventional aim. His topics bring him into almost closer association with the expiring efforts of French mediaevalism. There are indications that he closely studied the poetry of his English predecessors, Chaucer, Gower, and Lydgate. But it was in no spirit of disloyalty to the poetic practices of those masters that he supplemented

---

[1] Tarlton's *News out of Purgatory*, 1590.

their tuition by French instruction. He mainly devoted his
pen to allegorical romance on the old French pattern, which
the *Roman de la Rose* had created for Europe as well as for
France, and to which the ' rhetoriqueurs' were giving in his
time a new popularity. Hawes's seven-lined stanza is of
stubborn antiquity, but his allegorical machinery closely
reflects the current French standards. Hawes's *Example of
Virtue* shows Youth's adventure in pursuit of Wisdom, much
as Le Maire portrays the like struggle in *Le Temple d'Honneur et de Vertu*. Hawes's chief work, *The Pastime of
Pleasure, or the History of Graund Amour and La Bel
Pucel*, although it expounds minutely the academic curriculum
of the day and personifies the topics of academic study as
well as virtues and vices, has very few features to distinguish
it from the rhetorical type of French allegory.   Hawes's hero
and heroine, Graund Amour and La Bel Pucel, bear French
names, and that circumstance goes far to support a theory
which Warton advanced on wide grounds of style and sentiment, that the allegory has a French original which lies concealed in manuscript.[1] The whole title and treatment have the
ring of the long-lived French convention to which even Marot
as a youth subsequently paid court in his *Temple de Cupidon*.
Alexander Barclay was translating Pierre Gringoire's *Château
de Labour* near the same date as Hawes was engaged on his
Pastime. Hawes marches in Gringoire's regiment. His allegorical figures of Correction, Falsehood, Perseverance, are
of near kin to Gringoire's Chastisement, Tricherie (i.e. Treachery), or Talent de bien faire.   It is easy to perceive how
busily French allegorical ingenuity was fertilizing the English
soil whence Spenser's *Faerie Queene* was in due time to
spring.

[1] Very early in the sixteenth century numerous editions appeared in Paris
of a French didactic poem called *Le Passe-temps de tout homme et de toute
femme*, by Guillaume Alexis, prieur de Buzy, a voluminous poet, who
died in 1486. The word ' pastime' of Hawes's title seems to have been
one of Caxton's many anglicizations of the French. It reproduces the
French ' passe-temps'.

VIII

MAROT AND ALAMANNI: WYATT AND SURREY

Twenty years may be reckoned as the interval of time which separates the flourishing day of Skelton and Hawes from the epoch of Wyatt's and Surrey's poetic activity. The later scene differs much from the earlier. In the work of the younger Tudor poets we are in the presence of a new element of which their precursors knew little or nothing. French influence is by no means absent, and new harmonies were sounding in France, yet a virgin impulse coming from Italy gives an unprecedented colour to the younger Tudor poetry. The precise force which the new foreign element acquired in Tudor England and the avenues of its entry give room for discussion, but the Italian note is not to be mistaken in the work of Wyatt and Surrey.

Elizabethan critics claimed that the poetic labour of Wyatt and Surrey began a new era in English literature, and that their innovating tendency owed its virtue solely to liberal draughts of the poetic inspiration of Italy. The Elizabethan critic, Puttenham, in his *Arte of English Poesie*, penned these familiar sentences in 1589:

In the latter end of the same king's [Henry VIII's] reign sprung up a new company of courtly makers, of whom Sir Thomas Wyatt the elder and Henry Earl of Surrey were the two chieftains, who having travelled into Italy, and there tasted the sweet and stately measures and style of the Italian poesy, as novices newly crept out of the schools of Dante, Ariosto, and Petrarch, they greatly polished our rude and homely manner of vulgar Poesy, from that it had been before, and for that cause may justly be said to be the first reformers of our English metre and style.

There is obvious evidence of Wyatt's and Surrey's indebtedness to Italian effort, notably to the muse of Petrarch. The influence of Dante and Ariosto is not apparent. The sonnet, to which Petrarch's endeavours first lent popular favour, was introduced by Wyatt and Surrey into England. They translated or paraphrased many of Petrarch's quatorzains.

No poetic instrument was subsequently to achieve greater glory at English hands than the sonnet, and the pioneers are not to be denied their meed of honour, if their experiments are for the most part crudely and harshly modulated. Surrey was also the first English writer of blank verse. That form of poetic endeavour has played in English literature an even nobler part than the sonnet, and the debt to Surrey is enhanced proportionately. But Surrey has no better claim to the invention of blank verse than to that of the sonnet. Blank verse was another Italian invention.

The invasion of France by Italian culture began under Francis I but bore its ripened literary fruit in the reigns of his son and grandsons. Not until the reign of the French king Henry II, the contemporary of the English sovereigns Edward VI and Mary Tudor, did either the sonnet or blank verse become familiar to France. Yet Italian culture·made its primary assault on French taste in the generation of Wyatt and Surrey, even if it was during the succeeding epoch that the Italian spirit helped to refashion French poetry.

The signs of Wyatt's and Surrey's Italian inspiration are not to be mistaken, but there are subsidiary aspects of the Italian influence which link Wyatt's and Surrey's work with contemporary France more closely than Puttenham perceived. They learned much of the poetic art of Italy from an Italian poet who was domiciled in their day in Paris and was bringing to French notice the new modes of poetic satire, of blank verse and the sonnet; while the English poets' debt to the indigenous poetry of France calls for a fuller acknowledgement than has yet been rendered.

Both English poets had intimate personal acquaintance with France. Wyatt alone of the pair went to Italy, and his sojourn was not prolonged. Surrey never passed the Alps, save in the fictions of the critics. Surrey and Wyatt alike spent much time at the French court. The former as tutor of Henry VIII's natural son, the Earl of Richmond, lived for nearly a year at Paris or Fontainebleau with Francis I and his family. Wyatt was repeatedly in the French capital on diplomatic missions, and he mixed in cultivated French society.

The ambitious English votaries of the muse were not likely to resist the alluring appeals which contemporary literature in France made to their allegiance.

It was in France rather than in Italy that both Wyatt and Surrey acquired a substantial measure of the Italian taste and sympathy which were reflected in the manner and matter of their poetry. The two Englishmen occasionally translated or paraphrased sonnets and odes direct from Petrarch or from his Italian disciples. Yet, while Wyatt and Surrey sojourned in French territory they had opportunities of studying current Italian literature which was in course of publication in France at the time. Thus in all probability were Wyatt and Surrey most effectually brought in Paris under the Italian literary yoke. At every turn in our story, Paris presents itself as the chief mission-station of Renaissance culture.

The voice of the native muse of France also gained the two English poets' ear, while they were at the French court. Clément Marot was the king of French poets in the epoch of Wyatt and Surrey, and comparison of them with him is inevitable. In his own country Marot's fame largely suffered eclipse with his death in 1544. The Ronsardian dynasty of the ripened Renaissance was inclined to identify him with mediaeval barbarism. In England his original reputation lingered longer. It began at the call of Wyatt and Surrey, and expanded later. Wyatt caught inspiration from the versatility of Marot, and Spenser echoed some of his strains.

His father, Jean Marot, a poetaster of the rhetorical school, edited the work of the mediaeval master, Alain Chartier, whose name Caxton had made familiar to English ears. Clément's boyish breeding roused in him lasting affection for the past or the passing literature of his country. Beginning life as a nobleman's page, and accompanying his master to the wars in Italy, he enjoyed in youth a fleeting glimpse of Italian culture, but the foreign influence left small impress on his staunch Gallic spirit. Some sparse translations from Petrarch are almost all that his muse owed to Italy. He drank deeper of the classical learning of the Renaissance, and paid tribute to the apostle of Renaissance scholarship by

turning into French verse two of Erasmus's colloquies.
He knew no Greek, but his study of Latin coloured his
imagery.   He interpreted in French translations a portion of
Ovid's *Metamorphoses*, and, through the Latin, the Greek
Musaeus's poetic fable of Hero and Leander.   Marot's
modernization of Musaeus's beautiful idyll had a numerous
progeny, and included, half a century afterwards, the English
version which Marlowe began and Chapman completed.
Marot translated, too, an eclogue of Vergil, but his native
vivacity is seen to better advantage in original eclogues from
his pen.   There he followed in Vergil's path, but classical
poetry only lightly moulded his fancy.   The original notes
of his eclogues were robust enough to lend inspiration to
Spenser's *Shepheards Calender*, the earliest flower of great
Elizabethan poetry.   Marot wrote epigrams in which at times
there is an echo of Martial, but far more often the sting is the
Frenchman's own inspiration.

Marot's Muse in her most characteristic phase was nurtured
at home.   She was steeped in the Gallic spirit of blitheness
and of banter.   With much of his wonted airiness Marot in
early days paid tribute to the exigent convention of mediaeval
France by penning a pleasant allegory of love's supremacy
over life, called *Le Temple de Cupidon*.   There the poet, in
the vein of the old *Roman de la Rose*, makes adventurous
search for Jeune Amour, whom he finally meets in Cupid's
temple amid flowers and birds which gaily haunt the adorable
shrine.   In less ambitious efforts, however, he achieved his chief
triumphs.   Marot worshipped at Villon's shrine and edited his
poetry.   Many of Marot's rondeaus, ballades, and chansons
might have been written by Villon in his more refined mood.
The ballade of the selfish reprobate, Friar Lupin, rings with
that tranquil sort of laughter which is rarely heard outside
France.   The fable of the *Lion and the Rat* breathes a buoyant
simplicity and a rhythmical ease, which are thoroughly French
and gave La Fontaine a model.   A martial note of patriotism
also sounds at times in Marot's lyric verse, and the stirring
ballade which he addressed in 1521 to the Duke d'Alençon
when leading the armies of France against the Low German

troops of the empire is in a dithyrambic strain which adumbrates the animated chant of the Marseillaise.[1]

Marot's poetry in its normal guise has the charm of good conversation. He does not strain the note. He is spontaneous, intelligible, and melodious. He gossips fluently in poetical epistles to patrons and friends over his servant's pilferings or his creditors' importunities. An unpretentious grace and a cheerfulness which mocks at sorrow rarely forsake him amid his voluble confessions of poverty and misfortune.

Grief was indeed familiar to the Gallic bard, and it mainly came from a cause which could but evoke sympathy in England. The Reformed faith appealed to his idiosyncrasy. Although he denied that he was a 'Luthériste', he openly censured Papal doctrine, and his patron, Francis I, could not protect him from persecution in Paris at the hands of the guardians of the Catholic creed. The French king's sister, the cultured Queen of Navarre, offered him an asylum in that court of arts and letters at Nérac over which she presided for some two and twenty years (1527–1549). Marot requited the hospitality of his royal mistress in charming eulogies, but even his patroness could not give him lasting security, and he left France to become the guest in Italy of Queen Margaret's sister, the Duchess of Ferrara, who reflected her kinswoman's curious union of evangelical piety and liberal humanism. But Marot was a Parisian whose spirit drooped when he was absent from his beloved city. He obtained permission to return home on condition that he abjured his heterodoxy. Before long, however, he involuntarily renewed his old offence by the bold innovation of versifying in French some fifty of the Psalms. Marot's French renderings of the Psalms are not great poems, although they rank with the best vernacular versions in any language. In poetic temper they are far superior to the famous English version of Hopkins and Sternhold, which was undertaken six or seven years after. Marot's phraseology is not defaced by the homely tameness of the English. His metre is perhaps too jocund,

[1] Marot, *Œuvres*, ii. 71–2.

too merry for the solemnity of the theme; but therein Marot
was loyal to his native temperament. Like many of his
countrymen, he could reconcile piety with cheerfulness. In
any case Marot's version of the Psalms won him notoriety
which brought him unlooked for rewards and penalties. Set
to popular tunes, the French verses became almost national
anthems. Frenchmen of every religious belief got them by
heart. Even Francis I hummed them in the galleries of Fontainebleau. But the doctors of the Sorbonne were suspicious
of their fascination. The sour dogmatists deemed Marot's
versification of the scriptural poems an incitement to heresy,
and their threats of vengeance exiled Marot once again from
his native country. This time he was not to return. For
a short while he took refuge in Geneva. There the austere
atmosphere proved uncongenial. He was guilty of the sin of
playing the game of backgammon, and retreated before the
scandal to Turin, where he died at the age of 47, in 1544.
He was a late survival of old France, and one of the
greatest of the old French poets. Death silenced his lyre
just before French poetry openly gloried in the yoke of
ancient Greece and modern Italy. Half a dozen years later
the tide of Renaissance sentiment reached its flood, and Marot
was driven from his place of pre-eminence in the French
Parnassus. But his influence continued to work in Tudor
England after it was stilled in France.

Marot was the chief French poet with whom Wyatt and
Surrey were contemporary, but his labour was not done in
isolation. Poetasters of the period were legion, and despite
their crabbed power often engaged in more or less friendly
rivalry with Marot. Occasionally a promising experiment
was made by a contemporary in fields into which Marot did
not venture. Such a one was Antoine Heroet, a protégé of
Queen Margaret of Navarre, whose chief poem was a philosophic disquisition on Plato's conception of love, which was
entitled *La Parfaicte Amye* (The Perfect Mistress). This
was published by the scholar printer, Dolet, at Lyons in 1542.[1]

---

[1] Heroet became Bishop of Digne in 1552, and died in 1568, aged
about seventy-six. An admirable edition of his *Œuvres Poétiques*, edited

The tone is for the most part prosaic ; but there are oases of ethereal fancy and refinement, which anticipate by half a century Spenser's fervid portrayals of heavenly love. Heroet's motto might well be Spenser's lines :

> Such high conceit of that celestial fire,
> The base-born brood of blindness cannot guess,
> Nor ever dare their dunghill thoughts aspire
> Unto so lofty pitch of perfectness.

But Heroet's pure aspirations passed for the time unnoticed in England.   Marot easily ruled the French Parnassus in the era of Spenser's predecessors, and by them his supremacy went unquestioned.   Only one writer was reckoned even among his own countrymen to approach his throne—Melin de Saint-Gelais (1491–1559), a fashionable courtier and ecclesiastic of the orthodox type, who acknowledged less grudgingly than Marot the seduction of Italy. His early biographer indulgently credited the sweet Italian air with conveying a rare refinement and a classical purity to the crudity of Melin's native temperament. Melin seems responsible for the earliest French experiment in Italian sonneteering, and he has the distinction of adapting his words to lute accompaniments of his own composition. But he hardly merited his temporary vogue. His verse is, for the most part, pedantic artifice, and his obscenity passes permissible bounds. He lacks Marot's fresh wit and airy fluency. Wyatt gives occasional signs of acquaintance with his work, but Melin had little stimulus to offer foreign students.[1]

A living figure of an alien race, an Italian poet, loomed larger than Melin in the literary world of France, as Wyatt and Surrey knew it. Although Marot preserved a patriotic independence, Italian sentiment was freely sown in his day in Parisian fields. Italian authors were esteemed there, and to

by Ferdinand Gohin, was published by the Société des Textes Français Modernes in 1909.

[1] Melin de Saint-Gelais is rarely mentioned in Tudor literature. Puttenham, in his *Arte of English Poesie* (1589), notes that Melin, like Marot and 'Salmonius Macrinus', was rewarded by Francis I with office at court on account of his poetic excellence. Salmonius Macrinus or Jean Salmon Macrinus (1490–1557) was a Latin poet, and a friend of Rabelais and Marot.

one of them, Luigi Alamanni, Francis I offered an asylum
when a political revolution drove the Italian poet from his
Florentine home.   Alamanni published at Lyons, under the
French king's patronage and at his expense, a mass of
Italian poetry, which caught the ear of France.   Every
form of poetry which the Italian Renaissance encouraged—
sonnets, didactic poems, satires, eclogues, romantic tales in
blank verse, and plays—engaged Alamanni's pen.   No
strong poetic feeling stirred his muse, but versatility and
ingenuity lent some distinction to his irrepressible industry.
Alamanni's perseverance and ingenuity lacked no honour in his
land of exile.   Francis I not only proved a munificent patron,
but the king's daughter-in-law, Catherine de' Medici, made
him her *maître d'hôtel*.   His work attracted attention in
England as well as in France by its metrical deftness and
variety of topic.   With Alamanni's activity Surrey's and
Wyatt's efforts alike have undoubted affinity.[1]

Some of Surrey's and Wyatt's poetic experiments were
immediately suggested by the Parisian Florentine.   Surrey
was perhaps in warmest and closest sympathy with the
Italian's zeal for innovation in a direction which has
singular importance in English literary history.   Alamanni
was the first modern writer to employ blank verse in narrative poetry.[2]   It has been claimed for him somewhat
doubtfully that he was the inventor of that metre.   Two Italian
dramatists, Giovanni Trissino and Giovanni Rucellai, tried experiments with *versi sciolti* (i. e. blank verse) either just after or
just before him.   The chronology is not certain, but Alamanni
is more likely to have followed than to have preceded them.
Yet Trissino and Rucellai only used blank verse in tragic
drama.   While the likelihood may be admitted that one
or other of these two Italians was Alamanni's inspirer, his
pretension to originality is far from cancelled.   There is no

[1] For an estimate of Alamanni's place in French literature see
Francesco Flamini's admirable essay ' Le Lettere Italiane alla Corte di
Francesco I re di Francia' in his *Studi di Storia Letteraria Italiana
e Straniera*, Livorno, 1895, pp. 270 seq.
[2] *Alamanni, sa vie et son œuvre*, par H. Hauvette, Paris, 1903,
pp. 215 seq.

precedent for the employment of blank verse in narration, as
Alamanni habitually employed it. He proved his command
of it to signal effect in his Eclogues, in his tales of Atlas and
Phaethon, and in his curious poetic description of the inunda-
tion of Rome by an overflow of the Tiber in 1530 (*Il Diluvio
Romano*). Alamanni was conscious of the novelty of his
usage, and feared that it might rouse conservative censure.
When dedicating to his patron, Francis I, in 1532, his *Opere
Toscane*—the standard collection of his works—most of
which were written in Florence many years earlier, he
modestly defends himself against the charge of defying
the accepted law by employing ' verse without rhyme '. He
justifies his novel endeavour largely on the ground that
rhyme lacks classical sanction. There is an originality about
Alamanni's theory and practice in regard to blank verse that
was well calculated to attract a poetic aspirant of Surrey's
eager temperament. Francis I, a recognized arbiter on points
of literary taste, approved Alamanni's experiment. Alamanni's
royal patron was also personally acquainted with the English
poet. The Italian's appeal to the French king for a sympathetic
judgement on his metrical innovation attracted Surrey's
notice.

Alamanni's original experiment in blank verse as a vehicle
of poetic narrative was accessible to Surrey some years before the English poet first showed in his translation of the
second and fourth books of Vergil's *Aeneid* how the English
language adapted itself to unrhymed verse. Italian authors
other than Alamanni were at the time applying the new
metrical device to Vergil's epic. But they frankly acknowledged their discipleship to Alamanni. In France his repute
as the inventor of unrhymed verse was never doubted. When
the poetic masters of the French Renaissance were subsequently
discussing crucial laws of metre, they cited ' Seigneur Loys
Aleman ' as the sole champion, *de nostre tens*, of the free
rhymeless line, and if they questioned the fitness of his *vers
libres* for general use, they commended his bold originality.[1]

---

[1] Du Bellay's *Deffense et illustration de la langue françoyse*, 1549,
p. 132.

There are many grounds for ranking Surrey among
Alamanni's pupils.[1] Blank verse never flourished on French
soil, although it engaged in the next era the platonic affection
of Ronsard and some of his friends. A different fortune
awaited in Elizabethan England Alamanni's metrical innovation of which Surrey was the first Englishman to make trial.

Surrey's literary ally, Sir Thomas Wyatt, acknowledged
more openly Alamanni's tuition. Wyatt followed the Florentine's guidance in two most characteristic performances
—in his satires and in his poetic rendering of the Penitential Psalms. Wyatt's three satires on a courtier's life,
which recall the gentle vein of Horace, are often reckoned
the first examples of poetic satire in England. They are to
a large extent paraphrases of Alamanni's satires. Here and
there they sink to literal translation. When Wyatt is explain-
ing to 'mine own John Poins' why he flies 'the press of
courts' and ' cannot honour them that set their part with Venus
and Bacchus all their life long', he is repeating verbally the
assurances that Alamanni gave his familiar friend ' Thommaso
mio gentil' in the satires which he published in Paris under
Francis I's auspices very few years earlier. Nor does Wyatt's
assimilation of Alamanni's unexceptionable sentiment exhaust
the debt. He borrowed Alamanni's satiric metre, which, although the English adapter did not know it, is indistinguishable from Dante's *terza rima*, and was already applied to
satire by the earliest of Italian satirists, Antonio Vinciguerra,
and by his more famous successor, Ariosto.[2] Wyatt's rhymes

[1] The famous Italian author Aretino, writing to Alamanni June 10,
1542, mentions a translation of Vergil by one of Aretino's friends *secondo
l'uso de' vostri versi sciolti.* Surrey's blank verse translation of Vergil's
Aeneid, Books II and IV, was not published until 1557, ten years after
his death. It was probably written about 1538. The second book of
the *Aeneid* in Italian blank verse was first published at Castello in 1539,
and the first six books in the same metre at Venice in 1540.

[2] Flamini, *Il Cinquecento*, pp. 206-7 (in *Storia Letteraria d' Italia*).
Le Maire de Belges claimed to have first used in France (about 1503)
this metre, which he calls *vers tiercets à la façon Italienne ou Toscane.*
But the *terza rima*, although the poets of the Pléiade made some experiments with it, did not become common in France ; cf. Prof. L. E. Kastner,
French Versification, pp. 167 seq. Prof. Saintsbury calls Wyatt's satiric
verse 'intertwined decasyllables', and seems puzzled to account for their
intricacy (*Hist. of Prosody*, i. 311-12).

in his decasyllabic satires look to the English eye curiously
intertwisted.   The first and third lines rhyme together; then
the second, fourth, and sixth; then the fifth, seventh, and
ninth; then the eighth, tenth, and twelfth, and so on:

> I cannot honour them that set their *part*
>   With Venus and Bacchus, all their life *long*;
>   Nor hold my peace of them, although I *smart*.
> I cannot crouch nor yield to such a *wrong*,
>   To worship them like God on earth *alone*,
>   That are as wolves these sely lambs *among*.
> I cannot with my words complain and *moan*,
>   And suffer nought; nor smart without *complaint*;
>   Nor turn the word that from my mouth is *gone*.

The following quotation shows how precisely Wyatt follows
here Alamanni's metrical as well as his verbal guidance:

> Non saprei reuerir chi soli *adora*
>   Venere & Bacco, nè tacer *saprei*
>   Di quei che 'l uulgo falsamente *honora*.
> Non saprei più ch' a gli immortali *Dei*
>   Rendere honor con le ginocchia *inchine*
>   A più ingiusti che sian, fallaci, & *rei*.
> Non saprei nel parlar courir le *spine*
>   Con simulati fior, nell' opre *hauendo*
>   Mele al principio, & tristo assentio al *fine*.[1]

Nor, again, is it likely to be an accidental coincidence that
Wyatt should be the first to versify in English the Penitential
Psalms, and that Alamanni while at the French court should
render the *Salmi Penitentiali* a like service in Italian just
before. The choice of the same sacred topic by the two
secular pens has corroborative value in the argument.

Little doubt remains that France in her wonted rôle of
missionary introduced to Wyatt's and Surrey's notice that
mass of Italian poetry which the Florentine Alamanni penned,
or at any rate published, while he was domiciled in Paris.

Alamanni included in his work centuries of Italian sonnets. As soon as Alamanni's sonnets, which are themselves

---

[1] Alamanni, Satira X, *Opere Toscane*, 1532, p. 401. Wyatt's debt to
Alamanni is well estimated in Carlo Segrè's 'Due Petrarchisti inglesi
del secolo XVI' in his *Studi Petrarcheschi*, 1903, pp. 335 seq.

largely echoes of Petrarch and his early disciples, are
closely compared with the Englishmen's small harvest,
they suggest a partial source of English inspiration.[1] The
living Alamanni at any rate stood beside their desks to interpret the sonneteering practice of Petrarch, Ariosto, and
Sannazzaro. France could not otherwise give them much
help there.

Ronsard and his disciples were to convert the Italian
fashion of sonneteering into a French vogue. But French
literature in the pre-Ronsardian era caught only a first fleeting glimpse of the Italian sonnet. At most a dozen French
sonnets were in circulation while Wyatt and Surrey were
active. Clément Marot and his contemporary Melin de Saint-
Gelais tentatively translated or adapted a few Italian examples
in the third decade of the century. It was a few years after
Wyatt's and Surrey's effort that France completely naturalized
the Italian sonnet. When the English Muse awoke at the end
of Elizabeth's reign from that slumber which befell her on
Wyatt's and Surrey's death, she discerned in the sonneteering
activities of France an almost keener stimulus than in those
of Italy. Wyatt and Surrey found as sonneteers little assistance in French poetry.

It may even be doubted if the English pioneers owed any
thing to this sparse effort of the first French sonneteers.
Both Englishmen and Frenchmen often had independent
recourse to the same Italian originals. It is curious to note
that one of Wyatt's sonnets, in which a lover's life is somewhat clumsily compared to the Alps—

> Like unto these immeasurable mountains
> Is my painful life the burden of ire—

nearly resembles that French sonnet by Melin de Saint-Gelais
which is often reckoned the first sonnet to be penned in
France:

[1] Both Surrey and Wyatt variously modify the Petrarchan scheme, and
invariably employ the terminal couplet, which was rare in Italy. The
metrical characteristics of the English sonnet of the sixteenth century are
discussed at p. 264 *infra*. Alamanni prefers a somewhat original form of
tercet, *cde, cde.*

Voyant ces monts de veue ainsi lointaine,
Je les compare à mon long deplaisir.

But it is unquestionable that both Wyatt and the French poet
had here independent recourse to an original Italian sonnet
by Jacopo Sannazarro, a Neapolitan sonneteer of a little
earlier date, who is best known as author of the pastoral
romance of the *Arcadia* and was one of Alamanni's masters.
Sannazarro's sonnet opens with the lines :

Simile a questi smisurati monti
È l'aspra vita mia colma di doglie.

Wyatt's rendering of the Italian is more literal than the
Frenchman's version.[1]

In other branches of Wyatt's verse an influence of pure
French stamp can be traced. The clues graphically illustrate
English receptivity to current tendencies of the French muse.
Wyatt's varied lyric experiments passed far beyond the scope
of the sonnet or the *terza rima* of Italian satire. At times he
affects a simple stanza of six octosyllabic lines of which the
first four rhyme alternately and the last two form a couplet ;
this stave was already familiar in English verse, and although
it is also frequent in French *chansons*, no immediate foreign
source is to be suspected. But often Wyatt's lines vary from
four to eight syllables in length, and are combined in
quite new intricacies. The diversity is suggestive of contemporary France rather than of contemporary Italy. Many
of Wyatt's lyric measures clearly reflect the rhythms of
Clément Marot and his school, and the points of identity leave no doubt that the Englishman was often a
direct borrower from Marot.[2] Both poets occasionally

---

[1] Cf. *Gl' imitatori stranieri di Jacopo Sannazaro*, Ricerche di Francesco Torraca, Rome, 1882, pp. 31–2.

[2] There are extant in the Harington MSS. of Wyatt's work twelve
French poems in his own handwriting. (See Nott's edition of Wyatt's
Poems, p. 589.) The first lines are :

1. *Si la bonté se vouloit esmander*
2. *Ma maitresse a je ne scai quoi de bon*
3. *Dames ! a qui de ces eaux crystallines*
4. *Si par memoire amour, et le devoir*
5. *Plume qui fus du ciel predestinée*
6. *Extreme mal qui le desir renforce*

employ a stanza eight lines long, and although there are
slight variations in the length of line, the rhymes are in both
French and English cast in an identical mould of unusual
type—ababbcbc.[1] Wyatt's little six-line and eight-line poems
repeatedly catch the note of the *sixains* or *huitains* of
Marot or of his rival, Melin de Saint-Gelais. The *sestinas*
and *ottavas* of the Italians are in a somewhat different
key. By Tudor Englishmen such fragmentary verse was invariably associated with France. In the opening days of
Queen Elizabeth, George Gascoigne, the author of the
earliest English treatise on prosody, employed the French
terms *dixains* and *sixains* to designate poems of ten and six
lines long, of which he knew little save that they were ' commonly used by the French '.[2]

Again, Wyatt's fondness for irregular lines of Skeltonian
brevity echo a French predilection to which Marot was no

> 7. *Si vous pensez ue ma mie heust que faire*
> 8. *Frere Thibaud séjourné gros et gras*
> 9. *Un jour ma mie etoit toute seulette*
> 10. *Je ne veux rien qu'un baiser de la bouche*
> 11. *Une belle jeune epousée*
> 12. *J'ai vu le corps qui honore notre age*

The first is Melin de Saint-Gelais's poem, ' Au Roy François' (*Œuvres*, ii.
144), and the eighth is an epigram of Clément Marot (No. XLIV). The
sources of the others have not been traced, but all are probably tran-
scripts by Wyatt of contemporary French poetry.

[1]
> Si au monde ne fussiez *point*,
>   Belle, jamais je *n'aymerois*;
> Vous seule avez gaigné le *poinct*
>   Que si bien garder *j'esperois*;
>   Mais quand à mon gré vous *aurois*
> En ma chambre *seulette*,
>   Pour me venger, je vous *ferois*
> La couleur *vermeillette*.
>   (Marot, Chanson XVIII, in *Œuvres*, ii. 185.)

> I shall assay by secret *suit*
>   To show the mind of mine *intent*;
> And my deserts shall give such *fruit*
>   As with my heart my words be *meant*;
>   So by the proof of this *consent*
> Soon out of doubt I shall be *sure*,
>   For to rejoice or to *repent*,
> In joy or pain for to *endure*. (Wyatt, *Works*, p. 160.)

[2] *Certayne Notes of Instruction* in Gascoigne's *Posies* (Cambridge,
1907, p. 472).

stranger.[1] The light French note seems also struck by Wyatt
in both the metre and the sentiment of such a familiar poem as
' The Careful Lover Complaineth and the Happy Lover Coun-
selleth '.[2] More significant is the fact that Wyatt's muse
loved that form of lyric known as the rondeau, which was
a petted child not only of the mediaeval muse of France, but
of her latest disciples of the early sixteenth century. Occasionally the rondeau had been tried in England by Chaucer and
Lydgate, but old English experiments were rare and crude.
The metre of the French rondeau was only brought to perfection in the epoch of Marot, and mainly by Marot himself.
Marot, following a hint offered by his father, first purged the
rondeau of older irregularities and, by making the refrain the
central feature, invested the poem with a new and stimulating
charm. The length was sternly reduced to fifteen lines, and
the refrain became the keynote of the melody. The rondeau
on Marot's delightful plan invariably consists of two stanzas,

[1] Compare

> Such fire and such heat
> Did never make ye sweat;
> For without pain
> You best obtain
> Too good speed and too great.
> Whoso doeth plain
> You best do feign
> Such fire and such heat,
> Who now doth slander Love.   (Wyatt, *Works*, p. 139.)

> J'ay grand desir
> D'avoir plaisir
> D'amour mondaine ;
> Mais c'est grand' peine,
> Car chascun loyal amoureux
> Au temps present est malheureux ;
> Et le plus fin
> Gaigne à la fin
> La grace pleine.
>   (Marot, Chanson XXVIII, in *Œuvres*, ii. 189.)

[2] This song, which Shakespeare parodies (*Twelfth Night*, IV. ii. 79-80),
begins

> Ah! Robin!
> Jolly Robin!
> Tell me how thy Leman doth.

Marot in his *Eclogues* calls himself ' Robin', a common appellation of
French pastoral poetry, and applies the name to licentious shepherds in
two epigrams (cf. Nos. CCLXXXIV and CCLXXXV). Wyatt's brief
poem in its later stanzas takes the form of a dialogue in which the alternate
speeches are headed by the French words *réponse* and *le plaintif*.

one of eight lines with a marked pause after the fifth line, and
the other of five lines, while each stanza closes with a refrain
formed of the three or four opening words of the poem.[1]
Wyatt's rondeaus invariably respect that reformed scheme
which enjoyed Marot's peculiar sanction.   Though there is
nothing in Wyatt's bathetic cadences to recall the felicities of
Marot's best harmonies, the resemblance between Marot's and
Wyatt's rondeaus is too close in shape and often in topic to be
fortuitous.   Wyatt's refrains are clearly of Marot's invention.[2]

[1] Marot's notable triumph in the refrain of the *rondeau* is especially
commended by Boileau, the poetic censor of early French poetry, when
he mentions Marot's metrical inventiveness:
> Marot bientôt après fit fleurir les ballades,
> Tourna les triolets, rima les mascarades,
> *Et des refrains réglez asservit les rondeaux*
> Et montra pour rimer des chemins tout nouveaux.

[2] It is interesting to compare from the metrical point of view two
rondeaus respectively by Wyatt (*Works*, p. 81) and Marot (*Œuvres*, ii.
157), in both of which the fortunes of a lover's heart form the main topic.
The rhyming schemes compare thus : aabba aabc aabbac (Marot) ; aabba
bbac bbaabc (Wyatt). The specimen of Marot's art is a poor one, but
Wyatt is at his normal level :

MAROT.	WYATT.
Tant seulement ton amour te de- mande,	*Help me to seek!* for I lost it there ;
Te suppliant que ta beauté com- mande	And if that ye have found it, ye that be here,
Au cueur de moy comme à ton serviteur,	And seek to convey it secretly,
Quoyque jamais il ne desservit heur	Handle it soft and treat it tenderly,
Qui procedast d'une grace si grande.	Or else it will plain, and then appair.
Croy que ce cueur de te congnoistre amande,	But pray restore it mannerly,
Et vouluntiers se rendroit de ta bande,	Since that I do ask it thus honestly,
S'il te plaisoit luy faire cest honneur	For to lese it, it sitteth me near ;
Tant seulement.	*Help me to seek!*
Si tu le veulx, metz le soubz ta commande ;	Alas! and is there no remedy :
Si tu le prens, las ! je te recom- mande	But have I thus lost it wilfully.
Le triste corps : ne le laisse sans cueur,	I wis it was a thing all too dear
Mais loges y le tien, qui est vain- queur	To be bestowed, and wist not where.
De l'humble serf qui son vouloir te mande	It was mine heart! I pray you heartily
Tant seulement.	*Help me to seek!*

With the close of Surrey's and Wyatt's poetic careers, poetic ambition in England subsided for a generation. In France, too, ' le style Marotique ' was soon to be dethroned. Ronsard, a far nobler genius than Marot, was ready to scale the French Parnassus by a new Graeco-Italian path. The French Muses under Ronsard's rule redoubled their energy and gathered without pause new strength and fame. In England there was no contemporary of Ronsard's royal calibre to tread in Wyatt's and Surrey's somewhat faltering steps. Their ventures were not pursued. They had no genuine disciples, and poetry was for the moment silenced in England.

Yet Wyatt and Surrey do not lack all links with the Elizabethans, and it is curious to observe that the links are largely of French texture. When the poetic spirit of Elizabethan England first grew articulate in Spenser's early verse, it re-echoed for a short season the old-fashioned key of Marot which Wyatt had emulated. Only later did English poetry aspire to borrow notes from Ronsard's more accomplished lyre. Spenser's boyish endeavour of *The Visions of Petrarch* comes straight, not from an Italian source, but from Marot's *Les Visions de Pétrarque*. Two of the eclogues or pastorals in Spenser's *The Shepheards Calender* paraphrase with literalness poems by Marot. Spenser's friendly contemporary and commentator, ' E. K.', tells how the English poet called himself Colin because Marot had assumed the like pastoral name. Spenser's poetic shepherd, Thenot, is drawn, too, from Marot's tuneful page. Marot, in another of his pastoral names, that of Robin, makes confession to the shepherd-god, Pan, of the poetic aspirations of his innocent childhood :

> Sur le printemps de ma jeunesse folle
> Je ressemblais l'hirondelle qui vole
> Puis ça, puis là. L'âge me conduisait
> Sans peur ni soin où mon cœur me disait,
> En la forèt, sans la crainte des loups.

Spenser, under the pastoral name of Colin, echoed the strains of the French Robin and paid his addresses to Pan in Marot's accents. (*Shepheards Calender,* xii, ll. 19-24.)

> Whilome in youth, when flowered my joyful spring,
> Like swallow swift, I wandered here and there.
> For heat of heedless lust me so did sting,
> That I of doubted danger had no fear.
> I went the wasteful woods and forest wide,
> Withouten dread of wolves to be espied.

Marot's appeal—

> Escoute un peu, de ton vert cabinet,
> Le chant rural du petit Robinet —

sounds oddly in Spenser's rendering:

> Hearken awhile from thy green cabinet,
> The rural song of careful Colinet.

Thus Elizabethan poetry betrayed no reluctance to exercise its prentice hand in 'le style Marotique' after that vogue in France was dead. The Elizabethan muse while approaching maturity cast many a backward glance on old French literature, as if to seek counsel there for future progress. Marlowe followed Marot in versifying in his own tongue Musaeus's poetic tale of Hero and Leander. Adaptation of Marot's fancy was indeed pursued on occasion throughout the Elizabethan era. More than one instance is found in so representative a miscellany of the epoch's verse as Davison's *Poetical Rhapsody*, which was first published in 1602. The English adapter was prone to amplify his French original, but the source of his inspiration cannot be ignored by any student of Marot's work.[1]

---

[1] The following typical specimen of the turning of a *dixain* by Marot into a sonnet of Davison's *Poetical Rhapsody* may be examined with advantage. The four italicized English lines are original interpolations by the English versifier:

MAROT. *De Diane,* Epigram lxii, (1524).

> Estre Phebus bien souvent je desire,
> Non pour cognoistre herbes divine-
>   ment,

DAVISON. Ed. A. H. Bullen, 1891, i, p. 92.

TO MISTRESS DIANA.

> Phoebus of all the Gods, I wish to
>   be ;
> Not of the world to have the over-
>   seeing ;
> *For of all things in the world's*
>   *circuit being,*
> *One only thing I always wish to*
>   *see.*

IX

THE INTERREGNUM IN TUDOR POETRY

Between the ending of the first half of the sixteenth century and the opening of the Elizabethan period of English poetry there lies a dreary interregnum, on which France still shed light, although the glow was intermittent. Marot's influence, which was not yet exhausted, was supplemented by that of Marot's patroness, the Queen of Navarre (1492–1549). The ' tombeau ' or elegiac tribute which the daughters of the Protector Somerset paid her memory on her death,[1] illustrates the impression which her literary activity left on the England of Queen Elizabeth's youth.

No Englishman who took note of literary progress across the Channel failed to observe the noble service rendered to humanism by Marot's mistress, whom Michelet has called ' the beloved mother of the French Renaissance '. If, in the day of Wyatt and Surrey, Marot was the Apollo of the French poetic firmament, Queen Margaret was its Pallas Athene. Although English poets paid her less notice than they paid Marot and some of his predecessors, although the versatility

Car la douleur qui mon cœur veut occire	Not of all herbs the hidden force to know,
Ne se guerist par herbe aucunement ;	For ah ! my wound by herbs cannot be cured ;
Non pour avoir ma place au firmament,	Not in the sky to have a place assured ;
Car en la terre habite mon plaisir ;	For my ambition lies on earth below ;
	Not to be prince of the celestial quire,
	For I one nymph prize more than all the Muses ;
Non pour son arc encontre Amour saisir,	Not with his bow to offer love abuses,
Car à mon Roy ne veulx estre rebelle :	For I love's vassal am, and dread his ire,
Estre Phebus seulement j'ay desir,	But that thy light from mine, might borrowed be,
Pour estre aymé de Diane la belle.	And fair Diana might shine under me.

[1] See p. 45, supra.

of her pen was imperfectly recognized by Tudor Englishmen, she was reckoned by students the sole example in the century of a truly literary queen.   ' Queens,' wrote Puttenham in his work on poetry, ' have been known studious and to write large volumes.'   But the only name he can call to mind ' in our time ' is that of ' Lady Margaret, Queen of Navarre '.   Very surprising was her industry in authorship.   Verse and prose constantly occupied her graceful and thoughtful pen.   Her collected poetry, entitled *Les Marguerites de la Marguerite la Princesse* (1547), gave her a title only below that of Marot among the best poets of her day.   She excelled in epigram, madrigal, and elegy.   Nor did she eschew morality plays or farces. Many of her poetic themes were pious and scriptural, but her evangelical sentiment did not narrow the range of her literary sympathies.   A mysticism, which owed much to study of paraphrases of Plato, often coloured her speculations on spiritual and emotional questions, on the nature of perfect love. She was no prude, and among prose authors the Italian Boccaccio chiefly appealed to her.   She not only caused Boccaccio's *Decameron* to be translated into French, but composed a work herself on the same model, which she christened the *Heptameron*.   There she narrated seventy-two stories or anecdotes, all of which she claimed to be true. They were not always free of the taint of lubricity.

But perhaps more notable than the Queen of Navarre's literary activity, with her varied leanings to Platonism, piety, and profanity, is the record of her patronage of literature. Every scheme for the promotion of learning received her sympathy and active support.   Not only did she extend a generous hospitality to every scholar or man of letters who visited her court, but she was an energetic supporter of Universities in the south of France.   The University of Nîmes was founded by her, and that of Bourges, which gained immense repute in the days of the Renaissance, was largely expanded by her munificence.   In Tudor England no woman proved quite so versatile a benefactress of culture.   The only Tudor Englishwoman with whom comparison is possible belongs to that earlier generation which saw a first delusive ray of humanism on the nation's horizon. Henry VII's mother and Henry VIII's grandmother, the Lady Margaret Beaufort (1443-1509), founded Lady Margaret Professorships of Divinity at both Oxford and Cambridge Universities (in 1502), besides endowing two colleges at Cambridge—Christ's and St. John's. Her piety was cast in a sternly orthodox mould, but she sedulously encouraged the new art of printing. Her own contributions to literature were limited to the translation of portions of the *Imitatio Christi*, and of other works of devotion from the French. In the annals of humanism the English Lady Margaret is a slender prototype of her French namesake, and save possibly in the person of Queen Elizabeth herself, the English Renaissance presented no other patroness of culture who could compare with the French queen in versatile accomplishment and active benevolence in the humanist cause.

Adored by cultured ladies of Tudor England, the Queen of Navarre owed something of her English reputation to the infant zeal of Queen Elizabeth while she was princess. At the age of eleven the English princess translated a pious poem from Queen Margaret's pen.[1] On the French queen's death, in 1549, the daughters of Protector Somerset penned those elegies which won Ronsard's admiration.[2] But it was the Italian affinities of the literary queen which chiefly took the fancy of the Elizabethan pioneers. Queen Margaret's great endeavour to continue Boccaccio's work in her *Heptameron* was more loudly applauded by early Elizabethan authors than her French verse. Fifteen of the queen's tales figure in Painter's *Palace of Pleasure* (1566), the first collection of short stories which came from the English press. Painter's *Palace* formed the favourite reading of English ladies in the first decades of Elizabeth's reign, and the French queen of culture found ardent worshippers in Elizabethan boudoirs.

But in spite of such foreign stimulus and example as Queen Margaret and Marot offered, the Elizabethan awakening was slow in coming. Torpor lay heavy on the English mind in the generation which succeeded the poetic lispings of Henry VIII's

[1] See p. 39.   [2] See p. 45.

courtiers.   In the dark days which intervened before the true
illumination, voices of lament were heard that England lacked
the enlightened ardour of France.   While Henry VIII was
yet alive, Sir Thomas Elyot, the industrious author of *The
Governour*, a treatise on higher education (1531), imputed
to his fellow countrymen negligence and sloth in comparison
not only with Frenchmen but with Italians and Germans,
all of whom were bringing the learning and wisdom of
Greece and Rome into their countries by way of translation.
Early in Queen Elizabeth's reign Roger Ascham, in his *Schoolmaster* which he began in 1563, complains of the neglect of
literature and learning among the English gentry, and warmly
denied them the consolation that gentry in France shared
their own disdain of things of the mind.   Such acknowledgement of the active spirit of the French Renaissance was faint
and imperfect.   Yet few other rays of hope for the future were
discernible in the mid-century gloom of Tudor England.

BOOK III

FRENCH INFLUENCE ON ELIZABETHAN PROSE

TENDENCIES OF FRENCH AND ENGLISH PROSE

ENGLISH critics have often confessed themselves inappreciative of French poetry and have pronounced the French genius to be better adapted to prose. The English ear is wont to miss the rhythmical cadences of the French measures and to impute to the melody a ring of monotone. English critics often complain that sonorousness is lacking and that the tonic effect rarely rises above that of a pleasant jingle. Insular prejudice or ignorance seems largely responsible for this grudging verdict. There is a mass of French poetry of which the rich harmony or the profound thought could only be questioned by deafness or dullness. The lyric versatility and the imaginative range of Ronsard, who was born within a generation of Villon's death and was followed in due season by Racine, Chénier, and Victor Hugo, prove that France has yielded song which belongs to the world's poetic wealth. The harmonies of French metre are not those of English or Italian metre, but they are often equal to either in beauty and originality, if not in volume of sound. The Ronsardian lute was strung with Apollo's hair as surely as the lute of Shakespeare and the lute of Tasso. ' One star differeth from another star ' only in the kind of ' glory '.

Yet that active and living ' faith in light and motion ' which animated the French Renaissance was ambitious of perfection in prose no less than in poetry. France owed the vast scope of her foreign influence to her interpretative faculty, and that idiosyncrasy often found in prose its fittest agency. Elizabethan England eagerly absorbed the teaching which lay at her disposal in the prose-writing of contemporary France, some time before she exacted tribute of the ripest fruit of French poetry.

The service that France rendered Elizabethan prose requires care in definition. Other influences besides the French were actively at work and claim due acknowledgement. But French example was probably more pervasive than any other, and was earlier in the field. France led the way in the general application of the vernacular to serious literature, and Tudor England recognized there the force of French instruction. The character and scope of the literary labours of Caxton, and of his successor Lord Berners, illustrate how large was the part that French influence played in the early process of substituting English prose for Latin in ordinary exposition. Caxton and Berners, and other prose-writers of their generations, looked almost exclusively to France for their literary provender. Not that they confined their attention to original French literature. Early Tudor workers studied French translations from Latin or Greek, Italian or Spanish, with little less zeal than original French writing. The first vague gleams of genuine style came to English prose through English translation of French versions of the classics. Yet the early Tudor enthusiasm for French prose left its English counterpart a partially developed instrument. The literary savour was faint. Sentences were disjointed. The literary use of the vernacular, although widely spreading, was, too, far from universal. It was not quite habitual through the half-century following the introduction of printing. The tide which Caxton set flowing owed most of its impetus to fifteenth-century France, but it needed the deliberate enlistment of other sources of energy before it attained full flood.

Direct study of Latin and Greek, of Italian and Spanish, grew in England as the century aged, and reinforced the foreign notes which early Tudor translators caught from the French. French influence was not exorcized, but formidable competitors were at hand to challenge any French monopoly.

Elizabethan prose, of which the main aim was recreation, proved more catholic in its affinities and affiliations than the prose of serious exposition. Serious prose remained more or less loyal to French example, even if the French influence was materially modified by growth of Latin erudition; but recreative prose sought much nurture in fields outside France or classical Rome—notably in Italy and Spain. The habit of Caxton and Berners in relying on French romances of chivalry for literary amusement was discountenanced by the Elizabethans. Italian influence predominated in their recreative prose. Italy was the original home of the short story, of the little novel, of the art of fiction in any modern sense. The French *fabliau* or *conte* did not pass beyond the primitive stage of the anecdote, and the French tale of knightly adventure, while it made small attempt to respect methodical principles of construction, transgressed the limits of length which the art of story-telling required for its full effect. Boccaccio was the founder of the novel in the fourteenth century, but his sixteenth-century disciple Bandello greatly extended the vogue and range of fiction. Renaissance France energetically imitated Boccaccio and translated Bandello, but she did not obliterate the Italian hall-mark from the imported wares. Many Elizabethan loans were levied on Italian fiction through the French, but the transaction was at times effected without an intermediary. In any case the Italian flavour retained much of its zest. Spanish literature also exerted subsidiary influence on the lighter forms of Elizabethan prose literature. The affectation of Lyly's *Euphues*, the earliest specimen of original recreative work in a distinctive literary cast of prose, was coloured by Spanish pomposity and pedantry. Nashe's novel of *Jack Wilton* reflected the swaggering tone of the Spanish story of roguish adventure, which Nashe may have read at first hand. Some popular Elizabethan experiments in romantic fiction mingled numerous simples in varied proportions, but the French element was usually less perceptible than other ingredients. Sidney's *Arcadia* owed most of its diffuse matter and manner to the late Greek novel, and to the current pastoral romance of both Italy and Spain. The Greek novel probably reached the English author in French translation or in English translation from the French. The Italian and Spanish pastoral romance was doubtless intelligible to Sidney in the original texts.

William Painter's *Palace of Pleasure* is the earliest collection of short stories which an Englishman compiled. It was published in London early in 1566. The book makes no pretension to originality, and a summary analysis of its sources well illustrates the general distribution of the foreign influences on the Elizabethan prose of recreation. Of Painter's hundred and one little novels, fifty are drawn from the tales of Boccaccio or from those of his sixteenth - century Italian disciples Bandello or Cinthio. More than thirty come direct from the Latin or Greek historians. Fifteen of the remainder are translated from the French of Queen Margaret of Navarre's *Heptameron*, and one is described as being drawn ' out of a little Frenche booke called *Compte du Monde Avantureux* '. Queen Margaret's volume is itself an imitation or development of Boccaccio's *Decameron*; but in any case France holds among Painter's authorities a place far less conspicuous than that of Italy or even of Greece and Rome. It should be acknowledged that the Italian novelist Bandello, on whom Painter levied liberal loans, was known to the English collector only in a French translation. Painter, in a preliminary list of French ' authhours out of whom these nouelles be selected ', specifies the French translators of Bandello—' François Belleforest ' and ' Pierre Boaistuau, surnamed Launay '. Yet when all allowance is made for French aid, the French influence which Painter acknowledged is impregnated with a pronounced ' Italianate' sentiment. On almost all the recreative prose of Elizabethan England the like judgement may be passed. The Elizabethan romance, in the final form which Greene and Lodge favoured, is marked by a diffuse floridity of style, while the theme is presented with an artificial sensuousness which has little relation to life or nature. The mode is of Italian lineage, with an occasional infusion of the artificial solemnity of Spain and a slender tincture of French clarity.

Outside the bounds of Elizabethan fiction, Latin influence came to compete with French in moulding Elizabethan prose literature. A reviving zest for Latin scholarship stimulated the progress of English composition during the middle years of the sixteenth century. Latin influence helped to quicken the development of English prose.

But Latin tuition, while it gave a more businesslike regularity to syntactical structure, was touched by no warmth of feeling, by no artistic expansiveness, by small originality or exuberance of thought. Sir Thomas Elyot's *Governour* (1531), Thomas Wilson's *Arte of Rhetorique* (1553), and Ascham's *Schoolmaster* (1570) are substantial experiments in serious prose. Elyot and Ascham's books are technical treatises on education. Wilson's volume is a practical manual of composition. On each of the three works much reading of Latin authors has left a deep impress. Personal sentiment is for the most part lacking ; the argument is largely derivative. The practical ends of instruction are sought too coldly and too dispassionately to bring the volumes within the literary arena. Elyot, Wilson, and Ascham, who were all efficient classical scholars, bear cumulative testimony to the spreading habit of making English instead of Latin prose the expository implement of educated Englishmen. Wilson deprecated the employment of French or Italian words in place of English, and betrayed a certain insularity of sentiment, although he borrowed freely from Quintilian and Cicero. Elyot and Ascham were closer observers of the progress of humanism in France, and were conscious of its breadth of spirit and of its hostility to scholasticism. Scholars of the French Renaissance were among their heroes. If Tudor scholars did less in the middle years of the century for the ductility of English prose than contemporary French masters for French prose, their immediate resort to Latin fostered new virtues of cohesiveness and solidity.

But, in the heyday of the Elizabethan era, serious prose writers freely acknowledged the claims of French models to allegiance or to respectful study. Most of the Elizabethan works which dealt with philosophy, theology, and biography pay more generous tribute to French than to Latin culture. Contemporary French authors were the efficient tutors of serious writers of Elizabethan prose in its last and best phases.

The French masters were worthy of their Elizabethan pupils. In the course of the century serious French prose acquired a new directness and dignity, a grace and facility, which may be traced in the first place to the French scholar's persistent habit of translating Latin and Greek classics into his own tongue, and in the second place to the breadth of his interest in the world outside scholarship. Scholarship and liberality of outlook absorbed the old French instinct for vivacious narrative, purged it of incoherence or abruptness, and expanded its range of theme. A small but quite distinct and fruitful influence on the French development of literary form and subject is traceable to French translations of the Bible. England sought to adapt to her earnest purposes all these clarifying, liberalizing, and fertilizing strains of French influence. The balanced rhythm of serious Elizabethan prose in its final manifestations, its fervour and its argumentative versatility, owe much to the modulating tendencies newly at work in prose across St. George's Channel.

The directness and dignity of Sir Thomas North, and even of Hooker and Bacon may, together with the orderly presentment of their copious thought, be largely set to the credit of France. Classical suggestion was still operative without immediate French agency, while the English version of the Scriptures lent an independent measure of warmth and intensity. But even in these collateral directions France gave much help. French zeal for the vernacular translation of the Bible as well as for classical study communicated itself to England, and stimulated the Hebraic as well as the classical affinities of English writing. As for the special forms of prose literature—biography and the essay—in which North and Bacon won respectively their chief laurels, they are of purely French parentage. Biography of the intelligent vivid type first came to Elizabethan England through the French version of Plutarch. The essay was a form of literary effort directly imported from France. The mingling of theology and political philosophy, which gave Hooker his fame, is of more complex origin. The union has precedents in mediaeval scholasticism. But the Frenchman Calvin may well claim the main credit of laying the foundation on which Hooker built. While every allowance should be made for the progress of Latin scholarship in Tudor England, it is clear that the Elizabethan

essay and the biographic and speculative triumphs of Elizabethan prose are either of French descent or of French
kinship. The missionary energy of France explains much of
the lucidity of manner in serious Elizabethan prose, as well as
its catholicity of matter.

To four writers the development of French prose of the
sixteenth century is mainly due, — to Rabelais and Calvin
whose chief work was done in the first half of the century,
and to Amyot and Montaigne whose chief work was done
in the second half. Elizabethan England will be found to be
under obligation in different degrees to all these authors.
Rabelais, Calvin, Amyot, and Montaigne are the dominant
figures in the history of sixteenth-century French prose. But
the writings of these literary heroes do not quite exhaust the
scope of the present inquiry. The French Bible calls for
complementary recognition.

II

THE BIBLE IN FRENCH AND ENGLISH

Ardent study of the Bible in the vernacular began, more
or less under the stimulus of Germany, in both France and
England at much the same time. The enthusiasm of English
students, despite the primal debt to Germany, was soon
whetted by the French piety which, born in Paris, developed
in Antwerp, and ultimately found a permanent abode in
Geneva. The biblical influences on English prose were
fostered by personal and literary intercourse between the
religious leaders of London and those of Paris, Antwerp, and
Geneva.

From Germany there reached Tudor England the first
effective spur to the study of the Scriptures in English.
Wiclif, who translated much of the Bible into an artless prose in
the fourteenth century, was wellnigh forgotten. The German
chieftain of Protestantism, Luther, brought home to Tudor
Englishmen, by his precept and practice, the obligation of
making the Old and New Testaments accessible to the people
in the people's language. But to the development of the

vernacular study of the Bible in England, France of the Renaissance lent active help.

France was very early in the field of biblical translation. A mediaeval French version—in part a paraphrase and in part an epitome—belonged to the thirteenth century. Based on the Vulgate, it was a hundred years older than the endeavour of Wiclif. Of this French rendering the New Testament alone came from a Lyons press as early as 1477; both Old and New Testaments were printed in Paris in 1487. Nearly two generations passed away before any endeavour of a like kind was made in England. Not only the French and the German, but the Italian and Spanish presses also issued vernacular translations of the Scriptures half a century before the English press approached this sphere of activity.

The story of the original editions of the French Bible provides suggestive comment on the first English efforts. The mediaeval paraphrase, although constantly reprinted, was soon discountenanced by scholars. The first translator on scholarly lines of the whole Bible into French was Jacques Lefèvre d'Étaples,[1] an accomplished humanist, who began theological research long before the Huguenot Church was organized, before indeed Luther, his junior by twenty-eight years, had formulated his doctrine. As early as 1512 Lefèvre d'Étaples published a statement of his religious opinion which anticipates at many points the principles of the coming Reformation. In a Latin commentary on St. Paul's Epistles, he claimed the right of freely interpreting the scriptural text by the aid of unfettered reason. The royal humanist Francis I was at this period so unsuspicious of heterodoxy, or so fascinated by speculative originality, that he made Lefèvre tutor to a younger son. Only towards the close of his long life, which was mainly devoted to a French translation of the Bible, did Lefèvre rouse orthodox hostility. The first instalment of Lefèvre's Biblical enterprise, which, like the mediaeval para-

[1] Hallam, in his *History of Literature*, confusingly calls Lefèvre d'Étaples by his Latinized name Faber Stapulensis. Born at Étaples (Pas-de-Calais) in 1455, of parents named Lefèvre, the French translator died in 1537.

phrase, was largely based on the text of the Vulgate, appeared in Paris in 1523. Two years later the Parlement of Paris, at the bidding of the obscurantist Sorbonne, condemned the liberal tendency of the design. But Queen Margaret of Navarre encouraged the translator to continue his labour, and other portions followed. Lefèvre's whole Bible in French was finally printed in a single volume at Antwerp in 1530 by Martin de Keyser (or Martin l'Empereur), a Fleming, whose press enjoyed a cosmopolitan repute. Lefèvre's perseverance was ultimately well rewarded. French Catholics, despite the misgivings of the weaker brethren, were indisposed to reject permanently the fruits of his industry. After undergoing some revision, Lefèvre's translation became the authorized French Bible of the Catholic Church, and enjoyed a wide esteem.

Meanwhile Lefèvre's work underwent correction at Huguenot hands of a thorough and scholarly kind. The Huguenot recension was undertaken by Pierre Robert Olivetan, under the auspices of Calvin, who was a near kinsman of the editor. Both were natives of Noyon in Picardy. Olivetan's version was published in Neufchatel in 1535, the expenses being defrayed by a subscription of the Vaudois of Piedmont. It became the Authorized Version of the French Protestant Church, and the foundation of Authorized Versions of Protestant churches elsewhere. Thus by 1535 two adequate French translations of the Bible were in general circulation among Frenchmen, while the mediaeval paraphrase, although its credit was fast fading, then reached the dignity of a sixteenth edition. In no other vernacular did the Bible enjoy at the moment quite the same advantage.

Englishmen trod the path of Lefèvre and Olivetan at a slower pace. In her biblical as in almost all other enterprises England long leaned heavily on foreign props. Tyndale, the first of the Tudor translators of the Bible, began his pioneer labours almost at the same time as Lefèvre. Coverdale, the second of the Tudor translators of the Bible, was at work simultaneously with Olivetan. The French and English undertakings were bound together by stronger links than chronological ties, but the chronological association is worth emphasizing. It was not at home, it was on the continent of Europe, that the first Tudor translators of the Bible found the means of putting their work into type. Henry VIII's government shared the antipathy of the Sorbonne to a vernacular version of the Scriptures. It was at German or Flemish presses that Tyndale's translation of the Pentateuch and New Testament—the parent contributions to the Tudor Bible—were first printed. Two years after Lefèvre's New Testament in French was issued at Paris, Tyndale's New Testament in English came out at Cologne (1525). Tyndale subsequently, in 1530, published his anglicized Pentateuch with a German printer, apparently of Wittenberg; that event synchronized with the issue at Antwerp of the whole Bible in Lefèvre's French. In the German edition of his English Pentateuch Tyndale nearly reached the limit of his labour. He did not, like Lefèvre, complete his task, but in his remaining effort he came into more intimate relation with his French competitor. At the identical Antwerp press of Martin l'Empereur, which gave Lefèvre's finished venture to the world, Tyndale printed in 1531 a rendering of the Book of Jonah. This was the last contribution to his unfinished Old Testament which the Englishman sent to press. His association with Lefèvre's Antwerp printer continued longer. Under the same auspices there came forth two years later a second improved edition of Tyndale's New Testament. The Antwerp printer, Martin l'Empereur, forms a personal bond between the first complete French Bible of the French Renaissance and the first English Bible which Tyndale began and failed to finish.

Tyndale's successor, Miles Coverdale, retrieved his defeat. Coverdale compiled the first English translation of the whole Bible. It appeared in 1535, again at Antwerp, although at Jacob van Meteren's and not at Martin l'Empereur's press. Lefèvre had brought his great task to an end five years before, and Olivetan's second French enterprise belonged to Coverdale's year. Two years later there was a reprint of Coverdale's Bible in Southwark. No English translation of the Bible was printed in England earlier. In 1537, sixty years after the work of publishing the Scriptures in the vernacular had been successfully inaugurated in Paris, England made a first entry into the field.

It is abundantly clear that the early English translators of the Bible were cognizant of the contemporary French efforts, and owed them an appreciable stimulus. That the same printer at Antwerp should be simultaneously engaged on the two biblical manuscripts of Lefèvre and Tyndale does not exhaust the evidence of association. The second complete version of the English Bible, which was known as Matthew's Bible, was a composite compilation of both Tyndale and Coverdale's work. This was again published at Antwerp by van Meteren, and appeared in 1537. The Apocrypha was now first included, and that section of the volume offered signal proof of English knowledge of the French activity. A part of the Apocrypha was avowedly translated from Olivetan's Protestant version of the French Scriptures, the Neufchatel revision of Lefèvre's great work. Matthew's Bible, which was the first Bible to be fully legalized for sale in England, was under a direct obligation to France.

Nor was it only as far afield as Antwerp that the biblical trans-lators of the French Renaissance and of Tudor England formed personal alliances. In Paris itself the partnership was pursued. Coverdale was a frequent visitor to Paris, and there, at the well-equipped press of François Regnault, he superintended in 1539-40 the printing of the Great Bible—the third complete English version—which was constructed of earlier English translations. The process was interrupted by the French government, which scented heresy in the growing enthusiasm for the vernacular Scriptures, but Regnault's French types and presses were transported to England, and the work was completed in London. The Great Bible, which is virtually a specimen of fine Parisian typography, was the earliest version of the Bible to receive in England official ecclesiastical recognition.

Nor does the account of the debt of the English Bible to French exertion by any means end here. When, during Queen

Mary's reign, English Protestants sought an asylum in Geneva, they came directly under the personal influence of Calvin. The Frenchman then ruled the Swiss city with despotic rigour. His chief lieutenant, another Frenchman, Theodore Beza, was, despite his stern Puritanism, the most cultured humanist among French religious reformers. The English exiles at Geneva devoted their energies to a new recension of the English Bible, and Calvin and Beza both encouraged them in the work. On this version the English Puritans grafted in both notes and text the theological doctrine and exegesis of the French chieftains of their city of refuge. Olivetan was a chief authority for the English scribes. Calvin and Beza were their trusted guides. The Genevan Bible, which was compiled under French auspices, was first printed in 1560 in the French atmosphere of Geneva. Elizabethan Puritans treated the book for half a century with superstitious reverence. Two hundred early reissues of the Genevan Bible attest its popularity in England. Nor did Scotland escape the contagion. The first Bible to be printed in the vernacular in Scotland followed the Genevan version. It was issued in Edinburgh in 1579. The influence of the Genevan version is hardly capable of exaggeration. Its pronounced pietistic sentiment gave the cue to many devotional idiosyncrasies of Puritan prose, and riveted Hebraic fervour on the style of much profane writing. The French energy of Geneva greatly stimulated English love of the Bible.

The connexion of the Genevan version of the Bible with its place of origin and with the French ruler of the Swiss city, was kept well in mind by successive English editors. Into the preliminary almanac there was introduced at an early date and there was retained in permanence the entry under the day May 27, 'Master John Calvin, God's servant, died 1564.' Shakespeare was a month old at the moment of Calvin's death. A few years later the Genevan version gave him his first knowledge of the Scriptures. The dramatist on one occasion in adult life acknowledged the pertinacity of the French in translating the Bible by quoting a verse in

its French garb. In *Henry V* (III. vii. 70) the Dauphin cites
2 Peter ii. 22, in an early French version : ' Le chien est
retourné à son propre vomissement, et la truie lavée au
bourbier.' The dramatist's compliment was well deserved.
France is well entitled to share with Germany the honour of
promoting in England biblical study and knowledge. The
influence of the Genevan version was especially long-lived.
The English Bishops' Bible of 1568 and King James's
Authorized Version of 1611 betray at many points the
French influence of Geneva.

III

CALVIN

Huguenot writers claim for Olivetan, the translator of the
Bible, a great advance on the efforts of his precursor Lefèvre,
and credit him with an influence on French prose which out-
distances that of all other writers of the epoch. But it is
doubtful if such pretensions can be justified. Olivetan's merits
consist of literal and simple accuracy, which, while it well
served the cause of piety, exerted small effect on the artistic
development of literature. As a writer of French prose, Calvin
(1509–1564), Olivetan's cousin and leader, has an insistent individuality which gives him a commanding place in the history
of style to which the French translators of the Bible can sub-
stantiate no claim. Calvin was far more than a translator.
He was an original thinker of the highest power, and a man
of immense learning. There is little of the exuberance of
Hebraism in Calvin's French temperament. The influence
which he exerted on the literary development of French
writing comes from the majestic sobriety of his original
thought. His greatest work in French prose, his *Institution
Chrétienne*, was first written in Latin, and then translated by
himself into French. Constantly revised in many successive
editions, the book circulated far and wide in the two languages
with ever-growing authority. Calvin's *Institution* opens
with a manly dedication to the royal apostle of French
humanism, Francis I. Calvin tells his sovereign that he writes

for Frenchmen, for his fellow countrymen. It was in their interest that he compiled his encyclopaedic plea for the philosophic and practical recognition of God's will as the sole director and controller of man's life.

Calvin's influence owes as much to his literary temper as to his doctrine. Trained in youth in the classics, and studying law under Alciati at Bourges, he inaugurated his literary career with an edition of Seneca's ethical tract ' On Mercy ' (*De Clementia*). Until death Calvin cherished a deep reverence for the achievements and tradition of classical literature which he credits with bringing varied light to the intellect of man. In a noble passage in his *Institution Chrétienne* he applauds the pagan writers' ' admirable lumière de vérité '. In the Roman jurisconsults he detects ' grande clarté de prudence en constituant un si bon ordre et une police si équitable '. To Latin literature he traces the invention of the art of logical debate—' l'art de disputer, qui est la manière de parler avec raison.' Calvin treats the endowments of his Latin heroes as manifestations of God's will and power, and declares neglect or contempt of the benefits which their writings offer to be worthy of condign punishment.

An almost legal precision and lucidity are Calvin's supreme literary virtues. The Latin source of the fine qualities of his French style is never obscured. Much of his work was indeed penned in crisp, clear Latin. It has been said of him that he thought in Latin when he wrote in French. Yet his French writing gives him his literary fame. His fluent ease in vernacular composition, the copious yet pertinent flow of his dialectic, invested the French language under his hand with a suppleness and tractability which were almost new to it. His tone ranges over many keys. At times he rises to a chastened eloquence ; at times he sinks to a dry sarcasm which is coloured by a Gallic turn of wit. His attacks on ' the sophisters of the Sorbonne ', on the champions of what he regards as Roman superstition, are alive with Gallic raillery and badinage. In the result he gave French prose a versatility and facility the merit of which can hardly be over-estimated. His vocabulary and the turn of his sentences have a modern ring which no other of the great practitioners of his century rivalled. Compared with Calvin's general manner of writing, even Montaigne's style is archaic and unfamiliar.

Calvin's doctrinal influence on the religious reform of England is an immense tribute to the fascination of his dialectical energy. It was the fruit of his literary power no less than of his theological ardour. Much personal intercourse took place between the master and his English disciples, and greatly increased his authority. When, on Henry VIII's death and Edward VI's accession, ecclesiastical reform was carried to its completion in England, the chief organizers of the Protestant movement, Protector Somerset and Archbishop Cranmer, were in repeated correspondence with Calvin. They urged him to visit England for the purpose of healing differences of opinion among English reformers, and of removing the last obstacles to the national acceptance of his teaching. The Frenchman declined the invitation on the score of failing health, but his refusal was followed by a gift to the boy-king of copies of his books.

Nor during a great part of Elizabeth's reign was Calvin's reputation and authority seriously questioned by the leaders of the English Church. Regard for him and his writings was a link binding together mutually hostile parties of English Protestants. Archbishop Grindal and Archbishop Whitgift both respected his spiritual theory and the clarity of his reasoning, if they disagreed with one another in their attitude to his ritual. Calvin was to a large degree the doctrinal oracle of the Elizabethan people, and the technical language of his creed—predestination, election, reprobation, grace, faith without works—was absorbed by popular English speech. Archbishop Cranmer and Archbishop Whitgift were both writers of pithy and forcible English, and they were more deeply versed in Calvin's vocabulary than any other Churchmen of their day. They came under the irresistible influence of his direct and dignified diction, and spread respect for it among their fellow countrymen. 'The reverend fathers of our Church call M. Calvin one of *the best writers*,' wrote approvingly some Protestant clergymen of the Church of England in a manifesto on Anglican dogma in 1599.[1]

All Calvin's writings, whether in Latin or French, were translated into English. Some of his French sermons were published in London as early as 1560. Between that year and 1610— a period of fifty years—there came out in England at least seventy-five editions of English translations of various French or Latin works of Calvin. Calvin's standard treatise, *The Institution of Christian Religion,* which his admirers reckoned the chief jewel in his literary crown, originally appeared in England in 1561, and before the end of the century the English version went through at least five editions, which embodied its author's successive revisions and bulky amplifications. Thomas Norton, the Elizabethan translator, well typified in his varied activities the temper of the epoch. A successful barrister and an energetic member of the House of Commons, Norton sought sober recreation in secular literature as well as in theological debate. He lacked any gift of brilliance. Three of the five acts of *Gorboduc,* the first regular tragedy which the English language knew, are from his leaden pen, and he contributed to the clumsy metrical version of the psalms by Sternhold and Hopkins. Strong puritan sympathies led him to set immense store by the doctrine of Calvin's *Institution of Christian Religion.* At the same time the merits of the Frenchman's exact style made a strong appeal to his intellectual temper. Calvin's habit of packing 'great plenty of matter in small room of words rendered the sentences', according to Norton, 'so full as nothing might well be added without idle superfluity and again so nighly pared that nothing could be minished without taking away some necessary substance of matter therein expressed.' Norton lacked Calvin's command of the literary arts, and his effort runs lamely after the original. It is unfortunate that Norton should have preferred Calvin's Latin to his French text. But Norton's opaque leaves fail to exclude Calvin's luminosity altogether. Here is the guise (in modern

[1] Cf. Hooker's *Ecclesiastical Polity*, the Fifth Book, ed. Ronald Bayne, 1902, p. 621.

spelling) in which Norton presented to Elizabethan readers
Calvin's rational plea for the study by Christians of pagan
classical literature. The rhetorical flow has, however faintly,
the right current.

So oft therefore as we light upon profane writers, let us be
put in mind by that marvellous light of truth that shineth in
them, that the wit of man, howmuchsoever it be perverted
and fallen from the first integrity, is yet still clothed and
garnished with excellent gifts of God. If we consider that
the spirit of God is the only fountain of truth, we will neither
refuse nor despise the truth itself wheresoever it shall appear,
except we will dishonourably use the spirit of God. . . . Shall
we deny that the truth shined to the old lawyers which have
set forth civil order and discipline with so great equity?
Shall we say that the philosophers were blind both in that
exquisite contemplation and cunning description of nature?
Shall we say that they had no wit, which by setting in order
the art of speech have taught us to speak with reason? Shall
we say that they were mad which in setting forth Physic have
employed their diligence for us? What of all the mathematical
sciences? Shall we think them doting errors of madmen?
No, rather we cannot read the writing of the old men concerning these things without great admiration of their wit.
But shall we think anything praiseworthy or excellent, which
we do not reknowledge to come of God? Let us be ashamed
of so great unthankfulness, into which the heathen poets fell
not, which confessed that both philosophy and laws and all
good arts were the inventions of Gods.[1]

Despite its debt to Latin, Norton's great volume is associated
with France beyond risk of forgetfulness. Norton's labour
begins with Calvin's long preliminary address to Francis I,
so that in the English book the headline of the first seventeen
pages bears the suggestive legend 'The preface to the
French King'.

Another imposing venture of like kind may be cited by way
of illustrating how, in the dark years preceding the dawn of
the Elizabethan era, the nascent literary taste joined hands
with religious zeal in paying honour to Calvin. Arthur
Golding, the friend of Sir Philip Sidney, and himself a leading

[1] Calvin's *Institution*, London, 1582, f. 81.

figure in the first generation of literary Elizabethans, made his earliest fame by versifying in English Ovid's *Metamorphoses*. He fully sustained his reputation in later years by his industry in translating direct from the French many hundreds of Calvin's sermons. Golding's giant volumes found ready purchasers. Typographical skill was freely lavished on them. There are few finer folios of the period than Golding's rendering from the French of two hundred ' Sermons of M. John Calvin upon the fifth book of Moses called Deuteronomie '. Nashe, the Elizabethan satirist and critic, enters Golding's name on a ' page of praise ', not merely for his toil on Ovid, but for ' many exquisite editions of divinity turned by him out of the French tongue into our own '.[1] Nashe, who was more addicted to blame than praise of dogmatic theology, only bestowed the complimentary epithet of ' exquisite ' on volumes of divinity which were of French parentage.

Calvin's lieutenant and successor, Theodore Beza, and his pamphleteering aide-de-camp Pierre Viret were equally familiar names on the title-pages of Elizabethan translations. The style of clerical authors in England as a result caught much dominant colour from the abounding Calvinist literature. The greatest of all Elizabethan theologians, Richard Hooker, despite his antagonism to the Calvinist polity and to much of Calvin's doctrinal theory, proved in his *Ecclesiastical Polity* that he closely studied the works of Calvin and of Calvin's friend Beza. More direct and obvious was Hooker's dependence on the patristic researches of Beza's disciple Simon Goulart, a native of Senlis, who became pastor of the Genevan church in Hooker's youth (1572) and was, after Hooker's death, ruler of the Genevan state in succession to Beza from 1605 to 1628.[2] Yet to Calvin himself Hooker owed more than lies on the surface. His English style is far more cumbrous, complicated, and resonant than Calvin's French. He absorbed

---

[1] Nashe's preface to Greene's *Menaphon*, 1589, in Nashe's *Works*, ed. McKerrow, iii. 319.

[2] Goulart, the third occupant of the Genevan throne, survived Hooker, who was some nine years his junior, by twenty-eight years.

much of the sonorous grandeur of the English version of the
Bible and was greatly influenced by his reading in St. Augus-
tine and the early fathers, and in the masters of Latin prose.
His massiveness and ampleness are more imposing than
Calvin's simplicity. But the ceaseless flow of the sentences,
high sounding and rhythmical, with the uniformly logical
arrangement of argument, absorbs something of the facility
and clarity of Calvin's measured tones. At any rate, in
regard alike to matter and method, Calvin's *Institution
Chrétienne* is the French book which best deserves a place
beside Hooker's *Ecclesiastical Polity*.

IV

AMYOT

Whatever the potency of the French influence on Elizabethan
theology, French prose of the Renaissance worked with even
more stirring effect on the secular stream of serious Elizabethan
literature. From this point of view no Frenchman deserves
a larger measure of attention from Elizabethan students than
Jacques Amyot (1513-1593). Junior by some four years to
Calvin and surviving him by as many as twenty-nine, Amyot
was an ecclesiastic of a very different theological school. He
was a Catholic of unquestioned orthodoxy, if of a wide
tolerance. His religious opinions are, however, immaterial to the present issue. Here he comes into the arena
as a liberal humanist, a typical scholar of the French Renaissance. A competent Greek scholar, he recovered much
Greek literature from manuscript sources and cherished a
passion for literary research. His main energies were devoted
to translating Greek literature into French, to disseminating
Greek literature among his fellow countrymen who were no
scholars. French Renaissance scholars deemed it incumbent
on them to share their knowledge with the French people,
and they placed the art of accurate translation from the classics
high among branches of literary endeavour. Amyot brought
the art of translating Greek prose into French near the pitch

of perfection. His efforts rendered his unlearned countrymen two services. On the one hand he familiarized them with new and stimulating Greek ideas. On the other hand, French prose style was brought by his pen many steps nearer the neatness, the briskness, and suppleness of the Greek idiom, with which it always had general affinity. Amyot's largest labour, his translation of Plutarch's *Lives*, was rendered into English, and thereby English minds and English prose were made sharers in Amyot's intellectual gifts to France.

Amyot's career is worthy of attention. He came of the humblest parentage, of poor working-class people. His native place, Melun, lay within thirty miles of Paris. As a poor student he studied Greek at Paris University and then obtained an appointment as private tutor. In that employment he came under the notice of Queen Margaret of Navarre, the motherly patroness of humanism. She appointed him teacher of Greek in the University of Bourges, a university of fifteenth-century foundation, which was famous for its devotion to law and to the classics. The young teacher's first literary undertaking, which he completed at Bourges, was a translation of the *Aethiopica* of the Greek novelist Heliodorus. Already in holy orders, he received from Francis I, when the king was nearing death, useful preferment to an ecclesiastical sinecure, to the abbacy of Bellozane. The emoluments of the benefice he spent on a four years' tour in Italy in search of Greek manuscripts. He worked in the library of St. Mark's, Venice, and in the Vatican Library at Rome. At Venice he discovered manuscripts of as many as five hitherto unknown books of Diodorus Siculus, the Greek historian. Characteristically he translated these books into his own tongue, before publishing the recovered text. On returning to France he was made tutor to Francis I's grandsons, two sons of the new king, Henry II. His pupils afterwards succeeded in turn to the throne of France as Charles IX and Henry III, and their names loom large in the literary annals of the French Renaissance.

While engaged at court Amyot completed the work by which he gained his fame, his French translation of Plutarch's

Lives (1559). His French rendering of a second Greek novel, *Daphnis and Chloe,* by Longus, also gained much popularity, and for his royal pupils he prepared a treatise on rhetoric, which gives evidence of educational sagacity. When his elder pupil ascended the throne as Charles IX, Amyot in 1560 obtained the high office of Grand Almoner to the king, and ten years later he owed to the same patron the bishopric of Auxerre. The see lay amid vineyards some 109 miles southeast of Paris. He lived on as bishop for twenty-three years from 1570 to 1593. The days of his episcopate were troubled by the religious wars, which he deplored, and by litigation with his chapter. Yet one literary labour of no mean value or extent belongs to the closing epoch of his life: it is a translation into French of Plutarch's philosophical works. Amyot's career covered the best part of the sixteenth century. He died at the ripe age of eighty in 1593, when Shakespeare was twenty-nine years old.

Save for his work on Diodorus, the Greek historian, which attracted small notice, Amyot's literary efforts in translation enjoyed an immense reputation and influence. He transformed the Greek novels of Heliodorus and Longus into living and lasting French fiction. Beneath his wand Plutarch the biographer and the moralist became indistinguishable, with the mass of French readers, from an original French author. Plutarch's *Lives* had attracted little attention from the humanists before Amyot turned the book into French. The skill with which the conversion was effected awoke a responsive chord in the French mind which has never ceased to vibrate. Plutarch the biographer owes his modern fame chiefly to Amyot.[1]

Amyot has himself described his method as a translator and his aim as a writer. 'Take heed,' he bids us, 'and find the words that are fittest to signify the thing of which we mean to

---

[1] A minute critical analysis of Amyot's method as translator of Plutarch's *Lives* will be found in a recent monograph by M. René Sturel, entitled *Jaques Amyot, traducteur des Vies parallèles de Plutarque,* Paris, 1908. M. Sturel's learned study is issued in the *Bibliothèque Littéraire de la Renaissance,* dirigée par M. P. de Nolhac et M. Dorez. (Première série. Tome huitième.)

speak. Choose words which seem the pleasantest, which sound best in our ears, which are customary in the mouths of good talkers, which are honest natives and no foreigners.' The conditions of first-rate prose are hardly capable of more satisfactory definition. Amyot practised as he preached, and Amyot's Plutarch remains one of the best renderings of the Greek into a modern language.

Plutarch's style was a good model. He is clear, simple, and concise. Amyot's translation largely respects Plutarch's tone. The period is of moderate length, and when the sentence is prolonged there is an adequate balance in the sequence of the clauses. There are no awkward inversions nor elisions of articles and prepositions which were frequent blemishes of mediaeval French prose. His vocabulary too is peculiarly French, and it presents the language of cultured circles, stripped of Italianisms. Nor did Amyot favour latinized or archaic terminology. He is said to have spoken his own language with singular polish and purity, and to have written as he spoke. At the same time Amyot although a sound scholar was not impeccable. He travels occasionally from his text. He is less severe than the Greek, somewhat more redundant in his epithets and adverbs. But his amplifications tend to picturesqueness. In the result Amyot was accepted by the French Academy of the seventeenth century as the first French writer of prose who deserved academic recognition.

Amyot's choice of theme merits no less applause than his style. In lifting the curtain on the ancient experience garnered in Plutarch's *Lives* and in his *Morals*, he rendered vast service not to France alone but to the world at large. Plutarch's *Morals* consists of miscellaneous ethical essays which display a broad-minded sagacity and charity. But it is the chief glory of Amyot's Greek master to have placed biography in the category of the literary arts. Plutarch's method may not at the first glance promise any very pregnant result. He is in essence an anecdotal gossip. He loves to accumulate microscopic particulars of men's lives, the smallest traits of character, the least apparently impressive habits. But he arranged his ample and seemingly trivial details with so magical a skill as to evolve a speaking likeness of his chosen heroes, all of whom were of dignified stature.

The sentiment which Amyot's labour on Plutarch's *Lives* evoked among his countrymen is well expressed by his most eminent disciple in France, by Montaigne. 'I do with some reason, as me seemeth,' wrote Montaigne, 'give prick and praise unto Jaques Amyot above all our French writers, not only for his natural purity and pure elegancy of the tongue . . . but above all, I con him thanks that he hath had the hap to choose, and knowledge to cull-out so worthy a work [as Plutarch's *Lives*] and a book so fit to the purpose, therewith to make so invaluable a present unto his country. We that are in the number of the ignorant had been utterly confounded, had not his book raised us from out the dust of ignorance . . . It is our breviary.' Montaigne's enthusiasm for Amyot's labours as Plutarch's interpreter was undying in France. Madame Roland re-embodied it in her famous salutation of Plutarch's work as 'la pâture des grandes âmes'. Through Amyot's exertion Plutarch's *Lives* made a wide and an enduring appeal, and the unlettered reader proved as enthusiastic an admirer of their worth as the scholar.

Religious differences barely touched the attitude of Frenchmen to classical revelation. Catholic and Protestant worshipped side by side at Plutarch's shrine. The French apostle of Plutarch's art of life was an orthodox Catholic bishop. Yet Plutarch's vogue was never confined to Catholic circles. The Huguenots absorbed the story and teaching of Plutarch's *Lives* with a vehement avidity. There is hardly a Huguenot general or statesman (whose memoirs are extant) who does not pay tribute to the moral stimulus he derived in youth from reading Amyot. In a well-known letter which Henry IV of Navarre wrote to his queen from the field of battle during his fiercest struggle with the league, he addressed her in terms like these: 'Living God, you could have announced to me nothing which was more agreeable than the news of the pleasure which you have derived from reading Plutarch. Plutarch always offers me a fresh novelty. To love him is to love me, because he has been for long, from my infancy, my tutor. My good mother, to whom I owe everything, put this book into my hands when I was hardly more than a sucking babe.'

The influence of Amyot's achievement illustrates better than any other the moral and intellectual elevation which the humanists of the French Renaissance fostered by their study of the classics. The scholars and men of letters not merely appreciated the aesthetic quality of Greek and Latin literature, but they were led and they led their students instinctively to apply to current purposes of life the wisdom of the golden past.

Elizabethan men of letters quickly yielded to the fascination of Plutarch's *Lives*. But they owed the introduction to Amyot, the excellence of whose style ranked him, in the opinion of Elizabethan critics, with the Renaissance masters of prose throughout Europe. Gabriel Harvey, the Cambridge scholar, declared him to be as fine a writer in French, as Bembo was in Latin, Machiavelli in Italian, or Guevara in Spanish.[1] Sir Thomas North's English translation of Plutarch's *Lives* wholly came from the French version. It produced on England something of the effect which Amyot produced in France. North was a country gentleman whose only public service, apart from local county administration, was to accompany his elder brother, Lord North, on a special embassy to Paris to congratulate Amyot's pupil, Henry III, on his accession to the French throne in 1574. It was four years after this visit to France that North published in a massive folio his Plutarch's *Lives* in English. North's dependence on Amyot is undisguised. On the threshold of his book he sets a translation of Amyot's address to the reader, in which the Frenchman expounds the value of Plutarch's biographies. A comparison of North's rendering with the French version shows an admirable fidelity. There is hardly an epithet or adverb of Amyot's invention which North omits. Amyot's redundant embellishments or expansions of his Greek text are all reproduced in the English. In the two sentences, for example, in which Amyot describes the heroic efforts of Cleopatra and

---

[1] Gabriel Harvey, *Pierces Supererogation*, 1593, quoted in *Elizabethan Critical Essays*, ed. Gregory Smith, vol. ii, p. 276.

her women to drag the dying and helpless Antony into their secret place of refuge, the Frenchman introduces thirty-two words which the Greek text fails to authorize. Thirty of these superfluities are duly reproduced by North.[1] In the result, North is a step further removed than Amyot from the simple directness of the Greek. Occasionally he misunderstands Amyot and makes complete havoc of Plutarch's meaning. But North reproduces the French, if not the Greek, style as closely as the English idiom allows. Amyot's picturesqueness of expression gains rather than loses in the English version.

North's work fills a most important place in the development of English prose. It is the largest piece that had yet been contributed to our secular literature; it is the primordial monument of ripe literary composition, and one of the richest sources of our literary language. For the unaffected vivacity which is its most salient feature, Amyot must be allowed the main responsibility.

Of the influence exerted by North's work on Elizabethan development of style and thought, no apology is needed for quoting the instance that is most familiar to students.

---

[1] The passages referred to are here quoted in parallel columns. The italicized words in each quotation arc those for which the Greek gives no authority. The words between square brackets in North's sentences are additions of his own.

AMYOT.

'Car on tiroit ce *pauvre homme* tout souillé de sang tirant aux traicts de la mort, et qui tendoit les deux mains à Cleopatra, et se soublevoit *le mieulx qu'il pouvoit.* C'estoit une chose *bien* malaisée *que de le monter, mesmement* à des femmes, toutefois Cleopatra en grande peine *s'efforceant de toute sa puissance,* la teste courbee contre bas sans jamais lascher les cordes, *feit tant à la fin qu'elle* le monta *et tira à soy,* à l'aide de ceulx d'abas qui luy donnoient courage, et tiroyent autant de peine *à la voir ainsi travailler,* comme elle mesme.' (Amyot, ch. lxxvii.)

NORTH.

'For they plucked up *poore* Antonius all bloody [as he was], and drawing on with pangs of death, who holding up his hands to Cleopatra, raised up him selfe *as well as he could.* It was a hard thing for these women to do, *to lift him up*; but Cleopatra stowping downe with her head, *putting to all her strength to the uttermost power,* did lift him up *with much adoe, and never let go her hold,* with the helpe of the women beneath that bad her be of good corage, and were as sorie *to see her labor so,* as she her selfe.' (North's *Plutarch,* Tudor translations, vol. vi, p. 80.)

Plutarch in North's version was an inspirer of Shakespeare. Shakespeare's observant eye detected in Plutarch's *Lives*, as revealed to him by North through Amyot, a stimulating source of inspiration. No depreciation of the working of Shakespeare's genius attends a frank recognition of the immense debt which his Roman plays owe to Plutarch's suggestion. The character of Theseus in *A Midsummer Night's Dream* is a first faint echo of North's voice. But the three Roman plays, *Julius Caesar*, *Antony and Cleopatra*, and *Coriolanus*, mark the consummation of Shakespeare's debt. The Greek biographer and his translators are worthy of their disciple.

The English dramatist was not the first to perceive in Plutarch a rich mine of material for drama. For the moment I will only state the fact, commonly overlooked in our literary histories, that some years before Shakespeare turned Plutarch's *Lives* of Roman heroes to dramatic purposes at least five French dramatists had levied similar loans on the same source. Plutarch's lives of Julius Caesar, Brutus, Mark Antony, and Coriolanus had been wrought into tragedies on the French stage before Shakespeare approached those themes.[1] Here it is only pertinent to notice how North's prose was frequently converted by Shakespeare with the smallest possible change into vivacious blank verse and genuine poetry. The process illustrates not only Shakespeare's ingenuity, but the singular strength lurking in North's style which is in so marked a degree the gift of Amyot's French. The perfected prose of the French Renaissance was one of the many influences working at a short remove on Shakespeare's dramatic language. The close of Antony's dying speech in Plutarch's life of Mark Antony is rendered by North from the French, in *oratio obliqua* thus: 'And as for himself, he entreated that she [Cleopatra] should not lament nor sorrow for the miserable change of his fortune at the end of his days, but rather that she should think him the more fortunate for the former triumphs and honours he had received, considering

---

[1] See *infra*, pp. 386 seq.

that while he lived he was the noblest and greatest prince of the world, and that now he was overcome not cowardly, but valiantly, a Roman by another Roman.' Shakespeare transforms this passage into *oratio recta*. Shakespeare's Antony with his last breath bids Cleopatra—

> The miserable change now at my end
> Lament nor sorrow at; but please your thoughts
> In feeding them with those my former fortunes
> Wherein I lived, the greatest prince o' the world,
> The noblest; and do now not basely die,
> Not cowardly put off my helmet to
> My countryman; a Roman by a Roman
> Valiantly vanquished.

There are slight inversions, and about half a dozen words are added. But Amyot may almost be held responsible for one of the most tragic utterances penned by the English dramatist. Shakespeare's Roman plays offer a hundred similar examples of his loans on English prose which is of French inspiration. Amyot is a hero of English as well as of French literature.

V

RABELAIS

Rabelais (1495–1553) was born within five years of the close of the fifteenth century. He is the senior of Calvin by fourteen years and of Amyot by eighteen years. He died ten years earlier than the French reformer, and forty years earlier than the translator of Plutarch. Rabelais is of the era of Sir Thomas More and the Earl of Surrey, both of whom he outlived, rather than of the epoch of Spenser and Hooker, whose lives just began when the Frenchman's closed. Yet his influence failed to invade England before Elizabethan literature was ripening. His arrival on the English stage is not only later than that of his two great contemporary masters of French prose, but its results are, contrary to what his boisterous expansiveness might suggest, far smaller and less conspicuous.

It is difficult to place Rabelais's work in any of the recognized literary categories. His *Lives, heroic deeds and sayings of Gargantua and his son Pantagruel*, was begun as a burlesque continuation of a mediaeval romance of bombastic and impossible heroism. His disorderly style, and his incurable habits of digression, closely link him with the crudities of the past. Yet in truth Rabelais is a brilliant child of the Renaissance, a man of vast reading and close observation, bent on proving that mediaeval thought and custom had outgrown the needs of society and that new ideals had arisen to challenge the old conceptions of life. No aspect of human existence does he omit to place beneath his satiric microscope. Religion, philosophy, law, politics, education, are all scrutinized, and the chaff sifted from the grain with droll animation. Rabelais's career is as paradoxical as his theme and style. Successively a Franciscan friar, a Benedictine monk, a physician, a corrector of the press, a cañon, and a curé, he corresponded in Greek with Budaeus, and was suspected of heresy by the obscurantist clergy. He was favoured alike by the heterodox Queen of Navarre and by the orthodox Cardinal du Bellay. All the knowledge of his age was at his disposal; yet he met death with the grim pleasantry that he was on his way to seek 'the great Perhaps' (*le grand Peut-être*).

Rabelais writes with such extraordinary exuberance, he runs riot in such grotesque exaggerations, he indulges in such obscene buffoonery, that his contribution to the progress of thought stands in danger of neglect. Sagacious reflections on education, on the vice of ignorance and the value of scientific knowledge, on the true sanctions of religion and politics, are mingled almost inextricably with nonsensical burlesque and offensive obscenity. The discursive plot brings Rabelais's heroes after much devious travel to the shrine of the Divine Bottle, where the priestess of the oracle greets the pilgrims with the exhilarating injunction 'Drink'. The priestess delivers the genuine message of the Renaissance: 'Let every man possess his soul with cheerfulness, sing, laugh, and talk, enjoy the golden sunshine and the purple wine, and live according to the laws of the world, but at the same time study nature, learn patiently and hopefully all that is to be known of her, and never lose faith in a Divine Creator.' This is Rabelais's philosophy, however it be disguised in his wild vocabulary; a philosophy redolent of a full-blooded humanity; an amalgam of the philosophy of Falstaff and that of Prospero. The seeing eye detects earnestness in Rabelais's aim. There is more significance than appears on the surface in the paradoxical apophthegm of a French poet and critic of the Renaissance: ' Rabelais laid the eggs which Calvin hatched.'

Rabelais's writings were originally published in five books, of which the first came out in 1532, and the last posthumously in 1562. No part of his work is extant in any English translation of the Elizabethan era. *Gargantua his Prophecie* was, according to the London Stationers' Registers (ii. 607, 613), the title of a publication of the year 1592, but no copy has been met with, and it can only have presented a fragment of Rabelais's achievement. It was not till the seventeenth century was well advanced that Rabelais came forth in English dress. The eccentric Scotchman, Sir Thomas Urquhart, who had much in common with Rabelais's riotous temper, published his admirable version in 1653.

Like Rabelais himself, Urquhart has some title to be regarded as an elder brother of the Elizabethans. Rabelais's name was not unfamiliar to the Elizabethans, but they showed unaccountable reluctance in plainly recognizing the relationship. References to him in Elizabethan literature are sparse, and suggest that he was barely understood by Englishmen of the sixteenth century. Very often the allusion is of derogatory tone. The satirist Joseph Hall writes of ' wicked Rabelais's drunken revellings '. The scholar Gabriel Harvey complains of his lying extravagance. Rarely is the sign of acquaintance with the French humorist appreciative. Donne mentions Rabelais's burlesque hero Panurge as a mighty linguist of humble birth, and quotes Rabelais's tale of words that freeze in winter and thaw in the spring. Sir John Harington, in his cloacinean satire, *The Metamorphosis of Ajax*, cites ' the reverent Rabbles *quem honoris causa nomino* '. Bacon calls him 'the great jester of France' and a 'master of scoffing', but shows no full knowledge.[1] Enthusiasm is wanting, and there is no clear sign of close study.

Shakespeare probably knew as much of Rabelais as the average Elizabethan. The schoolmaster Holofernes in *Love's Labour's Lost* is reminiscent of that famous doctor of divinity Tubal Holofernes, to whose care the boy Gargantua was for a season confided. When Celia is about to tell Rosalind in *As You Like It* (III. ii. 238 seq.) the great news of her meeting with Orlando in the forest, she says: 'You must borrow me Gargantua's mouth first: 'tis a word too great for any mouth of this age's size.' The giant Gargantua was the hero of a mediaeval story-book before Rabelais re-created him. Yet Celia seems to be recalling Rabelais's own description of Gargantua's mouth, which was of such abnormal size that he put into it five pilgrims with their staves, who accidentally fell into a salad that the giant was eating. Elsewhere Shakespeare proves that he well knew Rabelais's peculiar vein of pleasantry. In *Twelfth Night* (II. iii. 23 seq.) the simple knight Sir Andrew Aguecheek recalls some very gracious fooling with which the clown of the play had solaced him in his cups in the small hours of the previous morning. Sir Andrew commends his companion's wit in speaking unintelligible nonsense about 'Pigrogromitus, of the Vapians passing the equinoctial of Queubus'. ''Twas very good, i' faith,' says the simple knight. This is the mystifying kind of jargon which Rabelais loved. The words are not to be found in Rabelais's text, but poor rabbit-witted Sir Andrew is hardly likely to report correctly in the morning a difficult verbal quip which he had heard at a convivial debauch at a late hour the night before. Again when Edgar (in *King*

---

[1] Bacon mentions Rabelais and his mock-library of St. Victoire at Paris in his Essay *Of Unity in Religion* (Essay III): 'There is a master of scoffing; that in his catalogue of books, of a feigned library, sets down this title of a book: *The Morris Dance of Heretics.*' In the *Apophthegms* Bacon tells the apocryphal story of Rabelais's death: 'When Rabelais lay on his death-bed, and they gave him the extreme unction, a familiar friend of his came to him afterwards, and asked him, How he did? Rabelais answered: Even going my journey, they have greased my boots already.' (*Works*, ed. Spedding Ellis and Heath, vii. 131.)

Lear, III. iii. 7), in his disguise of madman, mutters how ' Nero is an angler in the lake of darkness ', Shakespeare is confusedly recalling Rabelais's original and uncorroborated discovery that Trajan was in hell as an angler for frogs, while Nero was there as a fiddler.   But Shakespeare's echoes of Rabelais are hardly more distinct than those of Donne and Bacon.

On only one of Shakespeare's contemporaries, Tom Nashe, is Rabelais's influence defined with absolute clearness.   Thomas Nashe, the reckless prose satirist who tried his hand at drama and romance as well as pamphleteering, approaches nearest of any Elizabethan writer to the Rabelaisian type.   Nashe's prose style and temperament come as near Rabelais as anything with which one meets in Elizabethan English.   But Nashe wrote nothing on so large a scale as his master, for no such extended outlook on the world lay within his ambition or power.   He was a lampoonist, who filled up his vacant hours with a short novel of adventure, and some lyrics and plays.   He made his fame chiefly by a bitter controversy with the Cambridge scholar, Gabriel Harvey, on whom he turned all his artillery of unlicensed abuse.   But he was always comical in his scurrility, and his sense of the ridiculous was strong and lively.   One of his denunciations of the pedantic Harvey he dedicates with mock gravity to the barber of Trinity College, Cambridge, and his love of irresponsible fooling and grotesque humour led him at the extreme end of his life into an hilarious panegyric of the red herring, which he dedicated to a friendly tobacconist.

Nashe formally admits his discipleship to Rabelais.   The indebtedness was recognized by Nashe's critics.   Gabriel Harvey deplores that Nashe cast his work in ' the fantastical mould of Rabelais, that monstrous wit ', and he denounces his adversary as a Gargantuist who seeks to devour his enemies in salads. Nashe's breezy insolence of speech has affinity with another foreign author, the Italian Aretino, who defied proprieties with almost as great a gusto as Rabelais.   To him also Nashe makes obeisance.   But, in spite of tuition gained from other quarters, it is his reading in Rabelais which accounts for most of the peculiar eccentricities of Nashe's prose style, for most of his contumacy of phrase. Like Rabelais, he depended largely on a free use of slang for his best burlesque effects. So too his habit of inventing grandiose words is a gift of Rabelais. When he found no word quite fitted to his purpose, he followed the example of his foreign master in coining one out of Greek, Latin, Spanish, or Italian. 'No speech or words,' he wrote, ' of any power or force to confute or persuade, but must be swelling and boisterous,' and he was compelled to seek abroad, he explained, his boisterous compound words, in order to compensate for the great defect of the English tongue, ' which of all languages most swarmeth with the single money of monosyllables.' The Elizabethan poets also went, as we shall see, to contemporary France for aid in remedying the monosyllabic tendency of their own tongue, but Nashe is franker than they in the admission. Like Rabelais, too, Nashe sought to develop emphasis by marshalling columns of synonyms and by constant reiteration of kindred phrases. His writings have at times something of the fascination of Rabelais's rough tongue, but as a rule his themes are of too local and topical an interest to appeal to Rabelais's world-wide audience. His bursts of joviality are not linked with Rabelais's penetrating sagacity. Nashe's influence on language and literature is not profound. He was hardly great enough to have disciples.

Nashe plays a somewhat isolated part on the Elizabethan stage, but Rabelais did not pass from the English horizon with Nashe's death. Like Bacon, Sir Thomas Browne knew that ' bundle of curiosities', Pantagruel's burlesque catalogue of the library of the abbey of St. Victoire at Paris. The French humorist's ebullient note was more often detected by contemporaries in the Jacobean hero, Tom Coryat, the bombastic narrator of marvellous pedestrian feats on the European continent. A friendly versifier, by way of jest, bestowed on the giant walker, who was known as the Odcombian from his native village of Odcombe in Somerset, the Rabelaisian title of ' cet Heroique Geant Odcombien nommé non Pantagruel mais Pantagrué', while his volume of *Crudities* was hailed as worthy of a place in the library of the abbey of St. Victoire between ' Marmoretus de Baboinis et cingis ' and ' Tirepetanas

de optimitate triparum '. Coryat's *Crudities* was indeed re-
christened by a Rabelaisian enthusiast in his master's dialect
' La Caberotade de Coryat ou l'Apodemistichopezolie de l'Odcombien Somerseti '. But Coryat did less than Nashe for the
Rabelaisian tradition. Few passages of his farcical rhodo-
montade approach Nashe's Rabelaisian swagger. Surly Doctor
Donne in some commendatory verses compares Coryat's story
of travel with Rabelais's report of his hero's wonderful voyages.
But Coryat cannot sustain the blustering vein, and usually
ambles on tamer levels. Readers who recalled the whimsical
voyages which Rabelais assigned to Pantagruel and Panurge,
likened Coryat to the French comedian from the grotesque-
ness of his pedestrian adventures rather than from his ordinary
manner of reporting them. The popular association of Coryat
with Rabelais shows how Rabelais's English reputation grew
after Nashe had confirmed its footing. Nashe's Rabelaisian
accents, which added an iridiscent touch to Elizabethan humour,
helped to keep alive in the next age some interest in the
exploits of the French master of the comic spirit.

VI

MONTAIGNE

The fourth of the great French prose masters of the
sixteenth century, and the most fascinating, is Michel de Montaigne (1533–1592). A Gascon, cheerful and self-possessed,
he was son of a squire or small nobleman living on his estate
not far from Bordeaux. Brought up to the law, he practised
as a youth in local courts, and obtained a clerkship in the
provincial Parlement of Bordeaux. At the age of thirty-eight
his father died, and he retired from his profession to the
castle and farm of his patrimony. He thenceforth lived for
the most part the life of a country gentleman, though he left
home for occasional visits to Paris, and once made a prolonged
foreign tour through Italy, Germany, and Switzerland.
Towards the end of his career he acted, too, as Mayor of
Bordeaux. But the main interests of his later years were his
farms, his country neighbours, and, above all, his books. His

library, which filled the upper chamber of an octagonal tower of his house, was his earthly paradise, and the Latin and Greek classics were unfailing fountains of delight. He set the pleasures of reading above those of writing, although, happily for posterity, he fell into the habit of recording his thought.

As in the case of so many contemporary humanists, his first contribution to literature was a translation. He tried his hand at literary composition by turning from the Latin into French an outspoken speculation on natural theology by a Spaniard, Raymond de Sebonde. It was in 1580, when he was nearing fifty years, that he published the greater part of the work which gives him all his fame—the first two volumes of his *Essais*. The third and last book came out in 1588, the year alike of the Spanish Armada, and of the outbreak of the last civil war of the century between Catholics and Protestants in France. He died at Bordeaux in 1592, in his sixtieth year. Shakespeare was then twenty-eight years old, and was acquiring his earliest repute. Bacon was a year older.

Montaigne is the first of modern essayists in point alike of time and quality. Although he probably owed some suggestion for the form to one of his favourite classical books, Plutarch's *Morals,* the essay may fairly be reckoned Montaigne's invention. Montaigne's essays—107 in all—are desultory personal reflections on various aspects of life and experience. They are put together without method. In theme and style they are incurably rambling and digressive. The titles give one a notion of their scope. Some taken at random run : idleness, the punishment of cowardice, pedantry, friendship, names, age, books, thumbs, anger, the incommodity of greatness, vanity, experience. The field is wide as life.

Montaigne's supreme virtue is his egotism. He is the prince of egotists. His charm lies in his irrepressible faculty for gossip about himself. ' I speak to paper,' he says, ' just as I would to a man I meet. My thoughts slip from me with as little care as if they were quite worthless.' He writes just as he feels, without ceremony and without concealment. His want of premeditation not infrequently leads him to con-

tradict himself.   But the contradictions preserve the living
semblance of reality.   Human nature is a bundle of incon-
sistencies.   'All the contraries,' says Montaigne, 'are to be
found in me in one corner or another.'   Montaigne's language
faithfully reflects unconstrained conversation.   It always
maintains an easy flow, rarely rising and rarely sinking.   He
ambles along, serenely satisfied with himself, and he infects
others with his self-satisfaction.   But as he talks volubly from
his easy chair, he does not suffer his reader to forget that he
is in his library and that books are at his side.   The classics
were his intellectual fare from boyhood.   He was deeply
read as a youth in Seneca, Cicero, and, above all, in Plato and
Plutarch.   Plutarch as a biographer and as a philosopher
chiefly moulds his thought, and to Plutarch's French apostle
Amyot he extends the adoration which that scholar paid
the Greek master.   The enthusiastic eulogy which he passes
on Amyot, Plutarch's French translator, may prepare
us for the knowledge that his fluent French style bears
eloquent testimony to Amyot's influence.   Montaigne betters
Amyot's instruction in facility of phrase and easy wit, but
not in syntactical regularity.   Yet it is among Amyot's titles
to fame that he was Montaigne's master in French prose.

Montaigne is the latest and the most seductive champion of
the spirit of the French Renaissance.   To greater effect than
any of his predecessors he adapted the flower of ancient
wisdom to the needs and notions of modern times.   Montaigne
in effect converts into current coin all the emancipating
aspirations of the Renaissance.   The passion for extending
the limits of human knowledge, and for employing man's
capabilities to new and better advantage than of old, the
resolve to make the best and not the worst of life upon earth,
the ambition to cultivate as the highest good the idea of
beauty, the faith in man's perfectibility on the physical as
well as on the spiritual side—these fundamental aspirations of
the era found no more convincing exponent than Montaigne.
Very characteristic of his intellectual temper is this passage:—
'There is nothing in us either purely corporeal or purely
spiritual. 'Tis an inhuman wisdom that would have us despise

and hate the culture of the body. 'Tis not a soul, 'tis not a body, we are training up, but a man; and we ought not to divide him. Of all the infirmities we have, the most savage is to despise our being.'

In his attitude to religion, Montaigne was a sceptic or agnostic. 'Que sais-je?' ('What do I know?') was his motto.[1] Of the mysteries of heaven he thought no man could know anything, and he was content to be ignorant. He tries, he tells us, to sit through life on the stool of the Christianity of utter ignorance. He had no claim to the stool of the Christianity of perfect knowledge. The first stool is his natural seat. He does not deny that the received opinions may be true. He simply says he does not know whether they be true or false. The mysteries of faith are not comprehensible by reason, therefore his reason leaves them alone. For current controversies between Huguenot and Catholic he cared nothing. The theological points at issue seemed to him superficial or trivial. Shakespeare sums up Montaigne's mental temperament when he calls ' modest doubt the beacon of the wise', and Hamlet speaks in Montaigne's accents when he ejaculates:

There are more things in heaven and earth, Horatio,
Than are dreamt of in our philosophy.

It is a practical, worldly wisdom which Montaigne preaches. But his argument is always coloured by gentlemanly feeling, which restrained him from unseasonably parading his opinions to the wounding of others' susceptibilities. He calls himself in one place a creature of convention; the common customs and usages are good enough for him. On his death-bed he was quite ready to accept the priest's offer to celebrate Mass, not because he had belief in the efficacy of the ceremony, but because it was more civil to accept the priest's ministrations than to refuse them.

---

[1] It was in admiring discipleship to Montaigne that Byron wrote (*Don Juan*, c. ix. st. 17):

'Que sais-je?' was the motto of Montaigne,
As also of the first academicians.
That all·is dubious which man may attain,
Was one of their most favourite positions.

But however easy-going and garrulous was Montaigne's habit of mind and speech, he was never a mere laughing commentator on human affairs. At heart he was an earnest moralist. He seriously recognizes the defects of human nature, and sagaciously seeks to explain them without excusing them. There is, for instance, much vicious work, he points out, in politics; base tricks, bribes, diplomatic lying infect the political sphere. He suggests that these vices may be like poisons, which are employed in maintaining the health of one's body. Though they are bad things in themselves, they may prove useful in their application. Their baneful quality may thus be deprived of its effect. But, he adds, with ironical frankness, he has no personal liking for poisons, and has no intention of mixing in the business in which they are needful solvents. With a somewhat cynical smile he adds :—' Let us resign the acting of this political part in life to hardy citizens, who sacrifice honour and conscience, as others of old sacrificed their lives, for the good of their country.'

Almost every subject of social economy he illuminates with similar sprightly wit, in which irony clothes insight. At times the sportive note predominates and obscures the serious intention. His remark on marriage is proverbial. He will say no more about the merits of that institution, of which he had personal experience, than that it presents itself to his mind like a cage. ' The birds without despair to get in—the birds within despair of getting out.' Montaigne found *l'esprit gaulois* not always easy to bridle.

In spite of the tendency to mask his penetrating observation with badinage, Montaigne's fascinating flow of wit and wisdom, of gravity and seriousness, succeeded in bringing an ethical view of social duty down to the level of the popular and worldly intelligence. Montaigne's work also inaugurated a new form of literature. The matter and manner alike exerted a vast influence on European thought and taste.

Montaigne's *Essays* were soon known in England. The final edition was published in Paris after his death. All his manuscript corrections were there incorporated by Mlle de Gournay, a young lady of great cultivation, who brought to her editorial work an enthusiastic worship. The volumes were published in 1595. The Parisian edition of that year gives the authorized text of the *Essays*. It is significant of the closeness with which French literary effort was watched in Elizabethan England that on October 20 of that same year, 1595, a licence was issued by the Stationers' Company in London for the publication of an English translation.[1] A second printing licence was dated some five years later. No English translation earlier than 1603 is extant. But there are indications that a manuscript translation was in circulation some years before. Montaigne's name indeed became a household word in Elizabethan England very soon after he had become the idol of French enlightenment.

The first English translator of Montaigne's *Essays* was a well-known figure in Elizabethan society. John Florio was son of a Florentine Protestant who settled in England while Edward VI reigned and before his son's birth, to escape persecution at home. John became well known in Oxford as a teacher of Italian, and then pursued the same vocation in London. His pupils included Shakespeare's patron, the Earl of Southampton, and at a later date James I's queen, Anne of Denmark. He mixed freely in the best literary circles, and he reckoned Shakespeare among his acquaintances. An industrious compiler of aids to English students of Italian, he published useful Italian-English dialogues, and a copious Italian-English dictionary which he called ' A World of Words ', a work of lexicographical value. His most important literary effort was his translation of Montaigne's *Essays*. That piece of work, which has been highly praised for its style, certainly conveys something of the ease and flow of the French original. Yet it has too many clumsy and confused clauses to rank it with the best of the Tudor translations. North's *Plutarch* is a superior venture in perspicuity.

---

[1] Arber's *Transcript of the Stationers' Company*, iii. 50:—' 20 of October [1595]. Edward *Aggas*. Entred for his Copie vnder the handes of the Wardenes *The Essais* of MICHAELL Lord of Mountane . . . vjd.' On June 20, 1600, another stationer, Edward Blount, ' received a license to print ' The *Essais* of MICHAEL lord of Mountaigne translated into English by John Florio' (Arber, iii. 162).

The later English translation of Montaigne by Charles Cotton, the friend of Izaak Walton, has some claim to rank above Florio's. The archaic flavour which sometimes attaches to Montaigne's own manner of speech seems unduly accentuated by Florio. Yet his success in familiarizing Shakespeare's England with the wealth of Montaigne's genius was in no way prejudiced by defects in his literary accomplishments.

In England the finest fruit of Montaigne's effort is Bacon's *Essays*. Bacon's genius was too original to make him a servile imitator. The brevity of Bacon's essays distinguishes them at a first glance from the majority of Montaigne's, although a few of Montaigne's essays are of Bacon's modest dimensions. There is no garrulity about Bacon, no genial exchange of confidence with his readers, no digressions. He rivets his reader's attention by the incisiveness of his utterance and by the aptness of his illustration. He is impatient of levity and sternly avoids it. Yet Bacon follows Montaigne in the general design of bringing home to the untrained mind the leading truths of experience. The word ' Essays ' in the sense of informal comments on things at large, was first introduced by Bacon into the English language, and came direct from Montaigne. Bacon's ambition to bring wisdom informally and occasionally ' home to men's business and bosoms ' was the inspiration of Montaigne.

Bacon admits that Montaigne taught him to be an essayist. In the opening essay, *Of Truth*, he enforces his denunciation of the vice of lying with a long quotation from Montaigne's essay on ' giving the lie '. With some quaintness Bacon notes that Montaigne writes on the topic ' prettily '. Montaigne's topics are often borrowed by Bacon, and Bacon's style, flowing for the most part, but sometimes abrupt in its turns, catches frequently a note of Montaigne's homely naturalness.

Literary historians appear to have overlooked a curious personal link between Bacon and the great French essayist, which may well have drawn the Englishman into the circle of Montaigne's disciples. Bacon had opportunities in his own household of learning much of Montaigne. Bacon's elder brother, Anthony, with whom he cherished life-long ties of close affection, spent twelve of his forty-three years of life in the south of France. Much of his time between 1583 and 1591 was passed at Bordeaux, where he made the acquaintance of Montaigne and of all enlightened Huguenots and Catholics of the province. With Montaigne he formed a close intimacy and maintained a correspondence. Anthony Bacon returned to England after his long absence in the early spring of 1592. On September 13 of that year Montaigne unexpectedly died. A letter from his English friend was the last piece of writing which reached the great Frenchman's hand or caught his eye. Within a month the sad news was sent to Anthony by Montaigne's neighbour and close friend, Pierre de Brach.

Brach, a poetic aspirant of the school of Ronsard and the warm admirer of his fellow-Gascon Du Bartas as well as of Montaigne, enjoyed some reputation as a poet and sonneteer. A tolerant Catholic lawyer and squire, who patriotically deplored the civil wars of his country, he is chiefly remembered as the loyal friend and eulogist of three men greater than himself—of Montaigne, of Du Bartas, and of a foreigner, Justus Lipsius, the Leyden professor of classical scholarship. Anthony became an intimate of Brach's social circle at Bordeaux, and a close personal friend of the well-to-do poet. Classical repute already attaches to Brach's letter to Justus Lipsius, giving the authoritative account of Montaigne's death. The communication to Lipsius has often been printed; it was written on February 4, 1593. Yet it was four months earlier that Brach sent the melancholy tidings to Anthony Bacon in a letter which still remains in manuscript among Anthony Bacon's papers at Lambeth.

The communication is worthy of more attention than it has yet received. After expressing regret for Anthony's continued ill-health and reminding him that, in his anxiety to breathe again his native air, he had neglected warnings against the dangers of the sea, Brach laments the strife which infects France and tells of his retirement to his estate near Bordeaux, there to pen elegies on his recently deceased wife. The Frenchman continues, for the benefit of his English correspondent, with these memorable words:

But I am so touched to the quick by a new grief, by the news of the death of M. de Montaigne, that I am not myself. I have lost the best of my friends; France the completest and liveliest wit that she ever had; all the world the true patron and mirror of pure philosophy, so that the world has borne tribute to the shock of his death no less than to the writings of his life. According to what I have heard, this last great event has little in it to discredit his lofty writing. The last epistolary missive that he received was yours which I sent him. He did not answer, because he had to answer Death who has seized only on what was mortal in him. The rest and the better part—which is his name and memory—will only die with Death itself.[1]

---

[1] The original letter is among Anthony Bacon's manuscripts at Lambeth. Dr. Birch prints a summary in his *Memoirs of the Reign of Queen Elizabeth*, 1754 (i. 88). The following is Dr. Birch's full transcript, now in the British Museum (Additional MSS. 4110, f. 123):—

Monsr. De Brach to Mr. Bacon: 'Monsr.; Il me souvenoit tant de l'estat ou vous estiez quand vostre despart vous desroba de nous, qu'aussitost que je vy le sieur, qui me rendist la vostre lettre je luy demanday comment il vous alloit, sans que je prins le loisir de l'apprendre par vous mesme. Ainsi s'enquiert-on, suivent de sçavoir & de voir, ce que le plus souvent nous trouverons contre nostre desirs comme contre mon desir & avec grande desplaisir je sçeu la continuation de vostre mauvais portement. Il me souvient bien, que je me deffiois qu'en une saison si facheuse vous peussiez supporter le travail de la mer, qui vous devoit porter. Mais vous estiez si affamé de vostre air natural, que ce desin vous faisoit mespriser tout danger. Vous aviez raison de vouloir s'éloigner le nostre pour la mauvaise qualité, qu'il a prins par les evaparations de nos troubles, qui l'ont tellement infecté, qu'il n'a nous laissé rien de sain, & nous enmaladé autant de l'esprit que du corps. Quant à moy, monsieur, je me suis retiré en ce lieu, ayant tout à faict quitté Bourdeaux, pour ce que Bourdeaux ne me pouvoit rendre ce que j'y ay perdu, & je continue en ma solitude de rendre ce que je dois à la memoire de ma perte. J'ay icy dressé un estude aussi plaisant à mon desplaisir que nouveau en ses peintures & devises, qui ne sortent point de mon subject. Je les vous descriray, si j'avois autant de liberté d'esprit que de volonté. Mais je suis touché si au vif d'un nouvel ennuy par la nouvelle de la mort de Monsr. de Montaigne, que je ne suis point à moy. J'y ay perdu le meilleur de mes amis; la France le plus entier & le plus vif esprit, qu'elle eut onques, tout le monde le vray patron & mirroir de la pure philosophie, qu'il a tesmoignée aux coups de sa mort comme aux escrits de sa vie; & à ce que j'ay entendu ce grand effect dernier n'a peu en luy faire dementir ces hautes parolles. La dernière lettre missive, qu'il receut, fut la vostre, que je luy envoiay, à laquelle il n'a respondu, pourcequ'il avoit à respondre à la Mort, qui a emporté sur luy ce qui seulement estoit de son gibier; mais le reste & la meilleure part, qui est son nom & sa memoire, ne mourra qu'avec

It is of interest to learn that, as far as extant information goes, it was to an Englishman that the first posthumous tribute to Montaigne's eminence was addressed either inside or outside France. It is not, too, without significance that when in 1597 Francis Bacon published the first edition of his *Essays*, he dedicated them to Anthony, his 'dear brother loving and beloved', who was Montaigne's friend and an early sharer of the grief evoked at Bordeaux by his death.

Bacon, the essayist, in his dependence on Montaigne, did not long stand alone. He initiated the vogue of the English essay on Montaigne's pattern, and he soon had a large following. Ben Johnson declares, in a notable passage in his comedy of *Volpone*, that 'all our English writers . . . will deign to steal . . . from Montaigne',[1] and in his miscellany of criticism which he called *Timber* he describes Montaigne as master of all essayists, but rather crabbedly complained that men who, like Montaigne, write discursively tend to self-contradiction. At any rate, there quickly arose in England a school of essayists under Montaigne's banner. The second writer either to use the term or to practise the *genre* was Sir William Cornwallis, who brought out a first volume called *Essays* in 1600. Sir William was a country gentleman and a member of parliament, following a career not wholly unlike that of Montaigne. For thirty years he was a prolific essayist. With a frankness exceeding Bacon's acknowledgement, he admits familiarity with Montaigne's work; but he only knew it in the English version. He is liberal in the recognition of his debt, and praises the pregnant force of Montaigne's style and thought, albeit his familiarity with it did not extend beyond the English translation. 'For profitable recreation, that noble French knight, the Lord de Montaigne, is most excellent, whom though I have not been so much

---

la mort de ce tout, & demeurera ferme comme sera en moy la volonté de demeurer tousjours, Monsr., Vostre très humble & affectionné serviteur, De brach.

'De la Motte Montassan près Bordeaux ce 10 Octob. 1592.'

[1] Act III, Sc. ii. Here Jonson puts Montaigne on a level with Guarini's *Pastor Fido*, as a ready object of pillage for English authors. Jonson's comedy, which was first produced in 1605, was published in 1607.

beholding to the French as to see in his original, yet divers of his pieces I have seen translated : they that understand both languages say very well done, and I am able to say (if you will take the word of ignorance), translated into a style, admitting as few idle words as our language will endure : it is well fitted in this new garment, and Montaigne speaks now good English.' The Elizabethan essayist often literally copies Montaigne's language and sentiment with scant ceremony. But he amply atones for his servility by the enlightened tribute which he pays the French master. Montaigne, continues Cornwallis—

speaks nobly, honestly and wisely, with little method, but with much judgement; learned he was, and often shows it, but with such a happiness, as his own following is not disgraced by his own reading ; he speaks freely, and yet wisely ; censures and determines many things judicially, and yet forceth you not to attention with a hem, and a spitting exordium ; in a word he hath made moral philosophy speak courageously, and instead of her gown given her an armour ; he hath put pedantical scholarism out of countenance, and made manifest that learning mingled with nobility shines most clearly.[1]

These appreciative sentences were published, it should be borne in mind, three years before the first extant issue of Florio's translation of Montaigne's *Essays*. Cornwallis clearly read Florio's work in manuscript. His testimony confirms the evidence which is offered by the Stationers' Registers that as soon as the authentic edition of the *Essays* came from the press in Paris, English curiosity was active. How far-reaching in England was Montaigne's influence as the creator of a new literary mode will be obvious to any one who recalls that the essays of Cowley, Addison, and Charles Lamb all own kinship with the French endeavour.

The final proof of Montaigne's influence in Elizabethan England is to be deduced, as in the case of Amyot, from

---

[1] Cornwallis's *Essayes*, No. 12, Of Censuring.

Shakespeare. Some critics have strained to breaking-point the filial theory of literary parallels, by adducing numerous passages from Shakespeare and Montaigne in which the general identity of sentiment is not to be questioned. But many of these parallels bear witness to an intellectual sympathy or to an affinity between the two writers which may well have come independently from the temper of the times—from the all-pervading spirit of the Renaissance, and no debt on Shakespeare's part to Montaigne can be often safely pleaded. When Shakespeare calls 'modest doubt the beacon of the wise', or when he pleads for the free use of 'godlike reason', or when he expatiates on 'what a piece of work is man', he is giving voice to sentiments which Montaigne, like all the great prophets of the epoch, fully shared and effectively expressed. But it is hazardous to conclude from such general resemblances that Shakespeare was Montaigne's personal disciple. The language as well as the thought must come within measure of identity before our road is absolutely clear. There are instances in which a *prima facie* case for borrowing may possibly be made out, but where it is unsafe to dogmatize.[1] Very characteristic of Montaigne is the observation, 'feasts, banquets, revels, dancings, masks and tourneys rejoice them that but seldom see them, and that have much desired to see them: the taste of which becomes cloysome and unpleasing to those that daily see, and ordinarily have them.' Shakespeare twice makes the like reflection in terms that seem to reflect Montaigne's words. No monopoly may be claimed for the opinion that feasts and holidays to be enjoyed must be rare. Yet the circumstance that Shakespeare more than once lays a curious emphasis on the fact in something like Montaigne's language is consistent with a reminiscence of his reading. In the *First Part of Henry IV*, I. ii. 226-8, says Prince Hal:

> If all the year were playing holidays,
> To sport would be as tedious as to work;
> But when they seldom come, they wished for come.

[1] Many passages of this kind are collected by Mr. J. M. Robertson in his interesting volume *Montaigne and Shakspere* (new ed., 1909).

So again in the *Sonnets* (lii. 5-7) Shakespeare talks of the danger of blunting the fine point of ' seldom pleasure ' :

> Therefore are feasts so solemn and so rare,
> Since, seldom coming, in the long year set,
> Like stones of worth they thinly placèd are.

Another parallel between Montaigne and Shakespeare may be set in the same category.   Cowards, says Julius Caesar (II. ii. 32-7) :

> Cowards die many times before their deaths :
> The valiant never taste of death but once.
> Of all the wonders that I yet have heard,
> It seems to me most strange that men should fear ;
> Seeing that death, a necessary end,
> Will come when it will come.

So Montaigne (i. 19) :

Since we are threatened by so many kinds of death, there is no more inconvenience to fear them all than to endure one : what matter when it cometh, since it is unavoidable.

It is possible that such parallels may mean nothing more than the accidental community of independent thought.   Yet analogous passages are numerous enough to give, when they are examined collectively, a *prima facie* justification to the theory of direct indebtedness.

The inference is corroborated by the presence of a few passages in Shakespeare which literally echo Montaigne's deliverance, and leave no doubt of the English dramatist's immediate dependence. In *The Tempest* (II. i. 154 seq.), Gonzalo, the honest old counsellor of Naples, indulges his fancy after the shipwreck, and sketches the mode in which he would govern the desert island, if the plantation were left in his hands.   He would establish a reign of nature, a socialistic community, in which all things should obey nature, all things should be in common :

> I' the commonwealth I would by contraries
> Execute all things ; for no kind of traffic
> Would I admit ; no name of magistrate ;
> Letters should not be known ; riches, poverty,
> And use of service, none ; contract, succession,
> Bourn, bound of land, tilth, vineyard, none ;

No use of metal, corn, or wine or oil,
No occupation;—all men idle, all.
And women too, but innocent and pure ;
No sovereignty . . . . . .
All things in common nature should produce
Without sweat or endeavour : treason, felony,
Sword, pike, knife, gun, or need of any engine,
Would I not have ; but nature should bring forth,
Of its own kind, all foison, all abundance,
To feed my innocent people.

Montaigne, in a rambling essay on cannibals (bk. ii.
chap. 30), had already described an island where the inhabitants, unsophisticated by civilization, lived according to nature.
Montaigne's cannibals are not eaters of human flesh, but
savages who obey instinctive feeling and are innocent alike
of the vices or the virtues of civilization. Montaigne describes
this Utopian people thus (I quote Florio's version) :

It is a nation that hath no kind of traffic, no knowledge of
letters, no intelligence of numbers, no name of magistrate nor
of politic superiority; no use of service, of riches or of
poverty; no contracts, no successions, no partitions of
property; no occupation, but idle; no respect of kindred,
but common; no apparel, but natural; no manuring of lands,
no use of wine, corn, and metal. The very words that import
lying, falsehood, treason, dissimulations, covetousness, envy,
detraction, and pardon were never heard amongst them.

Shakespeare transfers much of Montaigne's vocabulary and
assimilates the abrupt turn of the language. There is no
room for doubt that Gonzalo is citing Florio at first hand.

Thus we reach the conclusion that French prose exerted
no small influence on both the form and substance of
Elizabethan literature. Elizabethans knew least of Rabelais,
the earliest master in prose of the French Renaissance. Yet
to him the pamphleteers of Shakespeare's day owed some
suggestions for their swaggering satire. From Calvin the
Elizabethans drew precision in expounding theological doctrine, and the habit of discussing the dark mysteries of the
faith in the domestic language. From Amyot came the
briskly balanced period, and the enthusiasm for biographic

detail. From Montaigne came pointed fluency and a cheerful habit of reflecting detachedly on life. The matter and manner of French prose helped to mould Elizabethan thought and expression. There were other threads in the skein—classical, Italian, and Spanish threads—but many of these were dyed in French colours before they were put to English uses. France, whether as principal or agent, was the predominant element in the serious branches of the literary art. If Elizabethan fiction sought sustenance further afield in Italy or Spain, France taught Elizabethan prose most of that bold vivacity and freedom which Elizabethans acknowledged to be a distinguishing trait of the French language. Familiarity with the themes of French prose—with the theology of Calvin, the ribald sagacity of Rabelais, the classical idealism of Amyot, the worldly ethics of Montaigne—signally helped to draw Elizabethan minds into the main currents of European thought and culture.

BOOK IV

FRENCH INFLUENCE IN THE ELIZABETHAN LYRIC

1

THE COMING OF RONSARD

THE general course that English poetry followed in the sixteenth century has been described already. The main historical or chronological fact is that there was no flow of true poetry through the first eighty years of the century. French and Italian influence wrought together on the wellnigh isolated ebullition of Wyatt and Surrey in the early years with evanescent effect. The lyrists of Henry VIII's court created no school of English poetry. The period of helpless doggerel which followed gave no hint of the future.

Between the death of Surrey in 1547 and the poetic birth of Spenser in 1579, only one poetic endeavour deserves attention from the artistic point of view—Sackville's 'Induction' to *The Mirror of Magistrates*. In that poetic allegory, published in 1563, the poet, guided by the personification of sorrow, visits, after the manner of Vergil or Dante, the abodes of the great dead. Sackville's faculty is impressive, but it is doubtful if his small and isolated output does more than attest a craving for a heightened standard of poetic art. It is a ray of light which failed to disperse the prevailing gloom.[1]

---

[1] Although Sackville's verse betrays little sign of French influence, the poet, like most cultured Englishmen of his day, was well acquainted with France and Frenchmen. Just before the publication of his 'Induction' he was making a tour of the continent, and soon after his return he was twice in Paris on diplomatic business. In 1568 he was much in the society of Queen Catherine de' Medici, and sought to overcome her objections to the proposal that her son the Duc d'Anjou should marry Queen Elizabeth. Early in 1572 he revisited France to convey the congratulations of the English court to the French king, Charles IX, on his marriage, and he performed the duty with ceremonial magnificence, giving and receiving lavish entertainments in Paris (Stow's *Chronicle*, p. 668). He wrote to Queen Elizabeth of the Italian comedies which he witnessed at the French court (Baschet, *Les Comédiens Italiens à la Cour de France*, 1882, pp. 15, 16). Four years later Sackville hospitably received the Huguenot envoy, Cardinal Châtillon, at his palace at Sheen.

Spenser's *Shepheards Calender,* published in 1579, must for aesthetic purposes be viewed as the starting-point of the Elizabethan tide. Spenser lived on till 1599, steadily developing in poetic genius for the best part of twenty years. With Spenser's early work was associated in point of time that of Sir Philip Sidney and Thomas Watson. The trio, in the order in which their names are mentioned, presents a descending scale of merit. Sidney was no match for Spenser. Watson was very inferior in power to Sidney, but he deserves to be greeted as a modest herald of the coming summer, for he laboured in new lyric fields with Sidney's industry, if with little of his poetic feeling. He survived Sidney by some six years, dying in 1592. It was not, however, until these two pioneer-companions of Spenser had left the scene that the lyric inspiration gained its full fervour or strength in Elizabethan England. The highest lyric triumphs are identified with such names as Lyly and Daniel, Lodge and Drayton, and high above the rest with Shakespeare; all flourished in the last decade of the century.

In that darkest age of poetic effort which followed the burial of Wyatt and Surrey, Tudor England vainly turned anew for tuition to Clément Marot, the master of French poetry in the first half of the sixteenth century. Wyatt, who had adapted Marot's characteristic rondeaus, had acknowledged Marot's sway. The crew of doggerel poetasters, who ambled across the English stage between the exit of Wyatt and the entry of Spenser—men like Turberville and Gascoigne—are stated by a contemporary critic to have ' come near unto Marot, whom they did imitate'. Fresh scraps of Marot's verse were translated into halting English. Gascoigne in the preliminary verses before his ' Posies ' (1575) excuses himself for occasional impropriety by the example of Marot's ' Alyx ', an epitaph of brutal grossness on an unchaste woman.[1] The

---

[1] Marot, *Œuvres,* ii. 219. Gascoigne's lines run :
Read *Faustoes* filthy tale, in *Ariostoes* ryme,
And let not *Marots Alyx* pass, without impeach of crime.
These things considered well, I trust they will excuse
This muse of mine, although she seem such toys sometimes
    to use.

Marotic tradition was still flickering in England in the *annus mirabilis* 1579. Spenser paid tribute to Marot's vogue in his earliest poetic endeavours. Of his *Shepheards Calender*, the title translates the name of a popular French tract *Le Kalendrier des Bergiers*, and two sections of the English poem paraphrase Marot's old-fashioned eclogues. That interesting act of homage was a belated courtesy and it was occasionally repeated. But it was on French poetry of more modern fibre and more nearly contemporary date that Spenser and the adult Elizabethans fixed their steadiest gaze.

In the gloomy interval between Wyatt and Spenser, Marot was himself dethroned in France. A new king of poetry arose. France came under a new poetic dispensation, of which the chief apostle was Ronsard. Ronsard was, if not the inaugurator, the acknowledged master of a new poetic school in France, a school of unprecedented wealth in melody and fancy. The temple of French poetry was crowded with a new generation of worshippers of Apollo who eagerly accepted Ronsard's priesthood. There is justification for the contemporary vaunt that the Muses from 1550 to 1580 treated France as their consecrated home. ' Never before,' truthfully writes the literary chronicler of the era, ' had France such a plenitude of poets (*telle foison de poètes*). Every province, every city, sent its poets to enrol themselves under the standard of the new chieftain, Ronsard.' [1]

It is for us to study the impression which this re-birth of the poetic art in France left on English poetry, to estimate how far the Elizabethan lyric was coloured by the ideals and modes of the French poetry, which came to birth with the second half of the century. The sonnets and all short lyric poems lie within the scope of this survey. The English poetic development was too tardy to offer any strictly contemporary outburst with which to compare the great French uprising. It was a generation of a date later than that of Ronsard which first saw the lyric sentiment of Elizabethan England acquire genuine force. The new French spirit was active

[1] Étienne Pasquier's *Lettres*, 1555, in *Œuvres*, Amsterdam, 1723, ii, p. 11.

in France long before the Elizabethans were garnering their first poetic sheaves. But the French inspiration was slow to lose its vigour. It had not lost all its freshness in the halcyon days of Elizabethan energy. The Elizabethan song and sonnet are reckoned among the fairest flowers of Elizabethan literature. There is nothing depreciatory in the admission, if facts warrant it, that much of their fragrance breathes the freshly scented air of France, or that, to use a robuster metaphor which has Elizabethan sanction, Elizabethans quaffed copious draughts of the new French Helicon.

II

THE BIRTH OF THE PLÉIADE

In 1549, five years after Marot's death, five young men of literary ambition and of high classical attainments, were attending at a college—le Collège de Coqueret—in Paris the classes of an eminent humanist, Jean Dorat. He inspired his pupils with a fiery enthusiasm for the great writers of Greece, especially for Homer and Pindar, Aeschylus and Sophocles. The young men, all of good family and from cultured homes. also read for themselves much recent Italian literature. When, in the confidence of ambitious youth, they compared the literary masterpieces of Greece and modern Italy with the efforts of Marot and of Marot's precursors which still enjoyed a vogue, they boldly pronounced the poetic literature of their own tongue to be clumsy, insipid, thin, inartistic, bucolic. Thereupon they deliberately set themselves to reform or re-create the literature of their country. They would assimilate in fullest measure the artistic refinement and restraint of Greek literary art on the one hand, and the warm sensuous melody of modern Italian poetry on the other. There was in the resolve a note of insolence which only success could excuse.

Viewed in all its aspects, the episode is a singular passage in literary history. These young men, with the serene arrogance of budding manhood, said in so many words, 'French poetry is spiritless and crude; it is no credit to

our nation. We intend to clean the slate and start afresh.'
The young men deliberately formed themselves into a society
to refashion the poetry of their country, and, contrary to
expectation, they succeeded in giving triumphant effect to
their conscious aim. Change in the temper and tone of
poetry has been in this country an unconscious development,
notwithstanding Wordsworth's preface of 1798, when he
announced a design to bring poetry down from the heights
of pomposity to the plains of simplicity. Very rarely has
the development of poetry been in other countries than
France a consistently conscious movement. But the new
school of French poetry in the middle of the sixteenth
century was consistently and consciously planned in minute
detail. The victory has led to experiments of similar calibre
in France at a later date. The romantic movement—*le
Romanticisme*—of the early nineteenth century arose in very
like fashion.

The creed of the new sixteenth-century school was set forth
in a preliminary manifesto from the pen of the oldest of the
revolutionary spirits—of Joachim du Bellay, aged twenty-four
The manifesto was published in 1549 under the title *La Deffense
et Illustration de la langue françoise*. The main argument
runs thus : The French language was not to be scorned. In
the hands of great writers it might reach the level of Latin
and Greek. But to give it its needful lustre, it must be
fertilized anew by foreign importations. Hard work and long
nights must be devoted to study of the Italian, the Latin, and
the Greek. The Italian had enriched itself by thefts from the
Latin. Latin had ennobled itself by thefts from the Greek.
The French could only find salvation by thefts from all the
three. The old forms—rondeaus, virelays, et autres épiceries—
must be abandoned. Chansons or songs must be replaced by
odes ; comic fables by satire ; mystery-plays by comedies and
tragedies ; dixains by sonnets, 'that cultured and charming
Italian invention.' Mediaeval fancies and childish ineptitudes
must be dismissed to the Round Table of a played-out
age. There was need of a more elevated poetry drawn from
sources of real antiquity—from the antiquity which conserved

enlightenment, not from the antiquity which cloaked obscurantism.

From end to end Du Bellay's plea was permeated by the broad humanism of France. He deprecated sympathy with those who despised the French language and deemed it incapable of ultimate perfection. He was no less hostile to scholars, who treated Latin and Greek poetry and prose like sanctified relics, which must be looked at in sacred places through panes of glass, and must never be touched with one's own hands. Greek and Latin books ought rather to come out of their dead shells. They ought to wing their way daily through the mouths of men in modern speech. But while the revolutionary leader commended as true patriotism the labours of translation, he pointed out that translation had spiritual limitations. The dangers of constraint and ungracefulness were never negligible. It was not to be expected that all translators could satisfy the supreme test of raising in their readers' minds the precise feeling evoked by the originals. Vernacular adaptation of the aesthetic spirit of the classics was the safest road to emancipation.

The names of the five young men who organized the new school were Pierre de Ronsard, Joachim du Bellay, Remy Belleau, Jean Antoine de Baïf, and Étienne Jodelle. Baïf and Jodelle were only seventeen years old, Belleau was twenty-one, and Ronsard and Du Bellay twenty-four. To the five there were soon added a more mature student, Pontus de Tyard, aged twenty-eight, and the Greek professor, Jean Dorat, aged forty-one. This band of seven, buoyant with youthful hope, was first content to be known as *le docte brigade*. But it soon gave itself the more distinctive name of the Seven Stars, the Pléiade, after a company of Greek poets at the court of Ptolemy Philadelphus at Alexandria, which had assumed the same designation. The French Pléiade is the best known constellation in literary history.

The work of the Pléiade was voluminous and varied. The new poets tried every manner of literary experiment in their effort to acclimatize Greek and Italian forms of poetry, in their resolve to give French poetry new grace and refinement. But save Dorat, whose work being in Latin hardly concerns us, all devoted their best energies to lyric or elegiac verse, to short poems of love or reflection, among which the imitation of the Italian sonnet filled a commanding place. The drama and the epic were not ignored. Jodelle, one of the seven chieftains, did his main work as a dramatist and in that capacity exerted influence at home and abroad. But the lyric note predominated and gave the Pléiade its widest fame. A new style of lyric elegance and lyric melody was the most characteristic fruit of the great poetic movement.

III

RONSARD

The acknowledged chief of the Pléiade was Pierre de Ronsard, who deserves to rank with the poetic artists of the world. His poetry presents nearly all the characteristics of his school in their perfection. While he lived he was the dictator of French literary taste. He is the poetic master of the French Renaissance. Born on September 11, 1524, at his father's Château de la Poissonnière, near Vendôme, in the valley of the Loire, he was son of a steward of Francis I, and after a brief education in Paris, became in boyhood page to the king's son, the Duke of Orleans, who died young. From the age of ten to twenty-four he served in royal or noble households. Many of his masters were engaged in foreign diplomacy, and the youth visited foreign countries—Scotland and England, Flanders and Holland—in the ambassadors' train. Ill-health, which resulted in permanent deafness, compelled him in early manhood to abandon the active life of the court and diplomacy. It was then that he renewed his studies with extraordinary ardour, and joined his tutor Dorat and his fellow students, Du Bellay, Baïf, Jodelle, Belleau, Tyard, in their efforts to re-create French poetry. Thenceforth Ronsard consecrated his life to the Muses and to culture.

No one is entitled to question Ronsard's declarations that he sang from boyhood because he must. The genuineness of his inspiration admits of no doubt. Of the spontaneity and the fluency which comes of the divine fount Ronsard has no lack. Yet he is far removed from the poetic children of nature who sing but as the linnets sing. He was a man of learning, and although his sympathy with nature and with humanity often invests his verse with an unaffected simplicity, his style was deliberately fashioned in moulds of scholarship and art. Poetry was for him ' la belle *science* '. Like Horace, he wrote much of the Art of Poetry, and the broad principles on which he lays emphasis in his critical essays throw light on the general character of the Pléiade and explain its far-reaching influence.

In the first place Ronsard framed the rule that the vocabulary of poetry was of right far removed from that of prose. The verse that could readily be turned into prose was bad verse, and the prose that could readily be turned into verse was, according to Ronsard, bad prose. The bounds of the one rarely, if ever, encroached on those of the other. In the second place the French poet preached the close affinity of music and poetry. He judged that poetry which did not lend itself with facility to musical setting was without sure signs of excellence. 'La musique,' he said, 'est la sœur puisnée de la poësie, et les poëtes et musiciens sont les enfans sacrez des Muses ; sans la musique la poësie est presque sans grace, comme la musique sans la melodie des vers, est inanimée et sans vie.' [1] New turns of language, which removed verse from common speech, and new turns of metre which gave prosody the melody of music, are among Ronsard's main contributions to poetic art.

Like his allies, Ronsard, though an innovator in literary matters, was a conservative in religion and politics, a lover of law and order, a faithful adherent of the catholic king, and a foe to the doctrine of the Huguenots. One of his colleagues, Pontus de Tyard, became Bishop of Châlons. He himself took minor orders, and was rewarded with Church preferment freed of clerical duty. He held the pleasant priories of

---

[1] *Œuvres*, ed. Blanchemain, viii, p. 51.

St. Cosme near Tours and of Ste. Croix-Val, both in Touraine.
The religion of their ancestors was good enough for Ronsard
and his fellow servants of the Muses. Belief in a beneficent
Creator, 'le père de tout bien,' satisfied their spiritual
aspiration ; niceties of dogma failed to move their interest.

To Ronsard and his friends the austere ideals of a Huguenot
dispensation were repugnant. In 1563 Ronsard replied to
fellow countrymen of the Reformed faith who reproached
him with self-indulgence. He warmly denied their allegations
that he was an atheist or a drunkard or the victim of vicious
disease. But with splendid self-confidence he exposes the
futility of life without art. He claims that his religious
beliefs are as simple as those of his censors, and that by his enthusiasm for the reformation of art he renders his countrymen
as high a spiritual service as they by the reformation which they
are devising of Christian doctrine. He rejoices in the confession that he loves laughter and women's smiles, music and the
masque, a cup of wine, a walk beside a river, or a book in
season beneath a shady tree. He is proud to assert that the
Muses have adorned his brow with myrtle, and that he wears
the laurel of Apollo.[1]

The souls of Ronsard and his friends sought indeed
poetic sustenance in other revelations than those of the
orthodox Church. Ronsard's temperament was largely
pagan. Greek sentiment swayed his being. He invoked
Apollo and Pallas to protect him from worldly distractions.
He worshipped at the shrine of Aphrodite and her son Eros.
His poetic ritual was devised in honour of Pan and Bacchus.
His genius sought the companionship of Naiads and Dryads.
The brightness and joyousness in his nature found their
closest affinity in the atmosphere of a pagan world.

A regal belief in himself and in his work is another dominant
feature of Ronsard's character. His self-assurance was fostered by the circumstances of his life. He never lacked
royal patrons. Four kings of France paid him the highest
honours, and he received their marks of respect with an

[1] *Œuvres*, vii, p. 26.

admirable assurance. Mary Stuart prided herself on his friendship, which found expression not only in beautiful verses from her own pen, but in the gift of a silver model of Mount Parnassus, inscribed ' A Ronsard l'Apollo de la source des Muses '. He was at one time the guest of the English queen, who acknowledged his eulogies of herself and of her favourite the Earl of Leicester, as well as of her minister, Sir William Cecil, with the gift of a diamond, which, she deplored, was less lustrous than his poetry. Ronsard was never sparing in compliments of exalted persons.[1] Soon after France and England made the great treaty of peace at Troyes within a few weeks of Shakespeare's birth in 1564, the poet confirmed the instrument, almost as though he were one of the high contracting parties, by dedicating to the English queen a new volume of *Elégies, Mascarades et Bergeries*. His patroness, Queen Catherine de' Medici, approved his

---

[1] Queen Elizabeth's beauty and accomplishments lose nothing at Ronsard's hand. Like so many who paid personal court to the English queen, Ronsard is specially delighted with her power of speaking many languages. He looks for the day when swans on the river Thames will proclaim that the Muses have deserted Parnassus to greet in poetry the sovereigns of England, but the day of the swans of the Thames had not yet dawned. In complacent mood Ronsard regrets that God has denied England the joy of the vineyard, with which his own country was bountifully endowed, but bids her take comfort, Bacchus had not refused Britons all his gifts; the merry god had joined Ceres in creating beer (*Le Bocage Royal*, 1567, in *Œuvres*, ed. Blanchemain, iii. 331). Cecil, whose name and lineage Ronsard fancifully derives from Sicily, he praises for his politic diplomacy and his courtesy to strangers (*Œuvres*, ed. Blanchemain, iii. 393). 'Milord Robert Dudley, Comte de Leicester,' is credited with almost divine faculties,—the beauty of Venus, the wit of Mercury, and the wisdom of Minerva. His triumphs in the tournament, the chase, and the dance are beyond compare. Ronsard declared that he risked the perils of the ocean to cast his eyes on so noble a prodigy. Ronsard's opinion of Leicester changed as years rolled on, and with characteristic frankness he adapted his verse to his altered views. When he reprinted the poem he removed all reference to Leicester, substituting for the Earl's name that of King Arthur, and representing his laudation of the English nobleman as Merlin's mythical description of the old British king. Finally Ronsard suppressed the panegyric altogether (*Œuvres*, ed. Blanchemain, iv. 382). The French poet elsewhere shows his early interest in Leicester by reporting the rumour of his coming marriage with Queen Elizabeth. He mentions among extraordinary prophecies—

Et qu'un Anglois si fortuné sera
Que sa maitresse un jour espousera.

Œuvres, vi. 262.

interposition. In the dedicatory epistle the poet contentedly
professes to commend his name and fame for all future time
to Queen Elizabeth's care.[1] Yet impatience of claims
to glory which he did not share, made it congenial to him
to keep before the mind of royal and noble patrons the
truths that poverty and lowly rank are surer roads to happiness than pomp and state, and that rich and poor will both
alike come to dust.

> Toutes choses mondaines
> Qui vestent nerfs et veines
>   La mort égale prend,
> Soient pauvres ou soient princes ;
> Car sur toutes provinces
>   Sa main large s'estend.[2]

The estimate which Ronsard formed of himself as well as of
others won general authority, despite the evergrowing range of
his pretensions. He claimed, when denouncing the Huguenots,
that the poet—not the preacher—confers greatness on a people.
His poetic work, he asserted, had set the Frenchman on the
level of the Romans and the Greeks, and had given his fellow
countrymen a reputation that they never enjoyed before.
The credit which the French settlers in Geneva claimed was
part of his gift to his nation. ' Vous estes,' he tells the wrang-
ling theologians, the Zwinglians, the Lutherans, the Ana-
baptists, the Calvinists, and ' les autres Puritains ',

> Vous estes tous issus de ma Muse et de moy :
> Vous estes mes sujects, je suis seul vostre roy :
> Vous estes mes ruisseaux, je suis vostre fonteine.[3]

The dignity with which he often received and distributed
flattery yielded at times to his thirst for extravagant and

---

[1] This dedicatory epistle seems only to appear in a rare first edition of
Elégies, Mascarades et Bergeries (1565). The epistle is not to be found in
any reissue of the volume, but it is reprinted in Marty-Laveaux's edition
of the Pléiade, vi. 446. (Cf. Paul Laumonier's *Ronsard, Poète Lyrique*,
1909, pp. 214–15.) The volume includes poems addressed to the Earl
of Leicester and Sir William Cecil as well as to Queen Elizabeth, all of
which reappeared in *Le Bocage Royal* (1567).

[2] Ronsard, *Odes*, Bk. IV, Ode v (*Œuvres*, ii. 253).

[3] *Œuvres*, vii, p. 128. Ronsard's poem was first published in 1563.
The word ' Puritan ' would seem to have been used familiarly in France
before it was generally accepted in England.

pompous adulation. He liked to be told that the deafness
from which he suffered resembled the blindness of Homer.
Finally he summed up his attitude to the world in the
haughty line :

Je suis Ronsard, et cela te suffice !

The expression was taken seriously by his admirers, and was
deemed by a contemporary biographer to be a fitting epitaph.

Ronsard's last years were spent in retirement, which he
divided between his two abbeys of Ste Croix-Val and of St.
Cosme.   There library and garden gave him contentment.
A gentle melancholy lends a peculiar pathos to his latest
works and his declining days.   Although he had no misgivings
of the immortality of his renown, he was nervous of neglect,
and the praises of younger men caused him, in spite of his
disclaimers, discomfort.   Disease had turned his hair gray at
thirty, and the further ravages of age dejected him.   The
miseries of civil and religious strife oppressed him like
personal sorrows.

Yet Ronsard died in the fullness of his fame.   Two months
after his death at St. Cosme (on December 27, 1585), a
pompe funèbre was celebrated in the chapel of the
Collège de Boncour at Paris, and its splendour might have
reconciled him to his dying anxieties.   The crowd of royal
and noble mourners was so great that even princes and lords
of Church and State were turned from the chapel doors.   The
English ambassador of the day, Sir Edward Stafford, had
small sympathy with literature and much suspicion of all
Catholic ritual.   He probably made no effort to attend, but it
is permissible to conjecture that the ambassador's chaplain,
Richard Hakluyt, whose mind was alert to every intellectual
influence, was not willingly absent from the great ceremony.
The *oraison funèbre* was pronounced by the most cultured
preacher of the day, Jacques du Perron, who next year did
a like service to the memory of Queen Mary Stuart, and later
presided at the ceremony of Henry IV's abjuration of the
Protestant faith.   Finally a cardinal, Du Perron won fame
as a poet as well as a Catholic controversialist and pulpit-
orator.   His funeral *éloge* of Ronsard is a model of elegiac

eloquence, and still preserves that living grace which gives enduring freshness to so much of the fruit of the French Renaissance.

'He will live,' the preacher prophesied of the mighty poet, 'he will be read, he will flourish, he will be cherished in the thought and memory of men, so long as there shall be any signs and any memorials of the realm of Frenchmen, so long as the French tongue has currency and sound among foreign peoples, so long as letters shall enjoy reverence and esteem. . . . Time will only serve to increase his fame. . . . Vials full of perfumes and scents, coming to be broken, spread their odour further than they did before.'[1]

Ronsard was laid to rest soon after he completed his sixty-first year. Shakespeare, his junior by thirty-nine years, came of age while the French poet was still alive. As far as chronology goes, the sovereign genius of English Renaissance poetry might have been son to the emperor of French Renaissance poetry on whom the preacher passed a just verdict. Although much of Ronsard's voluminous work is tedious pedantry, his fine achievements are many, and they deserve the eulogy passed on the French queen Marie Antoinette by Burke, when he described her at the zenith of her career as 'glittering as the northern star, full of life and splendour and joy'.

---

[1] Ronsard, *Œuvres*, viii, p. 213. 'Il vivra, il sera leu, il fleurira, il se conservera dans la pensée et dans la souvenance des hommes, tant qu'il y aura quelques enseignes et quelques marques de l'empire des François, tant que la lange françoise aura quelque cours et quelque son parmy les nations estrangeres, tant que les lettres seront en estime et en reverence. . . . Il ne craindra aucune suitte de temps ny aucune antiquité, il frequentera spirituellement et invisiblement avec nous, et plus il ira en avant et plus il verra croistre et augmenter sa renommé; . . . ny plus ny moins que les phioles pleines de parfums et de senteurs, lesquelles venant à se casser, espandent leur odeur encore beaucoup plus loin qu'elles ne faisoient auparavant.' The simile of the broken scent-bottle adumbrates Shakespeare's contempt for sealed vials of rose-water, 'a liquid prisoner pent in walls of glass' (*Sonnets*, v. 10).

IV

THE THEMES OF THE PLÉIADE

The subject-matter of the Pléiade's songs and sonnets strikes various notes. The poetry in its more serious strain voices patriotic elation, political ambition, religious zeal, dread of death, sympathy with suffering, and an almost romantic feeling for nature. But the theme to which the canvas owes its sparkling radiance is the pagan delight in life's fleeting joys. The doctrine that the present is all that counts, the worship of love and youth, the faith in women and wine, are main articles in the poetic creed of the Pléiade. The parentage of these blithe conceptions deserves attention.

French adaptations of the Pindaric ode were the first achievements of the bold innovators, but a quite unexpected stimulus of a somewhat different calibre came at the outset from the discovery by Henri Étienne, the great scholar-printer of France, of a manuscript containing a series of Greek poems ascribed to Anacreon. That lyric poet was known to have lived and written in the sixth century before Christ. Early Greek grammarians mention Anacreon's work, but, until Étienne discovered in a unique manuscript the collection of lyrics which he set to Anacreon's credit, Anacreon's verse was unknown. Étienne's unique manuscript formed an appendix to an isolated codex of the Greek anthology. Other manuscript copies of the Greek anthology had been recovered earlier. That poetic miscellany had been printed early in the sixteenth century; but Anacreon's work was not associated with it, before Étienne's discovery of 1552. Since Étienne's day scholars have proved conclusively that the poems assigned by him to Anacreon are of a date later than Anacreon's era, that they were probably penned at Alexandria early in the Christian era, and that they are spurious imitations of the poet's genuine work, specimens of which have since come to light. Only a minute criticism can differentiate the true Anacreon from the false Anacreon. Both present gay lyrics of love and pleasure in blithe lilting measures.   True or false Anacreon is far lighter in tone than most of the Greek anthologists.   The latter often treat pathetically of solemn themes, and move to tears as often as to laughter.   Anacreon is the poet of joy.

The school of the Pléiade was fascinated in its infancy by the Anacreontic verse which Étienne brought first to his country-men's notice.   Written copies of the Greek text must have been in their hands even before Étienne's book was published. For Ronsard and his friends printed avowed imitations in French of Anacreon's poems before 1554, the date of Étienne's publication.   Within a year of the issue of Étienne's volume a translation of the whole into French verse came from the pen of Remy Belleau, one of Ronsard's colleagues, and thence-forward adaptations, translations, imitations abounded.   The Pléiade laid the deeper-toned anthologists also under con-tribution.   But Anacreon's jocund temper and short, dancing metre were worshipped by them almost idolatrously.   Well might Ronsard fill high the flowing bowl and chant the toast (*Odes*, Bk. v, Ode xv)—

> Verse donc et reverse encor
> Dedans ceste grand' coupe d'or ;
>   Je vay boire à Henry Estienne
> Qui des enfers nous a rendu
> Du vieil Anacreon perdu
>   La douce lyre teïenne.

The poets of the Pléiade were the first not only to trans-late Anacreon's Greek into modern speech, but to make the Anacreontic vein current coin of modern poetry.   The French Renaissance failed on its advent to deprive of its old predominance the solemn and hortative allegory which had ruled the mediaeval realm of French poetry.   But that sad and serious form of poetic endeavour retired dis-comfited at the bidding of a newly revealed tuneful Muse, who lightly and naïvely declared in song that life owed its zest to women and wine, to roses and honey, to kisses and sighs.

Under Anacreontic influence, airy reminders to

> Gather ye rosebuds while ye may,
> Old time is still aflying,

became a recurrent refrain of the lyric of the French Renaissance. None of Ronsard's voluminous poetry is more often
cited or is more characteristic of the lyric temper of his school,
than the sonnet in which he pictures his indifferent mistress in
old age grieving after his death over her youthful obduracy,
or the song of lament over the fading at dusk of a rose which
had bloomed in the morning. The sonnet ends with the lines:

> Vivez, si m'en croyez, n'attendez à demain :
> Cueillez dès aujourd'huy les roses de la vie.[1]

The last stanza of the song runs—

> Donc, si vous me croyez, mignonne,
> Tandis que vostre âge fleuronne
> En sa plus verte nouveauté,
> Cueillez, cueillez vostre jeunesse :
> Comme à ceste fleur, la vieillesse
> Fera ternir vostre beauté.[2]

In these two poems we have the Anacreontic message fitted
to the sentiment of the new age. A cheerful recognition of
the inevitable conditions of mortality gives, in the verse of the
Pléiade, piquancy to the passing beauty of the world.

All aspects of nature which please the eye or ear are
portrayed by the Pléiade poets, not only with delicate
charm, but with accuracy in detail which testifies to close
observation. Ronsard's poems about the four seasons, the
lark, the hawthorn, or the hollybush, are close studies of
natural life as well as vignettes of poetic accomplishment.
Salutations of Spring, and especially of the months of April
and May; exultant cries of delight at the gushing of fountains,
at the song of birds, at the glint of precious stones; apostrophes
to roses and lilies, to violets and daisies, to carnations and
marigolds, embroider the Pléiade's airy canvas with brilliant
schemes of life-like colour. Blithe feasts of love and wine are
pictured in flowering glades lit with the summer sun.

It is an ethereal atmosphere which often envelops the scene.
At times, the slightest movement in life or nature suffices for

---

[1] Sonnets pour Hélène, xlii, in Œuvres, i. 340.
[2] Œuvres, ii, p. 117 (Odes, Book I, Ode xvii. À Cassandre). The first
line reads, 'Mignonne, allons voir si la rose . . .'

the poet's theme. Very characteristic of one aspect of the movement is the most popular of the poems of Ronsard's colleague Du Bellay, whose poetic nature was more deeply imbued with serious sentiment than that of any of the band. The topic is an appeal of a peasant to the wind to drive into motion the grain beneath his winnowing-fan. The representative value of the effort is all the greater when we learn that the poem is a magical translation from Latin of a nearly contemporary Italian poet, Navagero, who himself was influenced by the Greek anthology. In the last verse the peasant offers a parting prayer to the winds thus:

> De vostre douce haleine
> Eventez ceste plaine,
>   Eventez ce séjour:
> Cependant que j'ahanne [*i. e.* travaille]
> A mon blé que je vanne
> A la chaleur du jour.

The charm here, as Mr. Pater pointed out, is all pure effect. Nearly all the pleasure in the silvery grace of fancy lies in the surprise at the happy way in which an incident insignificant in itself is handled. Such a comment does not apply to the whole work of the Pléiade, but it is suggestive of much and explains its range and variety.

The lyre of the Pléiade is not always so lightly strung Life in its presentation by Ronsard and his allies is not wholly free from complexity or grief. Notes of sadness are present, and they on occasion strike home. The cruelties inflicted by fickle mistresses rarely touch the reader's feelings. The lovers' melancholy has a somewhat hollow echo. Nevertheless the thought that ' l'amour et la mort n'est qu'une même chose ' is at times invested with a poignancy that is disconcerting, and grief for loss of friends is nearly always of pathetic earnestness. No elegies strike a sincerer note of sorrow than many of the lamentations of the Pléiade on the death of their associates. Melancholy was curiously dominant in the nature of Du Bellay, who proudly claimed and was duly accorded the honour of first domesticating the Italian sonnet in France. Seldom has more touching regret for the decay of greatness, for the defacement ' by Time's fell hand ' of

> The rich proud cost of out-worn buried age,

found poetic expression than in Du Bellay's sequence of
sonnets called *Les Antiquités de Rome*, which he penned
while on a visit to Italy.   The series is a poet's reverie amid
ruins.   A lively historic sense overwhelms him with despair.
Rarely, too, has a patriot's affection for his motherland
sounded a more touching note than in Du Bellay's series of
sonnets called *Les Regrets*, which he penned while serving
as secretary to the French ambassador at Rome :

> France mère des arts, des armes et des lois,
> Tu m'as nourry long temps du laict de ta mammelle :
> Ores, comme un aigneau qui sa nourrisse appelle,
> Je remplis de ton nom les antres et les bois.

Du Bellay's *Les Regrets* form an intimate poetic journal of
that homesickness which patriotism fosters in the heart of
a sensitive exile.

The practical outlook of the Pléiade often went indeed far
beyond the worship of love and lilies.   The poets did not live
aloof from the social and political interests of ordinary life.
They loved their country, rejoicing in her political and
military triumphs, and grieving over her misfortunes.   Ronsard
himself at times abandoned his complacency amid political
anxiety and bitterness of party spirit.   In the four books of his
unfinished epic, called *La Franciade*, he gives ample rein
to his patriotic ardour, and furiously denounces the foreign
and domestic enemies of France.   The religious wars at home
roused in his and the other poets' hearts despair and shame,
and on England—the prison of the venerated Queen of Scots
—they came to reflect with scurrility and to heap maledictions
in a fiercely tragic key.

Of passing events further removed from their own country
than Queen Mary's martyrdom, the poets of the Pléiade were
most deeply impressed by the discovery of America and the
devastation of Greece by the Turks.   Ronsard rejoiced to be
alive in an age which had witnessed the glorious revelation by
a Spanish fleet of a new continent, a new ocean, new peoples,

and new languages.[1]   The aboriginal tribes of America excited immense curiosity in France.   Ronsard hailed them as survivors of the golden age of purity, as men free from the sophistications of Europe, as human beings who were captains of their own souls (*seuls maîtres de soi*):

> Ils vivent maintenant en leur âge dorée,
> Vivez heureusement, sans peine et sans souci,
> Vivez joyeusement, je voudrais vivre ainsi.

The love of Greek literature mainly inspired the Pléiade with a burning zeal for the political regeneration of Greece, which the Turks were laying waste.   With all Byron's or Shelley's poetic rage Ronsard called upon his patron Charles IX, King of France, to deliver the Greeks from the tyranny of the Turks :

> Bref, ceste Grèce, œil du monde habitable,
> Qui n'eust jamais n'y n'aura de semblable,
> Demande, hélas! vostre bras très-chretien
> Pour de son col desserrer le lien,
> Lien barbare, impitoyable et rude,
> Qui tout son corps genne de servitude
> Sous ce grand Turc.[2]

Ronsard entreated Venus, the 'amoureuse Cyprine', to seek the aid of Mars in defending her island of Cyprus from the barbarous seignory of Mahomet's viceroy.[3]

V

THE MANNER OF THE PLÉIADE

Ronsard and his friends were before all else great metrists. They practised with admirable deftness almost every variety of rhyming stanza, combining short lines with long lines in strophes of varying lengths and numberless mutations.   It is

---

[1] *Œuvres*, i. 368.
[2] *Œuvres*, iii. 321.
[3] *Œuvres*, i. 385. 'Vœu a Venus pour garder Cypre contre l'armée du Turc.'

202 FRENCH INFLUENCE IN ELIZABETHAN LYRIC

said that Ronsard tried his hand at sixty-three metres or strophes. One of the many innovations of the school was that four-lined stanza of Tennyson's *In Memoriam*, in which the first line rhymes with the fourth, the second with the third. But despite their bold claims to complete originality, the Pléiade showed as much ingenuity in refashioning old metrical forms as in inventing new ones.

Abundant experiment was made by Ronsard at the outset of his career in the Greek Pindaric ode, with its classical distribution into strophe, antistrophe, and epode.[1] But the strict classical divisions were soon exchanged for the simpler scheme of the Horatian ode. Hymns, eclogues, and elegies were of like classical lineage, but they rarely came nearer the classical pattern than rhyming decasyllabics could bring them. Such efforts as the Pléiade made in the epic and narrative fable were also clothed as a rule in decasyllabic rhyme—the measure which filled in the new French prosody the place alike of the Greek heroic hexameter and the Latin elegiac couplet.

At the same time all the poets of the fraternity brought their ingenuity to bear on the metrical inventions of Italy. The sestina, the madrigal, and even blank verse left some trace on the work of the Pléiade—yet none of these peculiarly Italian innovations took deep root in French soil. Very different was the fortune of the sonnet, which was openly borrowed by the Pléiade from Italy and became the chief badge of the new poetic movement.

The harvest in France of the Italian sonnet—often a literal translation from the Italian—was boundless. The three most prolific members of the Pléiade—Ronsard, Du Bellay, and Baïf—are reckoned to have penned together 3,516 poems, of which 1,686 are sonnets:

> Graves sonnets que la docte Italie
> A pour les siens la première enfantés.

---

[1] Most of the new technical terms of the poetic art, e. g. *lyrique*, *épique*, and *ode*, come direct from the Greek ; some come from the Greek through the Italian, e. g. *tragédie*, *comédie* ; while others are of direct Italian parentage, e. g. *sonnet*, *madrigal*, *stance*; but Greek nomenclature predominates.

Ronsard easily leads with 709 sonnets out of a total of 1,396 poems.[1]

It was one of the principles of the school to avoid popular metrical devices of bygone France. Yet their broad conceptions of art led them involuntarily to adapt to their purpose some veteran metrical fashions. While they rejected the rondeau and the ballade, they proved themselves susceptible to the influence of the past by the invention on an old pattern of the villanelle, or rustic song, which depends for its charm on the refrain. They revived, too, the more ancient Alexandrine and gave it a new cadence and pliancy. One of the band, Jodelle, was the first to employ the Alexandrine in tragedy, and he it was who made the hexameter for all time the standard type of dramatic verse in France. But it was in song, ode, and sonnet that the Pléiade wrought its main triumphs.

Never before was there such mingling of metrical strains. The keynotes were struck by Greece and modern Italy, and in the revolutionary ardour of classical zeal, Baïf, a chief member of the band, took a metrical step in a wrong direction, which is worth notice as an indication of a danger threatening the new movement. Baïf urged by precept and practice an innovation which seemed for the moment likely to lead the reforming movement to disaster. He sought to revive the quantitative rhymeless metre of Latin poetry, with its short and long syllables, its spondees and dactyls, its iambs and anapaests, its hexameters and elegiacs, its sapphics and its alcaics. He condemned alike rhyme and accent—the principles which had hitherto held undisputed sway over French verse. He would set in their place the unrhymed 'quantity' of *vers mesurés*. With unflinching thoroughness Baïf preached the

---

[1] Although Ronsard is entitled to the invention of the Theban ode, Du Bellay of Angers was never willing to forgo his right to the sonnet:

> Par moy les Graces divines
> Ont fait sonner assez bien
> Sur les rives Angevines,
> Le sonnet Italien.

A disciple, Vauquelin (*Divers Sonnets*, 3), addressed Du Bellay thus:

> Ce fut toy, Du Bellay, qui des premiers en France
> D'Italie attiras les Sonets amoureux.

classicization of French prosody as well as of French style.[1]
But his experiments proved the shallowness of his argument.
His hexameters and unrhymed anacreontics were openly
scorned, and with reluctance Baïf returned to the beaten
track. Ultimately he followed a friendly critic's advice :

> Baïf, suis le chemin que chacun va,
> Car tu ne verras point réussir l'emprise de ton temps.

The classical prosodists were slow to quit the field. They came
to concentrate their artillery on rhyme, and urged that rhyme
should be banished. Baïf argued that musical accompaniment
was the needful complement of *vers mesurés*, which ought to
be sung and not spoken. To prove his allegation to be practicable, he founded in Paris, with royal sanction, and under the
auspices of the University of Paris, an academy in which unrhymed quantitative verse should be fitted by musical composers
with appropriate musical notation. The professed aim was ' de
renouveler l'ancienne façon de composer des vers mesurés pour
y accommoder le chant pareillement mesuré selon l'art métrique'.
The effort made no real advance. Disciples of Baïf modified
the tactics of the campaign and belied their main principles
by adding rhyme to the *vers mesurés*. Rhymed hexameters,
rhymed elegiacs, and rhymed sapphics found a more charitable
reception than those measures without rhyme. ' The French
honey' of rhyme sweetened the classical pill of quantity. But
there was no relish of salvation in the mixture, and after a
brief trial it was dismissed, to join in oblivion the experiments
which preceded it. The sharp controversy was, we shall
find, loudly echoed in Elizabethan England. The danger to
which Baïf exposed the new poetic development in France
darkened the dawn of Elizabethan literature. In both
countries *tabulae solvuntur risu*, and the perils of classical
prosody were averted by force of ridicule.

Apart from metrical innovation the Pléiade sought to realize

---

[1] For a good summary of the history of Baïf's experiments see Kastner's
History of French Versification, Oxford, 1903, pp. 295-308, and *Poésies
choisies de J.-A. de Baïf*, ed. L. Becq. de Fouquières, 1874, pp. xv sq.

its reforming aim by differentiating the phraseology of French poetry from that of French prose. With that end in view new words were invented or were imported from foreign languages. From Greek they freely borrowed a large vocabulary. Some pure Greek words took permanent root in France, e.g. *mathématique*, *sympathie*, and *patrie*. Others which were as deliberately imported were wisely given short shrift, e.g. *entéléchie*—the Aristotelian word for 'innate perfection'.[1] Later, Ronsard and his disciples grew sensible of the need of restricting the employment by French poets of Greek words, and were sparing of the practice.

A second mode of creating a distinctly poetic vocabulary was to naturalize the terminology of Greek and Latin myth. With hands of unprecedented liberality the poets of the Pléiade scattered over the poetic page names of heroes, heroines, and places of classical mythology or mythical history and freely derived epithets from them. Natural phenomena were described as the actions of god or goddess. The rising and setting of the sun was associated with fifty adventures of Phoebus or Phaeton. Seas and rivers, woods and gardens, hills and fountains were presented as the abodes of nymphs. The titles of Homeric warriors were cited as synonyms of manly virtue. The French poets' earth, heaven, and hell were peopled with great Greeks or Latins, human or divine, and were credited with the mythic attributes of classical tradition.

In original method of word-composition the Pléiade under Ronsard's leadership distinguished itself mainly by its fertility

---

[1] It is usual to cite as an example of Ronsard's extravagant employment of Greek words his lines embodying the strange expressions 'ocymore', 'dispotme', 'oligochronien', &c. In his famous elegy on Queen Margaret of Navarre (*Le tombeau de Marguerite de France*), which belongs to the poet's early years, he wrote—

> Ah ! que je suis marry [grieved] que la Muse Françoise
> Ne peut dire ces mots comme fait la Gregeoise :
> Ocymore, dispotme, oligochronien ;
> Certes je les dirois du sang Valesien,
> Qui de beauté, de grace et de lustre ressemble
> Au lys qui naist, fleurit et se meurt tout ensemble.

Ronsard cites these three words as examples of Greek which are beyond his skill to Gallicize (*Œuvres*, vii. 178).

in inventing diminutives, and by its creation of compound epithets. The plenteous employment of diminutives reinforced
the impression of delicacy, which the French reformers of
poetry highly valued, but diminutives had been used already,
if in modest measure, by Ronsard's precursors. Their employment by the Pléiade was largely a revival or an expansion of
a pre-existing habit. The second device of compound epithets
was new to modern poetry and exerted a worldwide influence.
There is nothing in old French poetry with which comparison is possible. Ronsard personally claimed the sole glory
of the innovation which his disciples developed with grotesque
extravagance. Ronsard's 'vocables composez', by which he
set infinite store, were only remotely framed on the Homeric
pattern. This final embellishment of poetic speech he vaunted
as a triumph, which entitled him to no ordinary gratitude from
his country.[1] It is capable of proof that Elizabethan poetry
is hardly less indebted to him for this usage than the poetry
of sixteenth-century France.

VI

THE HEIRS OF THE PLÉIADE

The six active members of the Pléiade—Ronsard, Du Bellay,
Baïf, Tyard, Jodelle, and Belleau—were not only most prolific
poets, but all quickly gathered about them a host of disciples
who shared in varying degrees their qualities, and made all
France, to the end of the century, a nest of singing-birds.
The note of melody grew thinner with the advancing years.
But the music did not altogether fail. Italian influences
tended as the years sped to rival and outstrip the Greek; pedantic conceits and affectations grew.   Yet the lyric charm died

---

[1] Cf. *Œuvres*, vii. 127 :

> Indonté du labeur, je travaillay pour elle [*i. e.* France],
> Je fis des mots nouveaux, je r'appelay les vieux,
> Si bien que son renom je poussay jusq'aux cieux.
> Je fis, d'autre façon que n'avoient les antiques,
> *Vocables composez*, et phrases poëtiques,
> Et mis la poësie en tel ordre, qu'aprés
> Le François fut égal aux Romains et aux Grecs.

hard.   The generation of French poets who were busiest
in the first working days of Daniel and Drayton, of Chapman
and Shakespeare, included in the rank and file men like
Vauquelin de la Fresnaie, Jean Passerat, and Gilles Durant.
It was Vauquelin who invoked Phillis, in an almost endless
flow of tuneful song on such a pattern as this:

> Entre les fleurs, entre les lis,
> Doucement dormoit ma Philis.

Gilles Durant struck many a simple note in the melodious
key of his address to the souci, or marigold, which he prefers
to violet, pink, pansy, or rose:

> J'aime la belle violette,
> L'œillet et la pensée aussi,
> J'aime la rose vermeillette,
> Mais surtout j'aime la souci.

Few poets counselled youth more musically to snatch the
pleasures of the hour than Jean Passerat in his ode to May
Day—' du Premier Jour de May ':

> Laissons ce regret et ce pleur
>   A la vieillesse ;
> Jeunes, il faut cueillir la fleur
>   De la jeunesse.
> Or que le ciel est le plus gay
> En ce gracieux mois de May,
>   Aimons, Mignonne ;
> Contentons nostre ardent désir ;
> En ce monde n'a du plaisir
>   Qui ne s'en donne.

It is not easy to match in lightness of touch Jean de la
Taille's reproach of the damsel who scorns love:

> Elle est comme la rose franche
>   Qu'un jeune pasteur, par oubly
> Laisse flestrir dessus la branche
> Sans se parer d'elle au dimanche,
>   Sans jouir du bouton cueilly.

The Pléiade movement only drew its last melodious breath
on crossing the threshold of the seventeenth century.   Ronsard's

mantle of chieftain was worn on his death by a fashionable
ecclesiastic, a wealthy pluralist, a kindly patron of poor men of
letters, Philippe Desportes, who was born in 1545. His life
ended in 1606, a year which Drayton, Chapman, and Dekker
made memorable in England by exceptional activity. He
echoed Ronsard's voice in a somewhat halting key, and was
steeped in contemporary Italian influences. His abundant
lyrics, elegies, satires, and pious verse all stood high in
public esteem. To the vogue of the sonnet he paid conspicuous tribute; four hundred and forty-three of his seven
hundred and eighty-one poems are quatorzains. He caught
the sonneteering note of the bastard followers of Petrarch
while on a visit to Italy in youth, and he never freed himself
of the *genre's* debased affectations. He often relied on a silent
process of direct translation from his Italian masters, and
sincerity is usually lacking to his sentiment. His ceaseless pro-
testations of all-absorbing love—' Douce est la mort qui vient
en bien amant '—are apt to weary. But he was a good crafts-
man, and could, in his love-songs, mingle on occasion a light
touch of pathos, with a little piquant raillery. The faithless
Rozette, in spite of vows renewed amid tears at every
leave-taking, has yielded to a new admirer. The jilted
poet tells her that he has consoled himself with a new mistress, but he ends each of the valedictory verses with the
half-jesting, half-tearful refrain—

> Nous verrons, volage Bergère,
> Qui premier s'en repentira.

Towards the close of Desportes' career, the tradition of the
Pléiade was maintained by another clerical poet, Jean Bertaut,
who ended his career as bishop of Séez at the age of 59, in
1611. In Bertaut the lyric fervour of song and sonnet is
colder than in Desportes; his vows of gallantry and his regrets
for youth's passage tend to more conventional conceits, and
the sacred topics, to which he devoted his later years, are treated
on lines which sacrifice charm to orthodoxy. Yet his metrical
dexterity is great; he handles the *In Memoriam* stanza with
exceptional effect:

Pourquoy voudroy-je encor d'un idolatre hommage
    Sacrifier ma vie aux rigueurs de son œil,
    Et par un lâche espoir de fléchir son orgueil,
Perdant la liberté, perdre aussi le courage ? [1]

There are, too, touches of feeling in the more familiar poem
beginning—

Félicité passée
Qui ne peux revenir

In lines like these there is ethical insight—

La crainte de perdre une chose si chère
Fait que je ne sens point l'heur de la posséder.

But the inspiration seems more often on the point of exhaustion. With Bertaut's death, in 1611, the era of the Renaissance
lyric may be said to terminate in France. In the same year
Shakespeare retired from the active exercise of his profession.

Bertaut, like Desportes, boasted of discipleship to Ronsard
and the Pléiade, and both lived long enough to witness signs of
reaction against the leading principles of that great school. The
idolatry of Greece and Italy, which was a main creed of the
Pléiade faith, awoke in due time a patriotic revulsion of feeling.
The great scholar, Henri Étienne, in *La Précellence du
langage françois*, first raised the banner of revolt with a
declaration that the French language was rich enough to pass
current without foreign alloy. The cry against alien influences
gathered force early in the seventeenth century, and the Pléiade
was at length convicted by public opinion of worshipping false
gods. But the school had done its work ; it had cradled a new
conception of lyric theme ; it had created a new standard
of poetic vocabulary and, above all, a new temper of poetic
melody. Malherbe, the next ruler of the French Parnassus,
repudiated with vehemence the authority of the Pléiade and
heaped impatient scorn on its mythological imagery and its
classical terminology. Yet the new master, in his search
after a greater simplicity and regularity, was largely influenced by the aesthetic ideals and ambitions of those whose
fame he sought to displace. Much truth lurks, too, in the

---

[1] *Œuvres poétiques*, Paris, 1891, p. 326.

epigram entitled (in Boileau's phrase) ' Enfin Malherbe vint ', by
Banville, the romantic leader of the nineteenth century :

> Les bons rythmeurs pris d'une frénésie,
> Comme des Dieux gaspillaient l'ambroisie
> Si bien qu'enfin, pour mettre le holà,
> Malherbe vint, et que la Poésie,
> En le voyant arriver, s'en alla.

VII

THE PLÉIADE IN ENGLAND

Long before the day of Malherbe, the voice of the Pléiade
in all its variety—in the note of Desportes and Bertaut as
well as in that of Ronsard and Du Bellay—had caught the
Elizabethan ear. As soon as a careful inquiry is instituted, there
is no mistaking the amplitude of the debt which Elizabethan
England owed to French poetry of the second fifty years
of the sixteenth century. The Pléiade influence is visible in
Elizabethan metre, in turns of phraseology, in sentiment, in idea.
In some instances the influence works through a process of
adaptation which leaves ample room for the independent
activity of Elizabethan individuality or idiosyncrasy. In other
instances it works through a process of translation which is
for the most part unavowed and is a mysterious feature of
the inquiry.

In estimating the force of the French influence on the
Elizabethan lyric, due allowance must be made for the strength
of other streams which fed the tide of song. Elizabethan poets
often studied Greek, Latin, and Italian verse at first hand, and the
debts directly due to Anacreon and Horace, to Petrarch and
Ariosto, to Guarini and Tasso are not safely neglected. But
these writers were not invariably known to Elizabethans in their
original language. Much classical and Italian poetry circulated in England more freely in a French dress than in its
native garb. Doubt is at times inevitable whether Elizabethan lyrics which assimilate classical or Italian fancy are to be
reckoned among vicarious gifts of French writers or among
the direct donations of poets of more distant lands. It should

be admitted that the Elizabethan lyric acquired and preserved an indigenous flavour, despite its eager absorption of
foreign sustenance by way alike of adaptation and translation.
The harmony has often, at any rate to English ears, a richer
melody; the fancy presents a more pointed significance, and
the thought is of a robuster substance than the foreign
masters seem to command. Yet a comparative study pro-
claims a foreign cue for a vast deal of the blitheness, music,
and fragrance of the Elizabethan lyric, and proves the foreign
suggestion to be more often of French than of classical or Italian
origin. The inspiration of the Pléiade was more penetrating
than that of any other school, and it left on English song a
mark which was more lasting. It would be easy to trace the
influence of the Pléiade far beyond the Elizabethan era. The
French airs are echoed in the poetry of Wither and Herrick;
even the lyres of Charles II's day were attuned to them. Here
we do not carry our inquiry beyond the close of the sonneteering vogue in Elizabethan England, which synchronizes with
the publication of Shakespeare's sonnets in 1609. On the
Elizabethan sonnet French influence wrought with exceptional
energy and a very evenly sustained strength.

The evidence within the Elizabethan field is voluminous,
and can only be indicated in outline. It is the internal proof
which comes of setting Elizabethan poems at the side of
earlier French examples, that throws full light on the situation.
Less can be gleaned from the external evidence which is supplied by Elizabethan writers' familiar mention of the work
of Ronsard, Du Bellay, Desportes, and other 'brave wits'
of the Pléiade army. The outward marks of recognition
are important, but they fail to indicate the completeness of the
Elizabethan discipleship.

Ronsard and Du Bellay were popular names in England
in Shakespeare's youth. At the very outset of the Elizabethan activity the earliest leader of the great poetic movement,
Edmund Spenser, hailed Du Bellay as

First garland of free Poësie
That France brought forth, though fruitful of brave wits,
Well worthy thou of immortalitie.

Thomas Watson, the second writer of verse to enter the true Elizabethan fold, was adjured by an admirer to note how the French tongue was garnering the wealth of Parnassus and luxuriating in the new achievements of Ronsard.[1] There was no obscurity in the hint as to the quarter whence enlightenment was coming. Popular literature of the day paid its tribute to the French Apollo. In 1590, in a satiric tract, *Tarlton's News out of Purgatory*, a large company of poets is described as assembled in Purgatory to hear ' old Ronsard ', who died five years before, recite a description of his mistress, Cassandra, one of the heroines of his sonnets. The verses which are set on the French poet's lips are intended for sarcasm. But they ridicule Ronsard's English imitators rather than the French poet. In 1594 Michael Drayton deplored that it was ' a fault too common in this latter time ' to ' filch ' from the page of Desportes, Ronsard's successor on the throne of French poetry. In 1595 a patriotic critic who was desirous of protecting his own countrymen's poetic efforts from disparagement argued that ' France-remarked Bellay ' and ' court-like amorous Ronsard ' were currently overpraised. But this note was not repeated. A year later Thomas Lodge, one of the most popular of Elizabethan lyrists and one of the heaviest debtors to the Pléiade, penned a notable tribute to Desportes, Ronsard's heir. Lodge used words, of which the full significance will appear later : ' Few men (he wrote) are able to second the sweet conceits of Philip Desportes, whose poetical writings [are] for the most part Englished, and ordinarily in everybody's hands.'[2] At the extreme end of the century, in the Cambridge University play, the *Returne from Parnassus* (*c.* 1600), an amorous youth employs a friend to write sonnets for his lady-love, and he suggests to his poetic aide-de-camp as an acceptable pattern, not merely the verse of Chaucer, Spenser, and Shakespeare, but lines from Ronsard, of which he offers an English parody.

[1] Gallica Parnasso coepit ditescere lingua
Ronsardique operis luxuriare nouis.
(Watson's *Hecatompathia*, 1582, ed. Arber, p. 34.)
[2] *Margarite of America*, 1596.

But suggestive as are the notices of the work of Ronsard and his friends in Elizabethan books, no adequate testimony is furnished there to the extent of the French influence on the lyric fertility of Elizabethan England. The relations between the two schools of poetry are not fully discernible until the work of both is studied word by word in conjunction. Clearly inscribed sign-posts on the long road are few. Elizabethans rarely made open confession of translation from the Pléiade. Only one work by Ronsard seems to have been published in his lifetime in an English version with a quite plain and unequivocal acknowledgement that it was a translation. Ronsard's *Discours des Misères de ce temps à la Royne mère du Roy* was issued in Paris in 1562. It is the poet's fervid denunciation of Calvin. It is his refutation of Huguenot slanders, and a valuable piece of autobiography; although penned with a convincing eagerness and brilliant volubility, it has indeed more personal than aesthetic value. Thomas Jenye, a Yorkshireman, who was in the service of Sir Henry Norris, the English ambassador in Paris from 1567 to 1569, turned Ronsard's controversial poem into English verse while he was at the Paris embassy. The effort was published at Antwerp in 1568, with a dedication to the translator's diplomatic chief.[1] Equally halting were other undisguised tributes of the kind which were paid to Ronsard. Thomas Watson, the popular contemporary of Spenser, whose muse was overweighted by his learning, publicly stated that four of his hundred poems of passion — his *Hecatompathia* — which appeared in 1582, adapted specified poems of Ronsard. Two years later a very clumsy practitioner in verse, 'John Soothern, Gentleman,' in a volume which he christened *Pandora: the Musique of the Beautie of his Mistresse Diana*, gave in discordant doggerel, and in a vocabulary freely strewn with French words and idioms,

---

[1] Jenye's book bears this title: 'A Discours of the Present Troobles in Fraunce, and Miseries of this Tyme, compyled by Peter Ronsard Gentilman of Vandome, and dedicated unto the Quene Mother. Translated into English by Thomas Jeney, Gentilman. Printed at Andwerpe. 1568, 4to.' Only one copy seems to have been identified in modern times. It belonged to the great collector, Richard Heber, and its present whereabouts seem unknown.

a series of sonnets, odes and 'odelettes' which crudely adapt Ronsard's lyrics. The source, though imperfectly admitted by Soothern, was generally recognized by English readers. None could doubt that Soothern's clumsy boast,

> Never man before
> Now in England knew Pindar's string,

was a mere anglicization of Ronsard's repeated vaunt,

> Le premier de France
> J'ai Pindarisé.[1]

Ronsard's chief lieutenant, Du Bellay, enjoyed a somewhat fuller measure of open acknowledgement. In 1569, a year after Jenye's rendering of Ronsard appeared, Edmund Spenser, while little more than a schoolboy, issued by way of a first poetic experiment a literal translation into unrhymed English verse of some fifteen of Du Bellay's French sonnets. Du Bellay called these sonnets, which freely paraphrased the Apocalypse, *Songes ou Visions sur Rome*. The English youth entitled his rendering *The Visions of Bellay*. Du Bellay remained one of Spenser's acknowledged poetic heroes. Twenty-two years later the English poet reissued his *Visions of Bellay* in a rhymed revision, and added to them a sequence of thirty-two sonnets which were drawn from the same French treasury. *The Ruines of Rome, by Bellay*, are a literal rendering by Spenser of Du Bellay's characteristically pathetic *Antiquités*

---

[1] Puttenham, in *The Arte of English Poesie* (1589), writes of Soothern's effort to naturalize Ronsard's work in England: 'Another [writer] of reasonable good facilitie in translation finding certaine of the hymnes of *Pyndarus* and of *Anacreons odes*, and other Lirickes among the Greekes very well translated by *Rounsard*, the French poet, and applied to the honour of a great Prince in France, comes our minion and translates the same out of French into English, and applieth them to the honour of a great noble man in England (wherein I commend his reuerent minde and duetie) but doth so impudently robbe the French Poet both of his prayse and also of his French termes, that I cannot so much pitie him as be angry with him for his iniurious dealing, our sayd maker not being ashamed to use these French wordes *freddon, egar, superbous, filanding, celest, calabrois, thebanois* and a number of others, for English wordes, which haue no maner of conformitie with our language either by custome or deriuation which may make them tollerable. And in the end (which is worst of all) makes his vaunt that neuer English singer but his hath toucht *Pindars* string which was neuerthelesse word by word as Rounsard had said before by like braggery.' (Puttenham, ed. Arber, 1869, pp. 259-60.) The words which follow in Puttenham's text are quoted *infra* on page 249.

de Rome. Spenser's sole original embellishment here is his 'envoy' saluting Bellay as the earliest of the new wits of France, whose glory it was to have summoned ' old Rome out of her ashes ', and to have earned for himself ' never-dying fame'. Ronsard excited no such overt demonstration of respect. Among his disciples, only the Huguenot poet Du Bartas, who soon seceded from the Pléiade ranks, was honoured by Elizabethan translators with a frank avowal of their obligation to his work. The sole English volume which bore Desportes' name on its title-page during Shakespeare's life-time was an uncouth English translation of the Frenchman's free rendering into his own tongue of a poem by Ariosto.[1]

The genuine influence of the Pléiade operated more subtly. Elizabethan poets in the heyday of their energy rarely declared in the market-place their debts to foreign masters. The main obligations of Elizabethan poets are to be traced in poetry which they offered the world without any hint of dependence on foreign tuition.

The fact that poets of two countries write at much the same time in the like strain, must be examined in many lights before an inference of affiliation can be safely deduced from it. Coincidence in the expression of vague universal sentiments is often fortuitous. Everybody is familiar with such lines as these from Horace:

> Omnes eodem cogimur: omnium
> Versatur urna serius ocius
>   Sors exitura, et nos in aeternum
>   Exsilium impositura cymbae. (*Odes*, ii. 3. 25–8.)

or his

> Pallida mors aequo pulsat pede pauperum tabernas
> Regumque turres.   (*Odes*, i. 4. 14–15.)

It may be that Horace suggested to Ronsard the stanzas which he playfully addressed to a dead lap-dog named Courte:

---

[1] The English translator was Gervase Markham. His volume *Rodomonths Infernall*, licensed for the press in 1598, was published in 1606. Desportes' version of Ariosto, which Markham 'paraphrastically translated', is entitled *La Mort de Rodomont et sa descente aux enfers*.

> Par la vallée
> Où tu es, Courte, devalée,
> L'Empereur, le Pape et le Roy,
> Marcheront aussi bien que toy.
> Car telle voye, froide et brune,
> A tous les peuples est *commune*,
> D'où plus jamais on ne revient,
> Car le long oubly les retient.
> (Ronsard, *Œuvres*, ed. Blanchemain, vii. 252.)

Again Ronsard wrote in much the same vein :

> La Mort, frappant de son dard,
>   N'a égard
> A la majesté royale ;
> Les empereurs aux bouviers,
>   Aux leviers
> Les grands *sceptres* elle égale.   (*ibid.*, ii. 192.)

And again :

> Celuy qui est mort aujourd'huy
> Est aussi bien mort que celuy
> Qui mourut au jour du deluge.
> Autant vaut aller le premier
> Que de sejourner le dernier
> Devant le parquet du grand juge.
> (*Odes*, iii. 22 ; *Œuvres*, ii, p. 236.)

At many turns Shakespeare recalls the language of both Horace and Ronsard :

> Thou know'st 'tis *common*; all that live must die,
> Passing through nature to eternity. (*Hamlet*, I. ii. 72–3.)

> The *sceptre*, learning, physic, must
> All follow this, and come to dust.
> (*Cymbeline*, IV. ii. 268-9.)

> It seems to me most strange that men should fear,
> Seeing that death, a necessary end,
> Will come, when it will come. (*Jul. Caes.* II. ii. 35-7.)

Yet the English poet may well have reached these general assurances, for all their kinship to those of Horace and Ronsard, by way of his own intuition.

There must be a more definite measure of identity between language and sentiment, there must be coincidence of more peculiarly distinctive thought, before any conclusion of indebtedness on the part of one writer of genius to another could win acceptance.   But the bonds of thought and style which link numerous lyrics of the Elizabethans with those of the Pléiade and its disciples are positive and unquestionable. The Elizabethans' proved familiarity with the French language, and their acquisitive tendencies, constantly proclaim coincidences between distinctive idea and expression in Elizabethan and contemporary French poetry to be direct debts on the part of Elizabethans to the French poets.

VIII

THE ELIZABETHAN RENDERING OF FRENCH LYRIC THEMES

The Pléiade influence on Elizabethan metre and vocabulary will demand close study, but the coincidence of theme and sentiment is the most fascinating feature of the story and claims preliminary notice.[1]   The evidence is of embarrassing wealth, and clearly establishes the substantial measure of the debt which the Elizabethans incurred to the poetry of the French Renaissance. The degrees of kinship which link the Elizabethan lyric with preceding efforts of France are varied.   They will be seen to range from acceptance of suggestion to literal translation.   Each degree of relationship is capable of liberal illustration.   The claims of Elizabethan originality are not seriously in question.   The process of borrowing went hand in hand with abundant exercise of creative power, and the borrowed thought or phrase sometimes underwent a subtle mutation which bore witness to independent inventiveness and ingenuity. But no Elizabethan poet seems to have altogether escaped the contagion of French influence.   Little doubt is possible that Shakespeare himself at times accepted the suggestion of the French lyric, while Elizabethan stars of less magnitude drew floods of light from the French constellation of the Pléiade.

The songs of Anacreon and the Greek anthologists, the idylls of Theocritus and his school, supplied the threads of

---

[1] Consideration of the relation of the French and English sonnet is postponed to section XII of this Book.

which many Elizabethan lyrics were woven. Conceits of the Greek lyric streaked Elizabethan poetry almost as richly as the verse of the French Renaissance. But the Greek imagery is very often a direct reflection of the Pléiade temper. French adaptation of Greek lyric or idyll is frequently the immediate source of the Elizabethan inspiration. The Greek sentiment is not seldom expanded or diversified by the Elizabethan adapter. Yet signs of dependence on France lie as a rule near the surface. Hellenist fancies which find a place in Elizabethan lyrics are usually more closely allied with the French texts than with the original Greek.

Lyly may be reckoned the earliest and one of the most original of English workers in Anacreontics. His musical songs celebrate Daphne's brow, Pan's pipe, Apollo's lyre, Bacchus's revels, or Cupid's tricks. In his adaptations of the Greek conceits Lyly preserved his independence. He manipulated with freedom the classical themes. No precise Greek original can be assigned to his song of *Cupid and Campaspe*, in which Cupid makes a wager with Campaspe and loses to her all his weapons of offence. It is significant that the main topic was very recently anticipated in a sonnet of Desportes (*Diane*, I. xv), where Cupid bets away his bow in a contest with ' Diane et ma maîtresse '. Although the fancy is developed differently in the French and is less epigrammatic, Desportes' words, ' Amour gaigea son arc. . . Las! ma dame gaigne,' adumbrate Lyly's words (of Cupid): ' He stakes his quiver, bow and arrows . . . She won.' Again, Lyly's bacchanalian chants, although they may owe something to Horace, fuse, with admirable spirit, Elizabethan feeling and the Greek sentiment of the Pléiade. Lyly's

> Iô Bacchus! To thy table
> Thou callest every drunken rabble . . .
> Wine, O wine!
> O juice divine! . . .
> O the dear blood of grapes
> Turns us to antic shapes.

was the oft-heard cry of Ronsard's frolic muse when apostrophizing the god of wine in his *Chant de folie* :

Ta fureur me jette
  Hors de moy.
Je te voy, je te voy,
  Voy-te-cy,
  Romp-soucy !
Mon cœur, bouillonnant d'une rage,
En-vole vers toy mon courage.
Je forcene, je demoniacle ;
  L'horrible vent de ton oracle
J entens ; l'esprit de ce bon vin nouveau
  Me tempeste le cerveau,
    Ïach, ïach, Evoé,
    Evoé, ïach, ïach ! [1]

Again, Moschus's famous idyll of ' The Hue and Cry after Cupid ' was turned into French many times before Lyly's era of activity. *Amour Fuïtif* is the title of two most popular French adaptations of the Greek idyll (by Baïf and Amadis Jamyn respectively). The French renderings gave the Greek poem its Elizabethan vogue. Lyly's song of *Cupid Bound* wears much new raiment, in which French tones mingle with Greek. Here and elsewhere Lyly foreshadows future Elizabethan developments. A few years later Ben Jonson re-handled Moschus's theme to splendid effect in his beautiful lyric of *Venus's Runaway*. There Ben finally naturalized the French poets' *Amour Fuïtif* among Shakespeare's contemporaries.

Spenser shows like signs of sympathy with that Greek lyric vein which French poetry absorbed. There is a charming trifle by him in six ten-lined stanzas which under the generic designation of ' epigram ' amplifies the Anacreontic fable of Cupid and the bee. The boy-god, according to the Greek poem, is stung by the bee, and in tears complains to his mother. Venus, while curing the wound, draws the moral

---

[1] Ronsard's *Œuvres*, vi, p. 380. Cf. *Œuvres*, ii, p. 471—
    Voy-le-ci, je le sen venir,
  Et mon cœur estonné ne peut
    Sa grand' divinité tenir,
  Tant elle l'agite et l'esmeut.

Lyly's ' Cupid, monarch over kings ' opens with Anacreontic blitheness on the note of Desportes' chanson (*Œuvres*, ed. Michiels, p. 107)—
    Amour, grand vainqueur des vainqueurs,
    Et la Beauté, royne des cœurs.

that the pain is small compared with the griefs habitually caused the human heart by the infant god of love. At least six French renderings of the slight theme, more or less paraphrastic, were published in France before 1573. The most graceful rendering is by Ronsard. Spenser, while he adds touches of his own, accepts some developments of French ingenuity. His version approaches far more closely to that of Ronsard or Baïf than to Anacreon's original Greek. There is little doubt that he wrote under French rather than Greek inspiration. There is nothing in Anacreon to suggest Spenser's laughter of Venus, 'who could not choose but laugh at his [i. e. her son's] fond game.' That is one of the trifles in which Baïf and Ronsard anticipated Spenser. When, too, Spenser makes Cupid call the bee a 'fly' he doubtless has in mind the French poet's expression, '*mouche* à miel,' i. e. the honey-bee.

Of Shakespeare's Anacreontic adaptations probably the most striking example is met with in *Timon of Athens* (IV. iii. 442–8), where the dramatist wrote:

> The sun's a thief, and with his great attraction
> Robs the vast sea; the moon's an arrant thief,
> And her pale fire she snatches from the sun:
> The sea's a thief, whose liquid surge resolves
> The moon into salt tears: the earth's a thief,
> That feeds and breeds by a composture stol'n
> From general excrement: each thing's a thief.

Here Shakespeare handled in his own manner a famous Anacreontic ode in its French form. The Greek verse draws a natural justification for drinking from the fact that heavenly and earthly bodies reciprocally seek liquid sustenance. The fancy was thoroughly acclimatized by the Renaissance in France, and the Anacreontic poem was popular in independent versions of Ronsard and Remy Belleau. Ronsard's version opens thus:

> La terre les eaux va boivant,
> L'arbre la boit par sa racine,
> La mer éparse boit le vent,
> Et le soleil boit la marine;
> Le soleil est beu de la lune:
> Tout boit, soit en haut ou en bas.[1]

[1] *Œuvres*, ed. Blanchemain, ii. 286.

Shakespeare invests the suggestion of the reciprocal relations
of sun, moon, and ocean with a poetic luxuriance which
was peculiar to his genius. There is a new purpose
in Shakespeare's use of the imagery. But as soon as the
French and English lines are studied side by side their kinship
becomes unmistakable.

The study of Ovid, chiefly in Golding's translation, is a
main source of Elizabethan knowledge of classical mythology.
But contemporary French feeling would seem to have largely
stimulated the classical sympathies of the Elizabethan lyrists,
and their mythological touches constantly pursue distinctive
hints of the Pléiade. It does not seem to have been noticed
that, in the year of Shakespeare's birth, Ronsard anticipated
Shakespeare's poetic version of the Ovidian story of Venus
and Adonis. The evidence of literal borrowing on Shakespeare's part from Ronsard's poem on the subject may not
go far. Ronsard's *Venus and Adonis* has a more pronounced mythological setting than Shakespeare's work.[1]
Yet Shakespeare's descriptive imagery is often of Ronsardian
temper. When Shakespeare's goddess tells how she conquered the god of war, 'leading him prisoner in a red rose
chain,' the English poet echoes a familiar line in one of
Ronsard's Anacreontics.[2] In the pathetic appeal to Adonis's
hounds and to Echo, which Shakespeare sets on Venus's
lips, he seems to follow Ronsard's guidance. The fact at any
rate that the 'first heir' of Shakespeare's invention should
concern itself with one of Ronsard's themes, and should bear
resemblance to Ronsard's treatment, suggests an imaginative
bond which might well develop closer relationship later.[3]

[1] There are signs that both the French and English poet had made
some independent study of earlier poetic versions of the fable in Italian.
[2] Cf. Ronsard's *Œuvres* (ed. Blanchemain, ii. 285) —

Les Muses *lièrent* un jour
De chaînes de roses Amour.

Ronsard's poem was universally popular, and had already been cited (in
1582) by Watson as the source of his 'Passion', LXXXIII.
[3] In Ronsard's poem Mars's jealous anger leads the God of War to
seek Diana's aid, and it is the divine huntress who contrives Adonis's
death by means of the boar. With beautiful effect Ronsard again and
again repeats with slight modification this refrain :

Perhaps the most remarkable of all instances of identity of fancy between Ronsard and the great English dramatist finds illustration in a classical outburst of wonderful energy in Shakespeare's *Antony and Cleopatra* (IV. xii. 50-4). In that great tragedy, which shows Shakespeare's power at its zenith, Antony, on hearing the false report of Cleopatra's death, exclaims in an ecstasy of poetry, of which Plutarch gives no hint, that he will be her companion in Hades:

> I come, my queen! Stay for me;
> *Where souls do couch on flowers*, we'll hand in hand,
> And with our sprightly port make the ghosts gaze:
> *Dido* and her Aeneas shall want *troops*,
> And all the haunt be ours.

Nowhere does Shakespeare strike quite so vividly Ronsard's precise note. In his impassioned *Chanson* III the French poet had already greeted his mistress Hélène in the identical key. Together he and his beloved Hélène, Ronsard declares, will pass to the Elysian fields:

> Là, morts de trop aimer, sous les branches myrtines
> Nous verrons tous les jours
> Les anciens Héros auprès des Héroïnes
> Ne parler que d'amours.[1]

All the divine 'troop' of past lovers ('*la troupe* sainte autrefois amoureuse') will come to offer greeting, and none will refuse to quit their seats for the new comers, who will 'couch on flowers' in midst of all:

> Ny celles qui s'en vont toutes tristes ensemble,
> Artemise et *Didon*:
> Ny ceste belle Grecque à qui ta beauté semble,
> Comme tu fais de nom.[2]

> Hélas, pauvre Adonis, tous les Amours te pleurent,
> Toi mourant par ta mort, toutes délices meurent.

Ronsard's poem closes in a key which echoes, with a delightful freshness, *l'esprit gaulois*. He slyly mentions at the end that the goddess of love, despite her wailing, soon set her heart on the Phrygian shepherd Anchises. The French poet takes leave of the theme with a reflection that women's love, like April flowers, only lives a day. Shakespeare is more loyal to the sentiment of the myth.

[1] *Œuvres*, ed. Blanchemain, i. 383.

[2] Ronsard is addressing a lady named after Helen, the fair Greek.

Puis, *nous faisant asseoir dessus l'herbe fleurie,*
   De toutes au milieu,
Nulle en se retirant ne sera point marrie[1]
   De nous quitter son lieu.

Shakespeare in his maturity was at any rate faithful to the classical sentiment which animated the poetry of the French Renaissance.

No comparative student can ignore the resemblance, whatever the precise deduction to be drawn from it, between the buoyant notes with which both Pléiade and Elizabethan schools of lyric poetry greeted the months of April and May and the floral pageantry of spring and summer. Chaucer had caught something of the same exuberance, in part at least from French lyres, more than two centuries before. But the fresh delight of Shakespeare and his contemporaries in the painted meadows and in the brilliant colours of bud and blossom seems to proclaim another mark of affinity with Ronsard and his disciples. A hundred lines or stanzas could be quoted from the French poets in terms such as these :

   Avril, l'honneur des prés verts,
     Jaunes, pers (*i. e. azure*),
   Qui d'une humeur bigarrée
   Émaillent de mille fleurs
     De couleurs
   Leur parure diaprée.[2]

It was of ' ce mois Avril ' that Ronsard wrote—

Il peint les bois, les forêts et les plaines [3]

with rainbow hues—

   le bel esmail qui varie
  L'honneur gemmé d'une prairie
  En mille lustres s'esclatant.[4]

Shakespeare also likened ' flowers purple, blue, and white '

---

[1] This is Ronsard's final reading. The line read originally ' Nulle, *et fût-ce Procris*, ne sera point marrie' [i. e. grieved or offended].
[2] Belleau, *Œuvres*, ed. Gouverneur, ii. 43.
[3] Ronsard, *Œuvres*, i. 132.   [4] *ibid.*, ii. 342.

to 'sapphires, pearls, and rich embroidery' (*Merry Wives*, v. v. 75), and graphically presented spring as the season—

> When daisies pied and violets blue
> And lady-smocks all silver-white
> And cuckoo-buds of yellow hue [1]
> Do paint the meadows with delight.
>> *Love's Labour's Lost*, v. ii. 902–5.

There is moreover no spring flower to which the two schools denied much the same poetic honours. Not only the rose, the lily, and the daisy (*de Mars la blanche fleurette*), but the violet, the pansy, the gilliflower, hawthorn, eglantine, thyme, and above all the marigold repeatedly receive the poets' joint homage. The language of flowers which was current in the Pléiade school closely resembles that of the Elizabethans.

At the very opening of the Elizabethan movement Spenser developed to pleasant effect a floral inventory which is distinctly of Ronsardian affinity. In a ditty in his *Shepheards Calender* (Aegloga IV, April), where he adapts both the style and metre of the Pléiade, Spenser wrote—

> Bring hither the pink and purple columbine
>> With gelliflowers:
> Bring coronations (i. e. carnations) and sops-in-wine,
>> Worn of paramours:
> Strew me the ground with daffadowndillies,
> With cowslips, and kingcups, and loved lilies.
>> The pretty paunce
>> And the chevisaunce
> Shall watch with the fair fleur de lice.[2]

With Spenser's catalogue it is worth comparing the following strophes, which pay tribute in the like strain to most of Spenser's flowers:—

> Les uns chanteront les œillets
>> Vermeillets,
> Ou du lis la fleur argentée
> Ou celle qui s'est par les prez
>> Diaprez
> Du sang des princes enfantée.[3]

---

[1] Cowslips were known in France as 'brayes de *cocu*'.
[2] Spenser has no warrant for using the old French word 'chevisaunce' to designate a flower. In French it means 'a mercantile transaction'.
[3] Ronsard, *Œuvres*, ed. Blanchemain, ii. 430.

L'aubépin et l'églantin
Et le thym,
L'œillet, le lis et les roses,
En cette belle saison,
A foison,
Montrent leurs robes écloses.[1]

Many of the specific fancies with which the Elizabethans played in their allusions to particular flowers belong to domestic folklore. But others are drawn from the classical imagery which was more efficiently naturalized in France than anywhere else. Some of the most delicate songs of the French Renaissance celebrate the charm of the marigold. Ronsard in an Ovidian strain depicted the flower as a tearful lover of the sun, which drooped its head in pallor and dismay at sunset, and opened its eyes to welcome sunrise. In one long poem which he wrote in 1573 and called by the flower's name (Le Souci du jardin) Ronsard develops the conceit, addressing the marigold thus (Œuvres, vi, p. 111):

Quand le soleil, ton amoureux, s'abaisse
Dedans le sein de Tethys son hostesse,
Allant revoir le pere de la mer,
On voit ton chef se clorre et se fermer
Palle, défait ; mais quand sa tresse blonde
De longs cheveux s'esparpille sur l'onde
Se réveillant, tu t'éveilles joyeux,
Et pour le voir tu dessiles tes yeux,
Et sa clarté est seule ton envie,
Un seul soleil te donnant mort et vie.[2]

---

[1] Belleau, Œuvres, ed. Gouverneur, ii. 44. Cf. Shakespeare's *Midsummer Night's Dream*, II. i. 249-52 :

I know a bank whereon the wild *thyme* blows,
Where oxlips and the nodding violet grows
Quite over-canopied with luscious woodbine,
With sweet musk-*roses*, and with *eglantine*.

[2] Cf. Ronsard's *Amours*, I. cciv, and also *Œuvres*, vi, p. 333, where the poet likens himself to a marigold :

En mesme temps me fust avis aussi
Que j'estois fleur qu'on nomme du soucy,
Qui meurt et pend sa teste languissante
Quand elle n'est plus du soleil jouissante ;
Mais aussi tost que l'Aurore vermeille
Hors de la mer la lumiere reveille,
Elle renaist, sa vie mesurant
Au seul regard d'un beau soleil durant.

A very modest follower of the French master, Gilles Durant, expressed the same fancy in an apostrophe to the marigold of more touching simplicity :

> Toujours ta face languissante
> Aux raiz de son œil s'épanit,
> Et, dès que sa clairté s'absente,
> Soudain ta beauté se fanit.[1]

In similar strain Shakespeare wrote of—

> The marigold, that goes to bed wi' the sun,
> And with him rises weeping. (*Wint. Tale*, IV. iii. 105-6.)

and how at dawn—

> winking mary-buds begin
> To ope their golden eyes. (*Cymb.*, II. iii. 26-7.)

The turns of phrase differ in France and England, but the conceits are almost identical.

The lyric play of amorous fancy constantly runs in a mould which, whatever its ultimate origin, was reckoned by Elizabethans among French types. Elizabethan poets were wont to speculate interrogatively on the origin of love, and all seem to ring variations on a famous sonnet of Desportes (*Diane*, I. xxxvii, ed. Michiels, p. 28) :

> Amour, quand fus-tu né ? Ce fut lors que la terre
> S'émaille de couleurs et les bois de verdeur.
> De qui fus-tu conçeu ? D'une puissante ardeur
> Qu'oisiveté lascive en soy-mesmes enserre. . . .
> De qui fus-tu nourry ? D'une douce beauté,
> Qui eut pour la servir jeunesse et vanité.
> De quoy te repais-tu ? D'une belle lumière.[1]

---

[1] Desportes adapts an Italian sonnet by Pamphilo Sasso, which was published as early as 1519 at Venice. Sasso's sonnet opens :

> 'Quando nascesti, amor ? quando la terra
> Si reuesti de uerde : e bel colore
> Dhe che sei generato ? dun ardore
> Che occio lasciuo in se rachiuda :' &c.

Before Desportes' time Sasso's poem was independently turned into Latin by the Scotsman, George Buchanan, while domiciled in France.

> Quis puer ales ? Amor. Genitor quis ? Blandus ocelli
> Ardor. Quo natus tempore ? Vere novo.
> Quis locus excepit ? Generosi pectoris aula.
> Quae nutrix ? Primo flore iuventa decens.

(Cf. *Un modèle de Desportes non signalé encore : Pamphilo Sasso*, par MM. Vaganay, et Vianey, Paris, 1903.)

To like effect runs the Earl of Oxford's popular ditty:

When wert thou born, Desire? In pomp and prime of May.
By whom, sweet boy, wert thou begot? By fond Conceit,
    men say.

Shakespeare's

> Tell me, where is fancy bred,
> Or in the heart or in the head?

is in a kindred key. Shakespeare's 'fancy' is 'love'.

There are indeed few lyrical topics to which the French
and English writers failed to apply on some occasion or other
much the same language. Juliet admonishes Romeo not to
swear by the moon:

> O! swear not by the moon, the *inconstant moon*,
> .   .   . Swear by thy gracious self,
> Which is *the god of my idolatry*. (II. ii. 109 sq.)

Some twenty years before, Ronsard had given a like warning
to his mistress Hélène (Livre II, Sonnet xv):

> Je ne veux comparer tes beautés à la lune,
> *La lune est inconstante*, et ton vouloir n'est qu'un; ...
> Tu es toute ton Dieu, *ton astre et ta fortune*.

In a detached poem which Ronsard wrote before 1567
as epilogue of a dramatic performance at the royal palace
of Fontainebleau, he played effectively on a classical figure,
and gave it a new vogue (*Œuvres*, iv. 184):

> Le Monde est le theatre, et les hommes acteurs;
> La Fortune, qui est maistresse de la Sceine,
> Appreste les habits, et de la vie humaine
> Les Cieux et les Destins en sont les spectateurs.
>   En gestes differens, en differens langages,
> Roy, Princes et Bergers jouent leurs personnages
> Devant les yeux de tous, sur l'eschafaut commun.

The famous dialogue on the like theme in which the banished
Duke and the melancholy Jaques engage in Shakespeare's *As
You Like It*, II. vii. 137 *seq*., opens on Ronsard's note:

> *Duke.* This wide and universal theatre
>   Presents more woful pageants than the scene
>   Wherein we play in.
> *Jaq.*   All the world's a stage,
>   And all the men and women merely players.

Jean Bertaut, one of the youngest of Ronsard's disciples, penned at the extreme end of the sixteenth century a poem of which the first stanza runs thus :—

> On ne se souvient que du mal,
>   L'ingratitude regne au monde :
> *L'injure se grave en métal,*
>   *Et le bien-fait s'escrit en l'onde.*

Bertaut, *Œuvres*, ed. Chenevière,
Paris, 1891, p. 365.

The last two lines are barely distinguishable from the familiar words in *Henry VIII* (IV. ii. 45-6):

> Men's evil manners live in brass; their virtues
> We write in water.

Rather more characteristic of the temper of the Pléiade is Lorenzo's beautiful eulogy of music in the *Merchant of Venice*, v. i. 70 seq. All the French poets paid similar tribute to the power of music. Ronsard more than once, alike in prose and in verse, affirmed that a fit appreciation of music was the true test of a good character, while want of appreciation was proof of vicious feeling. ' Celuy,' Ronsard wrote, ' lequel oyant un doux accord d'instrumens ou la douceur de la voyx naturelle, ne s'en resjouist point, ne s'en esmeut point, et de teste en pieds n'en tressault point, comme doucement ravy, et si ne sçay comment derobé hors de soy ; c'est signe qu'il a l'âme tortue, vicieuse, et depravée, et du quel il se faut donner garde, comme de celuy qui n'est point heureusement né.' [1]

---

[1] The passage continues thus:—'Comment se pourroit-on accorder avec un homme qui de son naturel hayt les accords ? Celuy n'est digne de voyr la douce lumière du soleil, qui ne fait honneur à la Musique, comme petite partie de celle, qui si armonieusement (comme dit Platon) agitte tout ce grand univers. Au contraire celuy qui lui porte honneur et reverence est ordinairement homme de bien, il a l'âme saine et gaillarde, et de son naturel ayme les choses haultes, la philosophie, le maniment des affaires politicques, le travail des guerres, et bref en tous offices honorables il fait tousjours apparoistre les estincelles de sa vertu.' (*Œuvres*, ed. Blanchemain, 1866, vii, pp. 337-8.) The passage comes from a 'Preface sur la Musique' by Ronsard to a book called 'Mélanges de cent quarante-huit Chansons tant de vieux auteurs que demodernes, à cinq, six, sept et huit parties, avec une préface de P. de Ronsard' (Paris, Ad. Leroy et Rob. Ballard, 1572, 4to). It is worth noting that the modern French writer Romain Rolland in *Jean*

Shakespeare only slightly varies the language when he repeats the Ronsardian sentiment in the familiar lines—

> The man that hath no music in himself,
> Nor is not mov'd with concord of sweet sounds,
> Is fit for treasons, stratagems, and spoils,
> The motions of his spirit are dull as night,
> And his affections dark as Erebus.
>
> *Merch. of Venice*, v. i. 83-7.

Shakespeare's 'concord of sweet sounds' is Ronsard's 'accord de doux sons'. Ronsard's 'L'âme tortue, vicieuse, et depravée' adumbrates Shakespeare's 'motions' of 'spirit', 'which is fit for treasons.'

Aubades were peculiarly characteristic of French lyric effort. Hundreds of French songs ring variations on Ronsard's lines (*Œuvres*, i. 164):

> Mignonne, levez vous, vous estes paresseuse;
> Ja la gaye alouette au ciel a fredonné, . . .
> Sus! debout! allons voir l'herbelette perleuse,
> Et votre beau rosier de boutons couronné,
> Et vos œillets mignons ausquels aviez donné
> Hier au soir de l'eau d'une main si soigneuse.

Almost daily was the dawn saluted thus (Ronsard, *Œuvres*, vi. 364):

> Iô, que je voy de roses
> Ja décloses
> Par l'Orient flamboyant :
> A voir des nües diverses
> Les traverses
> Voicy le jour ondoyant.
> Voicy l'Aube safranée
> Qui ja née
> Couvre d'œillets et de fleurs
> Le Ciel qui le jour desserre,
> Et la terre
> De rosées et de pleurs.
> Debout doncq', Aube sacrée. . . .

Christophe à Paris, Dans la Maison, 1909, p. 179, makes a character (Arnaud) quote the sentences of Ronsard given in our text. The quotation is followed by this conversation : 'Je connais cela, dit Christophe : c'est de mon ami Shakespeare.—Non, dit Arnaud doucement, c'est d'un Français qui vivait avant lui, c'est de notre Ronsard.'

Shakespeare seems to have subtilized the essence—melody and sentiment together—of this blithe form of French song with its Anacreontic lilt, in such a glorified ebullition as this:

> Hark! hark! the lark at heaven's gate sings,
>   And Phoebus 'gins arise
> His steeds to water at those springs
>   On chalic'd flowers that lies;
> And winking mary-buds begin
>   To ope their golden eyes:
> With every thing that pretty is,
>   My lady sweet, arise; Arise, arise!

Shakespeare's original genius worked here in all its freshness. Yet there is hardly a syllable in Shakespeare's far-famed greeting of the dawn which cannot be independently matched in the verse of the Pléiade. The song of the lark at heaven's gate, the mythological touch about the watering of Phoebus's steeds, the marigold's or mary-buds' welcome of the sun, the drops of dew in the cups of flowers, the enveloping air of sweetness and light, all breathes a note more characteristic of a French than of an English atmosphere. Differences of expression might be consistent with accidental coincidences, were the poem considered in isolation. But the circumstances of environment offer powerful hint of nearer kinship.

Thus far, I have dealt with assimilation of French suggestion in Elizabethan lyric verse (outside the scope of the sonnet). But the situation cannot be fully appreciated without some examination of the many short poems of lyric character, which, in spite of tacit avowals of originality, belong to the category of literal translation from the French. The Elizabethan sonnet offers a rich harvest in this branch of comparative study; it is other forms of verse which are at present under survey. The poet Lodge is the chief worker in the literal manner of conveyance. But he does not stand alone. Samuel Daniel laboured in the same medium, and a writer of the learning of George Chapman is a third conspicuous practitioner in this misty field of literary labour, while Drummond of Hawthornden, whose Elizabethan affinities are unquestioned, is a brilliant member of the plagiarizing brother-

hood.   The serious Chapman's activity in this branch of effort
is as notable as any.   In one of Chapman's earliest volumes
entitled *Ovid's Banquet of Sence* there figures a poem
in thirty six-line stanzas entitled *The Amorous Zodiacke*.
It is a pedantic love-poem portraying celestial influences
on phases of the poet's passion.   Although Chapman gives
no hint of his indebtedness, no word of his text is original.
Throughout, he is anglicizing a French poem with the same
title and in the same metre by Gilles Durant.   Durant calls
his mistress Charlotte; Chapman preserves her anonymity by
calling her 'gracious Love'.   There is hardly any other change.
Durant, a lyrist who showed elsewhere no mean grace or
facility, published this rather clumsy piece in Paris in 1588,
only seven years before Chapman printed his version in London
in 1595.   The latter's method may be gauged by citation of
the concluding stanza in the two languages [1] :

Gilles Durant.	Chapman.
Charlote, si le ciel ialoux de mon enuie	But, gracious Love, if jealous heaven deny
Par si beau changement ne veut heurer ma vie,	My life this truly-blest variety,
Tu ne lairras pourtant de luyre à l'univers ;	Yet will I thee through all the world disperse ;
Sinon dedans le Ciel entre les feux celestes,	If not in heaven, amongst those braving fires,
Pour le moins icy bas tes beautez manifestes	Yet here thy beauties (which the world admires)
Comme les feux du Ciel luiront dedans mes vers.	Bright as those flames shall glister in my verse.

Lodge's activities in the like direction are, as far as his
French debt is concerned, more varied.   Desportes is his chief
quarry.[2]   But Ronsard and Baïf lie within the scope of his raids.
At times he puts his lyric gifts to effective purpose, even in the
process of transference.   The following English stanza is a
manifest improvement on Desportes' original :—

[1] Both poems are printed at length in Appendix II.
[2] In his *Romance of Rosalynd*, Lodge places a song in the French
language in the mouth of his shepherd Montanus, and gives no hint that
it is other than his own composition.   It is a 'chanson' literally tran-
scribed from the first book of Desportes' *Amours de Diane* (ed. Michiels,
p. 30): 'Hélas! tyran plein de rigueur', &c.

DESPORTES, *Diane*, II. xviii (ed. Michiels, p. 110).

On verra défaillir tous les astres aux cieux,
Les poissons à la mer, le sable à son rivage,
Au soleil des rayons bannisseurs de l'ombrage,
La verdure et les fleurs au printemps gracieux :
Plutôt que la fureur des rapports envieux
Efface en mon esprit un trait de votre image.

LODGE, Verses from *Rosalynde*, 1590 (1819 ed., p. 80).

First shall the heavens want starry light,
The seas be robbed of their waves ;
The day want sun, and sun want bright,
The night want shade, the dead men graves ;
The April flowers and leaf and tree,
Before I false my faith to thee.'

Yet often Lodge refrains from adding anything to his French original. Thus, he turns two famous sonnets by Desportes— one on a hermit's life and the other of Love's shipwreck— into English songs without substantial change of thought or word.[1]

DESPORTES, *Diane*, II. viii (ed. Michiels, p. 71).

Je me veux rendre hermite et faire penitence
De l'erreur de mes yeux pleins de temerité,
Dressant mon hermitage en un lieu deserté,
Dont nul autre qu'amour n'aura la connaissance.

LODGE, *Scillaes Metamorphosis*, 1589 (1819 ed., p. 59).

I will become a hermit now,
And do my penance straight
For all the errors of mine eyes
With foolish rashness filled.
My hermitage shall placed be
Where melancholy's weight
And none but love alone shall know
The bower I mean to build.

Diane I. xviii (ed. Michiels, p. 40).

Ma nef passe au destroit d'une mer courroucée,
Toute comble d'oubly, l'hiver à la minuict ;
Un aveugle, un enfant, sans souci la conduit,
Desireux de la voir sous les eaux renversée.

Verses from *Rosalynde*, 1590 (1819 ed., p. 102).

My boat doth pass the straits
Of seas incensed with fire,
Filled with forgetfulness,
Amid the winter's night ;
A blind and careless boy,
Brought up by fond desire.
Doth guide me in the sea
Of sorrow and despite.

Again, Desportes' greeting of Spring is handled by Lodge after the same fashion :

[1] Only the first stanzas of the poems are given here. The whole appears in French and English in Appendix I.

DESPORTES (ed. Michiels, p. 84).	LODGE, 1589 (1819 ed., p. 63).
La terre, nagueres glacée,	The earth late choked with showers,
Est ores de vert tapissée,	Is now arrayed in green:
Son sein est embelly de fleurs,	Her bosom springs with flowers;
L'air est encor amoureux d'elle,	The air dissolves her teen;
Le ciel rit de la voir si belle,	The heavens laugh at her glory,
Et moy j'en augmente mes pleurs.	Yet bide I sad and sorry.'[1]

Probably the most notable of Lodge's work in this branch of effort is a long poem in fifteen stanzas on the joys of a simple life. Here Desportes' original is far more deftly turned than Lodge's barefaced plagiarism. The following stanza in the two versions is characteristic of the whole:—

DESPORTES (ed. Michiels, p. 432).	LODGE (1819 ed., p. 44).
Dans les palais enflez de vaine pompe	Amidst the palace brave puffed up with wanton shows
L'ambition, la faveur qui nous trompe,	Ambitions dwell, and there false favours find disguise,
Et les soucys logent communément;	There lodge consuming cares that hatch our common woes;
Dedans nos champs se retirent les fées,	Amidst our painted fields the pleasant Fairy lies,
Roines des bois à tresses décoiffées,	And all those powers divine, that with untrussed tresses,
Les jeux, l'amour et le contentement.	Contentment, happy love, and perfect sport professes.

' Untrussed tresses ' is hardly a felicitous version of ' tresses décoiffées '.

No variation of Lodge's dependent method is discernible in his treatment of Ronsard's shorter poems. Ronsard's song of the swallow is rendered with very inadequate acknowledgement by Lodge thus :

RONSARD, Odes, V. xx (1553); Œuvres, ii, p. 358.	LODGE, William Longbeard, 1593. 'Imitation of a Sonnet in an ancient French poet' (1819 ed., p. 114).
Si tost que tu sens arriver	As soon as thou dost see the winter
La froide saison de l'hyver,	clad in cold,
En septembre, chère arondelle,	Within September on the eaves in
Tu t'en-voles bien loin de nous ;	sundry forms to fold,
Puis tu reviens, quand le temps doux	Sweet swallow, far thou fliest, till to our native clime
Au mois d'Avril se renouvelle.	In pleasant April Phoebus' rays return the sweeter time.

[1] See A. H. Bullen, *Lyrics from Elizabethan Romances*, 1890, pp. vii–ix.

The precise extent to which Lodge's and Chapman's mode of literal transference spread in Elizabethan literature cannot be determined till all the voluminous poetry of Italy as well as of France has been thoroughly ransacked. Almost infinite time must be devoted to a searching comparison before the full truth will be known.

The vogue which the practice enjoyed among the Elizabethans stoutly maintained its hold in the next generation. Early in the seventeenth century, William Drummond of Hawthornden, the Scottish poet whose lyric genius seems steeped in Elizabethan tradition, bore exceptionally convincing testimony to the persistence of the Elizabethan habit of secret borrowing from contemporary French verse. Very often do Drummond's lyrics appear to echo the genuine Elizabethan strain, and very curious is it to learn that the affinity usually comes of almost direct translation from the French. Drummond's debts to the poets of the Pléiade and to Desportes are conspicuous; but more worthy of notice is his dependence on less famous French poets whose activities were strictly contemporary with his own. Of these Jean Passerat has habitually perhaps the lightest touch and best lyric faculty. A chanson by him in the form of a dialogue between La Pastourelle and Le Pastoureau was turned by Drummond into a lyric idyll which seems to present almost all the essential features of Elizabethan song. The two poems should be closely compared. The opening and closing lines run thus in French and English :

PASSERAT, *Les Poesies Françaises* (ed. Blanchemain, i. 141).

La Pastourelle. Pastoureau, m'aimes-tu bien?
Le Pastoureau. Je t'aime, Dieu sçait combien.
La P. Comme quoi?

Le P. Comme toi,
Ma rebelle
Pastourelle.

DRUMMOND OF HAWTHORNDEN, *Phyllis and Damon* (Poems, ed. W. C. Ward, ii. 159).

Phyllis. Shepherd, dost thou love me well?
Damon. Better than weak words can tell.
Ph. Like to what, good shepherd, say?
Da. Like to thee, fair, cruel may.

La P. En rien ne m'a contenté
Ce propos trop affetté,
Pastoureau, sans moquerie
M'aimes-tu? di, je te prie.
Comme quoi?

Le P. Comme toi,
Ma rebelle
Pastourelle.

La P. Tu m'eusses répondu mieus,
Je t'aime comme mes yeux.

Le P. Trop de haine je leur porte :
Car ils ont ouvert la porte
Aus peines que j'ay receu,
Des lors que je t'apperçeu :
Quand ma liberté fut prise
De ton œil qui me mais-
trise . . .

La P. Comme quoi?

Le P. Comme toi,
Ma rebelle
Pastourelle.

La P. Laisse là ce 'Comme toi' :
Di, je t'aime comme moi.

Le P. Je ne m'aime pas moy-
mesmes.
Di moi doncques, si tu
m'aimes

La P. Comme quoi?

Le P. Comme toi,
Ma rebelle
Pastourelle.

Ph. O how strange these words I
find !
Yet, to satisfy my mind,
Shepherd, without mocking me,
Have I any love for thee,
Like to what, good shepherd,
say?

Da. Like to thee, fair, cruel may.

Ph. Better answer had it been
To say thou lov'd me as thine
eyne.

Da. Woe is me, these I love not,
For by them love entrance
got,
At that time they did behold
Thy sweet face and locks of
gold . . .

Ph. Like to what, good shepherd,
say?

Da. Like to thee, fair, cruel may.

Ph. Leave, I pray, this 'Like to
thee',
And say, I love as I do me.

Da. Alas! I do not love myself,
For I'm split on beauty's
shelf.

Ph. Like to what, good shepherd,
say?

Da. Like to thee, fair, cruel may.[1]

In all probability French poetry was put by the Elizabethan lyrists under heavier contribution than the Italian, but the exact ratio is yet to be ascertained. The poet Daniel laid impartial hands on contemporary verse of both countries. Drummond was no less liberal or catholic in his concealed translation of foreign verse. By way of evidence that the contemporary mode of appropriating Italian poetry was indistinguishable from that which was applied to French poetry, extracts may be cited from Daniel's melodious ode

---

[1] This discovery of Drummond's indebtedness is one of the many debts that students owe to Prof. Kastner. (See his 'Drummond of Hawthornden and the French Poets of the Sixteenth Century' in *The Modern Language Review*, vol. v, No. 1, January, 1910, p. 49.)

(on the Golden Age) which literally translates without any acknowledgement the metre and words of a lyric chorus in Tasso's pastoral play of *Aminta*.

TASSO, *Aminta*, Atto I. Sc. 2 (last chorus).

DANIEL, *Delia*.

TASSO	DANIEL
O bella età de l'oro,	O happy golden age!
Non già perchè di latte	Not for that Rivers ran
Sen' corse il fiume, e stillò mele il bosco,	With streams of milk, and Honey dropt from Trees;
Non perchè i frutti loro	Not that the earth did gage
Dier da l' aratro intatte	Unto the Husbandman
Le terre, e gli angui errar senz' ira, o tosco,	Her voluntary fruits, free without Fees,
Non perchè nuuol fosco	Not for no cold did freeze,
Non spiego allhor suo velo,	Nor any cloud beguile
Ma, in Primavera eterna	The eternal flowering Spring,
C' hora s'accende, e verna,	Wherein lived every thing;
Rise di luce, e di sereno il Cielo	And whereon th' heavens perpetually did smile;
Nè portò peregrino	Not for no ship had brought
O guerra, o merce, à gli altrui lidi il pino.	From foreign shores or wars or wares ill sought.
. . . .	. . . .
Amiam, che 'l Sol si muove, et poi renasce.	Let's love—the sun doth set and rise again,
A noi sua breve luce	But when as our short Light
S'asconde, e 'l sonno eterna notte adduce.	Comes once to set, it makes Eternal night.

IX

THE METRICAL DEBT OF THE ELIZABETHAN LYRIC OTHER THAN THE SONNET

In an inquiry into the relation of the Elizabethan lyric or short poem with the work of the Pléiade, form and sentiment, thought and style, metre and vocabulary, all come within the limits of the survey.[1]

The significance of the metrical debt may be at the outset inferred from the circumstance that the technical terms of the lyric art, although of Greek origin, reached the Elizabethans directly from France. The word 'lyric' itself, like 'ode' and 'hymn' (in its original secular sense), is an Elizabethan loan from the French, and was unknown to England at any

---

[1] Detailed notice of the sonnet is postponed to section XII *infra*.

earlier epoch.   The same story is to be told of the word
'sonnet'.   Although of Italian origin it was thoroughly
gallicized by the Pléiade.   'Amour,' which enjoyed a wide
vogue in France as a synonym, was also adopted by the
Elizabethans.   Drayton, like Ronsard and Desportes, called
his sonnets 'Amours'.[1]   But the alternative title was short-
lived.   The term 'sonnet' came to prevail in England no less
than in France.[2]   'Complainte' is another French poetic
term, which was often used in the sense of elegy.   A section
of Marot's work is headed *Complaintes*, and separate poems
are thus designated throughout the work of the Pléiade.
Spenser or his editor had the French terminology in mind
when he called one of his collection of miscellaneous poems
Complaints.

A peculiar episode in the early day of Elizabethan prosody
shows the closeness with which metrical developments at
home marched in foreign footsteps.   A warm controversy
respecting the adaptation to lyric poetry of the rhymeless
quantitative metres of Latin and Greek opened in Elizabethan
England just as the like debate was closing in France.   The
strenuous plea for 'vers mesurés' which Baïf, a leader of
the Pléiade, had raised in Paris, was soon reflected in an
effort to acclimatize hexameter and pentameter, sapphics and
alcaics, in Elizabethan London.[3]

---

[1] Another Elizabethan sonneteer, Thomas Watson, fancifully rendered
the French word 'Amour' in this connexion by the English word 'Passion'
(i. e. love), and dubbed his quatorzains 'passions'.

[2] The use of 'air' in the sense of song or melody first reached England
from France in Elizabeth's time.   The French word which was derived
from the Italian *aria* does not seem to have been known in France before
the middle of the sixteenth century, and Adrien Le Roy, the composer of
the famous French music book *Livre d'airs de cour miz sur le luth* (1571),
calls attention in the dedication to the fact that light songs which had
hitherto been known as 'voix de ville' had now first changed their name to
'*airs* de cour'.   Shakespeare appears to have been the first English writer
to use the word in a musical sense in the phrase 'your tongue's sweet *air*'
(*M.N.D.* i. i. 83).   Shortly afterwards the term was in common employment.   The musician Morley, in his 'Introduction to Music', 1597,
remarks that 'all kinds of light music except the madrigal are by a
generall name called *ayres*'.

[3] Some echoes of the French controversy over 'vers mesurés' in
Elizabethan England are very distinct.   Lodge heads one of his earliest

Gabriel Harvey, who shared Baïf's pedantry without his poetic sentiment, repeated Baïf's adventures on English soil. With Baïf Harvey denounced rhyme and accent as ungainly barbarisms. He himself not only practised the quantitative principle, but pressed his argument on his admiring disciples, Sir Philip Sidney and Edmund Spenser, the true heralds of the Elizabethan triumph. Under Harvey's auspices a literary club was formed at a nobleman's house—at the Earl of Leicester's house—in London, and was christened the 'Areopagus'. The chief members of the club—Harvey, Spenser, and Sidney—, all for a time discussed approvingly the classical theory of prosody, and upheld it on much the same grounds as had called into existence, a dozen years before, Baïf's poetic Academy of Paris. Like Baïf's pupils, Sidney and Spenser gradually perceived the underlying fallacy of Harvey's pedantry, and breaking away from Harvey's toils they brought the Areopagus and its ideals to an early end. In Elizabethan England no less effectively than in sixteenth-century France, the ineptitude of experiments in unrhymed classical metres disposed of the claims of classical prosody to regulate modern poetry. When the claims of quantity to take the place of accent were finally dismissed, the classical champions in England, as in France, concentrated their attack on rhyme. Thomas Campion, himself a master of rhyming melody, pleaded for the rejection of rhyme as late as 1602. He was answered by Samuel Daniel in his *Defense of Rhyme*, but Campion's own command of rhyming harmonies is the best confutation of his argument. George Chapman, a finished classical scholar, spoke a wise word on the general controversy in one of his earliest poems:

lyrics *Beauties Lullabie* (1589), for which he doubtfully asserts complete originality, with the suggestive words 'non mesurée'. Most of Ronsard's odes have the same heading by way of warning that he refused to write in 'vers mesurés' in accordance with the classical scheme of quantitative prosody. The French phrase 'vers mesuré' is not uncommon in Elizabethan literature in the form 'measured verse'. Some belated experiments figure in Davison's *Poetical Rhapsody*, 1602, which is said to contain 'Diuerse Sonnets, Odes, Elegies, Madrigalls, and other Poesies, both in Rime and *Measured Verse*'.

> Sweet poesy
> Will not be clad in her supremacy
> With those strange garments, Rome's hexameters,
> As she is English: but.in right prefers
> Our native robes put on with skilful hands—
> English heroics—to those antique garlands.
> *Shadow of Night,* ii. 86-91.

Baïf's censorious critics in France brought no surer logic than lurks in these lines of Chapman to bear on the metrical heresy of a pedantic classicism. Little doubt is possible that the English controversy is a pale reflection of the French.[1]

The versatility which Ronsard and his disciples betrayed in the rhyming schemes of their lyric stanzas on the accentual principle early attracted the notice of Elizabethan poets, and doubtless contributed to the discomfiture of classical pedantry. Almost all the new rhyming strophes of Elizabethan song were in earlier use by the poets of the Pléiade, before they were planted on English soil. The permutations of rhyme in five- and six-lined stanzas of the Pléiade are wellnigh infinite. Elizabethan prosodists were far less enterprising, but their echoes are numerous and varied. Drayton imitated one of the most familiar French schemes of rhyme *aabab* in the five-lined stanzas of his ode *To Himself and the Harp*.[2] Again, among Ronsard's many personal inventions was a five-line stanza rhyming *ababa*. With admirable effect Shakespeare employed this melodious scheme

---

[1] Ronsard's friend, Cardinal du Perron (1556-1618), condemned Baïf's prosodic principles of quantity (i. e. long and short syllables) in terms which have a qualified application to English verse: ' Notre langue n'est pas capable de vers mesurez, premièrement parce qu'elle n'a point de longues, et se prononce quasi tout d'une teneur sans changement de voix.' (*Perroniana,* ed. 1669, Paris, p. 249.)

[2] The metre of Drayton's lyric may be compared with that of an ode of Baïf in his *Amours de Francine,* Bk. iii (*Poésies Choisies,* ed. Becq de Fouquières, 1874, p. 147).

DRAYTON.

And why not I, as *he*
That's greatest, if as *free,*
    In sundry strains that *strive,*
Since there so many *be,*
    Th' old lyric kind *revive.*

BAÏF.

Amour, voulant à mon des*tin*
Metre une fois heureuse *fin,*
    M'a mené voir la *belle*
A qui deu je vivois, à *fin*
    D'estre serviteur d'*elle.*

with slight variation of the length of line, in his far-famed song, 'Who is Sylvia?' Ronsard contrived the strophe thus :

> Versons ces roses en ce *vin*,
>   En ce bon vin versons ces *roses*,
> Et boivons l'un à l'autre, *afin*
> Qu'au cœur nos tristesses *encloses*
> Prennent en boivant quelque *fin*.[1]

Shakespeare worked the French scheme of rhyme to this purpose :

> Is she kind as she is *fair* ?
> For beauty lives with *kindness* ;
> Love doth to her eyes *repair*
> To help him of his *blindness*;
> And, being helped, inhabits *there*.
>   *Two Gent. of Verona*, IV. ii. 45–9.

Another invention of the Pléiade was the four-lined stanza of Tennyson's *In Memoriam*. The French poets commonly composed it of eight-syllable lines, as in the standard Tennysonian version, but six-, ten-, and even twelve-syllable lines are also occasionally found. It was Sir Philip Sidney who inaugurated English experiments with the stanza, and he loosely imitated the normal octosyllabic version of contemporary France : but the eight syllables of the first and fourth lines dwindle to seven in the second and third. One of Sidney's stanzas runs thus :

> Have I caught my heav'nly jewel
> Teaching sleep most fair to be?
> Now will I teach her that she
> When she wakes is too, too cruel.

The English poem catches the metre and sentiment of such an effort as Du Bellay's *Baiser* :

> Quand ton col de couleur de rose
> Se donne à mon embrassement
> Et ton œil languist doucement
> D'une paupière à demi close, &c.[2]

---

[1] *Œuvres*, ed. Blanchemain, ii. 291.
[2] One of the best examples of the Pléiade's employment of this metre in octosyllabics is Ronsard's well-known ode *Magie, ou délivrance d'Amour*. Jean Bertaut, the youngest disciple of the Pléiade school,

Only less prominent than the 'sonnet' (which is to be considered hereafter) in the history of the Elizabethan lyric, is the 'ode', of which the French kinship is never much concealed. The 'odes' which won widest favour among the Elizabethans might often be justly entitled 'songs'. Their affinity with Horatian poetry is unquestionable, but it was the French adaptation of the Horatian vogue which explains the entry of the 'ode' into Elizabethan England. One of Ronsard's early boasts was that he was the first of Europeans to adapt to a modern language the Pindaric ode, with its division into epode, strophe, and antistrophe. But this elaboration was quickly dropped, and Ronsard and his friends, following the example of Horace's 'carmina' or 'epodae', reduced the 'ode' to an uninterrupted series of regular brief stanzas, varying in number at the will of the poet, but uniform in construction through the length of each poem. Odes, short or long, on this simple plan fill the pages of the Pléiade, and in the last decade of the sixteenth century they were eagerly imitated by Shakespeare's fellow countrymen.

The poetaster Soothern introduced the word and the form into the English language in 1584 when he published his volume of crude imitations of Ronsard. Barnabe Barnes was the first Elizabethan of any real promise to publish a collection of 'odes' in 1593. The prosody of Barnes's varied stanzas is nearly allied to France. The metrical versatility of his 'odes' cannot be matched elsewhere. The truer poet Drayton was the most vigorous contriver of Elizabethan 'odes', and his efforts again followed current French usage. Horace, to whom he pays vague tribute, gave him added suggestion at first hand, and there is originality in the development of his themes and in the manipulation of his strophes. But Drayton repeatedly accepts a French cue for both topic and metre, although he stops far short of plagiarism. His 'ode', *To Himself and the Harp*, echoes Ronsard's ode *A sa lyre*

employed Alexandrines in this four-lined stanza. Ben Jonson and Lord Herbert of Cherbury, who both used the stanza, seem to have borrowed it anew direct from the French, and to have known little of Sidney's pioneer effort.

more closely than Horace's *Ad lyram* (I. xxxii). As heir of 'Apollo and the Nine' Drayton here claims with Ronsard the praise of reviving 'th' old lyric kind' which Pindar and Horace dignified. But the English poet, unlike Ronsard, made no trial of the Pindaric ode. Drayton's praise of Pindar, 'that great Greek,' is merely a pale reflection of Horatian eulogy of Pindar as it was enshrined in Ronsard's verse. Drayton's companion salutation of Horace strikes boldly a French note.[1] Drayton's ode, *To the New Year*, is of similar kinship to Du Bellay's ode, *Du premier jour de l'an*, and he introduces the poem with Du Bellay's apostrophe to the statue of double-faced Janus. Ronsard's Anacreontic enthusiasm for the rose, which inspired at least three of his most tuneful odes, as well as many fine sonnets,[2] is the obvious source of Drayton's Anacreontic ode in praise of the same flower. Here Drayton plays slight variations on Ronsard's metre, but Ronsard's sentiment fully retains in its English garb its Anacreontic fragrance. In the English poet's ode, *To the Virginian Voyage*, the topic travels far from French bounds; but the rhyming involutions respect a French metrical scheme.

Occasionally an Elizabethan 'ode' renders with absolute literalness both the words and metre of Ronsard. There is no mistaking the source of Lodge's 'ode' in his romance of *William Longbeard*, which he published as an original composition. The first stanza in French and English runs thus:

---

[1] Acknowledgements to 'les deux harpeurs', Horace and Pindar often figure conjointly in Ronsard: cf.

> 'Je pillay Thebe et saccageay la Pouille (i. e. Apulia),
> T'enrichissant de leur belle despouille.' (*Œuvres*, ii, p. 128.)

Drayton, in the same 'ode', commends Soothern, the first imitator in England of the Ronsardian ode; he calls Soothern 'An English lyrick'.

[2] Cf.:—
> Sur toute fleurette déclose
> J'aime la senteur de la rose. (*Œuvres*, ii, p. 342.)
> Dieu te gard, l'honneur du Printemps. (*ib.* ii, p. 430.)
> Douce, belle, gentille et bien-flairante Rose. (*ib.* i, p. 152.)

Drayton's eighth 'ode' opens—
> Sing we the rose
> Than which no flower there grows
> Is sweeter:
> And aptly her compare, &c.

All the members of Ronsard's school pay like tributes to the rose.

Ronsard, *Odes*, v. 17 (1553); *Œuvres*, ii, p. 356.	Lodge, 'An ode' from *William Longbeard*, 1593. (1819 ed., p. 117.)
Puis que tost je doy reposer	Since that I must repose
Outre l'infernale rivière,	Beyond th' infernal lake,
Hé! que me sert de composer	What vails me to compose
Autant de vers qu'a fait Homère?	As many verses as Homer did make?[1]

Elizabethan ears were captivated by the varied charms of French prosody. Tributes to its seductive melody occasionally took, in the Elizabethan lyric, the shape of a refrain in the French language. Robert Greene, one of the earliest song writers of the genuine Elizabethan stamp, has more than one song on this pattern, which recalls many a popular villanelle or chansonnette of Ronsard's school:

> Sweet Adon', darest not glance thine eye,
> *N'oserez-vous, mon bel amy?*
> Upon thy Venus that must die,
> *Je vous en prie*, pity me;
> *N'oserez-vous, mon bel, mon bel,*
> *N'oserez-vous, mon bel amy?*[2]

X

The Pléiade Vocabulary in Elizabethan Poetry

In adorning his verse with snatches of French, Greene was pursuing a custom which was congenial to Elizabethan poets. The poets' familiarity with the language of the Pléiade may well be illustrated from Shakespeare's usage. The three

---

[1] The whole poem is quoted in Appendix I.

[2] Greene's *Works*, ed. Churton Collins, ii. 289. Less pleasing is *Mullidore's Madrigal*, a poem similarly constructed (in Greene's *Never too late*, 1590), of which the second stanza runs—

> Thy beauty, my love, exceedeth supposes,
> Thy hair is a nettle for the nicest roses,
> *Mon dieu, aide moy,*
> That I with the primrose of my fresh wit
> May tumble her tyranny under my feet,
> *Hé donque ie sera un ieune roy,*
> *Trop belle pour moy, hélas hélas,*
> *Trop belle pour moy, voilà mon trespas.*

Greene's *Works*, ed. Churton Collins, ii. 304.

scenes penned in the French tongue in *Henry V*, though defi-
cient in idiomatic grace, indicate facility in speaking and writing.
But the most convincing proof of his own and his fellow
writers' indulgent regard for the French language is found
in their occasional employment in an English context of pure
French words which had never been anglicized. The habit
was of old standing, but Shakespeare especially gave it a new
vogue. No importance attaches to his fondness for French
words like ' foison ' (i.e. plenty, harvest), or ' carcanet ' (a
diminutive of ' carcan ', necklace), or ' sans ', the French pre-
position (meaning without), because earlier English writers had
already shown these expressions much favour. The crucial point
is that Shakespeare grafts on his own English speech for the
first and only time numerous French colloquialisms. In one of
the best-known passages in *Macbeth* (II. i. 46) the hero descries
' *gouts* of blood ' on the blade and dudgeon of the phantasmal
dagger. ' Gouts ' is the French ' gouttes ' (i.e. drops). No
Englishman is known to have used the word, either before or
since save in quotation from this passage. In like manner
Othello, in his traveller's tale (I. iii. 140), speaks to Desdemona
of ' *antres* vast '. ' Antres,' which is another ἅπαξ λεγόμενον
in English, is prominent in the latinized vocabulary of the
Pléiade. It is the word which solemnly ushers in one of the
most famous and touching of Ronsard's poems, his world-
renowned *De l'Élection d'un Sépulcre* which has for its
first line : ' *Antres* et vous fontaines.' Again, ' *scrimers* ,' in
Hamlet, is Shakespeare's unique anglicization of the French
' escrimeurs ' (i. e. fencers) which is claimed as an invention of
Ronsard.[1] Robert Greene seems to have been the first to
employ the common French word ' *œillade* ' (i.e. glance or
wink). Shakespeare employed it twice, and with him its
English use for the period ended. The many Elizabethan

---

[1] The mention in *All's Well*, I. iii. 57, of ' Young Charbon the Puritan
and old Poysam the Papist ' betrays the same predilection for French
words. ' Charbon ' is no doubt an intentional corruption of ' chair bonne '
(i. e. good flesh) and ' poysam ' is a corruption of ' poisson ' (i. e. fish).
There is an ironical reference to the Lenten fare of Puritan and Papist,
the Papist's parade of a fish diet during Lent impelling the Puritan to
insist on a meat diet at that season.

substantives ending in *-ure* (the French *-eur*)—'rondure,'
'defeature,' 'rejoindure,' 'enacture,' 'recomforture '—are borrowed from France. These words Shakespeare employed
more liberally than any contemporary.

At times Shakespeare adapts a French phrase to English
speech. Twice he echoes the French 'grand jour' or 'grand
matin ', and writes of ' great morning' where he means 'broad
day '. When Autolycus in *Winter's Tale*, IV. ii. 9, sings of
' the lark that tirra-lirra chants', he borrows the French
onomatopoeic rendering of the lark's note, to which Ronsard
first gave a general vogue in his splendid ode, *L'Alouette* :

> Tu dis en l'air de si doux sons
> Composez de *ta tirelire*,
> Qu'il n'est amant qui ne desire,
> T'oyant *chanter* au renouveau,
> Comme toy devenir oyseau.[1]

But the vocabulary of the Elizabethan poets owes to the
Pléiade a more impressive debt than scattered words and
phrases. A novel principle of word-composition was borrowed from France. Of none of his innovations was Ronsard
prouder than of his introduction into French poetry of
compound words or double epithets. His fancy was caught
in youth by the compound epithets of Homer, and he framed
the rule that a poet should freely invent and employ such
formations provided that they could be made graceful and
pleasant to the ear. Ronsard quickly learnt the trick

---

[1] *Œuvres*, ed. Blanchemain, vi. 348. Du Bartas, after his wont,
bombastically exaggerated Ronsard's identification of the word 'tire-lire'
with the lark: cf.

> La gentille Alouette avec son *tire-lire*
> Tire l'ire à l'iré ; et *tire-lirant* tire
> Vers la voute du ciel ; puis son vol vers ce lieu
> Vire, et desire dire, 'àdieu Dieu, àdieu Dieu.'
> *Semaine I—Cinquiesme jour* (ed. 1615), p. 124.

'Tire-lire' is rarely found in English, although Thomas Muffet in his
Silkworms and their flies (1599) absurdly calls larks, after Du Bartas's
manner, 'tyry-tyry-leerers.' In the lines—

> the lark whose notes do beat
> *The vaulty heaven* so high above our heads.
> (*Romeo and Juliet*, III. v. 21–2.)

Shakespeare comes near Du Bartas's ' L'alouette tirelirant *vers la voute
du ciel*', but here the English poet ignores the bird's 'tire-lire'.

and taught it far and wide. Occasionally but rarely in old French, double words were used figuratively as proper nouns, chiefly in comic verse or in satiric prose, like our own 'Chicken-heart' or 'Hot-spur'. But the practice was rare, and was unrecognized in serious literature. Ronsard proceeded on different lines. He was the first modern European writer to create adjectives and epithets out of combinations of two separate words which were often different parts of speech, and he claimed that his 'vocables composez' sufficiently differed from any antique pattern to secure for them the credit of originality. Examples abound : To gold he applies such epithets as *chasse-peine* (trouble-chasing), *donne-vie* (life-giving), *oste-soin* (care-dispersing). The sea he describes as *embrace-terre* (earth-embracing). A mistress is distinguished as *aime-joie* (joy-loving) ; or *humble-fière* (humble in pride) ; Jove as *darde-tonnerre* (thunder-darting); Love as *doux-amer* (bitter-sweet).

Ronsard's 'vocables composez' are to be reckoned by hundreds, and follow any number of systems. Now he joins together two nouns, now two adjectives, elsewhere a verb and a noun or a noun and an adjective. He is extremely fond of prefacing substantives with the verbs *aime-*, *porte-*, and *garde-*. As many as 125 of the second formation and 50 of the first and third have been catalogued. Adverbial prefixes, *bien-*, *mal-*, *non-*, *demi-*, or *tout-*, are even more common. The practice was accepted loyally and eagerly by Ronsard's disciples, and some greatly extended its use. In Du Bartas's religious poem of *La Semaine* these compound epithets are to be counted by the gross, and descend to grotesque extravagances.

The compound epithet came to be recognized in France as a peculiar badge of the Pléiade and a chief element in its reform of poetic speech, but there were early signs that the method of word-formation was capable of abuse. When in 1579 the affectations of the school were submitted to fierce criticism on patriotic grounds by Henri Étienne, in *La Précellence du langage françois*, he bitterly complains of the excess to which the new process of epithet-making had been carried. Étienne regarded the practice, when worked with discretion and moderation, as an ornament to the language. 'But,' said Étienne, quoting an old Greek proverb, 'Ronsard and his friends had sown with the sack and not with the hand.'[1]

The vogue soon spread to England. The compound epithet is one of the most conspicuous gifts which the lyric effort of the Pléiade made to the vocabulary of Elizabethan poetry. Nothing resembling it is found in English literature of an earlier date, and on its arrival in Elizabethan England it was greeted as a stranger from France. The satirist Joseph Hall noticed how Sir Philip Sidney, who liberally assimilated Ronsardian as well as Petrarchan thought and expression, 'drew new elegance from France.' Hall specified the English poet's habit 'in epithets to join two words in one' as the chief French device of his adoption. Hall sagaciously deprecates exaggeration of the habit, which is readily marred by excess of 'liberty'.[2] Nashe similarly made it a chief reproach against the English tongue that of all languages it most 'swarmeth with the single money of monosyllables'. Nashe argued that the defect could only be remedied by the admission of 'compound words' from abroad. The Pléiade furnished Shakespeare's contemporaries with the chief remedy for cure of monosyllabic tendencies, and they availed themselves freely of the French corrective.

Sidney may claim the honour of first introducing the English reader to Ronsard's 'vocables composez'. In his

---

[1] *La Précellence*, ed. Edmond Huguet, 1896, p. 163.
[2] Hall's *Satires*, vi. 255 (of the modish Elizabethan poet).

> He knows the grace of that new elegance
> Which sweet Philisides fetch'd of late from France,
> That well beseem'd his high-styled Arcady,
> Though others mar it with much liberty,
> In epithets to join two words in one
> Forsooth, for adjectives cannot stand alone :
> As a great poet could of Bacchus say
> That he was Semele-femori-gena.

The double epithet was unknown to Lyly, whose *Euphues* introduced many other affectations into English, and, although he is sometimes loosely credited with the innovation of the compound epithet, he shows no knowledge of it. Sidney is the pioneer without question.

sonnets to Stella many epithets are found on such models as :
love-acquainted (eyes) ; sour-breathed (mate) ; past - praise
(hue) ; and rose-enamelled (skies).

The *Arcadia* is only a little less liberally sprinkled with like
ornaments. In his *Apologie for Poetrie,* Sidney strongly
urged ' compositions of two or three words together ', and
described the fashion as ' one of the greatest beauties there can
be in a language '. At his bidding the French practice rapidly
spread in Elizabethan poetry. It is met with in Spenser's sonnets,
and in the *Faerie Queene.* 'Storm-beaten' and 'heart-piercing'
are two of many compounds of Spenser's invention which have
passed into common speech. Among the poet Daniel's contributions to the long list of Elizabethan ' vocables composez ' is
the far-famed epithet ' care-charmer ', which he first applied
to sleep. There the English poet directly translates the French
' chasse-soin ' or ' chasse-souci '—epithets which Pléiade sonneteers repeatedly linked with ' sommeil '. The like use by Greek
poets of the word λυσίπονος suggests the ultimate source of
French inspiration, but Daniel, loyal to the custom of his age,
was content to take the gift direct from his French neighbours.

The highest historic interest which attaches to this Ronsardian device lies in Shakespeare's liberal adaptation of it to
purposes of both lyric and dramatic verse. Every reader of
Shakespeare's text will recall the frequency of double epithets
which, in the best original editions, are, as in the French books,
carefully hyphened by the printer. Very familiar are such
examples as (our) past-cure (malady) ; (my) furnace-burning
(heart) ; honey-heavy (dew) ; giant-rude ; fancy-free ; marble-
constant. These compounds are typical of a hundred others.
Occasionally Shakespeare somewhat betters Ronsard's instruction, and constructs an epithet out of three words instead of
two, as in ' a *world-without-end* bargain ', 'the *always-wind-
obeying* deep '. But the scheme never far departs from the
lines laid down by the Pléiade. Like Henri Étienne, Shakespeare perceived the vice of excess in the usage, and in *Love's
Labour's Lost* he ridicules its exaggeration.[1] But his practical

[1] Armado's stilted letter to the king (I. i. 219 seq.) contains the ten following compound epithets: sable-coloured, black-oppressing, health-giving,

recognition of value in the discreet application of the process is a notable tribute to the influence wrought by France on the vocabulary of Elizabethan poetry.

XI

THE RENAISSANCE THEORY OF 'IMITATION'

A large harvest of Elizabethan poetry is clearly seen to assimilate French sentiment, language, and metre. Even more notable is the circumstance that many leaders of the literary profession in Elizabethan England should have put forward as original compositions and as declarations of personal feeling, a number of poems which prove on examination to be literal translations from the French or Italian. Before we extend our comparative inquiry to the Elizabethan sonnet, which will accentuate the borrowing tendencies of the Elizabethan muse, it may be prudent to estimate the ethical significance which attached at the time to unavowed practices of plagiarism.

Unacknowledged borrowing, in the shape of literal translation either of complete poems or of substantial extracts, stands on a footing very different from that of assimilation, which is a universal law of poetry, and though it invites study, requires no excuse. Plagiarism of foreign authors has been shown to be common enough among Elizabethan lyrists to call for judicial inquiry. Contemporary critics recognized that the habit was widespread, and at times condemned it with little reservation. Of Soothern, the clumsy but tacit translator of Ronsard's *Odes* in 1584, the author of *The Arte of English Poesie* (1589) wrote :—' This man deserues to be endited of pety *larceny* for pilfering other men's deuises from them and conuerting them to his owne use.'[1]   Other offenders on the like

---

snow-white, ebon-coloured, curious-knotted, low-spirited, small-knowing, ever-esteemed, heart-burning. Although Shakespeare was gently satirizing the process here, it is curious to note that three of these invented compounds, viz. health-giving, snow-white, and low-spirited, found a permanent place in the language.

[1] Puttenham, *Arte of English Poesie*, ed. Arber, 1869, p. 260 ; passages which precede these words are quoted on page 214, note.

lines, including men of the calibre of Daniel, were charged with ' filching ' or with ' theft '.

The like habit was well known abroad. French poets borrowed from classical and Italian work as unceremoniously as the Elizabethans borrowed from French and Italian poetry. Montaigne is severe on authors who endeavoured to misrepresent as their own what they stole from others. The French essayist imputed to such procedure not merely injustice but cowardice. Yet Montaigne admitted that personally he could never resist the temptation of pillaging a favourite author. Of Plutarch he wrote :—' He can no sooner come in my sight, or if I cast but a glance upon him, but I pull some leg or wing from him.' The plagiaristic tendency both in England and France, when it was detected, was condoned in literary circles as often as it was denounced. It was held capable of defence.

There was frequently urged in mitigation of censure, if not in justification, an excuse which, while it savours of special pleading, cannot be refused weight. Ben Jonson, who ranked high among the Elizabethan giants, borrowed wholesale without specific acknowledgement. Dryden called him ' a learned plagiary ' of all other authors. ' You track him everywhere in their snow.' ' But ' (Dryden adds elsewhere) ' one may see he fears not to be taxed by any law. He invades authors like a monarch.' [1] In general terms Jonson denied offence in the habit. With frank self-complacency he explained: ' Whatsoever I pawned with my memory while I was young and a boy, it offers me readily and without stops [in my old age].' [2] But the process of unconscious cerebration hardly accounts for the details of the practice in the case either of Ben Jonson or of his comrades. More illuminating is Jonson's further argument that it was an essential requisite in a poet to be able consciously to convert the substance or riches of another poet to his own use, even to the extent of a literal adoption of the foreign poet's language. This second plea offers a practicable key to the problem.

[1] Essays of John Dryden, ed. W. P. Ker, i. 43, 82.
[2] Ben Jonson, *Discoveries*, ed. Schelling, p. 18.

There was abroad a scholastic conception of the art of poetry which minimized, if it did not cancel, the apparent reproach of the plagiarizing tendency. The truth of the familiar late Latin adage, ' orator fit, poeta nascitur,' was not questioned. The great poet was held to be divinely inspired. But something more was expected of him than to be, with the lunatic and the lover, ' of imagination all compact.' A current gloss on the proverb presumed (in Ben Jonson's words) that 'the good poet 's made as well as born '. The Renaissance critics reached their conclusion that good poetry was in part an article of manufacture, through a somewhat perverted interpretation of the classical doctrine of μίμησις, or *imitatio*, as applied to literary composition. The term was assumed to connote not merely imitation of life or nature, but also and often primarily imitation of pre-existing literature.

Renaissance critics in all countries acknowledged without much demur that in Greek literature human genius reached its zenith, and that Latin literature owed its value to habitual imitation of the Greek. There followed, not quite logically, the scholastic inference that the merit of literatur' grew in proportion to its dependence on what went before. In most authoritative handbooks on literary composition a section on ' imitation ' filled a chief place, and pressed this assumption to the uttermost.[1] It was never denied that other elements went to the making of poetry. Ben Jonson defined poetry as a compound mingled of four simples: first a goodness of natural wit (*ingenium*); second, exercise of native powers (*exercitatio*); thirdly, imitation (*imitatio*); fourthly, an exactness of study and multiplicity of reading (*lectio*). But his comment on the fourth element (*lectio*) brings it near the third element (*imitatio*); and when he warns the poet against thinking ' he can leap forth suddenly a poet by dreaming he hath been in Parnassus, or having

[1] Roger Ascham in his *Schoolmaster*, 1570, devotes many pages (ed. Mayor, pp. 135–9) to the discussion of ' Imitation'. Ascham mainly embodies the instruction of the Strasburg humanist Johann Sturm in his *De Imitatione*. Ascham argues that perfect style is the exclusive property of Greek and Latin, and must be sought there by writers in all other tongues. (*Schoolmaster*, ed. Mayor, p. 167.)

washed his lips as they say in Helicon ', he implies that poetic inspiration is of small service without both erudition and imitation.[1] The authority of the Frenchman Scaliger, the greatest critic of the Renaissance, was well recognized in Elizabethan England. It was he who summed up the dominant conception of poetic imitation in the maxim that 'every poet is something of an echo ', ' nemo est qui non aliquid de Echo.' From such a premise there not unnaturally followed the deduction that copying was not necessarily inconsistent with the fundamental elements of poetic art or the essential conditions of poetic success.[2] Translation was invariably regarded in continental Europe as one of the worthiest forms of scholarship, and it was generally accounted no less glorious adequately to turn foreign verse or prose into one's native tongue, than to write anything new.[3] ' Imitation' was capable of many gradations in the judgement of the critics, but no form need on principle be other than an honourable handmaid of genius. However perilous or sophistical the argument, it is needful to bear it in mind when we detect Elizabethan lyrists of repute circulating as of their own invention poems which they had translated with fidelity from the work of Ronsard, his friends or his disciples.

XII

THE ASSIMILATION OF THE FRENCH SONNET

An examination of the Elizabethan sonnet-sequence shows the assimilative and imitative processes to which all Elizabethan lyric was more or less subject, in an activity that is more penetrating and comprehensive than elsewhere. The English sonnet, which came to birth in Henry VIII's reign, was

[1] Jonson, *Discoveries*, ed. Schelling, pp. 75–8.
[2] A good summary account of the doctrine of imitation is given by Prof. J. E. Spingarn in *A History of Literary Criticism in the Renaissance*, New York, 1899, pp. 130 seq.
[3] Vida, the leading critical authority of the Italian Renaissance in his *De Arte Poetica* (1527), well sums up the situation thus :

> Haud minor est adeo virtus, si te audit Apollo,
> Inventa Argivûm in patriam convertere vocem,
> Quam si tute aliquid intactum inveneris ante.

born of Italian effort. But the sparse sonneteering experiment of Wyatt and Surrey was an isolated episode in our literary history. The Elizabethan sonnet was no mere fruit of the early Tudor stock, although in course of later development it borrowed thence a metrical suggestion of importance. The Elizabethan sonnet was practically a fresh development in Elizabethan England. At the outset it was independently imported not from Italy but from France. Edmund Spenser, the father of the Elizabethan quatorzain, introduced in boyhood the sonnet into Elizabethan England with a translation of sonnets by Du Bellay. The seed was slow to fructify. At first the Elizabethan growth was scanty and occasional. Not until Queen Elizabeth's reign was nearing its last decade did it acquire luxuriance. Then the scene changed, and sonneteering became an imperious vogue, a fashionable recreation, a modish artifice of gallantry and compliment. No poetic aspirant between 1590 and 1610 failed to try his skill on this poetic instrument. During those twenty years probably more sonnets were penned in England than in all the ages that followed.

The harvest of Elizabethan sonneteering is a strange medley of sublimity and pathos. The workers in the field included Sidney, Spenser, and Shakespeare, who, in varying degrees, invested this poetic form with charm and beauty. Shakespeare, above all, breathed into the sonnet a lyric melody and a meditative energy which no writer of any country has surpassed. It is the value attaching to the sonneteering efforts of this great trio of Elizabethan poets, and to some rare and isolated triumphs of their contemporaries, Daniel, Drayton, and Constable, which lends the Elizabethan sonnet its aesthetic interest. The profuse experiments of other Elizabethan sonneteers rarely touched high levels of poetic performance. Very few were capable of any sustained flight in the lofty regions of the imagination. The most prolific pens betrayed indeed a normal crudeness and a clumsiness of thought and language which invited and justified ridicule.

Despite the miraculous masterpieces of Shakespeare and the occasional successes of other English pens which were rarely matched abroad, the general standard of performance in points of grace and melody was higher in France, if not in Italy, than in England. The grotesque cacophonies which characterized much Elizabethan effort were unheard across the Channel. Vast, too, as was the output of Elizabethan sonneteers, they produced far less than their French or Italian neighbours. Probably ten times as many sonnets were penned by the chieftains of the Pléiade and their followers, or by the masters of the Italian school of the sixteenth century, as by Shakespeare and his contemporaries.

The sonnet in Elizabethan England of all degrees of merit or demerit never lost altogether the savour of a foreign origin. In the sentiment and imagery no less than in the metrical shape a foreign parentage is commonly traceable. France and Italy are the joint progenitors. Soon after Spenser had inaugurated the sonneteering vogue on a French model, Italian influence came afresh upon the English stage. The revived Italian influence proved a formidable rival to the French, but it never extinguished the French sway. Elizabethan sonneteers came to absorb at first hand much of the poetry of Petrarch, Ariosto, and Tasso; yet they were never neglectful of Ronsard, Du Bellay, and Desportes. Some of the Italian inspiration was drawn indirectly from French adaptation or translation of the Italian. The Elizabethan sonneteers threw their nets widely in both French and Italian waters. The sonneteering rank and file in France and Italy fell within range of the Elizabethan aim, and many obscure disciples of Ronsard or Tasso became as large creditors of the Elizabethans as those masters themselves.

The debt of the Elizabethan sonnet to Italian poetry cannot be debated here. But the omission does not seriously diminish the efficiency of the present argument. Frequently as was the work of Petrarch, Ariosto, and Tasso, and of smaller Italian poets pressed into the Elizabethan service, the Elizabethan sonneteers more often and more freely took their cue from the work of Ronsard, Du Bellay, Desportes, and other Frenchmen. Shakespeare owed more to French than to Italian tuition. His lyric poetry lay under far smaller obligation than that of his fellows to foreign masters. His indebtedness is slight when it is contrasted with the repeated dependence of his fellows on the precise phraseology as well as on the precise ideas of the Pléiade. But thought and expression in Shakespeare's sonnets reflect too often and too closely a French strain to justify the theory of fortuitous coincidence. In many other Elizabethan sonnet-sequences there figure not merely separate quatrains, but whole sonnets which are silently and unblushingly translated from foreign, and more especially from French collections. When some Elizabethan sonnet-sequences are fully analysed, they are found to be haphazard mosaics of French or Italian originals. Constable, Daniel, and Lodge, who all enjoyed high repute as Elizabethan sonneteers, were the most conspicuous offenders. Even Spenser falls at times under the same indictment. The habit of literal transference without acknowledgement spread further in the sonneteering work of the Elizabethans than in any other direction. There are occasional deviations from the French text in the borrowed poems; but the alterations often merely suggest a temporary failure of ingenuity on the part of the Elizabethan translator in anglicizing the French language.

It was when the sonneteering rage was at its full height in England, between 1591 and 1597, that the indebtedness to the Pléiade is most apparent. After Spenser's boyish translations from Du Bellay's sonnets, which came out in 1569, thirteen years intervened before a further attempt was made to popularize the sonnet in England. Then there appeared Watson's *Hecatompathia, or Passionate Centurie of Love*, a volume which, although it is introduced by a few regular quatorzains, mainly present as 'sonnets' short poems of eighteen instead of fourteen lines each. Lyric pieces of this pattern constantly interrupt, under the Italian name of madrigal, the continuity of contemporary sonnet collections of France as well as Italy. Watson in a prefatory note to each of his poems quotes Latin, Italian, or French sources for them all. Ronsard is duly named among his authorities. Watson's dependence on foreign effort is too widely distributed; he is too negligent of the metrical rules of the sonnet, and the quality of his work is too halting to claim much notice. Watson's successor as poet and sonneteer was of far higher calibre. Sir Philip Sidney's collection of sonnets called *Astrophel and Stella* gives the first sign of the English sonnet's poetic capacity. Sidney's sonnets were composed in the last years of Sidney's life, which ended in 1586, and after circulating widely in manuscript were first published in 1591. It was with their publication that the rage for sonneteering in Elizabethan England caught fire, and the flame burned briskly till near the close of the century.[1]

None who is widely read in the sonnets of Ronsard or

---

[1] It is necessary to bear in mind some dates in the history of the Elizabethan sonnet. The chronology of the Elizabethan sonnet-sequence opens with the publication of Spenser's sonnet-renderings of poems by Du Bellay and Marot in *A Theatre for Worldlings*, 1569. Thomas Watson's *Hecatompathia, or Passionate Centurie of Love*, a collection of irregular 'sonnets', came out in 1582, Sir Philip Sidney's *Astrophel and Stella* in 1591, and Spenser's rendering of Du Bellay's sonnet-sequence called *The Ruins of Rome*, with a revised version of his earlier rendering from Du Bellay, in *Complaints* in the same year. Samuel Daniel's *Delia* and Henry Constable's *Diana* first appeared in 1592, both to be revised and enlarged two years later. Three ample collections followed in 1593; they came from the pens respectively of Barnabe Barnes (*Parthenophil and Parthenophe*), Thomas Lodge (*Phillis*), and Giles Fletcher (*Licia*), while Watson's second venture (*The Tears of Fancy*) was then published posthumously and for the first time. Three more volumes, in addition to the revised editions of Daniel's *Delia* and Constable's *Diana*, appeared in 1594, viz. William Percy's *Coelia*, an anonymous writer's *Zepheria*, and Michael Drayton's *Ideas Mirrour* (in its first shape). E. C.'s *Emaricdulfe*, Edmund Spenser's *Amoretti* and R. Barnfield's *Cynthia with certaine sonnets*, came out in 1595, and Griffin's *Fidessa*, Linche's *Diella*, and William Smith's *Chloris* in 1596. Finally, in 1597, the procession was joined by Robert Tofte's *Laura*, a pale reflection of Petrarch's effort (as the name implied), travelling far from the metrical principles of the genuine form of sonnet. To the same period belongs the composition, although the publication was long delayed, of the Scottish poet Sir William Alexander's *Aurora*, and of the *Coelica* of Sidney's friend, Sir Fulke Greville, besides the sonnets of William Drummond of Hawthornden and Alexander Montgomerie. Various dates have been assigned by the critics to Shakespeare's sonnets, which were not published till 1609. The majority of them, in the present writer's opinion, were written well before 1600 (see his *Life of Shakespeare*, 6th ed., 1908, and the Introduction to the Oxford facsimile of the first edition, 1905). In addition to these secular, and, for the most part, amorous sonnet-sequences, there were published during the same period large collections of devotional or spiritual sonnets, as well as an immense number of detached commendatory sonnets, addressed by poets to their patrons.

Du Bellay fails to perceive the foreign echoes in Sidney's sonnets. The appeals to sleep, to the nightingale, to the moon, to his bed, to his mistress's dog, resemble the apostrophes of the foreign sonneteers too closely to make their foreign inspiration doubtful. Echoing Persius, Sidney protests, ' I am no pickpurse of another's wit.' Yet the spirit no less than the form of his sonnets attests his foreign discipleship. But on the whole, Sidney's work is more reminiscent of Petrarch than of the Pléiade, and his indebtedness to both stimulated rather than dulled the vivacity of his poetic powers.[1]

It is in the sonnet collections that follow the publication of Sidney's *Astrophel and Stella* that the French influence becomes full-fledged. But the bond of union between the French ' amours ' and the later Elizabethan sonnet-sequences is not announced on English title-pages. No debt is acknowledged in English prefaces. The Elizabethans usually gave the fictitious mistresses after whom their volumes of amorous sonnets were called the names that had recently served the like purpose in France, but they silently adopted the nomenclature. Daniel followed a somewhat early French versifier, Maurice Scève, in christening his collection *Delia*; Constable followed Desportes in designating his collection *Diana*; while Drayton, who applied to his sonnets on his title-page, in 1594, the French term ' amours ', bestowed on his imaginary heroine the title of *Idea*, which seems to have been the invention of Claude de Pontoux, although it was employed by other French contemporaries. Pontoux, a poet-physician of Châlons, published in 1579 an ample collection of sonnets under the title *L'Idée*, and Drayton's ' Divine Idea ', his ' Fair Idea', is nearly akin to Pontoux's ' Céleste Idée fille de Dieu' (Sonnet X).[2] Again, *Phillis*, the rustic heroine of Lodge's sonnets and lyrics, had already received the airy addresses of much

[1] The general history of the Elizabethan sonnet has already been treated by the present writer in his Introduction to *Elizabethan Sonnets* (Constable's *English Garner*, 1904) and in the chapter on the Elizabethan Sonnet in the *Cambridge History of Literature*, vol. iii, pp. 247 sq.

[2] The name of Pontoux and Drayton's heroine symbolizes the Platonic ἰδέα of beauty, which was often apostrophized in the sonnets of Du Bellay and Pontus de Tyard, two leaders of the Pléiade.

French verse, notably from the tuneful pastoral muse of Vauquelin de la Fresnaie. The ultimate classical source of all these appellations of poetic mistresses does not weaken the evidence that they entered English poetry through French avenues.

In all the sonnet collections of the professional men of letters of Elizabethan England not only do proofs of assimilation abound, but the instances of literal transference and of paraphrase without acknowledgement are embarrassingly numerous.[1] A few illustrations of the process of direct 'imitation' are all that can be cited here. I give first five examples of how the work of Du Bellay, Ronsard, and Desportes was directly rendered into English by men of the literary reputation of Daniel, Lodge, and Constable, all of whom enjoyed in their day a high repute as original writers of sonnets.

Du Bellay, *Olive*, x.	Daniel, *Delia*, xiv.
Ces cheveux d'or sont les liens, Madame,	These amber[2] locks are those same nets, my Dear!
Dont fut premier ma liberté surprise,	Wherewith my liberty thou didst surprise!
Amour, la flamme autour du cœur éprise,	Love was the flame that fired me so near:
Ces yeux, le traict qui me transperce l'ame.	The dart transpiercing were those crystal eyes.
Forts sont les nœuds, aspre et vive la flamme,	Strong is the net, and fervent is the flame;
Le coup, de main à tirer bien apprise,	Deep is the stroke,[3] my sighs do well report.
Et toutesfois i'ayme, i'adore, et prise	Yet I do love, adore, and praise the same
Ce qui m'estraint, qui me brusle, et entame.	That holds, that burns, that wounds in this sort;

[1] The reader should study the evidence of Elizabethan indebtedness to the French which Prof. L. E. Kastner has brought together in five valuable papers which he contributed to the *Modern Language Review*. The papers are entitled respectively 'The Scottish Sonneteers and the French poets' (October, 1907), 'The Elizabethan Sonneteers and the French poets' (April, 1908), 'Spenser's Amoretti and Desportes' (January, 1909), 'Drummond of Hawthornden and the poets of the Pléiade' (April, 1909), and 'Drummond of Hawthornden and the French Poets of the Sixteenth Century' (Jan. 1910).

[2] The original reading, which Daniel afterwards altered to 'snary'.

[3] The original reading, which Daniel afterwards altered to 'wound'.

Pour briser doncq', pour esteindre et guérir
Ce dur lien, ceste ardeur, ceste playe,
Ie ne quiers fer, liqueur, ny médecine :
L'heur et plaisir que ce m'est de périr
De telle main, ne permet que i'essaye
Glaive trenchant, ny froideur, ny racine.

And list not seek to break, to quench, to heal
The bond, the flame, the wound that festereth so,
By knife, by liquor, or by salve to deal :
So much I please to perish in my woe.
Yet, lest long travails be above my strength,
Good Delia ! loose, quench, heal me, now at length !

DESPORTES, *Cleonice*, lxii.

Je verray par les ans, vengeurs de mon martire,
Que l'or de vos cheveux argenté deviendra,
Que de vos deux soleils la splendeur s'esteindra,
Et qu'il faudra qu'Amour tout confus s'en retire.
La beauté qui, si douce, à présent vous inspire,
Cedant aux lois du temps, ses faveurs reprendra ;
L'hiver de vostre teint les fleurettes perdra,
Et ne laissera rien des thresors que j'admire.
Cet orgueil desdaigneux qui vous fait ne m'aimer,
En regret et chagrin se verra transformer,
Avec le changement d'une image si belle,
Et peutestre qu'alors vous n'aurez déplaisir
De revivre en mes vers, chauds d'amoureux désir,
Ainsi que le phénix au feu se renouvelle.

DANIEL, *Delia*, xxxiii.

I once may see, when' years may wreak my wrong,
And golden hairs may change to silver wire :
And those bright rays (that kindle all this fire)
Shall fail in force, their power not so strong.
Her beauty now the burden of my song,
Whose glorious blaze the world's eye doth admire,
Must yield her praise to tyrant Time's desire ;
Then fades the flower, which fed her pride so long.
When if she grieve to gaze her in her glass,
Which then presents her winter-withered hue,
Go you my verse ? go tell her what she was !
For what she was, she best may find in you.
Your fiery heat lets not her glory pass,
But Phoenix-like to make her live anew.

RONSARD, *Amours*, I. xxxii.

Quand au premier la dame que
    j'adore
  De ses beautez vint embellir
    les cieux,
  Le fils de Rhée appela tous les
    dieux
  Pour faire encor d'elle une autre
    Pandore.
Lors Apollon richement la décore,
  Or' de ses rais luy façonnant les
    yeux,
  Or' luy donnant son chant melo-
    dieux,
  Or' son oracle et ses beaux vers
    encore.
Mars luy donna sa fiere cruauté,
  Venus son ris, Diane sa beauté,
  Pithon sa voix, Cerés son abon-
    dance,
  L'Aube ses doigts et ses crins
    deliés,
  Amour son arc, Thetis donna ses
    piés,
  Clion sa gloire, et Pallas sa
    prudence.

LODGE, *Phillis*, xxxiii.

When first sweet Phillis, whom I
  most adore,
'Gan with her beauties bless our
  wond'ring sky,
The son of Rhea, from their fatal
  store
Made all the gods to grace her
  majesty.
Apollo first his golden rays among,
  Did form the beauty of her boun-
    teous eyes ;
  He graced her with his sweet
    melodious song,
  And made her subject of his
    poesies.
The warrior Mars bequeathed her
  fierce disdain,
  Venus her smile, and Phoebe all
    her fair,
  Python his voice, and Ceres all
    her grain,
The morn her locks and fingers
  did repair,
  Young Love his bow, and Thetis
    gave her feet ;
  Clio her praise, Pallas her science
    sweet.

RONSARD, *Amours*, I. cxix.

Franc de raison, esclave de fureur,
Je vay chassant une fere sauvage,
  Or' sur un mont, or' le long d'un
    rivage,
  Or' dans le bois de jeunesse et
    d'erreur.
J'ay pour ma laisse un long trait de
  malheur,
  J'ay pour limier un trop ardent
    courage,
  J'ay pour mes chiens l'ardeur et
    le jeune âge,
  J'ay pour piqueurs l'espoir et la
    douleur.
Mais eux, voyans que plus elle est
  chassée,
  Loin, loin, devant plus s'enfuit
    élancée,
  Tournant sur moi leur rigoureux
    effort,
Comme mastins affamés de re-
  paistre,
  A longs morceaux se paissent de
    leur maistre,
  Et sans mercy me trainent à la
    mort.

LODGE, *Phillis*, xxxi.

Devoid of reason, thrall to foolish
  ire,
I walk and chase a savage fairy
  still,
Now near the flood, straight on
  the mounting hill,
Now midst the woods of youth,
  and vain desire.
For leash I bear a cord of careful
  grief ;
For brach I lead an overforward
  mind ;
My hounds are thoughts, and
  rage despairing blind,
Pain, cruelty, and care without
  relief.
But they, perceiving that my swift
  pursuit
My flying fairy cannot overtake,
With open mouths their prey on
  me do make,
Like hungry hounds that lately lost
  their suit,
  And full of fury on their master
    feed,
  To hasten on my hapless death
    with speed.

DESPORTES, *Diane*, I. xxvi.

Mon Dieu! mon Dieu! que j'aime
  ma déesse
  Et de son chef les trésors pré-
  cieux!
  Mon Dieu! mon Dieu! que
  j'aime ses beaux yeux,
  Dont l'un m'est doux, l'autre
  plein de rudesse!
Mon Dieu! mon Dieu! que j'aime
  la sagesse
  De ses discours, qui raviroient les
  Dieux,
  Et la douceur de son ris gracieux,
  Et de son port la royale hautesse!

Mon Dieu! que j'aime à me res-
  souvenir
  Du tans qu'Amour me fist serf
  devenir!
  Toujours depuis j'adore mon
  servage.
Mon mal me plaist plus il est vio-
  lant;
  Un feu si beau m'égaye en me
  brûlant,
  Et la rigueur est douce en son
  visage.

CONSTABLE, *Diana*, Decade VI,
    Sonnet x.

My God, my God, how much I love
  my goddess!
  Whose virtues rare, unto the
  heavens arise.
  My God, my God, how much I
  love her eyes!
  One shining bright, the other full
  of hardness.
My God, my God, how much I love
  her wisdom!
  Whose words may ravish heaven's
  richest 'maker';
  Of whose eyes' joys, if I might be
  partaker,
  Then to my soul, a holy rest
  would come.
My God, how much I love to hear
  her speak!
  Whose hands I kiss, and ravished
  oft rekisseth;
  When she stands wotless, whom
  so much she blesseth.
Say then, what mind this honest
  love would break;
  Since her perfections pure, with-
  outen blot,
  Makes her beloved of them, she
  knoweth not?

In none of these examples is there genuine originality in diction or sentiment on the part of the Elizabethan sonneteer. Constable's final sestet here strays somewhat from the original. But he atones for any freedom at the close by his servility at the opening. Lodge is probably most loyal to his original, but Daniel runs him hard. Hardly a sonnet that Lodge published cannot be traced to a foreign source.[1]

This literal method is often exchanged for imitative paraphrase which improves on the original. In Spenser's case no imputation of slavish borrowing can be sustained. But Desportes was clearly a dominant master of Spenser's sonneteering muse, and the relationship between the French tutor and his English pupil may be deduced from a careful comparison of the two sonnets which follow:

[1] Besides Ronsard and Desportes, Lodge pillaged with equal freedom sonnets by Ariosto, Petrarch, Sannazaro, and Bembo, as well as by a very little-known Italian sonneteer Lodovico Paschale.

DESPORTES, *Diane*, I. xxxii.

Marchands, qui *recherchez* tout
le rivage more
Du froid septentrion, et qui, *sans
reposer*,
A cent mille dangers vous allez
exposer
Pour un gain incertain, qui vos
esprits devore,
  Venez seulement voir la beauté
que j'adore
Et par quelle *richesse* elle a sçeu
m'attiser :
Et je suis seur qu'après vous ne
pourrez priser
*Le plus rare tresor dont l'Afrique
se dore.*
  Voyez les filets d'or de ce chef
blondissant,
L'éclat *de ces rubis*, ce coral rougis-
sant,
Ce cristal, cet ebene, et *ces graces
divines*,
  Cet argent, cet yvoire ; et ne vous
contentez
Qu'on ne vous montre encor mille
autres raretez,
Mille beaux diamans et *mille perles
fines.*

SPENSER, *Amoretti*, xv.

Ye tradeful *merchants*, that *with
weary toil*
Do seek most precious things to
make *your gain*,
And both the Indies of their trea-
sure spoil,[1]
What needeth you to seek so far in
vain ?
  For lo, my love doth in herself
contain
*All this world's riches that may far
be found ;*
If sapphires, lo, her eyes be sapphires plain ;
If *rubies*, lo, her lips be rubies
sound ;
  If *pearls*, her teeth be pearls,
both pure and round ;
If *ivory*, her forehead ivory ween ;
If gold, her locks are finest gold
on ground ;
  If *silver*, her fair hands are silver
sheen :
But that which fairest is, but few
behold,
Her mind adorned with *virtues
manifold.*

DESPORTES, *Diane*, I. xliii.

  Solitaire et pensíf, dans un bois
ecarté
Bien loin du populaire et de la
tourbe espesse,
Je veux *bastir un temple à ma fiere
déesse*,
Pour apprendre *mes vœux à sa
divinité*.
  Là, *de jour et de nuit*, par moy
sera chanté
Le pouvoir de ses yeux, sa gloire et
sa hautesse ;
Et, *devot*, son beau nom j'invoqueray
sans cesse,
Quand je seray pressé de quelque
adversité.

SPENSER, *Amoretti*, xxii.

This holy season, fit to fast and
pray,
Men to *devotion* ought to be inclined :
Therefore I likewise, on so holy
day,
For my sweet saint some service
fit will find.
Her temple fair is built within my
mind,
In which *her glorious image* placed
is,
On which my thoughts do *day and
night* attend,
Like *sacred priests* that never
think amiss !

[1] Spenser probably also bore in mind here Ronsard's sonnet (*Amours*, I.
clxxxix) :

Ny *des Indois la gemmeuse largesse*,
Ny tous les biens d'un rivage estranger,
A leurs tresors ne sçauroient eschanger
Le moindre honneur de sa double richesse.

Mon œil sera la lampe ardant continuelle,	There I to her, as th' author of my bliss,
Devant *l'image saint* d'une dame si belle ;	Will *build an altar* to appease her ire ;
Mon corps sera *l'autel*, et mes soupirs les vœux.	And on the same *my heart will sacrifice*,
Par mille et mille vers *je chanteray l'office*,	Burning in flames of pure and chaste desire :
Puis, espanchant mes pleurs et coupant mes cheveux,	The which vouchsafe, O goddess, to accept,
J'y feray tous les jours *de mon cœur sacrifice*.	Amongst thy dearest relics to be kept.[1]

Not merely is the thought the same in these two pairs of efforts, but Spenser draws many of his phrases from the French.

So general was the resort of Elizabethan sonneteers to French verse that, in some instances, we find two English poets making independent raid on the same French sonnet, and producing two different English versions. Both Daniel and Spenser worked about the same time on the eighteenth sonnet in Desportes' *Amours d'Hippolyte*, which begins—

> Pourquoy si folement croyez-vous à un verre,
> Voulant voir les beautez que vous avez des cieux ?
> Mirez-vous dessus moy pour les connoistre mieux,
> Et voyez de quels traits vostre bel œil m'enferre.

Daniel rendered the passage thus (*Delia*, xxxii) :

> Why doth my mistress credit so her glass,
> Gazing her beauty, deigned her by the skies ?
> And doth not rather look on him, alas !
> Whose state best shows the force of murdering eyes ?

Spenser's version is freer and runs thus (*Amoretti*, xlv) :

> Leave, lady, in your glass of crystal clean,
> Your goodly self for evermore to view :
> And in myself, my inward self, I mean,
> Most lively like behold your semblance true.

---

[1] The cognate words are italicized throughout. Spenser's opening quatrain (No. xxii) suggests a reminiscence of another of Desportes' sonnets in *Diane* (II, No. xlvi), beginning ' Je m'estoy dans le temple un dimanche rendu '. The poet describes how he saw his mistress at prayer in church on Easter Day. Spenser, in *Amoretti* (No. lxviii), also treats of Easter Day, with an eye apparently both on the sonnet of Desportes and on four on the same theme by Du Bellay (*Olive*, cviii–cxi).

In their metrical scheme the Elizabethan sonneteers played variations on their foreign models. They sought to lighten their task by relaxing the continental laws of rhyme. Some discretion was permitted abroad. But a standard type was formally adopted at Italian suggestion by the Pléiade, and departures from it did not travel very far. The fourteen lines of the French, like the Italian, sonnet were invariably distributed into two more or less independent sections. An octave formed of two quatrains was separated by a marked pause from a succeeding sestet or sixain consisting of two tercets. The quatrains of the octave usually followed the rhyming arrangement of *abba*, *abba*, which were technically known as 'vers embrassés'. Alternate or cross rhymes in the octave *abab*, *abab*, grew common early in the seventeenth century, but were rare at earlier dates. The sestet was less uniform. A new set of rhyming syllables always found a place in the two tercets of the sestet. Usually the rhymes were three in number. But two were at times found adequate. Whether there were three or two rhymes, several permutations were sanctioned in their sequence. A common type of tercet in Pléiade sonnets presented four lines alternately rhymed and a closing couplet with a third rhyme *cdc*, *dee*. Or there might be six alternately rhymed lines with only two rhymes *cdc*, *dcd*. The favourite pattern of Ronsard and his chief allies was, however, three rhymes thus arranged, *ccd*, *eed*. In the majority of French sonnets the octave and sestet were thus constructed in combination on the model *abba*, *abba*, *ccd*, *eed*.

The metrical systems which were practised in Elizabethan England also fluctuated. That which was accepted by Shakespeare and enjoyed the widest vogue was less intricate than anything known in France, and may have been a legacy from Surrey's primitive experiments. The strict division into octave and sestet was often neglected. In contemporary language the fourteen lines of the Elizabethan sonnet were distributed thus :—' The firste twelve do ryme in staves of foure lines by crosse meetre, and the last two ryming togither do conclude the whole.'[1] In other words the first twelve lines

---

[1] Gascoigne, *Certayne Notes of Instruction*, ed. Arber, 1868, p. 39.

rhymed alternately on six different syllables, *abab, cdcd, efef*, and these lines were followed by a couplet with a seventh and new rhyme *gg*.[1] A main difference between the French and English normal types lay in the increase in the number of rhyming syllables from four or five to seven. The four alternate rhymes of the English octave were not found outside England. But the cross rhymes and the terminal couplet of the English sestet, though not encouraged in France, were known there. One of the most familiar of Ronsard's sonnets, although its octave observes the normal formula *abba abba*, has a sestet fashioned on Shakespeare's invariable pattern (*Œuvres*, i. 397):

> Le temps s'en va, le temps s'en va, ma *dame*;
> Las! le temps non, mais nous nous en-al*lons,*
> Et tost serons estendus sous la *lame.*
> Et des amours desquelles nous par*lons,*
>   Quand serons morts, n'en sera plus nou*velle.*
>   Pour ce aimez-moy cependant qu'estes *belle.*

With this rhyming scheme may well be compared that of the sestet of Shakespeare's first sonnet:

> Thou that art now the world's fresh orna*ment*
> And only herald to the gaudy sp*ring,*
> Within thine own bud buriest thy con*tent,*
> And, tender churl, mak'st waste in niggar*ding.*
>   Pity the world, or else this glutton *be,*
>   To eat the world's due, by the grave and *thee.*

Other Elizabethan sonneteers kept closer than Shakespeare to the normal foreign lines. Sir Philip Sidney showed a higher respect that any of his English contemporaries for the foreign canon. As a rule he observed the orthodox scheme of the octave or double quatrain *abba, abba.* In the first eight lines of Sidney's sonnets only two interlaced rhymes were permitted. In the sestet he usually presents four lines alternately

---

[1] Surrey anticipated the Shakespearean arrangement with its six cross rhymes and the terminal couplets, and he must be regarded as the English inventor of this system. Wyatt's rhyming scheme, on the other hand, is usually loyal to the Italian vogue in the octave, *abba, abba,* though new rhymes occasionally make their appearance in the second quatrain *abba, cddc.* The sestet has invariably a terminal couplet. But in the preceding four lines Wyatt usually prefers the principle of ' vers embrassés ' *cddc* to that of cross rhyming.

rhymed and a concluding couplet (*cdc, dee*). Yet in more than twenty of his sonnets the sestet is faithful to Ronsardian orthodoxy *ccd, eed*. Sidney's sonneteering work is thus metrically in closer harmony with continental prosody than that of Shakespeare or any other Elizabethan. Some of Sidney's successors, while adhering as a rule to the loose English model, at times pursued the strict lines of foreign orthodoxy. Daniel on one occasion adopted so stern a foreign model as this: *abba, abba, cdcdcd*, where the rhymes did not exceed four. Spenser was less adventurous, but he often subtly developed the foreign principle. While his sestets are on the Shakespearean pattern, the rhymes of the octave are disposed thus: *abab, bcbc*, and the first rhyme of the sestet repeats the last rhyme of the octave *cdc, dee*. Spenser never exceeds the five rhymes of the foreign canon.

XIII

SHAKESPEARE AND THE FRENCH SONNET

Most of the topics of Shakespeare's sonnets had been handled by the Pléiade before him, and though his original development of their poetic and emotional capacities is not in question, the parallelisms between his sonnets and those of Ronsard's school have a higher critical interest than other branches of such comparative study. In Shakespeare's sonnets no instances of exact translation or direct imitation appear. But thought and expression occasionally resemble French effort closely enough to suggest that the processes of assimilation wrought at times on Shakespeare's triumphant achievement in much the same way as on the mass of the sonneteering efforts of his day. Constantly Shakespeare seems to develop with magnificent power and melody a familiar theme of foreign suggestion.

Like Spenser, Shakespeare makes oft-repeated play in his

early sonnets with the thought which he turned thus in his earliest poem *Venus and Adonis* (131-2):

> Fair flowers that are not gathered in their prime,
> *Rot and consume themselves in little time.*[1]

This is here a plain reflection of the words as well as the vein of Ronsard, who never tires of warning his mistress—

> Que vos beautez, bien qu'elles soient fleuries,
> *En peu de temps cherront toutes flaitries,*
> Et, comme fleurs, periront tout soudain.[2]

When Shakespeare reminds his lover (Sonnet civ. 3-8)—

> Three winters cold
> Have from the forests shook three summers' pride . . .
> Since first I saw you fresh, which yet are green.

—the words resemble those of a minor sonneteer of contemporary France, Vauquelin de la Fresnaie:

> La terre ia *trois fois* s'est desaisie
> De sa verdure, et ia de leurs vertus
> Se sont *trois fois* les arbres devêtus,
> Depuis qu'à toi s'est mon âme asservie.[3]

But more important than similarity of detached passages is the broader adumbrations in French sonnets of Shakespeare's leading themes. The English poet's warning that youthful beauty will utterly perish unless it propagate itself,

---

[1] Spenser rhymed on the same words when he treated the common theme (*Amoretti*, lxx):

> Make haste, therefore, sweet love, whilst it is *prime*;
> For none can call again the passed *time*.

[2] Ronsard, *Œuvres*, ed. Blanchemain, i. 397: 'Cherront' in the second line, for which 'seront' is often substituted, is the future of 'cheoir', to fall, to tumble. 'Déchoir' is the modern French form of the verb.

[3] *Les Foresteries* (1869 ed., p. 137). Three years is the conventional period of a sonneteer's love-suit both in France and England. Cf. Desportes (*Cleonice*, lvii 'Du premier jour d'Octobre'):

> Amour, s'il t'en souvient, c'est *la troisième année*,
> Le jour mesme est le point qu'à toy je fus soumis.

So Ronsard, *Sonnets pour Hélène* (No. xiv):—

> *Trois ans* sont ja passez que ton œil me tient près.

and his impassioned appeals to a highborn patron in the name
of friendship, strike a note that is heard in the inner circle of
the Pléiade. Shakespeare's denunciations of a false mistress
of black complexion were, too, already very familiar to
French sonneteers.

It is the less known French poets who approximate most
closely to Shakespeare's manner when he dwells on the duty
of fair youth to continue its succession. With great delicacy
Amadis Jamyn, a favourite disciple of Ronsard, presents his
argument of 'unthrifty loveliness', and counsels his mistress
to transmit the light of her beauty:

> Si la beauté périst, ne l'espargne, maistresse,
> Tandis qu'elle fleurist en sa jeune vigueur:
> Crois moi, je te supply, devant que la vieillesse
> Te sillonne le front, fais plaisir de ta fleur.
> On voit tomber un fruit quand il est plus que meur,
> Ayant en vain passé la saison de jeunesse:
> La feuille tombe après, jaunissant sa verdeur,
> Et l'hiver sans cheveux tous les arbres delaisse.
> Ainsi ta grand' beauté trop meure deviendra,
> La ride sur ta face en sillon s'étendra,
> Et soudain ce beau feu ne sera plus que cendre.
> N'espargne donc la fleur qui n'a que son printemps:
> La donnant tu n'y perds, mais tu jouis des ans:
> C'est une autre lumière une lumière prendre.[1]

---

[1] Amadis Jamyn, in Fouquière's *Poètes Français du XVIᵉ Siècle*, p. 133.
To much the same effect runs a sonnet by Jean de la Taille:

> Veux-tu doncques laisser en sa fleur la plus verte
>   Ton bel âge flestrir par une nonchallance?
>   Ne veux-tu point gouster au fruict de la Jouvence,
>   Qui, perdue, jamais ne sera recouverte?
> Veux-tu donc espargner ce dont on n'a point perte
>   Quand encor tout le monde en auroit jouissance?
>   Pourquoy n'acceptes-tu ceste tant bonne chance,
>   Puisque l'occasion nous a sa porte ouverte?
> Crois-tu tousjours fleurir en beauté desirée?
>   Ne crains-tu point qu'Amour avec deuë vangeance
>   Ne punisse ta mine & ton orgueil farouche?
> Mais comme les grisons du mont Hyperborée
>   Veux-tu garder soingneuse un thresor d'excellence,
>   Dont tu ne jouïs point & ne veux qu'autre y touche!

> *Œuvres de Jean de la Taille*, ed. Maulde, 1880, vol. iii,
> p. clxxix.

The French lines will recall such verses as these from Shakespeare's sonnets:

> Thou that art now the world's fresh ornament
> And only herald to the gaudy spring,
> Within thine own bud buriest thy content
> And, tender churl, mak'st waste in niggarding.
>
> i. 9–12.

> Look in thy glass, and tell the face thou viewest
> Now is the time that face should form another. . . .
> But if thou live, rememb'r'd not to be,
> Die single, and thine image dies with thee.
>
> iii. 1–2, 13–14.

> Unthrifty loveliness, why dost thou spend
> Upon thyself thy beauty's legacy? . . .
> Thy unus'd beauty must be tomb'd with thee,
> Which used, lives the executor to be.[1]
>
> iv. 1–2, 13–14.

The ecstatic praise of friendship, which fills so many of Shakespeare's sonnets, only finds occasional and detached expression in the poetry of Ronsard and his friends. Yet in one series of sonnets, which a leader of the Pléiade addressed to a noble patron, there is concentrated a depth of feeling which anticipates Shakespeare's language of devotion. The poetic vivacity and emotional subtlety of the English poetry are wanting to the French verse. But little distinction can be drawn between the general sentiment of the French and the English poet. Étienne Jodelle, one of the seven poetic stars of the French Pléiade, whose unhappy career was likened by Elizabethan critics to that of Marlowe, addressed a sequence of eight sonnets to a noble patron, M. le Comte de Fauquemberge et de Courtenay. These were first published with a long collection of 'amours' chiefly in sonnet form in 1574. In the opening address to the nobleman Jodelle speaks

---

[1] The argument was common in Renaissance literature from the days when Erasmus presented it in his colloquy *Proci et Puellae*. Shakespeare's modification of the plea by making the poet address it to a patron instead of to a mistress was anticipated by Sir Philip Sidney in his *Arcadia* (bk. iii) in the address of the dependant Geron to his master Prince Histor, and by Guarini in his *Pastor Fido* in the addresses of the old dependant Linco to his master the hero Silvio.

of his desolation in his patron's absence which no crowded company can alleviate—

> Quand seul sans toy je suis, car rien que ton absence
>   Ne me fait trouver seul, tant que quand je serois
>   Avecq' tous les humains seul je me jugerois,
> Car plus que tous humains m'est ta seule presence.[1]

Yet when his friend is absent, the French poet in the intensity of his soul's yearning fancies him present—

> Present, absent, je pais l'ame a toy toute deue.[2]

Some twenty years later Shakespeare was writing to the beloved 'subject of his sonnets—

> Thyself away art present still with me;
> For thou not farther than my thoughts can move.
> xlvii. 10-11.

Jodelle, as he developes his argument, anticipates at almost every turn the tenor of Shakespeare's sonnets. Jodelle's patron, whose genius puts labour and art to shame, is endowed by Nature with virtue and wealth and all sources of happiness. None the less the greatest joy in the Count's life is—the poet asserts—the completeness of the sympathy between the patron and his poetic admirer, which guarantees them both immortality. True and perfect friendship is the solvent of all human ills, and two friends who are joined together in real bonds of friendship acquire godlike attributes, after the manner of the union of Castor and Pollux. The poet hotly protests the eternal constancy of his affection. His spirit droops when the noble lord leaves him to engage in the sports of hunting or shooting, and he then finds his only solace in writing sonnets in the truant's honour to while away the heavy time. Shakespeare in his sonnets, it will be remembered, did no less—

---

[1] Jodelle, *Œuvres*, 1870 ed., ii, p. 174.
[2] Throughout these sonnets Jodelle addresses his lord in the second person singular, as Shakespeare does in all but thirty-four of his one hundred and fifty-four sonnets.

Nor dare I chide the world-without-end hour
Whilst I, my sovereign, watch the clock for you,
Nor think the bitterness of absence sour
When you have bid your servant once adieu.

Sonnet lvii. 5-8.

O absence! what a torment wouldst thou prove,
Were it not thy sour leisure gave sweet leave
To entertain the time with thoughts of love,
Which time and thoughts so sweetly doth deceive,
  And that thou teachest how to make one twain,
  By praising him here who doth hence remain.

Sonnet xxxix. 9-14.

Elsewhere the poet declares that he, a mere servant, has
passed into the relation of a beloved and loving friend. The
master's high birth, high rank, great wealth, and intellectual
endowments, interpose no bar to the force of the friendship.
The virtues of friendship and servitude rest alike on loving
obedience. The great friends of classical antiquity, Pylades
and Orestes, Scipio and Laelius, and the rest, lived with one
another on terms of perfect equality. The rigorous tests of
adversity, which strengthened ties of friendship in the old days,
are not needed to confirm the love which binds to his highborn lord the poet-servant who has become the master's friend.[1]

---

[1] Cf. Étienne Jodelle's Sonnet iv to his patron (Œuvres, ii. 176):

Combien que veu ton sang, ton rang, ton abondance,
Seruiteur ie te sois: i'ose prendre enuers toy
Vn nom plus haut, plus digne, & plus grand, puis qu'à moy
Tu daignes t'abaissant en donner la puissance.
Ie suis donc ton ami, mais tel que l'excellence
Du beau mot n'orgueillit mon deuoir ny ma foy:
Car plus que mille serfs ie puis ce que ie doy
Payer, & croy qu'amour doit toute obeissance.
Thesee & Perithoe, Pylade & Oreste,
Scipion & Lelie, & si quelque autre reste
Des couples des amis furent, ce croy-ie, esgaux:
Mais l'alliance ainsi d'hommes pareils vnie
Ne pourroit rien gaigner en l'espreuue des maux
Sur mon amitié serue & seruitude amie.

A literal translation in English prose might run thus:

' However much thy birth, thy rank, thy wealth show me to be servant
to thee, I dare to take in relation to thee a name loftier, worthier and
greater, since thou deignest to humble thyself and give me that power. I
am then *thy friend*, but in such fashion that the excellence of the beautiful
word induces no insolent neglect of my duty or my loyalty, because I

He credits the patron in his fifth sonnet with every intellectual grace as well as with—

Une bonté qui point ne change ou s'espouante.

Jodelle's words recall Shakespeare's commemoration of his patron's 'birth, or wealth, or wit' (Sonnet xxxvii. 5), as well as his 'bounty' (Sonnet liii. 11), and his 'abundance' (xxxvii. 11). One is reminded, too, how Shakespeare was his patron's 'slave'—

> Being your slave, what should I do but tend
> Upon the hours and times of your desire?
>   Sonnet lvii. 1-2.

Jodelle's sentiment is again recalled in such lines of Shakespeare as—

> That god forbid that made me first your slave,
> I should in thought control your times of pleasure.
>   Sonnet lviii. 1-2.

Jodelle wrote of his patron :

> Et si lon dit que trop par ces vers je *me* vante,
> C'est qu'estant tien je veux *te* vanter en mes heurs.[1]

Similarly Shakespeare greeted his 'lord of love' with the words—

> 'Tis thee, myself,—that for myself I praise.
>   Sonnet lxii. 13.

Jodelle confesses much of Shakespeare's experience of suffering and, like the English sonneteer, grieves that he was the victim of slander. Although Shakespeare's note of yearning pathos and self-torture is beyond Jodelle's range,[2] yet the emotional phase which is revealed in these French sonnets clearly adumbrated that of Shakespeare's sonneteering triumph.

---

better than a thousand slaves can pay what I owe, and what love owes in my belief is all obedience. Theseus and Pirithous, Pylades and Orestes, Scipio and Laelius, and whatever other pair of friends there be, they were, I am sure, on a perfect equality. But no alliance of such united men shows under the trial of adversity superiority to my serf-like friendship and my friend-like servitude.'

[1] *Œuvres*, ii. 176.

[2] Sonnet xxxvii should be compared with Jodelle's sonnets v and vi.

Even closer resemblances with dominant features of the French vogue appear in those sonnets, which Shakespeare addressed to a woman. His praise and dispraise of his ' dark lady ' for her black complexion reflects a very distinctive French note. Here is Amadis Jamyn's sonnet in eulogy of his ' dark lady ' :

> La modeste Venus, la honteuse et la sage,
> Estoit par les anciens toute peinte de noir,
> Et pour veuuage, dueil, loyauté faire voir
> La tourtre[1] aussi fut faitte aveq vn noir plumage.
> La sommeilleuze nuit qui noz peines soulage,
> Qui donne bon conseil, se fait noire aparoir ;
> Les mysteres sont noirs, profonds à conceuoir,
> Noire est la vérité cachée en vn nuage.
> Mille corps et non corps d'vn excellent effet
> Ont ce teint, et sans luy nul portrait n'est bien fait :
> Chacune autre couleur l'vne en l'autre se change.
> Luy seul est sans changer, signe de fermeté,
> De regret, de sagesse : aussi je l'ay chanté
> Pour une qui sur toute en merite louange.[2]

To like effect wrote Shakespeare :

> Then will I swear beauty herself is black,
> And all they foul that thy complexion lack.
>
> > Sonnet cxxxii. 13-14.

There was earlier employment in Elizabethan sonnets of this new conceit which identified blackness with ' beauty's name '. Sir Philip Sidney in Sonnet vii of his *Astrophel and Stella* noted how the ' beams ' of the eyes of his mistress were ' wrapt in colour black ' and wore ' this mourning weed ', so

> That whereas black seems beauty's contrary,
> She even in black doth make all beauties flow.

Shakespeare, too, had employed the fancy himself in his early comedy, *Love's Labour's Lost* (IV. iii. 247–53), where the heroine Rosaline is described as ' black as ebony ' with ' brows decked in black ', while her lover exclaims admiringly : ' No face is fair that is not full so black.' This judgement was in full accord with that of the French sonneteer.

---

[1] i. e. *tourterelle*, turtle.
[2] Jamyn, *Œuvres*, i, p. 129, No. xcv.

There may be an original touch in Shakespeare's note of regret that blackness should lose its traditional association of ugliness:

> In the old age black was not counted fair,
> Or, if it were, it bore not beauty's name.
>
> Sonnet cxxvii. 1–2.

But when Shakespeare turns to denounce his 'dark' mistress's disloyalty, and substitutes for his praises of his mistress's complexion vituperative abuse, he plainly re-echoes the voice of the French sonneteer. Jodelle feigns remorse for having lauded the black hair and complexion of his mistress:

> Combien de fois mes vers ont-ils doré
> Ces cheveux noirs dignes d'une Meduse?
> Combien de fois ce teint noir qui m'amuse
> Ay-je de lis et roses coloré?
> Combien ce front de rides labouré
> Ay-je applani? et quel a fait ma Muse
> Ce gros sourcil, où folle elle s'abuse,
> Ayant sur luy l'arc d'Amour figuré?
> Quel ay-je fait son œil se renfonçant?
> Quel ay-je fait son grand nez rougissant?
> Quelle sa bouche, et ses noires dents quelles?
> Quel ay-je fait le reste de ce corps?
> Qui, me sentant endurer mille morts,
> Vivoit heureux de mes peines mortelles.[1]

The self-reproach, which Shakespeare feels or affects, for having borne false witness to the beauties and virtues of his mistress, is a constant burden of the sonnet of the French Renaissance. Desportes is very prone to blame himself for over-praising his love, and on occasion denounces her as a bundle of deceptions. Her complexion is the fruit of a Spanish cosmetic, and her hair is false:

> Ceste vive couleur, qui ravit et qui blesse
> Les esprits des amans, de la feinte abusez,
> Ce n'est que blanc d'Espagne, et ces cheveux frisez
> Ne sont pas ses cheveux: c'est une fausse tresse.[2]

---

[1] Jodelle, 'Contr'Amours,' vii, in *Œuvres*, ii, p. 94.
[2] Desportes, 'Diverses Amours,' Sonnet xxix, in *Œuvres*, ed. Michiels, p. 398.

Again Desportes writes:

> Le bruit de ses beautez, volant par l'univers,
> N'est qu'un conte à plaisir que j'ay feint en mes vers,
> Pour voir si je pourroy bien chanter une fable;
>   Bref, je n'y reconnois un mot de verité,
> Sinon quand j'ay parlé de sa legereté,
> Car lors ce n'est plus conte, ains discours veritable.

> Sonnet xxxviii, *ib.* p. 404.

Shakespeare echoes the note when in Sonnet clii. 13–14 he tells his 'dark lady':

> For I have sworn thee fair; more perjur'd I,
> To swear against the truth so foul a lie!

as well as in Sonnet cxxxvii, 13–14:

> In things right true my heart and eyes have err'd,
> And to this false plague are they now transferr'd.

Nor is there need to illustrate here the invective which Shakespeare and his fellows in both plays and poems often launched like Desportes against the artificial disguises of ladies' toilettes. 'These bastard signs of fair,' 'the living brow' decorated with 'the golden *tresses* of the dead', constantly moved Shakespeare's indignation (cf. Sonnet lxviii. 3–7).[1] 'The curld-worne *tresses* of dead-borrowd haire'

---

[1] Two other expressions of the same category in Shakespeare's vituperative sonnets have French parallels. In No. vi of his *Contr'Amours* Jodelle, after reproaching his 'traitres vers' with having untruthfully described his siren as a beauty, concludes:

> *Ja si long temps faisant d'un Diable un Ange,*
> Vous m'ouvrez l'œil en l'iniuste louange,
> Et m'aveuglez en l'iniuste tourment.

With this should be compared Shakespeare's sonnet cxliv. 9–10:

> And whether *that my angel be turn'd fiend*
> Suspect I may, but not directly tell.

Again Desportes summons to repentance abandoned women who sin for money:

> Qui avez preferée
> A la sainte amitié la richesse dorée,
> Le vice à la vertu, l'ignorance au sçavoir,
> Et l'orde convoitise au fidelle devoir,
> Et n'avez estimée estre chose vilaine—
> *Du revenu du lict* accroistre son domaine.

> Élégies, I. ix, in *Œuvres*, ed. Michiels, Paris, 1858, p. 258.

The phrase in this context 'Du revenu du lict' seems echoed in Daniel's

formed the text of many a biting Elizabethan satire.[1]
Desportes' words—

> ces cheveux frisez
> Ne sont pas ses cheveux : c'est une fausse *tresse*

—were almost as good English as they were good French.

More than one view is held as to the precise significance of
Shakespeare's sonnets. But those who deem them auto-
biographic confessions can hardly deny that Shakespeare at
times took his cue from contemporary French literature.

XIV

The Poetic Vaunt of Immortality

The dissemination through Elizabethan verse of the poetic
vaunt of immortality may serve as a final illustration of the
general influence which was exerted by the Pléiade on the idea
or sentiment of the Elizabethan lyric—both song and sonnet.
Very much of the work of the Pléiade is infected by that tone
of arrogance which Ronsard exemplified in his boast—

> Je suis, dis je, Ronsard, et cela te suffice,
> Ce Ronsard, que la France honore, chante et prise,
> Des Muses le mignon ; et de qui les escrits
> N'ont crainte de se voir par les âges surpris.

With a superb confidence Ronsard and his friends and
disciples repeatedly claimed immortality for their names, for
their poetry, and for all whom they celebrated in verse.

The pretension was a classical legacy. The veteran pleas
of Pindar, Horace, and Ovid nurtured the longing for eternal
renown in the hearts of the French poets. But the Pléiade
revived the classical aspiration with an assurance which ex-
ceeded that of their Greek and Latin masters. Ronsard's

Complaint of Rosamond (1594), 755-6, where it is said of vicious women
that they

> In uncleanness ever have been fed
> By the *revenue of a wanton bed*.

Shakespeare employs the same expression when he denounced his false
mistress for having

> Robb'd *others' beds' revenues* of their rents.

(Sonnet cxlii, line 8.)

[1] Cf. Goddard's *Satyricall Dialogue*, 1615, sig. Bb.

spirited rendering of Horace's familiar ode (III. xxx) seems to
accentuate the egoism of the Latin original:

> Plus dur que fer j'ay fini mon ouvrage,
> Que l'an, dispos à demener les pas,
> Que l'eau, le vent ou le brulant orage,
> L'injuriant, ne ru'ront point à bas.
> Quand ce viendra que le dernier trespas
> M'assoupira d'un somme dur, à l'heure
> Sous le tombeau tout Ronsard n'ira pas,
> Restant de luy la part qui est meilleure.
> Tousjours, tousjours sans que jamais je meure,
> Je voleray tout vif par l'univers,
> Eternisant les champs où je demeure,
> De mes lauriers fatalement couvers,
> Pour avoir joint les deux harpeurs [1] divers
> Au doux babil de ma lyre d'yvoire,
> Que j'ay rendus Vaudomois par mes vers.
> Sus donque, Muse, emporte au ciel la gloire
> Que j'ay gaignée, annonçant la victoire
> Dont à bon droit je me voy jouissant,
> Et de son fils consacre la memoire,
> Serrant son front d'un laurier verdissant.[2]

In the same vein Du Bellay turned into his own tongue
the famous vaunt with which Ovid brings his *Metamorphoses*
to a close.   Du Bellay's version runs thus:

> Un œuvre j'ay parfait, que le feu ni la foudre,
> Ni le fer ni le temps ne pourront mettre en poudre.
> Cestuy-là qui sera le dernier de mes jours
> De mon age incertain vienne borner le cours
> Quand bon luy semblera; sans plus il a puissance
> Dessus ce corps qui est mortel de sa naissance.
> Ce qui est meilleur de moi me portera
> Sur les astres bien haut, et mon nom ne pourra
> Jamais estre effacé; quelque part où se nomme
> Le nom victorieux de l'empire de Rome
> Je seray leu du peuple.   Et s'il faut donner foy
> Aux poëtes devins, qui predisent de soy,
> A jamais je vivray et la durable gloire
> De mes œuvres sera d'éternelle memoire.[3]

---

[1] Pindar and Horace.
[2] Ronsard, 'A sa muse,' Bk. v, Ode xxxii.
[3] Du Bellay, *Œuvres Choisies*, ed. Fouquières, pp. 162–3.

The French poets clothed their passionate desire for eternal fame in a rich variety of tones, which has no precise parallel elsewhere. Sometimes they are calmly precatory; sometimes they are aggressively or defiantly confident; at other times their self-assurance is almost regal in its complaisance. In one very beautiful ode Ronsard invokes all the gods of Greece and Rome, and entreats them to help him to realize his immortal longings. In the last verse he addresses himself to the Dryads, meek recluses of the forests:

> Ornez ce livre de lierre,
> Ou de myrte, et loin de la terre
> Sil vous plaist enlevez ma vois;
> Et faites que tousjours ma lyre
> D'âge en âge s'entende bruire
> Du More jusques à l'Anglois.[1]

It is no mere recognition by his own people that satisfies the French poet's aspiration:

> Mon nom, dès l'onde atlantique
> Jusqu'au dos du More antique,
> Soit immortel tesmoigné,
> Et depuis l'isle erratique
> Jusqu'au Breton esloigné,
> A fin que mon labeur croisse
> Et sonoreux apparoisse
> Lyrique par dessus tous,
> Et que Thebes se cognoisse
> Faite Françoise par nous.[2]

Elsewhere the master of the Pléiade (in a sonnet) bids his page bring him a hundred leaves of paper on which to write words which are to last like diamonds and to be studied deeply by all future ages.

Ronsard's colleagues betray no greater moderation. Perhaps the most buoyant expression of the valorous theme is that of Du Bellay in his lyric on the immortality of poets ('De l'Immortalité des Poëtes'). The animated melody of the verse no less than its imperial vanity renders the poem hard to match, despite its Horatian affinities:

---

[1] Ronsard, Odes, IV. xv, in Œuvres, ii, p. 272.
[2] ibid., Odes Retranchées, Œuvres, ii, pp. 443–4.

Arriere tout funebre chant,
Arriere tout marbre et peinture,
Mes cendres ne vont point cherchant
Les vains honneurs de sepulture,
Pour n'estre errant cent ans à l'environ
Des tristes bords de l'avare Acheron.

Mon nom du vil peuple incognu
N'ira sous terre inhonoré;
Les Sœurs du mont deux fois cornu
M'ont de sepulchre decoré
Qui ne craint point les Aquilons puissans,
Ni le long cours des siecles renaissans.[1]

With these professions go oft-repeated assurances to patrons
that the poet's praises can alone make their reputations
enduring:

C'est un travail de bonheur
Chanter les hommes louables,
Et leur bastir un honneur
Seul vainqueur des ans muables.
Le marbre ou l'airain vestu
D'un labeur vif par l'enclume
N'animent tant la vertu
Que les Muses par la plume.[2]

In the heyday of the Elizabethan outburst the identical
vaunts were naturalized in Elizabethan poetry. The proofs
are overwhelming that here, if anywhere, the Elizabethan
employed the language of the Pléiade. The note was of
classical strain, but the English writers echoed it in a
distinctively French key. Sir Philip Sidney in his *Apologie
for Poetrie* (1595) wrote that it was the common habit of
poets 'to tell you that they will make you immortal by their
verses'. 'Men of great calling,' asserted Nashe in his *Pierce
Pennilesse* (1598), 'take it of merit to have their names
eternized by poets'. In the hands of Elizabethan sonneteers
the 'eternizing' faculty of their verse became a staple topic.
Spenser wrote in his *Amoretti* (1595, Sonnet lxxv):

My verse your virtues rare shall eternize,
And in the heavens write your glorious name.

---

[1] Du Bellay, *Œuvres choisies*, ed. Fouquières, p. 118.
[2] Ronsard, Odes I. vii, *Œuvres*, ed. Blanchemain, ii, p. 58.

Again, when commemorating the death of the Earl of Warwick in the *Ruines of Time* (*c.* 1591), the same poet assured the Earl's widowed countess

> Thy Lord shall never die the whiles this verse
> Shall live, and surely it shall live for ever;
> For ever it shall live, and shall rehearse
> His worthy praise, and virtues dying never,
> Though death his soul do from his body sever;
> And thou thyself herein shalt also live;
> Such grace the heavens do to my verses give.

Drayton and Daniel developed the conceit with unblushing iteration. Drayton, who spoke of his efforts as 'my immortal song' (*Idea*, vi. 14) and 'my world-out-wearing rhymes' (xliv. 7), embodied the vaunt in such lines as:

> While thus my pen strives to eternize thee (*Idea*, xliv. 1).
> Ensuing ages yet my rhymes shall cherish (*ib.* xliv. 11).
> My name shall mount unto eternity (*ib.* xliv. 14).
> All that I seek is to eternize thee (*ib.* xlvii. 14).

Daniel was no less explicit:

> This [*sc.* verse] may remain thy lasting monument (*Delia*, xxxvii. 9).
> Thou mayst in after ages live esteemed,
> Unburied in these lines (*ib.* xxxix. 9–10).
> These [*sc.* my verses] are the arks, the trophies I erect
> That fortify thy name against old age;
> And these [*sc.* verses] thy sacred virtues must protect
> Against the dark and time's consuming rage (*ib.* l. 9–12).

Shakespeare, in his references to his 'eternal lines' (xviii. 12) and in the assurances that he gives the subject of his addresses that the sonnets are the young man's 'monument' (lxxxi. 9, cvii. 13), boldly accommodated himself to the French canon of taste. Characteristically he more than once invested the topic with a splendour that was not approached by any other poet (lv. 1–2):

> Not marble, nor the gilded monuments
> Of princes, shall outlive this powerful rhyme.

Elsewhere Shakespeare more conventionally foretells that his friend amid the oblivion of the day of doom

> shall in these black lines be seen,
> And they shall live, and he in them still green.[1]

> Your monument shall be my gentle verse,
> Which eyes not yet created shall o'er-read . . .
> You still shall live,—such virtue hath my pen.[2]

Here we have Ronsard very slenderly qualified :

> Donne moy l'encre et le papier aussi,
> En cent papiers tesmoins de mon souci
> Je veux tracer la peine que j'endure :
> En cent papiers plus durs que diamant,
> A fin qu'un jour nostre race future
> Juge du mal que je souffre en aimant.[3]

> Vous vivrez et croistrez comme Laure en grandeur
> Au moins tant que vivront les plumes et le livre.[4]

Ronsard and his friends never tired of the text that their pens, their papers, and their tablets were the base implements of a poetic spirit which through such poor agencies was winging its way to eternity.   The lyric expression of this boast in Elizabethan England was the most persistent of all the clear echoes of the Pléiade's phrase and aspiration.

---

[1] Shakespeare, Sonnet lxiii. 13–14.
[2] *ibid.* lxxxi. 9–10, 13.
[3] Ronsard, *Amours*, I. cxciii (*Œuvres*, I. 109).
[4] *ibid.*, *Sonnets pour Hélène*, II. ii.

BOOK V
THE MESSAGE OF THE HUGUENOTS

I

Characteristics of the Huguenot Movement

FRENCH Humanism in its early days set out in quest of
a mildly rationalized theology. It approved of biblical
study; efforts to strip the Church worship of what looked
like superstitious ceremonies were encouraged; there was
hope of diminishing ecclesiastical interference in the affairs
of the laity. But those who directed the main movements of
the French humanist army left Christian dogma much as they
found it. Liberty of belief or of unbelief satisfied the intellectual ambitions of the centre of the humanist forces. A left
wing, however, discerned elemental defects in the Roman theory
of religion. Under the leadership of Calvin a new theological
and ethical creed was evolved, and open war was declared on
the established Catholic codes. The Calvinist organization,
though it very slowly lost its humanist tinge, travelled far from
the humanist ideals. Expelled from France by the governing power, the Calvinist theocracy exercised from Geneva a
spiritual tyranny far more rigorous than anything it displaced.
In set terms it ultimately pronounced liberty of conscience
a diabolical dogma, and purely aesthetic or intellectual endeavour ungodly impropriety. Calvinist literature of the
sixteenth century, whether it were produced in France or
Switzerland, helped to endow literary prose with logical precision; but the doctrine checked among the faithful imaginative
activity or originality; poetry was banished to the outer courts
of the temple, and only there admitted, if heavily laden with
piety.

In France the humanist enthusiasm was too strong to commend Calvinism to the bulk of those who cherished early hopes
of religious reform. Most of the humanist reformers resented
Calvin's drastic revolution and his antagonism to secular culture.
Dread of the chilling atmosphere of Calvin's demesne tended

to draw moderate men of literary feeling back to the more genial air of the old Catholic fold.   Under Calvinist pressure, humanism in its main line of development more or less perfunctorily reconciled itself with Catholicism.   Profane French literature of the lighter kind in the middle of the sixteenth century was chiefly the work of professedly Catholic and anti-Calvinist pens.   The greatest writers in sixteenth-century prose and poetry—men like Rabelais, Montaigne, and Amyot among prose writers, or like Ronsard, Du Bellay, and Desportes among poets—were in name loyal Catholics, and in act and deed foes of Calvinist theory and practice.

Yet at the side of the poetic Pléiade and of the great Catholic artists in prose, there flourished within France a notable band of humanists who, calling themselves Huguenots, remained faithful to the early hopes of religious reform, but did not abandon liberal culture while they accepted Calvinist teaching.   Some French poets, some dramatists, some writers of eloquent prose succeeded in reconciling a substantial measure of Calvinist belief with aesthetic and intellectual aspirations. Their allegiance was divided between the Hebrew scriptures and the profane classics, and drawing mental and spiritual sustenance from both, they won distinction in many intellectual fields.   Among these enlightened Protestants were the poets Du Bartas and Aubigné, the scholars Étienne and Scaliger, the dramatists Grévin and Montchrétien, and the philosopher Ramus.   Huguenot soldiers and statesmen, under the leadership of Gaspard de Coligny and Henry of Navarre, cultivated literary enthusiasms, which did the spirit of the Renaissance no discredit ; they acknowledged discipleship to Plutarch and Seneca, as well as to Homer and Vergil, the Hebrew prophets and Christ's Apostles.   From this broad-minded Huguenot school there issued influences which powerfully helped to mould the course of English thought and culture.

The Huguenot movement at its maturity played many unexpected and hardly consistent parts in the history of France.   Its spirit took the Protean shapes which were bred of the mingling, on a generous scale, of Hebraic and classical, of sacred and profane conceptions of human life and endeavour.

The movement boasted at once of religious, intellectual, political, military, philosophic, and poetic achievement. Although the organization of Church consistories and synods, and the new theology of election and predestination exhausted the interests of the orthodox Calvinist, yet the Huguenot of the broad school watched with keen attention secular developments of philosophy and learning. He loved to debate first principles of logic and ethics; he was fascinated by the study of law and history; he cherished conceptions of political regeneration; he advocated with an emphasis which none had anticipated the rights of the people to control government; he pleaded for the sanctity of liberty in matters of conscience, and for the virtue of toleration. While the Huguenot of every type was in theory a votary of peace, he always cherished a firm faith in war as the last resort of those who suffered for conscience' sake, and the more enlightened section of the fraternity was prepared to fight for principles of philosophy and politics as well as of religion.

The ripened creed of Huguenot France was thus composed of simples culled as liberally from philosophy, literature, and political theory as from theology. Its piety was deep and lasting. The literary and philosophic activity of the movement rarely cooled its religious ardour. Love of poetry or art, enthusiasm for liberty of conscience, failed to breed in the Huguenot fold religious indifferentism. Literature and philosophy from Huguenot pens accepted, without demur, the main tenets of the faith. The stress of political or military conflict exposed Huguenot convictions to greater dangers. At the Huguenot head-quarters political exigencies often menaced principle, and there were among the practical strategists of the party backsliders who finally sacrificed their creed to political ambition.

The Huguenot movement, when it is viewed in its full scope, is consequently seen to split as it grew into three main divisions. Something of a centrifugal tendency was inevitable in a busy school of thought and activity, which drew much of its first strength from a predilection for dissent and controversy. On the left flank lay the zealots for Calvin's spiritual bondage, whose literary labour was confined to dogmatic themes. In the centre stood the enlightened champions of liberty of conscience, who contrived to harmonize love of their creed and courage on the battle-field with wide literary sympathy and philosophic originality. On the right flank there gathered a company of ambitious advocates of political ascendancy, who were prepared to go further than the centre in the name of expediency, and at times succumbed to the temptation of purchasing peace or profit by surrender of the spiritual citadel. In the moderate centre are to be found the great Huguenot authors, and their attractiveness resides as much in their fine traits of character and temperament as in their written word. The twofold devotion to the Bible and the classics seemed to generate in this middle party a noble type of integrity which was incapable of corruption, and while it was prepared to sacrifice non-essentials in the cause of toleration and liberty was stedfast in all else. Nor did this idiosyncrasy of the golden mean fail in a whole-hearted worship of the Muses.

II

The Civil Wars in France

Civil war was the most conspicuous and engrossing of the practical issues of the Huguenot movement. Some study of the politico-military annals of the French civil wars is needed to an appreciation of the influence of the movement abroad as well as at home. It is not only the literary and philosophic achievement of France that riveted the attention of England, when Elizabethan poetry and drama were coming of age at the end of the sixteenth century. There were in less ethereal spheres of activity events which stirred powerful emotion through two generations. Elizabethan Englishmen of all ranks and capacity were deeply moved by the religious and political conflicts which for nearly fifty years kept France in turmoil. While Ronsard and his friends were busily effecting their reformation of French poetry, France was in the early throes of that intestine strife which continued intermittently for great part of a century, though it only blazed in full ferocity at intervals, and was punctuated by prolonged truces. The warfare was pursued in its most brutal rigour while the Elizabethan poets were in early manhood. Pitched battles and sieges formed only one feature of the furious struggle. When the armies returned to their tents there were alarums and excursions in the shape of massacres or assassinations which caused in England hardly less horror than in France herself. The domestic dissensions of our neighbours found expression in deeds of violence, so cruel and startling as to shake the nerve of Europe.

Owing to the volatility of the national genius, the politico-military convulsions of France affected the tone of general literature less powerfully than might have been anticipated. The main lyric stream of poetic energy was rarely ruffled by the ferment. A man of Montaigne's literary genius could survey the scene of tumult without prejudice to his philosophic temper of detachment. French thought calmly evolved much political theory which bore no obvious trace of the storms of violence. Yet the civil warfare was bound on occasion to disturb the current of literary effort. Political and religious argument was often charged with revolutionary passion and a new strength of invective. Huguenot poetry, too, caught at times the menacing tone of Hebraic prophecy and roared imprecations on the heads of the Catholic foe. Satire in verse was driven by political and ecclesiastical rancour to scurrilous excesses. The atmosphere of literature could not always escape the vibrations of the world outside.

The questions at issue between Protestant and Catholic were submitted comparatively early to the arbitrament of force. If the ruling powers of France allowed in the dawn of the Renaissance freedom of religious thought, they only countenanced criticism which touched more or less academic theories of theology. As soon as Protestant disaffection questioned ecclesiastical practice and polity, the active leaders of the Church replied to the challenge in terms of persecution or decrees of exile. The secular government quickly accepted the sacerdotal counsel of coercion ; Protestant resistance proved stubborn ; the result was frank rebellion, political as well as religious.   The ground of quarrel often tended to shift from a difference between Romanism and Calvinism to one between unlimited monarchy inclining to absolutism and constitutional monarchy inclining to Republicanism.   But the controversy, whatever its immediate colour, was waged with assured reliance on the persuasive power of sword and cannon.

The persecution of French Protestants as heretics began in 1535.   A year before a fanatical body of Reformers had challenged the indulgence of the State by placarding Paris with a broadside abusing the Mass and its celebrants.   Paris and the chief cities of central France soon witnessed many Huguenot martyrdoms.   Seeking encouragement in such French poetry as was available, the martyrs went to the stake chanting Marot's tuneful version of the Psalms.   The Psalms were thenceforth the battle-songs of the Huguenots.   The persecution was pursued until 1560.   Then the stalwart Protestants were strong enough to organize military resistance.

The strength of the Huguenots first lay in the small cities among the small tradesmen and artisans of the lower middle classes, who had at the bidding of Calvin formed themselves into congregations, consistories, and synods.   Towns like Caen, Meaux, Poictiers, and the prosperous port of La Rochelle eagerly accepted the new faith at the outset.   But the infection steadily spread in many districts of France from the lower to the upper ranks of society.   The south-west, reaching from the river Loire to the Pyrenees, soon became the most compact of Huguenot strongholds, and there the rich bourgeoisie grew more ardent in the cause than the poor.   In Normandy, in Dauphiné, in Lower Languedoc, and in many scattered districts of Anjou, Maine, Champagne, and Burgundy Protestantism spread evenly through every class.   In Brittany the nobility alone encouraged religious reform, which the people at large stoutly opposed.   The city of Meaux, in the neighbourhood of Paris, where the flag had been raised in early days, was always faithful to the cause through all ranks.   Paris had a resolute but comparatively small Huguenot contingent.   With such notable exceptions, the centre and north-east of France, which were more densely populated than the rest of the country, showed only sparse signs of wavering in devotion to the old religion.

The Huguenot cause attracted men who loved fighting and adventure. It was reckoned that, out of every three members of the lower nobility who were capable of bearing arms, one was pledged to the new religion and served as an officer in the Huguenot armies. The rank and file were recruited from the trading and artisan classes, who cherished a spirtual earnestness which it was difficult to daunt on the field of battle. Huguenot officers and private soldiers reached a total exceeding 100,000. The Catholics claimed a force ten times as large. But superiority of zeal and generalship on the part of the Huguenots proved an effective compensation for inferiority of numbers.

When war grew imminent, Huguenot aspirations for political liberty and freedom of conscience won powerful adherents within the king's council, and schemes of toleration which were promulgated in the king's name, postponed for a season the outbreak of hostilities. There seemed a likelihood that the destinies of France would be guided by statesmanship, which had caught something of the magnanimity that gave the Huguenot centre its best title to respect. Hopes of conciliation on lines of comprehension conquered the mind and heart of an adviser of the crown. Although his efforts at an accommodation failed, they drew tributes of admiration from Englishmen no less than from enlightened Frenchmen. In 1560 Michel de l'Hôpital became chancellor of France. He was no avowed Huguenot; he seems to have attended mass; but his wife and children accepted the proscribed creed, he acknowledged the reasonableness of the Huguenot plea, and Protestants often reckoned him one of themselves. He stood indeed outside the range of religious or political party, and his religion was of that indefinable quality which is proverbially allotted to the faith of all sensible men. His philosophic calm and humane temper gave him his fame. It was said that his countenance resembled that of Aristotle on Greek medals, and his tone of mind that of Cato the

Censor.   A skilful orator and a fine scholar, he enjoyed the
affectionate regard of all men of culture.   L'Hôpital was a
writer of admirable Latin verse, and Ronsard greeted him
as—

> Ce divin l'Hospital
> En mœurs et en sçavoir, qui si doctement touche
> La lyre et qui le miel fait couler de sa bouche.

To him Ronsard dedicated the greatest and the longest of
his Pindaric odes.   There the poet describes how the chancellor's virtues and accomplishments have fitted France for the
Muses' lasting home.   But it is his moral excellence which,
in the opinion of the poet, chiefly glorifies his country :

> Mais veritable il me plaist
> De chanter bien haut, qu'il est
> L'ornement de nostre France,
> Et qu'en fidele equité,
> En justice et verité,
> Les vieux siecles il devance.[1]

L'Hôpital figures in an even more heroic light in Brantôme's
gallery where he is likened to Sir Thomas More, chancellor
of England, despite the obvious discrepancy between their
religious sympathies.

At the turning-point in his country's fortunes, L'Hôpital's
magnanimity seemed well fitted to mediate between the rival
hosts into which his fellow countrymen were divided.   Tran-
quilly and sanguinely he set forth to heal dissensions.   'Patience,
patience, tout ira bien,' were words often on his lips, but his
eloquent appeal for mutual tolerance succeeded only in delay-
ing the final breach.   When he saw how his manful strivings

---

[1] Ronsard, Odes, Bk. I, Ode x (Œuvres, ed. Blanchemain, ii. 95).
Some of Ronsard's friends were irritated by L'Hôpital's exemplary fair-
ness of mind and his obvious sympathy with the Huguenots.   Jodelle in
a bitter satire denounced in a very characteristic vein of controversy the
ambiguities of his opinions :

> Sa vertu est d'estre un Prothée,
> Sa neutralité d'estre Athée,
> Sa paix deux lignes maintenir :
> Changer les loix, c'est sa pratique,
> Sa court les pedants soustenir,
> Et son sçavoir d'estre heretique.

(Œuvres, ed. Marty-Laveaux, Paris, 1870, ii. 349.)

for peace were of no avail against the dominant forces of bigotry and unreason, he with calm dignity resigned the seals of office.   In words that have become classic, he declared that he had followed the ' great royal road ' which turns neither to the right hand nor the left, and had given himself to no faction.   Amid all the evils of the time the up-right statesman preserved, in the contemporary phraseology, 'the lilies of France in his heart,' but the crushing blow which the massacre of St. Bartholomew's Day soon dealt to his last hopes of pacification cost him his life (March 13, 1573). Of the impression which such a type of culture and integrity left on the Elizabethan mind, noble testimony is borne by Sir Philip Sidney, the knightly champion of the Huguenot cause in England.   In his *Apology for Poetry* Sidney numbers L'Hôpital among statesmen to whom the cause of sweet poesy was dear, and who made it prevail.   Sidney credits the French chancellor with a ' more accomplished judgement more firmly builded upon virtue, than had yet come to birth '.[1]

It was the noble family of the Guises, who controlled the most bigoted wing of absolutist Catholicism.   Their astuteness was mainly responsible for the impotency of L'Hôpital's great endeavour.   The Guises gained control of the action of the queen-mother, Catherine de' Medici, who as regent for her young son Charles IX dominated affairs of state.   Their influence made a stern and unflinching policy of repression finally to prevail.   The hope of compromise or conciliation was extinguished by the flame of brutal fanaticism, which the Guises fanned.   The Huguenots eagerly accepted the challenge, and in 1562 there was fought at Dreux, on the borders of Normandy, the first pitched battle between French Catholics and Huguenots.   Elizabethan England sent men, money, and guns to the aid of her French co-religionists. Although Huguenots cherished misgivings of foreign inter-

[1] Sidney's *Apology*, ed. Shuckburgh, p. 48.   Sidney is here inquiring into the causes of the low repute of poetry in England, and attributes the foreign superiority to the practice habitual to men in high position abroad not only of befriending poets, but also of writing poetry for themselves. Among such foreign champions of the poetic art he reckons ' before all, that *Hospitall* of Fraunce. '

ference in the field and showed some suspicion of their English allies, the fortunes of the war were scanned almost as anxiously in England as in France. There was no lack of sensation. The assassination by a Huguenot of the head of the Guise family, Francis, the second duke, while the Catholics were besieging Orleans, gave a foretaste of the weapon which was to be freely used in future frays (Feb. 18, 1563). A hollow peace between the combatants then gave them a brief breathing space. But campaign was to follow campaign in quick succession.

In 1567 there broke out the second war, during which the great battle of St. Denis was fought under the walls of Paris. In these early encounters the Catholics were victorious, but the undismayed Huguenots sanguinely began a third war in 1569 and lost no ground during its progress. At the well-contested fight of Jarnac in the western province of Saintonge, the Huguenot general, the Prince of Condé, Henry of Navarre's uncle, was captured and shot. The supreme command devolved on an officer of even larger skill and experience, and one whose character was as lofty,—Gaspard de Coligny. Coligny's first battle of Moncontour failed to retrieve the neighbouring disaster of Jarnac. But there followed in 1570 a third peace—that of St. Germain—which offered the Huguenots comparatively easy terms and greatly stimulated their hope of ultimate success.

It was in 1572, two years after the conclusion of the third war and the third peace, that Queen Catherine and the Guises, despairing of other means of crushing their enemies, planned and executed the ghastly massacre of St. Bartholomew's Day. Thirty thousand Huguenots in Paris and the provinces were put to the sword, and the victims included Coligny, the noble-hearted commander of the Huguenot forces, and Ramus, the intellectual chieftain of the movement. The barbarity outraged English feeling beyond all precedent. Loud and deep were the English curses of French Catholic cruelty. The fevered wrath of Queen Elizabeth's subjects was echoed on the Elizabethan stage, and Marlowe's lurid pageant of tragedy, which was entitled *The Massacre of*

Paris, was one of many testimonies to the unquenchable anger of Shakespeare's generation against the St. Bartholomew assassins of 1572.

The murderous manœuvre failed in attaining the object of its perpetrators. Surviving Protestants flew to arms with renewed spirit, and for the eight following years France had little respite from the wearing strife. At the outset of this period the Huguenot strongholds of La Rochelle and Sancerre were subjected to the tortures of desperate sieges. The chance of any early abatement of the vindictive stress seemed small. None the less a sense of impatience with extremists on both sides was steadily developing among the calmer sections of the people. Though compromise proved as yet impracticable the wish for it was growing articulate.

It was from the momentous year 1584 that there dated the latest and the longest campaign, or series of campaigns in the religious war of sixteenth-century France. Four years of delusive quiet preluded the final conflict. In that interval Queen Elizabeth encouraged, more actively than before, the addresses of a French suitor, the Duke d'Alençon, the French king's heir and brother, and her apparent earnestness in the matrimonial negotiation fostered a fallacious hope, both in England and France, of a religious and political settlement without further recourse to the sword. The death of Queen Elizabeth's French lover in 1584 abruptly revived the struggle in its fiercest shape. The French king, Henry III, was now brotherless as well as childless. The throne of France had lost its heir, and the process of choosing a successor brought into the struggle a new element of schism. Dynastic rivalry thenceforth embittered religious dissent. Henry of Navarre, who, despite his disposition to gallantry, was now the accepted leader of the Huguenot forces, was lineal heir of the childless king, and he fought henceforth for his crown as well as for his faith. Under such stimulus the passion for political ascendancy grew strong in the right wing of the Huguenot ranks.

Navarre's uncle, Cardinal Charles de Bourbon, whose Catholic fervour was unquestioned, was promptly put forward by the Guises as the royal Catholic heir. Catholics were adjured to acknowledge no title but his. A Catholic association was reorganized under the name of the Holy League to resist Navarre's claim to the French crown.

The Holy League's appeal to Spanish support ostensibly ruined the Huguenot chances of military success. But the foreign alliance had an effect opposite to that which was designed. Moderate Catholics and moderate Huguenots were drawn together by a patriotic sentiment which dreaded foreign dominion, and thus there was cradled the formidable party of ' Les Politiques ', whose most effective bond of union was hostility to the Guises. The French king, who chafed against the Hispaniolized sway of the Guises, bid boldly for the aid of the liberal Catholics, from whom ' Les Politiques ' were largely recruited. Thus the Catholics soon split into two militant factions. While the extremists rallied round the Guises, moderate men were inclined to support the reigning sovereign against all comers, and to leave the succession for time to settle. Huguenots of various complexions at the same time marched together in effectual harmony under the banner of the king of Navarre.

The moderate Catholic forces of the king opened the strife anew by rashly joining the advanced party of the Guises in an endeavour to drive Navarre from the field. The result was a surprise for Navarre's allied foe. He and the Huguenots won at Coutras, in Guienne, their first decisive victory in battle (October, 1587). Thenceforth the star of Navarre was in the ascendant. Murderous acts of private vengeance combined with natural processes of death to remove from his path his most formidable rivals, and to clear the road for his final triumph. In December, 1588, the French king contrived the assassination of the Duke of Guise and of his brother the Cardinal of Guise. Next month (on January 5, 1589) died Catherine de' Medici, the queen-mother, the inveterate foe of the Huguenots, and there followed at St. Cloud in the summer the murder, by the fanatic Dominican, Jacques Clement, of the French king (Henry III) (July 31).

Henry of Navarre thus advanced to the centre of the French political stage. The Elizabethan public had lately watched

his fortunes with intense sympathy and he was now their idol.
The Earl of Essex was an eager worshipper. English
volunteers crowded to Henry's camp. Shakespeare, in one of
his earliest comedies (*Comedy of Errors*, III. ii. 128), reflected
the popular interest when he wrote of ' France armed and
reverted, making war against her heir '. Henry's valour and
luck proved irresistible. He won the brilliant victory of Ivry
(March 14, 1590), and the Holy League could no longer bar
his passage to the French throne. Fate continued to fight
for him. His uncle, the Cardinal de Bourbon, who was
Catholic rival to the crown, and was known to his supporters
as King Charles X, was removed by death within two months
of the triumph of Ivry, and the royal pretender was soon
followed to the grave (December 8, 1592) by the great
Spanish general, Alexander of Parma, whose co-operation
was all-important to the League. That association was
thenceforth rent by internal jealousies. The moderate men
among Catholics and Huguenots preached peace with a new
energy. The cry of ' Les Politiques ' for compromise rang
with the note of both reason and expediency, and finally
grew irresistible.

But the Protestants were still a minority of the people, and
a nominal Catholic could alone win the allegiance of the
nation at large. Henry's religious convictions were not deep,
and he did not hesitate to cut the Gordian knot by choosing
the path of least resistance. He came to the conclusion that
a crown was worth a Mass. He was received into the bosom
of the Catholic Church at St. Denis on July 25, 1593, when
he solemnly abjured all protestant heresies, and was panegy-
rized by the preacher Du Perron, who had lately celebrated
Ronsard's funeral obsequies. Henry was anointed king of
France at Chartres on February 27, 1594, and Paris opened
her gates to him. Never was new-crowned monarch more
heartily greeted by his subjects.

' Les Politiques,' who were responsible for this happy issue,
found at the height of the crisis their most effective weapon
in literary satire. The dominion of the Catholic League received
its final blow from the pen and not from the sword. During

1593 there were put into circulation some flysheets of a journalistic pattern which effectively imputed to the enemies of Henry of Navarre the meanest motives and a total want of patriotism. The chieftains of the League were represented as cunning charlatans who gloried in a cynical contempt for the fortunes of their country. Part of the satire was cast in dramatic form. There were placed in the mouths of the Leaguers and of their satellites comically frank confessions of sordid principles. These ironies were followed by eloquent and serious statements of the case of 'Les Politiques'. The work was chiefly written in vigorous prose. But there were interludes of grotesque or flamboyant verse. The original flysheets were first collected and published with amplifications in the summer of 1594, under the title of *La Satire Ménippée*.[1] Additions were made in subsequent issues, which were numerous. The authorship was anonymous; but at least eight of the writers have been identified. Among them were the poets Jean Passerat and Gilles Durant, who were tuneful disciples of Ronsard, and the dramatist Florent Chrétien, who was at one time a convinced Huguenot. Few political pamphlets proved of greater effect. Elizabethan England welcomed with characteristic promptitude this sturdy assault on Catholic bigotry.

La Satire Ménippée helped to guide public opinion in England. Within a few months of the publication of the work in French an English translation was licensed by the Stationers' Company in London (September 28, 1594). The English version, which retained little of the polish of the original, duly appeared next year under the title, 'A Pleasant Satyre or Poesie. Wherein is discovered the Catholicon [i.e. the quack medicine] of Spayne, and the chiefe leaders of the League finelie fetcht over and laide open in their colours.' The French text greeted the accession of Henry of Navarre to the throne of France with a spirited enthusiasm which, despite the uncouthness of the English rendering, braced

---

[1] The name was suggested by the *Saturae Menippeae* of Varro, a voluminous Latin author of Cicero's epoch. Only fragments survive of Varro's work. It was an imitation of a lost treatise by the cynic philosopher Menippus of Gadara. See Teuffel and Schwabe, *History of Roman Literature*, 1891, i. 255-6.

Elizabethan sympathy. Some lines by Passerat, which were addressed to the new king, ran in the English volume thus:

> Unconquered prince, and of thine age the glorie eke
> alone,
> Euen God himselfe doth set thee up upon thy grand-
> sire's throne;
> And with a happy hand doth reach to thee two scep-
> ters braue,
> Which, taken from the Spanish foe, thou shalt uphold
> and haue.[1]

With Henry IV's coronation the politico-religious struggle in France was over for the century. The old religion then came to terms with the new. Spain made a strenuous effort to hamper the settlement, and war with her quickly broke out afresh. But Spanish aggression failed to restore the supremacy of extreme Catholicism. The French Church had always claimed much independence of the Papacy, and the recent progress of events intensified a desire for the conservation of Gallican liberties. The anti-national Jesuits were expelled from the country. The invasion of the Spaniards was arrested. Internal and external developments facilitated the emancipation of the Huguenots. The new king was able to secure, by the edict of Nantes, a practical measure of toleration for the French Protestants, at whose head he had fought. That edict was promulgated on April 13, 1598. Three weeks later peace was signed with Spain, and all clouds for the time vanished from the French sky.

By the edict of Nantes, the principle of liberty of conscience was secured to the Huguenots. Religious tests in the public service were abolished, and if restrictive clauses narrowed the practical scope of the enfranchisement, none could question that Protestantism had won a substantial triumph. Protestant England, which had been shocked by Henry IV's apostasy, was reconciled to him partly by his difficulties with Spain, her own inveterate foe, and wholly by his tolerant policy.

[1] *A Pleasant Satyre*, 1595, p. 196. The volume has the sub-title, *A Satyre Menippized*. The 'two sceptres' in the quotation are those of France and Navarre. 'Grandsire' is the English translator's inaccurate attempt to reproduce the French poet's allusion in a later line to Henry IV's distant descent from Saint Louis, who reigned in the thirteenth century.

The edict of Nantes was hailed on both sides of the Channel as a Magna Charta of Protestantism. Not that suspicion of the Reformed creed was extinguished in Catholic France by the great compromise. In the next century a strong Catholic reaction opened anew the sectarian controversy in its acutest form. The old faith regained its strength and the edict was revoked in 1685. Proof was then conclusive that, whatever the French affinity with the intellectual side of Huguenot enlightenment, something in the doctrine of Luther or Calvin was alien to the French national spirit. But though the Huguenot triumph of the sixteenth century proved in the end to be transitory, Elizabethan England reckoned it for the time a final miracle of God's grace. Sympathy with France deepened. At the end of Elizabeth's reign the governments of the two countries cherished in their diplomatic relations an unprecedented amity. There was a widening of the scope of French influence on English thought and literature.

III

HUGUENOT SETTLERS AND VISITORS IN ENGLAND

One effect of the vain effort of the French Catholic government to curb Huguenot dissent by persecution was to drive many French Protestants from their native land. Some found asylum in the Low Countries and some in Germany. But England was the land of promise which attracted the greater number of these Huguenot *émigrés*. The peaceful invasion of Britain began in the reign of Edward VI, a few years after the policy of coercion was openly proclaimed by the ministers of Francis I. The stream of immigration flowed continuously throughout the young king's reign. There was naturally a cessation during the Catholic reaction of Queen Mary's sovereignty, and the Protestant aliens retreated to kindlier havens in Holland or Switzerland. But Huguenot incursions were renewed in larger volume at the opening of Queen Elizabeth's reign, and were greatly encouraged by Archbishop Parker, who declared it a cardinal point of piety to befriend 'these gentle and profitable strangers'.[1] Till the end of the century English ports were freely opened to French refugees. Every critical disaster which befell the Huguenot communities at home quickened the tide of immigration into England. The massacre of St. Bartholomew's Day in 1572, and the temporary triumph of the Catholic League in 1585, sent ships crowded with Huguenot families to the coasts of Kent, Sussex, or Hampshire. The Huguenots well deserved a greeting of tolerance and charity. But the insular prejudice against aliens was never wholly silenced in Britain. In 1593, when a bill was introduced into the House of Commons prohibiting aliens from selling by retail any foreign commodity, the ancient cry against foreigners was raised at Westminster. Sir Robert Cecil, the Queen's Secretary, attacked the illiberal sentiment with fine spirit. In the name of the Queen's government he resisted any restriction on foreign traders, and gave voice to a feeling of rare enlightenment when he asserted that the relief afforded by England to strangers 'hath brought great honour to our Kingdom; for it is accounted a refuge for distressed nations, for our arms have been opened unto them to cast themselves into our bosoms'.[2]

The aliens of Elizabethan England were in constant process of reinforcement by visitors not only from France, but from Flanders, Germany, and even Italy and Spain. All these countries drove forth Protestant exiles for conscience' sake. But the French community in England remained more numerous and influential than the settlement of any other foreign nation. On Elizabeth's accession the French immigrants were presented by the sovereign with a church of their own, and the edifice, which was in Threadneedle Street, soon became a Huguenot cathedral of England, with daughter-churches scattered through the land. London was only one of the British

[1] Strype's *Life of Archbishop Parker*, 1821, i. 276. References to the French Protestant refugees in Elizabethan England abound in Strype's *Annals*. The subject is fully treated in Smiles, *The Huguenots . . . in England and Ireland*, 1880, and in Baron F. De Schickler's *Les églises du refuge en Angleterre*, 1547–1685, 3 tom., Paris, 1892. See also the publications of the Huguenot Society,—especially *Registers of the French Church, Threadneedle Street*, 1896–1906; *Returns of Aliens in London*, Henry VIII–James I, ed. R. E.G. and E. F. Kirk, 1900; *Letters of Denization . . . for aliens in England*, 1509–1603, ed. W. Page, 1893.

[2] Dewes' *Journals*, pp. 508–9.

cities of refuge. Huguenots abounded in the villages near the metropolis. Arras works at Mortlake, tapestry works at Fulham, bore witness to the presence of French-speaking residents. Tottenham was reported to have become a French settlement. Further afield, Huguenots were prominent at Southampton, Canterbury, in all the Cinque ports, and at Norwich. Everywhere they had their churches and schools, and at Canterbury they were suffered by Archbishop Parker to worship, from 1564 onwards, in the crypt or undercroft of the Cathedral. There is no means of ascertaining the precise numbers of the Huguenot population in the whole country during the sixteenth century, but it could hardly have fallen below the total of 10,000. At the end of the sixteenth century the baptisms in the chief French church of London—that in Threadneedle Street—averaged annually at least 100.

The settlers, who were invariably of small means, chiefly comprised skilled artisans—silkweavers, tapestry workers, printers, bookbinders—or doctors of medicine, and ministers of the faith. Normans were largely represented amongst them, but numbers came from Orleans, Poitiers, and the cities of the south. Many mechanical arts were greatly improved by these humble *émigrés*.[1] Their pastors often showed scholarly attainments, and their medical practitioners gave proof of unusual skill. It was no mere literary influence which the presence of these French sojourners exerted on the land of their adoption. They tended to raise the standard of intellectual efficiency and of material comfort in their English environment.

International sympathy was stimulated by the Huguenot invasion of England, and on occasion Huguenots were in a position to return in their own country the services of hospitality which their fellows received from English hosts. From an early date the port of La Rochelle, a chief stronghold of the Huguenots, was in close touch with the advanced

[1] Shakespeare was acquainted with a family of Huguenot refugees. In 1604 he was lodging in the house, in Silver Street, Cripplegate, of one Christopher Montjoy, a Huguenot tiremaker or wigmaker, and took part in a family quarrel. See 'New Shakespeare Discoveries' by Dr. C. W. Wallace in *Harper's Magazine*, March, 1910.

section of Elizabethan Puritans, and the printing presses of the French city were at times placed at the disposal of Elizabethan controversialists, to whose extreme opinions the English authorities refused the liberty of publication. The manuscripts of many Puritan theologians of the strictest type were sent across the sea to be printed. As early as 1574 Walter Travers, one of the most eminent of the school of English Calvinists, wrote his famous *Ecclesiasticae Disciplinae et Anglicanae Ecclesiae ab illa Aberrationis plena è verbo Dei et dilucida explicatio*, and caused it to be printed anonymously at La Rochelle. The same Huguenot citadel was at times the asylum of English publishers and authors who had incurred the wrath of the rulers of the Anglican Church. In 1589-90 the city was the home of a Puritan printer, Robert Waldegrave, who had been exiled from London for issuing attacks on the English bishops. After printing in 1588-9 some of the Martin Marprelate tracts, in which the endeavour was made to undermine episcopacy by force of ridicule, Waldegrave escaped late in 1589 from the fury of the bishops in London to La Rochelle. Subsequently he found a safe haven at Edinburgh, but he followed his trade during 1590 in the great Huguenot seaport. At least two of the Martin Marprelate pamphlets, which excelled in scurrility any of their companions,—Penry's *Appellation* in March, 1590, and Job Throckmorton's *M[aster Robert] Some laid open in his Colours* in April,—came under Waldegrave's auspices from a La Rochelle press. Very close was the intimacy between the active pamphleteers of the ultra-Puritan Revolution in London and the Huguenot leaders in the South of France.

Few Huguenot scholars settled permanently in Elizabethan England, but many figured prominently as occasional visitors. One of these, Antony Rudolf Chevallier, a Norman, was a temporary guest of Archbishop Cranmer in Edward VI's reign, and in the early years of Elizabeth's reign he returned to serve as Hebrew professor at Cambridge. Pierre du Moulin, the learned son of the Huguenot pastor of Orleans, fled before the Catholic League's predominance to study at Cambridge, earning his livelihood by instructing the boy-earl of Rutland and his brother. Of far greater note was Henri Étienne, the Huguenot scholar-printer and a chief apostle of Renaissance culture, who wandered about England during the middle years of the century. Toward the end of the period there came Joseph Scaliger—the younger Scaliger—a Huguenot scholar of supreme genius, who not only edited with infinite skill many classical texts, but with wonderful ingenuity determined the chronology of Greek and Roman history. According to Mark Pattison, Scaliger possessed 'the most richly stored intellect which ever spent itself in acquiring knowledge'. It is to be regretted that so eminent a guest formed a poor opinion of both the scholarship and the manners of his English hosts. He imputed indolence to the fellows at Cambridge ; he detected a narrow sectarianism in English churchmen, and deemed the disposition of the lower orders inhuman. But he admired the wealth of Church foundations despite diminution through Henry VIII's spoliation; he studied with interest border-ballads, and opened a correspondence with Camden, the great Elizabethan antiquary, and with Richard Thomson, a Cambridge scholar who greatly benefited by his erudition.[1] Scaliger's intimate friend and co-religionist, Isaac Casaubon, whose Greek culture was cast in his own mould, settled in England in James I's reign, and kept alive there Elizabethan memories of Huguenot scholarship.

Some Huguenot visitors to Elizabethan England suggest yet another sort of influence which came from Protestant France to colour English aspiration. In spite of the welcome offered by Elizabethan England to Huguenot refugees, the exiles rarely lost the sense that they were living under a foreign law and dispensation. Many times there flashed across the Huguenot mind, when the fortunes of the party sank low in France, the idea of a settlement across the Atlantic, where not only would threats of persecution be silenced, but where God's saints might reign in a peaceful autonomy free of all taint of foreign subservience. Twice a vigorous effort was made to give effect to this mirage of

[1] Mark Pattison's *Essays*, New Universal Library, i. 116–17.

an independent Huguenot province in America, and though the endeavours had no permanent result, they fostered, in England as well as in France, hopes of a colonial empire, which should be purged of all the political corruptions of the Old World and give liberty a fresh scope. The Elizabethan design of Virginia and the Puritan foundation of New England were ventures of Englishmen who more or less consciously followed in Huguenot footsteps.

The first Huguenot scheme of American colonization was tried in Brazil in 1555. The Huguenot leader, Nicholas Durand, Sieur de Villegagnon, had been one of Calvin's fellow students at the University of Paris. The expedition enjoyed the benediction of Calvin, and French pastors from Geneva were among the settlers. But Villegagnon's adventure came to early grief, amid discouraging omens. The second enterprise, which had a different destination in the vaguely defined district of Florida (in the northern continent) more forcibly impressed Elizabethan thought and aspiration. Jean Ribaut, a Dieppe captain of good family and strong Calvinist feeling, was its chief organizer, and he was for a time a refugee in Elizabethan England. It was at the request of Coligny, the Huguenot chieftain, who was an active patron of the Florida scheme of occupation, that Ribaut undertook his task in 1562.

Ribaut quickly formed a miniature Huguenot plantation on Floridan shores, and, leaving his fellow settlers there, he returned to Europe to consult the Huguenot leaders at home. But his native land was torn by civil war on his arrival, and his patrons were in no mood to give him a hearing. Retiring to England to formulate plans for the future, he remained there for two years. In London he wrote out in French his story of the Huguenot discovery and settlement of 'Terra Florida'. The book, which was a stimulating contribution to the literature of American exploration, had the fortune to be published in London in 1563 in an English translation. That rendering is the only form in which Ribaut's work has survived, for no copy of his original French is extant. While Ribaut lingered in England, his French settlement in Florida received notable reinforcements under René de Laudonnière, a Huguenot nobleman of sternest Calvinist convictions. Finally in 1564 Ribaut re-crossed the Atlantic ocean, but only to play on the other side the part of protagonist in a ghastly tragedy. Within five days of his arrival in Florida, he was slain by Spanish buccaneers, who massacred all but a handful of the Huguenot colonists.

News of Ribaut's tragic fate spread rapidly through Elizabethan England and moved anger and dismay. The Huguenot invasion of Florida riveted itself on Elizabethan attention. A few Frenchmen had under the leadership of Laudonnière evaded Spanish vengeance. These survivors landed, by an accident of navigation, after their hairbreadth escape, at Swansea, and travelled to London for the most part on foot. Most of them managed to return to France. But their misfortunes excited infinite pity in England. A vivacious report of Ribaut's massacre was quickly published in Paris by one of his surviving companions, Nicholas le Challeux, a carpenter, who, on his journey out to Florida, had spent nearly three weeks in the Isle of Wight. Le Challeux's statement achieved instant popularity in an English translation. Indeed, all the French literature concerning the Huguenot attempt on Florida enjoyed a general vogue in English versions. The colonial ambitions of Elizabethans were thereby quickened. Richard Hakluyt began his great career of literary advocate of Elizabethan colonization of America by publishing, in 1582, a volume of *Diuers voyages touching the discouerie of America*, in which Ribaut's early treatise filled the chief space. Hakluyt spent the next five years in Paris as chaplain to the English Embassy there, and before he came home he published in an English rendering another elaborate account of the Florida expedition, by one who played almost as prominent a part in its fortunes as Ribaut himself,—by René de Laudonnière. Laudonnière's work had just issued for the first time from the press at Paris when Hakluyt turned it into his own language.

Of the most cultured of Laudonnière's companions in Florida, an interesting story remains to tell. The artist of the expedition, Jacques Le Moine, made his permanent home in England, and the sketches of Florida, which he preserved, sowed seeds of colonial ambition in many English minds. Le Moine settled in Blackfriars, and Sir Walter Raleigh was among his patrons. Raleigh's effort of 1584 to people with Englishmen the American region which he christened Virginia owed much to the suggestion of the Huguenot experience. Virginia was a part of the district which Ribaut and his companions knew as Terra Florida. At Raleigh's expense Le Moine developed in colours his pictorial notes of his American observations. Sir Philip Sidney, the Paladin of Elizabethan benefactors of the Huguenot cause, likewise acquired from Le Moine some of his colonial aspiration. To Sidney's wife the Huguenot artist dedicated a published collection of drawings of birds, beasts, flowers, and fruits. The artist's fame, fanned by such patronage, spread far and wide. De Bry, the great Frankfort publisher and engraver, came to London to bargain with him for the purchase of his rich portfolio of sketches of Floridan life and nature. But the refugee declined to entertain the offer from a sense of loyalty to his English friends. After his death, his widow ignoring his scruples, made over his work to the German dealer, who at once gave engravings of it to the admiring world of Europe. Though Elizabethan England was slower than western countries on the continent to grasp new ideas and opportunities, the Huguenot zeal for colonial enterprise provoked a response in the Elizabethan mind. The presence of Huguenots on English soil proved an invigorating spur to action as well as to thought.[1]

IV

The Devotional Literature of the Huguenots

The Huguenots, despite their activity in other spheres of labour, were always energetic wielders of the pen. Little of their literary activity escaped Elizabethan notice. Their

[1] The connexion of the Huguenot Settlements with English endeavours of later date is treated by the present writer in the second article ('The Teaching of the Huguenots') of a series, called 'America and Elizabethan England', in *Scribner's Magazine*, 1907. Hakluyt's translation of Ribaut and Laudonnière's narratives is a main authority.

religious poetry evoked a paean of welcome. Nor were the political and theological views of the Huguenots less admiringly studied by Elizabethan Englishmen, and Huguenot prose played no inconspicuous part in the literary history of England through the eras alike of Queen Elizabeth and of her two immediate successors. The Huguenots' mingled hopes of theological and political reform led to a rich and varied harvest of both theological and political treatises and pamphlets. The Huguenot prose writers treated the theory and practice of politics with an originality and a disrespect for conservative convention, which especially attracted the attention of Shakespeare's fellow countrymen.

French Protestant theology for the most part, as far as style went, aimed at Calvin's lucid precision. Latin was its frequent vehicle of expression, but the French language was in common use, and lent many a touch of vivid colour to the arid wastes of religious controversy. Pierre Viret, one of Calvin's most active lieutenants, was a lively pamphleteer despite his dogmatic earnestness, and his works circulated in English translations among the faithful in Edward VI's and in Queen Elizabeth's reign quite as briskly as the more authoritative performances of his master. Of Calvin's leading disciples the name most familiar to Shakespeare's generation was that of Theodore Beza, who filled after Calvin's death his place as chieftain of the Genevan state, holding office from 1564 until his death in 1607. Beza's prolonged career of eighty-seven years, his versatile accomplishments as humanist and theologian, and his personal relations with Englishmen, gave his name and work an especial prominence in English life. For half a century he was in constant correspondence with English churchmen and puritan laymen, urging on both from the days of Edward VI the settlement of those religious differences which split Protestant England asunder. He declined a pressing invitation to settle in the country soon after Queen Elizabeth's accession, when France was no longer a safe abode. But he acknowledged the courtesy of the hospitable offer by presenting to Cambridge University one of the earliest extant codices of the Greek Testament,

which still enjoys universal repute as the *Codex Bezae*. Zest
for biblical scholarship was one of Beza's foremost interests,
and he pressed its claim to public endowment on Queen
Elizabeth's prime minister, Lord Burghley.[1] Beza's house at
Geneva was always open to English and to Scottish travellers
through the last four decades of the sixteenth century.
Among his guests midway through that epoch was Francis
Bacon's brother Antony, to whose mother, ' in testimonie
of the honour and reverence I beare to the vertue of you and
yours,' he dedicated on Nov. 1, 1581, his *Christian Meditations upon Eight Psalms*.[2] In 1588 he sent a congratulatory
message to Queen Elizabeth on the defeat of the Spanish
Armada, in the form of a Latin epigram, and it was published as
a popular broadside, not only in Latin, but with translations into
English, Dutch, Spanish, Hebrew, Greek, Italian, and French.

Probably Beza won his chief popularity in England and
exerted his widest influence as a translator into verse of
the Psalms. He was a chief promoter of psalmody in Protestant worship, which may be claimed as an invention of the
French Reformers. Luther based on a German translation
of certain psalms a few hymns which enjoyed a wide vogue.
But the general habit of psalm-singing did not come from
Germany to either France or England. It was the poet
Clément Marot who first stirred the Huguenot passion for
psalmody. Marot addressed the ladies of France in a poetic
preface to his translation of fifty psalms into French verse.
He foretold a golden age, when psalmody would deprive toil
of all its pain. The labourer would sing psalms beside his
plough, the carmen would chant them on the high roads, and

[1] Strype's *Annals* (Oxford, 1828), III. i. 110, 197-8.
[2] Beza's *Christian Meditations* were published in English in 1582. In
the dedication to Lady Bacon, Beza is made by the translator to state
that the manuscripts had long lain unused, ' where they had lyen still, had
not bene the comming of master Anthony Bacon your sonne, into these
partes : whom when I saw to take pleasure in this little piece of woorke,
and again knowing by the latin letters wherewith it hath liked you to
honour me, the great and singular, yea extraordinarie graces wherwith
God hath indewed you, and whereof I acknowledge a very paterne in your
said sonne : I perswaded my selfe that it should not be displeasing to
you, if this small volume carying your name upon the browe, were offered
to you.' Beza dedicated his *Icones* (1580) to James VI of Scotland, and
mentions the interest he felt in the Scottish students at Geneva.

the shopkeeper would hum them over his counter. Marot's prophecy almost came true in sixteenth-century France and Switzerland, not so much through his own effort as through Beza's energetic intervention. Marot's fragmentary work as French psalmist was completed by Beza. All the psalms, save those with which Marot had dealt, were turned by him into French verse. The tameness of his muse when compared with the vigour of that of his predecessor excited the ridicule of the critics,[1] but Beza's pious rhymes were welcomed with enthusiasm by the Calvinist rank and file. Popular French tunes were adapted to the completed French psalter under the sanction of Beza and the rulers of Geneva. They decreed that literal renderings of the Psalms were, with the biblical canticles, the only words fit for singing in divine worship. Many of Beza's and Marot's French renderings, set to brisk music, became not only the battle-songs of the Huguenot army, but the recreation of Huguenot households at work and play. Psalmody became as popular outside the Protestant temples as inside.

The psalmody of the Huguenots awoke the sympathy of English Protestants. The musical notation of the Geneva Psalter of 1551, to which Beza was the largest contributor of words, may be almost said to have called into being the psalm-singing proclivities of the Elizabethan Puritan. The psalm-tunes which enjoyed the widest popularity in Elizabethan England were for the most part of French invention. The 'Old Hundredth', which develops the harmony of an early French ballad, figured first in the French Psalter of 1551, and was transferred with many companion melodies of like origin to an English rendering of the Psalms which was published

---

[1] A contemporary epigram contrasted Beza's and Marot's psalms thus :
> Ceux de Marot, c'est d'Amphion la lyre,
> Ou du dieu Pan le flageol gracieux ;
> Mais ceux de Bèze un françois vicieux,
> Rude et contraint, et fascheux à merveilles.
> Donne à Marot le laurier gracieux,
> A Bèze, quoi ? de Midas les oreilles.

Beza in a clumsy answer retorted that he would borrow his ass's ears of his critic. (*La Bibliothèque d'Antoine du Verdier, seigneur de Vauprivas*, Lyons, 1585, p. 1172.)

ten years later. Psalm-singing failed to become quite so insistent a feature of life in Elizabethan England as in Huguenot
France, yet it largely owed to French example such scope as
it enjoyed among Shakespeare's fellow countrymen. When
Shakespeare imputed to Puritans as a distinctive mark the
habit of 'singing psalms to hornpipes', he obviously had in
mind some of the lively measures which Protestant Frenchmen
had adapted to purposes of religious exercise.

Beza, when his name loomed largest in England, was
a French pastor who was domiciled at Geneva, and was far
removed from the peril of current tumults in France. The
Huguenot layman who doggedly defended his creed with both
pen and sword near his own hearthstone through all the storms
of the civil war was a type of religious champion which
more nearly touched the Elizabethan heart. The heir of the
Huguenot fervour who stirred through Shakespeare's lifetime a vital sympathy was a cultured French nobleman,
Philippe de Mornay, Seigneur Du Plessis-Marly (1549-1623).
Du Plessis was a highly cultured humanist, who, if he accepted
without misgiving the Calvinist dogma, justified his convictions on liberally rational lines. He loved his country too
well to quit her soil, save on short visits to England, where
he sought practical and active aid for the Huguenot cause.
The political basis of the movement appealed to him as powerfully as the religious claim, and he was well equipped for the
vindication of both the theological and political sides of the
Huguenot position. He had at command an easy French style
and a fund of enlightened argument. The highest circles of
society welcomed him to England, whither he came for the
first time amid the crisis of St. Bartholomew's Day with
introductions from Sir Francis Walsingham, the English
ambassador in Paris. 'Il fut bien receu et embrassé de toutes
personnes de qualité et doctrine,' wrote his accomplished wife
of his first visit to England, 'et y fit des amys qui, depuis lors,
luy ont servi beaucoup en diverses négociations.'[1] Sir Philip
Sidney—'le plus accomply gentilhomme d'Angleterre' in

[1] *Mémoires de Charlotte de Mornay, Madame Du Plessis-Marly*,
edited by Madame de Witt (Société de l'Histoire de France), 1868-9, i. 71.

Madame de Mornay's phrase—soon numbered Du Plessis among his closest friends. Sidney's friend, Sir Fulke Greville, bore testimony, just after Sidney's death, to ' the respect of love between Du Plessis and him besides other affinities in their courses '. When the noble Huguenot and his wife were sojourning in London in the summer of 1578, a daughter was born to them. Sir Philip Sidney acted as a godfather and gave the infant the English queen's name of Elizabeth. It was Sidney's ambition to introduce to his fellow countrymen in their own language Du Plessis's authoritative and animated statement of the Huguenot beliefs. The design was not completed at the date of Sidney's premature death, but it was carried out, by way of tribute to his memory, by two near friends and fellow workers. They succeeded in placing at the disposal of the Elizabethan public admirable English renderings ot Du Plessis's chief endeavours in Protestant theology. His main contribution to Calvinist apologetics, *De la vérité de la religion chrétienne*, was an endeavour to justify Christianity of a Calvinist type on philosophic grounds and to confute the objections of all manner of infidels. A small part only was translated by Sidney. Nearly the whole came in 1587 after his death from the pen of Arthur Golding, a writer not unknown to Elizabethan students in other departments of literature; he won his chief fame as author of the standard translation of Ovid's *Metamorphoses*. Sir Philip's sister, the cultivated Countess of Pembroke, did complementary honour to her brother's name and to her brother's Huguenot hero. She devoted herself in her brother's spirit to translating into English from the French the second of Du Plessis's memorable religious treatises, *Excellent Discours De La Vie et De La Mort*. It is a pathetic meditation on the mysteries of existence which is almost worthy of Thomas à Kempis. The Countess's English version was published in 1600.

Huguenots ranked Du Plessis by virtue of his literary accomplishments along with Amyot, the Renaissance master of French prose, and with Ronsard, the Renaissance master of French poetry. The chief poet of the Huguenot camp, Du Bartas, described him as one—

qui combat l'Athéisme,
Le Paganisme vain, l'obstiné Judaïsme,
Avec leur propre glaive : & pressé, grave, saint,
Roidit si bien son style ensemble simple et peint,
Que les vives raisons de beaux mots empennées
S'enfoncent comme traicts dans les âmes bien-nées.[1]

These praises of Du Plessis were rendered into Elizabethan English thus :

And this Du Plessis, beating Atheism,
Vain Paganism, and stubborn Judaism,
With their own arms : and sacred-grave, and short,
His plain-pranked style he strengthens in such sort,
That his quick reasons winged with grace and art,
Pierce like keen arrows, every gentle heart.[2]

Du Plessis's literary piety was long remembered in England. James Howell in his *Instructions for Forreine Travell* reminded the English tourist that the ' pathetical ejaculations and heavenly raptures ' which distinguished Du Plessis's devotional treatises well fitted them for Sunday reading. The authority attaching among French Protestants to all Du Plessis's arguments and opinions won him the sobriquet of ' The Pope of the Huguenots '.

V

Huguenot Pleas for Political Liberty

The notion that personal liberty was a natural heritage of humanity and that evil rulers might be justly deposed flitted vaguely across many French brains before the Huguenot movement was fully organized. Classical study bred sympathy with the theoretic basis of republicanism, and there was formed a conception of constitutional monarchy which owes its sanction to, and is guided by, the people's will. Machiavelli's widely-disseminated plea in behalf of absolutism roused misgiving in many French minds, when the sceptre fell after Francis I's death into weak and unclean hands,

---

[1] Du Bartas, *La Semaine*, 1615 ed., p. 285.
[2] Sylvester's translation, 1613 ed., p. 332.

and the persecution of opinion became a normal weapon of sovereignty. The divine right of kings was freely questioned. As early as 1548 the new note of political liberalism was sounded in France by a young law student of Orleans, Étienne De La Boëtie. The youth wrote an eloquent dissertation entitled *Discours de la Servitude volontière, ou Contr'Un*. It is a scholar's denunciation of despotism penned in the old Roman spirit. The work, which is better known by its shorter alternative name of *Contr'Un*, long circulated in manuscript; it was first published in 1576. The argument adumbrates that of Shakespeare's Pompey in *Antony and Cleopatra* (II. vi. 14–19):

> What was't
> That mov'd pale Cassius to conspire? and what
> Made the all-honour'd, honest Roman, Brutus,
> With the arm'd rest, courtiers of beauteous freedom,
> To drench the Capitol, but that they would
> Have one man but a man?

But *Contr'Un* is an isolated effort, and was somewhat too academic in temper to generate practical attempts at revolution. The author, Étienne De La Boëtie, who was a Catholic, became a lawyer and a poet, but died prematurely in 1563, at the age of three-and-thirty. He is chiefly remembered as the close friend of Montaigne's youth, and as the inspirer of Montaigne's notable essay on 'Friendship'.

The classical conception of liberty which De La Boëtie first expounded in France, appealed to Huguenot sentiment, and, becoming a watchword among them, helped them in due time to justify their resort to arms.[1] The personal abuse of the Catholic leaders, which found free vent among Huguenot pamphleteers when the religious dissensions threatened war, was coloured by study of Roman history and politics. In the impassioned tract called *Le Tigre*, which flamed through France in 1560, and denounced with fury the Cardinal of Lorraine, the virtual head of the Guise family, the writer

---

[1] A useful summary of Huguenot opinion is given by Mr. E. Armstrong in *The Political Theory of the Huguenots* in *English Historical Review*, vol. iv (1889).

clearly emulated Cicero's denunciation of Catiline.[1] There is little doubt that the anonymous author of this lurid piece of invective was Francis Hotman (1524–90), a Huguenot jurist who succeeded Cujas as professor of law at Bourges and reached the highest eminence in his profession. The most accomplished Huguenot pens eagerly engaged in the task of denunciation.

Hotman was soon to develop the theory of political liberalism on broadest lines, and to win a hearing among Elizabethan thinkers. It was not until the massacre of St. Bartholomew hurled its desperate challenge against the stalwart minority that the Huguenot party-leaders openly advocated political doctrines of revolution, or sought to carry liberal arguments to all their logical consequences. The king who misgoverned his people was now declared in no veiled terms to have forfeited his right to reign, and the people were affirmed to be under a solemn obligation to deprive him of his throne. The matured liberalism of the Huguenots sounded many keys. Invective lost nothing of its initial virulence. But the calmness of philosophic inquiry was also fostered with a deadly earnestness, while irony, of a Gallic blitheness, was sometimes enlisted in the cause of political enlightenment.

After the massacre, Catherine de' Medici, who was held to be chiefly responsible for the crime, was the foremost target of Protestant philippics. No quarter was allowed her. Every weapon of literary abuse was reckoned legitimate, and volleys of undiluted scurrility were aimed at her. The *Discours merveilleux de la vie et actions et déportemens de Catherine de Médicis* was an unsparing exposure of what was alleged to be her Satanic villany. The blow clearly came from a trained hand, but the authorship is uncertain. The Huguenot scholar, Henri Étienne, has been groundlessly suspected, and the claim of Hotman has been also urged on doubtful grounds. An English version, *A marvaylous discourse upon the life, deedes and behaviours of Katherine de Midicis,*

---

[1] H. M. Baird in *The Rise of the Huguenots* (1880), i. 444–8, gives a full summary of this powerful piece of invective.

was at once in circulation,[1] and the Italian queen-mother
of France was set in Elizabethan calendars of infamy beside
Messalina or Queen Mary Tudor.

Whether or no Hotman be responsible for the biting
Discours merveilleux, his pen derived a new impetus from
the hateful massacre, which all but claimed him as a victim
at Bourges, and drove him thence for safety to Geneva.
Something more than a pamphleteering sensation was now
his object.   He designed a formidable assault on the fundamental principles, as well as on the practices, of absolutism.
He reasoned effectively from a review of the early history of
France.   His *Franco-Gallia*, which came out at Geneva in
1573, is an historical plea—sound in design if at times fantastic in its interpretation of events—for the recognition
of popular right and for the establishment of constitutional
checks on monarchy.   The work was translated from Latin
into French, under the title of *La France Gauloise*, by
Simon Goulart, a Huguenot scholar and pastor who busied
himself with theological as well as political study, and became a pillar of Calvinism at Geneva.   Hotman's work was
justly regarded as a new development of historical inquiry.
Elizabethan scholars and antiquarians entered into correspondence with him, and they honoured his name.

It was Hotman's example which drew into the arena of
political debate his intimate associate Du Plessis, whose
religious writing and whose friendship with Sir Philip Sidney
awoke among Shakespeare's contemporaries a widespread
interest in his personality.   Du Plessis made his political declaration soon after Hotman's serious appeal, in a Latin treatise,
Vindiciae contra Tyrannos, which seems to have been written
in 1574, although it was not published till 1579.   It proved
a masterly contribution to the politico-historical discussion
which Hotman inaugurated.   Du Plessis stated the case
against despotism with characteristic sobriety and moderation.   He neither championed republicanism nor tyrannicide.   The royal title, he argued, can only come from

[1] The English version was prudently published first at Heidelberg in
1575 and was reprinted at Cracow in 1576.

the people's sanction. Kings who lay waste the Church of God, who worship idolatrously, who defy their subjects' rights, forfeit their crowns. Deposition of the sovereign in such circumstances is the duty which the people owes to itself. But the people can only act through organized representatives, through parliaments or councils of state. Private persons are not justified in taking action on their own account. Though Du Plessis spoke respectfully of Brutus and Cassius, he seems to have held in abhorrence anything like assassination. He pleaded with dignity for popular liberties, and for the secure adaptation of monarchy to the purposes of freedom.

Du Plessis's manifesto was issued under the suggestive pseudonym of Stephanus Junius Brutus. Others were long suspected of the authorship, and consequently Du Plessis's responsibility for it was imperfectly recognized in his own day. The *Vindiciae contra Tyrannos* of Stephanus Junius Brutus enjoyed a European vogue. It circulated outside France, and nowhere more freely than in England and Scotland. The title-page of the first edition of 1579 gives the city of Edinburgh as its place of origin, but there is little doubt that though intended for circulation in Scotland it was printed at Basle. On the eve of the Spanish Armada—in the early summer of 1588—one section of the work appeared at London in an English translation. It bore the title, 'A short Apologie for Christian Souldiours: wherein is contained how that we ought both to propagate and also . . . to defende by force of armes, the Catholike Church of Christ.' In this section of his treatise Du Plessis more especially declared for organized resistance to monarchs who ignored the true principles of Christianity. His 'Catholike Church' was, of course, the church of the reformed dispensation. The monarch whom the English translator designed to hold up to English obloquy was Philip of Spain.

The authority of Machiavelli, the foremost advocate of absolute monarchy in Renaissance Europe, remained the chief obstacle with which champions of constitutionalism had to contend. Hotman and Du Plessis only inferentially sought to confute Machiavellian doctrine. Other Huguenots challenged it more directly; they denounced *Il Principe* as the political Bible of the hated queen-mother. The most famous of the challenges of Machiavelli's creed came in 1576 from the pen of another Huguenot lawyer, Innocent Gentillet, and his powerful indictment at once attracted English attention. A Cambridge student, Simon Patrick, who was travelling in France, soon turned the work into English under the title, 'A discourse upon the meanes of wel-governing and maintaining in good peace, a kingdome, or other principalitie . . . Against Nicholas Machiavell the Florentine.'[1]

Gentillet is mainly responsible for the notion, which rooted itself in the Elizabethan mind, that the great Florentine states-man was an embodiment of every public and private vice. Shakespeare's contemporaries knew little of Machiavelli's exposition of his political creed at first hand. The text of *The Prince* only circulated among them in French versions. There was no Elizabethan translation. The cult of Machiavellianism was invariably reckoned a French gift to Tudor England. 'Satan,' wrote Gentillet's translator, 'useth strangers of France as his fittest instruments to infect us still with this deadly poison sent out of Italy.' But by way of compensation France through the Huguenot pen of Gentillet helped to supply the antidote. It was Gentillet's

---

[1] Patrick's translation, though written in 1577, was not published till 1602. Another edition appeared in 1608. No English translation of *Il Principe* came out before 1640. For Gentillet's influence on Eliza-bethan literature see Edward Meyer's *Machiavelli and the Elizabethan Drama*, Weimar, 1897. Marlowe, who makes 'Machiavel' speak the prologue of his tragedy of *The Jew of Malta*, well attests English indebted-ness to France for the popular conception of Machiavellianism. Marlowe's 'Machiavel' exclaims:

> Albeit the world think Machiavel is dead,
> Yet was his soul but flown beyond the Alps;
> And, now the Guise is dead, is come from France
> To view this land, and frolic with his friends . . .
> I [i.e. Machiavel] count religion but a childish toy,
> And hold there is no sin but ignorance.
> Birds of the air will tell of murders past!
> I am asham'd to hear such fooleries.
> Many will talk of title to a crown:
> What right had Caesar to the Empery?
> Might first made kings, and laws were then most sure
> When, like the Draco's, they were writ in blood.

attempted confutation which turned Machiavelli's name among Elizabethan poets and dramatists into a synonym for a devil in human shape. The English people loyally accepted almost every vagary of Huguenot argument in favour of political liberalism.

Some Englishmen of Shakespeare's day intervened in the controversy over the right of rebellion with an ingenious perversity which clouded the issue. The cry against the divine right of kings was not confined to the Huguenots at the end of the sixteenth century. Devout Catholics, when they saw royal power securely held by Protestant heretics like Queen Elizabeth, by qualified supporters of the Papal authority like Henry III of France, or by Huguenots of the temporizing habit of mind of Henry of Navarre, criticized the monarchical pretensions no less eagerly than the Huguenots, although from an opposite point of view. Du Plessis's popular theory of constitutional government and of the right of rebellion was easily manipulated by astute controversialists, so as to serve the Catholic interest. Montaigne noted with characteristic impartiality how a general plea, which justified civil war in defence of religion, was capable of use by any dissentient from the religious views of a reigning sovereign, whether the monarch be Protestant or Catholic. The most daring endeavour to apply the argument of resistance to a support of the Catholic cause was made by an Englishman— a convert to Catholicism, one William Rainolds, whose brother, John Rainolds, was a well-known figure in Oxford society as president of Corpus Christi College. William Rainolds published at Antwerp, in 1592, under the pseudonym of G. Gulielmus Rossaeus, a tract in Latin entitled, *De iusta reipublicae Christianae in reges impios et haereticos authoritate.*[1] Here the tables were mercilessly turned on Protestant sovereigns and political liberals. Heretical kings and queens, all rulers who cherished heterodoxy, were declared to be fit objects of vengeance on the part of orthodox disaffection among their peoples.

[1] See J. N. Figgis's *Studies of Political Thought from Gerson to Grotius,* pp. 159 seq.

Such bold and uncongenial developments of the plea of political liberalism for a moment confused English opinion, and at the close of Elizabeth's reign national feeling in England was thereby excited against all censure of monarchical rights. Loyal sentiment was for the time alienated from advanced political theories of France. The theoretical attacks on absolutism could count on little English sympathy when they were found capable of employment by English Catholics who were plotting the assassination of Queen Elizabeth. To James I the liberalism of the Huguenot appeared to be too ambiguous to be tolerated. A stroke of irony condemned Du Plessis's *Vindiciae* after the Scottish king's accession to be burned at Cambridge as seditious heresy. The king had no hesitation in assigning the authorship of the Huguenot manifesto to the Jesuit Parsons, the chief plotter on the continent against the English crown.

Elizabethan Puritanism was indeed slow to drift into that aggressive propaganda of political revolution which the Huguenot doctrine easily ripened in France. The political pamphlets of Hotman, Du Plessis, and Gentillet struck a sympathetic chord in the Puritan mind, but they bred in England no active policy. The retort in kind of the English champions of the Catholic reaction awoke suspicion of the soundness of liberal argument. But under the Stuarts the Huguenot plea for popular right operated with practical effect. The process of assimilation worked somewhat sluggishly, but the Puritan revolution of seventeenth-century England owed much of its intellectual stimulus to the Huguenot assertion of political liberalism.

Political thought was active in France in other than professedly Huguenot circles, and bore outside their limits lasting philosophic fruit. At the very moment when Du Plessis and Hotman were, with an eye on passing events, seeking to justify Huguenot liberalism, a French professor of law, who was a stranger to the Huguenot camp, was surveying political problems with far greater thoroughness and detachment of mind. The religious opinions of Jean Bodin are undetermined. He has been credited with affinity with every religious creed, Jewish and Mohammedan as well as Protestant and Catholic. But his writings give little clue to his private convictions. His liberality of view links him with the advanced guard of the Huguenots, though he was free of any doctrinal prejudice, and cherished fewer personal animosities. Bodin made the ambitious attempt to trace the origin and growth of Government in civilized states, from the point of view of the sociologist rather than of the politician. Far more dispassionate and exhaustive than any of the Huguenot theorists in his treatment of political phenomena, he deduces monarchical rule from an implied primordial contract between sovereign and people. Monarchy in a limited form he regards as superior to republicanism, but in the internal regulation of states he asserts the need, above all else, of principles of toleration. History meant even more to Bodin than to Hotman, and he gave its teaching a wider scope. For the first time among modern European writers he assigned political phenomena and developments to climatic influences, a fruitful theory which Montesquieu restated and elaborated.

Bodin's chief work, *De la République* ('Concerning the State'), which appeared in 1576, was written in French, and was soon familiar in England. There it was read for some years in a Latin translation of local authorship. Ultimately it was translated into English (in 1606) by Richard Knolles, the Elizabethan historian of the Turks, who claimed that Bodin's political philosophy was to be 'preferred before any of them that have as yet taken so great an argument upon them'. Bodin's work was long a text-book for English students alike in its French, Latin, and English dress, and it guided the study of political theory for many a term in Cambridge University, as well as in the English realm of thought outside.[1] It can

[1] Gabriel Harvey, the Cambridge tutor, who carefully observed current academic feeling, wrote about 1579 of the general interest excited among Cambridge students by the political speculation of Bodin, and by French comment upon Aristotle's *Politics*: 'You can not stepp into a schollars studye but (ten to one) you shall likely finde open ether Bodin de Republica or Le Royes Exposition uppon Aristotles Politiques or sum other like French or Italian Politique Discourses.' (*Letterbook of Gabriel Harvey*, Camden Soc., 1884, p. 79.) Harvey made the personal acquaintance of Bodin, when the latter visited the University of Cambridge in 1579. Bodin, according to the Cambridge scholar's own account, likened him to

hardly be questioned that Hooker derived from Bodin the doctrine of contractual sovereignty which was developed by Hobbes from the same source, and was afterwards admitted to the political creed of the English Whigs.

But there were points in Bodin's argument which offended English sentiment and exposed it to frequent censure. His incidental warning against feminine monarchy caught the eye of many an Elizabethan, and was warmly contested by Elizabethan controversialists. The Frenchman's somewhat obscurantist advocacy of demonology and witchcraft also roused much hostility against him. In a second book entitled *Démonomanie des Sorciers* (1580) he fathered every superstitious fancy which science scouted. His conservatism on this topic left a curious impression on Elizabethan literature. It gave the cue to that fascinating piece of Elizabethan rationalism, Reginald Scot's *Discoverie of Witchcraft* (1584). The evidence is complete that Bodin was recognized as a thinker of authority by the subjects of Queen Elizabeth, and as one to be treated seriously both by those who accepted and by those who challenged his views.

Bodin's *magnum opus* stimulated speculative inquiry into all the conditions of social well-being. Among its many fruits in the seventeenth century must be numbered the science of political economy. That term was the invention of a Frenchman who may be reckoned an early disciple of the chief political philosopher of the French Renaissance. About the date of the publication of Bodin's treatise, *De la République*, in 1576, there was born to an apothecary at Falaise in Normandy a son Antoine de Montchrétien, who adhered through great part of a short life to the community of the Huguenots. At a precociously youthful age he devoted himself to the drama, but a turbulent disposition drove him in his adolescence to England and Holland. There, turning from literary study, he closely observed the

Homer. Harvey's enemy, Tom Nashe, states that Harvey addressed a highly complimentary letter to Bodin which drew from the Frenchman an 'answer in the like nature' which was hardly intended to be taken seriously (Gabriel Harvey's *Works*, ed. Grosart, i. 252, ii. 23, 24, 83; Nashe's *Works*, ed. McKerrow, iii. 116; iv. 360).

progress of commerce, and on settling anew in France he
sought to define the principles of mercantile prosperity. His
results were embodied in a work which he entitled *Le Traicté
de l'Œconomie Politique* (1615). None had combined the
noun and epithet before. Thus the French writer brought
into being a new branch of knowledge, which had for its aim
the discussion of 'la mesnagerie des nécessités et charges
publiques'. Montchrétien reached the conclusion that the
happiness of man chiefly depended on wealth, and that wealth
depended on labour. Well-being came partly from discipline
or organization, partly from art or invention, and in any case
life and labour were inseparably united. Montchrétien's argument may seem elementary from a modern point of view;
but it was the work of a pioneer to whose ingenuity the future
existence of economic science stood conspicuously indebted.

Nearly a century passed before news of Montchrétien's discovery of 'œconomie politique' reached England, where the
study was destined ultimately to reach its fullest development.

VI

PIERRE DE LA RAMÉE

No branch of knowledge escaped the active mind of the
Huguenot, and from ardent champions of the faith came
a thinker who questioned tradition in almost every branch
of knowledge, and sought to establish logic, ethics, and
philosophy on new foundations. His versatility marks him
out as a true son of the Renaissance. The war which he
declared in boyhood on the intellectual darkness of Rome
he pursued to the end. In Elizabethan England his eminence as an intellectual force went unquestioned for two
generations, and at Cambridge he was acknowledged to be
the only modern authority on logic, then the chief item in
the academic curriculum.

Pierre de la Ramée—Petrus Ramus—the son of poor peasants
of Picardy, was born in 1515, six years after Calvin and nine
years before Ronsard. Brought up in penury, he was gifted

from infancy with a passion for reading, and he attained a great position in the realms of thought by his bold originality and intellectual versatility.   He was credited by an impartial critic of the century with 'a universal mind'.   His fame was made in 1536, while he was a student at Paris University, by a thesis in which he professed to establish that Aristotle's views and conclusions on every topic were wrong. Aristotle had come to be treated by orthodox Catholic churchmen as one of themselves.   By a confusion of thought, which is rather difficult to explain, Aristotelian philosophy enjoyed ecclesiastical sanction.   Ramus's challenge of Aristotle's authority consequently exposed him to the suspicion of scepticism.   In 1543 he published the treatise on logic (*Institutiones Dialecticae*) which obtained worldwide repute.   There he aimed an almost fatal blow at the scholastic method of the syllogism.   He sought to convert logic, not perhaps with entire success, into an instrument of lucid thought.   The Sorbonne retorted by causing his book for the time to be suppressed. But in spite of persecution Ramus adhered to the road on which he had set his foot.   Although he avowed himself a Protestant, his gifts as a teacher secured for him even from those who disliked his views educational posts of dignity and emolument.   He became president of the Collège de Presles in Paris and regius professor of rhetoric and philosophy at the Collège de France.   But his colleagues, who resented his intellectual energy, made his life burdensome, and during the Civil wars he was expelled from all his offices.   After a tour through the German universities, where he was received with royal honours, he declined invitations to settle abroad and faced the risk of a retired life of study in his beloved Paris.

It was not only as a logician that Ramus proved his originality of mind.   Scarcely any subject of study failed to benefit by his alertness and industry.   He devised a mode of phonetic spelling, while his writings on grammar quickly acquired a European vogue.   His grammars, which became European text-books, dealt with the French, Greek, and Latin languages, and aimed at simplifying the rules and reducing their number. It was indeed as a grammarian no less than as a logician that the learned world acknowledged his pre-eminence. With characteristic versatility he also interested himself in mathematics and theology. He wrote a useful book on geometry, and greatly improved the place of mathematics in the educational curriculum. In theology he was a rationalizing Huguenot. He defined theology as *doctrina bene vivendi* and laid great stress on the Bible as the foundation of religion. One of his plans was a new translation of the whole Bible into French from the original languages. His religious aim was to restore Christianity to its primitive simplicity, and he condemned the refinements of Calvin's doctrine no less than the dogmatic pretensions of Rome. To the despotic power vested in the synod of the Protestant organization he raised objection on the ground that it menaced individual liberty. In the days of Ramus's misfortunes, Beza consequently discouraged him from seeking an asylum at Geneva.

There was indeed no direction of intellectual endeavour in which Ramus failed to show lively and practical interest. He sketched out an elaborate scheme of university reform at Paris in which he recommended the abolition of clerical qualifications for college offices, and the application of many cathedral endowments to the gratuitous education of poor scholars. It was a scandalous thing, he wrote, that the road to knowledge should be closed and barred against poverty. He had as a poor boy burned with eager desire of knowledge and always recalled with frankness his early struggles. By his will he founded with his scanty savings a mathematical lectureship at the Collège de France at Paris. The post was filled by men of distinction in later years, and greatly benefited mathematical study.[1]

Learning has to reckon Ramus among its leading martyrs. Superstition and intolerance prepared for him a violent end. Unhappily he was in Paris during the St. Bartholomew's massacre. His foes suffered him to lodge in the Collège de Presles, long after he had been deprived of professorial func-

---

[1] The chief authority is *Ramus (Pierre de la Ramée): sa vie, ses écrits et ses opinions,* par C. Waddington, Paris, 1885. See also John Owen's *The Skeptics of the French Renaissance,* 1893, pp. 493 seq.

tions. On the third day of the massacre, August 26, 1572, assassins, hired by 'the blockish Sorbonnists', burst into his study in the Collège and slew him with hateful barbarities. He was shot, stabbed, flung out of the window five stories high; then his lifeless body tied with cords was dragged through the streets and flung into the river Seine. There is no more ghastly episode in the records of fanaticism than Ramus's murder. The brutal outrage was represented on the Elizabethan stage in one of the crude scenes of Marlowe's *Massacre at Paris*.[1] Ramus's courage and noble temper from beginning to end of his chequered career may be gauged by one of the latest sentences from his pen: 'Je supporte (he wrote amid his distresses) sans peine et même avec joie ces orages, quand je contemple dans un paisible avenir sous l'influence d'une philosophie plus humaine les hommes devenus meilleurs, plus polis et plus éclairés.' Ramus might have said with Heine: 'I know not if I de-serve that a laurel wreath should be laid on my tomb . . . But lay on my coffin a sword; for I was a brave soldier in the liberation war of humanity.'

Ramus, although his writings became themes of fierce con-troversy, exerted a vast influence on Elizabethan thought. His Greek grammar and his elements of geometry were in general use in Elizabethan schools and colleges, and an English rendering of his manual of logic was issued in London within two years of his death. Roger Ascham valued Ramus as a great educational reformer, and corresponded with him on educational methods. Gabriel Harvey, the Cambridge tutor of Edmund Spenser, boasted of his worship of Ramus's genius.

[1] Act I, Sc. VIII :

Enter RAMUS *in his study.*

Ramus. What fearful cries come from the river Seine
That fright poor Ramus sitting at his book! . . .

Enter GUISE, ANJOU, *and the rest.*

Guise. Was it not thou that scoff'dst the *Organon*
And said it was a heap of vanities? . . .
Ramus. I knew the *Organon* to be confused
And I reduced it into better form . . .
Guise. Why suffer you that peasant to declaim? . . .
Anjou. Ne'er was there collier's son so full of pride.   [*Stabs him.*

In the University of Cambridge, which was then far more
sensitive to new ideas than Oxford, Ramus's system of logic
and philosophy dethroned Aristotelianism. His philosophical treatises became the authorized academic text-books
at Cambridge as at almost all the universities of Europe
save Oxford. When a press was for the first time permanently established at Cambridge in 1584, the first book
to be printed was an annotated edition of Ramus's *Dialectica*
in the original Latin. The editor was William Temple, a
young fellow of King's College. The volume was dedicated to Sir Philip Sidney. With characteristic enthusiasm
for Huguenot theory and practice Sidney had already
declared himself a Ramist, and now proved his faith in
Ramism by inviting the French philosopher's English
editor to become his private secretary. Subsequently young
Temple became an early provost of Trinity College, Dublin,
and spread in Ireland his enthusiasm for the new Huguenot logic. But Ramus's philosophical and logical theories
were closely studied by greater English thinkers than Sir
Philip Sidney or his secretary. Ramus's work was familiar
to Bacon from his Cambridge days. None can doubt, although the point is often overlooked or minimized, the
suggestive impetus given by Ramus to Bacon's exposition of
the defects of Aristotelian logic. Bacon's speculative originality engendered doubts of Ramus's efficiency at many points,
but Bacon admits that the Frenchman's intention was excellent.[1] Hooker, who resented Ramus's religious scepticism,
deemed his services to philosophy overrated, but at the end
of the sixteenth century, the Puritan writers proclaimed their
faith in him both as logician and educational reformer.[2]

It is worth adding that among other Englishmen whose minds

[1] Cf. Bacon's *Valerius Terminus* in Spedding's edition of *Works*, iii.
203–5, and his *De Augmentis, ib.*, iv. 453.
[2] A long story is told by Samuel Clark in his *Lives of Thirty-two
Divines*, 1677, p. 235, of how the well-known Puritan writer William
Gouge, when an undergraduate of King's College, Cambridge, at the first
entrance into his studies, in 1595, 'applied himself to Peter Ramus, his
Logick, and grew so expert therein' that he was able to defend him in
public argument from all assault. Clark names Richard Mather, the
famous New England Puritan, as an ardent worshipper of Ramus.

were fascinated by Ramus's liberal temper was Richard Hakluyt, the Elizabethan apostle of American colonization, who was long chaplain at the English Embassy at Paris. Hakluyt was then first urging on his countrymen the need of a more scientific study of navigation and mathematics in order to enable Englishmen the better to compete with French and Spaniards in the exploration and colonization of the new world of America. His argument sought sustenance in the example of Ramus. In the interest of his cause he implored Sir Francis Walsingham, the Secretary of State, to found two public lectureships—one in mathematics at Oxford and the other in the art of navigation in London. Hakluyt suggested as a model for the endowment the mathematical lectureship at Paris, which was founded by 'the worthy scholar, Petrus Ramus . . . one of the most famous clerks of Europe'.[1]

VII

HUGUENOT POETRY—AUBIGNÉ

The Huguenot thinkers covered a wide range of philosophy and theology. Their ordinary weapon was French prose, which they wielded with vigour and lucidity. To many Huguenot philosophers besides Du Plessis might be applied Du Bartas's description of that writer's leading characteristics —' Vives raisons, de beaux mots empennées'.

Ethical, political, theological topics engaged the pens of Huguenot writers in prose. The influence of the Huguenot philosophy on English thought chiefly worked through the direct process of literal translation. But there was at the

---

[1] Hakluyt's letter to Walsingham, dated April 1, 1584, which is in the Public Record Office, is printed with a facsimile in Hakluyt's *Navigations*, 1905 ed., vol. xii, pp. vii–x. Hakluyt says he encloses a printed copy of Ramus's will, which shows how 'the exceeding zeale that man had to benefit his country' led him to bestow ' 500 livres' on his lectureship, a sum more than twice as great as the rest of his estate which he divided among his kindred and friends.

same time a mass of Huguenot poetry of more general
scope which excited sympathy and attention on the part of
Elizabethan readers. There was much adaptation of Huguenot poetry as well as translation at English hands.

Huguenot poetry is a scion of the true Renaissance stock.
Ronsard was its acknowledged master, and many of its
peculiarities of style were learned in the school of the Pléiade.
But the Huguenot poet gave a new turn to the main principles
of the Ronsardian system. Ronsard and his brotherhood
endeavoured to breathe the classical form and spirit into
vernacular poetry. The Huguenot poets, while they respected
Ronsard's classical form, sought to imbue it with the spirit
of the Bible. The Huguenot poets sought to spiritualize
the classical temper of poetry, to make classical metre and
phrase handmaids of Protestant piety. The effort was an
innovation in modern European literature.

Two men are chiefly identified with this Huguenot endeavour, Theodore Agrippa d'Aubigné (1550–1630) and
Guillaume de Salluste, Seigneur du Bartas (1544–90). Both,
like Montaigne, belonged to the lesser gentry of Gascony,
both were classical scholars, and both fought valiantly
in the Huguenot army.

Of the two, Aubigné must be credited with the larger
measure of poetic genius. His literary range was exceptionally wide, and his work is memorable in prose as well as
in poetry. In lyric and epic, in satire and fable, in memoir
and history, he gave signal proof of an impetuous strength and
fire. From childhood Aubigné served the two causes of the
classical Renaissance and of the religious Reformation. His
father made him when a boy swear that he would avenge the
martyrdoms of his Huguenot co-religionists, and he was faithful throughout his long career to the oath of his youth. At the
same time he imbibed almost in his cradle the culture of the
Renaissance, translating Plato's *Crito* from the Greek before
he was eight. When he was of age he served in the
Huguenot army, and came into close personal relations with
the Huguenot leader, Henry of Navarre. His adolescence
was spent in camps and in hairbreadth escapes from death

in war. The story of his military life reads like a chivalric
romance. Yet in middle age, Aubigné was no less respected
in the council chamber than on the field of battle. He
became a diplomatist as well as a warrior, but he remained the
while a sturdy fanatic. His leisure was devoted to theology,
history, and poetry, which came to acquire the defiant note of
his soldiership.

Compromise of principle was impossible for him, and the
middle party of 'Les Politiques', which brought about the
religious peace at the end of the sixteenth century, moved
Aubigné's scorn. He likened the 'third party' to Purgatory,
which lies between Heaven and Hell. Loyal to his faith to
the end, he long survived the cruel grief of the conversion of
his old master, Henry IV, which he never ceased to deplore.
He grieved over the perversities of public life far away from
the court. His old age was spent in Geneva, where he died
in 1630, at the age of eighty.

Aubigné was born in 1550, a year after the new era of Renaissance poetry opened in France. The poetry of his early days,
which was collected under the general title *Le Printemps*,
closely pursues the new tradition of the Pléiade school. He
wrote sonnets in honour of a mistress whom he called by the
common title of Diane, in a style which has the merits and
defects of Ronsard's disciple, Desportes. To the memory
of the member of the Pléiade group who was not merely
the most heterodox, but also the most hostile to the
Huguenots, Étienne Jodelle, Aubigné a little paradoxically
addressed a poetic tribute of sympathy. His lighter verse
is more notable for its vigour than its grace; his imagery
constantly reflects his military temper. None the less his
literary sentiment at the outset betrays close affinity with
the Renaissance. A change came later. Under the stress of
religious warfare his poetry acquired in his maturity a
passionate rancour and a self-assurance which almost place it
in a category of its own. His *Les Tragiques*, the poetic
work which gives him his fame, was begun when he was
stricken down by wounds in 1577, and was continued at intervals for thirty years, but it was not published for yet another

ten years,—until 1617. *Les Tragiques* is a Covenanter's prolonged dirge over the sufferings of the faithful. His verses, he declares,

> Ne sont rien que de meurtre et de sang étoffés.

To the sweet delights of love and joy, his muse bids a stern farewell:

> Ce siècle, autre en ses mœurs, demande un autre style,
> Cueillons des fruits amers desquels il est fertile.[1]

In seven books, respectively entitled *Misères*, *Princes*, *La Chambre Dorée*, *Les Feux*, *Les Fers*, *Vengeances*, *Jugement*, he reviews the griefs of the age, the dissoluteness of the court, the cowardice of the Parlement, the tortures of the stake, the massacres of the sword, the vengeance of heaven on the persecutors of God's saints, and the final judgement passed by Almighty God on the sinners in authority. Traces of the author's classical training are not obliterated by his piety, but there is little coherence in the mingling of Greek mythology, moral allegory, and Scriptural theology. There are crudities and incongruities in the linking of sarcasms in the style of Juvenal or Horace, with reminiscences of Hebrew prophecy and of the Apocalypse. The tone varies from wrathful invective to calm trust in the divine will. The stream of inspiration often runs turbidly. Yet many passages reflect the sombre gravity of Dante and adumbrate the majesty of Milton. M. Faguet averred that the lyrical note of execration in Aubigné's *Les Tragiques* was an original experiment which has been only once attempted again with any success— in the well-known *Les Châtiments* of Victor Hugo.

Aubigné's prose work is less notable than his poetry. His *Histoire Universelle* and his *Mémoires* abound in curious details of his experience. The narrative never fails in nervous energy nor blunt sincerity. His descriptive power and insight into character are at times penetrating enough to recall the vivid pencil of St. Simon. But his record of personal reminiscence too often fails in the equability which is essential to artistic balance. Two ironical tracts, *La Confession Catho-*

[1] Aubigné, *Les Tragiques*, ed. Lalanne, 1857, p. 77.

lique du sieur de Sancy and *Les Aventures du baron de Fæneste*, are romances in the style of Rabelais; they deal shrewd blows at Catholic pretensions.

Much of Aubigné's literary work was penned in the sixteenth century, but until the death of Henry IV it circulated exclusively in manuscript. Little of it was published until after the king's death. Consequently Aubigné enjoyed a restricted reputation as a man of letters among his own countrymen during the early or middle periods of his long career. The eagerness with which Elizabethan writers studied printed Huguenot literature and poetry of inferior temper suggests how great would have been their debt to Aubigné had he proved less shy of publicity.

Such literary influence as he exerted on England belongs to the epoch of the Stuarts rather than to that of the Tudors. Early in the seventeenth century his energy and faculty as an historian were acknowledged by James Howell. One curious proof, too, is worth citing of the appreciative study which was given to Aubigné's poetry and prose by Englishmen who played in their country in the seventeenth century parts comparable to those filled by Huguenots in France half a century earlier. The great Lord Fairfax, the parliamentary general, who, like Aubigné, divided his allegiance between war and the muses, was a close reader of Aubigné's *Histoire Universelle*, and he rendered into English verse (without acknowledgement) the elegy on the death of Henry IV, which is one of several poetic interludes enlivening pathetically the progress of the grim prose chronicle.[1]

---

[1] I give by way of specimen two stanzas in both French and English :

AUBIGNÉ.	FAIRFAX.
Quoi ? faut-il que Henri, ce redouté monarque,	Ah ! is it then great Henry so famed
Ce dompteur des humains, soit dompté par la Parque ?	For taming men, himself by death is tamed !
Que l'œil qui vit sa gloire ores voye sa fin ?	What eye his glory saw, now his sad doom,
Que le nostre pour lui incessamment dégoutte ?	But must dissolve in tears, sigh out his soul,

VIII

SALLUSTE DU BARTAS

Guillaume Salluste du Bartas was the Huguenot poet who was identified beyond all risk of neglect with the cause of French Protestantism at home and abroad in Shakespeare's era. Born in 1544, Du Bartas was Aubigne's senior by six years, but predeceased him by forty. Like Aubigné, he was a squire of Gascony, and was amply endowed with the Gascon exuberance of speech and thought. A Huguenot warrior of soldierly instincts, he was at once a scriptural pietist and a classical scholar. Nor did his religious ardour damp his enthusiasm for the work of the Pléiade, to which he professed discipleship. Of Ronsard he wrote:

> Ce grand Ronsard, qui pour orner sa France,
> Le Grec et le Latin despouille d'éloquence;
> Et d'un esprit hardi manie heureusement
> Toute sorte de vers, de style, et d'argument.[1]

Et que si peu de terre enferme dans son sein	So small a shred of earth should him entomb
Celui qui méritoit de la posséder toute?	Whose acts deserved possession of the whole.
. . . .	. . . .
Il le faut, on le doit. Et que pouvons-nous rendre	Yes, it is fit; what else can we return
Que des pleurs assidus, à cette auguste cendre?	But tears as offerings to his sacred urn?
Arrousons à jamais son marbre triste blanc.	With them his sable marble tomb bedew;
Non, non, plutost quittons ces inutiles armes!	No, no such arms too weak, since it appears
Mais puisqu'il fut pour nous prodigue de son sang,	For us he of his blood too careless grew
Serions-nous bien pour lui avares de nos larmes?	Have we naught else for him but a few tears?

The indebtedness of Lord Fairfax to Aubigné was first pointed out by Mr. Edward Bliss Reed, whose valuable 'Poems of Thomas third Lord Fairfax from MS. Fairfax 40 in the Bodleian Library, Oxford' was published in the *Transactions of the Connecticut Academy of Arts and Sciences* (July, 1909). It is curious to note that Lord Fairfax's *Recreations of my Solitude* in the same collection is a literal metrical rendering of a famous contemporary French poem *La Solitude* (1650) by Marc Antoine de St. Amant (1594–1661), a popular member of Malherbe's school. Fairfax was also an unavowed translator of a poem of Malherbe.

[1] Du Bartas, *Les Œuvres Poétiques*, ed. 1615, p. 284.

But Du Bartas's strong Huguenot enthusiasm led him to modify his master's instructions in matters of moment.

Du Bellay, in his manifesto of the new poetic movement in France, had urged Frenchmen to cultivate the epic. Du Bartas eagerly accepted the advice. He deliberately attempted a series of long epic poems; but, contrary to the expectation of his mentor, he sought his themes, not in Greek or Latin history or mythology, but in the Bible. He was a precocious writer, and his earliest work was produced at the age of twenty-one. It was an epic called *Judith*. Here Du Bartas offered a poetic paraphrase of the book of the Apocrypha which tells how the fair Hebrew heroine murdered Nebuchadnezzar's general Holofernes in order to save from destruction her native town of Bethulia. Du Bartas, loyal to the Huguenot ambition of reconciling Hebraism with classicism, deliberately planned his *Judith*, he tells us, on the model of Homer and Vergil. From every point of view Du Bartas's first effort in poetry reflected the Huguenot temper. The cultured mother of his leader and master, Henry of Navarre, suggested the subject, which was suspected of a veiled intention of supporting the Huguenot plea of tyrannicide.

This first-fruit of Du Bartas's pious fancy was published in 1573, together with a second poem called after one of the muses, *L'Uranie*. There the poet versified his favourite argument for the regeneration of poetry by scriptural study. The volume containing the two poems was significantly and appropriately entitled *La Muse Chrétienne*.

But Du Bartas's full fame was won with a later performance of more imposing dimensions. His *magnum opus* is an elaborate description in verse of the creation of the world. This epic poem was called *La Semaine*, and was divided into seven books, or days. Each book, or day, described events of a day in creation. The work came from the press in 1578. A sequel, called *La Seconde Semaine* ('The Second Week'), was left unfinished by the author at his death in 1590. He intended to divide this second part also into seven days, in which he should describe the fortunes of mankind from Adam down to the end of the world. But only four days were

completed.   Again, all the topics belonged to Old Testament
history, and ranged from the felicity of Adam and Eve in the
garden of Eden to the fall of Jerusalem before the hosts of
Nebuchadnezzar.   Each day in the 'Second Week' is divided
into four books, so that the unfinished sequel reaches sixteen
books, and is nearly three times as long as the completed
'First Week'.[1] In point of size *La Semaine*, with *La Seconde
Semaine*, is a formidable contribution to poetic literature.
Ronsard, whom Du Bartas to the end claimed as master,
enigmatically remarked of his disciple's masterpiece, that
Du Bartas did in 'a week' what it took him his whole life
to accomplish.   Du Bartas's epic is only a little less voluminous than the complete works of Ronsard.

Despite his pious aim, Du Bartas's affinities with the
Pléiade remained to the end unmistakable.   Most of the
characteristic marks of the Pléiade style were assimilated by
Du Bartas, although he distorted recklessly some peculiarities
of the school.   With a zeal unknown to the fathers of the
Pléiade, Du Bartas, for example, pursued Ronsard's invention of the compound epithet.   The Huguenot poet employed

[1] The titles of the separate poems in *La Seconde Semaine* run as
follows :—

Le premier Jour   1. *Eden* (Story of Adam and Eve).
                   2. *L'Imposture* (Eve's temptations).
                   3. *Les Furies* (The expulsion from Paradise).
                   4. *Les Artifices* (The later history of Adam and Eve).

Le second Jour   1. *L'Arche* (Noah and the Ark).
                   2. *Babylone* (The tower of Babel).
                   3. *Les Colonies* (The dispersion).
                   4. *Les Colonnes* (A treatise on mathematics and
                      astronomy).

Le troisiesme Jour 1. *La Vocation* (The story of Abraham).
                   2. *Les Pères* (The story of Isaac).
                   3. *La Loy* (The story of Moses and the lawgivers).
                   4. *Les Capitaines* (The early history of the Jewish
                      state).

Le quatriesme Jour 1. *Les Trophées* (The story of King David).
                   2. *La Magnificence* (The story of King Solomon).
                   3. *Le Schisme* (The story of the kings of Judah and
                      Israel).
                   4. *La Décadence* (The story of the fall of Jerusalem).

An Appendix deals with the story of the prophet Jonah.

the device untiringly, sometimes pleasingly, but more often clumsily and cacophonously. Elemental fire he describes thus:

Le feu *donne-clarté, porte-chaud, jette-flamme,*
Source de mouvement, *chasse-ordure, donne-âme.*

Again, with more than Ronsardian licence he creates a number of words, mostly onomatopoeic. He has a habit, too, of duplicating the first syllable of common verbs, e.g. *floflottant* (waving) and *babattant* (beating), to emphasize a suggestion of movement. He is prolific in far-fetched and strange similes, often drawn from common objects which lie outside the ordinary range of poetry. The practice was not unknown to Ronsard, who is the inventor of Du Bartas's oft-repeated comparison of new-fallen snow on leafless trees to a periwig or covering of false hair. But Ronsard is sparing of eccentricities in which Du Bartas's muse revelled.

In his choice of metre Du Bartas works within narrower bounds than those in which Ronsard and his friends exercise their powers. Du Bartas restricted himself with rarest exceptions to Alexandrine rhyming couplets. The Alexandrine is an old French metre. But the Pléiade, when it condemned to limbo almost all the metrical forms of mediaeval France, reserved the Alexandrine for future use, and gave it a new and an improved lease of life. Du Bartas pursued the reformation of the ancient metre. He varied and multiplied the pauses, at times with rugged and abrupt effect, but often with a triumphant challenge of monotony. Not all his metrical innovations are commendable; he has a liking for tricks of rhyme, some of which were revivals of discredited fashions of an earlier epoch. After the manner of old *vers rapportés,* he has an odd habit of repeating at the opening of the second line of his couplet the last two syllables or words of the first line. His fluency of utterance was irrepressible and ill-regulated. Yet one cannot deny him a measure of the metrical ingenuity which is a constant characteristic of Ronsard's school.

In artistic presentation of his theme Du Bartas falls below the standard of his tutors. No nice faculty of selection or arrangement can be put to Du Bartas's credit in elaborating his sacred story. He sows his furrows with the sack, emptying into them a heterogeneous and multifarious mass of observation and information. His epic of the creation has points of resemblance to a crude encyclopaedia of scientific phenomena as well as of dogmatic theology. After describing in the first book the emergence of elemental light out of chaos, he pours into the second book a flood of ill-digested meteorological notes. In the third he pays like court to geology, mineralogy, and botany ; in the fourth to astronomy of an anti-Copernican pattern ; in the fifth to zoology and human physiology. In the last book, after a quaint picture of a very anthropomorphic Deity resting from his works and complacently contemplating them as a whole, the poet becomes doctrinal on the orthodox Huguenot lines.

Yet Du Bartas mingles with his scientific and theological reflections, which are often grotesque, descriptions of both animate and inanimate nature, which betray the vigour of poetic insight and a pictorial command of detail. He is catholic in his outlook on natural phenomena. A spring morning is portrayed with no less realistic energy than a storm at sea. Despite his warlike instincts, he was almost as sympathetic as Ronsard in his study of rural life, where sleep was undisturbed by drum, fife, or trumpet, and was soothed by the gentle murmuring of streams. He could define the points of a horse with an enthusiasm and an accuracy which seem to anticipate Shakespeare's treatment of the same theme.[1] The

---

[1] With Sylvester's faithful translation (1613 ed., pp. 286-8) of Du Bartas's account of ' a goodly jennet ' (*ce beau Ienet*) may well be compared Shakespeare's animated description of a ' courser' catching sight of a 'jennet' in *Venus and Adonis* (lines 271-4, 295-8, 301-4). Shakespeare probably consulted the French text.

SYLVESTER'S TRANSLATION.

With *round*, high, hollow, smooth, brown, jetty *hoof*,
With *pasterns short*, upright, but yet in mean ;
Dry sinewy shanks ; *strong*, fleshless knees, and *lean* ;
With *hartlike legs*, *broad breast*, and large behind,

VENUS AND ADONIS.

His *ears up-prick'd* ; his *braided hanging mane*
Upon his compass'd crest now stands on end ;
His nostrils drink the air, and forth again,
As from a furnace, vapours doth he send : . . .

movements of a spider were shown to the life, and his ear was so keenly attuned to the harmonies of nature that he could analyse the song of lark and nightingale with an admirable veracity. Even when he writes of the roaring of a lion, he gives his reader the impression that he has heard the note. His minute description of spacious landscapes shows that he possessed the eye of a painter for perspective. He presents mountains, meadow, sea, and streams in combination, and out of them constructs a background in lines like these :

> Un fleuve coule ici ; là naist une fontaine ;
> Ici s'esleve un mont ; là s'abbaisse une plaine ;
> Ici fume un chasteau ; là fume une cité,
> Et là flotte une nef sur Neptune irrité.[1]

The forefront and the middle distance of the scene are skilfully broken by charming vignettes of sportsmen aiming their guns at flying birds, of striplings wrestling on village greens, and of shepherdesses tending their flocks.

In the two decades following the St. Bartholomew's Massacre,

With body large, smooth flanks, and double chined :
A *crested neck* bowed like a half-bent bow,
Whereon a long, *thin, curled mane* doth flow ;
A *firmful tail*, touching the lowly ground,
With dock between two fair *fat buttocks* drowned ;
A *pricked ear*, that rests as little space,
As his light foot, a lean, bare bony face,
Thin jowl, and *head but of a middling size*,
Full, lively flaming, quickly rolling *eyes*,
Great foaming mouth, *hot-fuming nostril wide*,
Of chestnut hair, his forehead starrified . . .
As this light horse *scuds*, . . .
Flying the earth, the flying air he catches,
Borne whirlwindlike.

Round hoof'd, short-jointed, fetlocks shag and long,
Broad breast, full eye, small head, and *nostril wide*,
High crest, short ears, *straight legs* and passing *strong*,
Thin mane, thick tail, broad buttock, tender hide ; . . .

Sometimes he *scuds* far off . . .

To *bid the wind a base* he now prepares,
And *whe'r he run or fly* they know not whether.

----

[1] *La Première Semaine : le septiesme jour*, 1615 ed., p. 164.

Du Bartas's sacred poetry was warmly welcomed in France by the growing band of sympathizers with the Huguenot cause.   Thirty editions of *La Semaine* are said to have been issued within six years of its final completion in 1584. Simon Goulart, the successor of Calvin and Beza as ruler of Geneva, who had already offered his fellow countrymen a French version of one of Hotman's great political treatises, prepared early in the seventeenth century an elaborate commentary on Du Bartas's epic.   But, save in the straitest coteries, Du Bartas's triumph in his own country was short-lived.   Cultured taste quickly came to scorn his work.   Modern French critics have concentrated their attention on his many faults, and have condemned the incorrectness of his style, and the irregularities of his imagery.   He has been ridiculed as the *enfant terrible* of the Pléiade school, while a juster and more charitable verdict sneers at him as ' un Milton *manqué* ':

Greater indulgence has been extended to Du Bartas in recent years by both English and German critics, who detect both dignity and vivacity at many turns of his work.   Goethe saluted him as the king of French poets, and never ceased to emphasize the grandeur of his conceptions.

The truth seems to be that Du Bartas's obtrusive defects— his unmanageable erudition, his lack of artistic restraint, his ungenial pietism—were allied with an imaginative capacity which was too robust to sink under their weight.   His strenuous copiousness and his exalted faith in himself have suggested to an English critic a comparison between him and Victor Hugo, some touch of whose poetic fury a French critic quite independently detected in Du Bartas's Huguenot contemporary, Aubigné.   Undoubtedly both Du Bartas and Aubigné were capable of fusing Huguenot zeal and poetic ardour.   Nor did they lack intellectual energy.   Their temperaments begot, too, a power of flowing declamation which is rarely found in poetry outside the scope of drama.

IX

ELIZABETHAN DISCIPLES OF DU BARTAS

Du Bartas was the poet whom the Elizabethans mainly identified with the Huguenot movement. The honours which Shakespeare's generation paid him excelled those which were bestowed on any other foreign contemporary, and Ronsard's popularity waned in his presence. His fame passed like a comet over the literary firmament of France. In that of England it remained for near a century a fixed star. Du Bartas's ardent piety accounts for the fervour of applause, for the flood of eulogy. His critical shortcomings passed almost unrecognized. A rugged English translation to which he mainly owed his vogue across the Channel accentuated his tendencies to grotesque bombast. Justness of critical perception was sacrificed by Du Bartas's English admirers. Their estimates placed him above even Shakespeare and Spenser. The eager greeting of Du Bartas by the Elizabethans is a curiosity in the history of literary criticism. The generous tributes pointedly illustrate the occasional tendency of contemporary opinion to set what is second or third-rate in literature above what is first-rate. Owing largely to a widespread error of judgement, Du Bartas exerted a peculiar influence, which no other foreign writer quite equalled, on English poetic developments. Sacred poetry in our language has some title to be reckoned an offspring of his Huguenot muse.

The discoverer in Britain of this new constellation in the French sky of poetry was no other than James VI of Scotland. The reading of Du Bartas's early work *L'Uranie* filled the Scottish king with unbounded enthusiasm, and he turned it with his own pen into English or Scottish verse. A like service was rendered at King James's suggestion to Du Bartas's first epic, *Judith*, by one of the royal attendants at the Edinburgh court, Thomas Hudson. Hudson's translation of *Judith* appeared in 1584. Meanwhile Du Bartas had scaled the highest flight of his invention by the issue of his *La Semaine*.

James VI of Scotland, in perusing that poem, was moved to ecstasy, and to a passionate yearning to make the poet's personal acquaintance. He addressed urgent letters to Henry of Navarre and to the poet himself begging that Du Bartas should visit Scotland. James described himself as torn between sentiments of grief and desire, between grief that his own country had produced no such triumphal pyramid of literature, and desire to fix his gaze on the person of this new poetic Colossus.[1] Du Bartas yielded to the flattery,

[1] The letter of invitation which James VI addressed to Du Bartas, 'His Maiesties letter unto Mr. du Bartas' (MS. Bodl. 165, fol. 75), was printed by Mr. Rait for the first time in his *Lusus Regius*, 1901, pp. 60-1. It ran as follows:—

'Alexandre le grand ayant esté informé de la grande uertu & sagesse de Diogenes philosophe cinique en fut tellement rauy qu'il ne sceut contenter iusques tant qu'il eut communiqque auec lui, estimant d'aquerir non la moindre partie de contentement & renommée en se faisant *oculatus testis* des singulieres uertus de ce susdit personnage. La pareille occasion de rauissement, ô tres illustre poete, m'estant ministrée par la lecture de mon Homere (car de mesme facon ie me sers des menus-fruicts de nostre admirable muse comme ce susdit conquereur des Iliades) que jay esté agité de deux fortes passions dun mesme instant, à scauoir, iuste Douleur & insatiable Desir: Douleur que ce pais n'a esté si heureusement fertile que d'auoir produit un tell' colosse ou piramide triomfale triomfant urayement sur le monde d'un triomfe eternell, pour auoir le premier mis en œuure, & le seul puisé profondement iusques au fonds ce diuin subiect, chantant poetiquement la creation & conseruation aussi bien du grand monde que du microcosme par la sage puissance & soigneuse prouidence du tout puissant Createur, mais quant à l'extresme Desir, il me pousse sans cesse à l'imitation de ce Douleur du monde que comme iournellement i'oy le chant de l'Uranie ie puisse une fois obtenir la ueue de son fidelle secretaire. N'estimes, ô Saluste, qu'en usant ces epithetes enuers uous ie me ueuille seruir de la faulse flatterie ains du deu & uray louange de la uertu, le hault louange de laquelle ne doyt estre passée en silence habitante en personne quelquonque : & comme chacuns desireux de uoir la pourtraict de ceux qui ont surpasse le monde en quelque insigne vertu, d'autant qu'ill le remett en memoire des uertus si louables de mesme, ayie un ardant desir de ueoir le palais de la Muse vrayement celeste, puis que null mortell ne peut veoir l'host, pour ceste cause ie uous escrips cest present. Ie uous prie donques tres affectueusement de prendre tant de peine que de uenir icy au commencement de l' esté prochain, & mesme en may, sil est possible ; le uoyage n'est point long, uous pouues passer par terre, demeurer icy aussi peu de temps que uous uoudres, nonobstant les troubles, ie m'asseure que le roy de Nauar le trouuerra bon pour si peu de temps car ie luy ay aussi escript pour ce mesme effect, & ie m'asseure que uous uiendres le plus uolontiers puis que nous auons *communes deos* : puis donques que iay tant uœu uostre ombre en uos œuures une fois *da dextrae iungere dextram* ie uous prie de rechef de uenir, m'asseurant donques que puisque ma demande est *si iuste ex oratore exorator fieri* ie uous commets & uos estudes à la sainte tuition & inspiration du bon & uray dieu.'

and spent many weeks with the court at Edinburgh in the year 1587. He acknowledged King James's hospitality by translating into French a small original piece by his royal host—a poem on the great naval battle of Lepanto of October, 1571, when the Cross triumphed over the Crescent, and the Turks were routed by Spanish and Venetian fleets.

On the journey to and from Scotland Du Bartas paused in England, and the welcome of Queen Elizabeth and her courtiers was hardly less enthusiastic than that which was accorded him north of the Tweed. The fame of the great queen had already moved him to a panegyric. In his sacred epic he had expressed a hope that his writings might be read by 'la grand' Elizabeth, la prudente Pallas'. He had addressed her in strains which were well calculated to appeal to her idiosyncrasy:

Claire perle du Nord, guerriere, domte-Mars,
Continue à cherir les Muses et les Arts,
Et si iamais ces vers peuvent d'une aile agile,
Franchissant l'Ocean, voler iusqu'à ton Isle,
Et tomber, fortunes, entre ces blanches mains,
Qui sous un iuste frein regissent tant d'humains,
Voy les d'un œil benin, et favorable pense
Qu'il faut pour te louer, avoir ton eloquence.[1]

Of English literature Du Bartas had formed no clear conception before his visit. He had saluted Sir Thomas More and Sir Nicholas Bacon as pillars of English eloquence, and had paid a compliment to the sweet song of Sir Philip Sidney, whom he hailed as a unique swan adorning the current of the river Thames.[2] The Frenchman gave no proof that he

---

[1] *La Seconde Semaine : le second jour*, pt. ii, 1615 ed., p. 284.

[2]   Le parler des Anglois a pour fermes piliers
Thomas More, et Baccon, tous deux grands Chancelliers,
Qui seurant leur langage, et le tirant d'enfance,
Au sçavoir politique ont conioint l'eloquence.
Et le Milor Cydné qui, Cygne doux-chantant,
Va les flots orgueilleux de Tamise flatant,
Ce fleuve gros d'honneur emporte la faconde
Dans le sein de Thetis, et Thetis par le Monde.
  (*La Seconde Semaine : le second jour*, pt. ii, 1615 ed., p. 283.)

As early as 1592 Tom Nashe in his *Pierce Pennilesse* cited this passage as a notable praise of 'immortal Sir P. Sidney' whom, Nashe tells his

extended while in England his acquaintance with English literature. There was nothing reciprocal about the influence that he exerted on his hosts; he derived no help from them.

Unluckily, Du Bartas's visit could not be repeated, for he returned to France to wield his sword anew against the Catholics, with results fatal to himself. He fought bravely at the side of Henry of Navarre at the great battle of Ivry (March 14, 1590), and he celebrated the great victory in a spirited hymn or cantique. But in the engagement he received many wounds which within four months caused his death.

Shortly before Du Bartas arrived in England, Sidney, the gentle friend of all Huguenot activity, had acknowledged the high compliment which Du Bartas paid him, by embarking on a first translation into English of Du Bartas's verse.[1] Some portion of Sidney's tribute was completed before Sidney's death in 1586. It was admired in manuscript, but nothing of it has survived.

As in the case of Du Plessis, Du Bartas's presence in Great Britain greatly stimulated his literary reputation among Queen Elizabeth's subjects. Cultivated society in London was hardly slower than the Scottish monarch to acknowledge the fascination of the Huguenot epic. But it was not until its author had passed away that *La Semaine*, with some minor works of the author, which had not previously been translated, were offered in an English printed book to an eager and expectant public.

reader, 'noble Salustius (that thrice singular French poet) hath famoused, together with Sir Nicholas Bacon and merry Sir Thomas Moore, for the chief pillars of our English speech' (Nashe, *Works*, ed. McKerrow, i, pp. 193–4).

[1] William Ponsonby, the London publisher, obtained a licence for the publication of Sir Philip Sidney's *Arcadia* on August 23, 1588; at the same time he secured permission to print 'A translation of Salust de Bartas done by ye same Sir P. in the Englishe' (Arber's *Stationers' Register*, ii. 496). Sir Fulke Greville, writing to Sir Francis Walsingham in 1587, soon after Sidney's death, eulogizes his rendering of Du Bartas into English metre (State Papers Dom.). Florio in dedicating his *Montaigne* (Bk. ii, 1603) to Sidney's daughter, the Countess of Rutland, and to Sidney's friend, Lady Rich, notes that he had seen Sidney's rendering of 'the first septmane of that arch-poet Du Bartas', and entreats the ladies to publish it. Nothing further is known of Sidney's effort.

The chief Elizabethan translator of Du Bartas, Joshua Sylvester, was well versed in French. Born in 1563, a year before Shakespeare, he was educated at the Grammar School of Southampton, of which the headmaster was a French-speaking Flemish refugee. As a schoolboy he talked nothing but French. In early manhood he went into business as a clothier, joining a London corporation of merchants trading with Germany. His leisure was devoted to literature, and as early as 1592 he first declared his discipleship to Du Bartas by publishing an English version of the ' third day ' of Du Bartas's ' second week '—(the story of Isaac)—together with the fragment of the story of Jonah and the song of triumph over the victory of Ivry. Other portions of Du Bartas's work followed rapidly, and in 1605 there appeared a complete collection of ' Du Bartas His Devine Weekes and Workes translated '. Many reprints were issued between that date and 1641. Sylvester's literary services were rewarded by a pension and an honorary office in the household of Prince Henry, James I's elder son. But he never abandoned his association with trade, and his last five years were spent abroad—at Middelburg— where he died in 1618, two years later than Shakespeare.

Sylvester's version of Du Bartas, each instalment of which was welcomed by Elizabethans with shouts of applause, is in decasyllabic couplets. The Englishman is loyal to all the eccentricities of his French master's style, to the onomatopoeic duplication of syllables, to the tricks of jingling rhyme, to the abrupt pauses. The English poetaster is, above all, a slave to the compound epithet, which Sir Philip Sidney had first introduced from Ronsard's French. Sylvester's combinations of words were so clumsy as to lead sagacious critics to the opinion that the device was in conflict with the English idiom.[1] Sylvester, exaggerates, too, the grotesque surprises of the French imagery. On occasion, however, he inter-

---

[1] Dryden in his *Apology for Heroic Poetry and Poetic License* altogether condemns in English ' connection of epithets or the conjunction of two words in one '. He praises the habit as frequent and elegant in the Greek but blames ' Sir Philip Sidney and the translator of Du Bartas ' for having ' unluckily attempted [it] ' in the English (Dryden's *Essays,* ed. W. P. Ker, i. 187).

polates original lines. He adapts to an English environment Du Bartas's references to French personages and affairs, and appeals to his master for permission to weave into the rich garland flowers of his own growing. He shows to advantage in some of these developments. Now and then he even invents a compound epithet of peculiar charm, which there is nothing in Du Bartas to suggest. His ' *opal-colour'd* morn ' is a fine rendering of ' l'Aurore d'un clair grivolement '.[1] But in spite of oases of picturesqueness or felicity Sylvester's massive volume is a desert waste of cacophony and uncouth expression.

Here is a characteristic extract describing the end of the world, which reproduces the French with fair accuracy, and shows Du Bartas and Sylvester at their mean level:

> One day the rocks from top to toe shall quiver,
> The mountains melt and all in sunder shiver:
> The heavens shall rent for fear; the lowly fields,
> Puffed up, shall swell to huge and mighty hills:
> Rivers shall dry; or if in any flood
> Rest any liquor, it shall all be blood:
> The sea shall all be fire, and on the shore
> The thirsty whales with horrid noise shall roar:
> The sun shall seize the black coach of the moon,
> And make it midnight when it should be noon:
> With rusty mask the heavens shall hide their face,
> The stars shall fall, and all away shall pass:
> Disorder, dread, horror and death shall come,
> Noise, storms, and darkness shall usurp the room.
> And then the chief-chief-justice, venging wrath
> (Which here already often threatened hath)
> Shall make a bonfire of this mighty ball,
> As once he made it a vast ocean all.[2]

[1] Cf. *La Seconde Semaine: le second jour*, 1615 ed., p. 273. 'Grivolement' is defined by Cotgrave as ' pecklenesse, or a speckled colour '.

[2] Sylvester's translation, 1613 ed., pp. 11-12. Du Bartas's French original runs thus:

> Un jour de comble en fond les rochers crouleront;
> Les monts plus sourcilleux de peur se dissoudront;
> Le ciel se crevera: les plus basses campagnes
> Boursoufflées croistront en superbes montagnes:
> Les fleuves tariront, & si dans quelque estang
> Reste encor quelque flot, ce ne sera que sang.
> La mer deviendra flamme; & les seches balenes,
> Horribles, mugleront sur les cuites arenes:
> En son midi plus clair le iour s'espaissira:
> Le ciel d'un fer rouillé sa face voilera:

Perhaps Sylvester shows to better advantage in such a passage as this on the plurality of worlds :—

> I'll ne'er believe that the arch-architect
> With all these fires the heavenly arches decked
> Only for show, and with these glistering shields
> T'amaze poor shepherds watching in the fields.
> I'll ne'er believe that the least flower that pranks
> Our garden borders, or the common banks,
> And the least stone that in her warming lap,
> Our kind nurse earth doth covetously wrap,
> Hath some peculiar virtue of its own ;
> And that the glorious stars of heaven have none.

Sylvester is seen at his worst in the following passage, which startled Dryden as a boy into a spurious admiration :—

> But when the winter's keener breath began
> To crystallise the Baltic Ocean,
> To glaze the lakes, and bridle-up the floods,
> And periwig with wool the baldpate woods.
> Our grandsire shrinking, gan to shake and shiver,
> His teeth to chatter, and his beard to quiver.[1]

Sylvester shared the poetic adulation which was from the first showered in England on Du Bartas. The efforts of both Frenchman and Englishman were praised with the like solemn and sublime extravagance. Gabriel Harvey was early in the field with an ecstatic tribute of bombastic laudation.

> Sur les astres plus clairs courra le bleu Neptune:
> Phœbus s'emparera du noir char de la Lune :
> Les estoilles cherront. Le desordre, la nuict,
> La frayeur, le trespas, la tempeste, le bruit
> Entreront en quartier, & l'ire vengeresse
> Du juge criminel, qui ia desja nous presse,
> Ne fera de ce Tout qu'un bucher flamboyant,
> Comme il n'en fit jadis qu'un marest ondoyant.
> (*Semaine* i : *Jour* i, 1615 ed., p. 20.)

[1] Dryden quotes the first four lines in a dedication of his *Spanish Friar*, 1681, and adds the comment: ' I am much deceived if this be not abominable fustian, that is, thoughts and words ill-sorted' (Dryden's *Essays*, ed. Ker, i, p. 247). The French runs—

> Mais soudain que l'Hyver donne un froide bride
> Aux fleuves desbordez ; que, colere, il solide
> Le Baltique Neptun ; qu'il vitre les guerets,
> Et que de flocs de laine il orne les forets :
> Nostre ayeul se fait moindre ; il fremit, il frissonne,
> Il fait craquer ses dents, sa barbe il herissonne.
> Du Bartas, *Semaine* ii : *Jour* i, 1615 ed., pp. 238–9.

For elevation of subject and majesty of verse Harvey gave Du Bartas a place beside Dante. His wisdom excelled that of the seven sages of Greece. Euripides was his inferior. Only 'the sacred and reverend stile of heavenly divinity itself' could claim inspiration superior to that of this new 'French Solomon'.[1] But Harvey's standard of appreciation was nearly approached by abler pens. Poets of the highest standing, Spenser, Daniel, Drayton, Lodge, and Ben Jonson joined at the outset in the eulogistic hue and cry after both the Huguenot inventor of sacred poetry and his English satellite.

Spenser, who wrote while Du Bartas was yet alive, was comparatively restrained in associating Du Bartas with Du Bellay, and in noting that the Huguenot poet was beginning

high to raise
His heavenly muse, the Almighty to adore.

Drayton declared that—

Time could work no injury on the hallowed labours of the divine song in courtly French.

Thomas Lodge, whose last literary labour was to render into English Goulart's prose commentary on Du Bartas's epic, offers the opinion:

I protest that Du Bartas is as much delightful as any Greek, Latin, or French author that we can light upon, who ever hath bestowed his style and study to speak of God and his works. Moreover, I avow him in the first rank of writers either ancient or modern that ever intermixed profit with pleasure, and whose everlasting Genius discourseth itself to all posterity.[2]

More tuneful is William Browne's greeting:

Delightful Saluste, whose all blessed lays
The shepherds make their hymns on holy-days,
And truly say thou in one week hast penn'd
What time may ever study, ne'er amend.[3]

On the appearance of Sylvester's version, Ben Jonson greeted the reverend shade of Du Bartas in as respectful a key, but he

[1] Gabriel Harvey's *Works*, ed. Grosart, ii. 103.
[2] Lodge published in 1621 *A Learned Summarie upon the famous Poeme of William of Saluste, lord of Bartas*. Translated out of [Goulart's] French by T. L., D[octor] M[edicus] P[hysician] 1621, fol. The volume was licensed for the press March 8, 1620. It was reissued in 1638.
[3] Browne's *Poems*, ed. G. Goodwin (Muses' Library), i. 223.

sounded subsequently the only note of adverse criticism which
seems to have been heard in Shakespeare's generation. Ben
Jonson told Drummond of Hawthornden, when he visited him
at Edinburgh, that he thought Du Bartas was ' not a poet, but
a verser, because he wrote not fiction '.[1] Jonson doubtless
meant that the French Huguenot borrowed his subject-matter
from the Bible, and did not invent it.

French poetry, which was 'so generally applauded even of
the greatest and gravest of this kingdom', might well stir pens
of smaller eminence to salute—

> These glorious works and grateful monuments
> Built by Du Bartas on the Pyrenees.

The more habitual note of pedestrian admiration may be
gleaned from this sonnet of an Elizabethan poetaster :—

> Had golden Homer and great Maro kept
> In envious silence their admired measures,
> A thousand worthies' worthy deeds had slept,
> They reft of praise, and we of learned pleasures.
> But O ! what rich incomparable treasures
> Had the world wanted, had this modern glory,
> Divine Du Bartas, hid his heavenly ceasures,
> Singing the mighty world's immortal story ?
> O then how deeply is our isle beholding
> To Chapman, and to Phaer, but yet much more
> To thee, dear Sylvester, for thus unfolding
> These holy wonders, hid from us before.
> Those works profound are yet profane ; but thine
> Grave, learned, deep, delightful and divine.[2]

Nearly a century passed away before the trumpets of praise
ceased to sound. Dryden in boyhood deemed Du Bartas and
Sylvester far greater poets than Spenser, but at a maturer
age he denounced them both for 'abominable fustian ', as
' injudicious poets, who aiming at loftiness ran easily into the
swelling puffy style because it looked like greatness.'[3] The

---

[1] Drummond of Hawthornden's *Notes on Ben Jonson's Conversations*,
Edinburgh, 1831–2, p. 82.

[2] This sonnet is one of many such prefixed to the collected edition of
Sylvester's *Du Bartas*, 1605. It is signed R. N., doubtless Richard
Niccols, who brought out a revised version of *The Mirror for Magistrates*
in 1610. Chapman and Phaer are mentioned in the sonnet as the chief
Elizabethan translators of Homer and Vergil respectively.

[3] Cf. note on p. 344, *supra*.

poet Wordsworth echoed a still more recent verdict. 'Who is there that now reads the *Creation* of Du Bartas? Yet all Europe once resounded with his praise; he was caressed by kings; and when his poem was translated into our language the *Faery Queene* faded before it.'[1]

More important than the mighty eruption of panegyric are the traces which the worship of Du Bartas has left on the style and theme of Elizabethan poetry.[2] Occasional signs are not wanting that Shakespeare came under his spell.[3] Spenser, who was often compared to his disadvantage with Du Bartas, lightly echoes many of his phrases and his double epithets. The pseudo-scientific illustration is often the same in both poets. In Du Bartas's curious physiological notes Spenser clearly sought hints of his allegorical description of the human body, the lodging of the soul Alma, which appears in the *Faerie Queene* (Book II). Nor is some of his description of natural scenery easily freed of the imputation of indebtedness. Du Bartas showed especial sensitiveness to the song of birds, and in this regard there is a curious adumbration of the Spenserian temper. A note which is habitual to Du Bartas distinguishes the lines, which Sylvester renders thus:

> Arise betimes, while th' opal-coloured Morn
> In golden pomp doth May-day's door adorn,
> And patient hear the all-differing voices sweet
> Of painted singers, that in groves do greet
> Their love Bon-jours, each in his phrase and fashion
> From trembling perch uttering hi searnest passion.[4]

[1] Wordsworth's *Poetry as a Study*, 1815, in *Prose Works*, ed. Grosart, 1876, ii, pp. 111–12.

[2] The fullest estimate of Du Bartas's influence on seventeenth-century English poetry will be found in *The French Influence in English Literature*, by Alfred H. Upham, Ph.D., New York, 1908, pp. 145 seq. Mr. H. Ashton in *Du Bartas en Angleterre*, Paris, 1908, also gives quite independently a full critical estimate of Du Bartas's work, and describes the place that the French poet filled in Elizabethan literary annals.

[3] See note on p. 337, *supra*.

[4] The French of Du Bartas runs—

> Leue-toy de matin, & tandis que l'Aurore
> D'un clair grivolement l'huis d'un beau jour decore
> Escoute patient les discordantes voix
> De tant de chantres peints, qui donnent dans un bois
> L'aubade à leurs amours, & chacun en sa langue
> Perché sur un rameau, prononce sa harangue.

(*Semaine* ii : *Jour* ii, pt. ii, 'Babylone'; *Œuvres*, 1615 ed., p. 273.)

Spenser aims at the same effect with far greater splendour and success in the *Faerie Queene* (Bk. II, Canto xii..lxx–i), yet the sentiment of the Elizabethan poet is nearly anticipated by that of his Huguenot predecessor :

> Eftsoones they heard a most melodious sound,
> Of all that mote delight a dainty ear,
> Such as at once might not on living ground,
> Save in this Paradise, be heard elsewhere : . . .
> The joyous birds, shrouded in cheerful shade
> Their notes unto the voice attempted sweet ;
> Th' angelical soft trembling voices made
> To th' instruments divine respondence meet.

There is no possibility of mistaking the incitement which Du Bartas offered English poets to deal with sacred topics. It may be fairly said that almost all the sacred poetry of the last years of Elizabeth and the early days of James took its cue from *La Semaine*. The satirist, Hall, at the extreme end of the century described Du Bartas as 'a French angel girt with bays', whose divine strain was a holy message to Englishmen. Hall soon saw reason for lamenting that Parnassus should be transformed into a hill of Zion. The allegation was held by some of Hall's readers to reflect unfairly on 'Bartas's sweet Semaines' and on the current efforts to bring the French poet's 'stranger language to our vulgar tongue'. But the new vogue of religious rhyming readily lent itself to extravagance, and Hall was only warning the Huguenot poet's admirers against excesses. Many of those, too, who owed the inspiration of their sacred verse to the French muse carried into secular verse marks of their study of the French epic. Such a comment especially applies to two poets of the first order, Drayton and Donne, and to three voluminous poets of a secondary rank, Nicholas Breton, Sir John Davies, and John Davies of Hereford. From Spenser to Milton proofs are abundant of the impression which the Huguenot's amplitude of topic, and his curious striving after sublimity no less than his religious fervour left on serious English minds which fostered poetic ambitions. The Huguenot's matter and manner find faithful reflection in a mass of late Elizabethan and early Stuart verse.

When Drayton in 1604 published his paraphrase of scriptural story called *Moyses in a Map of Miracles*, he dedicated it to Du Bartas and his English translator, and he frankly admitted that the *Divine Week* was the source of his inspiration. Subsequently Drayton revised this poem and added two others, one entitled *Noah's Flood*, the other *David and Goliah*. In all the French influence is strong. The topics are identical with those of Du Bartas, and if Drayton adapts and imitates rather than translates Du Bartas's words, his decasyllabic couplets ring with Sylvester's cadence, while they loyally expound Du Bartas's cosmic theories. Truthfully did Drayton avow that his 'higher' poems of the divine grace came 'humbly' to attend 'the hallowed labours of that faithful muse' who 'divinely' sang 'this ALL'S creation' in 'courtly French'.

Similar relations are traceable in a pious poem, *The Soul's Immortal Crown*, by a facile lyrist, Nicholas Breton; in the metaphysical musings of Sir John Davies in his *Immortality of the Soul*, and throughout the voluble religious tracts of didactic John Davies of Hereford. To these men Du Bartas proved a false guide. John Davies of Hereford enjoys an unenviable notoriety by his clumsy copying of the least admirable tricks of Du Bartas or his translator. He duplicates prefixes to words, e.g. 'the super-supererogatory works'. He freely introduces compound epithets of singular awkwardness, and he falls into the grotesque habit of tame verbal jingles.

> Thy blissful-blissless blessed body O

is one of Davies's pious ejaculations. For many of his humbler English worshippers 'divine Du Bartas' proved an *ignis fatuus*. Small profit did they derive from his 'blessed brains', in spite of their ecstatic acknowledgement that thence

> Such works of grace or graceful works did stream,

that 'wit' could discover no more authentic 'celestial strains'.

Virile Donne's debt to Du Bartas is the most interesting fact about the French poet in the history of English poetry. Donne makes no avowal of dependence on Du Bartas. He pays him no hackneyed compliments. The only contemporary French book which Donne familiarly mentions in his

letters in early life is a very different example of French
poetry. He commends to a friend a book of satires, the
popular work of Régnier, which came out in Paris in 1612,
when Donne was a visitor to that city.[1] Régnier, a nephew
of Desportes, and a champion of Ronsard's falling reputation,
made his fame just after the Elizabethan period closed. As
a moral satirist in the manner of Juvenal and Horace, he
showed a keen insight into human vanities, adumbrating
something of the power of Molière. Satire on the Horatian
pattern had been recommended to French poets by the
masters of the Pléiade, and many efforts in that direction
were made in France from 1560 onwards.[2] Vauquelin de la
Fresnaie circulated much satiric verse in manuscript during
the last thirty years of the century. But he delayed publication of his endeavours till 1605. The authors of *La Satire
Ménippée* developed in 1593 a peculiar vein of irony, which
illustrated the national faculty for sarcasm. But Régnier's
pen first lent French satire poetic force. Donne is the only
Englishman who betrayed interest in Régnier's effort, and
English satire in Donne's hand owed something to the French
suggestion. Herein Donne was loyal to precedent. His
English predecessor in the satiric field, Joseph Hall, who
claimed, despite Wyatt's earlier experiment, to be the first
English satirist, acknowledged obligations to an anonymous
'base French satire', to whose identity there are several
claimants, as well as to Persius and Ariosto.

But whatever the measure of French influence which is
to be imputed to Donne's satires, it is other parts of his
work which bear conspicuous mark of French inspiration.
Huguenot sufferings left a deep impression on Donne's mind.
Once he constructs a most repulsive simile out of reports of the
tortures which Huguenots endured in the course of their war

---

[1] Writing from Paris in 1612 to his friend George Gerrard, Donne
wrote : ' I make shift to think that I promised you this book of French
satires. If I did not, yet it may have the grace of acceptation, both as it
is a very forward and early fruit, since it comes before it was looked for,
and as it comes from a good root, which is an importune desire to serve
you.' (Gosse's Life and Letters of Donne, 1899, ii. 10.)

[2] See Viollet-Le-Duc's *L'Histoire de la Satire en France* prefixed to
Régnier's *Œuvres Complètes*, 1853.

with the Catholics. The town of Sancerre, in the province of Berry, not far from Bourges, in the very centre of France, was a permanent city of refuge for Huguenots. The city won a terrible renown by its heroic defence when it was besieged by French Catholics in 1573. The extraordinary ingenuity with which the inhabitants reduced the pangs of famine by turning to culinary uses not merely horses, dogs, and cats, but cattle hide, old parchment, and all kinds of old leather, is described in minutest detail by one of the besieged, Jean de Lery.[1] No besieged city of antiquity was reckoned to have passed through a comparable ordeal. Donne graphically recalls the episode when he brutally compares 'the sweaty froth' on the brow of his enemy's mistress to

> The scum, which, by need's lawless law
> Enforced, Sanserra's starvèd men did draw
> From parboiled shoes and boots, and all the rest
> Which were with any sovereign fatness blest.[2]

The cited lines do far more than suggest that Donne closely studied Huguenot fortunes. They are in Du Bartas's least attractive vein, and they strike a note which is habitual to Donne's verse. The Huguenot poet or his English translator was clearly one of the influences at work on Donne's somewhat crabbed muse. The uncouth metaphor, the harsh epithet, the varying pause in the line, which are characteristic of Donne's rhyming decasyllables, all seem to mirror irregularities which dominate Du Bartas's or Sylvester's achievement. In his early work Donne frequently touches in Du Bartas's vein on episodes of the story of Creation. The metre is always that of Sylvester, Du Bartas's English translator.

> When nature was most busy, the first week,
> Swaddling the new-born Earth, God seemed to like
> That she should sport herself sometimes, and play,
> To mingle and vary colours every day;

---

[1] 'Discours de l'extrême famine, cherté de vivre, chairs, et autres choses non accoustumées pour la nourriture de l'homme, dont les assiégez dans la ville de Sancerre ont été affligez,' 1574.

[2] Donne's Poems, ed. E. K. Chambers (Muses' Library), i. 114.

And then, as though she could not make enow,
Himself his various rainbow did allow.[1]

As some days are, at the creation, named
Before the sun, the which framed days, was framed,
So after this sun's set, some show appears,
And orderly vicissitude of years.[2]

As all things were one nothing, dull and weak,
Until this raw disorder'd heap did break,
And several desires led parts away,
Water declined with earth, the air did stay,
Fire rose, and each from other but untied,
Themselves unprison'd were and purified;
So was love, first in vast confusion hid,
An unripe willingness which nothing did,
A thirst, an appetite which had no ease,
That found a want, but knew not what would please.[3]

Donne clothed elegies, eclogues, divine poems, epicedes, obsequies, satires in a garb barely distinguishable from this style of Du Bartas and Sylvester. The intellectual texture of Donne's verse is usually stiffer and subtler than that of Huguenot poetry. Yet the so-called metaphysical vein, which is usually said to have been inaugurated in English poetry by Donne, is entitled to rank with Du Bartas's legacies to this country. Donne's 'concordia discors', his 'combination of dissimilar images or discovery of occult resemblances in things apparently unlike', is anticipated by Du Bartas. In both poets 'the most heterogeneous ideas are yoked by violence together; nature and art are ransacked for illustrations, comparisons, and allusions; their learning instructs and their subtility surprises'.[4] Donne long survived the Elizabethan era, and he helped to extend Du Bartas's influence to the generation beyond.

The proof of such extended influence abounds. One later tribute to Du Bartas's 'eagle eye and wing' came from

[1] Poems, ed. E. K. Chambers, Muses' Library, ii. 116. 'An Anatomy of the World. The First Anniversary.'
[2] ibid., ii, p. 127. 'The Second Anniversary.'
[3] ibid., ii, p. 49. 'Letter to the Countess of Huntingdon.'
[4] Dr. Johnson's Lives of the Poets (Life of Cowley), ed. Birkbeck Hill, i. 20.

Spenser's disciple, Phineas Fletcher, in his *Purple Island*
(1633), and is an acknowledgement of an important source of
inspiration.   Nor was a greater poet than Fletcher free from
the infatuation to which the Elizabethans succumbed.   There
seems no reason to question the tradition that the boy Milton,
when living with his father in Bread Street, received in 1618
from a neighbour, Humphrey Lownes, who was Sylvester's
publisher, a new edition of the English version of Du Bartas,
and that the future poet read it with avidity while a boy of ten.
Milton's juvenile paraphrase of the Psalms abounds in verbal
and metrical coinage of Du Bartas's mint.   Sylvester could
hardly have improved on the boy poet's compound epithet,
' froth-becurled (head),' or on such a couplet with its disyllabic
weak endings as

Why fled the Ocean? And why skipt the mountains?
Why turnèd Jordan from his crystal fountains?

Paradise Lost has been claimed as one of the many offsprings
of *La Semaine*.   There is an undoubted kinship between the
great Puritan epic and the great Huguenot epic, and although
the degree of relationship is open to doubt and discussion, the
fact that marks of affinity are recognizable lends a singular
brightness to the poetic reputation of the Huguenot Homer.[1]

---

[1] The chief work on Milton's debt to Du Bartas is Charles Dunster's
*Considerations on Milton's Early Reading and the Prima Stamina of his
'Paradise Lost'*, London, 1800.   Cf. Masson's *Life of Milton*, i. 89 seq.

BOOK VI

FRENCH INFLUENCE ON ELIZABETHAN DRAMA

I

The Foreign Sources of Elizabethan Drama

The poetic and literary aspiration of Elizabethan England found its final triumph in drama. It is questionable if, apart from its drama, the Elizabethan era, despite its debt to Spenser, would rank with the supreme epochs of the world's literary or poetic activity—with the epochs of Sophocles or Vergil or Tasso or Wordsworth or Victor Hugo. With its drama the Elizabethan era has some title to rank above all the world's epochs of literary or poetic eminence.

The claim to precedence is mainly due to the giant genius of Shakespeare, but dramatic faculty of exceptional intensity, however inferior to Shakespeare's, is visible in Marlowe, Webster, Fletcher, and other of Shakespeare's contemporaries. The spirit of the age at its zenith was magically endowed with the power of interpreting passion and humour in terms of drama. Dramatic endeavour flourished from an earlier date in Italy and France, and was active in both countries through the age of Elizabeth, but the ultimate level of both tragic and comic energy in Elizabethan England was never reached in sixteenth-century Italy or France. In Spain dramatic ambition ran high while the Elizabethan fire was dying, and there drama breathed something of the versatile vigour and flexibility of the Elizabethan outburst, but even the Spanish drama at its *apogée*—the drama of Lope de Vega and Calderon—lacked the combined measure of poetry and passion, humour and intellectual strength, which glorified the work of Shakespeare. Yet in spite of the pre-eminence of Elizabethan drama, which the world's parliament of critics now acknowledges, its debt to foreign influence and foreign suggestion was hardly less than the debt of Elizabethan prose or Elizabethan lyric.

Elizabethan drama was no spontaneous emanation in the literary firmament. Neither its tragic, nor its comic, nor even its romantic manifestations were of native parentage. The whole conception of tragedy was a foreign gift—the gift to modern Europe of classical literature. Italy and France accepted the revelation long before it reached England, and England learned from early Italian or French experiments in tragic drama many of the practical aptitudes of the classical creed. Italian and French comedy was of less pure origin. While it traced its descent in part to the Latin plays of Plautus and Terence, it absorbed in both countries native elements of comic insight and satiric faculty. In the fifteenth and early sixteenth century, French comedy developed a peculiar briskness, breadth, and pliancy of original texture. The alertness of wit in French comic drama of this period owed little to classical influence and was superior in volatility to anything of previous date. As the sixteenth century advanced, the pure classical example fused itself with the indigenous gaiety of the nation, and there emerged a new and permanent standard of French comedy. Before the classical spirit had thoroughly mingled with the Gallic, France gave Tudor England early lessons in farcical comedy. The experience left traces on the perfected type of Elizabethan comedy, which also stood indebted to the growth in France of classical tendencies. Other foreign influences wrought on the final comic form of Elizabethan drama. There is no ground to question the substantial accuracy of the observation of a critic of Elizabethan drama in its early days : 'Comedies in Latin, French, Italian, and Spanish have been thoroughly ransacked to furnish the playhouses in London.'[1] Yet among these foreign stores the French tragedies and comedies, or French versions of classical and Italian comedies and tragedies were always the most abundant and accessible.

A notable modification of ancient orthodoxy in the sphere of tragedy and comedy is often reckoned peculiarly character-istic of the Elizabethan and notably of the Shakespearean

---

[1] Gosson's *Plays confuted in Five Actions*, 1579.

drama. Happy endings were allotted to dramatic renderings of poignantly pathetic romances, while comic episodes were introduced into tragedies. These amorphous developments gained admission early to the Elizabethan theatre, to the scandal of orthodox critics. Sir Philip Sidney, a champion of classical law, was especially scornful of his fellow countrymen's first attempts to 'match funerals with hornpipes'. Magnificently typical of the blending of tragedy with comedy is the irruption of the Porter after Duncan's murder into the tragedy of *Macbeth*. The romantic plot of Shakespeare's comedy of *Much Ado* hovers on the brink of tragedy. This fusion of type is an important feature of English drama and plays a larger part there than in any foreign literature. Yet such ambiguous broadenings of the bases of drama are no English innovations. However superior Shakespeare's performances in tragicomedy were to anything that preceded, or indeed succeeded them, Italians and Frenchmen and Spaniards were active in that field before him or at the same time as he. Endeavours of France and Italy in the field of dramatic romance lay well within Shakespeare's and his fellow countrymen's range of vision, and there again Elizabethan footsteps found guidance.

There is indeed no form of dramatic effort of which Elizabethan England, despite her triumphant handling of all, can claim the honours of the inventor. Her heavy debts to normal types of classical tragedy and Gallic or Italo-Gallic farce or romance do not exhaust her dramatic obligations to the foreigner. The pastoral and masque, with its mythological machinery, were importations from Italy, and the masque, as the French form of the word shows, grew up under French stimulus.

It was not merely the dramatic form which came to England from abroad. From foreign sources the plot or subject-matter of tragedy, comedy, and tragicomedy alike was widely drawn. Foreign novels were the richest mines of fable for Elizabethan drama. A foreign atmosphere often clung irremovably to the foreign story, and the foreign spirit of romantic intrigue coloured the foreign fiction in the Elizabethan theatre. The

harvest of novels was in Renaissance days most abundant in
Italy, and there the Elizabethan playwrights gleaned their
fullest sheaves. Bandello told the stories of *Romeo and Juliet*
and *Twelfth Night*, Cinthio those of *Measure for Measure*
and *Othello*. But France, true to her rôle of purveyor of
culture, offered ample stores of 'histoires tragiques', of
'plaisantes nouvelles', of 'contes facecieux'; of these a
few only were homegrown, the majority being culled from
Italian or classical authors or even from writers of less familiar
race. From a French cyclopaedia of fiction which embodied a chronicle of Danish history, England drew her first
knowledge of Hamlet's perplexed career. France rivalled
Italy in the quantity and the quality of the raw material of
tragedy, comedy, and romance which she provided for the
Elizabethan stage.

The Elizabethan dramatist sought his theme not only in
foreign fiction but also in foreign history, past and present.
Historical tradition of Greece and Rome, of the empires
of the East, of mediaeval and contemporary Europe, readily
served as the plots of drama in all countries which came
under the sway of the Renaissance. In providing England with historical topics France again proved a more valuable ally than Italy. Far earlier than Elizabethan dramatists,
French dramatists found themes for drama in Plutarch's
Lives which offered an exhaustive panorama of the whole
range of classical activity. France set England the fashion of
dramatizing Plutarch's histories of heroes of classical antiquity.
The English playwrights bettered the French instruction.
They handled Plutarch's narrative in the English version
with intensely dramatic vigour, but the Elizabethan translation
on which the English dramatists worked was wholly made
from a masterly French rendering of Plutarch's Greek. The
Roman plays of Elizabethan England rank with her best. Yet
they came to birth at French prompting.

Nor was it merely episode of classical history which
French example commended to the Elizabethan stage.
Recent or contemporary political conflict in France was also
eagerly scanned by Elizabethan playwrights and was adapted

by them to theatrical uses. Huguenot and French Catholic leaders were accepted heroes of Elizabethan drama. Neither Marlowe nor Shakespeare disdained suggestion from the pending warfare of religious and political factions in France, while dramatists of the rank and file drew thence a long series of dramatic incident. Of many of these topical efforts only the name survives; the text has vanished. The loss deserves mild regrets. For topical reviews of passing crises, whether in tragic or comic vein, rarely reach high levels of dramatic art. Such examples of the topical Elizabethan drama as have escaped destruction deal, however, with persons and places of contemporary France quite amply enough to attest a widespread tendency and habit among both the great and the small Elizabethan dramatists. The heights, as well as the plains, of Elizabethan drama are marked by many French features. France was generous in her supply of the threads of form and topic from which the many-coloured coat was woven.

For near a century France was in the van of the dramatic movement of the Renaissance, and England for the time was content to follow sluggishly behind her neighbour. Yet there was promise of originality in the Elizabethan disciples of continental drama. He who studies Elizabethan drama in its relation with French dramatic endeavour finds his chief profit in examining the early stages of the English movement. The first steps of the ascent have most in common in the two countries. The English road is paved at the outset with many French conceptions and French artifices from which the region of the summit is free.

Towards the end of the eighth decade of the sixteenth century, Christopher Marlowe framed what, in spite of signs of French affinity, was largely a new conception of tragedy. He imbued tragic diction with a new breadth and warmth which gave Shakespearean tragedy an immediate cue. Until the date of Marlowe's advent the growth of drama in fifteenth- and sixteenth-century France steadily anticipated the development of drama in England. Subsequently Elizabethan England broke away from leading-strings and passed unaccompanied ahead of her guides. When at a later epoch the consummated type of Elizabethan drama caught foreign attention it was condemned by foreign observers as barbarism. Even at home her final activity excited some critical misgivings, by reason of its defiance of pre-existing canons. A very deliberate effort was made in the heyday of the Elizabethan movement, by Elizabethan students of French drama, to recall Elizabethan drama to the classical paths on which Renaissance France ultimately concentrated her best energies. But the warning had small effect, and the Elizabethan drama refused to abandon its own independent lines. The links which bind Elizabethan drama with the dramatic efforts of the French Renaissance never altogether disappear, but they dwindle in significance and substance as Elizabethan drama approaches the final goal.

In a more marked degree than other forms of Elizabethan literature, the Elizabethan drama acquired in its progress to maturity a spirit of its own. A fire, which was undreamt of abroad, flamed into life on the Elizabethan stage, and soared into regions beyond continental bounds. France offered no parallel to the wealth of poetic colour and the breadth of dramatic sentiment which marked Shakespeare's final contribution to the dramatic achievement of Elizabethan England. Neither the previous nor the contemporary generation of French dramatists or of French actors can be credited with giving Shakespeare's genius any of its versatile touches of sublimity. Shakespeare's main elements of greatness—his insight into character, his width of outlook, his magical power of speech—owe little to French inspiration. None the less, Shakespeare like his fellows stands indebted to French instruction for much of his raw material, for much of the humble scaffolding of his art. Many of his ambitions were stimulated by French precedent. He learnt in French schools juvenile lessons in plot and dialogue. Italy was also among his tutors, but there, too, France lent him aid. Italian dramatists rank high among French masters, and the French were always ready to communicate teaching which they themselves derived from others as well as that of their own invention. French imitations of

Italian and classical plays joined original French comedy and tragedy in moulding some contours of Shakespearean drama.

II

THE BEGINNINGS OF FRENCH DRAMA

Drama of the popular kind is of greater antiquity in France than in England. The drama of Christian Europe was originally designed as a complement of divine worship, as a popular comment on the liturgy of the Church. Latin was the first vehicle of dramatic expression. It seems doubtful if the vernacular languages were deemed capable of dramatic usage before the twelfth century. France was the first to enter the field by at least two centuries before England. To the beginning of the twelfth century belong two extant French dramas of a primitive type, on the subjects respectively of Adam's fall and the Resurrection. To the thirteenth century are assigned some French specimens of dramatized hagiography as well as a primitive pastoral called *Robin et Marion*, which seems to challenge the claim of religion to monopolize the theme of drama. In the fourteenth century the miracle play in the vernacular was full-fledged and prolific in France. As many as forty pieces portraying miracles performed by the Virgin Mary are among surviving compositions of that era. There is no proof that England attempted to follow the French example at any earlier date, and sparse are the extant examples which can be dated with confidence before the fifteenth century.

Through the fifteenth century there was an active development of the religious drama in the two countries concurrently. On both sides of the Channel there was an abundant harvest of mystery and miracle plays which dealt in long cycles with Old and New Testament history and more detachedly with careers of popular saints. The English ventures betray frequent signs of indebtedness to French effort.

The primitive stream of sacred drama flowed with almost un-abated energy alike in France and England down to the middle of the sixteenth century. The popular religious play bore only rare and occasional traces in either land of the new influences of the Renaissance. But in sixteenth-century France the old sacred drama was accorded in literary circles a recognition which was denied it in sixteenth-century England. In England of both the fifteenth and sixteenth centuries the miracle or mystery play was cultivated by unprofessional pens of anony-mous scribes, and was ignored as a fit theme of work by professed labourers in literary fields. The labour was accorded a higher dignity in France. Queen Margaret of Navarre, in spite of her devotion to the New Learning, eagerly courted the popular dramatic tradition of the middle ages by penning new mysteries on such topics as the Nativity, the Adoration of the Magi, the Massacre of the Innocents, and the flight of the Holy Family into Egypt. The religious play of mediaeval France was not only of earlier birth than that of mediaeval England, but literary ability was moved in the early days of the French Renaissance to make the endeavour to prolong its life. As late as 1575 a French poet, who had drunk deep of the classical scholarship of the Renaissance, was urging on proficient dramatists, in a treatise on the art of poetry, the propriety of finding their tragic plots in the Old Testament or in hagiography which—

'montre de Dieu les faits admirables au monde'.[1]

In both France and England the morality play sprang immediately out of the miracle or mystery, and the new type, which was elder-born on French than on English soil, rid the popular drama to a large extent of religious fetters. The morality at first dealt with ethical problems on secular lines of allegory or symbolism. The characters were personifica-tions of virtues or vices. Surely and steadily, however, the morality loosened its allegorical bonds and escaped into the ampler air of personal action and experience. The moral or edificatory aim proved indeed readier of attainment in the

[1] Vauquelin de la Fresnaie, *L'Art poétique françois*, livre iii, 881-904.

presentation of individual men and women than in a procession of allegorical abstractions. The allegorical scheme of the morality easily gave way to mobile conventions of personality. Many experiences of everyday life were seen to be capable of pointing a moral quite as effectively as allegorical pantomime.

The French morality flourished in one shape or another from the fourteenth to the sixteenth century. Seeking at an early date material in the comic anecdote or *fabliau*, it quickly absorbed the comic spirit which was always indigenous to France, and had manifested itself from time immemorial in more or less ribald exhibitions of buffoonery by way of public pastime. Gaiety coloured the development of the native drama. The farce or *sottie*, the dramatic satire or *revue*, was a fruit of an alliance between the moral play and the irresponsible merriment of French bourgeois recreations. The term 'morale comédie', which was widely applied to specimens of the popular French drama early in the sixteenth century, marks a tendency of the nation's dramatic temper.[1] The serious note was not rejected, but jest became a needful environment and condiment. The precocity, the vivacity, the versatility, which attach to the manifold phases of the French 'morality', bear witness to a dramatic instinct in late mediaeval and early sixteenth-century France, to which England of the same period offers no parallel.[2]

[1] Rabelais describes a typical 'morale comédie' which he says that he and his friends acted about 1530, when students at the University of Montpellier. The piece was called 'La morale comédie de celuy qui avoit espousé une femme mute'. The husband wished his dumb wife to speak. A physician and a surgeon are summoned, and by a simple operation give the woman the power of speech. The cure proves so efficient and the wife grows so garrulous that the husband seeks medical advice for the purpose of restraining her volubility. But here medicine and surgery are baffled. The only palliation they can furnish is to render the husband deaf. The wife's irritation with a husband who cannot hear her voice causes her to go frantically mad, while the doctor who applies to the deaf man for his fee cannot make him understand his purpose. The doctor thereupon gives him a drug which renders him imbecile. At the end the insane couple set upon the doctor and surgeon, and nearly kill them. (Rabelais, bk. iii, ch. 34.)

[2] M. Petit de Julleville, in a series of volumes entitled generally *Histoire du Théâtre en France au moyen âge*, gives an admirable description of the

It is easy to illustrate the varied forms of the French
'morality' from infancy to maturity. To the fourteenth century
belongs a dramatic rendering of Boccaccio's tale of Griselda,
the patient but ill-used wife. Allegorical abstractions are
absent. Although the sole aim is to teach the lesson of
patience, the result is a dramatic romance in embryo.
Dramatic presentations in the fifteenth century of the fall
of 'Troie le grant' and of a recent 'Siege of Orleans'
illustrate the expansiveness of the dramatic topic of the
age. But the growth of the morality on its comic side was
chiefly of significance for the future. Comedy in France was
finally to win with Molière a renown which Shakespeare only
just outstrips. The blitheness of Gallic wit was ultimately
to give French comedy a world-wide empire. The seeds of
the comic triumph were sown by the morality.

During the fifteenth century the 'morality' engendered an
almost full-fledged example of the comic art in *Maître
Pathelin*. Although the Latin comedy of Plautus was
known to French mediaeval scholars, it was not thence, it was
from suggestion nearer home, that the author of *Maître
Pathelin* drew his inspiration. The familiar plot is an
anecdote of a briefless village lawyer who is duped of his fees
by a trick that he himself teaches a simple rustic client—
the device of bleating like a sheep whenever an inconvenient
question is put to him. On that slight foundation is reared a
little study of character and manners which has no shadow of
counterpart in England for some one hundred and twenty years.
The middle-sixteenth century *Gammer Gurton's Needle*
is the earliest English example of a comparable dramatic
experiment, but the English farce has little of the comic
gusto and insight of its veteran French precursor. Nor has
the English piece the clear-cut moral which the old French

early history of French drama. The individual titles of the separate volumes
run : *Les Mystères*, 2 vols., Paris, 1880 ; *Les Comédiens en France au moyen
âge*, Paris, 1885 ; *La Comédie et les mœurs en France au moyen âge*, Paris,
1886 ; *Répertoire du Théâtre comique en France au moyen âge*, Paris,
1886. The same author's *Le Théâtre en France : Histoire de la littérature dramatique depuis ses origines jusqu'à nos jours*, Paris, 1889, is a
useful summary,

farce had the faculty of emphasizing without prejudice to its humorous vivacity. *Maître Pathelin* graphically illustrates the popular maxim of ' the biter bit '. The popularity which the piece acquired during the fifteenth century never deserted it in France. The phrase of the judge ' revenons à ses moutons ' obtained at once proverbial currency. Rabelais echoed the language of ' noble Pathelin '. Pasquier, the far-famed critic of the French Renaissance, denied that Greece, Rome, or Italy had produced anything superior to it in the comic vein.[1]

Maître Pathelin, despite its exceptional fame, is no isolated phenomenon in the history of French mediaeval drama. French mediaeval drama owed most of its future influence to similar experiments in farce or satiric comedy. At the end of the fifteenth and opening of the sixteenth century the miracle and morality play were still pursuing active careers, but the most popular form of dramatic entertainment was the farcical type known as *la sottie*. The true subject-matter of the farce or *sottye françoyse*, was, according to an early sixteenth-century French writer, ' badinage, foolery, and everything that moves laughter and amusement.'[2] The *sottie* burlesqued the opinions or conduct of prominent living persons in church or state. Yet serious reflection and imaginative fancy occasionally diversify the theme. Sometimes the *sottie* touched the confines of social comedy and anticipated traits of Beaumarchais's *Le Mariage de Figaro*. The form varied. Not infrequently monologue sufficed. ' Un sermon joyeux ' insolently parodied the pious discourse of a popular preacher, or a braggart soldier made bombastic professions of courage with a humour of almost Falstaffian breadth. Dialogue was employed in energetic debate in which sharply contrasted opinions were presented with much point and adroitness.

The chief author of popular drama in the early sixteenth century was the actor and manager, Pierre Gringoire. His

---

[1] The farce of *Maistre Pierre Pathelin* was printed for the first time at Lyons in 1485. There were at least five editions before 1500 and more than twenty reprints in the sixteenth century.

[2] Sibilet, *Art poétique* (Paris, 1555), Livre II, ch. viii, p. 60 : ' le vray subject de la farce ou sottye françoyse sont badineries, nigauderies, et toutes sorties esmouvantes a ris et plaisir.'

facility and fertility knew no diminution through the first three decades of the epoch. His efforts took varied shapes. He was an adept at allegory in narrative poetry as well as in the morality play of the regular pattern. A mystery play on the royal saint of France, Louis IX, came from his versatile pen and enjoyed a wide vogue. But he won his chief fame by his insolent criticism of current life in *sottie* or *débat*. On the stages both of Paris and of the provinces Gringoire and his allies discussed in dramatic form pressing questions of politics, religion, and ethics. Social topics, especially the disadvantages of marriage or the foibles of the fair sex, were always welcome to author and audience. Personages of classical mythology were introduced at times, and there were occasional snatches of Latin. But the pieces had nothing in common with the method of classical drama. The text was continuous. There were no divisions into acts or scenes, and no limit was placed to the number of speaking parts.

Liberty of speech was in the sixteenth century a privilege of popular drama in France, and royal authority long forbore effective restraint. Louis XII found it useful in his struggle with Pope Julius II to patronize, if not to sanction, dramatic satire of the papacy. For a time Francis I raised no obstacle to the frank and impartial treatment on the stage of religious controversy. About 1523, in a farce called *Les Théologastres*, the orthodox doctors of the Sorbonne were mercilessly ridiculed and were represented as finally seeking the aid of ' Mercure d'Allemagne', a leader of the Lutheran Reformation, in an endeavour to rehabilitate their worn-out views. Shortly afterwards Queen Margaret of Navarre was herself brought on the stage as a Fury bearing a torch wherewith to set the kingdom on fire. Foreign sovereigns, including Henry VIII and Queen Elizabeth, were the more or less comic heroes and heroines of the dramatic entertainments of the French people.

As the years went on, both central and municipal authorities found it necessary, on moral and political grounds, to curb the growing licence of the popular stage. Danger was detected in the scurrilous tendency of the *sottie* or *débat*, while the sacred mystery to which popular esteem obstinately clung was held to incline to blasphemy. A decree prohibiting the religious drama in Paris was promulgated in 1548. Public or private performances of farces, comedies, songs, or other writings, which should in any way deal with sacred topics or ecclesiastical personages, were repeatedly forbidden by local magistracies through the middle years of the sixteenth century, while moralities and other pieces which were performed either for religious purposes or for honest popular recreation were proclaimed to be unlawful unless they were licensed by curé or magistrate. But these edicts were evaded. Religious themes were not banished. Mysteries as well as moralities still claimed a share of public favour. The *sottie* and satiric *revues* flourished in spite of censorship through all the period of the warfare of Huguenot and Catholic, and blows were aimed from the stage impartially at all the factions. The steady growth of the regular classical drama under the influence of the Pléiade failed to change the taste of the general public.

In England the progress of the popular drama was very sluggish in comparison with the activity of France. The English morality was far more reluctant than the French morality to transgress its original law of allegory. A personal element was by degrees grafted on the symbolic machinery, but the personifications of vice and virtue were not displaced. The English stage in the pre-Shakespearean era seemed likely to stagnate in crude conventions of ethical symbolism, when French example openly worked some tangible reform. The English morality of the fifteenth century often depended on French suggestion, but French influence directed almost singlehanded a fresh development of popular English drama. The Tudor invention of the interlude was no domestic evolution. It was an undisguised loan on the comic activity of the contemporary French theatre.

At the opening of the sixteenth century, English drama left contemporary life and society out of account. Moral allegory lacked genuine dramatic promise. John Heywood, a primitive Elizabethan, whose patriarchal length of life covers eighty-three years of the Tudor epoch, deserves the credit of having brought a ray of light into the dismal scene. He may be reckoned the creator of the interlude in England, the English writer who struck the first clear note of comedy. According to Warton he was the earliest English dramatist who 'introduced representations of familiar life and popular manners'. Recent research leaves no doubt that Heywood deliberately sought inspiration in the *sottie* and *débat* of contemporary France.[1]

The comic trend of the French stage had previously caught attention in England. The story of *Maître Pathelin* was narrated in a popular English jest-book of Henry VIII's reign.[2] French players had performed at the court of Henry VII, as well as at that of King James IV of Scotland.[3] But Heywood's interludes are far more substantial links. They are liberal adaptations of recent dramatic essays in France.

Heywood's chief works were satiric discussions or debates among humble ecclesiastics and humble laymen on the pattern of the *sottie*. The best known is, perhaps, that entitled *Four P's*, from the initials of the four interlocutors, a Palmer (or pilgrim), a Pothecary (or apothecary), a Pardoner, and a Pedlar. The efficacy of the various processes of salvation in which they each have a professional interest, is debated by the Palmer, the Pardoner, and the Pothecary, and the Pedlar is summoned to decide which of the three is the most extravagant liar. Again, in Heywood's *Merrie Play between the Pardonner and the Frere, the Curate and Neybour Pratte*, the Friar preaches salvation in front of a church, and is interrupted by the Pardoner, who displays

---

[1] 'The Influence of French farce upon the plays of John Heywood,' by Karl Young, in *Modern Philology*, vol. ii, pp. 97–124, Chicago, 1904.

[2] 'Mery Tales, Wittie Questions, and Quicke Answeres,' first printed by Thomas Berthelet about 1535, narrates Maître Pathelin's experience under the heading ' Of hym that payde his dette with crienge bea '. See Hazlitt's *Shakespeare Jest-books*, 1864, p. 60.

[3] The account books of Henry VII's household show payments to 'the Frenche pleyers' of 1*l*. on January 6, 1494, and of 2*l*. on January 4, 1495. The Scottish Exchequer Rolls note that on July 23, 1494, the king entertained French players at Dundee. Sir David Lyndsay's dramatic ' Satyre of the three estaitis ', which was performed in the open air at Cupar in 1535, and at Edinburgh in 1540, betrays the influence of contemporary French drama. Cf. Petit de Julleville's *La Comédie et les Mœurs de France au Moyen Age* (1866), Chap. v, 'Satire des Divers Etats.'

his relics.   After rallying each other with much briskness, they fight, until they are separated by the curate and a neighbouring villager, named Pratt.

Both these interludes are cast in the French mould, and clearly borrow much from a popular French *sottie*, *Farce nouvelle d'un Pardonneur, d'un Triacleur, et d'une Tavernière*. The French Pardoner, laden with relics, orates bombastically in a market-place on the spiritual efficacy of his wares. The *Triacleur*, or travelling apothecary, commends his drugs with like assurance. They abuse and ridicule each other, but are reconciled by the suggestion that they should visit a fair tavern-keeper in company.

A French source, is, too, responsible for Heywood's dramatization of a homely anecdote or fable in the *Merry Play between Johan the Husbande, Tyb the wife, and Sir Jhan the Priest*. This endeavour, which was new to England, reproduces a contemporary French interlude of domestic life, the popular farce *De Pernet qui va au vin*. In both English and French works a sharp-witted farmer's wife contrives to invite a secret lover to dinner and to keep her dense-witted husband from the dinner table by sending him on a derisive errand. The French husband is bidden fetch some wine and also melt a piece of wax before joining the feast. The English husband is bidden fetch water in a leaky pail and is given wax wherewith to patch the leak. In both cases a meat-pie, or *pâté*, forms the meal, and is eaten by the wife and her paramour before the husband completes his task. The identity of temper may be gauged by a comparison of the husband's complaint of the business with the wax in the two versions:

JOHN.	PERNET.
Mary, I chafe the waxe here,	Me faut-il donc chauffer le cire
And I ymagyn to make you good chere	Tandisque vous banqueterez?
	Corbieu, j'en suis marry :
That a vengaunce take you both as ye sit,	Je crois ce pasté est bon.
For I know well I shall not ete a byt.	
But yet in feyth yf I might ete one morsell	
I wolde thynk the matter went very well.	

Again, Heywood's dialogue, *Of wit and folly*, a quasi-dramatic dialogue or *débat* between the wise man and the fool as to which lives the better life, resembles a French *Dialogue du fol et du sage*. The French 'Dialogue', which is a typical example of the *débat*, is believed to have been performed at the court of King Louis XII, who was husband of Henry VIII's sister, Mary. At the close Heywood's adaptation travels somewhat beyond the French text. The English writer is faithful to French guidance in allowing the victory to the fool through the chief bouts of the encounter, but Heywood diverges from the French path in an original peroration which finally establishes the wise man's predominance.

Heywood's metre and sentiment are loyal to the *sottie*. The octosyllabic couplets which Heywood chiefly, but not invariably, uses is the habitual metre of the French. The cut and thrust of the burlesque dialectic is almost identical in temper, and at times in phrase, in English and French. Heywood's choplogic adumbrates that rough and tumble interchange of wit which is echoed by the clowns and serving-men of the perfected Elizabethan drama. Autolycus, the cheapjack pedlar, is in the line of succession. The stock comes of the *sottie* or *débat*. Heywood's crude efforts were popular and exerted much influence on one side of the coming dramatic development.

Heywood's introduction of the French *débat* into English literature was bearing English fruit when Shakespeare was beginning his professional career. The dramatist and romance writer, Robert Greene, Shakespeare's early foe of the theatre, took the trouble to translate as late as 1587 one of the most finished specimens of this rudimentary manner of drama. At the end of Greene's romance, called *The Carde of Fancie*, figures a prose piece entitled 'The debate between Follie and Loue. Translated out of French'. This is a literal rendering, with abbreviations, of a quasi-dramatic, half-comic, half-pathetic dialogue by Louise Labé, in which the mediaeval form and *naïveté* are touched, with an exceptional deftness, by the classical erudition of the Renaissance. The authoress was the most gifted and impassioned of all poetesses of the early French Renaissance. She was a native and resident of Lyons, and, being the daughter and wife of rope-makers, is known to literary history as La Belle Cordière. Her name has never lacked honour in her birthplace. There has always been a street in Lyons known as La rue de la Belle Cordière. Louise Labé's sonnets strike a curiously poignant note of despairing love. In her *Débat de Folie et d'Amour*, she treats the passion more lightly. There are six interlocutors, Folly, Love, Venus, Apollo, Jupiter, and Mercury. The argument runs thus :—Jupiter is giving a great feast to the gods. Folly and Love are among the invited guests, and dispute as to their precedence. Folly pushes Love aside and claims the first place, whereupon 'they enter into disputation of their power, dignity, and superiority'. The dispute waxes amusingly warm, when Love shoots an arrow at Folly. Love's rival avoids the aim by becoming invisible, but manages to deprive his enemy of his eyes, an action of which Love's mother, Venus, complains to Jupiter. Thereupon the royal god appoints Apollo and Mercury to plead before him the causes of the two combatants, and after hearing the long arguments he postpones his decision until ' 3 times 7 and nine ages be passed '. Meanwhile the disputants are to live in friendship together. Folly is to act as guide to blind Love, and Jupiter undertakes to invite the Fates to restore Love's sight. Greene reduces the five ' discours ', or scenes, of Labé's original to three ; he omits some of the French speeches and shortens others. But the dialectical fancy of the French authoress is unimpaired. Heywood was hardly quite so loyal to his French tutors' ingenious turns of thought. The tribute paid by Shakespeare's contemporary, Greene, to La Belle Cordière's experiment in the old dramatic *genre* of the *débat* is a curious illustration of the wide and active sympathy between French and English dramatic endeavour at the date of Shakespeare's entry into the literary arena.

III

THE GROWTH OF THE THEATRE IN FRANCE AND ENGLAND

There is another feature in the dramatic history of France which bears witness to the precocity of the nation's sympathy with drama. The French theatre was formally organized in the Middle Ages, and the organization, though it underwent development with the rise of new conditions, knew no disruption between its birth and our own time. The stage of the French Renaissance was a mediaeval institution. The playhouse of sixteenth-century Paris was no innovation; it was a survival of mediaeval dramatic ambition. No contrast is of greater significance than the differences in date and circumstance between the first establishment of a theatre in the French capital and in London.

From the fourteenth century there flourished in Paris as many as three guilds or brotherhoods whose aim was the organization of dramatic performances for purposes of either edification or amusement. These dramatic societies enjoyed the dignity of legal incorporation. The earliest and most important, *Les Confrères de la Passion*, was formed of laymen of all classes, more especially of the working classes. Their original function was to perform religious drama, but they soon conquered wider dramatic fields. *Les Confrères* boasted a fixed habitation or theatre in Paris as early as 1402, when they settled in the Hospital of St. Trinité, near the gate of St. Denis. There they remained for 137 years. In 1539 they removed to the Hôtel de Flandres, in the Rue des Vieux Augustins. Some nine years later, when the Hôtel de Flandres was demolished, they purchased the disused Hôtel de Bourgogne, in the Rue Mauconseil, in the quartier St. Denis, and built anew a rudimentary theatre on its site. This barn-like edifice, which continued to be known as the Hôtel de Bourgogne, remained the head-quarters of *Les Confrères* till the old fraternity was dissolved by royal edict in 1676.[1]

---

[1] M. Eugène Rigal's *Le Théâtre français avant la Période Classique*, 1901, is the chief authority; his bibliography is very useful.

Through the middle years of the sixteenth century acting rapidly developed into a profession, and the constitution of the amateur fraternity was modified.   After 1598 the brotherhood merely fulfilled the passive functions of proprietors of their theatre, which they leased out to well-organized professional companies of actors.   Yet the Hôtel de Bourgogne, for all the changes in its control, is a sturdy material link between the old and the new drama of France, and symbolizes its continuity of life.   The influence of *Les Confrères de la Passion* spread beyond Paris.   Provincial imitators formed themselves into local corporations, and at Angers, Bourges, Metz, Orleans, Poitiers, Rouen, Saumur, Tours, and Troyes there flourished similar dramatic organizations before, during and after the period of the French Renaissance.   The machinery of the theatre was from the first elaborate among *Les Confrères*. Scenery and costume were invariable features of the organized presentations of mysteries.   The stage was long, deep, and high and capable of divisions into compartments.   In the early days the various scenes were set up in three tiers or platforms which were known as 'mansions'.   The actors passed from 'mansion' to 'mansion', from scene to scene, as the evolution of the drama required.   This scenic device outlived the mediaeval era.   In the sixteenth century it developed into the system of 'le decor simultané'.   There two or three different scenes—for example, a palace, a prison, a landscape or a seascape—were painted side by side on the same canvas which hung round the stage semicircularly.   The actors took their stand in front of one scenic background after another in accordance with the progress of the dramatic action. Scenery in one crude shape or other was always a characteristic of the French stage.

The second mediaeval amateur dramatic society of Paris which received legal recognition was drawn originally from the upper classes, but soon attached to itself a full-fledged band of professional supporters.   This society was called *Les Enfants sans Souci*, or *Les Sots*.   Its rôle was frankly secular; it devoted its energies to farce—, to the *sottie*, the *revue*, and the *débat*.   *Les Enfants* in early days performed in the market halls and squares of Paris, at times under royal patronage. Ultimately *Les Enfants* entered into a working partnership with *Les Confrères de la Passion*, and were often to be seen at first at the Hôtel de la Trinité and later at the Hôtel de Bourgogne. Early in the sixteenth century the dramatist and poet Gringoire became manager and leading actor of *Les Enfants*, and under his command the fraternity perfected its professional organization. A third mediaeval dramatic corporation was formed of amateurs who were invariably lawyers. *Les Clercs de la Basoche*, as this legal-dramatic society was called, was formally authorized to produce moralities, and gave their chief dramatic performances in the hall of the Palais de Justice but occasionally acted in private houses. This legal brotherhood of the theatre lasted in name till the French Revolution, but its histrionic activity ceased early in the sixteenth century. Thenceforth, for the best part of a hundred years, Paris mainly depended for its public theatrical recreation on *Les Confrères* and *Les Enfants*, who lost by degrees all relics of their amateur origin, and grew indistinguishable from companies of professional actors.

The professional tendency of the old theatrical organization expanded steadily. Independent companies of professional players, which emerged from the ranks of the mediaeval dramatic corporations, wandered about the country, performing in municipal halls or in noblemen's mansions. The masters of the Hôtel de Bourgogne regarded the strolling actors as trespassers on their rights, and sought to shut the gates of Paris upon them. But the strollers flourished in the provinces, and in spite of the official opposition secured some foothold even in the metropolis. Travelling companies seem from the first to have been formed in Paris; they invariably started their provincial tours from the capital city, and journeyed back by well-marked circuits. In the middle of the sixteenth century the official prejudice against the wandering troops was powerful everywhere. But their popularity at large was increasing, and the official hostility lost its practical effect. Every town of importance came to be visited in a more or less regular sequence, and the tours not infrequently extended beyond France. French companies made their way into Holland, Germany, Piedmont, and even Spain, Denmark, and Sweden. At the close of the sixteenth century performances by French players were regular features of the great annual fair at Frankfort-on-Main. On occasion they were welcomed to the Imperial court at Ratisbon. The development of the touring companies in sixteenth-century France, in the face of official prohibition, was fruit of the fascination which the drama exerted on the people. The hold of the stage on public taste was never destined to lose its strength.

Cultured influences supported the dramatic advance, working through somewhat different agencies. In the early days of the Renaissance a predilection for amateur acting was encouraged at court, at the universities, colleges, and schools. Many subsidiary centres of histrionic activity thus came into being. At all the great educational establishments of France, notably at the Collège de Guienne in Bordeaux, and at the Collège de Boncourt, the Collège de Navarre and the Collège d'Harcourt in Paris, plays were regularly performed in halls fitted up for the purpose. Especially was the new classical drama of the Renaissance welcomed there. Scholars often gave dramatic performances in royal palaces or noblemen's 'hotels'. The Hôtel de Reims, the residence of the Cardinal of Lorraine, was frequently put to such uses. Servants in the royal houscholds at times took part in these entertainments. The growth of professional companies in Paris and the country, the academic organization of amateur acting, and the patronage of kings and noblemen, whose servants were suffered to practise the histrionic art,—all helped to extend general interest in the drama, and to hasten the reconstruction of the mediaeval theatre of France on modern lines.

In 1598, when the Hôtel de Bourgogne was permanently leased to a professional company whose experience had been gained in provincial tours, the dying tradition of mediaeval amateurism was banished for ever from the national theatre. Contrary to expectation, the complete installation of the professional actor on the national stage gave the death-blow to the mediaeval spirit of drama which the old fraternities had fostered. The new control reinforced the dramatic influences of the Renaissance, which had for a generation dominated academic circles and the higher social ranks. The classical drama enjoyed a freer scope for development and acquired a larger popularity after the French theatre was permanently organized on wholly professional lines.

The organization of the Elizabethan theatre and of the acting profession in Elizabethan England was no less momentous a factor in the development of Elizabethan drama, but the Elizabethan theatre was late-born as compared with France, and had fewer links with the past. The art of acting was far better and more widely organized in France during the Middle Ages than in mediaeval England. There were no actors' guilds in England during the fifteenth century of the organized strength or national authority of *Les Confrères, Les Enfants,* or *Les Clercs.* The histrionic art spread more readily in noble, academic, and legal circles under French than under English skies. Only during Shakespeare's boyhood did the tide of histrionic activity flow strongly enough in England to draw Elizabethan noblemen, lawyers, and university tutors into its current. That flood was anticipated in France by more than a generation. The ' profession ' of actor was born in France under the auspices of the ancient brotherhoods at least half a century before anything was heard of the acting vocation in England. The constant intercourse between French and English society suggests that the veteran histrionic traditions of France offered their stimulus to the Elizabethan innovation.

The assignment of a special building to theatrical purposes preceded in France the evolution of the professional actor. The distinctive theatrical edifice was a fruit in that country of mediaeval amateur effort, of amateur effort of the fourteenth century, which only acquired a professional status in the sixteenth century. The English theatre was inaugurated later and under different auspices. It was only during the last quarter of the sixteenth century that a theatre was first built in England, and the step was taken at the instance of her earliest professional actors.

The sequence in which the profession of acting and the theatre came into being in England reversed the order of the older experience of France. But such a discrepancy is immaterial to the main issues of English indebtedness. James Burbage, the promoter of the first regular acting company in England, built, in 1576, the first English playhouse in the Finsbury fields to the north-east of London. He was thus creating very modestly and tentatively an institution, which an amateur society had not only inaugurated on a far more imposing scale at the Hospital de la Trinité in Paris nearly two centuries before, but had throughout that long period maintained with a steadily increasing vogue. The seed sown by Burbage's theatre rapidly fructified in the English metropolis, and before the end of the sixteenth century there were in or near London six definitely organized theatres. But to none of the London buildings attached the venerable traditions which clung to the Parisian theatre of the Hôtel de Bourgogne.

IV

THE CLASSICAL DRAMA OF THE FRENCH RENAISSANCE

If the comic spirit in a primitive stage of strength was well alive in France in the first half of the sixteenth century, the tragic spirit was still unborn, nor had comedy of intrigue or romance given coherent signs of life. French tragedy, which blossomed in the last epoch of the French Renaissance, was the child of Greek and Latin parents, and grew up under the tutelage of classical scholarship. In Italy the development of dramatic art in all directions anticipated that in France by many years, and Italian example played an important part in exciting French interest in the classical conceptions which dominated the new birth of French drama.[1]

[1] As early as the fourteenth century classical drama was studied and imitated in Italy. To that era belong two original Latin tragedies on the Senecan model, *Ecerinis* and *Achilleis*, by Albertino Mussato of Padua. In the fifteenth century Seneca's tragedies and some contemporary imitations were frequently acted. Italian visitors to France early in the sixteenth century continued to press the classical drama on French notice. The elder Scaliger translated Sophocles' *Oedipus Rex* into Latin.

From the fifteenth century onwards, there was much study by Frenchmen of Seneca's Latin adaptation of Greek drama, which exaggerated the declamatory temper of the Greek and favoured sensational situations. Early in the sixteenth century Greek tragedy was disclosed in its original purity to scholars throughout France, and direct translations into French were among the first-fruits of the revival of classical learning. Lazare de Baïf, the father of Ronsard's ally, Jean Antoine de Baïf, rendered from the Greek Sophocles' *Electra* and Euripides' *Hecuba* line by line, in 1537 and 1544 respectively. Before the half century closed *Hecuba* was retranslated by another pen, and Euripides' *Iphigeneia* was added to the list of French versions of Greek tragedy.

Academic energy largely stimulated the new dramatic development. In French universities Greek drama awoke vast enthusiasm. Plays were often acted by the students in the original tongue. One or two college professors went a step beyond translating the Greek. From adapting the Greek texts to their pupils' histrionic capacities, they easily passed to writing original Latin tragedies on the classical pattern for their students to act. In this important development professors at the Collège de Guienne at Bordeaux bore a distinguished part. Latin tragedies were penned there by a Scottish teacher, George Buchanan, and by a colleague, Marc Antoine Muret, the professor of Latin, who subsequently wrote in French a commentary on Ronsard's *Amours*. Buchanan achieved great fame by a Latin drama on the biblical subject of Jephthah. Muret won only a little less renown by a Latin tragedy on the secular subject of Julius Caesar's assassination. Montaigne was a pupil of these scholars of Bordeaux, and he always recalled with pride how he had played leading rôles in their tragic work.

Alamanni, while at the Court of Francis I, rendered the *Antigone* into Italian. The Italian writer Trissino was the first to pen an original regular tragedy in any vernacular language of Europe. His Italian play of *Sofonisba* was written in 1515. It is in blank verse, and is the archetype of modern European tragedy. His comedy, *Simillimi* (a very liberal adaptation of Plautus's *Menaechmi*), which was written about the same time, is a notable landmark in the modern development of vernacular comedy. Shakespeare's *Comedy of Errors* is of its lineage.

Meanwhile classical comedy advanced along the same lines. Not only the Latin comedy of Plautus and Terence, but the Greek comedy of Aristophanes, received academic notice. While a schoolboy at the Collège de Coqueret in Paris Ronsard turned into French the Aristophanic comedy of *Plutus*, and his version was acted by himself and his companions under the auspices of the Greek professor Dorat. The chief hero of the Pléiade thus began his career with a precocious act of homage to Attic comedy.

Important as these first steps were, they ignored the living language of the country. It was not till the brotherhood of the Pléiade had formulated their national plea for a literary reformation that there arose in France the novel and revolutionary conception of original tragedy and original comedy in the French language, on a regular classical pattern. That conception was first defined by Du Bellay's manifesto of 1549. Du Bellay peremptorily bade Frenchmen banish farces and moralities and put in their place true tragedies and comedies which should re-create in the native tongue the archetypes of Greece.[1] It was at that call that French tragedy, which owed nothing to pre-existing French endeavour, was born, and that French comedy, in spite of its absorption of a measure of the old Gallic sentiment, came to acquire its modern shape.

A spirit of hostility to the old popular drama marked the new dramatic aims of France. Workers in the new field of tragedy lost no opportunity of denouncing the mediaeval aspiration. The classical drama was welcomed not merely as an innovation, but as an agent destined to destroy the indigenous mystery or morality. The old popular drama was not, however, easy to kill. It not merely survived the classicists' threats of extinction, but developed in presence of the enemy a new vitality and versatility.

---

[1] Cf. Du Bellay's *La deffense et illustration de la langue françoyse*, Bk. II, ch. iv, *ad fin.* : 'Quant aux Comedies et Tragedies, si les Roys et les republiques les vouloient restituer en leur ancienne dignité qu'ont usurpée les Farces et Moralitez, je seroy' bien d'opinion que tu t'y employasses, et si tu le veux faire pour l'ornement de ta langue, tu sçais où tu en dois trouver les Archetypes.'

A desperate strife long waged between the new dramatic development in France and the old theatrical organization. The new school regarded the Hôtel de Bourgogne with its enthusiasm for moralities and farces as a discredit to the national reputation. The actor of the Hôtel retaliated by imputations of dullness on the classical innovations, and the strolling companies fully shared the prejudice, which was rife at head-quarters. The new school had small hope of attracting the ordinary theatre-goer, and deemed the old theatrical organizations and their unlicensed touring offspring ill-qualified to present the classical drama.[1] Perhaps the grapes were sour. At any rate the party of progress appealed exclusively to cultured actors and auditors. They professed to be content if their pieces were performed by students in their college-halls or by personal friends in private mansions of patrons. The court showed much interest in the new development, and Ronsard's patron, King Charles IX, like his two successors on the French throne, Henry III and Henry IV, reckoned plays of the classical type among the pastimes of royalty. The kings encouraged members of the royal household to take part in dramatic performances. Queen Elizabeth and James I subsequently filled the like rôle of

---

[1] There has been much controversy as to the relations subsisting in the sixteenth century between regular classical tragedy and the actors of the public theatres. *Le Journal du Théâtre français*, a manuscript history of the French stage in the sixteenth and seventeenth centuries, which was drawn up in the eighteenth century and is now in the Bibliothèque Nationale (Nos. 9229-9235), represents the classical drama as entering into the public programmes day by day at the Hôtel de Bourgogne along with melodrama, farce, morality, mystery, and other kinds of popular drama. There seems, however, little doubt that *Le Journal* is an unauthentic compilation, and deserves no confidence. *Le Journal* is attributed to the Chevalier de Mouhy, and seems to form the materials from which he compiled *Un abrégé de l'histoire du théâtre français*, which was first published in 1752 and reissued, in an expanded shape, in 1780. *Le Journal* supplies the sole evidence that the sixteenth-century writers of classical French tragedy were habitual clients of the public theatre, and wrote their plays with a view to performance by the professional actors. Classical tragedies were, in all probability, produced only in the royal palaces, noblemen's houses, and college halls, where they were acted by amateurs. M. Faguet in his *La Tragédie Française au XVIe Siècle*, 1897, accepts with reservations the guidance of *Le Journal*. It would seem safer with M. Petit de Julleville to ignore it altogether. See E. Rigal's *Hardy et le théâtre français*, p. 688.

sponsors of a new drama across the channel. In both countries royal favour did much to encourage the dramatic advance in literary and artistic directions.

The French hero of the new dramatic development, Étienne Jodelle, came from the ranks of the Pléiade. Although Jodelle wrote much lyric verse, he alone of Ronsard's active lieutenants devoted his main energies to drama. His dramatic achievements were equally notable in both tragedy and comedy. He may be reckoned the father alike of French tragedy and of regular French comedy.

Jodelle's first dramatic essay was a tragedy on the subject of Cleopatra, Queen of Egypt, Antony's paramour.[1] The piece was performed, in the presence of Henry II and his court, at the Collège de Boncour in Paris in 1553, and was followed immediately before the same assembly by a comedy, *Eugène*, also from Jodelle's pen. The author and his literary friends were the actors. The enthusiasm with which the two pieces were received was celebrated in triumphal odes by Baïf and Ronsard. Ronsard greeted Jodelle as the inventor of French tragedy in the Greek manner as well as of the new style of French comedy (*Œuvres*, vi. 314):

> Le premier d'une plainte hardie
> Françoisement chanta la grecque tragédie,
> Puys, en changeant de ton, chanta devant nos rois
> La jeune comédie en langage françois.

After the performance the author with other members of the Pléiade, made a far-famed excursion to the rural retreat of Arcueil, and there amid Bacchanalian revelry pretended in mockery of Pagan rites to sacrifice a goat, garlanded with roses and ivy, to the god Bacchus. This celebration of the birth of classical drama on French soil is an event of supreme interest in the annals of both French and English literary history. It inaugurated a new era. But the ceremony of Arcueil excited bitterness in the hearts of the conductors of the old theatre at the Hôtel de Bourgogne as well as among the Huguenots. The dramatic revolution was credited with immoral tendency. Imputation of blasphemy menaced Jodelle and his

---

[1] The topic had already been dramatized in Italy.

friends. Against Jodelle especially there were levelled charges of atheism which clung to him during the rest of his unhappy life. His chequered experiences anticipated with singular closeness the ill-omened career of Marlowe in England during the next generation, and Elizabethan critics were quick to urge the parallel. Certainly Jodelle was of as impetuous a temperament as any Elizabethan. It was claimed for all his works that they were improvisations. He wrote according to his friends' account with the utmost rapidity, 'sans étude et sans labeur'—with the haste which Ben Jonson assigned to Shakespeare. The agility of Jodelle's pen was currently reckoned without example in the past or present.

Jodelle's *Cléopâtre*, the first French tragedy, is loyal to classical lines, but it is no translation nor adaptation of any pre-existing classical drama, and betrays signs of original interpretation and modification of the classical canons. The author dramatizes passages from Plutarch's *Life of Mark Antony*, and thus sets an effective example to those who sought afterwards tragic themes in Roman history. The dependence on Plutarch is a prominent feature of the theatre of the French Renaissance. There is little doubt that it was from France that the habit spread to Elizabethan England in the succeeding era.

It is worth noting how the French pioneer of tragedy handles the historical story of the Queen of Egypt half a century before Shakespeare approached the theme. Like the Englishman's, the Frenchman's debt to Plutarch is great, yet the biographical material is manipulated by him with a dramatic ingenuity. In the opening scene of Jodelle's tragedy the ghost of Antony—he is already dead—laments the ruin in which Cleopatra has involved him. The presence of the ghost betrays the influence of Seneca. In the next scene Cleopatra is dissuaded by her handmaidens from committing suicide ; and a chorus of Alexandrian women chant of the instability of human happiness. When the heroine first appears she is engaged in conversatio nwhich she has begun with her handmaidens before her entrance. This vivid device was familiar to Shakespeare. But before he made trial of it, it had lost the air of novelty which it enjoyed at Jodelle's hand. In the second act Octavian Caesar (Augustus), the conqueror of Antony, discusses with his councillors the sad fate of the hero, and the future of Cleopatra ; a chorus of men moralize on the emptiness of human pride. In the third act Octavian has a pathetic interview with Cleopatra. She begs for mercy for herself and for her children. One of her followers, Seleucus, has reported to Octavian that Cleopatra has made an imperfect disclosure of her wealth—has hidden some of her jewellery. Seleucus's revelation is communicated to Cleopatra ; she straightway summons him to her presence and, as he enters, she denounces his baseness to Octavian. Here the dramatic emotion rises to its full height. Although Cleopatra's angry remonstrance closely follows Plutarch's words, there are changes which are finely touched by Jodelle's dramatic instinct. The speech, which is in rhymed decasyllabics, runs thus :

Cléopâtre.   Mais quoy, mais quoy ?
  Mon Empereur, est-il vn tel esmoy
  Au monde encor que ce paillard me donne ?
  Sa lacheté ton esprit mesme estonne,
  Comme ie croy, quand moy Roine d'ici,
  De mon vassal suis accusee ainsi,
  Que toy, Cesar, as daigné visiter,
  Et par ta voix à repos inciter.
  Hé si i'auois retenu des joyaux,
  Et quelque part de mes habits royaux,
  L'aurois-ie fait pour moy, las, malheureuse !
  Moy, qui de moy ne suis plus curieuse ?
  Mais telle estoit ceste esperance mienne,
  Qu'à ta Livie et ton Octauienne
  De ces joyaux le present ie feroy,
  Et leurs pitiez ainsi pourchasseroy,
  Pour (n'estant point de mes presens ingrates)
  Envers Cesar estre mes advocates.[1]

[1] Jodelle's *Cléopâtre*, Act III. Shakespeare's version of the same speech of the Egyptian queen may profitably be compared with the French :

  Cleopatra.   O Caesar ! what a wounding shame is this,
      That thou, vouchsafing here to visit me,
      Doing the honour of thy lordliness
      To one so meet, that mine own servant should
      Parcel the sum of my disgraces by
      Addition of his envy. Say, good Caesar,

Cleopatra's outburst of rage and her characteristic excuse of her disingenuousness run in the same mould in the French and the English play. In both tragedies Octavian shows himself magnanimous, and promises to spare Cleopatra's life. In Jodelle's fourth act Cleopatra explains that she longs for death, and has dissembled with Octavian in order to protect her children. She quits the stage with her weeping hand-maidens to kill herself on Antony's tomb. In the fifth and last act Octavian's attendant, Proculeius, informs the people of Alexandria how Cleopatra died. The chorus of soldiers impartially applauds her heroism and the folly of contesting Octavian's supremacy.

Jodelle's scenes are for the most part a series of long declamations interspersed with choruses. There is the orthodox absence of action, but there is passion in the dramatic rhetoric and a lyric fervour in the choruses. The general effect is one of pathetic dignity although the dramatic vivacity is hampered by the choric interpositions. The choric functions are discharged not by one band of actors but by two; by Cleopatra's waiting-women as well as by Octavian Caesar's soldiers. Feeling and insight are brought to the portrayal of the heroine, and of her conqueror, Octavian Caesar. Truthfully, Jodelle wrote in the prologue which he addressed to King Henry II:

> Ici les desirs & les flammes
> Des deux amans; d'Octavian aussi
> L'orgueil, l'audace & le journel souci.

In some regards Jodelle aimed at a stricter adherence to ' classical ' method than Greek drama enjoined. French critics of the Renaissance, following in Italian footsteps, expanded Aristotle's law of unity of action or interest so as to cover in addition unities of time and place. This law

> That I some lady trifles have reserved,
> Immoment toys, things of such dignity
> As we greet modern friends withal; and say,
> Some nobler token I have kept apart
> For Livia and Octavia, to induce
> Their mediation; must I be unfolded
> With one that I have bred?
>   *Antony and Cleopatra*, Act V, Sc. ii, 158 seq.

of a triple unity was a gloss of Italian ingenuity on Aristotle's original canon, and was with modification accepted by the French writers of classical tragedy. In 1572 the new creed was embodied by the French dramatist, Jean de la Taille, one of Jodelle's disciples, in the critical edict : ' Il faut tousjours representer l'histoire ou le jeu en un mesme jour, en un mesme temps, et en un mesme lieu.' The context makes it clear that De la Taille's ' l'histoire ' and ' le jeu ' embraced both tragedy and comedy, in neither of which was the scene to change nor the time of the mimic action appreciably to exceed the hours of the theatrical performance. Jodelle, like many of his successors, transgressed the new law of unity of place by an occasional transference of the scene. But in *Cléopâtre* and in most of the French tragedies of which that piece was the progenitor, unity of time was acknowledged to be as binding an obligation as unity of action. Jodelle contrived to develop his tragic episode within the time which was occupied in the presentation of the drama.

The versification of Jodelle's first French tragedy is as significant of the future as its loyalty to the unities. The second, third, and fifth acts are in ten-syllable rhyming lines, but the first and fourth are in Alexandrines. The verse of six feet which closely resembled the Greek iambic line of Attic tragedy became the national type of dramatic metre in France.

Jodelle approached comedy in much the same spirit as tragedy. Classical correctness of form is, he declares, the primary aim of genuine comedy. But for the complete success of comedy elements of modernity, incidents of familiar life must be embroidered on the classical canvas. Jodelle's comic play, which is called *Eugène*, after its hero, tells a story of a rich abbé's disreputable intrigue with the wife of a foolish friend. In sentiment it is far less closely identified with the classical revival than the tragedy of *Cléopâtre*, but it is loyal to the classical form and its octosyllabic rhyming couplets are not out of harmony with classical metre. But the old French spirit of comedy, the temper of the old French *fabliau*, the love of broadly humorous anecdote, leavens in Jodelle's page the Roman wit of Terence. The Frenchman's intrigue is, moreover, coloured by Italian insolence. The first formal comedy in France, Jodelle's *Eugène*, is thus a cross between Terence's method of comedy and that of the author of *Maître Pathelin*, while there is at the same time a liberal infusion of Italian lubricity. It is a manner of composition which foreshadows much in the future development of French dramatic literature. It was in comedy that France was to produce in the seventeenth century her greatest literature of genius. French tragedy was never to scale the heights of French comedy, despite its majesty of diction and gesture. The comparative inferiority of French tragedy, with all its fine literary flavour, may be due to its failure to seek any sustenance in idiosyncrasies of national sentiment. A passion for classical feeling and for classical correctness dominated the tragic muse of France, and she pressed some classical canons to extremities of which Aristotle had not dreamed. In comedy, however, as Jodelle's pioneer effort showed, the 'esprit gaulois' claimed a control, and despite the critics' frown, successfully resisted eviction in the future.

Jodelle made only one other contribution to the drama. He was author of a second tragedy—on the subject of Dido. The plot was drawn from the fourth book of the Aeneid of Vergil. If in Cleopatra he anticipated a theme of Shakespeare, in Dido he anticipated a theme of Marlowe, who made Dido's misfortunes the subject of a tragedy. Jodelle's piece opens with the preparations for Aeneas's departure, and faithful to the unity of time, the fable is wholly confined to Dido's grief and suicide a few hours later. The speeches defy Seneca's generous standard of length, but Dido's expansive lamentations sound many a pathetic and piteous note. Again there are two choruses (one of Aeneas's companions and another of Phoenician women). *Didon* is the first French tragedy written (apart from the choruses) wholly in Alexandrines. In metrical facility Jodelle's second tragedy marks an advance on his first. Throughout his later Alexandrines, feminine rhymes alternate with the masculine on the approved modern pattern. The mellifluous utterances of the double chorus lend, too, lyric freshness to the scene.

Jodelle's example produced almost immediately a rich harvest of plays, both comedies and tragedies, on classical subjects and models. Jodelle's colleagues of the Pléiade gave him not only encouragement but the practical support of imitation. Baïf produced a comedy called *Braue ou Taille-bras* at the palace of the Duke of Guise in 1567. This was a spirited adaptation of Plautus's *Miles gloriosus*, to which Ronsard, Belleau, and Desportes added original choruses on classical lines, although the Latin text did not authorize them. Baïf was also responsible for quite literal renderings of Sophocles' *Antigone* and Terence's *Eunuchus*. His colleague, Remy Belleau, who died prematurely in 1577, showed greater inventiveness in a specimen of comedy which he called *La Reconnue*;[1] it is a sketch of contemporary society in Jodelle's classical manner with little of Jodelle's animation. Imitations of Seneca's *Medea* and *Agamemnon*, and two tragedies on the deaths respectively of Darius and Alexander the Great came likewise from pens of less eminent disciples of Jodelle. It was in tragedy that Jodelle's influence proved most fruitful. His effort in comedy bore comparatively small fruit. In that field his influence was soon eclipsed. But a long line of dramatists loyally took up his tragic parable.

Within a generation the new tragic art was set under Jodelle's guidance upon sure foundations throughout France. His capacities were soon surpassed, and two writers, Jacques Grévin and Robert Garnier, won superior tragic triumphs. Garnier's work helped more directly than Jodelle's to mould dramatic endeavour in England. If Jodelle deserve the honour of inventor of the classical type of modern drama Garnier should be credited with lifting it to a higher plane of art.

Grévin stands midway between Jodelle and Garnier. He is an interesting figure. A young French Huguenot, he twice visited England, and was well received by Queen Elizabeth. He addressed to her in 1560 a poetic epistle, entitled 'Le Chant du Cigne' ('The Song of the Swan'), in which, like

[1] The plot dealt with the Civil War of 1562 and showed how a young woman of Poitiers, after being rescued from death, defeated an uncongenial matrimonial plot to which her benefactor exposed her.

Ronsard, Du Bartas, and Aubigné, he grows dithyrambic over her linguistic faculty, which included Spanish, Tuscan, Latin, and Greek, in addition to French :

> Vous parlez promptement nostre langue françoise,
> L'espagnolle, et thuscane, et latine, et gregeoyse,
> Vous sçavez la vulgaire, et si avez cest heur
> D'entendre et de respondre à tout ambassadeur.[1]

Two comedies in verse and a tragedy in Jodelle's manner form Grévin's contribution to the regular dramatic movement. One of his comedies merely adapts Jodelle's *Eugène,* the other comes from the Italian through an earlier French version.[2] His tragedy in French, which deals with the death of Julius Caesar, is alone memorable. He wrote it while at the Collège de Guienne at Bordeaux for his fellow students to act. His tutor, Muret, had already penned a Latin tragedy on the subject, but Grévin passed beyond his tutor's scope. Muret found his material solely in Plutarch's life of Caesar. Grévin enlarged the theme by borrowing hints from Plutarch's lives of Brutus and Mark Antony in addition to the life of Caesar. Therein Grévin notably anticipated Shakespeare.

Nor does Grévin's dramatic feeling and insight into character discredit Shakespeare's splendid sequel. Calpurnia's fears and her appeal to Caesar to absent himself from the Senate on the fateful Ides of March are invested by Grévin with an air of mystery which adumbrates Shakespeare's tone. The emotional and choleric temperament of Cassius is forcibly contrasted with the equable tenor of Brutus's disposition. Most remarkable is Grévin's last act, which presents with spirit the harangues of Brutus and Antony to the fickle mob. Here Grévin shows a peculiar adroitness in handling Plutarch's narrative. The justificatory harangues of the assassins, Brutus, Cassius, and Decimus

---

[1] Le Chant du Cigne. A la majesté de la Royne dangleterre, 1560, lines 169-76 ; quoted in Appendix to Lucien Pinvert's ' Jacques Grévin (1538-70) '. Paris, 1899, p. 356.

[2] Grévin's *La Trésorière* or *La Maubertine* (1558) in verse is an imitation of Jodelle's *Eugène.* His *Les Esbahis* is very freely adapted from *Les Abusez,* Charles Étienne's earlier French version of the Italian *Gli Ingannati.*

Brutus, are heard by the soldiers in silence. But Mark Antony's address from the tribune quickly excites threats of vengeance. The orator holds up the blood-stained garment of the slaughtered dictator—

> Et vous, braves soldats, voyez, voyez quel tort
> On vous a faict, voyez ceste robbe sanglante,
> C'est celle de César, qu'ores je vous présente :
> C'est celle de César, magnanime empereur,
> Vray guerrier entre tous, César qui d'un grand cœur
> S'acquit avecque nous l'entière jouissance,
> Du monde maintenant a perdu sa puissance,
> Et gist mort, estendu, massacré pauvrement
> Par l'homicide Brute.

The leader of the soldiers responds—

> Armons-nous sur ce traistre,
> Armes, armes, soldats, mourons pour nostre maistre.

Antony resumes his speech by bidding his hearers follow him, and warns them against the fear of death in performing their vow to avenge their murdered leader.[1] Shakespeare touched with a pen of fire Plutarch's bare reports of the speeches in the forum at Caesar's funeral, and brought the events down to the disasters of Philippi. Grévin's work is a mere daub of drama compared with Shakespeare's living dramatic picture. Nevertheless Grévin's version, however bald, is an important anticipation of Shakespeare's masterpiece. Grévin's tragedy acquired a wide reputation, and it is significant that Shakespeare should have consciously or unconsciously developed the dramatic tradition of the oratory at Caesar's funeral which Grévin inaugurated.

Very notable developments of French Renaissance drama are associated with the name of Robert Garnier, whose power was recognized in Elizabethan England with greater eager-

---

[1] The first soldier thereupon recalls an augury of their beloved general's murder. The second soldier brings the play to a somewhat abrupt end with the somewhat enigmatic speech, which was a bold comment on the political philosophy of the Huguenots—

> Ceste morte est fatale
> Aux nouveaux inventeurs de puissance royale.

The rest is silence. But there is artistic finish in the slender indication of the issue.

ness than that of any other French writer for the stage. Garnier loyally obeys the rules of classical tragedy of the Senecan pattern. Monologues abound. Declamation is his chief weapon. Yet he brought to his work a larger measure of poetic sentiment and a greater command of tragic pathos than any predecessor. He showed too how classical sympathies could reconcile themselves with a new type of romantic drama. Garnier finally riveted on French tragedy the yoke of the Alexandrine, which he handled more skilfully than Jodelle. He was indeed a poet of no mean order, and the lyric note of his choruses has something of the grace and vivacity of his contemporary Ronsard. None of the Pléiade school save Ronsard were superior to him in variety of metre and imagery. He is equally at home in plaintive and merry keys. Nor does his charm lie merely in verbal harmonies. His graphic touches of description are equally attractive. In a chorus of huntsmen, in his tragedy of *Hippolyte,* he pictures all the incidents of the chase with a skill which gives the poetry the novel character of lyrical narrative. The stanza,[1] which portrays the crafty efforts of the hunted animal to escape the pursuing dogs, is worthy of comparison with Shakespeare's painting in *Venus and Adonis* of ' poor Wat ', ' the purblind hare ' tacking ' with a thousand doubles '.

Born in 1545 Garnier lived on till 1600, well into Shakespeare's middle life. He was a lawyer by profession, and no professional writer for the stage. Cultured society of Paris

---

[1] Cf. Garnier's *Tragédies*, Paris, 1582, p. 92 *b*:

> Lancés par les piqueurs ils rusent
> Ores changeant, ores croisant,
> Ore à l'écart se forpaisant
> D'entre les meutes qu'ils abusent.
> Ore ils cherchent de fort en fort
> Les autres bêtes qui les doutent,
> Et de force en leur lieu les boutent,
> Pour se garantir de la mort.
> Là se tapissant contre terre,
> Les pieds, le nez, le ventre bas,
> Moquent les chiens qui vont grand erre
> Dépendant vainement leurs pas.

The next stanza pictures the encounter with both boar and hare.

hailed him as the master-dramatist of the era. Ronsard echoed the prevailing opinion when he wrote (*Œuvres*, v. 353)—

> Par toy, Garnier, la scène des François
> Se change en or, qui n'estoit que de bois.

In the topics of his tragedies, he respected the classical tradition. Three of his plays—*Hippolyte, La Troade,* and *Antigone*—are to a large extent recensions of Seneca. His capacity may be better appraised in three tragedies drawn from Plutarch's biographies and developed on original lines. All three deal with the same historical epoch—the fall of the Roman Republic. Of one the heroine is Cornélie, the widow of Pompey, Caesar's rival ; the second revolves about the fortunes of Porcie (Portia), the wife of Brutus ; the third has Marc Antoine (Mark Antony) for its hero.

No dramatist before Garnier had brought the moving figure of Brutus's wife, Portia, on the stage. Baïf, a leader of the Pléiade, wrote—

> Au théâtre François, gentil Garnier, tu as
> Fait marcher grauement Porce à l'âme indomtée.

The story of Garnier's *Porcie* treats of the events after the death at Philippi of Brutus.[1] The dramatist warns the reader in his ' argument ' that he supplements Plutarch's information by that of Dion Cassius and Appian, besides introducing episodes of his own invention. The heroine has no competitor to share the dramatic interest, although her nurse has a prominence of which history knows nothing. The triumvirs Octavian, Antony, and Lepidus appear as Portia's jailers. All Garnier's tragic power is concentrated on the character and suicide of Brutus's noble-hearted wife and widow.

In his two other great tragedies, *Cornélie* and *Marc Antoine,* Garnier deals with Roman characters who had already figured in French tragedy. In his tragedy of *Cornélie* (the widow of Pompey) Garnier pursued much of the path which Grévin had trodden in his *César*, but the later dramatist invested with more dramatic significance

---

[1] Shakespeare errs historically in *Julius Caesar* in making Portia's death precede that of Brutus.

the characters not only of Julius Caesar, but those of Cicero, Mark Antony, Decimus Brutus, and Cassius. Cassius's speech glows throughout Garnier's drama of *Cornélie* with revolutionary ardour. Caesar is presented, at the zenith of his power, with a full consciousness of the revolutionary forces which his arrogance has brought into being to imperil his life.

In essaying in *Marc Antoine* the stirring theme of *Antony and Cleopatra,* Garnier followed in Jodelle's footsteps. But Jodelle had only dramatized the second half of the tragic tale. Garnier now tells the first half. His tragedy ends with the death of Antony. Through the first four acts he brings his energy to bear on the Roman hero, and the Queen of Egypt fills a subsidiary place. But in the last act Cleopatra becomes the protagonist with most pathetic effect. There is intensity of passion, there is the ecstasy of grief, in the long lamentations of Cleopatra over Antony's lifeless corpse.

> Antoine, ô pauvre Antoine, Antoine ma chere ame,
> Tu n'es plus rien qu'un tronc, le butin d'une lame,
> Sans vie et sans chaleur, ton beau front est desteint,
> Et la palle hideur s'empare de ton teint.
> Tes yeux, deux clairs soleils, où se voyoit empreinte,
> Luisant diuersement, et l'amour et la crainte,
> De paupieres couverts, vont noüant en la nuict,
> Comme un beau iour caché, qui les ténèbres fuit.
>
> Antoine, ie vous pry' par nos amours fidelles,
> Par nos cœurs allumez de douces estincelles,
> Par nostre sainct hymen, et la tendre pitié
> De nos petits enfans, nœud de nostre amitié,
> Que ma dolente voix à ton oreille arrive,
> Et que ie t'accompagne en l'infernale rive,
> Ta femme, ton amie : entens, Antoine, entens,
> Quelque part que tu sois, mes soupirs sanglotans. . . .
>
> Que dis-ie? où suis-ie? ô pauvre, ô pauvre Cléopâtre !
> O que l'aspre douleur vient ma raison abatre !
> Non, non, ie suis heureuse en mon mal deuorant
> De mourir auec toy, de t'embrasser mourant,
> Mon corps contre le tien, ma bouche desseichée
> De soupirs embrasez, à la tienne attachée,
> Et d'estre en mesme tombe et en mesme cercueil,
> Tous deux enuelopez en un mesme linceuil.[1]

[1] Garnier, *Tragédies,* Paris, 1582, pp. 201-2.

Compared with Cleopatra's magical words in the same situation in Shakespeare's *Antony and Cleopatra* Garnier may be judged turgid and strained :

Cleop.   Noblest of men, woo 't die?
Hast thou no care of me ? shall I abide
In this dull world, which in thy absence is
No better than a sty?   O, see, my women.
                                   [*Antony dies.*
The crown o' the earth doth melt. My lord!
O ! wither'd is the garland of the war,
The soldier's pole is fall'n : young boys and girls
Are level now with men ; the odds is gone,
And there is nothing left remarkable
Beneath the visiting moon.   (IV. xiii. 59-68.)

But Garnier, however faintly, adumbrates Shakespeare's inspired interpretation of the terrible scene. Both dramatists alike sought suggestion in Plutarch, and Jodelle had already marked out their road. Not once, but twice Cleopatra claimed rich toll of French drama before Elizabethan tragedy offered her its supreme tribute.

The two remaining dramatic works of Garnier, called respectively *Sédécie, ou Les Juives,* and *Bradamante,* diverge from the strict classical path. In *Sédécie,* the divergence touches not the form but the theme and sentiment, which have affinities with the middle ages. In *Bradamante* there is innovation in all directions ; its affinities are with the future.

Sédécie (the French name of Zedekiah) is a scriptural tragedy and has a backward link with the mediaeval drama. Garnier was not the first Frenchman to pen on the classical pattern a biblical tragedy which recalled the temper of the mystery-play. The ambition of clothing biblical history in classical form invaded the sphere of drama as well as that of epic. During the years immediately preceding the rise of the Pléiade, some scriptural dramas had been cast in either the Sophoclean or Senecan mould. But Latin and not French was then the vehicle of expression. The first author in France of a classical tragedy on a scriptural story was the Scotsman, George Buchanan, who was professor at the

Collège de Guienne at Bordeaux. His academic position and the excellence of his Latinity gave his Latin tragedies of *Jephthes* and *Baptistes* a wide vogue in both scholarly and religious circles. Translations of Buchanan's Latin plays into French stimulated the production of scriptural drama on the classical pattern in the French tongue. Saul and David were welcomed as heroes of French classical tragedy long after the Pléiade had anathematized the mediaeval mystery. Jean de la Taille, a disciple of Ronsard, contributed to the dramatic harvest of Renaissance France two sacred tragedies of strict classical orthodoxy, *Les Gabaonites* (1571) and *Saül furieux* (*c.* 1572). It was to this series of dramatic endeavour, which tried to reconcile the old religious aim of French drama with the new classical form, that Garnier's *Sédécie, ou Les Juives*, is a notable addition. It tells, with devotional fervour, the story of Nebuchadnezzar's victory over Zedekiah, king of Judah. Although the mediaeval method is rejected, the piece illustrates how the new school, despite its scorn of mediaeval influences, found it impossible to withstand all their assaults. Garnier's fame and abilities strengthened anew the hold of scriptural themes on French drama and gave the sway permanence. The tragic capacities of the story of Queen Esther were repeatedly proved by classical dramatists in the later part of the sixteenth century, and were finally developed by the master hand of Racine.

Garnier's seventh piece, *Bradamante*, marks a more original development in the history of French drama. It is a first experiment in quite a new dramatic type, and plainly indicates that whatever fetters the classical scholars were forging, the dramatic movement in France cherished hopes of expansion beyond classical bounds. *Bradamante* is described on the title-page as 'tragecomedie'. It is a play of romantic love and chivalry, with a happy ending. The chorus has disappeared, and there is no prologue. The story comes from Ariosto's *Orlando Furioso*. Garnier's tragi-comic plot runs in outline thus: Bradamante, sister of Rinaldo, the cousin and rival of Ariosto's hero Orlando, is a Christian Amazon, wielding a spear with irre-

sistible might.   Two friends, both knights of high repute,
Roger, a converted Saracen, and Leon, a son of the Greek
Emperor, sue for her hand, neither knowing the other's
intention.   The lady favours the Saracen, but her parents,
whose betrayal of worldly motives is in the comic vein, decide
in favour of the Greek Leon.   There is, however, no escape
for Leon from the immovable condition that the successful
aspirant to the lady-warrior's hand must first disarm her in
fair fight.   Leon, an ineffective fighter, recognizes the hope-
lessness of the attempt, and appeals to his friend Roger, an
invincible swordsman, to help him out.   Roger is under obligations to Leon, while Leon is quite ignorant that his friend's
heart is engaged in the same quarter as his own.   Roger
complacently accepts Leon's invitation to personate his friend
in the combat, and in his disguise he disarms the fair duellist.
Thereupon, after much involved incident, the visitor's earlier
passion for the lady comes to light.   Leon magnanimously
yields to his friend his claim on Bradamante, almost as suddenly
as Valentine surrenders his claim on Julia to his friend Proteus
in the *Two Gentlemen of Verona*.   In Garnier's romantic
drama, Leon at once matches elsewhere, and as he leaves the
scene for his friend Roger's hymeneal festivities with Bradamante, his own first love, he closes the play with the lines
(1582 ed., p. 42 *b*)—

> Quel heur le Dieu du ciel inspérément me donne!
> Oncq, ie croy, sa bonté n'en feit tant à personne.
> O que ie suis heureux! ie uaincray desormais
> L'heur des mieux fortunez qui n'esquirent iamais.

The ending is unqualified happiness all round.   The un-
reality of the theme is relieved by many natural touches
of character.   The dramatic tenor is new to France, and
although the note had been struck in Italy, Garnier sounded
it with a fresh vigour, which was soon to be echoed in England
in yet fuller tones.

V

IRREGULAR DRAMA OF THE FRENCH RENAISSANCE

Garnier's occasional deviations from the straight path of classical orthodoxy indicate that French national sentiment still craved a greater elasticity of dramatic method than the classical tradition provided or sanctioned. Not merely had the threat of the Pléiade to banish for ever from the French realm of drama the shapeless survivals of the past failed to take effect, but the irregular tendencies of popular taste were infecting the classical workshops. When one turns from the scholarly circles to the popular stage outside their bounds, one finds all manner of transgressions of classical law in unchecked operation. Religious feeling demanded the continuance of sacred drama in its old mould of mystery and not merely in Garnier's new shape of classical tragedy. Political feeling and interests of the moment claimed expression in tragedy and questioned the right of tragic writers to confine their topics to mythic history, which lacked relevance to current life. There was a yearning for 'les nouveaux arguments' which classical theorists scorned. Drama had entered into the life of the French nation to an extent quite unknown at the moment in England. In one of its unregenerate phases it had become an engine of public criticism and a disseminator of public intelligence. The classical reformers in seeking to restrict it to new channels of poetry and formal art, had misapprehended the force of popular opinion. A greater flexibility of form, too, than was reconcilable with the classical canons was required of drama which should serve purposes of general entertainment.

As a consequence, through the second half of the sixteenth century, while classical tragedy and classical comedy were winning notable triumphs in cultured ranks, flagrant breaches of the classical traditions were enjoying the nation's wholehearted suffrages. Popular applause was evoked in the public theatres not only by new experiments in the mediaeval mystery or the *sottie*, but by amorphous species of drama answering such lawless descriptions as these :—'tragédies

morales, tragédies allégoriques, tragi-comédies pastorales,
tragi-pastorales, fables bocagères, bergeries, histoires tragiques,
journées en tragédie, tragédies sans distinction d'actes ni de
scènes, martyres de saints et saintes.' Polonius's creator
might well have been studying theatrical programmes of
contemporary Paris when he asserted that actors of the day
were equally efficient in such miscellaneous diversions as
' pastoral-comical, historical-pastoral, tragical-historical, tragi-
cal-comical, historical-pastoral, scene - indivisible, or poem
unlimited '. (*Hamlet*, II. ii. 426-7.) Shakespeare's ' scene
indivisible' sounds like a literal reminiscence of the current
kind of French tragedy which was repeatedly described on
title-pages as ' sans distinction d'actes ni de scènes '.

The later history of the mystery is characteristic of the
general trend of events. The mediaeval form of the sacred
play was often reproduced even by those who were well
versed in classical drama. The law of 1548 which prohibited
the dramatization of scriptural topics was never strictly
enforced and by the end of the century had fallen into
desuetude. Such recognition of a past vogue made a
forcible appeal to the Huguenots, and Protestant scholars
encouraged the tendency, despite their classical training.
They knew that the scriptural tale was adaptable to the
classical shape of tragedy, but many deemed the mediaeval
mould freer of the suspicion of profanity. A pathetic piece
of drama entitled *Abraham sacrifiant*, by Théodore de Bèze
(or Beza), the Calvinist scholar, is mainly a dialogue between
Abraham and Isaac on wholly antiquated lines. It was acted
at the University of Lausanne in 1551, just before classical
tragedy had been turned to French uses. But even after the
advent of the classical drama in France and the production of
sacred five-act tragedies in Alexandrines and with choruses,
the method of the mystery still lived on. *David combattant*,
David fugitif, *David triomphant* (published in 1566),
are three notable pieces of literary merit, which form a
trilogy of mysteries; they are so loyal to conservative
principles that their scenic arrangement conforms to the
mediaeval stage-method of fixed ' mansions ' or unchange-

able tiers of set scenes. The author Louis des Masures was a Huguenot pastor at Metz and Strasburg successively, and his sole innovation on the mediaeval scheme was to graft on his dramatic endeavour the simple and joyous note of French Protestant psalmody. A lyric in his *David triomphant*, in which each stanza ends with the burden,

> Israel ramène en joie
> David triomphant!

is a fine contribution to Huguenot psalmody and as spirited a *réveil* as any that the poets of the Pléiade devised.[1]

Not that Huguenots monopolized the surviving mystery. In 1580 there was produced a new piece from a Catholic pen on the time-worn topic of Abel's murder by Cain, which, with much literary faculty preserves intact the mediaeval sentiment. A 'tragédie sainte, extraite de l'histoire de Judith', was published in Paris in the same year under the title of *Holopherne*, and was equally loyal to the old pattern. Its author, Adrien d'Amboise, was no Huguenot, but an ecclesiastic of the court. As late as 1601 there was produced in Paris a sacred play called *Joseph le Chaste*, which has all the irregular features of the old-fashioned mystery and was addressed to a Catholic audience.

But it was not only sacred topics that claimed free entry into the popular theatre. Outside the classical sanctuaries the dramatic prohibition of 'les nouveaux arguments' carried no weight, and war was declared on the canon which would limit drama to themes of classical history or mythology. Many writers, who were by no means destitute of classical learning, denounced the prejudice which cut off tragedy from national politics and affairs. On the threshold of the classical citadels there consequently

---

[1] One of the three stanzas runs thus:

> Réveillez-vous, réveillez,
> Réveillez vous tous;
> Ne gisez plus travaillés
> Sous le sommeil doux.
> Le jour chasse la nuit coie,
> Sorti du levant.
> Israël ramène en joie
> David triomphant.

arose a spacious French drama, for the most part in verse and embellished by choruses, which topically showed ' the very age and body of the time, his form and pressure '.

Nowhere is the resemblance between the French and English dramatic developments of the sixteenth century closer than in the growing reliance of dramatists in both countries on varied themes of national history and current political or social episode. National history of the past and present, tragic and comic incidents of current domestic life, contemporary crises in the affairs of foreign countries, were as freely turned to dramatic purposes by French as by Elizabethan authors in the last decades of the Renaissance era. Melodramatic crudities thereby came to permeate the French as completely as the English theatre. Scenes of violence were often admitted to the stage. There vanished the reticence of the classical drama, which relegated deeds of blood to the narratives of messengers. At the same time a rough form of tragi-comedy—a drama of romance, which lacked the literary quality of Garnier's prototype of *Bradamante*, grew rapidly in public favour. French drama of popular acceptance thus claimed a liberty of scope almost as versatile as the drama of Elizabethan England. A comparative survey indicates that French popular drama stimulated some measure of the Elizabethan licence, however the outcome of the two movements differed in artistic or poetic value. Difference in quality was quite compatible with identity of theme. No magic pen of genius was at work in France to invest the dramatic lawlessness with the vitality of great poetry or art. Therein England enjoyed a better fortune.

It is only possible here to select a few illustrations of the breadth of topic which, in defiance of the classical interdict against ' les nouveaux arguments ', characterize French drama of the epoch synchronizing with the dawn of Elizabethan drama. The national history was ransacked for plots. The titles of such popular French tragedies as *La Franciade* (a tale of the alleged Trojan invasion of France), *Mérouée* (son of King Chilperic and his wife Fredegonde), *Gaston de Foix*, *La Pucelle de Dom Remy, autrement d'Orléans* (Joan of Arc), adequately suggest the type of historical theme. Contemporary politics were even more prominent in the French theatre of the period. Recent events were loosely strung together to the neglect of all the unities save that of political feeling. In 1575 a crude tragic piece presented the assassination of the Huguenot leader, Coligny, which was one of the most revolting incidents of the massacre of St. Bartholomew three years before. During the final struggle in which the Holy Leaguers engaged from 1589 onwards with Henry of Navarre, leading members of the Guise family figured repeatedly as heroes on the French stage. Much popularity was accorded to a piece called *La Guisiade*, which dealt with the murder in 1588 of the Duke of Guise by the hirelings of King Henry III. The author, Pierre Matthieu, a political pamphleteer of repute, inclined to the *via media* of 'Les Politiques', and affects a very qualified sympathy with the murdered duke. But the house of Lorraine had its theatrical vindicators against both the house of Valois and the house of Navarre. *Le Guysien, ou Perfidie tyrannique commise par Henry de Valois*, in 1592 in five acts ('en vers avec des chœurs'), betrayed open hostility to the royal house. A somewhat similar production of a little later date, called *Le triomphe de la Ligue*, a five-act tragedy, again dealt, but in a more neutral vein, with the assassination of the Duke de Guise, slightly disguising his name and those of his fellows. A wide survey of current affairs here includes scenic presentments of Jesuit intrigues in England, of the fate of Mary Stuart, and of Henry of Navarre's victory at the battle of Coutras. A point of view which was more favourable to the house of Valois was taken in a tragedy called *Chilpéric le Second*, which satirized the subservience of King Henry III to the Duc de Guise, who figured in the play as Chilperic's mayor of the Palace.

Nor did the topical dramatists confine their attention to current history of their own country. *La Soltane*, which was acted with popular success as early as 1560, dealt with a very recent event in Turkish history, the execution by the Sultan Soliman the Magnificent of his son Mustapha in 1553. The fame of modern oriental heroes was soon to be no less securely enshrined in the Elizabethan drama. A 'tragédie nouvelle' of 1588 by a Franciscan of Mons is a dramatic version of the Duke of Parma's military campaigns against the Protestants in the Low Countries. The piece, although it is in five acts, borrows many of the features of the mystery. The Spanish general shares his prominent place in the *dramatis personae* with the three persons of the Trinity and the Virgin Mary, and there is a large crowd of Dutch 'heretics' in attendance. After the manner of mystery-plays, Christ, at the end of the last act, quits the stage with a rather ironical intimation that, disgusted with the wickedness of the faithful, He will no longer protect them from the ravages of the heretics.

The most striking and by far the most literary of all French tragedies of the age on contemporary foreign history closely touched English affairs. A tragedy, entitled *L'Escossaise*, portrayed the trial and execution at Fotheringay of Mary Queen of Scots. It was published in 1601, and loyally pursued the sixteenth-century habit of bringing politics on the popular stage. The author, Antoine de Montchrétien (1575–1621), was a believer in classical principles, and only deviated from the classical tradition in point of topic and sentiment. Of the school of Garnier, he was loyal to all the ancient canons of unity, of declamation, of choric interlude. Chorus and monologue are indeed developed beyond the common limit, and the interest attaching to the effort is mainly due to the author's bold endeavour to adapt to the classic mould the versatile demands of public taste. Montchrétien had literary and poetic gifts which give him a place beside his master. If Garnier may be regarded as the Corneille of the drama of the French Renaissance, Montchrétien deserves to be entitled its Racine. His lyric feeling sets him in the same category as the leaders of the Pléiade. In many choruses he sounds such delicate notes as this:

> Apres la feuille, la fleur;
> Apres l'espine, la rose;
> Et l'heur apres le mal-heur:
> Le jour on est en labeur
> Et la nuit on se repose.[1]

[1] *Sophonisbe*, Act II, last chorus.

406 FRANCE AND THE ELIZABETHAN DRAMA

Montchrétien's dramatic labours began with *Sophonisbe*, a regular tragedy on the Senecan model, the subject of which had already attracted classical dramatists of France as well as of Italy. There followed a like piece of work wrought out of Plutarch's life of Cleomenes of Sparta, entitled *Les Lacènes*, (i.e. *The Spartan Women*). Again turning to paths which had already been trodden by the classicists, Montchrétien next produced tragedies in classical form on the scriptural subjects of David and Haman, the prime minister of King Ahasuerus, respectively. *L'Escossaise* was Montchrétien's last and best contribution to the drama. It is, despite its orthodox construction, a moving dramatic picture of the almost contemporaneous sufferings of Mary Queen of Scots. Queen Mary and Queen Elizabeth are the protagonists. There are choruses of members of the English House of Commons as well as of Queen Mary's ladies in waiting. Between them they tell the story of Queen Mary's last days with pathetic accuracy. The play is a notable tribute to the modernizing influences which were working on the French drama when the English theatre was reaching its full splendour. There was much, too, in Montchrétien's career to enhance for English students the interest of his work. As a fugitive homicide, he, a Norman of humble Huguenot parentage, sought an asylum in England early in James I's reign. The English king was grateful to him for his portrayal of his royal mother's fate and successfully pleaded with Henry IV of France for the dramatist's pardon. After leaving England Montchrétien speculated on political problems in a liberal spirit, and invented the term 'Political Economy' (*économie politique*) to describe the purpose of his inquiries. But Montchrétien soon engaged in fresh exploits of violence in the Huguenot cause and was shot as a rebel, his body being torn on the wheel and then burnt. Montchrétien's stormy career and his crowning achievement in tragedy, in spite of its fidelity to the ancient tragic form, signally illustrate the yearning which was moving French sentiment to reconcile dramatic art with current life.

In every direction, if usually to crude effect, this tendency to imbue drama with topical interest was active. The

dramatization of reports of current murders in domestic life
was another popular feature of the topical tragedy of middle
and late sixteenth-century France. As early as 1551, there
was produced in Paris a 'tragédie françoise à huit personnages', by one Jean Bretog, who dramatized a recent
sordid episode of a manservant's adultery with his mistress.
The offender's trial and execution and the injured husband's
death of grief came within the dramatist's canvas. Allegorical figures of Venus and Jealousy figure among the
dramatis personae. The author in a prologue lays stress on
the truth of the incidents; he asserts that he witnessed the
adulterer's punishment, and that the whole is depicted 'sans
nulle fiction'. Here the anticipation of a certain class of
Elizabethan plays is singularly clear. Pieces like *Arden
of Faversham*, *A Warning for Fair Women*, and *Two
Tragedies in One*, which, towards the end of the sixteenth century, presented in London dramatic versions of
recent stories of murder and adultery, follow the precise lines
of this 'tragédie française' of 1551. Allegorical figures in
two of the English pieces, History, Murder, Lust, give, as in
the French play, positive assurances that the stories are true
and of recent date. Jean Bretog, in the Prologue of his *Tragédie
françoise à huit personnages* (1551), describes the events as—

> Depuis trois ans une histoire advenue
> Dedans Paris.

He writes of the punishment of the offenders as an eye-
witness—

> Je le dis d'assurance,
> Et avoir vu faire punition,
> Comme il est dit sans nulle fiction.

In the *Two Tragedies in One*, which anglicized a similar
theme in the Elizabethan theatre in 1601, Truth as prologue
says of the husband's murder by the wife and a servant-
paramour, that it—

> was done in famous London late
> Within that street whose side the river Thames
> Doth strive to wash from all impurity,—
> The most here present know this to be true.

Later, just before the guilty persons are hanged in sight of
the audience, Truth again enters and tells the spectators—

> Your eyes shall witness of the shaded types
> Which many here did see performed indeed.

A second French piece, which ostensibly belongs to the
same category of sensational veracity, is of more ambitious
design. It is called *Philonaire, femme d'Hippolyte*, was
first published in Latin, and after being translated into French,
was publicly acted in Paris in 1560. The tragedy professes to
dramatize a recent ghastly incident which took place in Piedmont. The repulsive motive adumbrates that of Shakespeare's
Measure for Measure. Hippolyte, the husband of the heroine
Philonaire, is in prison under sentence of death. In grief and
despair, the wife seeks an interview with the provost of the
town, and petitions him to release the prisoner. The provost
assents on the disgraceful condition that the petitioner shall
yield herself to his lust. Horror-stricken by the villany,
but unable to obtain any modification of the conditions, the
woman assents to the provost's proposal. But the provost
plays his victim false. Failing to cancel the husband's sentence of death, he sends in the morning the man's headless
body to the outraged wife. Nothing would seem capable of
surpassing the horror of the scene in which Philonaire learns
the grossness of the provost's treachery. But worse follows.
The governor of the province, hearing of the provost's
offences, insists that he shall at once marry Philonaire. Yet
no sooner is the marriage consummated than the governor
condemns the provost to death, and the play ends with
Philonaire's lamentations over her double widowhood. Probably no piece mingles in more revolting proportions intense
tragic sentiment with extravagant obscenity. Certainly
Philonaire had no sort of companion until John Webster
wrote *The White Devil*.

Meanwhile the progress of romantic tragi-comedy attracts
the attention of the student of French Renaissance drama.
Very significant is the appearance in 1576 of a romantic
comedy entitled *Lucelle* by one Louis le Jars. It was publicly
performed, apparently with success, and has more than one

new feature of moment. It is written in prose, and the author
in the introduction to the published text defends this innovation on the ground that prose alone can make drama real.[1]
He especially emphasizes the absurdity of putting verse into
the mouths of servants and persons of humble rank. He
insists that to such characters, at any rate, prose is alone
appropriate. Shakespeare's practice proves that he shared
Le Jars's conviction. Moreover, the serving-men in this
romantic French play freely indulge in a chop-logic, a loqua-
cious buffoonery, and a pedantry which anticipates the cut
and thrust of much Elizabethan comic dialogue.

The story of *Lucelle* is simple, and one or two of its
incidents curiously anticipate that of *Romeo and Juliet*.
Lucelle is the daughter of a banker, and is sought in
marriage by the Baron de Saint-Amour, a suitor who is
accepted with eagerness by the father. But the young lady
is already secretly betrothed to Ascagne, a clerk in her
father's office. Distressed by her father's bestowal of her
hand on the baron, she seeks consolation from her secret
lover, and is surprised in his company by her kindred. The
banker, roused to fury by the discovery, forces the clerk to
drink poison. Death to all appearance ensues, and the
heroine is copious in her lamentations over the supposed
corpse. A messenger arrives to announce that the clerk is
really the Prince of Wallachia in disguise. A quarrel with
his father had driven him to seek his fortunes abroad. The
father's death has just taken place, and the road to his
ancestral throne is now open to him. The astonished banker
appeals to the apothecary, who had supplied him with
the poison, for an antidote. The apothecary admits that the
drug is only a sleeping draught; the clerk quickly returns
to consciousness, and weds Lucelle. Save the Baron de
Saint-Amour, everybody is satisfied. The production of such

[1] In 1562 Jean de la Taille had written a comedy on the Latin model
which he called *Les Corrivaux*. It was in prose, in imitation of the Italian.
De la Taille's comedy was first published in 1573, but in spite of the
innovation of prose, it adhered so closely to classical form and sentiment
as to rank it with the classical school of French drama rather than with
the irregular popular school to which *Lucelle* clearly belongs.

a play adds one more plain proof that the French popular drama in Shakespeare's boyhood was capable of offering the Elizabethan theatre very valuable hints.

Meanwhile the farce or *sottie* renewed its life in the public theatres. Even when the main features of the programme were serious romance or history or melodrama or tragedy of the sanguinary pattern, the performance at the Hôtel de Bourgogne included ' un prologue drôlatique ' or ' un discours facétieux ', or ' un avant-jeu récréatif ' of which the coarseness was of more than mediaeval breadth. Actors in these buffooneries obtained popular honours which were rarely bestowed on performers in serious pieces. Early in the seventeenth century the chief heroes in the theatrical world of Paris were comedians, whose burlesque pseudonyms, Turlupin, Bruscambille, Gros-Guillaume, Gaultier-Garguille, Guillot-Gorju echoed their professional idiosyncrasies.

The anti-classical revolt which popular taste fomented and directed was, meanwhile, reinforced by a foreign agency, by the spread of Italian influence. Troops of Italian actors paid France frequent visits during the last half of the century, and under the patronage of the court obtained immense popularity in Paris. The theatre-going public was thus thoroughly familiarized with comic developments of Italian drama, and there was a cry for imitations of current Italian comedy in French. The pastoral drama and the masque were among dramatic inventions of Italy, which France also adopted late in the sixteenth century. She handled these delicate plants rather timidly, and made no sustained endeavour to modify the foreign type. Italy is mainly responsible for importing the masque and pastoral into Elizabethan drama; and the debt which England owed to her nearer neighbour's endeavours to naturalize these Italian products hardly passed beyond efficient encouragement to pluck fruit from the same tree.

It was in the comedy of manners, in domestic comedy, that Italian example wrought on French drama with more penetrating effect and thereby helped to bring new comic features into vogue abroad as well as at home. Pierre de Larivey

(1541–1612) was the chief writer of French comedy near the end of the sixteenth century,[1] and of the dozen comedies from his pen nine survive. Six were published in 1579, and the three others, which were written near the same date, only came from the press in 1611, the year before the author died. All are freely based on Italian originals, which themselves owe something to Plautus and Terence. But the Frenchman's style was more pointed than that of his Italian guides; there are new Gallic touches in the punning dialectic, and, though his intrigue abounds in offence, he slightly qualifies the Italian indecencies. He rebutted charges of obscenity on the ground that comedy is 'le miroir de la vie', and that the maxim 'castigat ridendo mores' regulates its purpose. Old men in love who are duped by their valets, girls disguised as men, husbands deceived by wives, are among Larivey's stock characters, and the tricks which they play on one another are the reverse of edifying. The sort of misconception as to the lady's identity which leads to Bertram's intimacy with Helen in Shakespeare's *All's Well*, and to Angelo's intimacy with Mariana in the same dramatist's *Measure for Measure*, is a frequent episode of unabashed merriment in Larivey's plays. A few of Larivey's misunderstandings are, however, quite innocent. In his comedy of *Les Tromperies*, which is drawn from a popular Italian piece, Secchi's *Inganni*, there is the same confusion between a brother and a sister in the disguise of a boy as in *Twelfth Night*, and the amorous complications which ensue are of like import in both comedies. One of Larivey's most interesting innovations is his exclusive and insistent use of prose. Larivey argued with greater force than Le Jars, and proved by more efficient practice, that verse was alien to first-rate comic dialogue. Molière may be regarded as one of Larivey's disciples, and from him Larivey's application of prose to French

[1] Though Larivey was born in Troyes his father was a near kinsman of the Giunti, the Florentine family of printers, and his surname, which was originally written L'Arrivé, literally translates the Italian participle *giunto*, i. e. come, arrived. Larivey obtained high church preferment in France, but devoted much of his time to translation from the Italian. His labours include a French rendering of the second book of Straparola's *Nights*, a popular collection of Italian romances.

comedy received its final sanction. In Elizabethan England the employment of prose in the comic scene is partly due to Italian tuition. But France must be credited with taking through Larivey's agency a direct hand in the instruction.

Larivey's best comedy, called *Les Esprits* (Ghosts), comes from an Italian comedy by Lorenzino de' Medici, entitled *Aridosio*, which itself borrows much from Latin comic writers for the stage. The leading characters are two old men, one genial and generous, the other gruff-tempered and avaricious, and the central episode is a trick played on the old miser, in the interest of an ill-used son and daughter, by an insolent valet who frightens the old man out of his house and out of his treasure by manufacturing a ghost. Character-studies of the two old men abound in the French in humorous flashes which made the French dramatist's influence world-wide. Ben Jonson, among Elizabethans, most closely caught Larivey's ambition to depict men's and women's humours. Molière's *L'École des Maris* is a descendant of Larivey's *Les Esprits*.

Larivey's conception of comedy was a liberal and expansive adaptation of the spirit of Latin comedy to the needs of popular French taste. In his own field of drama, he went some way towards effecting a reconciliation between the aims of the two rival dramatic schools in France— between the aims of the champions of classic conformity, and of popular licence. With an insolent disdain of each other's pretensions the rivals had been fighting for predominance through a generation, and Larivey's compromise pointed, in the sphere of comedy, the road to peace. At the very end of the sixteenth and at the opening of the seventeenth century, there seemed a likelihood of a similar accommodation in other regions of drama. A formal fusion was attempted between the classical form of tragedy and the popular conceptions of romance and melodrama. The endeavour was far more thoroughgoing than anything at which Montchrétien aimed. During the last half of Shakespeare's career, and for twenty years afterwards, France seemed to be pursuing the same dramatic ideal of romanticism and emancipated classicism which prevailed in England. The French

drama of the new type of tolerance was uninspired by poetic
and lyric fervour.   No French tragedy, no romantic comedy
of the epoch can be justly mentioned in the same breath as
any work of Shakespeare.   But there was alive in France for
a generation, which covered Shakespeare's middle and later
years, a theatrical instinct which appeared to be driving
drama towards the same goal as that which the Elizabethan
and Jacobean playwrights reached.   This newest dramatic
development of the French Renaissance proved transitory;
the classical laws soon reasserted their control of tragedy,
and ultimately refused all recognition to romance.   But the
passing effect on the French stage of the endeavour to fuse
the two divergent dramatic forms is well worthy of study.

It was from the independent ranks of professional actors
in France that the new movement of compromise sprang.   In
1598 there was installed at the Hôtel de Bourgogne a professional company of actors, which had gained experience in
provincial tours.   The newcomers developed the theatrical
machinery in many directions.   Scenery grew elaborate and
women were soon suffered to take part in the performances.   The company conferred on one of their number,
Alexandre Hardy, the post of playwright.[1]

Hardy repeated in some degree the exploits of the actor-
author Gringoire half a century before.   An even closer parallel
might be drawn between the outward facts, the mere external
circumstance, of Hardy's career and those of Shakespeare.
Born in obscurity and comparative poverty about five years
later than the great English dramatist, Hardy enjoyed little
education.   Like Shakespeare in England, he in France joined
while very young a company of professional actors, attending
on them at the outset in a servile capacity.   He accompanied
them on provincial tours, and finally settled with them
permanently in Paris.   Before he was twenty-four he had
developed an ambition to write for the stage.   Encouraged
by the manager he began pouring out, at an unexampled
pace, tragedies, tragi-comedies, masques, and pastorals.

It was in tragedies and tragi-comedies that he made his

[1] See Eugène Rigal, *Alexandre Hardy et le théâtre français*, Paris, 1889.

greatest fame. Comedy lay outside his scope. His masques and pastorals are lifeless echoes of Italy. Although he never rose far above the status of hack-writer, Hardy had original conceptions of drama. He had watched the recent classical development of French tragedy, and he knew that it defied current conditions of theatrical success. Destitute of literary grace or poetic fertility, stiff and bombastic in expression, Hardy sought to remodel French drama in the light of his theatrical experience. He did not disdain classical themes, which had been employed before. Dido, Meleager, Alcestis, Darius, Alexander, are among his heroes or heroines. He depended on Plutarch's *Lives* for many tragic plots. But Hardy sought to set tragedy adrift from the trammels of the unities and the chorus. He increased the number of actors; he deprived monologue of its old predominance; he put action and movement in its place. Classical fables remained, as in classical drama, favoured topics, but he sought to endow them with a ruder life and fresher colour than of old. At times he attempts psychological study in his characterization. In his best tragic drama *Mariamne*, the husband Herod's jealousy of his wife Mariamne is analysed with something of Shakespeare's penetration in *Othello*, and Herod's sister Salome fans the jealous flame in her brother's heart with something of the Machiavellian craft of Iago.

But it was on romance or tragi-comedy that Hardy bestowed his best energies. He eagerly raided novels of Italy and Spain, which he read in French translations. In his choice of tale, he and Shakespeare often by chance coincidence trod on one another's heels. Hardy's romantic comedy of *Félismene* tells a part of the story of *The Two Gentlemen of Verona*; the two plays both owed something to a translation of Montemayor's Spanish romance of *Diana*. A tragi-comic story, of a better sustained pathos, more powerfully appealed to Hardy's mature taste. He wrote a tragi-comedy, called *Pandoste*, on the same subject as Shakespeare's *Winter's Tale*—the most perfect tragi-comedy in the range of the Elizabethan drama. Like Shakespeare, Hardy had recourse to Greene's romance of *Pandosto*, which was popular in a French translation. Hardy's text of this piece is lost, but we know its character not only from the descriptive title which survives, but from an extant scenario which was prepared for the scene-painter of Hardy's company. These two romantic plays—*Félismene* and *Pandoste*—were probably penned by Hardy after Shakespeare's cognate efforts had seen the light, and the identity of effort merely illustrates the parallelism of aim in the dramatic activity of the two countries, when the Renaissance was reaching its close on both sides of the channel. Worthier of attention is Hardy's dramatization of Plutarch's story of Coriolanus, which he completed in 1607, just a year before Shakespeare dealt with the theme. Hardy stated in his preface that 'few subjects will be found in Roman history worthier of the stage'. None had tried to adapt the life of Coriolanus to dramatic uses before. Here Hardy adhered more closely than was his wont to classical canons of unity and monologue and chorus. His play of *Coriolan* opens with the banishment of the hero. Coriolanus's speeches, those of his mother, and the comment of a band of Roman citizens, practically constitute the whole dramatic theme. Yet the declamatory seed that Hardy sowed in *Coriolan* may have borne fruit in Shakespeare's *Coriolanus*, a tragedy of passion and action which was produced in London a year after its French prototype. Hardy's play caught firm hold of French taste; Coriolanus's relations with his mother strongly appealed to French domestic sentiment, and there have been at least twenty-three later adaptations of *Coriolan* on the French stage.

Hardy wrote his plays for the actors, and did not care that they should be published. There is evidence to show that before he died in 1632 he had produced as many as 700 pieces—a prodigious output. Of these only thirty-four survive. As Hardy's career was closing, he permitted, with hesitation and reluctance, the collective publication in six volumes of thirteen tragi-comedies, eleven tragedies, five pastorals, and five mythological masques.

For the task of permanently reforming the French drama, of modifying its classical tendency by mingling it with romanticism, Hardy was too weak. He lacked poetic strength or lyric power. Theatrical faculty and immense industry were his main assets. Although he had a few disciples, of larger literary capacity than his, his effort bore no permanent fruit. In spite of his example, French drama soon returned to the old classical road, with its strict observance of the unities and much choric elaboration. The genius of Racine and Corneille in the next generation finally gave the classical principle of tragedy a universal vogue in France, and deprived the reformers of their hold on public favour. Yet Hardy's energy, although fruitless, claims attention as the latest emanation of the versatile spirit of the Renaissance in the development of French drama.

VI

THE COGNATE DEVELOPMENT OF FRENCH AND ELIZABETHAN DRAMA

No one who scans the development of drama in sixteenth-century France can fail to be impressed by the points of resemblance with the dramatic progress of Elizabethan England. In both countries two mutually hostile forces were at work together. Reverence for the austere classical tradition was actively challenged in both countries by a craving for an ampler romanticism and realism. The relative strength of the two forces differed on the two sides of the Channel. The classical temper dominated the struggle in France and ultimately won the victory. The romantic temper finally gained an undisputed ascendancy in England. The fortunes of the warfare consequently varied in the two lands. But the same seed of strife was sown in the two countries, and bore abundant fruit in each. The true relation which subsists between the dramatic movements of France and England in the Renaissance era can only be diagnosed when due recognition is made of two features of the situation which are often ignored—namely, the classical influences which were operative in Elizabethan drama, and the romantic and realistic influences which were operative in the French drama of the sixteenth century.

Although the classical proclivities of tragedy and comedy were from the first more pronounced in France than in England, yet it was from classical soil that the Elizabethan drama also sprang. However boldly, too, Elizabethan drama defied in its maturity classical rule it continued to cherish pride in its early classical associations. The voice of scholarship never commanded in England the attention which was accorded it in France, but the scholars' cry for classical form and classical topic in drama was never silent among Shakespeare's countrymen. Scholarly critics of drama in both countries were at one in deploring the popular divergences from the classical paths. The alienation was condemned as a concession to barbarism by the critical schools of both nations.

Elizabethan culture endeavoured for a season to stem the rising tide of non-classical dramatic licence by a direct appeal to French classical example. Garnier's guidance seemed to offer Elizabethan lawlessness a means of regeneration. There were circulated English translations of Garnier's orthodox tragedies, and the translations were followed by independent imitation. But Garnier's authority only carried conviction to the critical clique of Elizabethan England. Professional playwrights of the Elizabethan era acknowledged, often with a show of regret, that public appetite demanded the less regular fare of romanticism or realism. Classical themes still found a home on the popular stage. Roman history provided the heroes of numerous Elizabethan tragedies. Even after the banishment of the classical formulae from the popular playhouse, the classical device of the Chorus survived in modified shapes. But the austere classical spirit was declared by the popular voice to be tame and lifeless beyond redemption.

There was much in the contemporary fortunes of the French theatre to stimulate and to justify the Elizabethan repudiation of classical law. The classical canons of unity, the prominence of the Chorus, the presence of declamation or narration in place of action, conflicted on both sides of the Channel in the last half of the sixteenth century with most of the conditions of popular taste. In French drama the classical ideal was often boldly challenged, and the struggle of the

French theatre for a larger liberty and complexity adumbrated many of the Elizabethan experiences. France, in the closing years of the Renaissance, showed much of England's impatience of the classical bonds ; tragi-comedy, in which romance defied the law of classical sublimity, was riveting its hold on the French stage.

The influence of French drama on Elizabethan England was by no means limited to propagating the orthodox classical creed. French drama of both classical and popular kinds presented many topics and situations which gave Elizabethan dramatists of the free romantic school serviceable hints. Some coincidences in the subject-matter of Elizabethan and contemporary French drama may be accidental. It is imprudent to assume invariably a direct indebtedness. Elizabethan and French dramatists occasionally sought their plots independently in the same Greek, Latin, or Italian sources. Euripides and Plutarch, Plautus and Seneca, Boccaccio and Bandello all fathered plays in both France and England. Cognate pieces abound, and the family resemblances often come from a community of ancestors rather than from any immediate lineal tie. France, however, long anticipated England in drawing on the old classical and Italian stock. The French precedent frequently proved the efficient cause of an Elizabethan tragedy or comedy on a Greek, Latin, or Italian topic which was previously naturalized in France. Like the French writers of irregular drama, the Elizabethans were especially attracted by the Italian romances of Boccaccio and of Bandello, his sixteenth-century successor. French renderings of Italian tales were more accessible to the Elizabethans than the original versions. It was either the French translations, or the French dramatizations, of Italian romance which repeatedly gave the Elizabethan playwrights their cues. Each case of coincident plot must be judged on its merits, and it is not always easy to pronounce a decisive verdict, but the probabilities are constantly in favour of French suggestion.

In regard to one category of dramatic topics which won popularity on both sides of the Channel, Elizabethan drama was obviously subject to the direct influence of France. Almost as free use was made, in the Elizabethan theatre as in the popular French theatre, of political and polemical incident of recent French history. French affairs were closely watched by those who provided the Elizabethan public with realistic or topical drama; French statesmen and generals who enjoyed contemporary fame were heroes of the realistic stage in London, almost as frequently as in Paris.

VII

ELIZABETHAN COMEDY AND FRANCO-ITALIAN DIALOGUE

We have already seen that Tudor England mainly borrowed from contemporary France the fashion of the interlude, which in the last years of Henry VIII's reign heralded the coming of Elizabethan comedy. Foreign guidance, other than French, was soon enlisted in the task of moulding the Elizabethan type of comedy, and of developing its satiric, farcical, and romantic lineaments. Through the middle years of the sixteenth century, Latin and Italian comedy was in sporadic process of adaptation to requirements of English taste. The archetypal English comedy *Ralph Roister Doister*, which was written about 1540 by Nicholas Udall, a head master of Eton, for his pupils to act, crudely paraphrased Plautus's Latin comedy of *Miles Gloriosus*. The piece was a pedagogic exercise in farce. The performance, which was for the time an isolated episode, belongs to the annals of the country's educational rather than of its literary progress. There is no link here between English and French dramatic endeavour. An adaptation of Plautus's play was attempted in France at a later date.[1] No French influence is discernible in Udall's comic crudities, which were a somewhat barbarous fruit of the revived interest in the classics.

But the next phase stands in a different light. George Gascoigne, rather than Udall, deserves the credit of inaugurat-

---

[1] For the French rendering, De Baïf, one of Ronsard's best-endowed lieutenants, was responsible. Baïf's *Brave, ou Taillebras*, which was performed in the Hôtel de Guise in 1567, presented Plautus's comedy with far more artistic feeling than is discernible in Udall's *Roister Doister*.

ing Elizabethan comedy, and he was wholly inspired by continental example. The first regular English effort in the comic branch of dramatic art was Gascoigne's *Supposes*. The play was produced in 1566 by lawyers of Gray's Inn. The London barristers were therein, consciously or unconsciously, emulating a prescriptive habit of the lawyers of Paris,—' Les Clercs de la Basoche.' Gascoigne's *Supposes*, which mingles romance with farce, was a translation from the Italian prose of Ariosto's *Gli Suppositi*, but French suggestion is apparent. Gascoigne, the English author, was a close student of current French literature. He was well versed in the poetry of Marot, and in a treatise on English metre—' Certayne Notes of Instruction '— he dwelt on the forms of verse ' commonly used by the French '. Ariosto's comedy was popular in France. As early as 1542 there had been published in Paris a French translation, which was printed side by side with the Italian. The French writer called his version ' La Comédie des *Supposes* '. In his prologue Gascoigne admits that his hearers may well be puzzled to know ' the meaning of our *supposes* ', and he interprets the strange and unauthorized noun as ' mystakings or imaginations of one thing for another '. His novel title came from the French model, which stirred his ambition to plant regular comedy on English soil.[1]

Gascoigne's effort proved popular in England, and one incident in the story of its vogue illustrates the bearing of French agencies on Shakespearean drama. Gascoigne's comedy supplied the underplot of Shakespeare's *Taming of the Shrew*. The disguises and mystifications which attended the amorous adventures of the shrew's younger sister, Bianca, are borrowed from the Italian comedy which Gascoigne paraphrased at the prompting of France. Shakespeare's responsibility for the subsidiary scenes of *The Taming of the Shrew*

---

[1] A free French metrical version by Jean Godard of Ariosto's comedy was printed under the title of *Les Desguisez* in 1594. On October 2, 1595, a year after, the English theatrical manager Henslowe produced a (lost) piece called *The Disguises*, which translates, there can be no doubt, the new French recension of *Gli Suppositi*.

has been questioned, but the continental affinities of the piece are not thereby affected.

Comedy of romantic intrigue in England was deeply indebted to Italian drama for its subsequent development, but English study of Italian effort continued to obey French guidance. The French stimulus in the field of comedy often lost little of its force, when it was itself tributary to the Italian. The triumphant career of Larivey, who planted Italian comedy firmly on the Parisian stage, quickened the Elizabethan progress alike in intrigue and in the fantastic conceits of comic dialogue. It is easy to show the process at work. One of Larivey's most popular efforts, *Le Fidelle*, was an adaptation of an Italian comedy of intrigue, *Il Fedele,* by a writer named Luigi Pasqualigo. The piece which was published at Venice in 1574 obtained more conspicuous fame abroad than in Italy. No sooner had the French adapter given it a Parisian vogue than at least two Elizabethan Englishmen sought to familiarize their fellow countrymen with it. The classical and the popular schools of Elizabethan England were both clearly attracted by the popularity which the Italian piece acquired in France. Abraham Fraunce, a strenuous advocate of the classical law of drama, turned Pasqualigo's effort into Latin under the title of *Victoria*, the name of one of the heroines. Anthony Munday, an active champion of the new romantic movement, produced as early as 1584 an English translation under the designation of *The pleasaunt and fine conceited Comedie of Two Italian Gentlemen*.[1] Munday's rendering is crude and clumsy. All is in verse, and for the most part in rambling lines of varying lengths which occasionally reach sixteen syllables.[2] Snatches of both

[1] Fraunce's Latin comedy was first printed from the manuscript at Penshurst by Prof. G. C. Moore-Smith in Bang's *Materialien zur Kunde des älteren englischen Dramas*, Band xiv, Louvain, 1906. Munday's English version was reprinted from the copy at Chatsworth by Fritz Flügge in *Archiv für das Studium der neueren Sprachen und Literaturen* (1909), xxiii (new ser.), pp. 45–80.

[2] The following incantation is a typical example of the normal metre (ll. 487–92) :—

This water and this oil I have, is conjured as you see,
In the name of those sprites that written on this image bee.
Now must I write the name of him whom you so much do love:
Then bind these sprites, him to the like affection for to move.

Latin and Italian occasionally adorn the dialogue. But the
English translator retains little of the sprightly temper of the
Italian original, and when we contrast the Elizabethan version
with the French adaptation, which is a free and idiomatic
expansion of the Italian text, we recognize how greatly the
spirit of comedy in France already excelled in point and
vivacity the comic forces that were operating at the moment
in England and Italy.

Shakespeare's efforts in romantic comedy bear abundant
signs of Italian influence. But it was rarely that he sought
direct access to the Italian sources. Italian inspiration usually
reached him through French or English translation. There
is evidence in the case of Pasqualigo's comedy of *Il Fedele*
that Shakespeare knew not only Munday's English version,
but Larivey's expansive adaptation in the French language
as well. Shakespeare, in *The Two Gentlemen of Verona,*
turned to account Munday's title of the Italian piece and
some of the incidents and phraseology of the English rendering. Shakespeare's 'Two Gentlemen', like the 'Two Italian
Gentlemen' of Munday, pay addresses to two Italian ladies
and in the evolution of the plot exchange their mistresses.
There is no question that that cynical episode of intrigue was
an invention of the Italian drama, which Munday conveyed to
Shakespeare.[1]

> I charge you as you mean to purchase favour in his sight :
> And by the virtue of mine art, tell me his name aright.

Occasionally the six-line stanza of *Venus and Adonis* is used :

> I serve a mistress whiter than the snow,
> Straighter than cedar, brighter than the glass.
> Finer in trip and swifter than the roe,
> More pleasant than the field of flow'ring grass.
> More gladsome to my withering joys that fade,
> Than winter's sun, or summer's cooling shade (ll. 216–21).

Shakespeare in his early dramatic works employs at times the same
stanza (cf. *Love's Labour's Lost*, I. i. 147–58, IV. iii. 210–15, and *Romeo
and Juliet*, I. ii. 45–50, 88–93, V. iii. 12–17, 304–9).

[1] The exchange in the Italian piece, as of the French version, is not
a temporary phase of the story, as in Shakespeare's comedy, but is the
final *dénouement*, while Victoria, the mistress of one of the two heroes, is
already another's wife, a debasing circumstance from which Shakespeare's
play is free. Shakespeare borrowed other hints for his *Two Gentlemen* from
the Spanish romance of *Diana*, by Montemayor, where Felismena's pursuit
in masculine disguise of her lover, Don Felix, adumbrates Julia's pursuit

Larivey's best defined contribution to the development of Shakespearean comedy touches a different issue. The conceited dialogue of Renaissance comedy was largely of Italian origin, but it was greatly developed by the French gift for badinage. Larivey has some claim to the title of European master of eccentric pedantry on the comic stage. Munday gives small indication of the dramatic capacity of pedantic humour. Larivey's versions of Pasqualigo's *Il Fedele* and other Italian comedies first invested the dialogue of subsidiary characters like gallants, schoolmasters, serving-men, and clowns with that note of quibbling whimsicality which became habitual to the Elizabethan theatre.[1] Shakespeare's comical ' chop-logic ' and punning by-play have a colour which is more French than Italian. Shakespeare's comedy of *Love's Labour's Lost*, probably his first dramatic experiment, reflects, as we shall see, much that was passing at the time in France. It illustrates the Elizabethans' tendency to weave into their plots actual incidents or personages which were exciting attention across the English channel. Here it is more pertinent to observe that the protagonists engage in a ' civil war of wits ' the temper of which has French analogues. The mock-learning of the French schoolmaster Holofernes in Shakespeare's *Love's Labour's Lost* and the later echoes of the same note on the lips of the Welsh schoolmaster, Sir Hugh Evans, in *The Merry Wives of Windsor*, as well as on those of the pretended tutor, Lucentio, in *The Taming of the Shrew*, approximate with astonishing closeness to the current French comic dialogue which expands or re-fashions Italian affectations. In Larivey's popular French play *Le Fidelle*, the pedant on whom the French author bestows the original name of M. Josse, talks a dialect which is indistinguishable from that

---

of Proteus in Shakespeare's play. But there is only one gentleman lover in the Spanish story ; the duplication, which is the essence of Shakespeare's play, is alone anticipated by Pasqualigo, Larivey, and Munday.

[1] John Lyly seems to have been the first Elizabethan comic writer to naturalize on a small scale this continental fashion. Lyly's comedies, which for the most part adapt themes of classical mythology, present detached examples of such quick repartee as Larivey actively developed under Italian tuition. Shakespeare passed early beyond Lyly's bounds.

of Shakespeare's Holofernes. Munday's bald language gives
a very imperfect notion of the pedantic vein of pleasantry.
A few quotations will bring home the debt which much
of whimsical dialogue in Elizabethan comedy owed to the
French bettering of the Italian instruction.

Some of M. Josse's phrases run thus:

Comme il est escrit d'Ulisse, on en peut autant dire de
moy: *Qui mores hominum multorum vidit et urbes* . . .[1]

Or, maintenant, je cognoy estre vray ce que dit nostre
Nason: *Littore tot conchae, tot sunt in amore dolores* . . .[2]

Si tu ne l'entend, tu es comme morte, *nam sine doctrina
vita est quasi mortis imago* . . .[3]

O fœminam acutissimam! elle contrefait encores sa voix
pour n'estre cogneue. Comme dit bien le bon Naso, *sapientem
faciebat amor.*[4]

In conversation with Babille, a maidservant, the pedant
acquits himself in a fashion which is peculiar to Larivey:

Babille. Le seigneur Fidelle sont-il en la maison?

M. Josse. *Fœmina proterva*, rude, indocte, imperite,
ignare, indiscrette, incivile, inurbaine, mal, morigerée, igno-
rante, qui t'a enseigné à parler en ceste façon? Tu as fait
une faute en grammaire, une discordance au nombre, au mode
appelé *nominativus cum verbo*, pour ce que Fidelle *est
numeri singularis*, et sont *numeri pluralis*, et doit-on dire:
est-il en la maison? et non: sont-ils en la maison?

Babille. Je ne sçay pas tant de grammaires.

M. Josse. Voicy une autre faute, un très grand vice en
l'oraison, pour ce que, comme dit Guarin, la grammaire estant
art *recte loquendi recteque scribendi,* jaçoit qu'en plusieurs
langues elle soit escritte, n'est pourtant sinon un seul art,
parquoy envers les bons autheurs ne se trouve *grammatice
grammaticarum*, ne plus encores que *tritica triticorum*, et
arene arenarum, car il se dit tant seulement au singulier . . .[5]

A scene in Larivey's *Le Laquais*—an adaptation of
Lodovico Dolce's *Ragazzo*—presents another schoolmaster
Lucian, in discourse with Maurice, a recalcitrant pupil:

Lucian (maître ès arts) . . . tu n'avois accoustumé passer

---

[1] Viollet-Le-Duc's *Ancien Theatre*, vi, p. 319.   [2] Ibid., p. 349.
[3] Ibid., p. 372. Cf. the dialogue between Malvolio and the Clown in
Twelfth Night, IV. ii. 40 seq.: 'I say there is no darkness but ignorance,' &c.
[4] Ibid., p. 445.   [5] Ibid., p. 371.

un jour sans me montrer quelque thème ou epigramme; *nunc vero, et credo quae luna quater latuit*, tu ne me montres *amplius* ny prose ny vers, et ne hantes les escoles, comme avois accoustumé, ou, si tu y vas, tu oy seulement une leçon, et puis adieu.

Maurice (élève). Ne sçavez-vous que dict Terence?

Lucian. Quid inquit comicus, noster fili? Il a une memoire tresaguë.

Maurice. Haec dies aliam vitam adfert, alios mores postulat, s'il m'en souvient.

Lucian. Ita est, mais tu ne penètres bien la mouelle de ceste tant belle sentence.

Maurice. Exposez-la.

Lucian. Terence veut inferer que, quand l'enfant est sorty de l'age pueril et entré en l'adolescence, comme tu es: *tunc* alors, *haec dies,* ce temps, *adfert* ameine, *aliam vitam* une autre vie, *et ipsa subintelligitur aetas vel dies, postulat* requiert, *alios mores* autres mœurs ou façons de vivre: *id est* qu'il devroi tretenir en soy-mesme un peu plus de gravité, et laisser *penitus,* du tout, les façons pueriles, &c. . . .

The dialogue takes a more comic turn, when Valère, an impudent serving-man, invites the tutor to let him share the instruction, and fails to distinguish between Latin words and French.

Valère. Cujum pecus, est-ce Latin ou françois?

Lucian. C'est tresbon Latin, et fut chanté par ce Mantuan, qui modula *Titire, tu patulae.*

A very narrow interval here separates the Elizabethan comic writer from the French. It is in the strain of Larivey's M. Josse or of his Lucian that Holofernes fashions his snatches of Latin and of affected English which he addresses indiscriminately to the ignorant constable Dull, to the villager Costard, to the wench Jacquenetta, and to the curate Sir Nathaniel, whose parishioner's sons he tutors. Shakespeare's note is at times more boisterous and exuberant, but the key is identical.[1] Holofernes' simi-

---

[1] The pedagogue Lydus in Plautus's *Bacchides* seems to be the archetype of the schoolmaster in the comedy of the Renaissance. But the conception was greatly developed first by the comic writers of Italy and then by those of France. Shakespeare's pedant, Holofernes, is of the type of Sir Philip Sidney's Rombus, in his fantastic masque *The Lady of the May* (a work which, although Sidney wrote it in 1579, was not printed till 1598). Rombus, a village schoolmaster, there talks in a vein which adumbrates

426 FRANCE AND THE ELIZABETHAN DRAMA

larity of phrase may be judged from the following passages:
'*Mehercle!* if their sons be ingenuous, they shall want no instruction . . . But, *vir sapit qui pauca loquitur*. . . . *Fauste,
precor gelida quando pecus omne sub umbra Ruminat*, and
so forth. Ah, good old Mantuan.'[1]

Here is a sample of the conversation in which Holofernes
engages with the curate Sir Nathaniel and the constable Dull:

Holofernes. The deer was, as you know, *sanguis*, in blood;
ripe as a pomewater, who now hangeth like a jewel in the
ear of *caelo*, the sky, the welkin, the heaven; and anon falleth
like a crab on the face of *terra*, the soil, the land, the earth.

Nathaniel. Truly, Master Holofernes, the epithets are
sweetly varied, like a scholar at the least; but, sir, I assure
ye, it was a buck of the first head.

Hol. Sir Nathaniel, *haud credo*.

Dull. 'Twas not a *haud credo*; 'twas a pricket.

Hol. Most barbarous intimation! yet a kind of insinuation,
as it were, *in via*, in way, of explication; *facere*, as it were,
replication, or, rather, *ostentare*, to show, as it were, his
inclination, after his undressed, unpolished, uneducated, un-
pruned, untrained, or, rather, unlettered, or ratherest, uncon-
firmed fashion, to insert again my *haud credo* for a deer.

Dull. I said the deer was not a *haud credo*: 'twas a
pricket.

Hol. Twice-sod simplicity, *bis coctus*![2]

Nor is any violent difference discernible between the
mannerism of Larivey's characters, M. Josse and Lucian,
and that of Sir Hugh Evans when, with digressive irrelevance
to the dramatic scheme, he asks his pupil William Page 'some
questions in his accidence' (*Merry Wives*, IV. i. *passim*).
Mistress Quickly's futile interruptions seem, too, to reflect the

that of Holofernes in Shakespeare's *Love's Labour's Lost*, which was penned
about 1591, seven years before the publication of *The Lady of the May*.
But Shakespeare's pedants, Holofernes and Sir Hugh Evans, seem cast
in the mould of Larivey rather than of the Frenchman's Italian prototypes
or of any English master.

[1] *Love's Labour's Lost*, IV. ii. 80-98.

[2] Ibid., IV. ii. 3-22. On Sir Nathaniel's poetic experiments Holofernes
comments (IV. ii. 125 sq.) in M. Josse's precise vein thus: 'Let me
supervise the canzonet. Here are only numbers ratified; but, for the
elegancy, facility, and golden cadence of poesy, *caret*. Ovidius Naso was
the man; and why, indeed, Naso, but for smelling out the odoriferous
flowers of fancy, the jerks of invention?'

burlesque misunderstandings of Larivey's maid-servant Babille
or of his lackey Valère in the presence of his pedants M. Josse
and Lucian.

> *Evans.* What is he, William, that does lend articles?
> *William.* Articles are borrowed of the pronoun, and be
> thus declined, *Singulariter, nominativo, hic, haec, hoc.*
> *Evans. Nominativo, hig, hag, hog;* pray you, mark:
> *genitivo, hujus.* Well, what is your accusative case?
> *William. Accusativo, hinc.*
> *Evans.* I pray you, have your remembrance, child; *accu-*
> *sativo, hung, hang, hog.*
> *Quickly.* Hang hog is Latin for bacon, I warrant you.

The likeness between Larivey's and Shakespeare's exercises
in pedantic quip may be best explained by the theory that the
Franco-Italian dialogue of comic pedantry caught the ear of
the great writer of Elizabethan comedy, and stirred him to
feats of emulation.

VIII

THE EARLY FORTUNES OF ELIZABETHAN TRAGEDY

The Latin writer Seneca deserves to be reckoned the father
of tragedy in England. It was under his exclusive inspiration
that *Gorboduc*, the first English tragedy, was written in 1560,
two years after Queen Elizabeth's accession. Two lawyers
of the Inner Temple were authors of the play, and it was first
acted by gentlemen of their Inn of Court. For tragedy as
for comedy English barristers rendered English dramatic literature a service very like that which Parisian lawyers—'Les
clercs de la Basoche'— had already rendered dramatic literature
of France.

At the date of the production of *Gorboduc* the Greek
drama was far less known in this country than in France.
The study of Seneca was rarely qualified by that of Aeschylus,
Sophocles, or Euripides. Greek guidance was, however, soon
sought at second hand. George Gascoigne, author of the first
regular English comedy of *Supposes,* is here again the pioneer.
The second English tragedy, *Jocasta*, came from his pen, and

it emulated at a distance the Greek type. *Jocasta* was an adaptation of Euripides' *Phoenissae*. But there is no ground for assuming that Gascoigne had direct recourse to the Greek original. Nor was there any French translation of the *Phoenissae* when Gascoigne adapted the theme to purposes of English drama. It was an Italian version by Ludovico Dolce which the English writer followed. The English tragedy of *Jocasta* obeys the classical canons of chorus, unity, and monologue more closely than its predecessor *Gorboduc*. Its mould is almost identical with that of Jodelle's *Cléopâtre* or Garnier's *Cornélie*, and it familiarized cultured society in England with the processes of tragic composition which were already in operation in France.

If English tragedy threatened at its birth to pursue a classical path under Italian rather than under French direction, it showed during its infancy a tendency to defy pre-existing convention for which France must be credited with a partial responsibility. There were early signs of deviation into those irregular by-ways which the popular French drama had begun to tread. The first steps which popular tragedy took in Elizabethan England were discouraging to cultured onlookers who hoped to identify it with classical traditions. The first results accentuated all the least admirable features of the popular movement in France. It was no real blemish that the plot, as in France, should be sought outside Greek myth or Roman legend, or that themes of romance or of modern history—'les nouveaux arguments'—should be presented with the frequency to which the popular stage of France gave its sanction. But the rise of the profession of actor and the first organization of the theatre in England seemed likely not merely to drive the infant Elizabethan tragedy altogether out of classical channels but to plunge it irretrievably into ignoble streams of coarse and extravagant sensation. The scenes of turgid rant and sanguinary violence discredited by their uncouthness the popular development across the Channel. The infant tragedy of Elizabethan England loved 'inexplicable dumb-shows and noise', and revelled in the accumulation of mysterious and blood-curdling crimes.

In its wholesale defiance of classical canons the construction of early popular tragedy in Elizabethan England went in
all directions beyond continental limits. The law of unity
vanished altogether; the Chorus dwindled to the dimensions
of prologue or epilogue of an Act; choric debates within the
play disappeared, and their place was often filled by digressions into farce. The London stage in Shakespeare's boyhood
made a grotesque effort to continue the allegorical tradition
of the old 'morality'. Allegoric symbolism had never been
wholly abandoned in Paris, but grim statuesque figures per-
sonifying abstractions like Lust, Jealousy, or Murder, walked
the London boards more often than the Parisian. The
boisterous encroachment of farce on the tragic domain had,
too, its foreign precedent; the professional rulers of the
Hôtel de Bourgogne encouraged it; it was a universal mark
of the popular revolt against the classical convention of
austerity. But the mingling of rough merriment with tragic
gloom won a wider vogue in England than anywhere else.
'Lamentable tragedies mixed full of pleasant mirth'—plays
which associated stories of revolting crime with scenes not
merely of romance but of horseplay—were incongruities which
were rare outside the early playhouses in England. The first
Elizabethan play-goers fed eagerly on such confused and
discordant fare which was inferior in literary dignity or
dramatic flavour to any of its continental analogues.

When Shakespeare was entering manhood, English tragedy
of popular acceptance, though so new a growth, gave little
artistic or literary promise. The worst French examples
were of a more hopeful design. Popular English tragedy
offered in its infancy few titles to respect. To rescue it
from a premature degeneracy needed strong hands of genius,
which happily were not wanting.

Two policies of reformation were initiated very soon after
Shakespeare's professional career opened about the year
1587. One policy sought to counteract the current sensational
extravagance and brutalities by infusion of poetic dignity and
romantic glamour. The other policy aimed at a return to the
laws of classical simplicity. The active champions of both

remedial policies turned to France for aid and support. The effort to enforce the classical ideal proved a failure ; the effort to fuse tragedy with poetry and romance won lasting triumphs. France more actively encouraged the classical movement than the poetic and romantic endeavour; but French influences were at work in both.

Marlowe led the way to a poetic reform of Elizabethan drama. He created the English art of tragedy. France only offered him subsidiary inspiration, but his pioneer effort has many links with what was passing in that country. His career and achievements bore a strange resemblance to those of Étienne Jodelle, the dramatic pioneer of the Pléiade school some forty years before. The likeness of the two men's fortunes and labours impressed Elizabethan critics, and Marlowe's name was from an early date associated with that of his French predecessor.

The striking similarity between the sensational ways in which the French and English creators of tragic art met death, especially helped to bring the dramatic movements of the Renaissance in the two countries within one perspective. Jodelle's career ended in 1573 at the early age of forty-one amid degrading disease and want. To him there clung the same suspicions of atheism as darkened Marlowe's sordid death, twenty years later, in a tavern brawl at the age of thirty. A Puritan schoolmaster, who was soon to reckon Cromwell among his pupils, called attention to the coincidence as early as 1597. He narrated how the French tragical poet Jodelle 'being an Epicure and an Atheist, made a very tragical and most pittifull end; for he died in great miserie and distresse, euen pined to death, after he had riotted out all his substance, and consumed his patrimonie'. A few pages onwards the same author tells how Marlowe, 'one of our own nation, of fresh and late memorie,' rivalled Jodelle not only in his atheism and impiety, but also in the manner of his punishment.[1] The parallel was not forgotten. A year later—in 1598—Francis Meres, an Elizabethan student of

[1] Thomas Beard's *Theatre of God's Judgements* (1597), 3rd ed., revised and augmented (1631), pp. 146, 149.

comparative literature, who pronounced Shakespeare to be the greatest genius of the age, drew more emphatic attention to the coincidence. ' As JODELLE, a French tragical poet,' wrote Meres, ' being an Epicure and an Atheist, made a pitiful end; so our tragical poet MARLOW, for his Epicurism and Atheism, had a tragical death.'[1] Marlowe and Jodelle shared the common fate of reformers whose vision was wider than that of their neighbours. Each was the father of tragic art in his own country.

Christopher Marlowe, the founder of Elizabethan tragedy, echoed the ambition of the French leaders of the Pléiade when in 1589 in the prologue of his earliest play, *Tamburlaine*, he declared war on the past age of drama with its 'jigging veins of rhyming mother wits, and such conceits as clownage keeps in pay '. Marlowe promised to show the world how ' high astounding terms ' were essential elements of tragedy. This was the spirit that awoke and flourished in France some forty years before, and led Du Bellay in the name of the Pléiade to decree the banishment of *sotties* and *badineries*, of farces and moralities, from the French theatre. The decree was only partially effective across the channel. The proclamation was often repeated there. Twenty years after Du Bellay's manifesto and twenty years before Marlowe's fulmination, the classical tragedian Jean de la Taille impressively warned the French theatre anew against ' telles badineries et sottises qui comme amères espiceries, ne font que corrompre le goust de notre langue'. Marlowe's aspirations had ample French precedent.

Marlowe showed faith in the main principle of classical tragedy by concentrating his energy on the portrayal in elevated language of colossal types of passion. Of classical law he was careless; he practically eliminated the Chorus; he neglected the unities; he presented violent action on the stage ; nor could he check his tendency to bombast. Yet the spirit of his work has classical affinities, and there are indications that he was familiar with current French developments not merely of classical, but of popular drama. Under such

[1] Meres, *Palladis Tamia* (1598) : Arber, *English Garner*, vol. ii, p. 103.

influences Marlowe sought to lift Elizabethan tragedy out of the depths which it touched before he began his campaign of poetic reform.

Marlowe, like Jodelle, wrote a tragedy of *Dido*. Although a comparison of the two pieces suggests little direct indebtedness on the part of the English author to his French predecessor, there are characteristic points of contact.[1] Both paraphrase Vergil freely. In some respects Marlowe is more loyal to the classical story. He, like the Roman poet, and unlike the French tragedian, introduces Juno, Jupiter, and Venus as effective controllers of the action. The hosts of heaven exaggerate in Marlowe's tragedy the magisterial functions of the old Chorus. Impatient of the unity of time, Marlowe expands Jodelle's narrow canvas by presenting Aeneas's amorous adventure from the hour that he is wrecked on the Carthaginian coast until his departure three or four weeks later and Dido's subsequent suicide. Poetic feeling reaches a loftier key in Marlowe's work than in the French. But the tone of passion is at times indistinguishable. Dido's parting cry in the two plays well illustrates both the similarity and dissimilarity of the styles in adapting the poetry of Vergil. The passage runs thus in Jodelle (*Œuvres*, Paris, 1868, i. 221):

Quant à vous Tyriens, d'une eternelle haine
Suiuez à sang & feu ceste race inhumaine !
Obligez à tousiours de ce seul bien ma cendre,
Qu'on ne vueille iamais à quelque paix entendre.
Les armes soyent tousiours aux armes aduersaires,
Les flots tousiours aux flots, les ports aux ports contraires.
Que de ma cendre mesme un braue vangeur sorte,
Que le foudre & l'horreur sus ceste race porte.
Voilà ce que ie dy, voilà ce que ie prie,
Voilà ce qu'à vous Dieux, ô iustes Dieux, ie crie.

[1] The topic of *Dido* was very familiar in Italy before and after Jodelle's time. A lost Italian tragedy of the name is assigned to the year 1510. Lodovico Dolce published a second piece called *Didone Tragedia* in 1547, and Giraldi Cinthio followed with yet a third in 1583. Cinthio closely anticipates Marlowe in his frequent introduction of Juno, Venus, Cupid, and Mercury. Cinthio's third act opens with a long monologue spoken by Fama, which owes much to Vergil, and seems to adumbrate many similar prologues of Rumour in Elizabethan drama.

In Marlowe, Dido's speech takes this form :

And now, ye gods, that guide the starry frame,
And order all things at your high dispose,
Grant, though the traitors land in Italy,
They may be still tormented with unrest;
And from mine ashes, let a conqueror rise,
That may revenge this treason to a queen,
By ploughing up his countries with the sword.

IX

CURRENT FRENCH HISTORY ON THE ELIZABETHAN STAGE

Dido holds a modest place in the catalogue of Marlowe's dramas. Its suggestion of the influence of continental classicism lends it its chief literary interest. Another of Marlowe's minor dramatic endeavours brings him into closer relation with the popular French drama which dealt with contemporary French affairs. His *Massacre at Paris* crudely but vividly presents not only the Bartholomew Massacre of 1572, but the sequence of stirring events in Paris which issued in the assertion of Henry of Navarre's claim to the French throne in 1589. Marlowe's piece, which has only three Acts, and is cast in the mould of the dramatic chronicle, echoes rapidly a series of French plays portraying the crimes of the Guises. In the First Act the opening scenes show Charles IX, the French king, in colloquy with the Duke of Guise, Coligny, and the Huguenot leaders; at its close the St. Bartholomew massacre is realistically pictured, together with the murders of Coligny and Ramus. In the Second Act Charles IX dies, and is succeeded by his brother Henry III, who quickly quarrels with the Guises. In the last Act the Duke of Guise and his brother the Cardinal are murdered, Henry III is assassinated, and Navarre reaches the throne. Eternal love is finally sworn by the new French king to the Queen of England ' whom God hath blest for hating Poperie '.

Marlowe's *Massacre at Paris* contributed little to the artistic development of Elizabethan tragedy. Its interest largely lies in its plain indication of the sort of dramatic theme and sentiment which uncultured taste was still exacting of Elizabethan playwrights, after the inauguration of the endeavour to lift drama to a high poetic plane. There is abundant evidence in the diary of Philip Henslowe, a prosperous manager of the popular stage, that Marlowe's topical play held the suffrages of the play-going public for the long period of ten years. Whenever French affairs attracted marked notice in England, Henslowe promptly revived Marlowe's lurid tragedy. The piece is a first message from the Elizabethan stage, of English sympathy with the cause of Henry of Navarre and the Huguenots.

Much in the same vein was to follow Marlowe's tragic comment on the French civil wars. Shakespeare's patrons, while they were giving sure signs of an improved taste, encouraged theatrical portrayals of sensational crises in French affairs. It is significant that Shakespeare himself courted in early life this topical predilection. The great dramatist's comedy, *Love's Labour's Lost*, which lightly satirizes many passing events at home and abroad, makes free with the names and character of important personages in contemporary France. The hero, the King of Navarre, in whose dominion the scene is laid, bears the precise title of the Huguenot leader in the civil war of France, which was at its height between 1589 and 1594. The fortunes of the true King of Navarre, who was supported on the battlefield by many English volunteers of social position, engaged, while Shakespeare was writing *Love's Labour's Lost*, much anxious notice in England. The two chief lords in attendance on the king in the play, Biron and Longaville, bear the actual names of the two most active associates of the Huguenot chieftain across St. George's Channel. 'Lord Dumain' is a common anglicized version of the name of that Duc de Mayenne, another French general and statesman, who had already played a small part under the like designation in Marlowe's *Massacre at Paris*. He was frequently mentioned in popular accounts of current French affairs in connexion with the King of Navarre's movements, and, although he belonged to the house of Guise, Shakespeare fantastically numbered him among his supporters. Shakespeare's comedy is in most respects a satiric 'revue' or 'sottie', a topical extravaganza. It is no serious presentation of history. But the dramatist attests in whimsical fashion the prevalent interest which current French politics excited in theatrical circles.

Many popular pieces, of which the text has not come down to us, are stated in theatrical records of the time to have dealt with the same theme as Marlowe's *Massacre at Paris*. The theatrical manager Henslowe who revived Marlowe's play under the name of *The Guise*, as well as under its original title, added to his repertory, in the autumn of 1598, a drama called *The Civil Wars in France*. This piece was in three parts, and was the fruit of pens so eminent as those of the poet Michael Drayton and the practised dramatist Thomas Dekker. Very early in the next century, on November 3, 1601, Henslowe produced yet another play called *The Guise*, which came from the more distinguished hand of John Webster. The extant French tragedies of the previous decade, *La Guisiade* and *Le Guisien*, clearly had a large English progeny. One of the latest playwrights of the Elizabethan school, Henry Shirley, brother of James Shirley, the last survivor of Shakespeare's generation, was responsible for a tardy recension of the well-worn story of the Duke of Guise, which is again no longer extant. The Guisian topic, indeed, became so embedded in the tradition of Elizabethan tragedy that John Dryden, the glory of English tragedy in the next era of the Restoration, brought his energies to bear on it anew, in collaboration with his disciple, Nathaniel Lee. A tragedy called *The Duke of Guise*, which appeared in 1682, was a joint production of Dryden and Lee. Nor did the succession stop there. A different version of the story by Lee alone came out in 1690 under Marlowe's old title of *The Massacre of Paris*.

The fascination which current French history exerted on dramatic effort of Shakespeare's own generation is signally illustrated by the work of George Chapman. An Elizabethan whose classical erudition was linked with a rugged force of expression, Chapman was deeply read in French literature, and he based no less than five five-act tragedies on more or less contemporary themes of French politics.[1] For the most

[1] Chapman's main authority was *A General Inventorie of the History of France*, 1607, a translation by Edward Grimestone from the French of

part he followed almost slavishly an English translation of a recently published French history. His tragedy of *Philip Chabot, Admiral of France*, dramatizes the pathetic story of a favourite of Francis I; the hero, a man of integrity, was wrongly suspected of disloyalty, and, though acquitted of the charge, died of a broken heart. The protagonist of Chapman's tragedy, *Bussy d'Amboise*, was a favourite of the Duc d'Alençon, who was familiar to Englishmen as Queen Elizabeth's French suitor. Bussy, in Chapman's tragedy, was slain, owing to a disreputable intrigue of his master. Chapman pursued the course of events in a sequel, *The Revenge of Bussy d'Amboise*, which told of the vengeance taken by Bussy's brother on his murderer. There the assassination of the Duke of Guise and his brother the Cardinal, in 1589, was once more handled on the English stage. The most interesting of these labours of Chapman were two further tragedies which dealt with the career of one of the best-known lieutenants of Henry of Navarre through the early years of his triumph. Monsieur de Biron, whose charming personality dominated under his actual name Shakespeare's *Love's Labour's Lost*, was a trusted counsellor and friend of the Huguenot leader until his death in 1594. But Biron's son was even more intimately associated with his sovereign's fortunes. Every dignity that it was in the French king's power to bestow on a subject, the younger Biron enjoyed, and when he paid a visit on diplomatic business to Queen Elizabeth in 1600, the English sovereign and her people accorded him an heroic welcome. But his ambition soon afterwards o'erleapt itself. He was charged with conspiring to depose his generous benefactor, and he paid for his treason on the scaffold. Chapman, in two tragic pieces, the one called *Biron's Conspiracy*, and the other, *Biron's Tragedy*, narrated the sad story of the unhappy nobleman's fall. The two plays transcribe passing events with a strange literalness. Henry IV of France, in Chapman's piece, describes

the Huguenot Jean de Serres (1597) with additions from Matthieu, Cayet, and others (see F. S. Boas in *Athenaeum*, 10 Jan. 1903, and *Modern Philology*, iii. 1906). Chapman shows his predilections for French topics and characters in his comedies, *Monsieur d'Olive* and *A Humorous Day's Mirth*. For Chapman's and other French dramatic themes, see F. E. Schelling's *Elizabethan Drama, 1558–1642*, i. 414 seq.

the hero's successive promotions with the baldness of a legal
record (*Biron's Tragedy*, Act I, Sc. i):

> When he was scarce arrived at forty years,
> He ran through all chief dignities of France.
> At fourteen years of age he was made Colonel
> To all the Suisses serving then in Flanders;
> Soon after he was Marshal of the Camp,
> And shortly after, Marshal General.
> He was received High Admiral of France
> In that our Parliament we held at Tours;
> Marshal of France in that we held at Paris.
> And at the siege of Amiens he acknowledged
> None his superior but ourself, the King;
> Though I had there the Princes of the blood,
> I made him my Lieutenant-General,
> Declared him jointly the prime Peer of France,
> And raised his barony into a duchy.

Elsewhere Chapman lays stress on Biron's patriotic service
in the days of his country's deepest distresses:

> When the uncivil civil wars of France
> Had poured upon the country's beaten breast
> Her batter'd cities; press'd her under hills
> Of slaughter'd carcasses; set her in the mouths
> Of murtherous breaches, and made pale Despair
> Leave her to Ruin; through them all, Byron
> Stept to her rescue, took her by the hand;
> Pluck'd her from under her unnatural press,
> And set her shining in the height of peace.[1]

---

[1] *Biron's Conspiracy*, Prologus. A curious endeavour to bring Biron's
historic position home to the Elizabethan audience is made by Chapman
in the closing scenes of *Biron's Tragedy*. The doomed hero contrasts
his position with that of Queen Elizabeth's favourite, the Earl of Essex,
after the latter's conviction of treason.

> *Biron.*   The Queen of England
> Told me that if the wilful Earl of Essex
> Had used submission, and but ask'd her mercy,
> She would have given it, past resumption.
> She, like a gracious princess, did desire
> To pardon him; even as she prayed to God
> He would let down a pardon unto her;
> He yet was guilty, I am innocent:
> He still refused grace, I importune it.
> *Chanc.* This ask'd in time, my lord, while he [i. e. Essex] be-
>   sought it,
> And ere he had made his severity known,
> Had with much joy to him, I know been granted.
>   (*Biron's Tragedy*, Act V, Sc. i.)

A note of genuine sympathy with recent sufferings of France and Frenchmen is sounded in these lines. That note is characteristic of all Chapman's dramatic handling of French political topics. Only a corresponding sentiment on the part of his Elizabethan audience would have justified his persistent devotion to the drama of current French history. From the period of Marlowe's rise to that of Shirley's fall, strong links in the chain which bound the France of Ronsard and Montaigne to the England of Shakespeare and Bacon are discernible in English by-ways of popular tragedy.

X

ROMANTIC TRAGEDY, AND OTHER IRREGULAR DRAMATIC DEVELOPMENTS

Active as were Elizabethan dramatists in treating contemporary French affairs, the theme only sustained a subsidiary current of the mighty dramatic movement. The main stream flowed in the broader channels of poetic sublimity or living action to which Marlowe's genius had pointed. Finally the reformed drama travelled far beyond the bounds which he had known, and absorbed in its onward course elements of penetrating introspection and romantic passion, of which he as pioneer had dim perception. The generation that succeeded Marlowe was swayed by his defects, as well as by his merits. There was room for purgation in the work of his disciples as well as for processes of broadening and of deepening. Marlowe interspersed his majestic efforts in poetic tragedy with much rant. Many of his successors were less richly endowed than he with poetic genius, and in their tragic work developed more of his extravagances than of his dignity.

Yet Marlowe's tragic aim of stateliness, which accorded with the classical canons of Europe, left an indelible impression on his own and the next generation. He excited a dread of the ignoble lowering of the tragic standard to the debased level of the previous era. Thomas Kyd, a pupil of Marlowe, whose sanguinary tragedies achieved even greater popularity than his master's on the Elizabethan stage, echoed, despite his inferior powers of execution, Marlowe's plea for elevation in tragic theme and treatment.

> Comedies [he declared] are fit for common wits; . . .
> Give me a stately written tragedy.
> *Tragedia cothurnata*, fitting kings,
> Containing matter, and not common things.[1]

Romance held an inconspicuous place in Marlowe's scheme of tragedy. His disciples endeavoured to supply this want. Kyd mingled scenes of romance with his tragic violence, and the popular drama of France was well qualified to help him there. Kyd was well acquainted with current developments of tragedy in Italy and France, and when, in his most popular piece, *The Spanish Tragedy*, he introduces the device of a play-scene in anticipation of the familiar episode in *Hamlet*, his characters profess knowledge and study of histrionic methods of both France and Italy. Kyd's hero insists on the need of rapidity in production to give impressive effect to tragedy, and he speaks of the French modes from personal experience.

> I have seen the like
> In Paris, mongst the French tragedians.[2]

Kyd's contemporaries raised no question that the French theatre could teach much to Englishmen.

Shakespeare's genius for romance was of too original a compass to owe much to foreign sustenance. But it is significant that Shakespeare's first original experiment in romantic tragedy, *Romeo and Juliet*, treated a theme which had already served theatrical purposes on the other side of the Channel. In 1580 there was performed at the French court before Henry III, a tragedy founded on Bandello's tale of Romeo and Juliet. The author was a professional actor in the royal service who held the honorary rank of royal *valet de chambre*.[3] It is curious to note that

---

[1] Kyd's *Spanish Tragedy*, IV. i. 156-60.
[2] Ibid., IV. ii. 166-7.
[3] According to *La Bibliothèque françoise* (vol. ii), by Antoine du Verdier, Sieur de Vauprivas, which was first published at Lyons in 1585, 'Cosme La Gambe dit Chasteau-Vieux a récité plusieurs comédies et

in England the king's players—of whom Shakespeare was one—received from James I the like titular recognition of 'grooms of the royal chamber'. The French tragedy of *Roméo et Juliette* is not known to be extant, but the contemporary evidence of its production is of undisputed authenticity. There is no ground for crediting it with the lyric splendour or tragic intensity of Shakespeare's effort, but a ray of reflected glory from that supreme masterpiece illumines the record of the French actor's earlier labour.

Tragedy, comedy, and romance did not exhaust the energies of the Elizabethan dramatists, and everywhere French precedent is recognizable. Mediaeval tradition, in England as in France, still encouraged fresh experiments on the pattern of the old moral or scriptural play, and the scriptural and moral drama of the Elizabethan age borrowed suggestion of the French theatre. Of the scriptural drama of the Elizabethan era a representative example is George Peele's *The Love of King David and fair Bethsabe, with the tragedie of Absalon.* This paraphrase of the Bible story is a continuous piece without division into acts or scenes, and was often acted in London before its publication in 1599. Peele's work, in spite of its superiority in dramatic movement and scenic construction, has affinities with the French presentation of the same scriptural theme in Des Masures' *David combattant, fugitif, triomphant* (1566). Montchrétien's *David, ou l'Adultère*, which is cast in the classical mould, was written almost contemporaneously with Peele's work; its production corroborates the affinities of dramatic aim in the two countries at the end of the sixteenth century.

The 'morality' of the ancient pattern was practically swept

tragédies devant le roi Charles IX et le Roi à présent regnant (Henri III), et en a composé quelques-unes, assavoir *Le capitaine Bonboufle* et *Jodès*, comédies, *Roméo et Juliette* et *Édouard roi d'Angleterre*, tragédies tirées de Bandel, Alaigre,' &c. The dramatic author, Chateau Vieux, who is thus seen to have penned two (lost) tragedies on Italian tales by Bandello, won great fame as an actor at court, chiefly in comic rôles. In Vauquelin de la Fresnaie's *L'Art poetique françois*, which was written before 1589, though it was not published till 1605, 'Chateau Vieux, le brave farceur,' is twice mentioned with great commendation. In one place he is credited with 'la douceur' both in writing and in speaking dramatic verse (Vauquelin, *Diverses Poésies*, ed. Travers, 1869, vol. i, pp. 26, 85).

away by the new dramatic movement, but a few Elizabethan survivals betray the activity of foreign influences. The general situation may be gauged by the history of two English specimens belonging respectively to the beginning and end of Queen Elizabeth's reign. About 1561 there was first published 'A certaine tragedie entituled Freewyl'. The work is a contribution to polemical theology on 'moral' lines. It champions allegorically Protestant doctrine against the papal creed. The original source of this controversial drama is an Italian *Tragedia del libero arbitrio*, which was first published in 1546. A French version, *Tragédie du Roy Franc-arbitre*, came out at Villefranche in the south of France in 1558, and a Latin translation of the French in the following year at Geneva. The English rendering holds the fourth place in the succession, at the head of which stand versions in Italian and French. The fact illustrates that England was still travelling slowly in the rear of her neighbours. In the case of the second typical moral play of the Elizabethan era, which was written at the extreme end of the sixteenth century, France supplies the sole inspiration. A 'farce nouvelle des cinq sens de l'homme', in which 'Bouche' (i. e. mouth) plays a chief part, was produced in Paris about 1550. This French 'morality' suggested 'Lingua, or The Combat of the Tongue, and the Five Senses for Superiority, a pleasant Comedie', which was written by Thomas Tomkis, fellow of Trinity College, Cambridge, before Queen Elizabeth died.[1]

Other dramatic experiments in Elizabethan England which were without ancient sanction, mediaeval or classical, were of foreign origin, but they came from Italy rather than from France. The new forms of masque and pastoral found at the extreme end of Queen Elizabeth's reign among her subjects a first audience which quickly grew in eagerness and number during the reign of her successor. The English pastoral drama was a direct offspring alike in France and England of recent Italian effort. Tasso's *Aminta* (1581) and Guarini's *Pastor Fido* (1590) are the parents of both French and English pastoral plays. Three French renderings of *Aminta* (of

---

[1] The French farce is printed in Viollet-Le-Duc's *Ancien théâtre français*, vol. iii. The English comedy was first published in 1607.

1584, 1593, and 1596) and one of *Pastor Fido* (of 1593)
chiefly brought the pieces to the knowledge of the Elizabethans. The French versions failed to modify the Italian
tone and colour, and the influence which they exerted was
predominantly Italian. The Elizabethan and Jacobean masque
is also the child of Italian parentage. The French form of
the English word bears witness to French agency in bringing
to England the Italian *maschera* or *mascherata*. But the
English masque embarked on its main career after the Elizabethan era—strictly speaking—closed, and it is not necessary
here to apportion the varied foreign influences—of Greece as
well as of France and Italy—which went to its final evolution.

XI

The Classical Reaction in Elizabethan Tragedy

The enthronement of Romance in the realm of Elizabethan
tragedy rendered irreparable the breach with classical tradition. But it was with misgivings that the classical law of
Tragedy was abandoned by scholarly Elizabethans, and the
triumph of Romance failed to still the doubts of conservative
culture. When Marlowe was preaching his new creed of
dramatic freedom and poetic dignity, an endeavour was made
to elevate English tragedy by a different process, by a revival
of the classical dispensation which frowned on romantic experiment. Although the attempt failed, it was slow to acknowledge
defeat. Its history bears interesting testimony not only to the
current state of critical opinion in England but to the inveterate reliance of cultured sentiment on French taste.

While Elizabethan tragedy was yet in its turbulent and
unregenerate infancy, Sir Philip Sidney, the chief Elizabethan
champion of the principles of the continental Renaissance,
waved with new energy the classical banner. In his *Apology
for Poetry* Sidney warned English dramatists of the peril
that they ran in neglecting classical rules of tragedy which
alone made for 'honest civility and skilful poetry'. Sidney's
ideal of dramatic perfection was the style of Seneca with
his 'stately speeches', his 'well sounding phrases', and his

'notable morality'. He even complained that *Gorboduc*, the archetype of English tragedy, was 'very defectious in the circumstances', and could not serve as 'an exact model'. 'The two necessary companions of all corporal actions' in the theatre were the unities of time and place, to which Elizabethan tragedy from the first paid scant respect.

Sidney admitted that the sins of *Gorboduc* were nothing in comparison with those of its defiant and decadent successors. There the action moved, he lamented, from Asia to Africa, and even to the under-kingdoms of the world. The stage was in quick succession a garden, a rock, a cave, a battle-field. Within two hours' space a child might be born and grow to manhood. Crimes of repellent brutality were, too, committed in sight of the audience. Especially bitter was Sidney's denunciation of mongrel tragi-comedy—of 'tragical mirth'—in which hornpipes were matched with funerals, to the sacrifice of the genuine spirit of comedy and tragedy alike. Sidney finally cited as best worthy of study and imitation the Latin tragedies on conventional classical lines of Buchanan, the Scottish scholar who had been a professor at a French University and had reckoned Montaigne among his pupils.

Sidney's counsel carried little weight with popular opinion. English tragedy found ultimate salvation in poetry and romance which ignored the classical canons. Marlowe devised the only path in tragic art that could satisfy the national sentiment. Yet while Marlowe's pen was active strenuous efforts were initiated to purify the turbid stream of Elizabethan tragedy by a liberal assimilation of classical theme and mould. The new school of conservative reformers sought the aid of Garnier, the latest and the best-endowed apostle of classical tragedy in France.

The inaugurators of the classical reaction inherited the literary feeling and ambition of Sir Philip Sidney who was patron-saint of the new movement. His accomplished sister, the Countess of Pembroke, and his intimate friend, Fulke Greville, were leaders of the classical champions, and their influence easily led professional men of letters to give their efforts some practical aid. The ablest adherent of the movement was the poet Samuel Daniel, while Thomas Kyd turned aside, at the prompting of the Countess of Pembroke, from his unlicensed pursuit of popular favour to supplement the countess's endeavours as a translator of Garnier into English. The popular irregularities inspired even the practised dramatists of the day with uneasiness.

The Countess of Pembroke took the first effective step. ' *The Tragedie of Antonie*, done into English by the Countess of Pembroke ' was the literary labour which occupied her leisure during the summer and autumn of 1590.[1] Marlowe was then in the full flush of his fame, and Shakespeare was just about to challenge fate with his *Romeo and Juliet*, a romantic type of tragedy, which was already known to France but was new to England. The countess translated the Alexandrines of Garnier's regular tragedy of *Marc-Antoine* into English blank verse, which was very literal and none too graceful. She cast the choruses into the six-, eight-, and eleven-lined stanzas of the French. The brief play, which is in four acts, brings events only as far as the death of Antony. The countess's crude English hardly did justice to the clear current of the French style, and its obvious inadequacy was not of good augury for the future of the classical reaction.

But the countess's energy stirred emulation in abler pens. Under her auspices Thomas Kyd forsook his full-blooded work in irregular tragedy of the stamp of his *Spanish Tragedy*, in order to give the English public a better taste of Garnier's quality. Kyd undertook to translate two of Garnier's tragedies—*Cornélie* (Pompey's widow) and *Porcie* (Brutus's wife). The promise of *Porcie* remained unfulfilled. Kyd's rendering of the French dramatist's *Cornélie* was duly published in 1594. The English tragedian in the preface expresses a warm admiration for ' that excellent poet, Ro: Garnier ', and apologizes for the ' grace that excellent Garnier hath lost by my default '. He commends the tragedy as ' a fair precedent (i.e. example) of honour, magnanimity, and love '. Kyd's style as a translator is more

---

[1] It was first published in 1592. A reprint, edited by Alice Luce, was issued at Weimar in 1897.

facile than that of his patroness. But his literal method, like the Countess of Pembroke's, emphasized unduly Garnier's tendency to a stilted convention.

Meanwhile the poet Samuel Daniel presented Cleopatra's fate afresh, on Garnier's lines but in English language of his own. Daniel brought to the classical revival far richer poetic gifts than Kyd or his noble patroness. He abandoned the method of literal translation from the French, and brought some original power to reinforce the countess's aspiration to free Elizabethan drama of the Gothic taint. Daniel's *Cleopatra*, his first contribution to the new classical school of drama, was avowedly a continuation of Lady Pembroke's *Antonie*; it carries the story from Antony's death to Cleopatra's suicide. In a dedication to the countess Daniel explains that his Muse would never have ' digressed ' into such a path—

> ' had not thy well graced Antonie,
> (Who all alone having remained long)
> Wanted his Cleopatra's company.[1]

Daniel was encouraged by his poet-friend, Edmund Spenser, whose sympathies were classical, to attune his lyre to tragic plaints. Daniel scarcely fulfilled Spenser's anticipations of success in the tragic sphere. He keeps close to French models. His *Cleopatra* at times is a mere paraphrase of Garnier's *Marc-Antoine*. Such a chorus as that in which both English and French dramatists apostrophize the Nile illustrates the general relationship of their sentiment and metrical scheme.[2] At no long interval Daniel took a second

[1] *Works*, ed. Grosart, vol. iii, p. 23.
[2] Cf. Garnier's *Marc-Antoine* (Act II, *ad fin.*).

Garnier's *Marc-Antoine* (Act II, *ad fin.*).	Daniel's *Cleopatra* (last chorus).
O vagueux prince de fleuues,	And canst, O Nilus, thou
Des Ethiopes l'honneur,	Father of Floods endure,
Il faut qu'ores tu espreuues	That yellow Tiber should
Le scruage d'un Seigneur :	With sandy streams rule thee ?
Que du Tybre qui est moindre	Wilt thou be pleas'd to bow
En puissance & en renom	To him those feet so pure,
Voises (i. e. ailles) reuerant le nom,	Whose unknown head we hold
Qui fait tous les fleuues craindre,	A power divine to be ?
Superbe de la grandeur	Thou that didst ever see
Des siens qui veulent enceindre	Thy free banks uncontrolled
De ce monde la rondeur.	Live under thine own care.
	Ah, wilt thou bear it now ?
	And now wilt yield thy streams
	A prey to other realms.

step along the classical road. His second tragedy dealt with the tale of Philotas, the friend of Alexander the Great, who was convicted of treachery. Here Daniel, again pursuing Garnier's path, dramatized an episode in Plutarch's *Life of Alexander*. He exaggerated every classical convention. The speeches run to inordinate length. A messenger narrates the catastrophe in tedious detail, and a long chorus on varied rhyming schemes brings each act to a close with gnomic platitudes.

The classical movement was continued by Sir Philip Sidney's friend, Fulke Greville. Greville, followed the Countess of Pembroke and Samuel Daniel in a design of dramatizing on ancient lines—for a third time in English— ' the irregular passions of Antonie and Cleopatra ', who ' forsook empire to follow sensuality '. The story of Antony and Cleopatra, which had fascinated Jodelle and Garnier, the founders of the tragedy of the French Renaissance, clearly exercised as magnetic an attraction on the advocates of a classical reform of Elizabethan tragedy. Greville's drama on the subject is not extant. It was ' sacrificed to the fire ' by his own hands.[1] Not that he doubted its literary merits, but that he feared that his treatment of the Queen of Egypt and her paramour might be suspected of aiming at ' vices in the present governors and government '.[2] Greville fancied some vague sort of resemblance between the relations of Queen Elizabeth and the Earl of Essex, and those of Cleopatra and Antony.

Greville's remaining dramatic work, which was not exposed to a suspicion of political libel, survives. Although it touched contemporary history more closely than classical, and its

[1] Greville's *Life of the Renowned Sir Philip Sidney*, 1552, p. 178.
[2] There was much to prejudice the classical dramatic revival in the eyes of the English public. Among the obstacles to progress was an unexpected and unfounded suspicion that its intentions were other than those of literary purification. Daniel's classical tragedy of *Philotas*, which was written quite innocently for amateur acting by gentlemen's sons at Bath, was suspected of ulterior political motives. There, as in Greville's lost tragedy, some likeness was presumed between the fate of the imperial favourite Philotas and that of Queen Elizabeth's Earl of Essex.

theme passed outside the strict classical confines, it was strictly loyal to the classical form. There was French precedent for an extension of the topic of regular tragedy beyond the boundaries of classical mythology and history. Greville sought his dramatic material in recent oriental history, and was thus in accord with French example. One of his two tragedies, *Mustapha*, dealt with the death of a Turkish prince of the name, who was slain in 1553 by his father, the great Sultan Soliman the Magnificent, at the instigation of the Sultan's wife Rossa.[1] Mustapha's story had already engaged the hand of a French dramatist. *La Soltane*, a tragedy which was published at Paris in 1561, presents in like form the incidents of Greville's piece, but the sultan's wife, as the title indicates, fills a rather larger space of the canvas than the sultan. The other of Greville's classical dramas, *Alaham, heir to the King of Ormus*, is a more crabbed presentment of an episode of Mohammedan history.

Enthusiastic praise was bestowed by contemporaries on Fulke Greville's endeavours to enshrine oriental heroes in classical English tragedy. A wish was expressed—

> To raise this buskèn-poet to the skies;
> And fix him there among the Pleyades,
> To light the Muse in gloomy tragedies.[2]

In point of gloomy solemnity at any rate Sir Fulke's work entitled it to share the fame of the tragedy of the French Pléiade.

The classical effort of the Countess of Pembroke, of Kyd, of Daniel, and of Greville, was continued at the beginning of the seventeenth century by William Alexander (afterwards Earl of Stirling), a young Scotsman, who at the end of the

---

[1] The great Sultan Soliman, who reigned from 1520 to 1566, was a familiar figure on both English and French stages. Shakespeare bears witness to his wide repute by a mention of him in *The Merchant of Venice*. The prince of Morocco swears (II. i. 24–6):
> ' By this scimitar—
> That slew the Sophy and a Persian prince
> That won three fields of *Sultan Solyman*.'

[2] John Davies of Hereford in *Scourge of Folly*, which was probably published before 1611.

previous century left Glasgow University to travel abroad. On his return home in 1603 he entered the service of James of Scotland, then newly king of England, and published a tragedy of *Darius* on the strict classical model. There followed in rapid succession three similar compositions: the tragedy of *Croesus, king of Lydia*, the *Alexandrean Tragedy*, which dealt with the struggle among Alexander's generals for Alexander's crown after his death, and finally the tragedy of *Julius Caesar*. The four pieces were published together in 1607 under the general title of *The Monarchicke Tragedies*. All but one of the plays had French precedents. No French writer seems previously to have dealt with the story of Croesus. The fate of Julius Caesar was repeatedly handled by French dramatists, and the Scottish dramatist failed to modify conspicuously the French treatment of the theme. The stories of Darius and Alexander were also thoroughly identified with the French theatre. Not only did Jacques de la Taille, one of the pioneers of classical tragedy, make his reputation by dramas on the same two heroes, but Alexandre Hardy, who tried to amend the old classical method of the French stage, dramatized both the Plutarchan topics anew early in the seventeenth century. In their treatment of Alexander the Great, Jacques de la Taille and Hardy were content to bring Alexander's career to its close. In the plot of his *Alexandrean Tragedy*, the Scottish dramatist pursued the story of the conqueror's influence beyond his death. But the Scotsman's dramatic scheme shows little variation on the foreign models. His speeches are of interminable length. The choruses are in a sombre monotone. William Alexander's pen was rarely touched by the Promethean fire. None the less, his discipleship to classical tutors constituted him, in the indulgent view of British scholars, ' the monarch tragick of this isle,' even in the era of Shakespeare's maturest achievement.

With Sir William Alexander's *Monarchicke Tragedies* the effort to acclimatize classical drama in Elizabethan England practically ceased. The active champions of the irregular drama had then won their final victory. The critics acquiesced in the inevitable issue with regret. Garnier's

failure to gain the popular ear in England was held to do no
credit to public taste.   It was deemed inglorious that Kyd's
tribute to 'tragicke Garnier—his poor Cornelia . . . should
stand naked upon every post', should suffer popularly humi-
liating neglect.   'Howsoever not respected in England,' Kyd's
endeavour was in critical judgement 'excellently done'.[1]

Such a view was widely held.   Many of the dramatists
who resisted classical authority viewed their revolutionary
courses with searchings of heart, and blamed the cruel
necessity which compelled them to serve a perverted public
opinion.   Ben Jonson constantly deplored the breaches of
classical decorum, of which his colleagues and himself were
guilty.   He reckoned among 'the ill customs' of the age
dramatic infringements of unity of time, which permitted
children to grow into old men in the course of a single play,
and he ridiculed the absurd excesses of violent action within
sight of the audience, which made 'three rusty swords'

Fight over York and Lancaster's long jars.[2]

John Webster, a master of the Elizabethan type of romantic
tragedy, whose powers were only second to those of Shakespeare, was even franker in his comment on the same text.
When publishing in 1612 his *White Devil*, a typical Elizabethan tragedy of lawless romantic passion, Webster sadly
acknowledges that it 'is no true dramatic poem'.   But he
explained that he had broken classical laws knowingly, and
attributed his default to the ignorance of the play-goer.
'Willingly and not ignorantly in this kind have I faulted; for
should a man present to such an auditory the most sententious
tragedy that ever was written, observing all the critical laws,
as height of style and gravity of persons, inrich it with the
sententious chorus, and as it were, life in death in the passionate
and weighty nuntius; yet after all this divine rapture, 'O dura

[1] William Clerke's *Polimanteia*, 1595.
[2] With significant irony Jonson describes the innovation of diversity
of place.   'How comes it,' asks a character in *Every Man out of his
Humour* (1599), 'How comes it then, that in some one play we see so
many seas, countries, and kingdoms passed over with such admirable
dexterity?'   The answer is: 'O that but shows how well the authors can
travel in their vocation, and outrun the apprehension of their auditory.'

messorum ilia,' the breath that comes from the uncapable multitude is able to poison it; and ere it be acted, let the author resolve to fix to every scene this of Horace—

Haec hodie porcis comedenda relinques.'

Garnier, throughout the Elizabethan and Jacobean era, enjoyed the critics' reverence, and was even credited with a truthfulness and vivacity which were superior to that discernible in the irregular Elizabethan drama. At the very close of the great period of English drama the poet William Browne, in his *Britannia's Pastorals*, ascribed to Garnier's 'buskined muse' capacity to 'infuse the spirit of life' into the 'very stones'. The verdict is of more archaeological than aesthetic interest, but it is a significant tribute.

XII

CONCLUSION

William Browne wrote when Shakespeare's professional career was just ended, when, save in the complacent language of courtesy, Garnier had finally lost his place of predominance in the world of dramatic art. It does not fall within the limits of the present study to describe those pre-eminent features of Shakespearean or Elizabethan drama which lay beyond the scope of French influence. There is nothing in the labours of the French dramatists of the sixteenth century which is comparable with Shakespeare's subtle portrayal of character, with his universal survey of life, with his all-embracing humour, or with his magical command of language. There is little or nothing in the French theatre of Shakespeare's own or the preceding generations to account for these dazzling radiations of English dramatic genius. We are here only concerned with the humbler constituent elements of English drama which owed support and suggestion to France, more especially while the Elizabethan movement was in the stage of experiment and on the road to its apotheosis. It is clear that within these limits active help and passive suggestion were real and substantial.

It is in the themes of tragedy and comedy that the closest

bonds of union between the dramatic work of the two countries are visible. Chronology leaves small doubt that this resemblance of topic is a debt on the part of the English movement to the French.

The Elizabethan theatre's impatience of classical restraint never diminished the demand for plots which had served in France the purposes of classical tragedy. It was no small benefit to Elizabethan dramatists first to learn from French tutors how adaptable Plutarch's *Lives* were to the contemporary stage. Each of Shakespeare's great Roman plays, *Julius Caesar*, *Antony and Cleopatra*, and *Coriolanus*, had its precedent in a French tragedy which had lately been fashioned out of Amyot's standard French version of the Greek biographies. Julius Caesar, Antony, and Cleopatra repeatedly figured on the tragic stage of Renaissance France, and were among the best-applauded *dramatis personae*. Coriolanus was a new-comer and a less familiar visitor to the French dramatic arena, but he was there before Shakespeare introduced him to his own clients.

In spite of the popular demand for dramatic licence in France through the Renaissance era, the classical conventions of drama were powerfully supported there, and well held their own. The breach which Elizabethan drama contrived with the old tradition was for the most part bold and complete. Yet the English dramatists viewed their revolutionary conduct with small exultation, and remained loyal to much subsidiary machinery of the old *régime*. The choric element, which survives in Shakespearean drama in a modified form, seems to reflect influences issuing from the classical reaction of his day in his own country,—a reaction which flowed directly from Garnier's predominance in the French theatre. Daniel, the most powerful and active of the reactionaries, laid stress on the importance of the Chorus to the due exposition of tragic motive:

> We, as the Chorus of the vulgar, stand
> Spectators here, to see these great men play
> Their parts both of obedience and command,
> And censure all they do, and all they say.

Such comment helps to explain the manifest reluctance with which the great Elizabethan dramatists of the irregular school parted with the chorus. The tragic chorus, which was so conspicuous a feature of classical tragedy, was indeed never rejected with the same completeness as the classical rule of unity and statuesque declamation. Traces of the Chorus are widely distributed over the Elizabethan drama, and are prominent survivals of the classical form in both Marlowe and Shakespeare. Not only did Shakespeare occasionally introduce choric prologues on which, as in *Henry V*, he lavished freely his lyric gift, but in some of his tragedies he allots choric functions to subsidiary characters. The choric note of independent exegesis is plainly sounded in some speeches of Friar Laurence in *Romeo and Juliet*, and when Shakespeare's tragic power was at its zenith—in his two Roman plays of *Antony and Cleopatra* and *Coriolanus*—he fully invests with the choric office the character of Enobarbus in the one case and that of Menenius Agrippa in the other. In his own original way Shakespeare pays weighty tribute to the worth of the ancient choric formula, and implicitly adopts Daniel's estimate of its purpose. Nor, again, did Shakespeare, in spite of his acceptance of the new dramatic principle of scenic presentation of violent crime, exclude altogether the classic method of the ' nuntius' or ' reporter' of acts of death and outrage. The descriptive reports of the murder of the princes in the Tower in *Richard III* and of Ophelia's death by drowning in *Hamlet* recall the speeches of messengers in classical tragedy.

It was not only the classical themes which had already inspired tragedy in the French theatres that figured anew in Shakespearean drama. The adapters of French history to the uses of the French stage had before Shakespeare's day dealt with the pathetic episode of Joan of Arc's exploit in the war with England. The Maid of Orleans was more than once an honoured heroine of French tragedy, and her association with the French theatre is not likely to have escaped the attention of Shakespeare's coadjutor, who treated her with scant courtesy in *1 Henry VI*. The foundations of Shakespeare's earliest comedy, his satiric *Love's Labour 's*

Lost, were openly laid on French soil. Nor in those paths of dramatic romance which Shakespeare's genius illumined with its own incomparable light can he be often reckoned a pioneer. Not only had the fortunes of Romeo and Juliet been during Shakespeare's youth adapted from the Italian story to purposes of romantic tragedy in France, but the Italian fables of his two romantic comedies, *The Two Gentlemen of Verona* and *Twelfth Night*, had suffered the like fate across the English channel. The French dramatic endeavour, as we have seen, was very often an Italian inspiration, and Italy must share with France the glory of guiding Shakespeare's steps. Like both romantic and comic intrigue, comic pedantry was a foreign importation on the Elizabethan stage, which came from Italy, chiefly through France. When all the circumstances of Elizabethan England's relations with the culture of the continent of Europe are carefully weighed, when the French tendency to assimilate Italian example and the English tendency to assimilate French example are each fairly estimated, the pretensions of France to instruct Elizabethan dramatists in the dramatic efforts of Italy as well as in those of her own people cannot be lightly dismissed.

In the study of the causes and the origins of English literature in the sixteenth century it must always be borne in mind that France stimulated England's intellectual energy in two ways—by imparting her own knowledge, ideas, and example, and by imparting the knowledge, ideas, and example which she herself derived from Greece and ancient and modern Italy. England benefited not merely by the original inventions of literary France, but by the French power of absorbing the spirit and forms of Greek, Latin, and Italian literature. Much came to Elizabethan England from Italy direct. Italy may well claim to have introduced the first English humanists, Linacre and Colet, to an intelligent study of the classics. Elizabethan men and women of culture were well read in Italian poetry and prose. Yet it was the French habit of translation, of which England took every advantage, that must be credited with making the subject-matter of Greek and Latin literature current coin of English thought and expression, while only slightly smaller was the service which Frenchmen rendered the general Elizabethan public by their interpretation of Italian literature.

In poetry the French influence is imposing. The Pléiade may almost be said to have taught the Elizabethan lyrists their trade. Much of the imagery and metre which is often regarded as most characteristically Elizabethan reflects the Anacreontic vein of Ronsard's school. Not merely did French metres attract the English poets, but welcome was extended to French phraseology of classical flavour, like compound epithets, and to the accepted French terminology of the poetic art. Nor was secular verse alone affected. Huguenot example was a moving cause of the sacred poetry, including the sacred epic, of both the Elizabethan and Jacobean epoch.

If Germany was first to instruct Tudor England in Protestant theology, France gave her the doctrine of Calvin, and presented it in language of so logical a precision that serious English prose caught thence a new coherence. In recreative prose the chief French gift to Elizabethan England was the essay. In drama the Elizabethan spirit winged a flight beyond the range of France, but even there French suggestion first disclosed the dramatic potentialities of Plutarch's *Lives* and the primary conception of tragi-comedy or dramatic romance. The English genius had no lack of robustness or originality; above all, it never lacked passion; but it worked early in the sixteenth century sluggishly and fitfully. It acquired the agility and facility, which spurred it forward to its Elizabethan triumphs, largely from its intellectual and social commerce with its more precocious and vivacious neighbour overseas. Thereby the Englishman's assimilative instinct was quickened to beneficent and enduring purpose. None who compare the two literatures are likely to question the justice of the conclusion that a knowledge of the literary activity of contemporary France is essential to a sound conception or estimate of the literary forces at work in England throughout the period of the Tudor sovereigns' rule, from the accession of King Henry VII to the death of Queen Elizabeth, and even through the generation beyond.

APPENDIX I

ADDITIONAL SPECIMENS OF ELIZABETHAN POETRY,
WHICH ARE BORROWED WITHOUT ACKNOWLEDGE-
MENT FROM CONTEMPORARY FRENCH SOURCES

IN order to give the reader further opportunities than space
allowed in Book IV of studying the Elizabethan method of
direct and unavowed transference from French poetry of the
Pléiade School, I print here in full in parallel columns seven
illustrative French and English poems. Two of the five
French poems are by Ronsard, three by Desportes, one by Du
Bellay, and one by Jean Passerat. The Elizabethan renderings
of Ronsard and Desportes, of each of which I have cited
a single stanza in the text, are by Thomas Lodge; Daniel
is the literal adapter of Du Bellay and Drummond of Hawthornden of Passerat. It would be easy greatly to expand
this section, but my purpose is confined to a general cor-
roboration by concrete evidence of my allegation that much
representative Elizabethan poetry was nothing more than a
more or less literal reproduction of current French poetry.

1. RONSARD, *Odes*, Bk. V.17 (1553);
   Œuvres, vol. ii, p. 356.

LODGE, *William Longbeard*, 1593.
   (1819 ed., p. 117.)

Puis que tost je doy reposer
Outre l'infernale riviere,
Hé ! que me sert de composer
Autant de vers qu'a fait Homere ?

Since that I must repose
Beyond th' infernal lake,
What vails me to compose
As many verses as Homer did
   make ?

Les vers ne me sauveront pas
Qu'ombre poudreuse je ne sente
Le faix de la tombe là bas,
S'elle est bien legere ou pesante.

Choice numbers cannot keep
Me from my pointed grave,
But after lasting sleep
The doom of dreadful judge I needs
   must have.

Je pose le cas que mes vers
De mon labeur en contr'eschange
Dix ou vingt ans, par l'univers,
M'apportent un peu de louange.

I put the case, my verse,
In lieu of all my pain,
Ten years my praise rehearse,
Or somewhat longer time some
   glory gain.

Que faut-il pour le consumer
Et pour mon livre ôter de terre
Qu'un feu qui le vienne allumer,
Ou qu'un esclandre de la guerre ?

What wants there to consume
Or take my lines from light,
But flame or fiery fume,
Or threatening noise of war, or
   bloody fight ?

Suis-je meilleur qu'Anacreon,
Que Stesichore ou Simonide,
Ou qu'Antimache ou que Bion,
Que Philete ou que Bacchylide ?

Excell I, Anacreon,
Stesichons, Simonides,
Antimachus, or Bion,
Philetes or the grave Bacchylides ?

Toutefois, bien qu'ils fussent Grecs,
Que leur servit leur beau langage,
Puisque les ans venus après
Ont mis en poudre leur ouvrage ?

All these though Greeks they were,
And used that fluent tongue,
In course of many a year
Their works are lost, and have no
    biding long.

Donque moy, qui suis né François,
Composeur de rimes barbares,
Hé ! doy-je esperer que ma voix
Surmonte les siècles avares ?

Then I, who want wit's sap,
And write but bastard rime,
May I expect the hap,
That my endeavours may o'ercome
    the time ?

Non-non, il vaut mieux, Rubampré,
Son âge en trafiques despendre,
Ou devant un senat pourpré
Pour de l'argent sa langue vendre,

No, no ; 'tis far more meet
To follow merchant's life,
Or at the judge's feet
To sell my tongue for bribes to
    maintain strife,

Que de suivre l'ocieux train
De ceste pauvre Calliope,
Qui tousjours fait mourir de faim
Les meilleurs chantres de sa trope.

Than haunt the idle train
Of poor Calliope,
Which leaves for hunger slain,
The choicest men that her attend-
    ants be.

2. RONSARD, *Odes*, Bk. V. 20(1553);
   Œuvres, vol. ii, p. 358.

LODGE, *William Longbeard*, 1593.
'Imitation of a Sonnet in an
   ancient French poet' (1819 ed.,
   p. 114).

Si tost que tu sens arriver
La froide saison de l'hyver,
En septembre, chère arondelle,
Tu t'envoles bien loin de nous ;
Puis tu reviens quand le temps
    doux,
Au mois d'Avril, se renouvelle ;

As soon as thou dost see the winter
    clad in cold,
Within September on the eaves in
    sundry forms to fold,
Sweet swallow far thou fliest, till to
    our native clime,
In pleasant April Phoebus's rays
    return the sweeter time.

Mais Amour, oyseau comme toy,
Ne s'enfuit jamais de chez-moy :
Tousjours mon hoste je le trouve ;
Il se niche en mon cœur tousjours,
Et fond mille petits amours
Qu'au fond de ma poitrine il couve.

But love no day foresakes the
    place whereas I rest,
But every hour lives in mine eyes,
    and in mine heart doth nest.
Each minute I am thrall and in my
    wounded heart
He builds his nest, he lays his eggs,
    and thence will never part.

L'un a des ailerons au flanc,
L'autre de duvet est tout blanc,
Et l'autre ne fait que d'éclore.
L'un de la coque à demy sort
Et l'autre en becquette le bord,
Et l'autre est dedans l'œuf encore.

Already one hath wings, soft
    down the other clads,
This breaks the skin, this newly
    fledged about my bosom gads.
The one hath broke the shell, the
    other soars on high,
This newly laid, that quickly dead,
    before the dam come nigh.

J'entens, soit de jour, soit de nuit,
De ces petits Amours le bruit,
Béans pour avoir la béchée,
Qui sont nourris par les plus grans,
Ét, grands devenus, tous les ans
Me couvent une autre nichée.

Quel remede auroy-je, Brinon,
Encontre tant d'Amours, sinon
(Puisque d'eux je me desespere),
Pour soudain guarir ma langueur,
D'une dague m'ouvrant le cœur,
Tuer les petits et leur mère ?

Both day and night I hear the
    small ones how they cry,
Calling for food, who by the great
    are fed for fear they die.
All wax and grow to proof and
    every year do lay
A second nest, and sit and hatch
    the cause of my decay.

Ah, Magdalen, what relief have
    I for to remove
These crooked cares, that thus pur-
    sue my heart in harbouring love.
But helpless of relief since I by
    care am stung,
To wound my heart thereby to slay
    both mother and her young.

3. DESPORTES, *Diane*, lxviii (1573);
Œuvres, ed. Michiels, p. 40.

LODGE, Verses from *Rosalynde*,
    1590;
Sonetto by Phoebe (1819 ed., p. 103).

Ma nef passe au destroit d'une mer
    courroucée,
Toute comble d'oubly, l'hiver à la
    minuict ;
Un aveugle, un enfant, sans souci
    la conduit
Desireux de la voir sous les eaux
    renversée.

My boat doth pass the straits
Of seas incensed with fire,
Filled with forgetfulness ;
Amid the winter's night,
A blind and careless boy,
Brought up by fond desire,
Doth guide me in the sea
Of sorrow and despite.

Elle a pour chaque rame une
    longue pensée
Coupant, au lieu de l'eau, l'esperance
    qui fuit ;
Les vents de mes soupirs, effroyables
    de bruit,
Ont arraché la voile à leur plaisir
    poussée.

For every oar he sets
A rank of foolish thoughts,
And cuts, instead of wave,
A hope without distress :
The winds of my deep sighs
That thunder still for noughts
Have split my sails with fear
With care and heaviness.

De pleurs une grand'pluie, et
    l'humide nuage
Des dédains orageux detendent le
    cordage,
Retors des propres mains d'igno-
    rance et d'erreur.
De mes astres luisans la flamme est
    retirée.

A mighty storm of tears,
A black and hideous cloud,
A thousand fierce disdains
Do slack the halyards oft :
Till ignorance do pull,
And error hale the shrouds,
No star for safety shines,
No Phoebe from aloft.

L'art est vaincu du temps, du bruit
    et de l'horreur.
Las ! puis-je donc rien voir que ma
    perte asseurée ?

Time hath subdued art, and joy is
    slave to woe :
Alas Love's Guide, be kind, what
    shall I perish so ?

4. DESPORTES, *Diane* II. viii (1573);
Œuvres, ed. Michiels, p. 71.

Je me veux rendre hermite et faire
    penitence
De l'erreur de mes yeux pleins de
    temerité,
Dressant mon hermitage en un lieu
    deserté,
Dont nul autre qu'Amour n'aura la
    connaissance.
D'ennuis et de douleurs je feray
    ma pitance,
Mon bruvage de pleurs; et, par
    l'obscurité,
Le feu qui m'ard le cœur servira
    de clairté

Et me consommera pour punir mon
    offance.
Un long habit de gris le corps me
    couvrira,
Mon tardif repentir sur mon front
    se lira
Et le poignant regret qui tenaille
    mon ame.
D'un espoir languissant mon baston
    je feray,
Et tous jours, pour prier, devant
    mes yeux j'auray
La peinture d'Amour et celle de ma
    Dame.

LODGE, *Glaucus and Silla*, 1589.
(1819 ed., p. 59.)

I will become a hermit now
    And do my penance straight,
For all the errors of mine eyes
    With foolish rashness filled.
My hermitage shall placed be
    Where melancholy's weight,
And none but love alone shall know
    The bower I mean to build.
My daily diet shall be care,
    Made calm by no delight;
My doleful drink, my dreary eyes,
    Amidst the darksome place
The fire that burns my heedless
    heart
    Shall stand instead of light,
And shall consume my weary life
    Mine errors to deface.
My gown shall be of spreading gray
    To clad my limbs withal,
My late repent upon my brow
    Shall plainly written be.
My tedious grief and great remorse
    That doth my soul enthrall,
Shall serve to plead my weary pains
    And pensive misery.
Of faintful hope shall be my staff
    And daily when I pray
My mistress' picture placed in love
    Shall witness what I say.

5. DESPORTES, *Bergeries* (1573);
Œuvres, ed. Michiels, p. 431.

O bienheureux qui peut passer sa
    vie
Entre les siens, franc de haine et
    d'envie,
Parmy les champs, les forests et
    les bois,
Loin du tumulte et du bruit popu-
    laire,
Et qui ne vend sa liberté pour plaire
Aux passions des princes et des
    rois.

Il n'a soucy d'une chose in-
    certaine,
Il ne se paist d'une esperance vaine,
Nulle faveur ne le va decevant,
De cent fureurs il n'a l'ame em-
    brasée,

LODGE, *Glaucus and Silla*, 1589.
(1819 ed., p. 42.)

Most happy blest the man that
    midst his country bowers
Without suspect of hate, or dread
    of envious tongue,
May dwell among his own: not
    dreading fortune's lowers,
Far from those public plagues that
    mighty men hath stung:
    Whose liberty and peace is never
        sold for gaine,
    Whose words do never soothe a
        wanton prince's vein.

Incertain hopes and vows do never
    harm his thought,
And vain desires do shun the place
    of his repose;
He weeps no years misspent, nor
    want of that he sought,

Et ne maudit sa jeunesse abusée,
Quand il ne trouve à la fin que du
  vent.

Nor reaps his gain by words, nor
  builds upon suppose :

Il ne fremist, quand la mer
  courroucée
Enfle ses flots, contrairement pous-
  sée
Des vens esmeus, soufflans hor-
  riblement ;
Et quand la nuict à son aise il
  sommeille,
Une trompette en sursaut ne
  l'éveille,
Pour l'envoyer du lict au monument.

The storms of troubled sea do
  never force his fears,

Nor trumpet's sound doth change
  his sleeps or charm his ears.

L'ambition son courage n'attise ;

D'un fard trompeur son ame il ne
  déguise,
Il ne se plaist à violer sa foy ;

Des grands seigneurs l'oreille il
  n'importune,
Mais en vivant content de sa fortune
Il est sa cour, sa faveur et son roy.

Ambitions never build within his
  constant mind,
A cunning coy deceit his soul doth
  not disguise,
His firm and constant faith corruptions never blind,
He never waits his weal from
  prince's wandering eyes ;
But living well, content with
  every kind of thing,
He is his proper court, his favour,
  and his king.

His will (restrained by wit) is never
  forced away,
Vain hopes and fatal fears, the
  courtiers common foes,
Afraid by his foresight, do shun his
  piercing eye,
And nought but true delight ac-
  quaints him where he goes,
No high attempts to win, but
  humble thoughts and deeds,
The very fruits and flowers that
  spring from virtue's seeds.

Je vous rens grace, ô deitez
  sacrées
Des monts, des eaux, des forests et
  des prées,
Qui me privez de pensers soucieux,
Et qui rendez ma volonté contente,
Chassant bien loin ma miserable
  attente,
Et les desirs des cœurs ambitieux.

O deities divine, your godheads I
  adore
That haunt the hills, the fields, the
  forests and the springs,
That make my quiet thoughts contented with my store,
And fix my hopes on heaven, and
  not on earthly things ;
That drive me from desires, in
  view of courtly strife,
And draw me to commend the
  fields and country life.

Dedans mes champs ma pensée
  est enclose ;
Si mon corps dort, mon esprit se
  repose,
Un soin cruel ne le va devorant.
Au plus matin la fraischeur me
  soulage ;
S'il fait trop chaud je me mets à
  l'ombrage,
Et, s'il fait froid, je m'échauffe en
  courant.

My thoughts are now enclosed
  within my proper land,
And if my body sleep my mind
  doth take his rest,
My simple zeal and love my dangers
  do withstand,
The morning's pleasant air invites
  me from my nest,
  If weather wax too warm I seek
    the silent shade,
  If frosts afflict, I strive for warmth
    by hunter's trade.

Si je ne loge en ces maisons
  dorées
Au front superbe, aux voûtes pein-
  turées
D'azur, d'esmail et de mille cou-
  leurs,
Mon œil se paist des thresors de
  la plaine,
Riche d'œillets, de lis, de marjo-
  laine,
Et du beau teint des printanieres
  fleurs.

Although my biding home be not
  imbossed with gold,
And that with cunning skill my
  chambers are not dressed,
Whereas the curious eye my sundry
  sights behold
Yet feeds my quiet looks on thousand flowers at least,
The treasures of the plain, the
  beauties of the spring
Made rich with roses sweet and
  every pleasant thing.

Dans les palais enflez de vaine
  pompe,
L'ambition, la faveur qui nous
  trompe,
Et les soucys logent communément ;
Dedans nos champs se retirent les
  fées,
Roines des bois à tresses décoiffées,
Les jeux, l'amour et le contente-
  ment.

Amidst the palace brave puffed up
  with wanton shows
Ambitions dwell, and there false
  favours find disguise,
There lodge consuming cares that
  hatch our common woes :
Amidst our painted fields the
  pleasant Fairy lies,
  And all those powers divine, that
    with untrussed tresses,
  Contentment, happy love, and
    perfect sport professes.

Ainsi vivant, rien n'est qui ne
  m'agrée :
J'oy des oiseaux la musique sacrée,
Quand du matin ils benissent les
  cieux,
Et le doux son des bruyantes fon-
  taines,
Qui vont coulant de ces roches
  hautaines,
Pour arrouser nos prez delicieux.

So living, naught remains my solace
  to betray,
I hear the pleasant birds record
  their sacred strains,
When at the morning's rise they
  bless the springing day :
The murmuring fountains noise
  from out the marble veins,
  Are pleasing to mine ears ; whilst
    with a gentle fall
  They fleet from high, and serve
    to wet the meads withal.

Que de plaisir de voir deux co-
  lombelles,
Bec contre bec, en tremoussant des
  ailes,

What sport may equal this, to see
  two pretty doves
When neb to neb they join, in flut-
  tering of their wings,

Mille baisers se donner tour à tour,
Puis, tout ravy de leur grace naïve,
Dormir au frais d'une source d'eau
    vive,
Dont le doux bruit semble parler
    d'amour.

And in the roundelays with kisses
    seal their loves?
Then wondering at the gifts which
    happy nature brings;
What sport is it to sleep and
    slumber by a well,
Whose fleeting falls make show,
    some lovely tale to tell?

Que de plaisir de voir sous la
    nuit brune,
Quand le soleil a fait place à la
    lune,
Au fond des bois les nymphes
    s'assembler,
Monstrer au vent leur gorge dé-
    couverte,
Danser, sauter, se donner cotte
    verte,
Et sous leurs pas tout l'herbage
    trembler.

Oh what content to see amidst the
    darksome night,
When as the setting sun hath left
    the moon in place,
The nymphs amidst the vales and
    groves to take delight
To dance, to leap, to skip, with
    sweet and pleasant grace,
    To give green gowns in sport,
    and in their tripping make
By force of footing all the spring-
    ing grass to quake.

Le bal finy, je dresse en haut la
    veuë,
Pour voir le teint de la lune cornuë,

Claire, argentée, et me mets à
    penser
Au sort heureux du pasteur de
    Latmie.
Lors je souhaite une aussi belle
    amie,
Mais je voudrois en veillant l'em-
    brasser.

Their dances brought to end, I lift
    my looks on high
To see the horned moon, and
    descant on her hue,
Clear silver shining bright, and eft-
    soons then think I
Upon that happy chance the Lat-
    mian shepherd knew:
    Then do I wish myself as far a
    friend as she,
But watching I desire she might
    disport with me.

Ainsi la nuict je contente mon
    ame,
Puis, quand Phebus de ses rays
    nous enflame,
J'essay encor mille autres jeux
    nouveaux;
Diversement mes plaisirs j'entre-
    lasse,
Ores je pesche, or je vay à la chasse,
Et or' je dresse embuscade aux
    oyseaux.

Thus midst the silent night myself
    I do content;
Then when as Phoebus' beams our
    hemisphere enflames;
A thousand change of sports for
    pleasure I invent,
And feast my quiet thoughts with
    sundry pleasant games,
    Now angle I awhile, then seek I
    for the chase.
And straight my limerods catch
    the sparrows on the place.

Je fay l'amour, mais c'est de telle
    sorte
Que seulement du plaisir j'en rap-
    porte,
N'engageant point ma chere liberté;

I like and make some love; but yet
    in such a sort
That naught but true delight my
    certain suit pursues;
My liberty remains, and yet I reap
    the sport,

Et quelques laqs que ce dieu puisse faire
Pour m'attraper, quand je m'en veux distraire,
J'ay le pouvoir comme la volonté.

Douces brebis, mes fidelles compagnes,
Hayes, buissons, forests, prez et montagnes,
Soyez témoins de mon contentement !
Et vous, ô dieux ! faites, je vous supplie,
Que cependant que durera ma vie,
Je ne connoisse un autre changement.

Nor can the snares of love my heedful thoughts abuse :
But when I would forego, I have the power to fly,
And stand aloof and laugh, while others starve and die.

My sweet and tender flocks, my faithful field compeers,
You forests, holts, and groves you meads and mountains high,
Be you the witnesses of my contented years ;
And you, o sacred powers, vouchsafe my humble cry,
And during all my days, do not those joys estrange ;
But let them still remain and grant no other change.

6. Du Bellay, *Olive* (1549), xxxvi.

Samuel Daniel, in *Sonnets after Astrophel* (1591), Sonnet IV.

L'vnic oiseau (miracle émerueillable)
Par feu se tue, ennuyé de sa vie :
Puis quand son ame est par flammes rauie,
Des cendres naist vn autre à luy semblable.

Et moy qui suis l'vnique misérable,
Faché de vivre, vne flamme ay suyuie,
Dont conuiendra bien tost que ie déuie,
Si par pitié ne m'etes secourable.

O grand' doulceur ! ô bonté soueraine !
Si tu ne veulx dure et inhumaine estre
Soubz ceste face angélique et seraine,

Puis qu'ay pour toy du Phénix le semblant,
Fay qu'en tous poinctz ie luy soy resemblant,
Tu me feras de moy mesme renaistre.

The only bird alone that Nature frames,
When weary of the tedious life she lives,
By fire dies, yet finds new life in flames ;
Her ashes to her shape new essence gives.

When only I, the only wretched wight,
Weary of life that breathes but sorrow's blasts,
Pursue the flame of such a beauty bright,
That burns my heart ; and yet my life still lasts.

O sovereign light ! that with thy sacred flame
Consumes my life, revive me after this !
And make me (with the happy bird) the same,

That dies to live, by favour of thy bliss !
This deed of thine will show a goddess' power ;
In so long death to grant one living hour.

7. JEAN PASSERAT, *Élégies*, I. xi;
Sur la mort d'un moineau.
Œuvres, 1606, ed. Blanchemain,
(1880, i. 56).

Demandez vous, Amis, d'où vien-
nent tant de larmes
Que me voyez rouler sur ces fune-
bres carmes?
Mon passereau est mort, qui fut si
bien appris:
Helas! c'est faict de luy, une Chate
l'a pris.
Ie ne le verray plus en sautelant
me suiure;
Or' le iour me deplaist, or' ie suis
las de viure.
Plus donc ie ne l'orray chanter son
pilleri;
Et n'ay-ie pas raison d'en estre
bien marri?
Il estoit passé maistre à croquer
une mousche:
Il n'estoit point gourmand, cholere
ny farousche,
Si on ne l'attaquoit pour sa queue
outrager:
Lors il pinçoit les doigts, ardent a
se vanger.
Adonc vous l'eussiez veu croüller
la rouge creste
Attachee au sommet de sa petite
teste,
Tel que lon veit Hector, mur de
ses citoyens,
Dedans les Grecques naufs lancer
les feux Troyens.
Toutesfois une Chate, espiant ceste
proye,
D'un sault, à gueule bée, engloutit
nostre ioye.
Le pauuret, pour certain, fut pris
en trahison,
Autrement de la Chate il eust eu sa
raison.
Le pasteur Phrygien ainsi vainquit
Achille,
Et le vain Geneuois la vaillante
Camille.
Ainsi le grand cheual que Pallas
charpenta
Contre le vieil Priam de soldats
enfanta.

DRUMMOND OF HAWTHORNDEN,
Phyllis on the death of her Sparrow.
(*Poems*, 1616, ed. W. C. Ward,
ii. 158.)

Ah! if ye ask, my friends, why this
salt shower
My blubber'd eyes upon this paper
pour,
Gone is my sparrow; he whom I
did train,
And turn'd so toward, by a cat is
slain.
No more with trembling wings shall
he attend
His watchful mistress; would my
life could end!
No more shall I him hear chirp
pretty lays;
Have I not cause to loath my tedious
days?
A Daedalus he was to catch a fly,
Nor wrath nor rancour men in him
could spy;
To touch or wrong his tail if any
dar'd,
He pinched their fingers, and
against them warr'd:
Then might that crest be seen shake
up and down,
Which fixed was unto his little
crown;
Like Hector's, Troy's strong bul-
wark, when in ire
He rag'd to set the Grecian fleet on
fire.
But, ah, alas! a cat this prey espies,
Then with a leap did this our joys
surprise.
Undoubtedly this bird was kill'd
by treason,
Or otherways had of that fiend had
reason.
Thus was Achilles by weak Paris
slain,
And stout Camilla fell by Aruns
vain:
So that false horse, which Pallas
rais'd 'gainst Troy,
King Priam and that city did
destroy.

Toy qui en as le cœur enflé de
vaine gloire,
Bien peu te durera l'honneur de ta
victoire.
Si quelque sentiment reste apres le
trespas
Aux espris des oiseaux qui trebu-
schent là bas,
L'ame de mon mignon se sentira
vengee
Sur le sang ennemy de la Chate
enragee.
Ie ne rencontreray ny Chate ny
Chaton
Que ie n'enuoye apres miauler
chez Pluton.

Thou now, whose heart is big
with this frail glory,
Shalt not live long to tell thy
honour's story.
If any knowledge resteth after
death
In ghosts of birds, when they have
left to breathe,
My darling's ghost shall know in
lower place
The vengeance falling on the cattish
race.
For never cat nor catling I shall
find,
But mew shall they in Pluto's palace
blind.

Vous qui volez par l'air entendans
les nouuelles
De ceste digne mort, tournez icy
vos œlles ;
Venez, pileux oiseaux, accompagner
mes pleurs,
Portons à son idole une moisson de
fleurs.
Qu'il reçoiue de nous une agreable
offrande
De vin doux et de laict, d'encens et
de viande :
Puis engrauons ces mots sur son
vuide tombeau :

Ye who with gaudy wings and
bodies light
Do dint the air, turn hitherwards
your flight,
To my said tears comply these notes
of yours,
Unto his idol bring an harv'st of
flowers ;
Let him accept from us, as most
divine,
Sabaean incense, milk, food, sweet-
est wine ;
And on a stone let us these words
engrave :

' Passant, le petit corps d'un gentil
Passereau
Gist au ventre goulu d'vne Chate
inhumaine,
Aux champs Elysiens son Ombre
se proumeine.'

' Pilgrim, the body of a sparrow
brave
In a fierce gluttonous cat's womb
clos'd remains,
Whose ghost now graceth the
Elysian plains.'

Catullus's well-known poem on the death of Lesbia's Sparrow (*Carmen* III) doubtless gave Passerat a faint cue. Drummond of Hawthornden depends solely on Passerat's verses.[1] The French poet, who died on September 14, 1602, at the age of sixty-eight, wrote most of his poetry in early life, but no collective edition was published before 1597, and no complete edition till 1606.

[1] See Prof. L. E. Kastner's article entitled ' Drummond of Hawthornden and the French Poets of the Sixteenth Century ', in *The Modern Language Review*, January, 1910.

APPENDIX II

GEORGE CHAPMAN AND GILLES DURANT [1]

A WRITER of the capacity of George Chapman is responsible for an example of the common Elizabethan habit of plagiarism from the French, which seems worth quoting separately. In 1595 Chapman published a little volume of verse bearing this title:

Ouids Banquet of Sence. A Coronet for his Mistresse Philosophie, and his amorous *Zodiacke*. With a translation of a Latine coppie, written by a Fryer, Anno Dom. 1400. *Quis leget haec? Nemo, Hercule Nemo, vel duo vel nemo* : Persius. [Printer's device of a gnomon rising from the sea waves, and casting a shadow on the water, with motto on a scroll in the sky above, 'Sibi Conscia Recti.'] At London. Printed by I. R. for Richard Smith, *Anno Dom.* 1595.

This volume seems to be the second that Chapman published. His first publication, also in verse, came out one year earlier under the title of *The Shadow of Night*. Great bibliographical interest attaches to *Ouids Banquet of Sence*. It is a very rare book. Only two perfect copies [2] seem known in England. Of these one is at the Dyce Library at South Kensington and the other was formerly in the Corser collection.[3] An imperfect copy is in the Bodleian Library at Oxford. I have made use of the perfect copy in the Dyce Library. It is a quarto of thirty-five leaves in admirable preservation. The signatures run from A to I_3.

The volume opens with a dedication ' To the Trvlie Learned and my worthy Friende, Ma. *Mathew Royden* '. Royden or Roydon was a little-known writer of verse, who reckoned among his intimate friends Sidney, Marlowe, Spenser, and Lodge, as well as Chapman ; all held him in high esteem and appreciated his critical powers. In conformity with the spirit of the quotation from Persius which figures on the title-page

---

[1] The substance of this section has already appeared in a paper entitled Chapman's *Amorous Zodiacke*, which I contributed to *Modern Philology*, Chicago, October, 1905.

[2] The British Museum Library contains only a copy of a reprint of 1639.

[3] Cf. Corser's *Collectanea*, Part IV, pp. 283-9.

of *Ouids Banquet of Sence,* Chapman complains in his address to Roydon of 'the wilfull pouertie' of public taste, which insists on excessive simplicity of style in poetry. Chapman argues that poetic art requires subtlety, and no mere 'plainness', in the presentation of ideas. He denies the right of 'the prophane multitude' to judge of 'high and hearty invention expressed in most significant and unaffected phrase'. The poems that follow are offered as a specimen of his 'high and hearty invention'.

Five sonnets follow the author's prefatory dedication. Of these the first is ascribed to Richard Stapleton, the second to Tho. Williams of the Inner Temple, and the fourth to I. D. of the Middle Temple (i. e. Sir John Davies), while the other two are anonymous. The general burden of the commendatory verse is that Chapman is an English poet of Ovid's rank.

A close examination of the volume puts a new complexion on the author's pretensions to originality, which his friends accepted. An appreciable part of the volume illustrates the Renaissance theory of 'imitation', and forms a graphic comment on its practical workings. It has not been suspected before that a third of the contents is a second translation from the French. In view of this revelation there seems almost a touch of irony in the printer's second motto at the extreme end of the volume: 'Tempore patet occulta veritas.'[1]

Four separate poems are included in the rare little book. The first, which bears the title of 'Ouids Banquet of Sence', is a somewhat licentious description of the poet Ovid's emotions on witnessing the emperor Augustus's daughter Julia (otherwise called Corinna) in the bath, and of his endeavours to gratify each sense in turn as he surveys the seductive scene. The second poem is a sequence of ten sonnets entitled 'A Coronet for his Mistresse Philosophie', in which the poet condemns the habitual celebration by contemporary sonneteers of 'love's sensual empery'.

The third poem, 'The Amorous Zodiacke,' is more

---

[1] The device at the end of the volume shows the figure of Time, with his scythe and hour-glass, dragging by the hand a naked woman from a rocky cave. The picture is encircled by a scroll bearing the motto, 'Tempore patet occulta veritas,' together with the initials of the publisher, R. S. (Richard Smith), at the bottom. Another instance of Chapman's habit of 'imitation' is perhaps more curious. Many of the most moving passages in his *Epicede or Funerall Song on the most disastrous Death of . . . Henry Prince of Wales* (1612) boldly adopt long extracts from Politian's *Elegia sive Epicedion In Albierae Albitiae immaturum exitum, ad Sismundum Stupham eius sponsum,* Opera, Lyons, 1546, tom. iii. 259 seq.

familiar than any of the others to students of Elizabethan literature.[1] In thirty six-lined stanzas, it is a translation, contrived with singular exactness, of a French poem entitled 'Le zodiac amoureux', by a living French author, who first published his work anonymously in Paris in 1587, reprinted it again anonymously in 1588, and published it for a third time, and then under his own name, in 1594, the year preceding the appearance of Chapman's English version.

The author of 'Le zodiac amoureux' was Gilles Durant, sieur de la Bergerie, to whom frequent reference has already been made. He was born at Clermont in the Auvergne, about 1550, and died at Paris in 1615, after a long and successful career at the Paris bar. Durant's leisure was devoted to poetry, mostly of an amorous kind. His verse was not always free from licentious coarseness, but some of his lyrics have grace and charm. A long sequence of sonnets which he addressed to an imaginary mistress, whom he called *Charlote*, abounds in conventional conceits. His best-known

---

[1] With regard to the fourth and last poem in the volume doubt is justifiable as to Chapman's authorship. It is avowedly no original composition, but a translation from the Latin. The title runs, 'The Amorous Contention of *Phillis* and *Flora* translated out of a Latine coppie, written by a Fryer, *Anno*. 1400.' The English writer is here translating with some literalness a mediaeval Latin poem, which was at one time wrongly attributed to Walter Mapes. The English verse is followed by ninety-five Latin verses, extracted from a Latin poem entitled 'Certamen inter *Phillidem & Floram*'. The Latin poem probably dates from the twelfth century; it is far earlier than the year 1400, to which the superscription assigns it. It seems to have been first printed from manuscript in the *Beyträge zur Geschichte und Literatur*, &c., von J. Christoph Freyherrn von Aretin, Part IX, pp. 301–9, Munich, September, 1806. There is a thirteenth-century copy in the British Museum, MS. Harleian 978, fol. 115 v°. This was first printed in 1841 in the *Latin poems commonly attributed to Walter Mapes*, edited by Thomas Wright for the Camden Society, pp. 258–67. The rhyming metre of the Latin is carefully followed in the English version in Chapman's volume. With regard to the authorship of the English rendering, it is noticeable that in 1598 it was separately reissued, and was then assigned to another's pen—to the pen of 'R. S. Esquire'. R. S. may very probably be Richard Stapleton, who prefixed commendatory verse to Chapman's volume of 1594. The title of the reissue of 1598 ran: 'Phillis and Flora. The sweete and ciuill contention of two amorous Ladyes. Translated out of Latine, by R. S. Esquire. Aut Marte vel Mercurio. Imprinted at London by W. W. for Richarde Johnes. 1598.' It is likely enough that Chapman had no hand in the translation of 'Phillis and Flora', but civilly rendered his friend Stapleton, whose work it was, the service of including it in his volume.

work was a spirited translation into French of *Pancharis*,
a series of Latin love-poems by his fellow-townsman and
close friend, Jean Bonnefons (1554–1614). To the first edition
of Bonnefons' Latin *Pancharis* (1587) Durant appended a
second part, which bore the title, ' Imitations tirées du Latin
de Jean Bonnefons, avec autres amours et meslanges poétiques,
de l'invention de l'Autheur' (i. e. Gilles Durant) ; and ' Le zodiac
amoureux' first appeared among these ' amours et meslanges
poétiques'. This volume was reissued in 1588 without change. In 1594 Durant's contributions reappeared
separately under the title of *Les Œuvres poétiques du
sieur de la Bergerie, avec les imitations tirées du Latin
de J. Bonnefons.*

Chapman is wholly dependent on Durant. It will be
seen from the reprint of the French and English poems,
which is given below, that not only is Durant's language
accurately, and indeed servilely, reproduced by Chapman,
but the Frenchman's metre is borrowed, and many of his
rhymes are anglicized with curiously halting effect. Chapman
omits five of Durant's stanzas towards the end of the poem,
but he scarcely gives any other indication of originality. He
does not reproduce the name of Durant's imaginary mistress,
' *Charlote* '; he contents himself with addresses to ' Deare
Mistres' or ' Gracious Loue '.

Chapman's endeavours to anglicize the French epithets of
Durant often cause him embarrassment. Durant's ' les neiges
Riphées' (stanza 21, l. 4) is a reference to the snows of the
Riphaean mountains in Scythia, which are familiar to classical
students. But Chapman's reproduction of this expression of
Durant in the English words, 'the white riphees,' is very
clumsy. Most of Chapman's English is clear and intelligible,
but ' the white riphees' has parallels, of which the following
are examples (I italicize in both the French and English the
words mainly concerned) :

Stanza 7.   M'empestrant parmy l'or de *tes beaux crepillons.*
              And fetter me in gold, *thy crisps implies.*

Stanza 8.   La Terre encore triste, *& feroit ouverture.*
              The Earth (yet sad) *and ouerture confer.*

Stanza 15.   *S'eschaufferoit encor'* dans le Signe suyuant.
              Should still incense mee in the following Signe.

Stanza 23.   *Au sortir de* ce lieu si brave & magnifique.
              To sort from this most braue and pompous signe.

Stanza 26.   De fait quand ie verroy les *iournées* s'accroistre.
              But when I see my *iournies* do encrease.

In the following reprint the spelling and punctuation of the originals have been respected :

THE AMOROUS ZODIACK
By George Chapman

From 'Ouids Banquet of Sence. A Coronet for his Mistresse Philosophie and his amorous *Zodiacke*. With a translation of a Latine coppie, written by a Fryer, Anno Dom. 1400 . . . . London. Printed by I. R. for Richard Smith, Anno Dom. 1595.' (In the Dyce Library at South Kensington.)
Sigs. F₃ recto—G₁ verso.

1. I Neuer see the Sunne, but suddainly
  My soule is mou'd, with spite and ielousie
  Of his high blisse in his sweete course discerned :
  And am displeasde to see so many signes
  As the bright Skye vnworthily diuines,
  Enioy an honor they haue neuer earned.

2. To thinke heauen decks with such a beautious show
  A Harpe, a Shyp, a Serpent, and a Crow ;
  And such a crew of creatures of no prises,
  But to excite in vs th' vnshamefast flames,
  With which (long since), *Ioue* wrongd so many Dames,
  Reuiuing in his rule, theyr names and vices.

3. Deare Mistres, whom the Gods bred heere belowe
  T' expresse theyr wondrous powre and let vs know
  That before thee they nought did perfect make
  Why may not I (as in those signes the Sunne)
  Shine in thy beauties, and as roundly runne,
  To frame (like him) an endlesse Zodiack.

LE ZODIAC AMOUREUX
By Gilles Durant

From 'Imitations Tirées du Latin de Jean Bonnefons, avec autres amours et meslanges poétiques de l'invention de l'Autheur.' . . . . Paris, printed by Abel L'Angelier, 1588. (In the British Museum.)
Page 44.

Iamais vers le Soleil ie ne tourne la veuë,
Que soudain, de dépit, ie n'aye l'ame émeuë,
En moy mesme jaloux de sa felicité :
Et porte à co[n]tre-coeur qua[n]d ie uoy tant de Signes
Luyre dedans le Ciel, ores qu'ils soient indignes
De iouyr d'un honneur qu'ils n'ont point merité.

Pe[n]sez qu'il fait beau voir deda[n]s les cieux reluire
Un serpent, un corbeau, un Nef, une lyre,
Et un tas d'animaux qui ne servent, sinon
De nous ramenteuoir les impudiques flâmes,
Dont Iupiter iadis abusa tant de femmes,
Qui font reuiure au Ciel leurs vices et leur nom.

Charlote, que les Dieux icy bas firent naistre
Pour mo[n]strer leur pouuoir, et no' faire cognoistre
Qu'ils n'avoient rien creé dauant toy de perfait ;
Que ne m'est-il permis, comme au Soleil du Mo[n]de, •
De luyre en tes beautez, et d'une course ronde
En faire un Zodiaque à iamais, comme il fait ?

4. With thee Ile furnish both the
   yeere and Sky,
   Running in thee my course of
   destinie :
   And thou shalt be the rest of
   all my mouing,
   But of thy numberles and perfect
   graces
   (To giue my Moones theyr ful in
   twelue months spaces)
   I chuse but twelue in guerdon
   of my louing.

De toy ie fournirois & le Ciel &
   l'année,
I'acheuerois en toy ma course
   destinée,
Tu serois le seiour de tout mon
   mouuement :
Mais du nombre infiny de tes graces
   perfaites
(Pour rendre en douze moys mes
   Lunes satisfaites)
Ie n'en voudroy choisir que douze
   seulement.

5. Keeping euen way through euery
   excellence,
   Ile make in all, an equall resi-
   dence
   Of a newe Zodiack; a new
   Phoebus guising,
   When (without altering the
   course of nature)
   Ile make the seasons good, and
   euery creature
   Shall henceforth reckon day,
   from my first rising.

Errant par ces beautez, d'une juste
   cadance,
Ie ferois en chacune égale residence,
   D'un nouueau Zodiaque, aussi
   nouueau Soleil :
Lors, sans rien alterer l'ordre de la
   Nature,
Je rendroy les Saisons : & chasque
   creature
   Se reigleroit le iour à mon premier
   resueil.

6. To open then the Spring-times
   golden gate,
   And flowre my race with ardor
   temperate,
   Ile enter by thy head, and haue
   for house
   In my first month, this heauen-
   Ram-curled tresse :
   Of which, Loue all his charme-
   chains doth addresse :
   A Signe fit for a Spring so
   beautious.

Pour ouurir du Printemps la saison
   redorée,
Et commencer mon cours d'une
   ardeur temperée,
I'entreroy par ton chef, & auroy
   pour maison
Durant le premier moys, ceste
   Tresse bessonne :
Tresse dont Cupidon tous ses liens
   façonne,
   Signe forte à propos pour si gaye
   saison.

7. Lodgd in that fleece of hayre,
   yellow, and curld,
   Ile take high pleasure to enlight
   the world,
   And fetter me in gold, thy
   crisps implies,
   Earth (at this Spring spungie
   and langorsome
   With enuie of our ioyes in loue
   become)
   Shall swarme with flowers, &
   ayre with painted flies.

Couché sur la toison de ceste
   Tresse blonde,
Ie prendroy grand plaisir à esclairer
   le monde,
M'empestrant parmy l'or de tes
   beaux crepillons :
La terre à ce Printemps, de morne
   & la[n]goureuse,
A l'enuy de nos ieux, deuenuë
   amoureuse,
   Seroit pleine de fleurs & l'air de
   papillons.

8. Thy smooth embowd brow, where
   all grace I see,
   My second month, and second
   house shall be:
   Which brow, with her cleere
   beauties shall delight
   The Earth (yet sad) and ouer-
   ture confer
   To herbes, buds, flowers, and
   verdure gracing Ver,
   Rendring her more then Summer exquisite.

Ton beau Front re-ŭouté, où toute
   grace loge,
Seroit mon second moys & ma
   seconde loge;
   Ce front resioüiroit de sa sere-
   nité
La Terre encore triste, & feroit
   ouverture
Aux herbes, aux bouto[n]s, aux
   fleurs, à la verdure,
   Et rendroit le Printe[m]ps plus
   gaillard que l'Esté.

9. All this fresh Aprill, this sweet
   month of *Venus*,
   I will admire this browe so boun-
   teous:
   This brow, braue Court for
   loue, and vertue builded,
   This brow where Chastitie holds
   garrison,
   This brow that (blushlesse) none
   can looke vpon,
   This brow with euery grace
   and honor guilded.

Le long de cest Auril, doux mois de
   la Cyprigne,
l'admireroy ce front plein de douceur benigne,
   Ce front braue palais d'Amour &
   de Vertu:
Ce front que Chasteté tient en sa
   sauuegarde,
Ce front que sans rougir iamais on
   ne regarde,
   Ce front de toute grace & d'honneur reuestu.

10. Resigning that, to perfect this
    my yeere
    Ile come to see thine eyes: that
    now I fcare;
    Thine eyes, that sparckling
    like two Twin-borne fires,
    (Whose lookes benigne, and
    shining sweets doe grace
    Mays youthfull month with a
    more pleasing face)
    Iustly the Twinns signe, hold
    in my desires,

Le quittant à la fin, pour acheuer
   ma route,
Ie viendroy voir tes Yeux qu'encores
   ie redoute,
   Tes yeux qui esclaira[n]s comme
   deux feux iumeaux
(Dont le regard benin & la douceur
   luysante
Rendroie[n]t du moys de May la
   face plus plaisante)
   Ont à bon droit le lieu du Signe
   des Gemeaux.

11. Scorcht with the beames these
    sister-flames eiect,
    The liuing sparcks thereof Earth
    shall effect
    The shock of our ioynd-fires
    the Sommer starting:
    The season by degrees shall
    change againe
    The dayes, theyr longest du-
    rance shall retaine,
    The starres their amplest
    light, and ardor darting.

Me brulant aux rayons de ces
   Flâmes iumelles,
La Terre en sentiroit les viues étin-
   celles,
   Le choc de nos deux feux feroit
   naistre l'Esté:
La Saison peu à peu deuiendroit
   alterée,
Les iours seroient aussi de plus
   longue durée,
   Tant ces Astres sont pleins d'ar-
   deur & de clairté.

12. But now I feare that thronde in such a shine,[1]
  Playing with obiects, pleasant and diuine,
    I should be mou'd to dwell there thirtie dayes:
  O no, I could not in so little space,
  With ioy admire enough theyr plenteous grace,
    But euer liue in sun-shine of theyr rayes.

Or' ie doute bien fort si estant en ce Signe,
Iouissant d'un obiect si plaisant & si digne,
  Ie me contenterois d'y estre trente iours:
Non, non, ie ne sçaurois en si petit espace
A mon aise mirer leur beauté ny leur grace.
  Ie croy que ie voudrois y demeurer tousiours.

13. Yet this should be in vaine, my forced will
  My course designd (begun) shall follow still;
    So forth I must, when forth this month is wore,
  And of the neighbor Signes be borne anew,
  Which Signe perhaps may stay mee with the view,
    More to conceiue, and so desire the more.

Mais ce seroit en vain : ma volonté forcée
Suyuroit bon gré mal gré sa course commencée :
  Sur la fin de ce moys il les faudroit quiter,
Et au signe d'aprés, soudain venir renaistre,
Signe, dont la beauté m'empescheroit peut-estre
  De plus penser en eux & de les regretter.

14. It is thy nose (sterne to thy Barke of loue)
  Or which Pyne-like doth crowne a flowrie Groue,
    Which Nature striud to fashion with her best,
  That shee might neuer turne to show more skill:
  And that the enuious foole, (vsd to speake ill)
    Might feele pretended fault chokt in his brest.

C'est ce beau Nez traitis, qui dedans ton visage
Paroist ainsi qu'un Pin au milieu d'un bocage,
  Que Nature (ce semble) en faisant à tasche
De bien former, afin qu'il n'y eust que redire
Et qu'un sot enuieux, coustumier de médire,
  Desirant s'en mocquer se trouast empesché.

15. The violent season in a Signe so bright,
  Still more and more, become more proude of light,
    Should still incense mee in the following Signe:
  A signe, whose sight desires a gracious kisse,
  And the red confines of thy tongue it is,
    Where, hotter then before, mine eyes would shine.

En un Signe si beau, la Saison violente
Tousiours de plus en plus deuenuë insolente,
  S'eschaufferoit encor' dans le Signe suyuant;
Signe qui, à le voir, desire qu'on le touche
D'un baiser gracieux, c'est ta mignarde Bouche
  Où ie me feroy voir plus chauld qu'auparauant.

[1] Misprint for ' sign '.

16. So glow those Corrals, nought
    but fire respiring
    With smiles, or words, or sighs
    her thoughts attiring
      Or, be it she a kisse diuinely
      frameth ;
    Or that her tongue, shoakes[1]
    forward, and retires,
    Doubling like feruent *Sirius*,
    summers fires
      In *Leos* mouth,[2] which all the
      world enflameth.

Aussi ces beaux couraux rie[n] que
feux ne respire[n]t
Soit qu'ils forment un riz, qu'ils par-
lent, qu'ils soupirent,
  Soit que mignardement ils se lais-
  sent baiser :
Soit que la langue encor' s'élance &
se recule
Pour redoubler l'ardeur, comme la
Canicule
  Brule, au Lyon, le Monde & le
  fait embrazer.

17. And now to bid the Boreall
    signes adew
    I come to giue thy virgin-
    cheekes the view
      To temper all my fire, and
      tame my heate,
    Which soone will feele it selfe
    extinct and dead,
    In those fayre courts with mo-
    destie dispred
      With holy, humble, and chast
      thoughts repleate.

De là, pour dire adieu aux Maisons
Boreales,
Ie viendroy visiter tes Ioües Virgi-
nales,
  Pour temperer mes feux & domp-
  ter mon ardeur,
Qui bien tost se verroit esteinte &
amortie
Dedans ce beau seiour, couuert de
modestie,
  Remply de sainte honte, & de
  chaste pudeur.

18. The purple tinct, thy Marble
    cheekes retaine,
    The Marble tinct, thy purple
    cheekes doth staine
      The Lilies dulie equald with
      thine eyes.
    The tinct that dyes the Morne
    with deeper red,
    Shall hold my course a Month,
    if (as I dread)
      My fires to issue want not
      faculties.

La pourprine couleur de tes Ioües
marbrines,
La marbrine couleur de tes Ioües
pourprines,
  Ces liz si proprement aux oeilletz
  égalez,
Ce taint qui fait rougir celuy-là de
l'Aurore,
Me retiendroient un moys : & si ie
crains encore
  Que mes feux au sortir n'en fussent dé-solez.

19. To ballance now thy more ob-
    scured graces
    'Gainst them the circle of thy
    head enchaces
      (Twise three Months vsd, to
      run through twise three
      houses)
    To render in this heauen my
    labor lasting,
    I hast to see the rest, and with
    one hasting,
      The dripping tyme shall fill
      the Earth carowses.

Aprés (pour balancer tes graces
plus secrettes,
Contre celles qu'on voit dessus to[n]
chef pourtraites)
  Ayant usé six moys à courir six
  maisons,

Pour rendre dans le Ciel ma peine
continuë,
Ie viendroy voir le reste, & tout
d'une venüe
  Aux humains ie rendroy les plus
  mornes saisons.

---

[1] i. e. ' shakes ' ; *var. lect.*, ' shoots.'   [2] Misprint for ' month '.

20. Then by the necke, my Autumne
   Ile commence,
   Thy necke, that merrits place of
   excellence
   Such as this is, where with a
   certaine Sphere,
   In ballancing the darknes with
   the light,
   It so might wey, with skoles[1] of
   equall weight
   Thy beauties seene with those
   doe not appeare.

Ie commenceroy donc par to[n] Col
   mon Autonne,
Col qui merite bien qu'une place on
   luy donne
Telle que celle-cy, ou d'un certain
   compas
En balançant la Nuit avecques la
   lumiere,
Il puisse balancer en semblable ma-
   niere
Tes beautez que l'on voit & que
   l'on ne voit pas.

21. Now past my month t' admire
   for built most pure
   This Marble piller and her
   lyneature,
   I come t' inhabit thy most
   gracious teates,
   Teates that feed loue upon the
   white riphees,
   Teates where he hangs his glory
   and his trophes
   When victor from the Gods
   war he retreats.

Ayant passé mon moys, à mirer la
   structure
De ce pilier de marbre & sa linea-
   ture,
Ie viendrois habiter tes Tetons
   gracieux:
Tetons qu'Amour poistrist[2] da[n]s
   les neiges Riphées,
Tetons où il append sa gloire & ses
   Trophées
Quand vainqueur il revie[n]t de
   co[m]batre les Dieux.

22. Hid in the vale twixt these two
   hils confined,
   This vale the nest of loues, and
   ioyes diuined
   Shall I inioy mine ease; and
   fayre be passed
   Beneath these parching Alps;
   and this sweet cold
   Is first, thys month, heauen
   doth to us vnfold
   But there shall I still greeue
   to bee displaced.

Tapy dans le Vallon d'entre ses
   deux collines,
Vallon Nid des Amours & des
   Graces divines,
Ie serois à mon aise; & auroy
   beau passer,
Sous l'abry de ces mons, la pre-
   miere froidure
Dont le Ciel en ce moys nous feroit
   ouuerture,
Mais aussi ie seroy fasché d'en
   deplacer.

23. To sort from this most braue
   and pompous signe
   (Leauing a little my ecliptick
   lyne
   Lesse superstitious then the
   other Sunne,)
   The rest of my Autumnall race
   Ile end
   To see thy hand, (whence I the
   crowne attend,)
   Since in thy past parts I have
   slightly runne.

Au sortir de ce lieu si brave & ma-
   gnifique,
Me destournant un peu de ma ligne
   Ecliptique
(Moins superstitieux que n'est
   l'autre Soleil)
I'iroy paracheuer le reste de l'Au-
   tonne
A voir ta belle Main, dont i'attens
   la couronne
Que i'ay peu merité en chantant
   ton bel oeil.

---

[1] Misprint for 'scales'.
[2] Mod. Fr. pétrit, *i.e.* kneads, handles.

24. Thy hand, a Lilly gendred of a Rose
That wakes the morning, hid in nights repose:
And from *Apollos* bed the vaile doth twine,
That each where doth, th' Idalian Minion guide;
That bends his bow; that tyes, and leaues untyed
The siluer ribbands of his little Ensigne.

Main qu'un Liz enge[n]dra d'une Rose vermeille,
Main qui resueille l'Aube alors qu'elle sommeille,
Qui du lit de Phoebus entr'rouure le rideau:
Main qui guide par tout le mignon d'Idalie,
Main qui bande son arc, Main qui lie & de-lie
Les ribans argentez de son petit bandeau.

25. In fine, (still drawing to th' Antartick Pole)
The Tropicke signe, Ile runne at for my Gole,[1]
Which I can scarce expresse with chastitie.
I know in heauen t'is called *Capricorne*
And with the suddaine thought, my case takes horne,
So, (heauen-like,) *Capricorne* the name shall be.

En fin, tira[n]t tousiours vers le Pole Antarctique
Ie viendrois attraper l'autre Signe Tropique,
Signe que ie ne puis chastement exprimer:
Ie sçay qu'icy le Ciel l'appelle Capricorne,
Et puisque en y pensant soudain mo[n] cas prit corne
Ie le veux, comme au Ciel, Capricorne nommer.

26. This (wondrous fit) the wintry *Solstice* seaseth,
Where darknes greater growes and day decreseth,
Where rather I would be in night then day,
But when I see my iournies do encrease
Ile straight dispatch me thence, and goe in peace
To my next house, where I may safer stay.

Ce lieu fort à propos tient l'hyuernal Solstice
Ou l'obscurité croist & le iour s'apetisse,
Aussi plus volontiers i'y seroy nuit que iour:
De fait quand ie verroy les iournées s'accroistre,
Ie le quiteroy là, et m'en iroy paroistre
En la maison suiuante où ie feroy seiour.

27. This house alongst thy naked thighs is found,
Naked of spot; made fleshy, firme and round,
To entertayne loues friends with feeling sport:
These, *Cupids* secret misteries enfold,
And pillers are that *Venus* Phane[2] vphold,
Of her dear ioyes the glory, and support.

Ceste Maison d'apres, ce sont tes Cuisses nuës
Nuës de toute tache, arrondies, charnües,
Qui servent aux Amans d'ébat & d'entretien,
Qui cachent le secret des amoureux mysteres,
Cuisses les deux pilliers du Temple de Cytheres,
Des doux ieux de Cypris la grace & le soustien.

---

[1] Misprint for 'goal'.

[2] Misprint for 'fane'.

28. Sliding on thy smooth thighs to
    thys months end ;
  To thy well fashiond Calues I
    will descend
  That soone the last house I
    may apprehend,
Thy slender feete, fine slender
    feete that shame
Thetis sheene feete, which Poets
    so much fame,
  And heere my latest season I
    will end.

Glissant au bout du moys sur ces
    Cuisses polies,
Ie me lairrois aller par tes Greues
    iolies
  Pour gaigner vistement la der-
    niere Maison :
Ce sont tes petis Pieds, petis Pieds
    qui font honte
Aux beaux Piés de Thetys, do[n]t
    l'o[n] fait tant de conte,
  En eux ie finiroy la derniere sai-
    son.

[Not translated by Chapman.]

Alors, assez recreu d'une si belle
    traite,
Au lieu de reposer & de sonner
    retraite
  (Pour rendre mon labeur tous-
    iours continuel)
Ie me r'efforcerois, et sans reprendre
    haleine,
l'iroy voir de rechef mon Mouton &
    ma laine,
  Poursuiuant sans repos ce trauail
    annüel.

L'ENVOY

29. Deare mistres, if poore wishes
    heauen would heare,
I would not chuse the empire of
    the water ;
  The empire of the ayre, nor of
    the earth,
But endlessly my course of life
    confining
In this fayre Zodiack for euer
    shining,
  And with thy beauties make
    me endles mirth.

Mignonne, si souhaits avoie[n]t lieu
    par le Mo[n]de,
Ie me souhaiteroy ny l'Empire de
    l'onde,
  Ny l'Empire de l'air, ny de la
    Terre aussi ;
Ie voudroy seulement, sans cesse,
    me conduire
Par ce beau Zodiaque, & tousiours
    y reluire
  Ioüissant à iamais de tes beautez
    ainsi.

[Not translated by Chapman.]

Cela m'estant permis : ces coureurs
    de Planettes
Qui font couler çà bas tant de vertus
    secrettes
  Et forgent (ce dit-on) les heurs &
    les malheurs,
N'y seroient plus logez : la seule
    mere nüe
Du petit Archerot y seroit bien
    venüe,
  Tous les autres iroient chercher
    logis ailleurs.

[Not translated by Chapman.]

Saturne est trop resueur: Iupiter
    est trop sage:
Ce grand Dieu belliqueur est de
    trop fier courage:
    Le messager des Dieux ce n'est
      qu'un babillard:
La deesse des bois elle est trop in-
    constante:
Venus demeureroit, son humeur me
    contante,
    Ie ne voudrois icy rien qui ne
      fust gaillard.

[Not translated by Chapman.]

N'elle ne moy n'aurions maisons
    particulieres,
Car indifferemment reluiroient nos
    lumieres
    En chasque station; mais si
      i'estoy forcé
D'en prendre une à mon gré que ie
    pourrois élire,
Souuent au Capricorne on me ver-
    roit reluire,
    Ce resueur de Saturne en doit
      estre chassé.

30. But gracious Loue, if ielous
    heauen deny
My life this truely-blest va-
    rietie,
    Yet will I thee through all
    the world disperse,
If not in heauen, amongst those
    brauing fires,
Yet heere thy beauties (which
    the world admires)
    Bright as those flames shall
    glister in my verse.

Charlote, si le ciel ialoux de mon
    enuie
Par si beau changement ne veut
    heurer ma vie,
    Tu ne lairras pourtant de luyre à
    l'univers:
Sinon dedans le Ciel entre les feux
    celestes,
l'our le moins icy bas tes beautez
    manifestes
    Comme les feux du Ciel luiront
    dedans mes vers.

INDEX

Addison, Joseph, 175.

Aeneas, Sylvius (Pope Pius II), 81.

Aeschylus, 17, 186, 427.

A'Kempis, Thomas, 312.

Alamanni, Luigi, 116-21, 117 n., 118 n., 381 n.

Alciati, Andrea (1492-1550), 19 and n., 146.

Alençon, Francis, Duke d': suitor of Queen Elizabeth, 38-40, 112, 295, 436.

Alexander, Sir William, Earl of Stirling, 256 n.; his classical *Monarchicke Tragedies*, viz.: *Darius, Croesus, The Alexandrean Tragedy*, and *Julius Caesar*, 447-9; their French predecessors, 448.

Alexandrines, 389, 394.

Alexis, Guillaume, prieur de Buzz, 108 n.

Amboise, Adrien d': his *Holopherne*, 402.

America, 7; Ronsard on, 200, 201; Huguenot settlements in, 304-7 and n.

Amyot, Jacques, 139, 151-9, 167, 175, 178-9, 286, 312, 451.

Anacreon, 16, 17, 196-8, 210, 214 n., 217-18, 220-1, 454.

André, Bernard, 44, 46.

Angelier, Charles L', 73 and n.

Anjou, Duc d', 183 n.

Anne of Bretagne, 92 n.

Anne of Denmark, 170.

Appian, 395.

Arber, Edward, 35, n. 3, 90 n.

Arden of Faversham, 407.

Aretino, Pietro, 23, 118, n. 2, 163.

Ariosto, Lodovico, 4, 6, 184 n.; influence on Wyatt and Surrey, 109; his satiric metre, 120; his influence in England, 210, 254; translated by Desportes, 215; Lodge's plagiarisms, 261 n.; Joseph Hall's debt, 352; *Orlando Furioso*, influence on Garnier, 398; his *Gli Suppositi*: French and English adaptations by Godard and Gascoigne, 420.

Aristophanes, 382; his *Plutus* translated by Ronsard, 382-3.

Aristotle, 291; his *Politics*, 321 n.; denounced by Ramus, 324; the dramatic unities, 388, 390.

Armstrong, Mr. E., viii; on Huguenot political theory, 314 n.

Arnold, Matthew, vi.

Arthur, Prince of Wales, 44.

Ascham, Roger, 130, 137; views on imitation, 251 n.; correspondent of Ramus, 326.

Ashton, H.: his *Du Bartas en Angleterre*, 349, n. 3.

Aubigné, Theodore Agrippa d', 328-32; his praise of Queen Elizabeth, 9 n., 391; Huguenot poet, 286; his wide literary range, 329; his culture, 329; warrior and diplomatist, 330; his *Printemps*, 330; *Les Tragiques*, 330-1: his prose works, *Histoire Universelle* and *Mémoires*, 331-2; influence in England, 332; Lord Fairfax's debt, 332 and n.; *see* 333, 339.

Auvergne, Martial d' (Martial de Paris), 104-5.

Aymon, the four sons of, 91.

Bacon, Anne, Lady, 309 and n. 2.

Bacon, Anthony: friend of Montaigne, 43, 172, 173 and n., 174; guest of Beza at Geneva, 309.

Bacon, Francis, Lord, 7, 166, 309; his travel in France, 43; his prose diction, 138; criticism of Rabelais, 161-4; his *Essays*, 171; dedicated to Anthony Bacon, 174; student of Ramus, 327.

Bacon, Sir Nicholas, 342 and n. 2.

Baïf, Jean Antoine de: member of French Pléiade, 188-9, 206; his sonnets, 202; his experiments with classical metres, 203-4; his *Amor fuitif*, 219-20; influence on Lodge, 231; initiates *vers mesurés* in France, 237; English metrical imitators, 238-9 and n. 2; his praise of Jodelle, 385; his *Braue on Taillebras*, an adaptation of *Miles Gloriosus*, 391; translates Sophocles' *Antigone* and Terence's *Eunuchus*, 391; his praise of Garnier, 395.

Baïf, Lazare de: translates Sophocles' *Electra* and Euripides' *Hecuba*, 382.

Bailey, John C., x.

Baird, H. M.: *The Rise of the Huguenots*, 315 n.

444-5 and *n.*; his *Sédécie*, 397-8; his *Bradamante*, 398-9; its debt to Ariosto, 398; the Corneille of the Renaissance, 405; champion of classical drama, 394, 400, 403, 417, 443, 451; his English disciples: Countess of Pembroke, Kyd, and Daniel, 443 *seq.*; his neglect in England, 448-9; Elizabethan reverence of, 450; praised by William Browne, 450.

Gascoigne, George: inaugurates comedy in England, 419; his *Supposes*; translation of Ariosto's *Gli Suppositi*, 420; influence on Shakespeare, 420; his *Certayne Notes of Instruction*, 122; 264 and *n.*, 420; his *Posies*, 184 and *n.*, pioneer of English tragedy, 427; his *Jocasta*, adaptation of Dolce's version of Euripides' *Phoenissae*, 428; obeys classical canons, 428; *see also* 122, 184 and *n.*, 264 and *n.*

Gaston de Foix, 403.
Gaulois, L'esprit, 13 *seq.*
Geneva Psalter, 310.
Gentillet, Innocent: refutes Machiavellian doctrines, 318; in English translation, 318, 320.
Gerrard, George, 352, *n.* 1.
Gerrard, Mark, 57.
Gilbert, Sir Humphrey, 7.
Giotto, 4.
Godard, Jean: his *Les Desguisez* and its English version, 420 *n.*
Goddard, William: his *Satyricall Dialogue*, 276 *n.*
Goethe, 339.
Golding, Arthur, 149, 150, 221, 312.
Gorboduc: first English tragedy, 427-8, 445.
Gosson, Stephen, 360 and *n.*
Goudimel, Claude, 28.
Gouge, William: student of Ramus, 327, *n.* 2.
Goujon, Jean, 5, 28.
Goulart, Simon, 150 and *n.* 2, 339; his summary of Du Bartas, 347, *n.* 1.
Gournay, Mlle. de, 169.
Gower, John, 107.
Grant, Edward, 77.
Greece, conquered by the Turks, 201.
Greek type in France, 87; in England, 87, 88 and *n.*
Greene, Robert, 136, 150 *n.*; his use of French, 243 and *n.* 2, 244; debt to Louise Labé, 374-5; his *Pandosto*, 414.
Gregory Smith, Prof. G., 156 *n.*
Greville, Fulke, 256 *n.*, 312, 343 *n.*, 443 *seq.*; his tragedy on Cleopatra, 446;

his loyalty to classical form, 446-7; his *Mustapha*, *La Soltane*, *Alaham*, 447; contemporary praise of, 447.
Grévin, Jacques, 286, received by Queen Elizabeth in England, 391; praises her linguistic powers, 9 *n.*, 392; his *La Trésorière* and *Les Esbahis*; debt to Jodelle and Charles Etienne, 392 and *n.* 2; his tragedy of *César*, 392-3, 395; compared with Shakespeare's, 393.
Gresham, Sir Thomas, 56.
Griffin, Bartholomew, 256 *n.*
Grindal, Edmund, Archbishop of Canterbury, 147.
Gringoire, Pierre, 98-100; his *Château de Labour* translated by Barclay, 100, 101, 108; his dramatic work, 369-70; 413; actor and manager of *Les Enfants*, 378.
Grolier, Jean, 28, 29.
Gruter, Jean, 34, *n.* 3.
Guarini, Giovanni Battista, 5, 210; his *Pastor Fido*, 174 *n.*, 269 *n.*, 441-2.
Guevara, Antonio di, 156.
Guicciardini, Francesco, 4.
Guilleville, Guillaume de, 103 and *n.*
Guise, François, Duc de, 294, 404, 433.
Guise, Marie de, 41.
Guise, The, 435.
Guises, The, 293 *seq.*; death of, 296, 433; tragedies on by Marlowe, Drayton, Dekker, Henry Shirley, Webster, Dryden, and Lee, 435.
Guisiade, La, 435.
Guysien, Le, 404, 435.

Hakluyt, Richard, 7, 194; account of Huguenot colonial discoveries, 306; admirer of Ramus, 328 and *n.* 1.
Hall, Joseph, 16 *n.*; on Rabelais, 161; on compound epithets, 247 and *n.* 2; on Du Bartas, 350, 352.
Hallam, Henry, 140 *n.*
Hardy, Alexandre: parallel with Shakespeare's career, 413; his versatility, 413; his tragedies, 413 *seq.*; use of classical themes, 414, 448; his *Mariamne*, 414; his tragi-comedies, 414; *Félismene*: its debt to Montemayor's *Diana*, 414; *Pandoste*: debt to Greene, 414; his *Coriolan* and French adaptations, 415; his dramatic output, 415; his influence, 415-16.
Harington, Sir John, on Rabelais, 161.
Harrison, William, 50, *n.* 2, 51, *n.* 2.
Harvey, Gabriel, 61 and *n.*; praise of Amyot, 156 and *n.*; advocacy of clas-